# FIGHT BACK & WIN

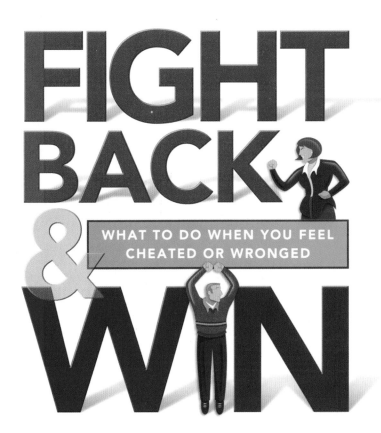

**WHAT TO DO WHEN YOU FEEL CHEATED OR WRONGED**

Reader's Digest

The Reader's Digest Association, Inc.
Pleasantville, New York/Montreal

# FIGHT BACK & WIN

Library of Congress Cataloging in Publication Data

Reader's Digest fight back & win: what to do when you feel cheated or wronged.
    p. cm.
  Includes index.
  ISBN 0-7621-0325-6
    1. Law—United States—Popular works. 2. Dispute resolution (Law)—United
States—Popular works. 3. Actions and defenses—United States—Popular works. I. Title:
Fight back and win. II. Reader's Digest Association.

KF387 .R42 2001
347.73'9—dc21

                                     00-047070

Printed in the United States of America.

Address any comments about Fight Back & Win to:
    Reader's Digest
    Editor-in-Chief, Illustrated Reference Books
    Reader's Digest Road,  Pleasantville, NY  10570

To order additional copies of Fight Back & Win, call 1-800-846-2100.
You can also visit us on the World Wide Web at: www.readersdigest.com

## Note to Readers

This publication contains the opinions and ideas of its contributors and is designed
to provide useful information to the reader on the subject matter covered. This
publication is sold with the understanding that the contributors and the publisher
are not engaged in rendering legal advice. Laws vary from state to state, and
readers with specific issues should seek the services of an attorney. Any references
in this publication to any products or services do not constitute or imply an
endorsement or recommendation. The publisher and the contributors specifically
disclaim any responsibility for any liability, loss or risk (personal, financial or
otherwise) which may be claimed or incurred as a consequence, directly or indirectly,
of the use and/or application of any of the contents of this publication.

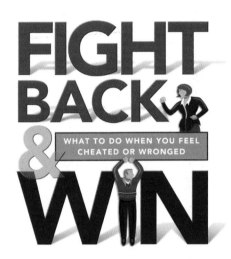

# FIGHT BACK

# &

WHAT TO DO WHEN YOU FEEL
CHEATED OR WRONGED

# WIN

# CONTENTS

# ABOUT THIS BOOK

**E**VERY DAY, THOUSANDS OF AMERICANS ARE ENGAGED IN BATTLE—contending with dishonest customers or incompetent merchants, combating con artists or swindlers, taking on city hall or Uncle Sam, or just trying to get a problem fixed or a promise kept. For some, the battle always seems to go smoothly and result in a successful outcome; these are the folks who know their rights and aren't afraid to stand up for them. They aren't always the most confrontational, and in some cases it's hard to say they've really been to battle at all; by calmly presenting their claims to those opposing them, they're often able to get everything they're entitled to—and to minimize stress and anger.

FIGHT BACK & WIN is designed to help you become one of those fortunate souls. In these pages you'll find hundreds of problems that people face daily. Also here are suggested strategies and methods designed to help you handle each situation, and resources you can enlist to help you "level the playing field" when faced with what may seem like overwhelming odds.

The vast majority of everyday problems are the result of honest misunderstandings or a lack of communication. But there are also plenty of scam artists ready to cheat honest individuals or to take advantage of the weak, the sick, and the elderly. You'll discover ways to recognize and protect yourself against these mischief-makers. And if you should suffer at the hands of a criminal, you'll learn how to testify against the offender, obtain restitution, and cooperate with police and prosecutors to see that justice is done.

## What About Litigation?

FIGHT BACK & WIN never suggests going to court until other potential avenues to justice have been exhausted. Litigation is time consuming, stressful, and usually expensive; even threatening a lawsuit at the wrong stage can shut off the possibility of a negotiated settlement. Here you'll learn how stating a problem clearly and proposing a workable solution can often mean avoiding the need for a fight. Taking advantage of mediation can also help you short-circuit a costly courtroom battle. Or, when your claim is relatively small, going to small-claims court can be an excellent course of action.

A lawyer's help will be indispensable in many situations. FIGHT BACK & WIN will help you find the kind of attorney you need and show you how to keep legal fees under control. One compelling reason to seek a lawyer's help is the fact that laws differ from state to state and city to city—sometimes subtly, in other cases substantially. In this book, every effort has been made to include only the most accurate and up-to-date information—but keep in mind that by the time you read it, some of the laws described may have changed and are no longer (or never were) the law in your community.

## Your Own Situation

While the scenarios in this book commonly occur in real life, some details may vary from your own plight—and even a very slight difference could lead to a dramatically different outcome. A lawyer is trained in obtaining all the facts and is required to investigate a client's claims before beginning a lawsuit. Knowing the specific details of your own situation can help your lawyer better fight for your cause or propose solutions short of going to court.

FIGHT BACK & WIN will help you weigh the pros and cons of your case. This way, you won't pursue a victory that will cost more than it is worth.

**Y**ou splurged when you bought your fiancée's engagement ring. Now she's called off the wedding and she refuses to return the ring.

**I**s it true that possession is nine-tenths of the law? Not in the case of an engagement ring, at least. This is a *conditional gift,* given on the understanding that the marriage will take place. If you don't get married, the condition no longer exists, and the ring should be returned. Not every ex-fiancée is so obliging, however, and many cases have been tried to determine the ownership of an engagement ring.

### ASK HER TO GIVE IT BACK

Obviously, the first thing you should do is simply ask your ex-fiancée to return the ring. If she refuses, write her a letter, telling her that the ring was given in anticipation of your marriage and asking again that she return the it. Specify a deadline, such as two weeks from the letter's date, by which time you expect the ring back. Send the letter by certified mail, return receipt requested, and keep a copy. If your ex-fiancée refuses to return the ring, you can go to court.

### GOING TO COURT

How you handle going to court depends on the ring's value in the state where you live:

■ **You may be able to go to small-claims court**. Small-claims courts hear cases about property disputes where the monetary value of the property is limited—too low, perhaps, if the ring you bought was expensive. In some states, however, a small claims court can rule on as much as $10,000.
■ **You can file a suit in the general trial court** if the limits of the small-claims court are lower than the ring's value. In this case, consider consulting a lawyer, because this kind of case is more complicated than a small-claims case.

When making a claim, you will need evidence that the ring was an engagement ring—an engagement announcement in the paper and a wedding invitation, for example. The court will not order the return of an *unconditional gift,* such as one given for a birthday or for Christmas.

If you win, your ex-fiancée will either be ordered to return the ring or repay you its value. If the ring is a family heirloom ask the court to specify that your ex-fiancée return it rather than pay. The ill will between you and your ex-fiancée is regrettable, but the ring is rightfully yours.

**Y**ou're excited that you're just about to get married. The next thing you know, your spouse-to-be asks you to sign a prenuptial agreement that you don't understand.

**W**hether this surprise comes out of the blue or not, be careful: This kind of agreement can take rights away from you that are otherwise guaranteed by law. By signing a prenuptial agreement, you are saying it's all right to have issues of property and money settled under the terms of that agreement, instead of the normal legal rules. For example, a prenuptial agreement may…

● Provide one spouse with less support in a divorce than the state law might allow
● Divide property less equitably
● Leave the widow or widower with a smaller share of the deceased spouse's estate than state laws would.

This rushed scenario is not an uncommon one. One party (almost always the one with more assets) asks the spouse-to-be to sign a prenuptial agreement shortly before the day of the wedding. What should you do?

- **Don't sign an agreement** that you don't understand or that seems unfair.
- **Postpone the marriage,** if need be, for a few weeks until you can have a lawyer look at the contract and explain it to you.
- **Don't count on the courts** to find that the agreement was signed under duress. While a prenuptial agreement made at the last minute could be found invalid, courts will look at the entire set of circumstances surrounding the agreement and may not find the case in your favor.

### DO-IT-YOURSELF AGREEMENTS

Couples draw up a prenup for several reasons, but usually to protect their individual money, property, or other financial assets. Those who marry a second time (or more) will often prepare a prenuptial agreement so that they can be sure that certain assets are passed on to their children and grandchildren from a previous marriage and do not become the property of the most recent spouse.

You can create your own prenuptial agreement using a kit, a book, or software. However, each party should hire his or her own lawyer (using the same one might lead to a conflict of interest) to review the agreement before it is signed.

State law determines what constitutes a valid prenuptial agreement. In order to be enforceable, these agreements must be in writing and

**SMART MOVES**

Have a prenuptial agreement created long enough before the wedding day to allow time to have it examined by a lawyer representing each party.

signed by the prospective bride and groom. In the agreement each must disclose his or her financial assets and property as well as the sources and amount of income he or she receives. An incomplete report may mean that a court will find that misrepresentation of one party's true financial situation makes the agreement invalid.

**TAKE NOTE** *Don't think that prenuptial agreements are just for the wealthy; many young couples who are anything but rich draw up and sign one of these (also called a premarital or antenuptial agreement) before they tie the knot. This contract sets out the rights and responsibilities of husband and wife, and can specify the amount of inheritance if one of them dies, or settlement in case of divorce.*

## WHAT TO DO IF YOUR SPOUSE ABUSES YOU

Since the late 1970s, both state governments and Congress have passed many laws designed to protect victims of domestic abuse. Unfortunately, spousal abuse remains a major problem. Abuse isn't limited to physical assault or marital rape. Pushing, slapping, stalking, and harassment are all acts of abuse. If you are ever a victim of spousal abuse, do the following:

■ **Call the police immediately.** The police can arrest your spouse and help get you and your children to a safe place.

■ **Have someone take photographs of your injuries** at the hospital or clinic where you are treated. These photos will be important pieces of evidence in any future legal proceedings.

■ **Get a temporary restraining order,** which will require your spouse to stay away from you and even leave the home you share. Your police department can explain how to get one.

■ **Go to court to obtain a permanent order of protection.** You have to follow up on the temporary restraining order. Your local court should have a victim's advocate program to help guide you through the legal process and provide emotional support. Your spouse has the right to be at the hearing and object to the permanent order of protection. *A permanent order of protection isn't really permanent,* but it is usually effective for several months up to a year or more. You may have to return to court to have the order renewed.

■ **Try to have a trusted friend or family member live with you,** if you are staying at the family home. Ask the police to increase their patrols in your neighborhood.

■ **Arrange to move to a shelter** if you need to leave home. Contact your local domestic violence support group for help. Be sure to take important possessions such as your...

✔ driver's license

✔ Social Security card

✔ checkbook

✔ medical records

✔ your children's school records

✔ jewelry

✔ photos

✔ prescription medicines

✔ address book

The police can provide protection for you while you collect these items.

■ **Follow up in court.** If your spouse has been charged with the crime of domestic violence, it's important to appear at the criminal trial to testify. Many abusers are able to escape punishment because the abused spouse won't cooperate with prosecutors.

For more information about protecting yourself from your partner's abuse and finding local resources, support groups, and crisis counseling, call the National Domestic Violence Hotline toll-free at (800) 799-7233.

The law is on your side. Whether you are married to him or not, the man who has fathered your child owes you child support. Unfortunately, many unmarried women don't try to collect child support from their ex-partners.

This may mean that these children will live at or below the poverty level and that their mothers will rely on government support instead of getting money from the absent parent. Although some progress has been made in enforcing child-support decrees in the last 10 years or so, thousands of mothers and children are not receiving the money they are due.

## WHO'S THE FATHER?

If you haven't already established paternity, you will need to if you want child support. Even if your ex-partner's name is on your children's birth certificates, courts do not consider this conclusive proof, as there is no requirement for the father to sign the birth certificate. As a result, a birth mother could write in anyone's name as the father of her child.

In some breakups, a man who has faithfully acted as a parent will suddenly register a doubt that he is actually the child's father. While he may truly question his blood relationship to the child, he may also be raising the issue merely to avoid paying child support.

## TESTING FOR PATERNITY

Ask the court to order testing for paternity if there is a question about the kinship of father and child. Hire a lawyer unless you feel confident that you can work directly with the clerk of the court. Either way, be sure that the order is filled out and served properly to your ex. If the court finds sufficient reason, it will order tests, including DNA testing, that will help resolve the question. You, the child, and the alleged father will have a saliva sample taken at a court-approved laboratory. The tests cost several hundred dollars or more, but if your ex-partner is found to be the father, he will probably be ordered to pay the bill.

Modern DNA testing is extremely accurate, and the court will find the results to be conclusive proof—unless there is evidence of tampering or contamination at the laboratory or if your ex-partner can show conclusively, with medical records or otherwise, that he was sterile when you claim he fathered your child.

## GETTING SUPPORT

Once the issue of paternity is settled, you can go to court to get custody of your children and get a court order requiring your ex-partner to make child-support payments. The court will decide how much support is due based on…

- The number of children you have
- The income of both parents
- Whether the children have special needs such as unusual medical expenses.

**TAKE NOTE** *If you find yourself having to rely on welfare to support your children without help from your ex-partner, the department of social services in your state may be able to help you get a child-support order.*

## WHEN CIRCUMSTANCES CHANGE

Even after a child-support award is made, you may find that your situation in life has changed and that you need—or are entitled to—more money. For example:

● You lose your full-time job or your part-time work hours are reduced significantly.

● Your child has a serious illness or is injured in an accident.
● Your ex-partner's income increases radically.

To get larger support payments each month, you will have to go to court for a modification order. The court will call another hearing, unless your ex-partner does not oppose your request.

---

*Y*ou've always wanted to adopt a child from another country. Now that the process has started, you find yourself caught in a snarl of government red tape.

---

Unless you are one of those people who enjoy the challenge of tangling with government systems, you'll find that adopting a child from another country is often as frustrating a process as it is rewarding. You have to deal with several bureaucracies, not just one: the other country's government, the U.S. government, and the social services agency that regulates adoptions in your state. To adopt a child from another country, the U.S. Immigration and Naturalization Service (INS; page 15) requires

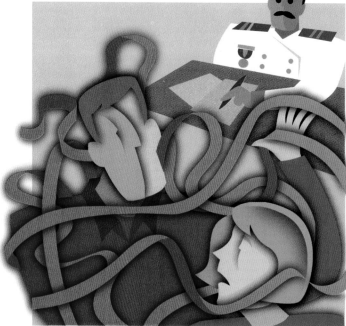

that you fill out more than a dozen forms. If you submit even one of these forms incorrectly, the entire adoption can be delayed or derailed. The requirements that foreign countries place on prospective American parents differ from country to country, and even long-standing regulations can change suddenly and without warning.

## KNOW FOREIGN LAW

Learn all you can about the country's regulations. It's essential that you follow them. In some countries you'll find that they...

● Have minimum and maximum age limits for adoptive parents
● Require adoptive parents to be willing to adopt a child of either sex
● Allow adoptions only by families with four or fewer children living in the home
● Require that you meet the child before an adoption takes place (others allow the adoption even if you've seen only a photo or a videotape of the child).

In addition, some countries in South America and eastern Europe are notorious for changing their adoption laws and regulations with little or no advance notice. If you are working with an international adoption agency, it should inform you of any changes as soon as they happen. If you are adopting without an agency, you will need to contact the country's embassy in the United States for advice and assistance. You can also find help on the Internet: Many support groups have Web sites where you can find specific solutions that help you deal with foreign bureaucracies.

## THE U.S. GOVERNMENT MAZE

The first step in a foreign adoption is to open a file with the INS and pay a fee. If you don't have a specific child in mind, you should fill out Form I-600A, the Application for Advance Processing of Orphan Petition. If you know of a particular child you want to adopt, you must complete Form I-600, the Petition to Classify Orphan as an Immediate Relative.

Next, you will have to undergo a series of investigations:

- **The FBI** will investigate your background, which can take several months.
- **The state social-services agency** or a licensed independent investigator will report on the quality of your home life. This includes both the physical environment and your family's day-to-day interaction.
- **The state will issue child-abuse clearance** stating your family has no record of abuse.

In addition, you must provide the INS with your birth certificate, financial statements, proof of employment, and letters of reference. Once these steps are completed, you should receive Form I-171H from the INS, indicating that your petition has been approved.

> **TAKE NOTE** *Sometimes adoptions don't go smoothly. If you run into a problem during the adoption process, keep in mind that you are ultimately responsible for making sure all documents are filed with the INS. Even if you have hired an agency, you should be certain that your application, home study reports, and supporting documents have been sent to, and received by, the INS. Be sure to keep copies of all documents. It is crucial to send all materials certified mail, return receipt requested, so you will have proof that the materials are in the hands of the INS.*

## LAST-MINUTE HURDLES

When a child is available, the steps you take will depend on the child's country of origin:

- **Picking up your child.** You will either travel to the country where the child lives or have the child escorted to the United States. In either case, you will need to pay for a medical checkup for the child before he or she can get a visa to enter the United States.
- **Getting final adoption clearance.** Sometimes you must adopt the child in the court system of the country of the child's birth. Or you may be able to leave the country with your child and adopt your child in your home state. If the adoption was completed in your child's country, you will need to readopt the child in your home state as well.
- **Considering citizenship.** Until recently, adoptive parents needed to apply for citizenship for children that they adopted from foreign countries. But a federal law enacted in 2000 now grants citizenship to these children upon adoption by parents who are U.S. citizens.

## HELP FROM UNCLE SAM

Patience is a virtue but also has its limits. If things appear hopelessly stalled, you can appeal to your U.S. Senator or Representative. In some cases, members of Congress have been able to unravel the red tape surrounding a foreign adoption. You can find the phone number of your senator's or representative's local or regional office in the government listings of your phone book.

Tell your story to a staff member, who will ask you to send in copies of the documents that you sent to the INS and the foreign government.

Stay in touch by telephone or over the Internet to ensure that the matter doesn't fall between the proverbial cracks. With some luck and a lot of persistence, you may find that your legislator's office has been able to clear the way.

**Your son's girlfriend is pregnant with his child. She says that she intends to put the baby up for adoption even though your son strongly objects.**

Your son has a legal right to keep his baby. However, if he presses his case, he has to provide for him, too. He cannot force his girlfriend to raise their child.

Many birth fathers choose not to take part in the adoption process, usually because either the birth mother refuses to say who the father is or because the father chooses not to acknowledge the child as his own.

### CONSIDER THE CONSEQUENCES

Your son must fully understand what will happen if he refuses to consent to the baby's adoption:

- If his girlfriend doesn't want the baby, he will have to raise the baby himself.
- If his girlfriend keeps the baby, he will have to provide support until the child turns 18, and perhaps even longer.
- He must also pay some or all of his girlfriend's pregnancy expenses.

While the thought of being a father may be very exciting, the long-term implications of this decision are enormous. If after careful consideration your son decides to fight the adoption, there are certain things he should get busy doing.

### MAKING A CLAIM OF PATERNITY

Your son should write his girlfriend a letter (sent certified mail, return receipt requested, keeping a copy for his records) acknowledging that the baby is his and offering to assist her. The next step depends on the state laws where he and the mother live, but most likely it is essential that he hire a lawyer immediately.

The laws regarding the rights of a birth father vary widely. In most states, he will be required to register with the state as the baby's *putative father*.

**SMART MOVES**

Your state's laws may place time limits on objecting to an adoption. With this in mind, urge your son to start taking the necessary steps for fighting the adoption as quickly as possible.

This will help him if his girlfriend claims that he is not the father; she may use this excuse as a ploy to proceed with the adoption. In other states, the birth mother's lawyer or adoption agency will have to prove that they tried to contact the birth father but were unsuccessful.

### NOTIFYING THE BIRTH FATHER

Not surprisingly, courts are usually reluctant to take away a birth father's rights without his knowledge. If your son's girlfriend refuses to name the father (or she says she truly doesn't know who the father is), her lawyer will need to contact the potential father and ask him for consent before an adoption can take place.

Some states allow a birth father to be notified of the intended adoption before the baby is born, while other states allow the notice to be given only after the baby is born. Your son has a specified time to contest the adoption, or his parental rights may be terminated and the adoption will proceed without his consent.

Even if your son tries to block the adoption, a variety of factors could keep him from being successful. He could lose his case if he has…

- A history of mental illness
- A history of drug or alcohol abuse
- A criminal record
- Been violent or abusive to his girlfriend.

### YOUR LAST RESORT

Adoptions occasionally take place without the birth father's consent. In these cases, when the birth father was able to show conclusively that he had been denied the right to block the adoption, the courts have ordered the adopted child to be returned to the birth father.

*You want to adopt a baby but the adoption agency refuses to consider your application because you are too old.*

Whether or not it is fair, adoption agencies often place age limits on prospective clients. Some agencies refuse to consider applications from anyone older than 40, for example; others will accept older applicants, but only for adoption of children with special needs, or for older children.

> *Pay expenses out of an escrow account so you have an itemized record for the court.*

### GETTING A PRIVATE ADOPTION

Happily, there are other options available for older couples and single people:

- **Independent adoptions** are those that take place without a state-licensed adoption agency. (Six states forbid them: Colorado, Connecticut, Delaware, Massachusetts, Minnesota, and North Dakota.)
- **Identified adoptions** are those in which the prospective adoptive parents find the birth mother, either by answering a newspaper ad or by contacting lawyers who represent birth

mothers. In states that don't allow independent adoptions, an agency must make the final arrangements for the prospective parents. These adoptions sidestep the age issue and have some other advantages as well:

- **More babies are available** for these adoptions than through agencies, so you will not have to wait as long for the child.
- **Prospective parents** can work with the birth parents to decide what kind of contact, if any, should take place between the child and the natural parents (a decision that's frequently imposed by an agency).
- **Adoptive parents** may watch the baby's birth and be able to bring the infant home immediately. In agency adoptions, adoptive parents are rarely present in the delivery room, and they may have to wait several days or more before they can receive their baby.

### HIRING A LAWYER

Whether you want to arrange an independent or identified adoption, it is essential to hire a lawyer who has a complete understanding of the process and the laws of your state. And before scheduling an appointment with a lawyer, be sure to ask about any fees. Unlike attorneys who specialize in some other areas of the law, adoption lawyers will rarely offer a free first consultation.

## WATCH WHAT YOU SPEND

No state allows a prospective adoptive parent to pay money that could be construed as a fee. Paying for the birth mother's education or giving her a lump sum of cash is considered by law to be baby-selling, which is illegal in every state.

Once you decide on an independent adoption and a birth mother is located, your expenses will be monitored by the court. Depending on where you live, you may be allowed to pay only for the birth mother's medical expenses and legal fees. In other states, you also may be permitted to pay other expenses, such as maternity clothes and the birth mother's housing. In any case, it's best to have your lawyer pay all expenses out of an escrow account, so you will have an itemized record that the court can review if needed.

## ADOPTING THE BABY

Shortly before the baby is born, or soon afterward, have the birth mother (and father, if he has been identified) sign papers that relinquish all parental rights. If the birth parents are minors, their parents may also need to sign the form.

The birth mother may want you to send her pictures of the baby or wish to visit the child from time to time. You should think about this very carefully. In some states, failing to live up to your agreement could allow the birth mother to reclaim her child, while in others she may be entitled to seek a court order to enforce the terms of your agreement.

After the consent is given, state laws typically give birth mothers a chance to withdraw their consent. In many states, the birth mother must take action within a few days, but in a few states she may have as much as six months to act. Your lawyer can tell you how long you have to wait. After that, it is extremely unlikely that an adoption will be overturned—unless there is strong evidence of duress, fraud, or a serious violation of the rights of the birth parents.

---

### HIRING AN ADOPTION LAWYER

Even though many lawyers run ads saying that they are experienced in adoption cases, not all are well qualified. Here are some questions to ask before hiring an adoption lawyer:

■ **How long has the attorney handled independent adoptions?** While a new lawyer may be capable, one with more experience is likely to have a better understanding of the process and an established network of contacts with court administrators, social workers, and judges that can help speed the process and avoid pitfalls.

■ **How much of the practice is devoted to independent adoptions** and how many have been handled this year? Look for more than half the cases to involve independent adoptions. Dozens of cases a year allow individual attention; hundreds of cases don't.

■ **What are the usual fees for handling an independent adoption?** Fees vary widely depending on the experience of the lawyer and where you live. For example, someone practicing in downtown Chicago is likely to charge a higher fee than someone in a rural area of Illinois.

■ **Can the lawyer handle an adoption if the birth mother lives in another state?** In this case, your lawyer must know the Interstate Compact on the Placement of Children (ICPC), a contract among all 50 states, the District of Columbia, and the U.S. Virgin Islands. Your lawyer's knowledge of the ICPC is critical; failure to meet its requirements can result in having an interstate adoption overturned and the child returned to his or her state of birth.

■ **Will the lawyer pursue a lawsuit if the birth mother changes her mind at the last minute, or will the case be referred to another lawyer?** If there is to be another lawyer involved, you will want to interview that lawyer, too, so you are prepared for any trouble ahead.

Discuss your concerns with the manager of the daycare center. It may be that these changes are only temporary: Staff numbers can fluctuate because of unexpected resignations, illness, or even a death in the family. If the manager assures you that the problem will be rectified in the near future, you may decide to wait awhile and see what happens.

Every state licenses its daycare centers and establishes the minimum requirements a center must meet in order to operate legally. While you are waiting for the problem to be fixed, you can do some research into your state's standards:

- **Learn the staff-to-child requirement.** This ratio varies according to state law and in many cases will depend on the ages of the children cared for at the center. In Colorado, for example, one staff member can be in charge of as many as 10 one-year-olds, but when children reach the age of three, there must be one staff member for every 6 children.
- **Learn your state's requirements for daycare centers** regarding whether they should provide a certain number of activities, such as outdoor play and regular nap time.

## PUT IT IN WRITING

If the situation continues, notify the center in writing of your concerns. Your letter should explain the nature of your complaint ("There are fewer staff members per child than when my child was enrolled") and mention your previous contact with the center's manager ("When we spoke last month, you assured me that this problem was only temporary, but as of today the situation has not changed").

Finish the letter by describing the actions that you demand the center take ("I expect that the staff will be increased to the appropriate number per child no later than next week"). Keep a copy of the letter and send the original to the center by certified mail, return receipt requested.

## YOUR LAST RESORT

If your letter doesn't work, you have two options:

- **Enlist the help of the state agency** that regulates daycare centers. You can get the agency's name, address, and phone number from the general information operator of the state government. In some states, you may have to make a complaint in writing; in others, a telephone call may trigger an investigation. In either case, you should get the name of the person who will handle your complaint. Provide him or her with copies of your correspondence about the problem.
- **You can move your child to another daycare center.**

> **TAKE NOTE** *Keep in mind that state agencies regulating daycare providers are very busy. It may take some time before the agency can act—unless the problem you describe poses an immediate danger to the safety of the children. You must be persistent in pressing your case.*

> **Y**our son has been expelled from school. You are upset because you don't think such a harsh punishment fits the "crime."

In the 1960s, '70s, and '80s, students who needed disciplining often were sent into counseling instead of being suspended or expelled from school. In the 1990s and beyond, however, student violence, sexual assault, and harassment have led to more and more kids being suspended or expelled from their schools. "Zero tolerance" has become the watchword of the day.

## Find Out the Facts

Although state laws vary, most school districts cannot expel a student immediately without notifying the student's parents first and providing them with an opportunity to respond. Here's what you can do:

- ■ **Make an appointment with the school's principal** if your son was severely disciplined.
- ■ **Find out why such action was taken** and whether he received any less severe disciplinary punishments before this.

## Attend Any Hearing

The length of expulsions differs. If the punishment is for more than a few days, a disciplinary committee must hold a hearing. The panel will review the charges and determine if the penalty is appropriate. You and your child should go to this hearing. He should be given the chance to respond to the charges, and you may also be given a chance to speak on his behalf.

If it is evident that your child feels remorse about what he did, or if it is clear that the punishment is inappropriate given the level of the offense, the hearing panel may reduce the punishment from expulsion to a less severe one, such as limiting or prohibiting participation in extra-curricular activities.

## Appealing Your Case

You have a right to appeal this decision to the full school board if you are dissatisfied with the results of the hearing. You must request the appeal hearing within a specific time period, usually 30 days. Although school-board hearings are less formal than a court proceeding, most states allow a student to have a lawyer or other spokesperson at this hearing. In cases where there may be a language barrier, a translator may be provided.

In most cases, the school board will not review the evidence at the appeal hearing. It will consider only whether the student was treated fairly in the earlier proceedings and if the school followed proper procedure in ordering the expulsion. (The only evidence that will be considered is anything that wasn't available earlier.) In most cases, unless there has been an obvious failure in the original disciplinary hearing, the school board is likely to uphold the decision. However, an appeal may be successful for several reasons:

- ● If the student and parents weren't informed of the discipline policies
- ● If the expulsion was based on actions unrelated to school activity

- If the parents weren't given adequate notice of the hearing
- If the hearing wasn't held within the time limits required by law.

If the school board finds in favor of the student, it has several options. It may overrule the expulsion, remand the matter to the committee that ordered the expulsion for reconsideration, or reduce the penalty based on its own findings.

## YOUR LAST RESORT

If you still feel strongly that your son has been treated unfairly, you can hire a lawyer and sue in state court to have your child readmitted to the school and have the expulsion deleted from his school record. Although courts tend to respect the decisions of administrators in disciplining students, the courts have ruled against school districts across the country in several cases. If your case is strong, your suit may succeed.

## WHEN CAN YOUR CHILD BE EXPELLED?

Because expulsion is such a serious matter, most states set out the specific grounds for expulsion in their statutes. Although these vary somewhat from state to state, expulsion can usually be ordered if a student does any of the following:

- Deliberately causes or attempts to cause physical injury to another student, a teacher, or other school personnel

- Brings a gun, knife, explosive, or other dangerous object onto school property

- Possesses, uses, sells, or attempts to sell controlled substances or drug paraphernalia on school property

- Engages in habitual profanity, obscenity, or other disruptive behavior in defiance of the authority of school personnel

- Commits or attempts to commit a robbery or engages in extortion

- Steals or tries to steal school property

- Possesses alcoholic beverages or is under the influence of alcohol on school property

- Causes or tries to cause serious damage to school property or the property of other students

- Engages in sexual harassment of other students or school personnel

*Y*our son has a disability, and his school
says it doesn't have the resources to educate him.

Disabilities come in many forms, from learning difficulties to physical impairment. If a school district really doesn't have the resources to give your child what he needs, the district is obligated to place him in a private school at no cost to you. In several instances, school districts have had to enroll disabled students in private residential schools—and pay for boarding and all educational costs.

## THE LAW IS ON YOUR SIDE

Remind the school district of its legal obligations to your child. Two federal laws, the Education for All Handicapped Children Act and the Individuals With Disabilities Education Act, set out the government's requirements for the education of disabled children. Under these laws, trained professionals must evaluate your child and create an *Individualized Education Program*

(IEP) for him. The school district may also be required to provide speech, language, and physical therapy; counseling; and other services to help your child get the most from his education.

---

*S*chool districts must place disabled students in the least restrictive environment.

---

In some cases, the law covers preschool children with disabilities, but generally it covers those who, by law, have to go to school (from age 6 to age 18). Older students are also entitled to transition services, such as vocational training and independent-living programs, designed to help them move from school to the outside world.

**TAKE NOTE** *The school should consult with you as it evaluates your child. It's important to remember that the law requires school districts to place disabled students in the least restrictive environment. This means that your child should be included in regular school programs as much as possible. In extreme situations, your child may need to have an aide help him do daily tasks, take care of himself, and go from class to class.*

## Your Right to an Appeal

Once your child's school district has created his IEP, it must notify you of…

- The results of the evaluation
- Where the school district has decided your child will be placed
- The services that must be provided.

You have the right to appeal any part of your child's Individualized Education Program. If you disagree with your child's program, you have the right to a hearing before the state education agency. It can revise the IEP, including ordering additional services and overruling the school district's placement decision.

## Your Last Resort

If you are still dissatisfied with the results of the appeals hearing, you have the right to file a lawsuit against the school district. You will need to hire a lawyer with specialized experience. An advocacy group, such as the National Information Center for Children and Youth With Disabilities, can provide information on local support groups and guidance in pursuing your appeal.

---

*Y*our teenage daughter is running with a wild crowd. You want to stop her misbehavior and fear being liable for the damage she does.

---

You have reason to be concerned. Recent cases in which children have committed serious crimes give parents reason to worry about their liability for their children's acts. In the 1999 Columbine High School shooting case in Colorado, for example, two teenagers murdered more than a dozen classmates and a teacher. The parents of the students had lawsuits seeking millions in damages filed against them.

Rebellious behavior is hardly new. In the '50s movie *Rebel Without a Cause,* the sullen teenager portrayed by actor James Dean was emblematic of a generation that questioned the authority of their parents and foreshadowed the counterculture of the '60s. But in those days, parents were stricter. Most not only believed that they had the right to spank their young children but were also more adamant about their teenagers' adherence to curfews and other rules.

Today the situation is different: Most parents wouldn't dream of striking their children (indeed, severe physical punishment can lead to charges of child abuse), and they allow teenagers more freedom. However, parents do have an obligation to watch over their children and to instill certain standards of behavior in the youngsters.

## TAKING CONTROL

As a parent, you have certain rights in bringing up your children:

- **A child's privacy at home,** according to the courts, is a privilege to be earned rather than an entitlement. You, as a parent, have a right (and perhaps a responsibility) to screen your children's phone calls, restrict their access to the Internet, and limit the programs that they watch on television, as well as censor the books that they read, the movies that they see, and the music that they listen to. Your child does not have a legally protected right to privacy in your home.
- **Search rights.** You may look through your child's room, drawers, closets, and backpack without legal interference.
- **Drug testing.** Although the law hasn't addressed the issue of home drug-testing, courts that have heard these cases have been reluctant to interfere when parents require their children to submit to testing.

## UNDERSTANDING A PROBLEM

It's important to try to understand why a youngster is behaving in a self-destructive way. Get professional help for your child if you suspect that he or she has a serious problem, such as drug addiction, depression, or an eating disorder.

In an extreme situation, you may have to admit your child to a drug rehabilitation facility or a mental hospital. The courts have held that you may commit your child without his or her consent in these instances:

- **If you have a doctor's opinion** that it is medically necessary
- **If a neutral investigator,** like a social worker, agrees with it. The opinion of such a professional must be based on what he or she has discovered about your child's background and relationships.

Your child's condition must be reevaluated periodically in order to determine if his or her confinement should be continued.

## ARE YOU LIABLE?

In situations where children are out of control without an identifiable medical condition, you won't have the option of medical treatment or confinement. And as long as your daughter is in your custody, you can be held liable for any intentional or malicious acts she commits, although state laws generally limit the amount you have to pay. (For example, Texas law makes the parent who has custody of a child liable for as much as $15,000 when the child willfully or maliciously damages property.) Parental liability typically continues until a child turns 18, although the age varies by a year or two in some states. Liability may also end when a child…

- Gets married
- Enters the military
- Runs away
- Refuses to submit to reasonable parental supervision.

## YOUR LAST RESORT

If your daughter consistently refuses to obey you, has been truant from school, has run away from home, or is frequently in trouble with the police or school authorities, you may want to consider filing what is known as a PINS petition. "PINS"

stands for Person in Need of Supervision. The juvenile court will hold a hearing to determine whether your daughter is out of your control and needs court supervision. Your daughter is entitled to have a lawyer represent her at the hearing.

A child who is declared a PINS by the juvenile court is ordered to follow rules set by the court and to report to a probation officer regularly. A child who refuses to comply with the court order can be taken into state custody and sent to a foster home or group home until her behavior improves or she reaches adulthood. A PINS petition is not to be taken lightly, and you should consult a lawyer or your local social services department before taking such a drastic step.

## YOUR CHILD AND DRUGS

Illegal drug and alcohol abuse by teenagers—and younger children—continues to be a problem in our society. A 1999 survey found that nearly 80 percent of the high school students who were polled reported that illegal drugs were being used, sold, or kept at school.

Young people begin taking drugs for a variety of reasons: to fit in with friends, to feel grown up, to relax, to satisfy curiosity, or to rebel against authority. Physical signs of drug use include changes in appetite, rapid weight gain or loss, poor coordination, slurred speech, shaking hands or other body tremors, and sleep problems. Behavioral signs include forgetfulness; excessive secrecy or paranoia; a decreased interest in school, hobbies, and family activities; truancy; stealing; and chronic dishonesty.

The best way to prevent the use of illegal drugs is to begin early. Pay attention to your children's behavior and to your own.

- **Don't come home from work** and announce that you need a drink to relax—you may be sending your child the wrong message.

- **Set limits for your child's behavior** and be consistent. Don't allow her to manipulate you into allowing her to violate curfew or engage in risky behavior "just this once."

- **Know your child's friends** and get to know their parents, too. Some parents see no harm in allowing their child to drink alcohol or use drugs, arguing that "he's going to do it anyway, so I'd rather he did it here at home." Don't let him go to homes where this attitude prevails.

- **Know where your children are,** what they are doing, and who they are with. You may want to have your child check in with you on a regular basis when she is away from home. A beeper and cell phone are a good way to keep in contact with her.

- **Let your child know that he can come to you** with a problem and that you will help him find a solution. A child who is afraid to share his concerns about academic or social problems may turn to his peers, who may encourage drug use as a way to get through a difficult time.

- **Don't try to be your child's friend.** Your youngster will have many friends, but only you and your spouse will be the child's parents. Be firm, be fair, be fun, but be responsible.

Getting a divorce without a lawyer is relatively easy—if your case isn't complicated or if the divorce is uncontested. In Arizona, for example, residents can use computers at their local courthouse to get divorce forms. In other states, the court clerk has the documents you need to file for divorce, obtain custody and support, and arrange parental visitation.

## NOT A GOOD IDEA IF...

Just because you can represent yourself, however, doesn't necessarily mean that you should. Before deciding to represent yourself in a divorce, you need to consider several factors. Do-it-yourself divorces are usually not a good idea if...

- You and your spouse are parents. Because issues of child custody and support can be complicated, it's best to get professional advice about the laws in your state that protect your children's interests.
- Significant assets need to be divided, such as an inheritance, a business, or pension benefits.
- You and your spouse own your home or other real estate.
- You have been married for a long time.
- You have been unemployed for years.
- You need professional help to determine how much support you should receive and how long it should continue.
- You have serious health problems that require expensive medical treatment.
- You and your spouse can't agree on the division of property.
- Your spouse has hired a lawyer to contest the divorce.

## DIVORCE WITHOUT A LAWYER

If you decide that you *can* get a divorce without a lawyer, follow these relatively simple steps:

- **You and your spouse should write and sign an agreement** stating how your property and other assets will be divided; this will become part of your divorce decree.
- **Cancel all credit cards or accounts that you and your spouse hold jointly,** and have new cards issued or new accounts opened only in your name. Even though your spouse may agree to pay bills on joint accounts, you can still be held liable if he or she doesn't follow through by making payments.
- **Fill out the appropriate summons and complaint forms** and file them in court. There is a filing fee, usually less than $100. You will need to hire a process server to have them delivered to your spouse. Your spouse will file a document known as an *answer,* responding to your complaint. If he or she has decided not to contest the divorce, the answer will essentially be a consent to dissolve the marriage.

The court will then review the papers you have filed and decide whether the agreement you and your spouse have reached is a fair one. State courts often require that you appear in court to verify the facts under oath.

Once the court has approved your agreement, a judgment will be entered into the court record and you will be granted a divorce decree. Keep in mind, however, that although you and your spouse are divorced, you may not be free to remarry immediately. Some states require a waiting period of several weeks to several months before your divorce decree becomes final.

## FREE AT LAST

Once your divorce has been granted, notify creditors and companies you do business with that you are no longer married. If you are a woman and have resumed using your maiden name or taken a new last name, you will need to notify several agencies, including...

- The Social Security Administration (do this immediately) to ensure that your earnings record continues to be credited accurately
- The Internal Revenue Service and the department of revenue in your state
- The U.S. Postal Service
- The Department of Motor Vehicles
- All major credit-reporting agencies.

Getting a divorce without a lawyer is its own reward. While the paperwork may be more than tedious, you have the satisfaction of achieving what seems to be a monumental and critical task at the lowest possible price.

## HOW TO HIRE A DIVORCE LAWYER

While many lawyers say that they handle divorce cases, many may have done only simple cases. Interview several candidates before you hire one. Here are some questions to ask:

■ **How long have you practiced law, and how much of your practice is devoted to divorce cases?** The more time spent on divorce cases the better, but this area of the law should account for at least half of the lawyer's practice.

■ **Do you represent both men and women?** A lawyer who represents only one sex or the other may lack insight into the mindset of the opposite sex, or may have some kind of personal ax to grind.

■ **Do you try to settle disputes before going to court?** Some lawyers are proud of their reputation for fighting over details. If that's your style, fine. But many clients want to minimize conflict and stress and like the fact that compromise lowers the cost of their divorce.

■ **Will you be handling my case, or will most of the work be done by an associate or paralegal?** If the lawyer you are speaking to won't be handling the bulk of the work, you are talking to the wrong person. Ask to speak to the people who will be representing you.

■ **When can I expect to have my telephone calls returned?** Most of the complaints that people make against lawyers concern unreturned telephone calls. As a rule, your lawyer should call you back within one business day—or have someone from the office contact you, if he or she cannot.

■ **How much will the divorce cost, and how will I be billed?** Once an experienced divorce lawyer knows your case, he should be able to estimate how much your divorce is going to cost. Keep in mind that estimates are just that; complications or a stubborn opponent can quickly raise costs.

■ **Can you handle this case for a flat fee?** Some lawyers will agree to represent you for a flat fee, especially if your case isn't too complex. If you have serious issues about custody, child support, or about dividing your property, however, don't be surprised if the attorney refuses to agree to a flat fee.

*Your divorce lawyer sends you bill after bill, but you don't see any progress in the case.*

Unless your divorce is an easy one (and many lawyers will tell you there is no such thing), the process can be expensive. Divorce lawyers can usually tell you how much it is going to cost before they represent you. But your legal bill will increase very quickly if…

■ **Your spouse's attorney** takes a confrontational approach to the divorce. She can file a lot of motions, each of which needs a response from your lawyer.

■ **You call your attorney** frequently with questions or concerns. Many lawyers charge in 10- or 15-minute increments. So each time you speak to your lawyer about your divorce, even if it's only for a moment or two on the telephone, you could find yourself billed for a full quarter hour of his time.

Don't be afraid to ask your lawyer to make your legal fees more affordable. When you hire your lawyer, he should draw up a document known as a *retainer agreement.* This letter explains that the lawyer agrees to represent you and states the fees that he will charge for his services. A retainer agreement should also list additional costs you will be billed for, such as photocopies, telephone calls, mileage for travel to interview witnesses, and fees you'll be charged for filing documents with the court.

## WAYS TO CUT COSTS

Keep in mind that this agreement isn't set in stone. You may be able to negotiate a less expensive divorce. Here's what you can do to cut costs:

- **Ask him to allow your telephone calls** shorter than five minutes to be free of charge.
- **Check to see how much your lawyer charges** for photocopies and faxes. Some law offices charge as much as 50 cents per page for copying and $2.00 per page for a fax. Ask the lawyer to lower these charges to what a local photocopy shop might charge. There's no reason for a lawyer to inflate the cost of providing these routine office services in order to pad his profit margin.
- **Make sure the agreement has a clause** that prevents your lawyer from charging for time spent responding to questions about his bill.
- **Make sure that your agreement provides for the return** of any unused retainer fee that you paid up front.
- **Ask your lawyer if other people can help** with your case as a way to reduce your fees. For example, in some states a summons can be served by any adult who isn't involved in the proceedings, rather than by a sheriff or a lawyer. And if your lawyer has a paralegal on staff, he or she may be able to do some of the paperwork at a reduced cost.

**TAKE NOTE** *Your agreement should state that your lawyer will give you your files if you should change lawyers and that he will not withhold them for payment. A lawyer who unreasonably refuses to release a client's files in order to collect fees may be in violation of the profession's ethical rules and can be reported to the state's attorney disciplinary body.*

## SMART MOVES

Keep a record of the dates, times, length, and nature of phone calls to your lawyer (and any other contact that you have with him) and check it against your legal bill.

## READ YOUR BILLS CAREFULLY

If you think your bill is higher than it should be, tell your concerns to your lawyer directly. Today most lawyers send itemized bills every month, but a few lawyers, especially some older ones, may send you a lump-sum bill "for services rendered." This is ethically unacceptable, because it doesn't allow the client to know how much work the lawyer has actually done and how long it took him to do various aspects of the work related to your divorce case.

If you aren't getting itemized bills, you should request them immediately. Review them carefully, referring to your record book as needed. You may find that what was a short telephone call is being billed as an office visit. If you are satisfied with your lawyer's performance, give him the benefit of the doubt. Call it to his attention as a clerical error, and the bill will probably be corrected immediately.

## YOUR LAST RESORT

Lawyers are ethically bound to charge reasonable fees, although what is reasonable is debatable. If you are still unable to get your legal bill corrected, or if your lawyer is extremely uncooperative, what action you take may depend on how far along you are in the divorce process. If it is nearly completed, you may want to keep your lawyer anyway. If your divorce is at an early stage, you may want to dismiss your lawyer and give your case to another who is more responsive and less expensive. However, you should never fire your attorney before you hire a new one. In the interval, you might inadvertently overlook a deadline for a motion or fail to attend a hearing and jeopardize your case or delay its progress unnecessarily.

In either case, you can file a complaint with your state's attorney disciplinary committee. (If you choose to keep your lawyer, wait until *after* the case is settled.) In some states, this panel is regulated by a department of the state's highest court; in others, it is part of the state bar association. The panel will consider factors such as the lawyer's experience, the difficulty of your divorce case, and the range of fees charged by other attorneys in your area. If it finds that your lawyer has violated the rules of professional conduct, he or she can be ordered to make restitution and could be suspended from practicing law or could even face being disbarred.

## Your ex-husband is behind on his child-support payments and seems to be unable to get back on track.

Bringing up baby often includes a struggle with your ex about child support. While Congress has passed a number of laws designed to help custodial parents collect child support, many of these laws are not very effective. You can improve the odds by being persistent and by taking some unconventional steps.

### COLLECTING HIS WAGES

Because so many parents don't make support payments, the law requires an automatic deduction of child-support payments from the noncustodial parent's paycheck, unless both parents agree to another arrangement. The employer sends the deducted money directly to the court, which then forwards the payment to the custodial parent.

**TAKE NOTE** *Wage deductions can only be made from the paycheck from a full-time job. If your ex-husband freelances, you are out of luck.*

If your ex changes jobs, he may not tell his new employer about the deduction order. If you find that he has a new job, contact the court so it can arrange for payroll deductions.

What can you do if your ex-husband changes jobs and refuses to disclose his new employer? Some mothers have gone so far as to hire a private detective to find out where the delinquent dad is working. But before you take such a step, there are a couple of other resources to tap:

- **If your ex-husband is a union member,** his local union may provide you with information about his new employer.
- **Ask your local child-support enforcement agency** to help you get the Internal Revenue Service to release information from your husband's tax return.

### GOING TO COURT

You can hire a lawyer to help you enforce payment through your state or district attorney's office—although the backlog of cases may mean your case is not a high priority. In some states, lawyers take child-support cases on a contingency basis. This means they take a percentage of the amount collected, but not every state permits lawyers to handle these cases on this basis. And while you will have legal fees, the court can order the delinquent parent to pay them.

Some collection agencies (listed in the Yellow Pages of the phone book) will also take on child-support collection cases. But they also usually charge a percentage of the money they collect as their fee.

**TAKE NOTE** *Never hire a collection agency that asks for a fee up front—it will likely do little or nothing for you, because it already has your money.*

### GETTING THE GOVERNMENT TO HELP

More drastic methods for collecting child support:

- **Seize his tax refund.** The court can notify the Internal Revenue Service and state tax department. Any refund owed to the nonpaying parent can be intercepted and sent to the court.

- **See to it that he loses his license.** In some states, a delinquent parent can lose his driver's license, and in a few states, any professional license he may have.

---

*The law requires an automatic deduction of child-support payments from the non-custodial parent's paycheck.*

---

- **Place a lien** against your ex-husband's personal property, such as his car, or against the real estate he owns. This can make it difficult for him to sell without first meeting his obligation and satisfying his child-support debt. State laws may limit the kind of property that you can file a lien against, so you should consult with your child-support enforcement agency or a lawyer to find out the specific rules in your state.

- **Have him sent to jail.** State and federal laws make it a crime when a parent who can pay court-ordered child support doesn't do so. In some states, this may be a felony, leading to a stint in state prison.

When a father who lives in one state fails to pay support to a child living in another, it is a federal offense. You'll have to work with your state attorney general to coordinate collection efforts. Be persistent.

### YOUR LAST RESORT

Many prosecuting attorneys feel that putting a deadbeat parent in prison defeats the purpose of child support: A parent in jail can't earn money to support his children. So if you think that the only way to get your ex-husband to pay is a threat of a criminal prosecution, you will have to be persistent. A number of mothers have sought the help of newspaper columnists and television reporters in bringing their problem to public attention. The unforgiving glare of the media spotlight can bring pressure on a reluctant prosecutor and the deadbeat dad.

---

*Your divorce decree states that you should be able to see your children according to a certain schedule. Now your ex-wife refuses to let you be with them.*

---

Child custody and visitation are white-hot issues for many divorced couples. Either the ex-spouses can't agree to an arrangement, or they are so hostile to each other that they cannot be civil long enough to transfer their children from one home to the other.

### REMIND HER FIRST

If your ex-wife refuses to follow the schedule, remind her of the agreed terms. (In some cases, especially when visits don't follow a regular pattern, parents can lose track of what is required.) Reiterate that visitation has been ordered because the court has ruled that it is in your child's best interest to spend time with you. Don't make the mistake of withholding child-support payments when you are denied visitation. In every state, the obligation to provide support is separate from the right to visitation. If you retaliate by cutting off child support, you might…

- Find yourself in court
- Have your wages garnished (payments are deducted directly from your paycheck)
- Have other collection agencies taking action against you
- Be fined or sent to jail for being in contempt of court.

### PUT IT IN WRITING

If you are still not able to see your child, write a letter (send it certified mail, return receipt requested) to your ex-wife stating that you are not being allowed the visitation required by the court. Indicate that you would prefer to maintain a cordial relationship for the sake of your child, but that you will not continue to allow the visitation schedule to be ignored.

**TAKE NOTE** *If your ex-wife had a lawyer in the divorce proceedings, he should also receive a copy of the letter.*

### YOUR LAST RESORT

If your ex continues to ignore the visitation schedule, you probably have no other choice but to hire a lawyer, return to court, and ask the court to enforce its order. The judge may find her in contempt of court for violating the schedule and give her a warning. If she continues to resist, there will be another hearing, and your ex-spouse could be held in contempt of court—and either fined or put in jail, or both.

---

> **You know that your ex-wife is neglecting your children and you want to step in. How can you get your custody agreement changed?**

---

What can you do if you know that your children are being mistreated? Courts can respond to changes in the lives of parents, but *only* when it is in the best interest of the children. In most states, the law requires courts to consider a joint-custody arrangement first (page 32). This permits both parents to be actively involved in making decisions that affect the children. Even in joint-custody arrangements, however, one parent may be granted physical custody, with the children living primarily with that parent.

So many parents use the threat of modifying custody against their ex-spouses that courts in most states have reduced the number of child-custody battles they review. For example, some states restrict these requests in the first year after divorce to those that claim the children are endangered by the current setup.

### TAKE CHARGE OF THE SITUATION

You may be able to talk to your ex-wife and tactfully suggest that the children move in with you. If the situation that alarms you is a temporary one (for example, as a result of a change in work schedule or a health problem), this is probably the best solution. When life returns to normal, the children can return to their legal home, and custody and visitation will resume as before.

**TAKE NOTE** *Without the court's knowledge or approval of the change, you still have*

*to continue support payments to your ex-wife even though the children are living with you.*

---

> **Think carefully about your motives, but do not hesitate to act if your children are truly at risk.**

---

Your ex-wife may not agree to let the children's live with you. If you think it is key for them to move, you will have to go to court. (Although you can do this on your own, you may find that hiring the lawyer who handled your divorce will make the process go more smoothly.) You will have to show that you are able to provide a more reliable and stable environment for your children than their mother can. In addition, if the divorce is relatively recent, you may have to show that the children are in danger, such as being exposed to drug or alcohol abuse, going without medical attention, or being physically abused. This may be easier to prove if your children are youngsters rather than teenagers.

### THE CHILDREN COME FIRST

If your children are older, the court may interview them. While the court may consider their wishes in the matter, it won't be bound by them. In each case the judge will make a decision that is based on what is in their best interest.

**TAKE NOTE** *Don't try to undermine the children's relationship with your ex. Criticizing the custodial parent, coaching the children about what to say in court, or bribing them with gifts almost guarantees that the current (and unsatisfactory)* *arrangement will be upheld. Judges who handle divorces have experience in custody disputes, and they won't be swayed by such behavior.*

Remember that your children's interests, not your own, should always come first. Before you challenge your ex in court, think carefully about your motives. Do not hesitate to act, however, if your children are truly at risk.

---

# Your ex-wife has custody of your children and you've just found out that she plans to move out of the state.

Your ex-wife may think she is a rolling stone and want to start looking for a new life. She has that right, but not, perhaps, if she is taking your children with her. Courts can intervene, especially when her move means that your children will lose contact with you.

## TRY TO COMPROMISE

Your ex-wife may be willing to work out a modified custody and visitation schedule that will allow you to spend the same amount of time—or even more time—with your children. If so, you can file your new agreement with the court that issued the original custody order.

## GOING TO COURT

If she won't cooperate, ask the court for a revision of the custody and visitation order (page 30). You can do this on your own, but you may wish to hire a lawyer. Courts will modify an existing order only if you can show there is going to be a major change in circumstances (for example, a move out of the country, not to a nearby state). The court is more likely to order a change in custody and visitation…

● If your ex-wife had interfered with your right to visit your children previously or had denied you visitation
● If the move will interfere with your children's education
● If the move will have a negative effect on their relationship with you and their other family members.

On the other hand, if your ex-wife has been cooperative about allowing you to visit your children, has been their primary caregiver, and is moving to pursue a financially rewarding job opportunity, it may be more difficult to change your custody arrangement.

If your children are 10 years old or older, the court may want to know their opinion about the move and how they feel it will affect their lives. The judge hearing your motion will usually interview the children in chambers—out of your presence—to encourage them to speak freely. While the court isn't bound to follow their wishes to continue living near you, it may do so if the children express concerns about disruptions in their lives or if they would prefer to stay in familiar surroundings. As a rule, the older the child, the more likely the court is to consider his wishes.

**TAKE NOTE** *Never attempt to bribe, coerce, or coach your children into claiming that they are opposed to a move, and don't encourage other family members to do so. Judges are alert to these tactics and are likely to dismiss your motion as a result of your actions.*

## WHAT THE COURT CAN DO

After hearing the evidence, the court can…

- **Allow your ex-wife to make the move** with the children, but increase the visitation time that you have with them.
- **Order you and your ex-wife to share the cost** of transportation between the two homes.
- **Change the child-custody order** and require that your ex-wife give you custody, and make provisions giving her liberal visitation rights.
- **Require you both to go into mediation** to work out a plan tailored to your individual situation and that is agreeable to both of you.

---

### CHILD-CUSTODY ARRANGEMENTS

As a rule, custody arrangements are to be in the best interests of the child—whatever that may mean. Here are typical arrangements that courts can choose from:

- **Joint Legal Custody**. Both parents make the important decisions regarding their child's welfare, such as health care, education, and religious training. This arrangement works best when both parents can put aside their personal differences and concentrate on what's best for their child. This can be a nightmare if parents are confrontational and unable to work cooperatively. Still, many states' laws require judges to consider this arrangement first. And more than 20 states permit a judge to order joint custody even when one parent objects.

- **Joint Physical Custody**. The child regularly alternates living with one parent and the other. Sometimes the child spends one week with one parent and the following week with the other parent. In a few situations, courts have allowed a child to change his or her living quarters every day. For joint physical custody to succeed, the divorced parents must live fairly close to one another so the child can go to one school. This arrangement works best when the divorced parents can coordinate schedules for school and extracurricular activities and agree on bedtimes and discipline.

- **Sole Custody**. One parent makes the important decisions about the child's life and takes daily care of him or her. The other parent has no say in these matters. Usually, the noncustodial parent has visitation rights on weekends and holidays and during school vacations.

- **Split Custody**. One parent has custody of one (or more) of the children, while the other children are in the other parent's custody. In some cases, one or more of the children may have a serious conflict with a parent, while the other children don't. In other cases, split custody may be awarded because the children have problems with each other. Split custody is not normally favored by the courts except in unusual circumstances.

*Your son and daughter-in-law rely on you to raise their children. Because your arrangement is informal, you have trouble coping and paying for your grandchildren's care.*

Today almost 4 million children live in households headed by their grandparents. Most of these arrangements have no court approval or supervision. And here is where the trouble lies. Without legal power, grandparents find themselves helpless…

- When a child needs the consent of a parent or legal guardian for any medical treatment
- When the school near the grandparent's house won't allow the child to enroll without a formal custody order
- When the school won't let the child participate in school activities that require a parent's or guardian's consent.

## GETTING CUSTODY

Before you go for custody, consider your own age, health, and financial circumstances. Ask yourself the following questions:

- Can you provide guidance and care for your grandchildren until they reach adulthood?
- Do you have the strength and stamina to care for them?
- Are you willing to engage in what may be a protracted legal battle over custody?
- Can someone else in the family step in and get custody?

If you can answer these questions to your satisfaction and decide to seek the legal custody of your grandchildren, keep in mind that the law in most states recognizes *parental preference* in child-custody disputes. This means that the law presumes that it is in the children's best interests to be in the custody of their parents rather than in the custody of their grandparents.

**SMART MOVES**

Your state's social-services agency may be able to help you get your daughter-in-law and son's consent for a change in custody, which could avoid a bitter court battle.

If the parents agree to it, however, you can get custody. Discuss the situation with them. If all's well, you can file a petition in court.

## WHEN THE PARENTS ARE UNFIT

If they don't agree, you will have to prove that your son and daughter-in-law are unfit to care for their children. For example, they have abandoned them or have serious problems with drugs or alcohol. You may have to show police reports, get a social worker to testify, and you may also testify.

While many parents who have abandoned their children don't contest a custody award, others—either because they resent what they see as interference or because they regret having left their children—will contest a petition for custody.

## STARTING THE LEGAL BALL ROLLING

Draw up a petition, either on your own or with the help of a lawyer, asking that the court give you custody and order your son and daughter-in-law to pay child support. You will also need to notify the parents that you have begun the proceeding by issuing a summons. Get the official summons form from the clerk of the court and work with the clerk to have it *served,* or delivered to them legally.

If your son and daughter-in-law have moved and you don't know where they live, you may have to place a notice of your petition in the newspaper. This is called *service by publication.* The rules governing this kind of notice vary from place to place, and you may need a lawyer or grandparents' rights organization to help you to do it legally. Otherwise your son and his wife can contest the custody decision later—a situation that will needlessly harm the children.

---

# Your former son-in-law has custody of your grandchildren and he refuses to let you see them.

To most kids, grandparents rule. But this important relationship is often overlooked in the upheaval of divorce or separation. The issue of a grandparent's right to visit his or her grandchildren is being tested by lawyers and judges alike. The Supreme Courts in several states have recently placed limits on grandparents' rights to see their grandchildren, and the U.S. Supreme Court has recently ruled on the matter (see box "The Shifting Sands of Grandparents' Rights," facing page).

## Why He May Be Denying You Visits

Before taking legal action, consider the reasons your former son-in-law may have for not letting you see your grandchildren:

- **He may be angry** with your daughter and be trying to punish her by denying you visitation.
- **Your daughter has lost her parental rights** (because she was found to be an unfit mother), and your son-in-law may feel that her loss includes you as well. Fortunately, most state laws make grandparent visitation a right separate from that of the noncustodial parent.
- **Your daughter has died,** and your son-in-law may believe that having you close to them will bring up painful memories.

In any case, it is always best to try to negotiate an arrangement in a friendly, nonconfrontational manner first. If you can't convince your former son-in-law that it is important for you to have a relationship with your grandchildren, you may have to go to court.

## Taking Action

To get a visitation order, you will need to file a motion in the appropriate state court (often it is the district court where the grandchild lives that has jurisdiction) and pay a filing fee—usually amounting to less than $100.

Your former son-in-law can oppose your motion, either because he does not want you to see the children or because he feels that the schedule you propose is unreasonable. If he files an answer that opposes visitation, a court hearing will be scheduled and you should probably hire a lawyer to represent your cause.

You and the children's father will each have a chance to present your side of the argument, and if the court finds that granting you visitation is in the best interests of your grandchildren, it will then grant an order. And if you win your case, the court may require your former son-in-law to pay your legal fees.

## When You See Your Grandchildren

Follow the schedule approved by the court. When you are with them, be sure that you...

- Don't discuss their father in a negative way
- Don't make statements about his lifestyle or his religious beliefs (or lack of them)
- Don't say or do anything that could be seen as undermining his authority as a parent.

You don't want the court to modify or terminate your rights as a result of how you act.

## Your Last Resort

Not all disputes of this kind have a satisfactory ending. If your former son-in-law refuses to comply with the order, you can go back to court and ask that he be held in contempt. The court can use its contempt powers to enforce your rights, and he could be fined or even jailed for refusing to allow you to be with your grandchildren.

## THE SHIFTING SANDS OF GRANDPARENTS' RIGHTS

The rights of grandparents to obtain court ordered visitation have long seemed to be established law. Every state had legislation granting visitation, usually when it was "in the best interest of the grandchild." But in 2000, a U.S. Supreme Court decision put the entire issue of grandparent rights up for grabs. The Court considered a Washington statute that gave any interested person (even one unrelated to a child) the right to petition for visitation. It ruled that the law was unconstitutional because it unduly interfered with a parent's right to make decisions about how to raise his or her child. In overturning the law, the Court held that great deference must be given to the rights of parents. Legislators in many states immediately began reviewing their own statutes and proposed new legislation designed to meet the requirements set out by the Supreme Court. Still, it's certain that additional challenges will be raised to these statutes.

*A con artist is encouraging your elderly mother to spend money on merchandise with the hope of winning a "sweepstakes" prize.*

Your mother doesn't have much to do during the day, and she enjoys responding to offers that come in the mail. One of the most prevalent schemes is *illegal* "sweepstakes." Here's how the scam works:

- The con artist convinces his victim that she has won a prize.
- In order to claim the prize, however, the "winner" must buy vitamins, office supplies, magazines, or other items.
- Once the purchases are made, the con artist follows up with a phone call. What was once a guaranteed prize suddenly becomes something less—it turns out that the buyer has only won a qualifying round and now has to buy more items before the grand prize can be awarded.
- If the "contestant" makes another purchase, the cycle repeats itself, until the person runs out of money or finally realizes that no prize money is ever going to be given out.

### FIGHT SWEEPSTAKES CON ARTISTS

You may find that it is impossible to locate these companies, as many of them operate only briefly, close up shop, and then reopen in a different city under another name. If your mother used a credit

card, you may be able to have the credit-card company give her a credit for recent purchases. For purchases made more than a few months ago, it is too late.

Go to your local police department and tell them about the company, the merchandise your mother received, and how much she paid. The police may begin an investigation, or add your information to one already in progress.

Writing letters to your state's consumer protection agency and the Federal Trade Commission (FTC) describing the scam may also lead to an investigation and prosecution.

### AVOID FUTURE PROBLEMS

Limit the mailings and telephone offers your mother receives. With her consent, you can…

- **Write to the Mail Preference Service** of the Direct Marketing Association (DMA; page 467) and ask that her name be added to its "Do not mail" list. Her name will be removed from the mailing lists of all its members. Remember that only legitimate marketers, not scam artists, can be members of the DMA.
- **Write directly to companies** that have sent misleading or confusing solicitations to your mother and demand that she be taken off their lists as well.
- **Write to the Telephone Preference Service** of the DMA (page 467) to have her name placed on its "Do not call" list.
- **Make sure that she tells** any telephone salespeople that she wishes to be put on their

company's "Do not call" list. After that, any more calls from that company can result in fines being levied against it. This also allows your mother to file suit for damages.
- **Have the telephone company install** a privacy feature on her phone, if it is available. For a few dollars a month, a recorded voice answers automatically, informs the caller that she does not accept calls from telemarketers, and instructs the caller to add your mother's name to the company's "Do not call" list.

### YOUR LAST RESORT

Despite all your efforts, your elderly mother may still make unnecessary purchases or not understand that she is being taken advantage of. If so, you may want to consider having yourself appointed as her conservator or guardian. This is a serious step and should not be taken lightly.

Before deciding to take over your mother's affairs, you will want to consult a lawyer who knows the probate laws and the elder-law issues in your state.

To start, you must petition the probate court to declare that your mother is incompetent to handle her own financial affairs. She can fight your petition in court, and the judge will order that she undergo a mental examination. The court will also consider her testimony and that of doctors, social workers, friends, and other relatives. If the court decides that she cannot manage her own financial affairs, it may name you—or someone else, such as another family member or even the state—to act as her guardian or conservator.

---

*Y*our second husband has just died. His grown children from a previous marriage are now trying to evict you from the home you and he shared.

---

**T**his is the age of so-called blended families, and one of the hazards of getting married more than one time is that there may be misunderstandings and bad feelings between the new spouses and the children from the previous marriages. This is one reason that prenuptial agreements (page 10) can be so valuable in setting out the rights of the new husband and wife

and in protecting the interests of the children, especially when the couple is older. In any case, you, as a widow, have a legal right to be protected in the event that your spouse dies.

### WHO OWNS THE HOUSE?

First, you have to analyze what rights you have to the house. Take a look at the title for the house to determine *joint tenancy with right of survivorship* or *tenancy by the entirety*.

- **Joint tenancy with right of survivorship** is a common situation when husband and wife buy the house together. If the title was worded this way when your husband died, his interest in the house passed on to you. You are now the sole owner of the house, and there is nothing his children can do to change that.
- **Tenancy by the entirety** is ownership based on the historic concept that a husband and wife are a single legal entity. Here, when one spouse dies, the other automatically becomes the full owner of the property.

**TAKE NOTE** *If your husband bought the house while you were married but failed to put your name on the title, you may still be entitled to stay there, depending on state law.*

## TAKE A LOOK AT HIS WILL

If your husband left the house to you in his will, the children will probably not be able to evict you. If they contest the will, they would have to show the following:

- Their father left the house to you as a result of fraud or duress.
- He was not competent to dispose of his property. However, the fact that he left the house to you disproves that claim. In a contested will, mental competence is determined by whether or not the person making the will recognized what is known as *the natural objects of his bounty,* including his wife, his children, other members of his family, and his friends. Leaving the house to you shows that he was mentally competent.
- He had revoked the will, or that the will was improperly executed. Here, too, the likelihood of success is slim.

They may well know that opposing a will contest is expensive for you. Their legal action may be intended to harass you into a settlement rather than a legitimate challenge. The children may tell you that it's cheaper for you to settle (meaning "Give us what we want") than to spend the time and money on a court case.

## A WIDOW'S RIGHTS

What if your husband died without a will, or actually left the home to his children? Once again, the law is usually on your side. In some states, a widow has what is known as a *homestead right* to the property where she lived with her husband. This right creates a *life estate,* meaning you can stay in the house for the rest of your life; the children will inherit the house when you die.

If your husband dies without a valid will, you may also be allowed to take an *intestate share* of his estate. In many states, this is one-third to one-half of your husband's total estate. In a few states, however, the share you are entitled to depends on how long you and he were married. Thus, a short marriage means you'd get a small portion of the estate; but after a long marriage, you would receive the full intestate share.

## ENLIST LEGAL HELP IF NECESSARY

While most states' laws protect you from the actions of your stepchildren, consult a lawyer for a clear understanding of your rights. In many cases, a letter from an attorney outlining the law and stating that the claims have no merit may be all it takes to put an end to their harassment. If they persist, or if they come to your house without your permission, you may want to get a restraining order against them, preventing them from contacting you or trespassing. And while you may also be able to bring criminal charges against them, this is a civil matter—it may not be easy to get the local prosecutor to act.

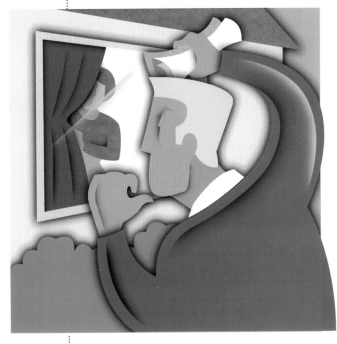

*Your elderly father is in a nursing home and you think that one of his caregivers is abusing him.*

It is hard to face the fact: Family members and home-care givers are threatening, hitting, and neglecting elderly people. Recently the National Survey on Elder Abuse found that about 1 in 20 people over the age of 60 have been abused (both at home and in nursing homes) and that most cases go unreported, many times because the victims fear reprisal.

## SOUND THE ALARM

If you believe that your father is being abused in his nursing home, it's important that you do something quickly. While you may be able to move him to a different home, this isn't always easy (many homes have waiting lists and you need to evaluate a new home thoroughly).

If you cannot move your father, you should contact your local police department to find out which government agency is in charge of protecting the elderly against abuse. Depending on the state, it may be the Department of Aging or the Department of Human Services or Social Services that bears the responsibility.

Many states have toll-free hotline numbers to encourage reports of elder abuse, or call the appropriate agency's main number. In most cases, calls reporting suspected elder abuse are confidential, and your identity will not be revealed to anyone outside the agency. The law in most states also protects you from any civil liability if it turns out that your suspicions of abuse were unfounded. Be prepared to report…

- Why you suspect abuse
- When and where you believe the abuse occurred
- Who you suspect may be the abuser.

Once you report the suspected abuse, the agency has to begin investigating your complaint within a certain time, usually two to three days. If the investigators discover that abuse has occurred, those who are responsible can be charged with several crimes, including assault, battery, and criminal neglect. If convicted, the abuser(s) can be imprisoned or fined, or both.

## SIGNS OF ELDER ABUSE

Here are some warning signs of elder abuse or neglect.

**If the resident...**
- Shows irrational or violent behavior
- Is extremely withdrawn or depressed
- Has poor hygiene
- Is malnourished or dehydrated.
- Has torn or soiled clothing, or soiled bed linens
- Has suspicious bruises, cuts, burns, or pressure sores
- Feels isolated from friends and family

**If the caregiver...**
- Forces residents to participate in unnecessary activity
- Uses physical restraints
- Forbids any conversation outside the presence of a caretaker
- Displays an attitude of indifference or hostility toward residents
- Becomes overly defensive or angry when concerns are raised about the quality of care being given

LIVING IN YOUR HOME

You bought the country retreat of your dreams, burbling brook and all. Now a neighbor has built a dam that's dried up the stream on your property.

Your right to have your neighbor remove the new dam and restore the water supply to your property depends on the state in which your property is located. There are essentially two sets of rules used to determine water rights. In most states, the law rests on what is known as a *reasonable use* rule. Under this rule, the neighbors who live along a stream or lake must use the water in a way that is reasonable and does not unduly harm others who are sharing the water supply.

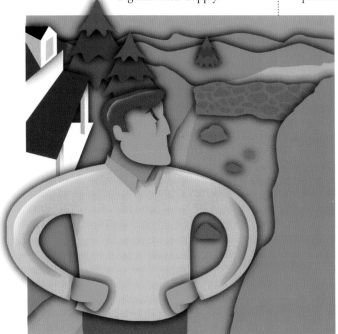

In western states, such as New Mexico, Arizona, and Colorado, where water is often scarce, water rights are determined by a *prior appropriation* rule. In these states, landowners may obtain a permit for water use. A permit holder generally has a right to use all of the water covered by the permit, leaving any neighbors without permits high and dry.

## STEPS FOR REASONABLE USE RULES

If you live in a reasonable-use state, your problem shouldn't be difficult to resolve. The steps you need to take are straightforward:

- ■ **Contact your neighbor** to explain the problem. A friendly phone call will do. Remember, your neighbor may not know that the dam has had any effect whatsoever on your property. Tell her about the situation; that may be all you'll need to do to get the problem corrected.
- ■ **Follow up with a letter** (sent certified mail, return receipt requested) if your neighbor doesn't offer to redress the damage after your first telephone contact. Politely spell out the problem and the solution you seek. The letter should state the situation clearly and show the thoughtfulness of your concern. It will often get results. Keep a copy of the letter and any replies you receive. This record of the dispute will be important if you have to take more drastic measures later.
- ■ **Have a lawyer write a letter** on your behalf, but only if your neighbor still refuses to act; this should not be expensive. A letter from a lawyer will explain in an authoritative way the law supporting your right to have the water to your property restored. Another benefit: The letter will indicate that you are serious about pursuing your complaint, and help to head off an expensive lawsuit.
- ■ **Consider going to court** if your neighbor is unwilling to cooperate with you. For this, you will need a lawyer familiar with local water law. A lawyer can get an injunction— a court order telling the neighbor to stop diverting water from your stream until your case has been settled.

A lawyer will also help you file suit in the appropriate court. You may also want to seek the assistance of your state's department of natural resources: (Call the general information number listed in the state government pages and ask for the agency responsible for regulating water rights.) The government can help you when a neighbor unlawfully diverts water from your stream. The state can order your neighbor to cease and desist, and may even fine her.

If you live in a prior appropriation (not reasonable use) state, you will need to do some research before you can consider any options:

- **Check the permit.** As a first step, contact your state's department of natural resources to see if your neighbor has a permit for use of the water. If she does, you may need to negotiate the purchase of water rights from her to have your stream restored.
- **Hire a lawyer** who has experience in cases that fall under your state's water law. After examining the state's records and the neighbor's permit, your lawyer may be able to discover a previously filed grant of water rights that would require your neighbor to modify or remove the dam and restore your stream's water flow. If this is the case, your lawyer should help negotiate these rights and record the appropriate documents in the effort to protect your stream.

**HOMEBUYER ALERT** *A country property may seem perfect in every way, but never buy it without checking who has water rights—especially in a state with prior appropriation rules.*

---

> **W**hen you first moved into your house, you had a wonderful view of the mountains. Now your neighbor's trees have grown so tall that they block your view.

**D**oes everyone have a right to a view? At one time, no. Today, possibly. More and more communities have enacted *view ordinances.* These ordinances are common where the view is considered an important part of the community's appeal, such as in mountain communities, at lake shores, and along the oceanfront. In addition, many planned communities protect views through their Covenants, Codes, and Restrictions (CC&Rs). Keep in mind, though, that most communities' view ordinances protect only the view you had from your property when you bought it or when the ordinance was passed. In other words, you can't complain about a fully grown tree that is already blocking the view when you purchase your house.

### SMART MOVES

When you buy a new house with a lovely view, take photographs to document it for future reference. Then when a neighbor's plants begin to obstruct it, you have clear proof.

### LOOK UP THE LAW

To find out if there is a local ordinance that protects your view, you can contact your city council representative or your local zoning office. To find out about protective CC&Rs, contact the management office of your homeowners association.

Once you determine that there is a legal basis for your complaint, write a letter to the property owner whose trees block your view. In your letter…

- Describe the nature of the problem.
- Enclose a copy of the relevant law or regulation.
- Suggest an appropriate solution.
- Give the property owner a deadline for taking action.

Be cordial, but firm. Keep a copy of the letter for your files.

### GETTING TOUGHER

You'll probably have more success if you ask your neighbor to trim or thin the trees (rather than demand they be removed) and indicate some flexibility about enforcing your proposed timetable. However, if your neighbor refuses to comply with your request or ignores it, you will need to take further action to have your view restored. If your situation is covered by a CC&R, approach your homeowners association to take action. (A homeowners association, which has the power to suspend community privileges —and sometimes to fine a non-compliant property owner—may be better at communicating your problem. The association can write a letter containing the following to the property owner:

- A reference to the relevant CC&R
- A request for compliance.

While some homeowners associations have the power to file a lawsuit to enforce CC&Rs, many are reluctant to do so because of the time and expense involved. And some communities that are subject to CC&Rs have no homeowners association at all, or only a very weak one. In this case, you may have to bring a lawsuit against your neighbor to have the CC&Rs enforced.

### TRY TO COMPROMISE

Before going to court, offer to pay some of the cost of having the trees trimmed. It may be that your neighbor can't afford to have the work done; if this is the case, paying a portion of the pruning bill will be far less expensive than paying the full costs of a lawsuit.

If your municipality has a view ordinance, you can file suit, but the city won't act on your behalf in the matter. Here, too, it may help if you offer to pay part of the pruning costs. In fact, some communities' view ordinances place the entire expense of trimming on the person whose view is obstructed (unless the tree was planted after the ordinance became law) or in cases where the tree's owner refuses to cooperate.

### GOING TO COURT

In your district or county court, you will need to present evidence about your view and the obstruction your neighbor's trees have caused. This could be accomplished with before-and-after photographs or through the testimony of neighbors.

The bathtub upstairs is leaking into the dining room below, or the foundation of the back porch needs bolstering. When you want a reliable contractor, interview several prospective contractors. Get recommendations from friends, neighbors, and real estate brokers.

- **Reliable contractors should be willing to visit your home, analyze the repairs to be made, provide a written estimate of the cost, and give references.** Check the references, and call the Better Business Bureau and your state consumer protection agency to inquire if any complaints have been made against any contractor you're considering.

Using a licensed contractor may provide additional protection; many communities use licensing fees to pay claims when a contractor goes out of business or fails to complete a job. Licensing doesn't guarantee work quality, however, because most communities don't test skills.

Always get a written contract that includes mechanic's lien safeguards (page 48) and these:

- The name, address, telephone number, and license number of the contractor

- The names, addresses, and telephone and license numbers of any subcontractors who will work on the project

- A description of the work to be done, the materials that are to be used, and a timetable for completion of the project and making payments

- A clause stating that any changes to the agreement must be in writing and signed by you and the contractor

- The contractor's promise to get all necessary permits before work begins

- A written guarantee of the contractor's work as well as a provision that the contractor will give you the warranties for products and materials

- A provision that requires the contractor to clean the work site on a regular basis and at the completion of the project

- Attached copies of the cover pages of the contractor's liability insurance and workers' compensation policies

- **Get results if a job goes awry.** Contact your contractor to give him a chance to make things right. If he is very busy and has not paid attention to your job, a telephone call may be all that's required. If he doesn't respond, or if you still aren't satisfied, send a written notice (by certified mail, return receipt requested). Describe the problem, propose a solution, and set a deadline for rectifying the matter. Keep a copy for your records.

- **Using Arbitration.** Many contractors include a clause in the agreement that requires such claims to go to arbitration. While arbitration is usually cheaper than going to court, it can have negative consequences. If it is binding, you may not be able to appeal the arbitrator's decision in court. If your contractor wants to include an arbitration clause in your agreement, ask that he be bound by the arbitrator's decision while leaving you free to take further action.

In any case, if you have a problem, you will need evidence of your claim against the contractor:

- ✔ Your contract

- ✔ Canceled checks

- ✔ Copies of all correspondence

- ✔ Photos of poor workmanship

- ✔ The testimony of experts about how the contractor's work is deficient

Having a written contract and clear evidence of the contractor's failure to meet its terms will make it easier for you to win when a contractor fails to do work as promised.

## HOME-REPAIR SCAMS AND SWINDLES

In just about every city and town across America, gangs of scam artists known as "travelers" pose as home-repair crews. These gangs are busy throughout the year, but especially in spring, cheating homeowners out of millions of dollars annually. As a rule, they are well-groomed, courteous, and considerate men, particularly when dealing with older homeowners. Here are some warning signs that you may have been targeted by a home-repair swindler:

■ **A construction crew arrives at your door** with "leftover material from another job" and offers to give you a steep discount if you agree to buy today.

■ **A "utility company worker" shows up at your home** to offer a free inspection of your furnace, water heater, or plumbing. Public utility companies *do not* send workers out unannounced to conduct such inspections. Ask the worker for identification and call the company while he stays outside. Don't let a stranger into the house before confirming his identity or you may find yourself missing cash or other valuables after he departs.

■ **A repair crew comes by shortly after a flood,** fire, or other disaster offering a "bargain price" for cleanup. Refer all offers to your insurance company's claims department.

■ **If you have any suspicions about an unsolicited home-repair offer,** you should contact your local police department immediately. Be prepared to give a careful description of the people who contacted you, what they were wearing, the kind of vehicle they were using, and its license-plate number.

■ ***Another warning:*** Someone telephones you offering a "fabulous discount" on siding, painting, or replacement windows if you agree to let your house be used in their company's advertising. Although a few legitimate businesses may operate this way, the discounts will rarely be as big as the telemarketer will claim.

*The new owner of a home in your historic neighborhood wants to tear it down and build one of a completely different style.*

If you want to keep a historic home from being replaced with a modern one, first find out what, if any, historic designation protects it. Call your local landmark authority or zoning board for that information.

**TAKE NOTE** *Homes in many historic areas, even those listed on the National Register of Historic Places, are not always protected from being altered or even torn down. But that doesn't mean you should give up the fight to keep a historic home from being replaced by a modern one.*

### LAYERS OF LAW

Laws to preserve the historic quality of a community have been passed at three levels of government—local, state, and federal. These laws and regulations are intended to help balance the private rights of property owners with the public's interest in maintaining the community's unique character, charm, and historic value.

■ **State and local laws.** State and local rules are usually more stringent than federal ones when it comes to preserving architecture and the character of the neighborhood. Many local landmark authorities, for example, prohibit any alteration (even a minor one such as painting the trim a different color) without a hearing and board approval.

■ **The NHPA.** At the federal level, the National Historic Preservation Act limits the government's role in the alteration or destruction of historic houses and buildings. Under this law, properties listed or eligible to be listed on the National Register of Historic Places are protected from actions of the federal government. No federal money can be used to alter, damage, or destroy one of these homes without a hearing. However, there is no guarantee that even with a hearing the federal government won't approve the demolition. And if the homeowner isn't using federal funds for the demolition or construction, the federal government can't stop him.

## HOW THE PROCESS WORKS

In general, the owner of a historic house protected by local laws must give the local zoning board or historic preservation committee advance notice of his intent to alter the home's appearance. The owner may also be required to post a notice on the property advising neighbors when and where a hearing on the proposed changes will take place. This hearing will be open to the public, and the owner will have the opportunity to present arguments on behalf of making the changes to his property. Generally, interested members of the community may also have an opportunity to address the hearing panel, either in support of or in opposition to the property owner's plans.

Once the board or committee has weighed the evidence, it will issue a ruling. In most communities, the ruling can…

- Grant the property owner the right to make the proposed alterations
- Reject his right to alter his house
- Suggest modifications to the owner's plans.

The owner has the right to appeal a decision, but once the decision has been made, the law presumes that it is valid.

Unless the homeowner can show that the restriction is unreasonable, or that the hearing panel violated its own rules or acted without proper authority, the decision will likely be affirmed. Frustrated property owners have argued that such limitations placed on their renovation plans by the community are unconstitutional, since they deprive owners of control of their own property without compensation. Historic renovation can be prohibitively expensive. Courts, however, have consistently found in favor of historic preservation districts, holding that the public good outweighs the individual owner's interest.

## DEFYING THE LAW

In a few cases, owners of historic properties proceed with alterations or demolition despite a ruling against them. Preservation laws generally give the local government power to fine a homeowner for each day such property is in violation, and homeowners can be required to restore their homes to their original appearance.

*You've come up with a handsome new color scheme for the exterior of your house, but your homeowners association refuses to approve it.*

Your homeowners association is a great ally—that is, until it gets in your way. The board has refused your plan because it believes you are violating one of the Covenants, Codes, and Restrictions (CC&Rs) put in place when a community or subdivision was developed. Generally, courts give these associations a lot of leeway in the interpretation and enforcement of the rules. As long as an association does not violate state or federal laws, courts are loath to overrule its decisions. Still, these associations can sometimes be arbitrary or violate their own rules.

### MAKE AN ACTION PLAN

Here is a plan of action for challenging the decision of a homeowners association:

- **Review the rules** or bylaws of the association. Most homeowners associations provide copies of their rules to new homeowners when they first arrive. If you didn't receive a set of rules or if you can't find them, you can go to the association's office and review them there. In many cases, the association will give you a copy, either for free or for a small fee.
- **Get prior approval.** The homeowners association may have objected to your choices of paint colors because you didn't apply for advance approval of them as stated in the bylaws. In many communities, you must get the association's approval of your color scheme before you repaint, even if you are repainting your home the same color; this is because the association may have changed the list of colors it approves. And it is within its rights: Courts across the country have been consistent in finding that homeowners associations have the right to amend regulations, provided they follow their own established rules for making the changes.
- **Ask the association to tell you why** it denied your request (if you provided your color choices for prior approval and they were rejected). Most homeowner associations allow members to appeal a decision that adversely affects them. Your appeal may be heard by an architectural or landscaping committee or by the board of directors of the association.

- **To appeal the decision,** prepare your case well in advance of the hearing. If a neighbor has recently received approval to paint her home in colors that are identical or close to the ones you want to use, take pictures of the home as evidence, noting its address and the name of the homeowner. (Or, if no similar color schemes have been used in the community in the recent past, you can enlarge a photograph of your house on a copy machine and color it with the proposed colors.)
- **Ask neighbors to testify** that they have no objection to the colors you want to use. Their testimony may persuade the association to grant an exemption to the rules. The association may even decide to add your colors to those on its approved list.
- **Submit your dispute to an arbitrator or mediator** if the association continues to stand by its earlier decision. Some homeowners associations' bylaws allow this as a way to avoid the cost and time involved in going to court. In some cases, arbitration may be binding on the association but not on you, while in others, both sides will be bound by the arbitrator's decision.

If you lose in arbitration, your immediate options are limited. To proceed with a legal claim against the association, you will have to show that its actions were arbitrary, unauthorized by the association's bylaws, or discriminatory. These can be tough standards to meet, and the burden of proof will be on you. Consult a lawyer who specializes in handling cases against homeowners associations for a candid evaluation of your case.

### A LAST RESORT

In most cases, homeowners association officers and directors are elected by members of the community. If you and your neighbors feel that these officials are not acting in the best interest of the community, you can sometimes recall them from office. This requires a petition drive and a special election. Or you may want to arrange for a slate of candidates to oppose the current officials when their terms expire. Your association's bylaws will contain the exact procedures you must follow.

If you are adding a room to your home, finishing your basement, or making other major improvements, you must make sure that the work conforms to local building codes. You can find out the building codes in your community by going to the local planning or building department. These codes vary widely from place to place even within the same state, so don't assume that a project that was approved in one place will pass muster in another.

### Working With the Building Department

Once you have the building code in hand, you can start negotiating with your community's building department by doing the following:

■ **Submit your plan.** First, you will need to take a set of plans for your renovation to the building department. The department will review them to see that they meet the local codes. You may have to make changes to satisfy the codes.

■ **Get a permit.** After the department approves your plans it will issue you a building permit for the project. You will have to pay a fee for the permit, usually based on the size of the job.

■ **Expect inspections.** Once you get the building permit, you can expect periodic visits from a building inspector, who will check the work to see that it is being done according to code, and that it follows the approved building plans. If you have violated any part of the code, the inspector can make you stop work until the violations are corrected.

■ **Receive written approval.** When the work is complete, the building inspector will issue a document known as a *certificate of occupancy*, which states that the renovation complies with the community's legal requirements.

### Can You Get Away Without a Permit?

What happens if you don't get a building permit for a major project? It depends on the community in which you live and the nature of the improvement. Finishing a basement may not draw the city's attention to your project, but building an addition to your house almost certainly will. The building department can bring your project to a halt and take action against you.

● The building department can obtain a court order requiring you to stop work until you receive department approval.

● It can require you to demolish any work that was done before a permit was obtained.

● It can issue you a fine on top of the cost of obtaining a building permit.

● In rare cases, it can have homeowners who persist in making improvements without obtaining a building permit arrested and jailed.

There's another important reason to get a permit, however. When you try to sell your home, the sales contract normally requires that you guarantee that the property meets all code requirements. If the buyer discovers that there are code violations, you could find yourself forced to make expensive repairs in order to have the sale go through. Worse still, the prospective buyer may even be able to back out of the deal. While it may seem like a hassle to go through the process of getting a building permit, proceeding without one could prove much more troublesome in the long run.

## How to Protect Yourself Against a Mechanic's Lien

Before tackling any major work on your house, guard yourself against a mechanic's lien, a legal claim against your property to satisfy the bill of one of your contractor's subcontractors.

■ **How a mechanic's lien works.** You hire a general contractor to renovate your kitchen. He commissions new cabinets from a subcontractor. You pay the general contractor in full, but he, for whatever reason, doesn't pay the subcontractor. The subcontractor then comes to you for payment. To pressure you, he puts a lien on your house that must be satisfied before you can refinance or sell the house. A mechanic's lien ensures that anyone who supplies materials or labor to build, repair, or improve a property will be paid.

● Some states require that you pay twice for the same work in order to have the mechanic's lien removed from your property. Depending on the state you live in, you would then need to sue the general contractor for reimbursement.

● Other states do not hold you responsible for the actions of the contractor. If you can prove that you paid the contractor, the lien will be lifted.

The subcontractor has to file his lawsuit within a certain time limit, usually six months to a year from completion of the job. You must settle the matter either by paying off the lien, proving you paid the contractor, or obtaining a release from the contractor or subcontractor. Until the matter is settled, your credit may be seriously damaged.

■ **Reducing the risk.** To protect yourself from a mechanic's lien, take these steps before you start any home project:

● Deal only with reputable, established contractors.

● Insist that your contractor sign a waiver of his right to file a mechanic's lien.

● Require the contractor to obtain a surety bond, a guaranty that a third party will pay for any of the contractor's obligations should he fail to honor them.

● Ask for a complete list of all suppliers and subcontractors.

● Include a provision in your agreement that the contractor will provide you with *lien waivers* from all suppliers and subcontractors before you make your final payment. Lien waivers state that all payments have been made in full, and they should be signed and notarized. You should also require that the contractor give you copies of all receipts to prove that he has paid all suppliers.

After work on the project begins, you can safeguard yourself by doing any of the following:

■ **Make checks payable to the contractor and the subcontractor or supplier jointly.** This way, neither can be paid without the agreement of the other. Your canceled checks will help serve as proof of payment to all parties if one of them later files a lien against your property.

● Don't make checks directly payable to subcontractors or suppliers, since doing so could make you liable for workers' compensation or unemployment insurance.

■ **Have the contractor give you a notarized affidavit saying that all bills have been paid.**

■ **Do not make final payment to the general contractor until you have proof that all subcontractors have been paid.**

**If the worst happens.** Should a lien be filed against your home, contact an experienced real estate lawyer immediately. If you fail to respond to the lien claim within the time limits set by state law, you could find yourself subject to a default judgment on behalf of the lien holder. In some states, a default judgment could mean your home will be subject to a foreclosure sale.

> *The contractor you hired to build an addition to your home took your deposit, but you haven't seen him for a month—and his phone is disconnected.*

While most contractors are honest and do a good job, there are some who are con men. These "contractors" will promise you anything, as long as they get a check before doing any work. They prey on your desire to save money and offer to complete a project for far less than an honest contractor would charge.

### A Disappearing Act

Once your check clears the bank, these con artists disappear. They'll change the name of their business and continue to sell the same scam again and again. And if you call the Better Business Bureau (BBB) to check their reputation, you'll probably be told that there are no complaints on file against them—they haven't been in business under their new name long enough for anyone to complain.

### When the Work Doesn't Get Done

When a contractor has breached his contract with you and shows no sign of correcting the situation, you can hire another contractor. If the cost is higher than your first contract, you can seek reimbursement from the original contractor for the extra costs.

Unfortunately, collecting money from a con artist, even with a court judgment, is often difficult. Hire a collection agency or a law firm that specializes in collections. They know how to locate resources and assets in ways the average citizen doesn't; they also work on a contingency basis, keeping a percentage of whatever they can collect.

If the contractor is licensed, you may be able to get some money *from the state.* Licensed contractors are often required to pay into a bond fund that reimburses consumers when a job isn't completed. Ask the state department of licenses if a fund is available and how to apply for a claim.

You should also tell the BBB and the state attorney general's office of consumer protection about your problem. While the BBB has no enforcement powers, it gathers information on contractors who consistently fail to complete work. The consumer protection office can also bring a civil suit on behalf of people who have been swindled and recommend filing criminal charges, especially when the victims are elderly homeowners. In such cases, contractors have actually been fined and jailed.

### What to Do Next Time

When you hire a contractor…

- Ask for a written contract that provides for payments tied to the completion of each work stage.
  - Never give the contractor a large advance payment.
  - Don't schedule payments on calendar dates instead of on completion of parts of the work. You may have to pay for the whole project before it's finished.

**SMART MOVES**

Get estimates from several contractors for a large job. That will help you recognize bids that are *too* low.

> *Your home's foundation is on the verge of collapse because it was built on "expansive" soil.*

You couldn't have been happier to move into your spacious new home. But months later, you are dismayed to find large cracks in the house's foundation.

---

## The law guarantees you the right to a home free of major defects and dangerous conditions.

---

How could this have happened? It's simple: After the last recession, home building had an unprecedented boom. Developers and builders often hurried to construct houses without having an adequate understanding of the special types of foundations needed for houses built on soil that undergoes considerable expansion and contraction as the weather changes. A foundation built on this kind of soil will crack during a dry month and buckle when a drenching rain arrives.

### CHECK THE WARRANTY

Whenever you have a problem with the structure of a new home, you should begin by checking the terms of the warranty given to you by the builder. If your home was constructed within the last four years, it's likely that you will be able to file a claim to have the foundation repaired free of charge. Many older homes are covered by 5- or 10-year structural warranties. Under some of these warranties, the foundation will be repaired at no charge to you; others are *prorated,* which means you may have to pay a portion of the repair bill, depending on the expensiveness of the work and the age of the house.

### WHEN THERE IS NO WARRANTY

If your home isn't covered by a warranty, don't despair. You may be able to bring a lawsuit against the builder for failing to comply with state laws that require a home to be soundly constructed. These laws provide what are known as *implied warranties of habitability.* This means that the law guarantees you the right to a home free of major defects and dangerous conditions.

Before filing suit, there are some preliminary steps you will need to take:

- **Notify the builder** of your problem as soon as possible. Write a letter describing the defect, and give the builder an opportunity to correct it. Be sure to include a reasonable deadline by which you expect the builder to act, such as 30 days. Also include copies of supporting documents, such as engineering reports and photographs that bolster your claim. Send your letter by certified mail, return receipt requested so you will have proof that you notified the builder.
- **Enlist the media.** If the builder refuses to rectify the problem, consider bringing the power of the media to bear on your behalf. In most communities, newspapers and broadcast media take real interest in serious consumer problems. Calling your local television or radio station's consumer affairs reporter or the city editor of your newspaper could lead to embarrassing publicity that will prompt the builder to repair your foundation quickly.
- **Go to court.** If the builder still refuses to fix the foundation, you can proceed with a lawsuit. Litigation regarding home defects is complicated, so you will need a lawyer who knows this area of law. (Because you've documented the problem, a lawyer should be able to evaluate your case quickly and inexpensively.) The lawyer may write a letter to the builder demanding that the company repair the foundation or face a lawsuit. If the builder still fails to respond, the lawyer can file the appropriate documents to bring your suit to court.

### GETTING YOUR REPAIR MONEY BACK

Before the trial, the builder may contact you with an offer to settle the case. This offer may not be for the full cost of the repair, meaning you are expected to bear at least some of the expense. You need to consider this offer carefully; it ultimately may be cheaper to agree to a compromise figure than to pursue the matter through an expensive full trial and the potential of appeals.

In some cases the builder may be bankrupt. In many states, builders pay into a fund to help pay a homeowner who has a claim against a builder who's gone out of business. You can find out about filing a claim through this fund by contacting your state's department of licenses.

### STRENGTH IN NUMBERS

If you live in a development or planned community, your neighbors may be experiencing similar problems with their house foundations. Ask your lawyer about filing a class-action suit against the builder. Class-action suits give people who are similarly affected by the misdeeds of another the chance to pool resources in pursuit of justice. Even the suggestion of a class-action suit may prompt a reluctant business to address problems it had previously ignored.

You also may want to bring your problem to the attention of the attorney general in your state. In some states, he or she can file suit on behalf of consumers who have been victimized by a single offender. Your state representative's office can put you in touch with the appropriate contact at the attorney general's office.

*The city landscaped a plot of land it owns next to your home. Now, whenever it rains, the water runs off the city's lot and floods your basement.*

Water probably causes more damage to homes than anything else, even fire. While the law generally makes a neighbor who causes water damage to your home liable for that damage, your local government is the "neighbor" in this case. This means you'll have to work harder to solve the problem.

### WHERE TO START

Start by reporting the problem to your insurance company. A claims adjuster will come and assess the damage to your property. He can help you get immediate assistance to prevent any further damage. Most insurance policies require you to take steps to correct the problem at least temporarily. Once you became aware of the water washing into your home, you can't just let the water continue to flood your basement and expect the insurer to pay for damages that could have been avoided .

The terms of your policy may limit how much you can recover from your own insurer. This is because many home insurance policies exclude coverage for flooding from an external source. (Consider whether it's worth your while to purchase a separate flood insurance policy.)

### ARE YOU ALONE?

Ask your neighbors if they are also being affected. It's usually more effective to have several people working to get a problem corrected rather than

acting on your own. This is especially true when dealing with government agencies, which may not be quick to respond to a single complaint but move more speedily when calls begin pouring in from a group of residents.

### FIRST PRIORITIES

No matter how many people are involved, contact the city clerk's office immediately.

---

**W**hile the city is permitted to make reasonable use of its land, it must do so without harming someone else's.

---

- Explain the nature of the problem and insist that the city send an employee to see the situation firsthand.
- Get the name of the employee you talk to, and if the response isn't satisfactory, ask to speak with the employee's supervisor. In any case, be persistent.
- Contact your city council representative if you can't convince the city's employees to come to your aid. A council representative can often bring enough pressure to bear to speed up the city's response time.

The city will eventually send someone out to make a report on your problem, but a report is not enough. You want the government to take action to eliminate the possibility of any future flooding as well.

As soon as possible, take an inventory of any damaged or destroyed property, and photograph or videotape the damage. You will need this documentation for insurance claims, and it will serve as evidence if you file a lawsuit against the city. If you can videotape water rushing into your property and trace its course to the government's lot, you'll have strong evidence.

### TACKLING THE CITY

Early in our history, government entities were able to walk away from the problems they created. Under the legal doctrine of *sovereign immunity,* governments couldn't be sued for their actions unless they gave their consent. Today most governments have waived this right, especially when a citizen claims that the government has damaged private property.

Some municipalities have liability insurance policies, while others are self-insured. Either way, the city will assign you a claims number and you will likely be contacted by a claims agent for the city, who will offer to settle your case. Your paperwork should include a list of damaged items with photographs, the cost of replacing each item, and receipts for any expenses you incurred while correcting the initial problem.

### UNDERSTANDING THE NEGOTIATIONS

Don't feel obligated to accept the first settlement figure the city offers. If you believe that the offer isn't adequate, say so. Remember that the claims agent's job is to save his company—or the city— money. If he can get you to accept a lower figure, he's done a good job. On the other hand, if he sees that you are prepared to pursue every available avenue to receive a fair settlement, he will realize that paying more on your claim is still less expensive than the cost of litigation.

If the city's offer is inadequate, think about the possibility of a lawsuit. But be aware that many cities give themselves an edge by requiring anyone considering litigation to notify the city well in advance of actually filing suit.

### TAKING THE CITY TO COURT

Before suing the city, consult a lawyer who has experience in dealing with lawsuits against government bodies. (Unfortunately, not many lawyers practice in this area of litigation.)

Happily, the law in most states is on your side. While the city as a property owner is permitted to make reasonable use of its land, it must do so without harming someone else's. If you can document that the source of the water that flooded your basement is the city-owned lot, the big question for a judge or jury to decide is likely to be the amount of damages to be awarded.

In some cases, you may be entitled to have the city pay your court costs and attorney fees, although many jurisdictions limit fee awards to cases in which the city acted unreasonably in failing to settle your case before trial.

*The city intends to widen the street in
front of your home but refuses to pay you what you think the
property you'll be losing is worth.*

One of the most cherished myths in America is the belief that the right to own private property is unrestricted. In fact, local, state, and federal governments all have the right to take your property for a variety of reasons, including appropriating it for public use.

When a government body takes property for a public project, such as a park, playground, or wider road, it is exercising its right of *eminent domain*. Under the Fifth Amendment to the U.S. Constitution, the government must provide just compensation when using its eminent domain powers. The trouble is, there is no hard-and-fast definition of what constitutes just compensation, and that is why governments are often challenged when they set a price for property that is below what the owner believes is fair.

The government exercises its power of eminent domain through a process of condemnation. Once your property is condemned, the government will make an offer of compensation based on what it believes is the fair market value of the condemned property.

## MAKE A DEAL

It's possible that you may be able to negotiate a better deal:

- **Propose a higher figure** if you don't believe that the city has offered you enough money. You may find that your counteroffer will be accepted.
- **Hire a private appraiser** to determine the value of the condemned property if the government rejects the figure you propose. An appraiser can compare the offer you received with those received by other property owners, adjusting for inflation if necessary and factoring in differences between communities.

## GOING TO COURT

If direct negotiation doesn't get you the amount of compensation you believe is fair, you will have to consider going to court. This route to the desired outcome is more complicated, of course, and will require more money and time.

- **Hire a lawyer.** You may want to hire a lawyer because condemnation proceedings are complicated, and the rules for challenging the government can be difficult to follow. Look for a lawyer who has experience in the field of condemnations. She will help you formally oppose the government's last offer at the condemnation hearing. Although these proceedings vary from state to state and community to community, most follow similar steps. You, as property owner, must be given a written notice of when and where the hearing will take place and be given sufficient time to prepare your case. You will be allowed to present evidence, such as your appraiser's report. Other evidence could be testimony from witnesses who can support your claim to greater compensation; these might be other property owners who received more money for similar property.

■ **Get a jury trial.** You may be entitled to a trial by jury to determine whether the government's compensation offer is fair, depending on state law. Experts suggest that a jury trial is more likely to work in your favor than a hearing before a judge in cases of this kind, since jurors will probably feel more sympathy toward you than toward the government. Remember, though, that the expense of a jury trial may be more than the increase in compensation you might win. The government will be represented by its own full-time attorneys in a trial by jury, while you will have to pay for your lawyer out of your own pocket.

## Keeping Your Home Safe and Secure

Keeping your home and family safe is a top priority, but not an expensive one. By following a few simple steps, you can protect your property and your peace of mind, and you may even save money on your homeowner's insurance.

■ **Make sure that front and back doorways are lighted at night.** Motion-sensing lights that turn on when someone approaches your property can be an effective deterrent to burglars who count on the cover of darkness.

■ **Trim shrubs and hedges around doors and windows** so that intruders won't be able to hide behind them.

■ **Have deadbolt locks installed** on exterior doors and use them, even if you are only working in the backyard or visiting a next-door neighbor.

■ **Install locks on ground-floor windows** and sliding-glass patio doors.

■ **Keep your garage door closed** and never leave your keys or valuables in your car.

■ **Never leave your house keys on the key ring** with your car keys at an auto-repair shop or an attended parking lot.

■ **Don't let newspapers pile up in the driveway or let mail accumulate** in your mailbox when you are away from home. You can stop deliveries while you are gone, but it's often a better idea to have a trusted neighbor collect mail and papers for you. In some cases, postal service employees and newspaper carriers have used their knowledge of a homeowner's vacation to burglarize a vacant home.

■ **Plug lights and a radio or television into timers** when you are away from home. Set them so they will turn on and off as if you were there.

■ **Consider installing a burglar alarm.** Check with your local police department for recommendations about reliable security companies in your area.

■ **Be wary of telephone and door-to-door solicitations.** You can't know when potential burglars are casing your house. Never admit to a caller claiming to represent an alarm company, for example, that you don't have an alarm. Never tell a stranger that you are home alone. (Be sure that your telephone answering machine message doesn't either.)

■ **Consider getting a dog.** A noisy dog may convince a burglar to try a quieter location.

You chose to buy a home in a new community because it promised a nearby park. Now you can look forward to neon and plastic signs, and driving miles to a playground.

Home builders know the value of open, recreational space; their brochures usually include a map showing the areas protected from commercial development. But builders and developers are out to make a profit, and sometimes the lure of money can lead even the best-intentioned ones to renege on a promise to keep certain property reserved for community use.

## LOOK FOR THE MASTER PLAN

In most parts of the country, builders must receive approval from the city or county government in order to develop a new community. The governmental body will base its approval on the master plan provided by the developer.

In some cases, however, the developer is given a certain amount of leeway in adapting the plan to changing conditions, including economic ones. If an economic boom goes bust, for example, areas that were reserved for single-family houses may be changed to allow for higher-density apartment complexes that can house more families at less expense.

Your first step should be to review any master-plan documents to determine if the developer has the right to make a change without the approval of the local government. (To locate these papers, check with the city hall or the office of the county commissioner.) Some plans allow the developer to substitute one piece of property for another (that is, to re-site elements of the plan), provided the percentage of property devoted to community space remains the same.

### CHECK THE ZONING

Even if the master plan allows leeway to the developer, local zoning laws may protect residents. Contact your county commissioner or city council representative to express your concern about the proposed change. If the community is zoned, restrictions may prohibit commercial development in a residential neighborhood. Your representative can help you identify zoning regulations that may stop the restaurant chain in its tracks.

Even if zoning appears to prohibit a new restaurant on the site, the restaurant chain may apply for a zoning variance that will allow it to operate a restaurant there. Before any zoning change can take place, however, the law requires a public hearing, at which you and your neighbors can express your opposition to the restaurant chain's proposal.

### PUTTING UP A GOOD FIGHT

You should have ample time to prepare your opposition before the zoning board hearing, but it's best to marshal your resources quickly:

■ **Petitions.** Circulate a petition in the community opposing the restaurant at the site it proposes. When you draw up your petition, first consult your county or city clerk to find out which local laws govern the situation. Have the clerk look over your document to be sure it addresses the correct issue; otherwise you risk having the petition disregarded.

■ **Witnesses.** Find expert witnesses to testify at the zoning hearing. A traffic engineer could provide evidence that the number of cars visiting the restaurant would pose a danger to children in the neighborhood; a noise-pollution expert could testify about the undesirable sound levels the restaurant would create.

■ **Media coverage.** Get the attention of the media. It's an effective tool in fighting a proposed zoning variance. Local newspapers and radio and television news programs love grass-roots movements. In some cases, media coverage alone has made businesses withdraw their applications for a zoning change for fear of seeming insensitive to the community.

■ **Zoning board meetings.** Attend the zoning board meeting with your neighbors to show the community's strong resistance to the project. Testimony by residents can go a long way toward obtaining a rejection of the restaurant's proposal.

### FIGHTING AN APPEAL

A truly determined business may not abandon its plans even in the face of governmental rejection or community opposition. It may decide to appeal the zoning board's decision to the city or county government or go to court in an attempt to overturn the board's decision. Your local government has an obligation to defend its decision on behalf of the community. But some governments are less than diligent in their defense; accordingly, you and your neighbors must continue to exert pressure on your elected officials so that they will defend the decision vigorously.

You and your neighbors may also want the help of a lawyer experienced in zoning law to guide you through the legal process and make sure that your voices are heard at court proceedings. Check to see if one of your neighbors is a lawyer willing to advise you on a pro bono (free of charge) basis; or, your lawyer neighbor might have a colleague who is knowledgeable in zoning law and who would be willing to assist you for a reduced fee.

*At a party you host, one guest gets into a fistfight with another. Now the second guest is threatening to sue you, saying the first guest was drunk.*

This is about as unpleasant a scenario as you can imagine, considering that what was intended to be a carefree and convivial evening ended in disaster. To decrease the chances of such conflict, you must act responsibly whenever you host a party:

● You must not continue to serve an inebriated guest alcohol.
● You should make sure a drunken guest doesn't drive a car home.
● You should have a drunken guest driven home early by someone else.

In addition, you may be liable for injuries if you invite a guest who is known to have a bad temper and another guest with whom the bad-tempered guest is likely to quarrel. Any injuries may be seen to be the result of your negligence.

### ARE YOU COVERED?

When you are threatened with a lawsuit, first check your homeowner's insurance policy. Some insurance companies now refuse to pay for alcohol-related injuries to guests unless you have purchased an endorsement to your standard policy that covers them. In fact, a few insurers have raised rates on, or even canceled, the policies of homeowners with a history of making claims involving alcohol-induced violence.

If you believe that your insurer will cover you, contact the claims department or your insurance agent and explain what happened. If the police were called, get a copy of the police report and provide it to the claims agent. Your insurance company may offer a settlement to the injured guest in return for his promise to accept the payment as full compensation for his injuries. If the guest refuses the settlement offer, your insurance company will take over your defense in any lawsuit that may be brought against you.

## A SIMPLE SOLUTION IF YOU AREN'T COVERED

If your insurance doesn't cover alcohol-related injuries, you must deal with the injured guest yourself. Offer to pay for any medical expenses incurred in the fight. If he agrees, ask him to sign a document releasing you from any further liability in return for the payment. This can be the easiest and least expensive solution, especially if the injuries are not serious. Your lawyer can provide you with the appropriate document for your injured guest to sign.

## MOUNTING A DEFENSE

If your guest was seriously injured or if he senses the possibility of a big payoff from you, hire a lawyer before you do anything else. In many jurisdictions around the country, the law makes the host responsible for alcohol-related injuries that take place on his or her property. You will need to work with your lawyer to defend yourself:

- **Are you really liable?** You may be able to show that the alleged assailant's actions were not the result of excessive alcohol consumption at your residence. For example, if he had arrived at the party in an intoxicated state right before the altercation, you can show that you didn't serve him any alcohol and may not have had time to recognize his inebriation and have him escorted home.
- **Was it self-defense?** If the alleged assailant was physically attacked or threatened by the second guest, he can claim self-defense.
- **Was he really drunk?** It is possible that the alleged assailant hadn't consumed any alcohol

at all, but the injured party assumed that he had. Check with the bartender or whoever was serving drinks at the party.

- **Are there witnesses?** You should provide your lawyer with a list of the guests at the party and their addresses and telephone numbers. Your lawyer will want to learn which guests, if any, saw the altercation, and whether a witness can support or refute the injured party's claims. While guests may be reluctant to talk about the event, in a lawsuit you can have them subpoenaed to testify about the events that they witnessed.

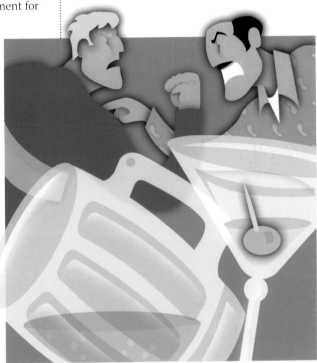

**HOMEOWNER ALERT** *If you entertain frequently and serve alcoholic beverages, check the related laws in your state so that you can be a responsible host. To protect yourself further, you may also want to consider a special endorsement to your homeowner's insurance.*

> *Y*our neighbor plays his stereo at
> full volume all hours of the day and night, with the windows
> wide open. It's intolerable.

Noisy neighbors can drive you crazy, and that's why most communities have laws designed to preserve peace and quiet. These laws vary but usually limit noise that is unnecessary, unreasonable, or that occurs late at

---

*O*rganizing the nearby community can be effective in quieting things down.

---

night or early in the morning. A snowblower clearing a driveway at noon probably isn't violating the local noise ordinance; at 4 A.M. it is. Similarly, if your neighbor's son practices his tuba at midday, it's much less likely that he's violating the law than if he were playing at midnight.

Some noise laws set out clear definitions of a violation, such as sounds exceeding a certain decibel level or that continue for an extended period of time. Others state that any noise that is "excessive" or "unreasonable" is prohibited, but do not define those terms. That means it's up to a police officer and ultimately a judge to decide if the law has been broken.

### SCOPE OUT THE SITUATION

Before you take any drastic steps, do some preliminary work:

- **Contact the offending neighbor** about the problem. It may be that he is unaware that the noise he is creating is offensive.
- **Find out if your neighbors are also irritated** by the nonstop rock-and-roll and enlist them to back up your complaint. Organizing the nearby community can be effective in quieting things down.
- **Call the police to find out what constitutes a noise-law violation** in your town and ask

how you can prove that your neighbor has gone beyond the limits.

### GETTING HELP

The next time the stereo is on full blast, call the police with your complaint. Unfortunately, in some cases the police will arrive after the noise has stopped. If that's the case, consider buying or renting a decibel meter, which can record the noise levels as they occur. If the readings exceed the legal limits, you will probably be able to convince the police to be more attentive to the situation. They may place their own decibel meter on your property before taking action.

### TURNING DOWN THE SOUND

If the noisy neighbor is found to have violated your local noise ordinance, he probably will

receive a warning for a first offense. After that, the neighbor will receive a citation and have to pay a fine—unless he decides to contest the matter in court. If the neighbor is found guilty, he may be fined and ordered to pay court costs.

Repeat offenses will lead to increased fines, and failure to pay the fines could lead to a citation for contempt of court.

If your neighbor continues to be noisy, even after he has been cited and fined, he may also be guilty of disturbing the peace or disorderly conduct. In most states, these are misdemeanors, and your neighbor could find himself facing as much as a year in county jail and ordered to pay increased fines and court costs.

Your neighbor's new fence is a few feet over your property line, but she refuses to move it.

This is one of the more common problems in the suburbs. Your neighbor's new fence is what the law calls an *encroachment* on your property. Encroachment is a kind of trespass that, left unchallenged, could end up permanently costing you a piece of your property.

## WHAT'S THE LAW?

Under a legal doctrine known as *adverse possession*, someone who comes onto your land, even a small portion of it, and plants a garden or puts up a swing set for his children may eventually gain ownership of that part of your property.

Similarly, a person who uses your land openly (as a shortcut to the bus stop, for example) but doesn't actually take possession of it may gain what is known as a *prescriptive easement.* Although it usually takes many years—10 or more—for a neighbor to gain legal rights to your property under either doctrine, it's smart to take action right away. You don't have to alienate your neighbors or even stop their use of your land, but you do need to legally establish your ownership.

> **TAKE NOTE** *The longer you put off responding to the encroachment, the more difficult asserting your ownership will be. As a result, your heirs might receive a smaller piece of property than you originally purchased.*

## ACTION PLAN

Be calm, be cool, and build your case:

- **Check your deed and county records** before talking to your neighbor. That way you'll be certain about your property's boundaries. If there's any question about the actual property line, have it surveyed.

- **Talk to your neighbor.** Show her clear proof of her encroachment. Ask your neighbor to move the fence back to her property.

## FACING UP TO OBSTINACY

If your neighbor refuses to remove the fence, you have several options:

- **If you are generally on friendly terms,** and you believe she made an honest mistake and cannot afford to have the fence moved, you can offer to give her permission to maintain the fence on your land. Create a simple written agreement describing the fence and its location and giving the neighbor your consent to have the fence on your property. Include a sentence that allows you to revoke your permission without her consent. Sign the agreement, have your neighbor sign it, and keep a copy with your real estate records.

- **If your neighbor refuses to sign** the permission agreement, stronger steps are in order. Hire a real estate lawyer to write a letter to your neighbor asking her to remove the fence before you file a lawsuit to settle the matter. Such a letter can often persuade an obstinate person to act. Of course, if you receive no response to the letter, your lawyer will help you to pursue the matter in court.

## DO-IT-YOURSELF JUSTICE

Can you simply tear down the fence yourself? You are usually entitled to dismantle any structure that was built on your property without your permission. Remember, however, that doing so risks long-term bad feelings with your neighbor. Before you start dismantling the fence, check the boundaries of your property one last time.

> You live in a seniors' community and are dismayed
> to find that the daughter and minor grandchildren of your
> next-door neighbor have now moved in with her.

The federal Fair Housing Act prohibits residential buildings and communities from discriminating against people based on their family status. A family with one or more children under the age of 18 can't be denied housing so long as at least one adult in the family is the parent or legal guardian of the children.

But there are exceptions to the Fair Housing Act for communities that consist primarily of older residents. Families with young children can be legally excluded from a community if the Department of Housing and Urban Development (HUD) finds that it was established for, and is occupied by, elderly persons under a federal, state, or local government program. For example:

- A community has only residents who are age 62 or older.
- A community has 80 percent or more of its residential units occupied by at least one resident age 55 or older, provides significant services and facilities for older people, and has a public policy stating its intent to house only those 55 or older.

## Prudent First Step

Before you involve your community association, talk to your neighbor about her expanded household. The situation may be temporary, due to a divorce, a family illness, or another set of circumstances that will end soon. In most senior communities, provisions are made for younger people to stay with a resident for a limited time. You may learn that the daughter and her children will be gone shortly.

If it appears, however, that the situation is more than a temporary one, you will need to contact the tenants or homeowners association that enforces the community's rules. It will probably write your neighbor a letter stating that she is in violation of community rules and giving her a deadline by which to have her daughter and grandchildren out of her home.

## Enlightened Self-interest

A community that bills itself as designed for seniors has an interest in seeing that younger people are consistently excluded; otherwise, the community jeopardizes its "seniors only" status.

If the association lets your neighbor's child and grandchildren stay, future attempts to keep younger applicants out of the community could lead to the community no longer being eligible for exemption from the Fair Housing Act.

> *A community that bills itself as designed for seniors has an interest in seeing that younger people are consistently excluded.*

## Enforcement Options

If your neighbor remains uncooperative, the association has several options:

- **If your neighbor owns the home** or residential unit she lives in, the association may fine her for failing to comply with community regulations. If she fails to pay the fine, the association can attach a lien against her property, which can restrict her ability to sell the property unless the lien is paid.
- **If she rents her unit** from another private individual, the association can notify the owner of the property and demand that he or she evict the young people.
- **If she lives in a rental unit owned by the community,** the association can begin eviction proceedings against her for violating the terms of her lease.
- **If nothing else convinces your neighbor** to send her daughter and grandchildren on their way, the association may have to go to court to obtain an order requiring them to leave the property. Don't hesitate to keep after the association to enforce the community's rules on age. It's the association's job to help preserve the nature of the community and protect your ability to enjoy peaceful, child-free property.

In most jurisdictions, you are financially responsible for any damage your pet causes to other people or their property (see "Pets and the Law," page 62). This means that you are probably liable for repairs to the bike and you may be liable for any medical bills that the youngster incurred from the spill.

Check with your local police for the laws in your community, and then check with your household insurance company. Your liability coverage may include your pet's misdeeds, and the insurance company will pay for the bicycle repairs.

Smart pet owners buy liability insurance that includes pet coverage. Unexpected events can cause even the best-trained pet to get excited, take up a chase, or run for cover, creating havoc in its wake.

## Dog Laws

Every state and municipality has ordinances dealing with dogs. Here's an overview.

- **Leash laws** require an owner to keep the dog on a leash when the dog is off the owner's property. Some communities now have special dog parks where a dog can run unleashed.

- **Poop-scoop laws** require dog owners to remove and properly discard any excrement their dogs deposit in any public or private place other than their own properties.

- **Dog-bite laws** in half the states hold owners liable for any injury caused by their dogs, whether it involves biting or not.

- **Barking-dog laws** call excessive barking a nuisance. If a neighbor complains about your dog's barking, you can be fined. If it continues, you may be forced to give up the dog.

- **Vicious-dog laws** may prohibit ownership of certain breeds considered to be dangerous. To have a dog declared dangerous, someone who has been hurt or threatened by it files a complaint; a judge then decides if the dog needs to be constrained, removed, or destroyed.

- **Dog-fighting laws** prohibit owners from provoking dogs to fight. Training or using an animal for organized dog fighting is a felony in most states, punishable by fines and imprisonment.

## PETS AND THE LAW

As rewarding as pets may be to those who love them, they can put careless owners at risk for medical bills, damages, and fines. Many apartment buildings and homeowners associations have their own rules about pets, which you should check into before you move in or take on a pet. In addition, most communities have laws stating…

- What kinds of animals you can keep as pets, barring some wild animals and vicious breeds of dogs (see page 61 for more on dog laws)

- Which pets need annual licenses and rabies shots (always dogs, and sometimes cats)

- How many pets you can legally have in your home at one time

■ **Damage laws.** Most states make you financially responsible for any damage your pet does to a neighbor's property.

■ **Pet's rights.** Your neighbor cannot harm your pet for digging up his rosebushes or soiling his lawn. As long as the person has not been threatened by the pet, the pet is protected. If the neighbor hurts the pet, you may be able to recover the costs of veterinary bills or even collect compensatory damages.

■ **Injury laws.** An owner of a wild animal is subject to a higher duty of care to protect others from harm from the animal and is responsible for any injuries or damages it causes, whether or not the animal is provoked.

■ **When your pet bites.** You may or may not be responsible. If a teenager pulls the tail of your gentle tabby cat and it nips her, you will probably not be liable. However, if your snarling dachshund attacks the postal-carrier's ankle, you will be held accountable. When your dog bites someone, report it to the police right away. Also provide proof from your vet that your animal has an up-to-date rabies shot; this will save the victim a series of painful anti-rabies injections. If your dog is overdue for a rabies booster, the animal will be impounded to make sure it doesn't have the disease. Offer to pay the victim for any medical costs and report the incident to your insurance company.

■ **If You Are the Victim.** Victims and pet owners often settle suits out of court. Do the following to protect your interests:

- Immediately get the name and phone number of the pet owner, and find out if the animal has had rabies shots. This may spare the victim the ordeal of anti-rabies injections.

- Get the names and addresses of any witnesses to the incident.

- Report the incident to the local animal control board; if you discover that there are previously reported incidents involving the same animal, you will have a stronger case.

- Save copies of any medical bills or other expenses connected to the injury.

- If your injuries are severe and the expenses substantial, contact a lawyer for advice.

BUYING & SELLING A HOME

> **Y**ou make an offer on a house and the owner agrees.
> Now, just before closing day, he is asking for more money.

**S**urprises like this are never welcome. Here's what you can do when you are just about to buy the house of your dreams and the owner suddenly wants to change the deal.

### TELL ME WHY

First of all, find out why the seller has raised the price after accepting your offer (see "Bidding on a House," page 68). If you are buying a house directly from the owner, you can talk to him. If a real estate agent is involved, go through her. Real estate agents can help—they take a dim view of last-minute problems that could delay or take away their commission.

The owner may be raising the sale price for a reason:

### SMART MOVES

A real estate agent usually works for the seller, who pays her fee. She therefore has responsibilities to the seller that she doesn't have to the buyer. Be cautious when you talk to her. If you make an offer of $150,000 for a home but tell her you could go as high as $175,000, she may be legally required to tell that to the seller.

- **Miscommunication.** The seller may think the house's swimming pool, for example, is worth extra money, while you believe it was included in the original price. Here's what to do:
  ● Read the terms of your purchase agreement to see if the pool was specifically included or excluded in calculating the offer price. If it was included, the seller has no case.
  ● Determine if the pool is removable (an aboveground pool) or a fixture (a built-in pool). An aboveground pool is the owner's *personal property,* if it is portable—not fastened or attached to the house or its surroundings. Personal property isn't part of the original price unless it was specifically described in your agreement. A built-in pool, on the other hand, is part of the purchase price unless it was specifically excluded.
- **He is trying to sell personal property.** If the

seller has upped his asking price because he wants to force you to buy his aboveground pool, you can do one of two things:
  ● Agree to buy the pool under a separate contract.
  ● Refuse to buy it and insist that the seller complete the sale as planned.

- **He is concerned about your finances.** You may have failed to meet the terms of the offer. If the seller is financing your loan, for example, he may discover that your credit is not as solid as he thought. As a result, he may want a bigger down payment or more money to make up for the increased risk. But unless the agreement you signed specifically states that he has this right, he cannot change the terms without your consent.

### YOUR LAST RESORT

If the situation continues, you can go to court to seek damages from the seller for his failure to honor the contract. In some cases, you may be able to get *specific performance* of the contract—the court orders the seller to complete the deal as originally agreed. Specific performance is used sparingly. If the seller's property has a unique design or special historic value, it's more probable that a court will order it. Otherwise, the court may award money damages, including the living expenses you incurred and higher costs you paid for a similar house as a result.

**TAKE NOTE** *Hire a qualified real estate lawyer as soon as the sale is in jeopardy. She will know the laws and how the court is likely to act.*

## A Checklist of Closing Costs

For most home buyers, closing costs (also referred to as settlement costs) can add a surprisingly large amount to the purchase price of a home. While these costs depend on how the home is financed and other factors, a buyer can expect to pay the following:

- **Title fees.** A title search ensures that no one else has recorded a claim to the property.

- **Title insurance.** This protects the buyer and the mortgage lender against claims challenging the buyer's ownership of the property. Often the seller will purchase the buyer's policy; the buyer usually pays for the lender's policy.

- **Recording fee.** This is the cost of recording the deed and mortgage in the county real estate records.

- **Inspection fee.** This is the cost of inspections required by local laws, such as termite and furnace inspections.

- **Survey fee.** Surveys of the property are often required by mortgage lenders as a condition of making the loan.

- **Loan discount fee.** Commonly known as points, this is the fee a buyer agrees to pay in order to get a loan. For example, a fee of two points on a $200,000 mortgage is $4,000.

- **Appraisal fee.** Lenders require an appraisal to guarantee that they are not lending more for the property than it is worth.

- **Legal fees.** In most states, buyers and sellers pay for their own lawyers. In some states, buyers may be required to pay their lender's legal fees as well.

> *Y*our real estate agent shows you homes
> only in a certain neighborhood. You want to look elsewhere.

You have worked hard, saved your money, and now you are ready to buy a house. The real estate agent, however, is showing only homes in certain neighborhoods and avoiding others, a practice known as *steering*.

This brand of discrimination is subtler than it once was, but you still feel demoralized. The good news: Federal and state laws make it illegal for real estate agencies to discriminate against clients based on race, creed, gender, national origin, disability, or even pregnancy.

### Be Your Own Advocate

Ask your real estate agent why he is doing this. Chances are, the agent will not have a ready answer to your question and will show you homes in your price range in several different areas. If the agent resists, contact the agent's supervisor and tell her of your concerns. You may be given a different, more cooperative agent.

### Be Proactive

If not, you can help yourself—and others—if you make a strident protest. If your agent is a Realtor (be aware that not all are), write a letter to the local Board of Realtors, describing how the agent acted and how he violated the fair housing laws.

Also send a letter to the agent's employer and to the fair housing enforcement agency in the community where you are looking. You can find the right agency by calling city hall or the county administrator's office.

Making your concerns known to as many regulators as possible puts pressure on the agent and his firm. The local Board of Realtors, for example, can remove the agent's designation as a Realtor. The fair housing board can discipline the agent and even the real estate firm.

You may also want to contact the U.S. Department of Housing and Urban Development (HUD). HUD can investigate your claim of discrimination, either directly or by referring your complaint to a state or local housing authority. Be aware that an investigation by HUD must begin within 30 days. A real estate agent who is found guilty of discrimination can be fined and lose his real estate license.

### SUING FOR DAMAGES

If you have been a victim of discrimination, you can hire a lawyer to find out if it is worth filing a lawsuit for damages. You must bring your suit, either in U.S. District Court or in state court, within 180 days of the discriminatory act.

## TAKING TITLE

Today most real estate comes with one of two kinds of deeds:

■ **Warranty deed.** This is the most common one, and the one that effectively protects a buyer. The seller promises that the title she is transferring to the buyer is "good," meaning that...

● The seller is the true owner of the property.

● The seller has the right to sell the property.

● There are no claims against the property.

If someone later claims to have an interest in the property, or if a lien against the property is discovered (page 48), the buyer can sue the seller for breach of the warranty.

■ **Quitclaim deed.** This deed is far less desirable from the buyer's point of view. The seller makes no promises or warranties to the buyer—not even the promise that she actually owns the property being transferred. In fact, this deed transfers only the interest the seller owns to the buyer. In some cases, the seller may not have any interest at all, and you could end up paying the seller for property that she doesn't even own.

● Understand that accepting a quitclaim deed is extremely risky for a buyer. If you want to buy a property and the seller will only offer a quitclaim deed, get the advice of a real estate lawyer before proceeding any further.

> *You discover that your mortgage lender is charging you a higher rate of interest than it charges in other parts of town.*

Although the practice is not as common as it once was, some mortgage lenders still redline certain neighborhoods. *Redlining* means using different lending standards in a community for racial or ethnic reasons, or because the area has a high crime rate. In the old days, lenders could justify it by claiming that…

- The risk of losses was higher in these neighborhoods because the borrowers were less likely to make payments.
- Homes were at greater risk of damage or destruction, leaving the lender without a house to resell if the owner defaulted.

## THE LAW IS ON YOUR SIDE

Two effective federal laws prevent redlining solely on the basis of race or ethnic background:

- **The Community Reinvestment Act** requires banks to provide lending services to people in the neighborhoods where the banks receive their deposits.
- **The Home Mortgage Disclosure Act** (HMDA) requires most mortgage lenders to

submit detailed information about the race, gender, and income of loan applicants. Community groups, civil rights organizations, and banks use this data to detect redlining.

---

> *Two effective federal laws prevent redlining solely on the basis of race or ethnicity.*

---

**TAKE NOTE** *No law requires a lender to make a loan to a borrower who isn't financially qualified. The bank's decision must be based on the family's creditworthiness.*

Before assuming that your higher mortgage rate is due to redlining, look for other reasons why your loan's interest rate may be higher. If you have a history of late payments, bankruptcy, or job instability, a lender can legitimately charge you a higher interest rate. Check your credit rating to be sure there are no errors that might be causing the problem. If there are errors, straighten them out in writing (page 111) as soon as you can.

### MAKING YOUR CASE

The HMDA data is available to everyone, but unless you are an expert in statistical analysis, it may be hard to use. You may be better off seeking help from a civil rights organization, such as the National Association for the Advancement of Colored People (NAACP), or a community group that promotes fair housing opportunities.

If you are convinced that you are a victim of redlining, call the bank and ask to speak to the senior mortgage lender. Express your concern over the phone, and then follow up with a letter. In the letter, make sure you do the following:

■ **Ask for a meeting with the senior lender.** When you go, bring all the information you have that supports your claim, such as HMDA statistics or bank advertisements promoting a specific interest rate that is lower than yours.

■ **Ask that your loan rate be reconsidered** based on your credit history and ability to pay.

Make sure that you record the names of all the bank employees you speak with and that you keep copies of your correspondence.

### GOING TO A HIGHER AUTHORITY

If the lender refuses you, file a complaint with the appropriate agency, usually the Federal Reserve System. Write to its Division of Consumer and Community Affairs and include…

✔ Your name, address, and telephone number
✔ The name and address of the bank
✔ Your account or loan number
✔ The names of bank employees you contacted about the problem
✔ A brief description of your complaint
✔ Copies of any letters and documents that can help the Federal Reserve System conduct its investigation.

Your complaint will be sent to a consumer affairs representative at the regional Federal Reserve Bank. He will contact the lending bank about your problem and request all records the bank may have in regard to your complaint. The representative may also contact you by mail or telephone for additional information.

Once the investigation is made, the Federal Reserve will tell you its decision. Just be patient: Your answer may take as long as one or two months. If the Fed finds the bank at fault, it will tell you what the violation was and what it has ordered the bank to do.

### YOUR LAST RESORT

If the Fed finds in the bank's favor, you can talk to an attorney who specializes in civil rights law, as well as to civil rights organizations and community groups. They may be interested in pursuing the matter if the evidence appears strong.

If you aren't afraid of being in the public eye, don't forget the power of the media. Present your case to the editors of your local newspaper and the producers of local radio and television news programs. Their influence, combined with pressure from local activists, could help convince an errant lender to change its ways.

## BIDDING ON A HOUSE

When you want to buy a particular house, make an offer to the seller using a form known as an *Offer to Purchase* or a *Residential Purchase Agreement*. State your bid price and the contingencies that must be met for you and the seller to come to terms. Your offer may be contingent on your selling your current home, getting financing, and having the property inspected for major defects or damage (see "Hiring a House Inspector," page 71).

Once the seller accepts your offer, the purchase agreement becomes a binding contract. The Offer to Purchase, however, seldom sets out all the details of the sale. Negotiate through the real estate agent or the seller and ask your lawyer to spell out…

■ **How property taxes** or assessments are to be prorated between buyer and seller

■ **Who will pay repair costs** to put the house in working order

■ **A contingency plan** if the home is appraised at less than the agreed-upon price, which can make it difficult for the buyer to obtain financing. (A lending institution may require an independent appraisal of the property's value before approving a mortgage.)

■ **Any personal property** included in the purchase, such as furniture, draperies, or an aboveground swimming pool

How annoying it is to have your bank let you down! Somehow, you think, it wasn't always like this. Remember the 1946 movie *It's a Wonderful Life*? Jimmy Stewart as George Bailey, the head of the local Building and Loan Society, lends money to the residents of Bedford Falls so they can build their homes. Their payments allow the Building and Loan to lend money to other homeowners in turn, and the money stays safely in the community.

That isn't the case today. Mortgages are sold to institutions outside the community and it is up to whoever has taken over the loan to make your insurance and tax payments (page 70).

Unfortunately, some banks don't service mortgage loans well. Trouble starts when…

- **The bank fails to pay your homeowner's insurance premium** on time. The insurer will send you and the lender a notice that your payment is late. The letter will tell you that you can either pay the premium or face cancellation of your policy.
- **The bank doesn't make property tax payments** on time. Unfortunately, the first time you are aware of this is when you receive a delinquency notice with a penalty for late payment.

In either case, immediately call the institution that is handling your mortgage. The payment may have already been made, and the check and delinquency notices crossed in the mail. If payment hasn't been made, find out when it will be. Write down the name and position of the person you speak to; note the date and time of your conversation.

## PAYMENTS LATE?

Whenever payments are late you need to act, and act fast:

- **If an insurance payment is late,** call your insurance agent to tell him when to expect the money, and give the name, posi-

tion, and phone number of the person you spoke to at the lender's customer service department. Be sure to ask your insurer to call you as soon as payment has been received.

- **If the property tax payment is late,** call your local tax collector a few days after the date that the lender says it sent the check just to be sure it has been received.

If there is a penalty fee for late payment, the loan servicer, not you, must pay it. Read your escrow statement to make sure that the lender didn't take the penalty fee out of your account.

## MAKE THEM PAY

If the lender deducted a penalty fee from your escrow account, contact the lender in writing immediately (send it certified mail, return receipt requested). You can find the address on your payment coupon or in your payment book. State the problem ("You deducted money from my escrow account to pay a penalty for late payment of property taxes"), the reason this is unacceptable ("It is your responsibility to pay my

taxes on time from my escrow account"), and the solution you want from the lender ("Please reimburse my escrow account for the penalty fee").

Under federal law, a loan servicer must reply to a written complaint in 20 working days. A lender can be forced to pay up to $1,000 in damages *each time* it fails to service your loan properly. To sue for damages, you can file a lawsuit.

**HOMEOWNER ALERT** *If you think that your loan has been sold, don't pay the new lender until you confirm the transaction. Scam artists sometimes send you a letter, hoping you'll make a payment to them before you discover the ruse. If your loan is legitimately transferred, you'll get a "good-bye letter" from the old lender and a "hello letter" from the new one.*

---

## UNDERSTANDING THE MORTGAGE BUSINESS

Most mortgage agreements give the lender the right to sell the mortgage, and chances are a lender won't keep your mortgage for the entire term of the loan. Today more than half of all mortgages are sold to large organizations shortly after the buyer purchases the house.

- **The Federal National Mortgage Association (Fannie Mae) and the Federal Home Loan Mortgage Corporation (Freddie Mac)** buy mortgages at a discount from their face value, giving lenders an immediate cash return.

- **To service the mortgages,** Fannie Mae and Freddie Mac contract with banks and other organizations that will collect payments and manage escrow accounts to pay property taxes and insurance. Mortgage servicing is a profitable business for large financial institutions.

To find out who is servicing your mortgage now, contact your original lender and ask which organization purchased your loan. For Fannie Mae, send a copy of your letter to the Public Information Officer there. For Freddie Mac, send a letter to the office that's closest to you. To get the address, call the Freddie Mac's New York City office at (212) 418-8900.

---

*Y*ou've signed all the papers on your new home. Now you discover a serious defect in the foundation that the seller didn't tell you about.

---

**H**appily, the watchword "buyer beware" no longer applies to new homeowners. A major shift in the law means that today people who sell their home must disclose problems about their property, not cover them up.

### YOU HAVE A CASE

If you're unlucky enough to discover a serious problem such as a collapsing foundation soon after you've closed on your house, write the seller immediately. Describe the problem and how much it will cost to repair, demand that he pay you back, and set a deadline for a reply; send it certified mail, return receipt requested.

If the house was bought through a real estate agent, you (or your lawyer) should send her a similar letter. Agents must ask about and disclose any known defects before a sale takes place. State in your letter that you hold the agent and her firm liable for failure to disclose the problem.

If you don't get the response you want by the deadline you impose, send a copy of your letters to the state licensing authority. It can investigate your case and may be able to impose penalties on the real estate agent. Those penalties could include the suspending or revoking of her license to sell real estate. In some states, the licensing authority may have a fund that can pay for some or all of the repairs, easing the financial burden.

## YOUR LAST RESORT

If all else fails, you can file a lawsuit against the seller and the real estate agent. Although you are allowed to represent yourself, a good real estate lawyer may be able to help settle your claim before it goes to trial—especially when the evidence and the law are clearly on your side.

## HIRING A HOUSE INSPECTOR

A house inspection before closing is always essential, but never more important than when the house is older. The inspector should look at...

- **The foundation** for cracks, water penetration, termite damage, rot, and general structural stability

- **The exterior of the house** for water damage and rotted siding, decks, or porches

- **Yard** for proper slope and drainage

- **Doors, windows, and screens** to see that they are intact and operate properly

- **Roof, gutters, and downspouts**

- **Chimney** to determine that it has structural integrity and is free of blockages

- **Attic** for proper insulation and ventilation. In addtion, ladders to the attic should be in good repair

- **Furnace, boiler, water heater, and cooling system** to see that they are working properly, ventilated, and in good repair

- **Plumbing** for leaks. Water pressure should be adequate, and drains should all function properly. If there is a septic tank, it should be inspected

- **Electrical systems** for adequate capacity and safety. Outlets, wall switches, and rheostats should be tested to see if they work properly; wiring should be examined for age and potential defects

- **Bathrooms and kitchen** for leaks or water damage to ceilings, walls, or flooring, and damaged tile or other floor coverings. Also, all fixtures and appliances should be in working order

- **Driveway** for cracks or buckling

- **Fences and retaining walls** for defects or damage

The price of a house inspection varies widely, and may be based on factors such as the size of the house and the type of its construction. You can expect to pay from $300 and up for a thorough house inspection.

A note of caution: Be sure the inspector is covered by errors-and-omissions insurance. Coverage of this kind will give you some additional protection in case the inspector overlooked a serious problem that you discover later.

*You're ready to move into your new house, and you discover that the seller has removed the cabinets and light fixtures.*

When a house is sold, you buy the land, the house, and its fixtures—even the kitchen sink. *Fixtures* are items that are permanently attached to the structure and cannot be removed without damaging the house and affecting its value, such as wall-to-wall carpet, built-in bookcases, wall ovens, and ceiling lights. Floor lamps, area rugs, or draperies are *personal property,* and the seller is free to take them with her when she vacates the house—unless they were specifically negotiated in the sale.

### ACT QUICKLY TO GET THEM BACK

In this scenario the seller has violated the terms of your sales contract. Call her on the phone and follow up with a letter (send it certified mail, return receipt requested). The letter should…

### SMART MOVES

Make sure your purchase agreement states all the financial terms and itemizes all of the household property that is to be sold.

- Demand that the fixtures be returned, and that they be reinstalled at her expense
- Say that you will hold her responsible for the cost of repairing any damage caused by her removal of the fixtures.

Send a copy of the letter to the seller's real estate agent or brokerage firm. The agent or firm may be able to persuade the client to return the fixtures.

**TAKE NOTE** *While you can file a police report, don't expect much help. The police might consider this a civil matter, not a criminal one.*

### MAKE THE SELLER PAY

If the seller refuses to restore the fixtures, hire a lawyer and ask him to write a letter to her. This may convince her to settle out of court.

If you find that you have to go to court, you are able to sue the seller for…

- **The cost of replacing** the items, including installation
- **The cost of any damage** caused by the items' removal.

You also may be able to recover lawyer fees and court costs. Unless the amount is small, choose the regular court system over small-claims court. You can represent yourself, but a lawyer may better negotiate the maze of complaints, summons, and motions that courts require.

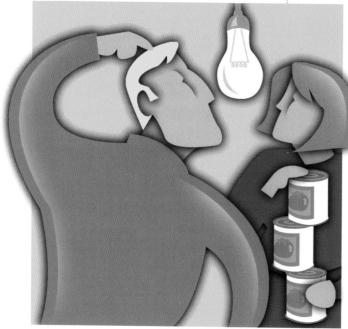

> *Y*ou want to buy a manufactured (mobile)
> home, but your bank won't lend you the money you need.

**G**etting a traditional mortgage to buy a manufactured home shouldn't be difficult if you are purchasing both the home and the lot where it will be placed.

Life becomes more difficult if you are only leasing the lot. To get financing similar to a traditional real estate mortgage, you will need to get a *chattel mortgage*—a loan secured by personal property, not real estate. Getting a chattel mortgage is similar to financing the purchase of a car, a boat, or a motorcycle. But such a loan comes with longer terms—typically 15, 20, or 25 years—and interest rates that are closer to those for traditional home mortgages than for auto loans.

## WHY A BANK MAY REFUSE

In some cases, your bank may have other reasons for refusing to accept your loan:

- **Your credit is questionable** and the bank therefore may not want to take a chance of lending you the money.
  - You have the right to see your credit report and object to inaccurate or incomplete information (page 111).
- **The appraisal of the home** shows that it is worth less than the selling price you agreed upon. The bank will thus lose money if you default on your loan. The bank should tell you if this is the reason for refusing your application.
  - Unlike traditional homes, which tend to increase in value over time in most places, older manufactured homes lose value.
- **The bank is guilty of discrimination,** especially if it has a record of not making loans for manufactured homes in areas with a large minority population.
  - You can file a complaint with both the Federal Reserve Bank and your state's office of consumer protection. If found guilty, the lender could be required to reconsider your loan or it could be fined.

## EXPLORE OTHER OPTIONS

Lending is a competitive business. You can look for financing in many places:

- **Call other banks and lenders in the community.** Some banks are more willing than others to make loans on manufactured homes—and know more about such homes.
- **Get financing through the manufacturer.** Some companies provide financing at competitive rates. Developers of mobile-home communities sometimes offer help as well, but these kinds of loans can be more expensive.
- **Negotiate owner financing.** Some homeowners are willing to take a down payment and then receive payments over time. This is especially true in cases where the homeowner can pay an interest rate that's a little higher than that which the seller might be able to get from other conservative investments.

In most cases, if your credit is good and the home is sound, you should be able to get financing to buy the home, no matter what.

*Your neighbor has begun using his back yard to store old cars and furniture. You want to sell your house but fear that the unsightly view will lower the price.*

While most homeowners and tenants take pride in the appearance of the house they live in, there are some who either don't care about the way their homes look or simply don't realize just how unattractive their property has become.

There are several ways you can fix the situation. Start by contacting your neighbor in person, if you feel comfortable doing so. If that gets you nowhere, put your complaint in writing (send it certified mail, return receipt requested), and keep a copy to prove you notified him.

Contact the zoning department of your town with your complaint. You will need to give the address of the offender's property, your neighbor's name if you know it, and any other information that will help a zoning inspector identify the property and determine what ordinances are being violated. A zoning inspector will pay a visit to the house, usually within a few days. The inspector will report to the zoning department management, which will contact the property owner and require that the property be brought into compliance.

### ZOOM IN ON ZONING

In most communities, zoning laws restrict the ways in which a homeowner can use his or her property. Residential codes, for example, usually prohibit owners from operating a junkyard or other business on their property that leads to increased traffic, noise, or pollution. Even if your neighbor isn't operating a business, zoning laws typically require that eyesores such as inoperable cars and abandoned furniture be screened or fenced so they cannot be seen from neighboring property and from the street.

### PLANNED COMMUNITIES

You may live in a development with its own restrictions on how property can be used. These restrictions, which are commonly referred to as Covenants, Conditions, and Restrictions (CC&Rs), give each homeowner a private right of enforcement against a neighbor who violates them.

In some communities a homeowners association has the right to act on behalf of the community in bringing offenders into compliance. If you belong to a homeowners association, you should make your complaint following the association's rules. Some associations, for example, will investigate a complaint made by telephone, while others require a written objection before taking action.

The association will investigate and then notify the person responsible for the violation and require corrective action within a specified period. If your neighbor refuses to comply, the association usually has the power to punish the offender by suspending access to community facilities or issuing a fine.

### PROVING A PRIVATE NUISANCE

If neither CC&Rs nor zoning laws prevent your neighbor from using his property for a junkyard, your last resort is going to district or county court to have the property declared a private nuisance, a circumstance that unreasonably or unlawfully interferes with your ability to use and enjoy your own property or to sell it at full price. Here are some ways to make your suit successful:

- **Contact other neighbors** who may have been affected by the unsightly back yard before you file a private nuisance lawsuit; they may want to join you as plaintiffs in the suit or even file their own lawsuits at the same time you file yours. Having multiple plaintiffs in one suit can reduce your overall legal costs, while the impact of facing multiple lawsuits may move your neighbor to clean up his property in order to avoid costly litigation.
- **Show that yours is a residential community** (provide photos of homes nearby) and that your neighbor's yard is a private nuisance. This proves that harboring the junk is not a reasonable use of his property, that others nearby do not pile up junk outdoors, and that this is not a proper way to manage the property.
- **Show how the yard full of junk interferes with your enjoyment** of your own property and your ability to sell it. Take photos of the yard as seen from your own. Ask a real estate appraiser for a statement that the neighbor's junk diminishes the value of your property.

- **Prove that the junk is there as the result of your neighbor's actions.** In one case, a property owner escaped liability for the junk that was on his property because it had been dumped there without his knowledge. In court, he showed that he began taking steps to clean up the property as soon as he became aware of the problem, and the court dismissed the lawsuit against him. (Now would be the time to present the letter you sent earlier. It is proof that your neighbor has been aware of the junk and has taken no action.)

### Happy Outcome

If your neighbor rents the property, you can file suit against both him and his landlord, and this could work to your advantage. Often a landlord who is served notice of a lawsuit will take steps to see that his tenant cleans up the yard. If the lease requires a tenant to maintain the rental property, the landlord can threaten eviction.

If you are successful in your lawsuit, you can sell your house and live happily ever after. You may also either be awarded damages or obtain a court order requiring the neighbor to clean up his yard. In some cases, a court may decide that both damages and a court order are appropriate, in which case you've hit a home run.

---

## Paying Taxes When You Sell Your Home

Since 1997, home sellers have benefited from a revision in the federal tax code. Today a single person can exclude as much as $250,000 of profits and a married couple can exclude a gain of $500,000 from the sale of their home. The only limitations are:

- The house has to have been the seller's principal residence for at least two of the five years immediately before the sale.
- The seller can take the exclusion only once every two years.

However, there are other taxes you can expect to pay when you sell your home:

- **Annual property tax** (a prorated portion) when you close the sale.
- **A transfer tax,** depending on your state and local laws. This pays for the cost of recording mortgage documents and the deed of sale in the county property records.
- **A sales tax** may be assessed, usually as a percentage of the home's sales price.

It may be possible to have the buyer pay some or all of these taxes, depending on local law and custom. Your real estate agent or lawyer can advise you.

---

**Y**ou've listed your house with a real estate
agent, but she isn't trying very hard to sell your home.

---

**W**hen you list your house—for what-ever reason—you may feel like a chorus girl in a Broadway play: It's hard to get anyone's attention. You are disappointed because you have signed an agreement with an agent and she soon shows little interest in your home. In fact, some agents get listings, and then rely on *other* agents to sell the home. (This is because the listing agent gets part of the commission no matter who makes the deal.)

### MAKE YOUR AGENT ACCOUNTABLE

Read the listing agreement you signed. The agent usually promises to "exercise reasonable efforts" or "use due diligence" in selling your home. Give her a call if she isn't following through. Explain your concerns and ask her to describe what she has done since you signed the agreement. Ask her what she plans to do in the next two weeks.

---

**W**hen you need to
sell your home quickly,
a lazy or
inattentive agent is
hard to tolerate.

---

She should be able to tell you what she has done ("I put your home in the Multiple Listing Service, placed two newspaper ads, and mailed brochures to agents I've worked with in the past") and what she is going to do ("I'm bringing the other agents from my firm on a tour, and I want to hold an open house next Saturday"). Otherwise she is going to have a hard time proving that she is doing what is required.

Keep in mind, however, that you *must* cooper-ate with the agent in selling your home. If you refuse to hold an open house, or if you consis-

tently say "No" when she wants to show your home to a prospective buyer, you can't expect her to have much success.

### SMART MOVES

When you list your house with a real estate agent, sign an agreement that lasts only for a few months. Then, if you are dissatisfied, you can switch to a more aggressive agent sooner rather than later.

### TURNING UP THE HEAT

If you've held up your end of the bargain and the agent has not, write her a letter outlining your dissatisfac-tion (send it certified mail, return receipt requested):

■ **Restate her contractual duty.** Make a copy of the con-tract and circle the relevant text.
■ **Say you expect a marketing program** within seven days, or you will consider the agreement breached.
■ **Send a copy of the letter to her firm.** Her supervisor may be able to get her to act.

### YOUR LAST RESORT

When you need to sell your home quickly, a lazy or inattentive agent is hard to tolerate. Chances are, you are eager to find another agent. What you should do next depends on the length of your listing agreement:

■ **If the remaining time is short,** wait it out.
■ **If the agreement has a longer term,** you can cite a breach of contract and cancel the agreement. Write the head of the firm and the agent a follow-up letter (send it certified mail, return receipt requested) that…
  ● Restates your dissatisfaction with her efforts.
  ● States that the brokerage has violated the terms of the contract by not making a good-faith effort to sell your house. Refer to the clause in your agreement.
  ● Includes copies of all correspondence. Note any lack of response as well.

The agent may claim that you cannot termi-nate the agreement or that you have interfered with her ability to sell your home; she may even threaten a lawsuit if you list your house with another agent. If she does, consult a real estate lawyer as soon as possible. If the lawyer agrees with you, hire another agent.

> **Y**ou find a buyer for your house after your listing agreement expires. The agent who had the listing now demands a commission for the sale.

**M**ake no mistake: Real estate agents will see to it that they get any commission they are due. In this case, if you had an Exclusive Right to Sell agreement (see "Listing Agreements," page 78) and sell your home to someone who saw the home while the listing was still active, chances are you still owe the agent a commission.

This provision protects the real estate agent from being cut out of a deal between buyer and seller. It is tempting for the buyer to offer a little less than the asking price and for the seller to save the agent's commission (typically around 6 percent). Both come out ahead on the deal.

### HANDLING A CLAIM

If the agent did not show the buyer the house, you have a case. Perhaps the real estate agent doesn't understand the law, doesn't realize that he didn't show the buyer your house, or mistakenly believes that a cooperating agency brought you and the buyer together. You should…

- **Deny his claim,** if he talks to you about it.
- **Respond in writing** (sent certified mail, return receipt requested) as soon as possible, if and when he sends you a written complaint, and in it…
  - Acknowledge the agent's letter.
  - Explain why the agent is mistaken in making his claim ("Jim Smith was never shown the property by you or by another agent during our listing agreement").
  - State that you consider the matter closed.

- Keep a copy for your files in case the agent decides to pursue the matter.

### GOING TO MEDIATION OR ARBITRATION

In some listing agreements, there may be a clause requiring that disputes about commissions be submitted to mediation or arbitration. If your agreement so specifies, this is the next step in your dispute. To get ready for the meeting, you should gather your evidence, including…

- Testimony from the buyer in the form of a written affidavit or by testifying in person at the proceedings
- Copies of any correspondence you had with the agent, brokerage, and their lawyer.

The agent will probably have an attorney present. While you don't have to have a lawyer in mediation or arbitration proceedings, it is helpful to get legal advice beforehand.

Mediation tries to get the parties to agree on a compromise solution. If you are still unhappy, you can go to court. Arbitration has stricter rules to follow and may be *binding* (you cannnot go to court if you lose). You may want a lawyer if the matter goes to arbitration.

**HOMEOWNER ALERT** *Negotiate the terms of your exclusive listing. For example, have agents keep a record, such as a sign-in sheet during an Open House, of who has been shown the house. This will reduce the possibility of the agent claiming a commission after the listing has expired.*

## LISTING AGREEMENTS

Before signing any real estate listing agreement when you're selling a house, it's useful to know what the different types of agreements are.

■ **Multi-listing agreement** allows your real estate agency to share the listing with other agencies. All of the agencies can arrange showings, and your agency will share the fee with whoever sells the house.

■ **Exclusive Right to Sell agreement** gives the agency the right to earn a commission no matter who sells your home *if* the sale takes place during the term of the agreement. Real estate firms and their agents prefer this agreement over all others, because even if you do all the work of finding the buyer and negotiating the contract, they can still claim their commission.

■ **Exclusive Agency agreement** requires the brokerage and its agents to make an active effort to sell the property. But it also allows the homeowner to avoid paying any commission if he sells the home on his own. Real estate firms and their agents are not enthusiastic about this kind of contract, and in a buyer's market (when selling a home is difficult) you may not get an Exclusive Agency agreement. Still, it doesn't hurt to ask, and you will almost certainly have to—few real estate professionals will tell you about this kind of agreement voluntarily.

■ **Open Listing agreement** allows a seller to list his home with several real estate agencies. The agency that sells the house is the only one to earn a commission. And if the owner sells without any help, no commission is owed to anyone. Open listings are seldom used for residential sales. You can ask, but it's unlikely you will get this kind of listing.

> *Your broker found a buyer, but he backed out before closing. The broker claims you owe her a commission anyway.*

Unless you did something—or failed to do something—that caused the buyer to back out of the deal, you don't owe a commission to the real estate agent.

### ACTING IN GOOD FAITH

Take a look at your listing agreement. You'll probably find a paragraph that requires you to act in good faith in selling the property. You must…

● Cooperate with the broker
● Review offers made for your property
● Follow through with the sale once you accept an offer.

You could be liable for the broker's commission, however, if you do any of the following:

● Accept an offer, and then decide to take your house off the market
● Agree to make repairs at the request of the buyer but then refuse to do so, giving the buyer no choice but to back out of the deal
● Fail to disclose a serious defect and cause the buyer to withdraw his offer as soon as the defect is discovered.

Ask your broker to write a letter explaining why she believes that you owe a commission. Remember, she may be bluffing.

### STAND UP, STAND UP

If you acted in good faith, you have the law on your side. Write the real estate firm, saying that you won't pay the commission. In the letter…

- Explain how her claims are unsubstantiated.
- Remind her that you have done what you could do to close the sale.
- Say that you still want her to try to sell your home (if your listing is still active).

Send a copy of the letter to her boss and to your state's real estate licensing authority (send it certified mail, return receipt requested), keeping copies for your file. If your agent is a Realtor (understand that not all are), she can be disciplined for failing to adhere to the organization's code of conduct.

If she persists in her suit or takes you to arbitration, hire a real estate lawyer. If you win, you may be able to have his fee paid.

---

*Your real estate agent convinces you to accept an offer on your home. After you sell it, you discover that another buyer was willing to pay a much higher price.*

---

When you list your home with a real estate agency, the agency has a *fiduciary* responsibility. It must…

- Act in your best interest, not its own
- Notify you of all offers they receive on your home, the low ones as well as the high ones
- Honor your decision about which offers you reject and which you will accept.

## WHOM CAN YOU TRUST?

Before you decide that your agent has acted in bad faith, you need to investigate. Who is claiming to have offered a higher price? Why are they telling you about it? Could that person have a grudge against the agent? A disgruntled former client, perhaps, or someone who has an unhappy personal relationship with the agent?

If you believe a higher offer was made, contact the agent and tell her; she may have an explanation that will satisfy you. For example, the potential buyer may never have made a formal written offer. Speculating in conversation about the price is not the same as putting an offer on paper. Keep a record of your contact with the agent.

## THE AGENT'S MOTIVES

On the other hand, the agent may have had a conflict of interest. For instance, she may have also been involved in selling the home of the people who bought your house. Their sale might have depended on their being able to buy a home

they could afford. Thus the agent may have seen a chance to "kill two birds with one stone." If she sells your house to these people at an affordable price (lower than another buyer might offer), she collects two commissions at once. This inspires her to talk you into the transaction—in spite of a lower commission.

### MAKE YOUR CLAIM

If your agent failed to meet her fiduciary responsibility, you should contact the firm and the real estate licensing board with your concern. You will need solid evidence of your claim, including…

- Selling prices of comparable homes
- The statement of the person who claims to have made the higher offer
- A log of the telephone conversations you had with the agent about the higher offer. Include the dates, time of day, and the substance of your conversation
- Copies of all correspondence between you and the agent.

The licensing board will investigate your complaint. Some boards hold a hearing where you and the agent can give your versions of the story.

Otherwise, they interview you and the agent individually and then provide you with their finding and what your appeal options may be. If the board decides in your favor, it may suspend or revoke the agent's license. In most states, however, the licensing board cannot order the agent to repay the commission on the sale and the additional money you might have received.

### YOUR LAST RESORT

In order to force the real estate agency to pay you any money, you will have to go ahead and file a lawsuit. But remember that the burden of proof is on you, and your evidence against the agent will have to be strong. For example, it may be hard to show conclusively that the agent didn't act in your best interest. Once the high-bidding buyer is under oath, he may not be as certain about what he did as when he was telling you the story in the first place.

If you're fortunate enough to win your case, you may be able to collect the full amount of damages from the real estate agency.

---

## HOW TO CHOOSE A REAL ESTATE AGENT

Be picky when you hire a real estate agent to sell your home. You should interview several and ask each one to supply the following, either verbally or in writing:

- **Information about experience.** How long has the agent been licensed to sell real estate? How long has she been employed by the current real estate agency? How many homes does the firm list each year, and how many does she sell (including those listed by other agents)?

- **A market analysis.** You'll want to find out about recent sales of comparable homes in your neighborhood and a listing of similar homes currently on the market. Look at the average listing time (the period between when a home was listed and when it sold).

- **A marketing proposal.** The agent should outline how she would sell your house.

- **Suggestions about ways to make your home more attractive to buyers.** Examples include painting the interior or exterior, or making repairs.

- **Suggestions for your asking price.** The agent should explain why that price seems right. For example, if you are looking for a quick sale, the agent may suggest pricing your home a little less than other homes in the area.

- **The agent's commission.** Historically, real estate commissions range from 5 to 7 percent. Commissions are usually negotiable, however, and you may be able to get the agent to agree to a lower one if your home is especially marketable.

- **The kind of listing agreement.** Ask if the agent will consider an *Exclusive Agency agreement* (page 78), which frees you from owing the agent money if you find the buyer yourself.

> **Y**our tenant is three months late with the rent, and despite his promises to the contrary, it's clear he has no intention of getting caught up on his payments.

**W**hen your patience runs out, it's time to begin eviction proceedings. You can hire a lawyer to help you. Or you can get advice from a landlords association. You can find an association by talking to other landlords or rental management companies, or by asking local departments of housing.

### STARTING STEPS

Procedures vary from state to state and even among communities within a state, but you should generally follow these basic steps:

**SMART MOVES**

If you have tenants, check with landlords associations in your community. You'll get advice, legal help, and sample leases and court filings.

■ **Provide your delinquent tenant with a Notice to Pay Rent or Quit.** The notice gives the tenant one last chance to set things right before legal proceedings begin. The deadline for the tenant to take action is set by law and is generally very short—three days in most states. (If the tenant is current on rent payments but has broken some other term of the lease, such as engaging in an illegal activity, you'll need a different form, one of which is called a Notice to Perform Covenant or Quit.)

■ **Start the eviction suit,** which is called a *forcible entry and detainer* or *unlawful detainer* action. Do this after the deadline has passed and if the tenant has not remedied the breach of the rental agreement. File a complaint with the court. It should…

● Give names of the parties in the dispute
● Set out your reasons for bringing suit
● Request the right to evict the tenant.

■ **Have the complaint served on (delivered to) the tenant,** along with a summons. The complaint and summons notify the tenant that an eviction proceeding has begun and the documents give him an opportunity to contest it. Depending on state and local law, the summons and complaint can be served by fastening them to the tenant's door; through delivery by the sheriff or a process server; or by sending them certified mail, return receipt requested.

**TAKE NOTE** *Failing to serve the complaint and summons properly is grounds for a tenant to contest eviction, so follow local statutes to the letter.*

### GOING TO COURT

Oftentimes a tenant will not contest an eviction; in this case, you win a *default eviction* judgment. If the tenant does challenge the suit, however, he has the right to proceed to a trial. If the evidence at the trial shows that the eviction is warranted, the court will issue an eviction order requiring the tenant to vacate the property within a few days or up to a few weeks.

### REMOVING THE TENANT

In the majority of evictions, the tenant will leave your property without incident, and before the deadline. However, if a properly evicted tenant refuses to vacate the premises by the required date, it's time to be firm: Call your local law enforcement agency and have them forcibly remove the tenant and his belongings.

**W**hen a home-based business brings more noise, traffic, or pollution into the neighborhood, it raises eyebrows—and the hackles of the people who live there. These types of commercial activities are also likely to break zoning laws and covenants. As a landlord, you are obliged to protect the community from a tenant's illegal activities. As a safeguard, do the following:

■ **Contact your tenants** and tell them to close the auto-repair business immediately. Simply talking to your tenants may solve the problem, but be prepared to check frequently to see that the business has stopped.

■ **Notify uncooperative tenants in writing** that you're aware of the business and that it violates zoning laws affecting the house. Tell them that they should cease immediately or face eviction. Send the notice by certified mail, return receipt requested (so you will have proof of delivery, or of attempted delivery if the tenant refuses to accept the letter).

■ **Begin eviction proceedings** (page 82). As the owner of the property, you are liable for the activities that go on there. In an extreme case of illegal activity by your tenant, such as the selling of controlled substances, you could lose your house under statutes that allow the government to seize property that is found to be a public nuisance.

## KEEP YOUR COOL

Once your tenants see that you are serious about evicting them, they may stop their business and may even ask for a second chance. Or they may decide to move out.

Whatever your tenants choose to do, there are some actions you should avoid:

■ **Don't take the law into your own hands**— you will only give your tenants an opportunity to put you on the defensive.

■ **Don't harass the tenants** while you are waiting for the court to come to a decision. If you win the eviction, the local police will physically remove the tenants on a given date if they have not already vacated the premises.

**LANDLORD ALERT** *Add a provision to the lease that prohibits tenants from violating the local zoning laws. This alerts tenants to zoning restrictions and gives you clear grounds for eviction proceedings if the tenants ignore the restrictions.*

## WHAT A RESIDENTIAL LEASE TYPICALLY INCLUDES

This is a sample agreement provided by landlords, with annotations. Before signing the lease, read it carefully and understand it. A lawyer can help if the wording is unclear or worrisome.

**The Undersigned Parties Agree as Follows:**

_____ ("Landlord") shall lease to _____ ("Tenant") the premises located at _____, in the City of _____, State of _____.

The landlord requires the name and signature of *every* tenant to be included on the lease.

**Occupancy:** The premises are to be used only as the residence of the Tenant(s) listed above, and by their minor children. No guests may occupy the premises for more than __ days without the prior written approval of Landlord.

In some communities, a guest who stays for more than a brief period can actually become a co-tenant in the eyes of the law. The landlord and even the other tenants might need to go to court to evict him.

**Term:** This lease shall be for a period of _____, beginning on _____, 20__, and continuing until _____, 20__, unless terminated earlier as provided for in this Agreement.

**Rental Payment:** Tenant shall pay to Landlord a monthly rent of $_____, payable in advance on the first day of each month. Payment shall be made to Landlord at ____ _____. Payment shall be made in the form of cash, money order, or personal check.

**Late Charges:** In the event Tenant fails to pay monthly rent within ____ days of the due date, Tenant shall pay Landlord a late charge of $_____, plus an additional charge of $_____ for each additional day rent remains unpaid. In no event shall the total late charge for any month exceed $_____. Nothing herein shall be interpreted as a waiver by Landlord of the right to payment in full on the due date.

The last sentence reinforces the landlord's right to be paid on time and not to accept late payment. A tenant can be evicted for consistently paying rent late.

**Security Deposit:** Tenant shall deposit with Landlord the sum of $_____ as security for Tenant's performance of the terms of this Agreement. Tenant may not apply this deposit toward last month's rent or any amount due under this Agreement. Landlord will return deposit to Tenant in full, or provide Tenant with an itemized statement of reasons for, and the amount of, any amount withheld by Landlord, along with a check for any balance due, within _____ days after Tenant has vacated premises, returned keys, and provided Landlord with a forwarding address.

Under this provision the landlord cannot keep your deposit longer than state law provides, but its terms may require the landlord to return it more quickly. Not every state has an absolute deadline, but 30 days is typical.

**Utilities:** Tenant shall pay all utility charges except the following, which shall be paid by Landlord:

_____

Landlords often pay for trash pickup and water; tenants usually pay for electricity, gas, and telephone service.

**Improvements:** Tenant shall not make any alterations or improvements to the premises without the prior written approval of Landlord. Alterations or improvements shall become the property of Landlord unless they can be removed without damage to the premises. Tenant shall not install or rekey any locks or install or alter any burglar alarm system without prior written approval of Landlord.

This means that if the tenant builds in bookcases or installs a light fixture, these items may become the landlord's property.

**Pets:** Tenant shall keep no animals on the premises without the prior written approval of Landlord.

**Assignment; Subletting:** Tenant shall not assign this Agreement or sublet the premises without the prior written consent and approval of Landlord.

**Landlord's Right to Access and Inspection:** Landlord or landlord's agents/employees may enter the premises in the event of an emergency, to make required repairs, or to show the premises to prospective tenants or buyers. Landlord may also enter the premises in order to inspect the property at any reasonable time during the term of this Agreement. Except in cases of emergency, abandonment of the premises by Tenant, or by court order, Landlord shall give Tenant _____ notice before entering the premises.

**Maintenance:** Tenant shall keep premises sanitary, clean, and in good condition, and upon termination of tenancy, return premises to Landlord in an identical condition to that in which it existed upon Tenant's occupancy, except for ordinary wear and tear. Tenant agrees to notify Landlord immediately of any dangerous conditions or defects in and around premises of which Tenant is aware. Tenant agrees to reimburse Landlord upon demand for costs of repairs for damage caused by Tenant, Tenant's family, or Tenant's guests. Tenant has examined premises, including carpets, drapes, and any appliances and fixtures, and has found them to be in safe, clean, good working order, except as may be noted in the Move-In Checklist attached to this Agreement.

**Default; Termination:** Failure of Tenant or any guest or invitee to comply with any provision of this Agreement shall constitute a default. Landlord shall give Tenant written notice of any such default, and Tenant shall have ___ days in which to correct it. Failure to correct the default shall be grounds for termination of this Agreement in accordance with state and local law.

**Additional Terms:**

_____

_____

_____

**Entire Agreement:** This document constitutes the entire Agreement between the parties, and no representations or promises, either written or oral, have been made by either Landlord or Tenant. Any modifications, additions, or alterations to the terms of this Agreement must be made in writing and signed by both parties.

Landlord: _____

Date: _____

Tenant:_____

Date: _____

---

If the tenant has a pet, this provision must be amended.

Some leases add that the landlord shall not unreasonably withhold approval.

Some state laws require a landlord to give 24 to 48 hours notice before entering your apartment, while others require only "reasonable notice." The tenant can negotiate a specified amount of notice for all but emergency situations.

The landlord may make his own checklist or may use a standard form. Here's where a tenant has to be careful. Make sure that every problem, no matter how small, is noted on the checklist. The tenant might also want to add a provision stating that the landlord will fix the problems within a short period of time, such as within 10 days. *No checklist?* Then a tenant should think twice about renting from this particular landlord.

An example of a representation: "Don't worry if the rent is late, I never collect a late fee." If there is a provision for a late fee in the lease, that's what counts.

(Signature)

(Signature)

*The couple you so carefully checked out to rent your apartment has moved out and a new couple has moved in, claiming that they sublet the apartment.*

Your tenants have flown the coop, arranging for another couple—about whom you know nothing—to occupy the apartment in their place. If there's no sublet clause in the lease, you don't have to let the new couple stay.

On the other hand, having rent-paying tenants in the apartment may be better than having the space empty—not to mention the expense and frustration of a month-by-month pursuit of the old tenants as you hunt for new ones.

### SUBLETS AND ASSIGNMENTS

A lease may contain a clause prohibiting tenants from subletting the apartment or assigning their obligations under the agreement without the landlord's written permission. These prohibited actions are defined as follows:

- *Subletting* takes place when a tenant lets someone else move into the apartment and pay the rent, while the original tenant remains liable under the lease.
- An *assignment* lets the original tenant out of the lease completely, with the new tenant taking over all the obligations of the lease for the remainder of its term.

Subletting or assigning a lease without your permission, when there is no such clause in the lease, is a violation of the lease agreement. In this situation you have the right to pursue eviction proceedings against the original tenants. The new tenants' rights depend on those of the old tenants, so you can have the sublet tenants evicted at the same time if you so choose.

### EVALUATING THE SUBLET TENANTS

Suppose you want to consider letting the new tenants stay as a convenience to everybody. First, you can ask the new couple to fill out a rental application (page 91), giving you permission to obtain a credit report and check their employment and personal references. If they agree, you should conduct the same kind of background investigation and credit check that you would conduct for any prospective tenant. If they refuse, you should begin eviction proceedings (page 82).

---

*Having tenants in the apartment paying rent may be better than having the space empty and facing the expense and frustration of pursuing your old tenants.*

---

- If your investigation indicates that the new tenants seem to be reliable and reputable, terminate the original tenants' lease and create one for the new couple.
- Evidence of credit problems or a history of questionable behavior should prompt you to evict the new tenants.

**TAKE NOTE** *Before signing a lease with the new tenants, you may have to notify the original tenants of the impending eviction proceedings against them, either by mail to their last known address or by publication (placing a notice in a local newspaper). Ask a lawyer or a local landlords association about the exact notification procedures required by local law, and then follow the procedures precisely. It's unlikely that the runaway tenants will contest their eviction. If they do appear, their violation of the lease terms will almost certainly prevent them from successfully challenging your eviction proceedings.*

You want to rent out your extra bedroom for income. You don't think it will work unless you're very picky about the person to whom you rent. Is that a problem?

You cannot refuse to rent to a prospective tenant on the basis of race, religion, age, or gender. State and local laws may also prohibit you from discriminating on the basis of sexual orientation. Furthermore, federal and state fair housing and antidiscrimination laws apply to all landlords.

In practice, asking a prospective renter an inappropriate question, such as "Do you go to church on Sunday or some other day of the week?," could get you into hot water with the law because it might be construed as asking the person to disclose his religion.

## PROTECT YOURSELF

There are several things you can do to protect yourself from renting to disruptive or irresponsible people.

- **Ask prospective tenants to fill out an application** form that allows you to check their financial and credit ratings, and character references (page 91). Carefully verify the information they've supplied; you certainly don't have to rent to a tenant who is financially unstable or who has a record of being unreliable or rowdy.
- **Think through the house rules** that you will be comfortable with. Provide a list that may include, for example:
  ● Kitchen privileges or no kitchen privileges, and the times of day they may use the kitchen.
  ● Whether he will have a separate bathroom, or share one. If a bathroom is to be shared, set up a schedule that will allow adequate time for all members of the household.

● An on-property parking space or street parking for the tenant's car.
● Separate telephone line for the tenant or shared phone. If the phone is shared, designate what the tenant should account for and pay for any long-distance or toll calls. You could ask that he use a calling card when making toll calls.
● Visiting hours for guests, the number of guests allowed at a time, and where the visitors can congregate—for instance, the living room, family room, or the tenant's room.
● Cleanup responsibilities, whether the tenant is expected to clean his room and bath, or if cleaning will be provided.

Include the house rules in the lease you draw up so that there is no misunderstanding between you and the tenant. As a reminder, you can post the rules in a visible place.

> ***W***e're moving to a new home but are having trouble selling our old one. What would we be getting ourselves into if we were to rent it out?

onverting a home into rental property can have real benefits—rental income; tax advantages such as writing off all the business expenses of renting the property (real estate fees, advertising, fixing the house up); and price appreciation of the property in a good market.

## A Good Tenant

You can reap a steady rental income without undue wear and tear on your house if you have reliable tenants. To find them, advertise in the paper or list the house with a real estate agent.

However you attract your potential tenants, have them fill out a tenant application form (page 91), and then thoroughly check their job histories, bank accounts, and personal references. To comply with federal fair housing and antidiscrimination laws, you can't reject tenants because of race, gender, or religion. But you can be picky about rental criteria. For example, you can require that the tenants earn three times the monthly rent and have held the same job for at least a year.

## A Landlord's Obligations

When you rent a house to tenants, your responsibilities are generally the larger ones—fixing a leaking roof, pumping out a basement that flooded in a downpour, and periodic painting inside and out. The tenants are responsible for day-to-day maintenance, such as cutting the grass, shoveling snow off the walks in winter, and putting on the window screens in summer.

This division of chores is not dictated by law, so you should spell out your responsibilities and those of the tenants in the lease, and be ready to negotiate with the tenants.

## Ask the Experts

Consult your household insurance company about whether or not you have adequate liability protection for the rental house, and take additional coverage if needed. You may also need to consult with a tax professional to help you take advantage of all the deductions that are associated with owning a rental property.

> ***Y***our building superintendent keeps entering your apartment to "make repairs" without giving you advance notice.

andlords sometimes seem to be under the impression that they can enter a rental property whenever they choose. But the law takes a different view. Once you lease an apartment, you have the right to exclusive possession. Although this right isn't absolute, it does put limitations on when your landlord or his agent or superintendent can enter your home.

## Check the Rules

First, check your lease for the clause that outlines the landlord's right to access. A landlord may be allowed to enter your apartment to…

● Make repairs
● Show the apartment to prospective tenants when your own lease is nearing an end
● Handle an emergency.

Except in the last case, the lease and most state laws require that the landlord give you "reasonable notice" before he or his superintendent enter your apartment. What's reasonable? Generally, 24 hours; sometimes 48 hours. They are also expected to enter only during normal business hours, and not late at night or early in the morning, unless you give them permission.

## Put the Landlord on Notice

Write a letter to your landlord describing the ongoing problem and remind him of your legal right to privacy and your right to be notified before the landlord or building superintendent enters your apartment. Send the letter (by certified mail, return receipt requested) to the landlord, using the "notices should be delivered to…" address in your lease.

In most cases, this should be all that's needed to rectify the situation, but if the building superintendent continues to enter your apartment unannounced, send another letter to your landlord, notifying him that despite your previous letter, the super is continuing to violate both the lease and the law.

If this doesn't work, contact the police. The building superintendent's actions make him a trespasser, and a visit from the police may convince him to stop such unwanted intrusions. Continued entry without notification could be considered harassment, and you would be entitled to obtain a court order against the super, which would prohibit him from having any contact with you in the future.

## Your Last Resort

Your lease and the law give you the right to exclusive possession of your apartment, and a landlord who fails to honor that right has breached his agreement. If after your earlier efforts he or his super continues to enter your apartment unannounced, you have the right to break your lease and move elsewhere. But contact a lawyer who is experienced in resolving these matters.

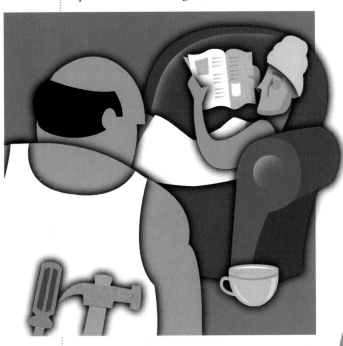

Your lawyer can advise you on specific local laws that govern such situations and send a letter to your landlord to help head off any retaliatory legal action. If you feel you have no choice but to move, you may be able to sue your landlord not only for damages but also for moving expenses.

---

*You moved out three weeks ago and your former landlord has yet to return your security deposit.*

---

Security deposits are a frequent cause of disputes when a tenant vacates rental property. While a landlord has a right to protect her property from damage caused by a tenant, the law restricts what a landlord can charge for damages; what deductions can be taken from the security deposit; and when the deposit must be returned to the former tenant.

## Look at Your Lease

The amount of your security deposit, its purpose, and the deadline by which it must be returned to you after moving should all be specified in the lease agreement. It may be that the landlord has not violated either the lease or the law. For example, your lease may give the landlord 60 days in which to return your deposit or to provide a detailed explanation of why she is keeping all or some of it. Ask the local housing authority about laws governing security deposits. If the lease gives the landlord 60 days in which to act, but local law provides for 30 days, local law prevails, and you can inform the landlord of this by letter.

Similarly, some landlords put provisions in their standard leases requiring tenants to make *nonrefundable deposits* for cleaning or redecorating. While a few states allow landlords to demand nonrefundable deposits, most states and many cities prohibit them. Ask your local housing authority if such deposits are legal.

### A FIRM REMINDER

Write the landlord a letter reminding her that you have not received a refund. State a date (in line with local law) by which you expect her to send it. Include a copy of the checkout list (page 91), if you have one, or copies of photographs you took at the time you moved out, which show that the apartment is in acceptable condition. You can also include a copy of the state law or local ordinance covering security-deposit refunds.

If you made an illegal nonrefundable deposit, ask for the return of this money as well.

### PUTTING TEETH IN YOUR CLAIM

Your landlord may reason that since she has your money (or doesn't, because she spent it for other purposes), it's up to you to fight for its return.

Hiring a lawyer and going to

court may cost you as much as the deposit is worth. But going to small-claims court can do the trick more affordably. Ask the small-claims court administrator to send you the forms you'll need

---

*P*hotograph or video tape the apartment showing that the rooms are empty and the walls and floors are clean and undamaged.

---

to make a claim against your landlord. You will have to file the complaint and have it along with a summons served on her (page 82).

### THE LANDLORD'S OPTIONS

The landlord will have a period of time (usually between 10 and 30 days) in which to respond to your complaint in writing by sending a letter to the court. She may deny your allegations or make her own counterclaim against you. Suppose, for example, your security deposit was $750. The landlord could claim that her cost for repairing damages you caused to the apartment was $1,000. As a result, her counterclaim would be for the amount of $250.

On the other hand, the landlord may ignore the summons and complaint. If you go to court on the appointed day, which is set by the court when you file your complaint, and your landlord does not show up, you can obtain a default judgment, which will allow you to take steps to collect your deposit (page 91).

If the landlord does appear in court, you will each have an opportunity to present your case to the judge. Have copies of your checkout list, your lease, correspondence between you and the landlord, and photos of the apartment for the judge to review. Stay focused on the issue (having the deposit returned according to the law). Be calm, don't interrupt, and think about what you want to say before answering questions.

## COLLECTING YOUR DEPOSIT

Winning the case in court doesn't guarantee payment. Get the necessary forms from the court clerk that you'll need to recover your deposit:

- A writ of garnishment allows you to receive payment from the landlord's employer.
- A writ of attachment allows you money from the landlord's bank accounts. You can find the name of the landlord's bank and her account number by looking on the back of a canceled rent check.
- A judgment lien allows you to file for judgment against the landlord's property.

Once you've filled out the relevant form, send it to the local sheriff or local police. They will deliver the writ on your behalf—for a fee.

## PROTECTIVE MEASURES

The best way to minimize disputes about a security deposit is to conduct a "walk-through" of your apartment with the landlord or her representative at the time you move out. By having the landlord's agreement that you left the apartment in good condition, you can minimize any later claims the landlord may make regarding damage to the unit. Many landlords have a checkout list, which they will use to indicate the condition of the apartment when you vacate it. Both you and the landlord sign the checkout list, and you keep a copy of it for your records.

If your landlord doesn't have a check-out list, or if you can't get her to inspect the apartment when you are ready to leave, there are other ways for you to protect yourself.

- **Photograph or videotape the apartment**, showing that the rooms are empty and the walls and floors are clean and undamaged.

- **Record the plumbing and electrical systems** with a videotape recorder. Turn on the water, flush a toilet, turn lights on and off. Such a videotape will provide evidence in the case of a serious dispute down the road.

## WHAT TO PUT IN A RENTAL APPLICATION

While you can obtain preprinted lease forms at office-supply and bookstores, not all applications are created equal. At a minimum, an application should contain blanks for the following:

- **Applicant information** includes the applicant's name, current address, and work and home telephone numbers. You may also want to get previous addresses where the applicant has lived if she's been in her current home for less than five years.

- **Employment information** includes the applicant's current employer (with address and telephone number), the job title, length of time on the job, and monthly income.

- **Personal references** includes addresses, phone numbers, and relationship to the applicant; names of additional occupants, including children, and their relationship to the applicant.

- **Financial stability information** includes names of banks and brokerage houses where the applicant has savings, investments, and checking accounts, as well as information about financial obligations, such as auto loans, student loans, and credit cards. The application should also ask if the applicant has ever filed for bankruptcy, been evicted, or been sued.

- **Authorization** allows the landlord to verify the information and to obtain a credit report.

- **Verifying statement** is an affirmation signed by the applicant that the information provided is true and correct, and includes a termination-of-lease provision if an applicant made intentionally false or incomplete statements on the application.

## Your landlord refuses to renew your lease after your new wife and her teenage children move in.

While most people know that state and federal fair housing laws prohibit discrimination based on gender, religious affiliation, and race, not everyone knows that these laws also prohibit discrimination against families with children. Although there are times when a landlord may be legally justified in refusing to renew a lease due to a change in family status, these exceptions are rare, and unless your landlord is following the law exactly, he may be guilty of discriminating against your newly expanded family.

### DOES THE LANDLORD HAVE A CASE?

Your first step: Review the terms of your original lease. Most leases give landlords the right to limit the number of occupants of a rental unit:

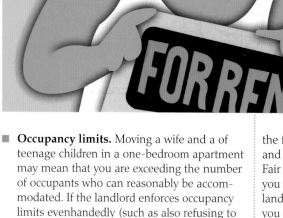

■ **Occupancy limits.** Moving a wife and a of teenage children in a one-bedroom apartment may mean that you are exceeding the number of occupants who can reasonably be accommodated. If the landlord enforces occupancy limits evenhandedly (such as also refusing to rent a one-bedroom apartment to four adults),

he is probably within his legal rights in refusing to renew your lease. Occupancy limits are usually based on the health and safety of the tenants and fit within guidelines set by both state and federal laws.

> *Most leases give landlords the right to limit the number of occupants of a rental unit.*

■ **Age-exclusive rentals.** If you live in an "age-exclusive" building or community, your landlord may have the right to deny your wife's children residency (page 60). Seniors-only buildings usually must meet stringent standards, such as providing housing only for those age 62 or older and services and facilities designed exclusively for older persons.

### IS THE LANDLORD BIASED AGAINST CHILDREN?

In some cases landlords simply don't want the perceived hassle of having children around. They may believe that the youngsters will be noisy and cause damage to the apartment.

If you suspect that this is the real reason behind your landlord's refusal to renew your lease, you should contact your local housing authority for information about legal occupancy limits in your community and to learn about the law that prohibits discrimination against family units. You can also contact the federal government's Department of Housing and Urban Development (HUD). By calling its Fair Housing Clearinghouse at (800) 343-3442, you can learn about the federal limits on your landlord's actions. Armed with this information, you can confront your landlord if she is illegally excluding children from her rentals.

## How to Follow Up

If your landlord still refuses to renew your lease, he faces charges of discrimination. You need to file a complaint with the local or state housing department, explaining the situation in detail. (To find the correct agency to handle your complaint, contact the mayor's office or your state representative.) The agency will investigate your complaint and, if it agrees with your conclusion that the landlord has acted in violation of the law, the agency will then order him to stop his discrimination against families.

You can also file a complaint with HUD. Information and a form for filing a federal complaint can be obtained from HUD by calling (800) 669-9777. A federal investigation can lead to the landlord being fined for failing to observe the Fair Housing Act. A first offense can result in a fine of as much as $10,000, while a repeat violator can be fined as much as $50,000.

---

## You move into your new apartment and find no heat or hot water.

It can be pretty upsetting to move into a new apartment and discover that the water heater doesn't provide hot water and the furnace is cold. If your landlord is not responsive to your complaints, the problem is compounded.

### Implied Warranty of Habitability

Fortunately, the law in most states is on your side when a landlord refuses to make repairs. That's because of a principle known as the *implied warranty of habitability*. This warranty states that a landlord has a duty to keep the residential property she rents fit for people to live in and to undertake repairs when they are necessary to make the property livable.

What constitutes "habitability" can vary from place to place, but generally the implied warranty of habitability means that your landlord is obliged to see that the apartment you rent…

- Is sound structurally
- Has adequate heat, water, and sewer service
- Is reasonably secure (doors and windows shut and lock properly).

A landlord violates the implied warranty of habitability when she is aware of a problem that affects the livability of the property and she knowingly fails to take action to correct it within a reasonable period of time.

What's considered a reasonable time for repairs to be made? That depends on the nature of the problem and can even vary depending on the time of year. A reasonable time to repair a furnace that stops working in the dead of winter is going to be shorter than that allowed for the same repair in late spring.

### How to Get Action

Your first step whenever you have a serious problem in your apartment is to contact the landlord and ask for repairs. Most landlords want to maintain their property and will respond quickly.

---

**When you withold part of your rent payment, put the money in a separate account.**

---

If your verbal request doesn't get any action, send a letter that defines the problem, reminds the landlord of your previous requests for repairs, and sets a deadline by which time you expect her to get things working properly. Your letter should also tell your landlord what you intend to do if the problem isn't fixed by the deadline. Generally, you have three options:

- Repair the problem and deduct the cost from your rent.
- Withhold rent until the landlord fixes the problem (called a *rent abatement,* page 94).

● Move out under what's known as the doctrine of *constructive eviction* (page 95).

### REPAIR AND RENT DEDUCTIONS

If the landlord doesn't meet your deadline, you have the right to hire someone to make the repairs and deduct the cost from your rent. Before doing so, however, you need to find out if your state or local laws limit the amount you can deduct and the kinds of repairs for which you can take a deduction in your rent. Contact your city's housing department for this information.

  ● Generally, you can't take a deduction for a problem you or someone living with you caused to the property. If your son broke a window with his baseball, for example, you are responsible for the cost of that repair, not the landlord.
  ● The repair must qualify as furnishing a basic need. Taking a deduction to fix a faulty water heater may be permitted, but doing so to replace a window air conditioner may not.

● Some states limit the number of times you can repair and deduct in a 12-month period; others limit the dollar amount of repairs to no more than a month's rent.

Once you've determined that you are entitled to take a deduction, have the repairs completed and get an itemized bill from the contractor.

When your next month's rent is due, reduce the amount by the cost of the repair and enclose a copy of the bill so that your landlord will understand the reason for the reduced payment.

### DON'T DO IT YOURSELF

Can you do the repairs yourself and take a deduction for your time and the cost of materials? It's not a good idea unless you are a licensed plumber or electrician. You may not do the work properly, or you might overcharge for your time, which could make you liable to the landlord. The law lets you deduct only the reasonable cost of repairs; having an outside licensed repair contractor do the work provides proof if the landlord challenges your deduction.

### RENT ABATEMENT

When a major repair is called for, you may not want to pay up front for the repair. In that case, you can withhold some or all of your rent payment until the repairs needed to return your rental unit to livable conditions are made. This is known as rent abatement.

  In most parts of the country, with rent abatement you can withhold only the amount of money by which the value of your apartment is reduced. Let's look at an example of how rent abatement works:

  You are paying $900 a month for a two-bedroom, two-bath apartment. For months, one of the bathrooms has been unusable because the pipes to that bathroom froze and broke during a winter cold spell. Repairing the pipes will cost $3,000; that is more than you want to pay out-of-pocket. The rental value of a two-bedroom, one-bath apartment in your community is $750 per month. You can probably withhold $150, which is the difference in value between a one- and a two-bath unit, until the landlord repairs the pipes to your second bathroom and restores it to usable condition.

### MAKING IT LEGAL

Before withholding any money, write to the landlord reminding her of the continuing problem, her failure to fix it, and your intent to withhold rent until she does so. Give her a specific period of time in which to make the needed repairs.

  When you withhold part of your rent payment, put the money in a separate account. If your landlord still refuses to fix the problem or tries to evict you, having the money in a separate account shows a court that you acted in good faith and didn't simply try to avoid paying all your rent. If your landlord fixes the problem shortly after the deadline passes, pay the amount you owe and close the account.

## DIRE MEASURES

Can you ever withhold your entire rent payment because of your landlord's failure to make your apartment livable? If the apartment is uninhabitable, yes. But unless the roof is falling in or you've gone months without heat or water, you may have a hard time convincing a judge that the landlord wasn't entitled to any rent at all.

Instead of staying in a rental home that's unfit for human habitation, you can simply move out. This is legal and is called *constructive eviction.* The premise behind the term is that the landlord's refusal to make your rental home habitable has the same effect as if she evicted you from it.

**TAKE NOTE** *Living conditions in the apartment have to be demonstrably bad for you to effect a constructive eviction. Consult a lawyer who specializes in landlord and tenant matters before taking such a drastic step. Your local bar association's referral service can help you find a lawyer who handles these cases.*

Not only can you move out of the apartment, but you can also sue your landlord to recover the cost of the move and the rent you paid while you lived in the uninhabitable apartment and the extra you have to pay during the remaining term of your original lease. For example, you had a two-bedroom, two-bath apartment at $900 a month. You are forced to move to another apartment with six months remaining on your original lease. Your new apartment costs $1,100 per month. You can sue your original landlord for the additional $200 per month, or a total of $1,200.

## REPORTING TO THE AUTHORITIES

Also contact your city's department of housing or the department of health and safety to report the substandard living conditions you were forced to endure at your old apartment. Most communities require landlords to obey regulations designed to safeguard the public from dangerous housing conditions, and your landlord could be fined for failing to meet the local standards of living.

---

**Your landlord has announced that your apartment building is being converted into condominiums. He wants to terminate your lease so that he can begin renovations.**

---

It seems as if you've lived there forever. Suddenly it looks like you may have to pull up stakes and find another, possibly more expensive, place to live. The first step is to find out what is legal and what is not. In many communities a landlord must protect your rights as a tenant.

## WHAT ARE YOUR OPTIONS?

To find out if you have to move, contact your local housing department to be sure that the landlord is following its requirements. If he is not, you can get a reprieve. You may find that…

● He may have to notify tenants at least 45 days before the conversion process can begin.

● He may have to file a registration form for the conversion with the state or local government, and the form must be reviewed and approved before any units can be sold.

● He may have to offer tenants a first right of purchase of their apartment. And you may be able to get favorable financing terms from the landlord, such as a lower down payment and lower interest rates, but this is usually negotiable rather than being legally required.

● The landlord may have to pay some or all of your moving costs if you choose not to buy.

● He may have to offer you the option of renewing your lease if you are a senior citizen or are disabled. The law varies state to state.

## STALLING FOR TIME

If your landlord is breaking *state laws,* contact your state's consumer protection office (begin with the office of the state attorney general). An investigator will review your complaint. If the agency finds that the landlord has failed to comply, it can require him to stop selling units until he brings his offer into compliance.

If there's been a violation of *local laws,* you should call the office of the mayor or the city manager to find out what it can do to delay, or even stop, the conversion process.

## YOU MAY BE ABLE TO STAY

If the landlord has violated your legal rights, the state attorney general may be able to get an injunction prohibiting the landlord from taking any action to remove you from your apartment.

In most states, tenants who choose to enforce their rights to remain in their apartment after a condominium conversion takes place are protected from any unreasonable rent increase. If you are in the dark about what to do, the state attorney general's office can tell you what your rights are.

> **Y**our bank has tacked a service charge
> on your account without your authorization.

The hard truth is that a bank doesn't have to get your authorization before raising its fees or hitting you with additional service charges. What it does have to do is notify you before doing so. And you can easily miss such notices, which often are not very clear or are presented in small print, or which may have been included with a credit-card offer or some other "junk mail" that you received from the bank.

Your first step toward getting the charges reduced? Call your bank to find out when notification about the fee increase was sent to you. If there was no notice, or if the notice was given less than 30 days before the fees were imposed, the fees should be removed and your account credited for any amounts you were charged. But if the bank can prove that it gave you proper notice, you'll probably have to pay the higher fee.

## What Else You Can Do

To discover how you can reduce your bank charges, ask the bank to give you a list of all the fees it imposes on your accounts. Then look for ways in which to minimize the charges:

■ **Make sure that all of your accounts are included to calculate your minimum balance.** Many banks charge a fee when a customer's balance on deposit falls below a certain minimum. Your bank may have neglected to combine your accounts when imposing the below-minimum fee. For example, one couple had their checking account under the husband's Social Security (SS) number and their savings account under the wife's SS number. They pointed out the discrepancy to the bank's customer service representative and asked him to correct the accounts and waive the fee and credit their account. He agreed.

■ **Check to make sure you have the right kind of checking account.** Some kinds of bank accounts pay interest but require a minimum balance; if you fall under the minimum, the penalty fee could be higher than the interest you are earning. In that case, it makes sense to switch to a no-interest account that requires no minimum balance.

■ **Switch to an account that provides "check safekeeping"** if your bank charges a fee for returning canceled checks with your monthly statement. In this type of account, your checks are not returned with your statement, but you can get them or copies of them on request.

■ **Check to see if your bank offers fee-free services to seniors** if you over 50. Some banks offer free checking, savings, and even safe deposit boxes to older customers, but you usually have to ask for these and other perks.

## Still Not Satisfied?

If your bank is uncooperative, or you think the fees charged are unreasonable, you can register a complaint with the government agency that regulates your bank. (The name, address, and other contact information for the appropriate regulatory agency are normally posted in the bank's lobby.)

If, after trying everything, you receive no satisfaction, you can always take your money somewhere else. Banking is a business, and a highly competitive one. Smaller banks tend to charge lower fees than big regional or national banks. And a local bank may be more likely to waive a fee for a bounced check or a deposit item returned for insufficient funds.

If you decide to change banks, take heed:

● Some banks charge you for using the bank's own ATM, while others allow you to use their machines at no charge.
● Some banks even charge your account a fee when you *don't* make deposits or withdrawals for a certain period of time.

A credit union may also be a good place to put your money instead of a bank—many credit unions charge lower fees and pay higher interest than banks or savings and loan associations.

**TAKE NOTE** *Internet banks, sometimes called virtual banks, often offer higher rates and lower fees, since they have no physical facilities to maintain. Be aware, though, that some customers have reported customer service problems with Internet banks. See page 102 for more about Internet banks.*

You'd be surprised to know how many people forget about parcels of property, small bank accounts, and safe deposit boxes, leaving them languishing in banks or at other businesses. Could this have happened to you or a relative of yours? If so, you may be in for a nice surprise. Legally, the state or business has to do the following:

● Notify you of the assets they have if the property belonged to someone you are legally entitled to inherit it from. But if you've moved, they may not be able to find you.

● Place advertisements in local newspapers in an attempt to locate the rightful owner of abandoned money and property. But if you live outside the state, you may not see the ads. (Some states now also post information on the Internet.)

In most states, forgotten assets must be turned over to the state after a legally specified period of time, such as five to seven years. But how do you learn whether you have any?

● Contact the treasurer's office in any state where you, a parent, or grandparent may have had bank accounts in the past to see if your name or theirs is listed in the state's records of abandoned property. It's worth a try.

● Be wary of any company that asks for a fee up front in order to help find or collect assets. Private companies often track down the owners of abandoned property in exchange for a percentage of the property's value. The company may take your money and then "discover" that the property it said was yours really belongs to someone else.

*Your salary is usually deposited directly into your bank account on the first of the month. This time your rent check bounced because the deposit wasn't credited until the fifth of the month.*

You are entitled by law to have access to funds that are directly deposited to your account *within one business day*. So in this case, either your pay check did not get to the bank when it was supposed to or your bank fouled up. You will have to find out which.

## TRACKING DOWN THE CULPRIT

Call your company's payroll department and find out if the deposit was made on time. There are several reasons it might not have been sent:

● The accounting department may have simply dropped the ball.
● If your company has been experiencing financial difficulties of its own, it may be that the money wasn't transferred on the first of the month because your employer's own funds wouldn't cover the payroll.
● Your company may use an outside payroll-service firm to handle paying employees. The payroll service may have failed to do its job.

If the deposit wasn't made on time, either your company or the payroll service should be liable for expenses, such as returned-check charges, collection charges, and penalties you may owe your landlord for late payment. Call the company or the payroll service and ask them to make restitution. Follow up with a *demand letter* (page 456) requesting the money. If that doesn't work, consider small claims court.

### If It Was the Bank's Fault

If you find that your pay check was in fact deposited on the first of the month, you will have to go after the bank. Get a letter from your employer, or the payroll service, stating that the funds were deposited into your account on time and giving the date of the deposit. Take this letter to the bank manager. Ask her to investigate the problem and to take steps to pay the extra expenses that resulted. Provide copies of the returned-check notice and any correspondence from your landlord or his check-collection service. Insist that the bank notify your landlord that the bounced check was due to its error, not yours.

**TAKE NOTE** *The bank should also get the check-collection agency to rectify its record of your credit (or lack thereof) so that future checks won't be refused. Today many merchants subscribe to these services, which warn them about customers who have had checks returned for insuffi-cient funds. Your bounced rent check to the land-lord could mean having other checks refused at a supermarket or a department store.*

Don't settle for the bank officer's assurances that she will correct matters. Insist that the bank provide you with copies of its letter to your land-lord. It may even be helpful to carry a copy with you in case you have a problem with a merchant.

### Mad At the Bank?

If you believe that the bank acted in bad faith by failing to credit your deposit on time, ask the bank manager for the bank's regulatory agencies. Write a letter to them explaining your concerns. The regulators may investigate and could impose fines and other sanctions on the bank if they discover a pattern of disregard for the legally imposed time limits on crediting direct deposits.

Finally, don't hesitate to move your account to another bank that provides better service.

---

**Y**ou make a deposit at your bank's ATM, but the machine doesn't give you a receipt.

---

**M**ost transactions at auto-mated teller machines (ATMs) go smooth-ly, but the ones that don't require quick action.

- **Get help from a bank employee** if you are using the ATM in your bank's lobby during regu-lar business hours. Explain the problem: without a receipt, you have no record of the amount deposited and you can't be sure the money went into your account and was not deposited into someone else's.
- **Use the phone near the machine** (directly connected to the bank's customer service department) if the bank is closed or if the ATM

isn't in your bank. (Chances are, however, that there won't be a phone, because fewer and fewer banks maintain phones at their ATMs. These telephones are easily vandalized and expensive to replace.)

*Once the bank confirms the deposit, it should take only a day or so to have your account credited with the amount of the deposit.*

- **No phone at the ATM?** Get to an outside phone and call your bank about the problem. You should provide the customer service representative with your name, address, account number (but *not* your PIN, or Personal Identification Number), the amount of the deposit, and the exact location of the ATM. Get the bank representative's name and the

address so that you can make an ATM complaint to the bank.

- **Follow up on your telephone call with a letter** noting the date and time of your conversation, the name of the person you spoke to, and all of the information you relayed on the phone. Send the letter to the bank by certified mail, return receipt requested so you will have proof that the bank received it.

**TAKE NOTE** *Just because you don't get a receipt doesn't mean your deposit won't be credited. But be sure to confirm that it was credited by contacting your bank.*

Generally, ATMs are balanced every day, and once the bank confirms the deposit, it should take only a day or so to have your account credited with the amount deposited. Ask the bank to send you a letter of confirmation. If the bank doesn't credit your account quickly, ask for a reason for the delay. If the bank claims that it could not confirm the deposit, contact the appropriate regulatory agency with your complaint.

---

### ATM DON'TS

We have grown very dependent on ATMs. But there are a couple of things you should never do:

- **Don't make a cash deposit at an ATM.** If the money isn't properly credited to your account, you'll have a hard time proving the money is yours even if the bank discovers the excess amount when it balances the machine. Always make cash deposits with a teller.

- **Don't make a deposit at another bank's ATM,** whether you're depositing a check or cash. Correcting a problem will be far more complicated and could take days or weeks to fix. In any case, it can take up to five business days for your deposit to be credited when you use a "foreign" ATM. And, to add insult to injury, you could end up paying two service charges (one to each bank) for the privilege of putting money into your own account.

## THE PROS AND CONS OF INTERNET BANKING

Internet banking is here to stay. Experts are now taking a more positive view of the practice, and more and more customers are putting their money into Internet banks. Some of these banks are offshoots of traditional institutions; others exist only as Internet businesses. Many of them pay higher interest rates on customer accounts than brick-and-mortar banks, and some offer added perks such as free checking and automated bill paying. Yet the industry is still young, and you don't want to plunge in without asking these important questions:

■ **Is the bank insured by the FDIC?** Don't rely on an FDIC logo on the bank's Web site as confirmation. Call the FDIC or visit its Web site at www.FDIC.gov to confirm that your accounts will be protected by federal insurance.

■ **How long has the bank been in business, and what are its assets?** Again, the FDIC should have this information.

■ **Where are the bank's headquarters located?** Some Internet banks are located outside the United States and may not be subject to the same level of regulation as those within the nation's borders.

■ **How secure is the bank's Web site?** While most Internet banks take serious precautions to protect their customers' transactions, some Web sites have had problems with hackers gaining access to account information. You want to be sure that the bank encrypts sensitive data—you'll see a window pop up on your computer screen telling you when you're entering or leaving a secured area.

■ **How do you make deposits in the bank?** Generally, you can use a check, money order, or electronic funds transfer. Sending cash is a bad idea.

■ **Is there a toll-free number that connects you to a customer service representative?** If you are limited to contacting the bank by e-mail or regular mail, you may wait days or weeks to have questions answered or problems resolved.

*Your latest bank statement shows a check cashed against your account that you didn't write. You call your bank to report a forgery. The bank claims it's too late to do anything about it.*

Finding a forged check in your bank statement is like having a robber break into your house. Fortunately, the bank is liable for the money within a certain time frame (usually two weeks), and it should put the money back into your account as soon as you prove the forgery.

### PROVING THE FORGERY

If you get your canceled checks back with your statement, you can tell right away, by looking at the signature, if the check was forged. If the bank keeps canceled checks in safekeeping, you must ask that the original check or a photocopy be sent to you. Either way, your first step is to call the bank immediately and explain your problem. Then, when you have the canceled check or a photocopy in hand, go to the bank and get them to compare the signature on the forged check with the signature card you signed when you opened the account.

- **Have a face-to-face interview with a bank officer,** not a teller. Explain the problem and request that the money be restored to your account. If the officer says it will take time to investigate the matter, ask how long the investigation will take and have her put the time limit in writing.

- **Pursue the matter** even if the banker tells you that you've waited too long to notify the bank. Many banks require notification of a forgery within 14 days of the date of the statement. But by not documenting this forgery, you may become liable for other checks that may have been forged.

- **Don't be intimidated** by a bank employee who claims that you are responsible for the loss because you didn't safeguard your checks properly. You are not responsible for loss due to forgery.

- **Follow up with a letter** after your interview with the bank officer. Send it by certified mail, return receipt requested, and address it to the bank officer you talked to. Describe your conversation, and restate your demand that the money fraudulently withdrawn from your account be replaced.

- **Tell your local police** about the forgery. It's likely that the police won't do much more than file a report, but they may also alert merchants and banks in the community about the problem.

- **Write to the agency that regulates the bank** if you don't get satisfaction. To identify the agency and find out how to reach it, you can either ask the bank manager or look for a sign posted in the bank lobby. Tell the regulatory agency that the bank didn't fulfill its responsibility. Send all the letters by certified mail, return receipt requested, and be sure to keep copies of your correspondence as well as the canceled check.

**SMART MOVES**

Always open and check your statement as soon as you receive it from the bank.

### IT COULD HAPPEN AGAIN

It is possible that whoever stole your check might try to forge more in the future. So look at your checkbook and extra checks to see if any other checks are missing. Some crooks will steal checks from the middle of a series or the back of a checkbook, hoping you won't notice that they are missing until they have had a chance to forge your signature and obtain cash or merchandise.

If checks are missing, you should close your account and open a new one to avoid a problem weeks or even months in the future.

## HOUSE RICH, CASH POOR?

If you own a home but are retired and no longer have much income, you may find yourself in a state of being "house rich and cash poor." In other words, most of your worth is in the house, which you want to keep living in, but you haven't enough disposable income to meet regular expenses such as property taxes and utility bills. You may well find a solution to your problem in a *reverse mortgage*. Here's how it works:

■ **The bank lends you a given amount** (either in a lump sum or in annual or monthly installments), based on the value of the house, your age, and where your house is located. You get the money, but you don't pay any interest on the loan because the interest is added to the amount of the loan and is paid off at the end of the loan. Depending on the terms of the loan, repayment isn't due until the last surviving borrower dies, sells the house, or moves out permanently. In effect, you are converting the value of your house, or a portion of its value, into cash for your elderly years; the bank gets its loan plus interest back when the house is finally sold. To qualify for a reverse mortgage, you must:

  ● Be at least 62 years old

  ● Either own your home outright (see below) or have a small existing mortgage so that a part of the reverse-mortgage proceeds can be used to pay off the existing mortgage debt.

■ **The bank is betting on the fact that when your house is sold it will be worth as much as, or more than, the amount the bank has paid to you, plus interest.** Any money left over from the sale of the house after the reverse mortgage has been paid off belongs to you or to your estate. But even if the house has declined in value over the term of the loan, the bank cannot claim from you or your estate any more than the house sells for. This means that while the reverse mortgage will indeed deprive you or your heirs of part or all of the value of the house when it is sold, it cannot put you or your heirs into any further debt. Here are other points to be aware of:

■ **Only single-family homes and condominiums** are eligible for a reverse mortgage. Cooperative apartments, mobile homes, and duplexes or multifamily residences do not qualify.

■ **Rural homes** qualify more often for smaller reverse mortgages than urban homes do.

■ **Proceeds from a reverse mortgage are *not* taxable.** And since the proceeds of a reverse mortgage don't count as income, but merely a loan, they don't normally count against certain government benefits, such as Social Security, Medicare, Medicaid, or Supplemental Security Income (SSI). It can affect these benefits, though, if you take the payment as a lump sum or fail to spend monthly payments as you receive them. In that case you could accumulate assets that would put you above the cutoff limits for Medicaid and SSI. Check with a lawyer who specializes in the field of Social Security law for advice about your situation.

■ **The reverse-mortgage plan should be federally insured** to protect your payments in case the lender defaults or goes bankrupt.

■ **Reverse mortgages aren't available everywhere,** so you will need to contact a bank or mortgage broker to see if they are authorized in your state.

> **Y**our bank has notified you that it is
> lowering the interest rate on your certificate of deposit.

**B**efore you fly off the handle, carefully check the terms stated on the certificate of deposit (CD) that you received from your bank. Most CDs offer a fixed rate of interest that cannot be altered for their entire term—but under certain circumstances the bank may have been justified in its action. Here's what may have happened:

■ **The CD is nearing maturity** and the bank is now offering you a renewal at a lower interest rate. By law, banks have to notify you when your CD is about to mature. Then you generally have 7 to 10 days from the date of maturity to withdraw your money or to tell the bank how to reinvest it. If you can find a higher interest rate elsewhere, or if your current bank is offering a CD with a higher rate for a different term (for example, if you deposit the money for 18 months instead of a year), it's a relatively simple matter to get the money out of the expiring CD and reinvest it.

■ **You didn't respond in time after the CD matured.** The bank may have automatically rolled your money over into another CD at the current—and now lower—rate. You can still get your money out of the CD, but you will probably have to pay a penalty, typically between 30 and 90 days' worth of interest. Before withdrawing, ask yourself: Is it worth paying the penalty? Compare the amount of money you will give up to the amount you stand to gain by investing your money elsewhere at a higher interest rate.

■ **You may have bought a *variable rate* CD.** This kind of certificate of deposit offers higher returns on investments when interest rates in general rise, but variable rate CDs may also yield less when the interest rates fall. In this case, the bank has done nothing wrong.

### SMART MOVES

Keep a record of when your CDs mature. If the bank's notification gets lost or if you don't read it, you can still take proper action when the CD matures.

■ **Your CD has a so-called *teaser rate*.** These certificates offer a high interest rate for a portion of the time you have your money on deposit, then lower the rate for the remainder of the term.

■ **Your bank has been taken over by another institution.** It is allowed under law to lower your CD rates to match current interest rates. It must notify you of the change, however, and you have the right to withdraw your funds without penalty.

■ **You may have bought something that *looks* like a CD but really isn't.** Some financial institutions offer notes that are known by three different names: *lobby notes, subordinated debentures,* or *retail debentures.* These are actually unsecured and uninsured notes, and they essentially represent the bank's promise to repay you money you are lending it.

**TAKE NOTE** *Some institutions that offer these notes may be having financial trouble, and you should be very wary of buying one. If one of these debentures was represented to you as a certificate of deposit, contact your bank's regulators immediately (look for a notice in the bank's lobby or ask the bank manager for the address). They may be able to require the bank to return your money and put an end to the misrepresentations.*

### NONE OF THE ABOVE?

If after investigating, you find that the bank did lower your interest rate without justification, you definitely have a case. Federal law requires banks to disclose the *annual percentage yield* (APY) on CDs. If the amount your bank says you will now earn on your CD is less than promised on the APY disclosure, notify the bank immediately, and be prepared to follow up with letters to the state agency that regulates the bank's business. It's also time to move your funds to another bank.

**Y**our 17-year-old son filled out a credit-card application.
Now he's run up $1,000 in debt and
the credit-card issuer wants you to pay the bill.

**A**s a parent, your first order of business is to make it clear to your son that his actions were irresponsible and could have serious repercussions for him well into future.

## PAY IT BACK TOGETHER

No matter what the situation, it's almost certain that your son's failure to pay will be noted with the major credit-reporting agencies, resulting in a black mark on his credit record.

You as a parent can use this as a lesson for your son. Swallow your anger and make a deal with him. Tell him that you'll pay off the debt on his behalf, and he'll pay you back. And don't forget to add any legal fees to the amount he owes you.

## MINIMIZE THE DEBT

If this is the first time your son has done this sort of thing, you may want to take steps to lessen the pain of the repayment for him.

Legally, you are not obligated to pay your son's debt because you did not co-sign his application for the credit card. But because your son is a minor, you can try to convince the credit-card

company to back off and write it off as an "uncollectible" debt. Here's how to proceed:

■ **Write to the card issuers**, by certified mail, return receipt requested, and tell them you will not accept responsibility for the credit-card bills your son ran up. In your letter state that you believe the company may have violated state laws by contacting you about your son's debt. In many states, it's illegal for a retailer, credit-card company, or other lender to contact someone other than the debtor.

■ **Send a copy of the letter** to your state consumer protection agency at the same time.

■ **Have your son write a letter** (certified mail, return receipt requested) canceling the credit card and disaffirming the debt. In most cases, the law protects your son from being liable for breaching a contract that he entered into as a minor. But it may also require him to return to the various merchants any items still in his possession that he purchased through the contract. The amount received for returned items should be credited to the card issuer in order to reduce your son's debt. In many cases, this will be enough to get the credit-card company to leave you and your son alone.

## WHAT IF IT DOESN'T WORK?

If the company doesn't back down, and especially if it threatens to sue your son over his debt, it's time to get a lawyer to help you. After that, all inquiries should be directed to your lawyer, and the credit-card issuer should stop any direct contact with you. Here's what the lawyer can do for you:

● Tell you whether state law permits a suit against a minor in this situation.
● Negotiate an agreement with the credit-card issuer for less than the amount that is owed in cases where a minor can be sued.

What the card issuer did in offering credit cards to students—who often don't even have to show any income in order to qualify—may have been legal, but it smacks of an unethical business practice. Your lawyer may be able to convince the company to reconsider its position because of the unfavorable publicity it could receive if it were to take your son to court.

## AVOID COURT

You should not pursue the matter in court—especially if your son lied about his age on the card application. In some states, a minor can be sued for causing monetary losses by his deceitful statements or behavior. If the credit-card company wins its case, your son may be forced to repay the money to the card company after he turns 18.

> **Y**ou have your bills paid automatically out of your checking account. Last month, the bank paid $1,000 in unauthorized charges to your credit-card issuer.

**Y**ou rely on the bank to pay your bills. All goes well until a company sends the bank a flawed statement. While automatic debit programs are convenient and usually reliable, mistakes can and do happen. These problems are almost always resolved in the customer's favor, but that doesn't make you feel better when you discover that checks you have written during this time have bounced as a result. Your account has been overdrawn through no fault of your own.

### SMART MOVES

It's important to open and review your bank statements, as well as the bills being debited from your account, as soon as you receive them.

### TAKE CHARGE

When you discover that your bank account has been debited to pay a credit card bill that you believe is in error, proceed as follows:

■ **Contact the credit-card issuer to challenge the charge to your account.** You can call the toll-free customer service number, but be sure to follow up with a letter. The company will investigate the claim. If it discovers that the charge was in error or fraudulent, the charge will be taken off your card account.
■ **Ask the merchant who billed you in error to pick up any costs** you incurred because of the bounced checks. You can also ask the bank

to waive those charges because of the unusual circumstances surrounding them. Some banks will do so in order to maintain their good customer relations.

If the bill is determined to have been issued in error, the money should be transferred back into your account.

**TAKE NOTE** *The bill you are disputing may indeed be a mistake—but then again, it might not be. For example, one consumer received an electric bill that was five times larger than normal. But the power company had been estimating his power usage, rather than reading his meter. When it did take a reading, it billed him for the difference between its low estimates and his actual use.*

### HEADING OFF FUTURE PROBLEMS

Ask the bank to schedule your automatic payments so you'll have plenty of time to review your bills before they are paid. For example, if your credit-card payment must be paid within 25 days of the closing date, some banks will pay that bill 10 days before it's actually due. A mail delay or a business trip could mean you wouldn't be able to check your bill for errors before the payment is made. It's better to have the bill paid at the last possible date to avoid late payment penalties.

## A GLOSSARY OF CREDIT-CARD CHARGES

It's hard to keep track of the different fees and charges that credit-card issuers have devised to increase their profitability. Here are some of them:

■ **Annual fees** are often assessed by cards that tie in to rewards programs, as well as those issued to cardholders who may pose a higher credit risk. In fact, your card issuer may also decide to charge an annual fee just because you don't carry a balance on your account. This is one fee you may be able to beat. Call the card issuer's toll-free number to see if you can have it waived. If you've been a good customer over the years, or if your card is issued by a financial institution where you have other accounts, you may be able to get this charge taken off your account. (Keep checking your statements, though, in case the fee is reapplied later.)

■ **Late payment fees** may be charged even if your payment is only one day late. These fees have risen to the $30 range. Note that it is the "pay by" date on the statement that counts here, not the "closing date," which is when your next statement will be issued. Also, be aware that for most credit-card issuers the "pay by" date refers to when the payment is received, not when it is postmarked (a controversial stance that has led to challenges from customers who claim to have mailed their checks in time but still were charged late fees). The late fee is probably negotiable—once. Call the customer service number on your bill about it; if it's the first time you've missed the pay-by date, chances are the representative can take the penalty off your next statement.

■ **Over-limit fees** are assessed if you exceed the card's credit limit. Again, these fees hover around $30. If you used your card for a major purchase or in an emergency, it's all too easy to go over your credit limit—especially if other family members are also using the account. You can try calling and asking to have this charge removed, but it's less likely you will succeed in this situation than with a late payment charge.

■ **Insufficient use fees** are charged by some credit-card issuers when you don't use your account often enough for the company's liking. Write a letter to the credit-card issuer and ask to have the fee removed. If the company won't do so, your best move is to cancel the card and get one from another issuer with better terms.

■ **Cash advance fees** are on the increase. Use a cash advance check, or use your card to get cash from an ATM, and you may be charged as much as $15 per transaction or 2% of the transaction amount, whichever is higher. Some cards also charge higher interest rates for cash advances than they do for purchases. As long as the issuer disclosed the information, you won't have much luck getting these charges reversed. Better to look for a new card issuer that offers better terms than you are currently getting.

■ **Interest rates** fluctuate widely from one card issuer to another issuer, but more and more the interest is being charged sooner than it once was. At one time, most credit-card issuers offered a grace period of 30 days from the time you made a purchase until they began charging you interest. Gradually, many companies reduced this period from 30 to 25 days, and then to 15 days. Today some card issuers begin charging you interest from the very minute you make a purchase using your card. And few, if any, card companies now offer a grace period when you use your card for taking out a cash advance.

Credit-card fraud is a bane of the electronic age, causing some $1 billion dollars in losses each year—and the cost of the crimes is passed on to consumers in the form of higher interest rates and finance charges.

In the bistro scenario, it's possible that someone who works at the restaurant used your card number to make the unauthorized calls. An unscrupulous waiter or cashier could easily make a copy of a card number and expiration date and use them later for transactions that don't require presenting the card in person.

### OTHER CULPRITS

On the other hand, it's possible that someone unconnected to the restaurant may have gained access to your credit-card number:

- Mailbox thieves steal credit-card statements or envelopes containing renewed cards and use the numbers to make fraudulent charges.
- "Dumpster divers" open trash bags in search of old statements, carbon-paper inserts, customer copies of receipts, and expired credit cards that weren't cut into pieces before being discarded. Some consumers make it easy for credit-card thieves to access their accounts by writing their Personal Identification Number (PIN) directly on the credit card.

### PHONE, THEN WRITE

What to do? First, review your credit-card statement as soon as you receive it. If it shows any unauthorized charges, proceed as follows:

- **Call the card issuer** immediately. Most card companies have 24-hour toll-free numbers listed on the back of the credit card or on the monthly statement.
- **Follow up with a letter** stating that you are disputing the charges. (Under federal law, a telephone call alone isn't enough to preserve your right to remain protected from unauthorized charges.) In writing, you must specify the charges you're disputing within 60 days of receiving the bill on which the charges first appeared. After being notified, the card issuer must then acknowledge your inquiry within 30 days, and then resolve the matter within the next 90 days.

### WHAT ARE YOUR RIGHTS?

While the matter is being investigated, you cannot be required to pay an amount in dispute—nor can you be reported as delinquent to a credit bureau for failing to pay the amount in question. (You must, of course, still pay any charges that you're not disputing.)

If the charges in question are large, the credit-card company will probably cancel your account number and issue a new card. (This helps protect you from having to file another written challenge if the card thief uses your old card number again.) Even if the charges are small, ask the company to cancel the number and issue another card.

**TAKE NOTE** *You cannot be held liable for any fraudulent use of your card that occurs after you've notified the issuer that it was stolen (or lost, for that matter), but you can be liable for the first $50 of unauthorized charges that were made prior to notification. So act fast! If the thief beats you to the punch, however, be aware that many credit-card issuers will routinely waive the $50 penalty fee when you ask them to do so.*

### IF THE ISSUER BALKS

If the company that issued the card decides not to correct your bill, it can assess finance charges on the disputed amount from the date of your inquiry to the date the bill is paid. If you refuse to pay, the issuer can report you as delinquent.

Once the card company informs you that it won't adjust the bill, you're allowed 10 days to state in writing that you still refuse to pay. The company must then 1) tell any credit-reporting agency that you dispute the bill; 2) tell you that your refusal will be cited on your credit report.

Fortunately, most cases of credit-card fraud are ultimately resolved in favor of the cardholder. You may be asked to provide an affidavit (a statement signed under oath) to the issuer stating that you did not make the purchases in question. Once the credit-card company receives the affidavit, your account usually will be cleared of the charges without further trouble.

### YOUR LAST RESORT

If it becomes impossible to resolve the matter with the credit-card issuer, or if you're dissatisfied with the way your inquiry is being handled, you can then proceed to file a complaint with your state's office of consumer protection.

If the issuer violated the federal Fair Credit Billing Act, you have more recourse: you can sue the company for the damages you've incurred, including the cost of trying to remove erroneous data from a credit bureau's records, as well as attorney fees and court costs.

The referral service of your local bar association should be able to help you find a lawyer with experience in this area.

---

**Your credit-card provider has raised the interest rate on your card from 8.9% to 23.9%.**

---

**W**hat your credit-card issuer has done may seem sneaky—but it probably is legal. Somewhere in the fine print in the terms of your agreement with the issuer (usually on an insert that came in the mail along with your card), you will find the justification for the card's interest-rate increase:

---

*Always read every piece of mail you receive from your credit-card company.*

---

■ **A low initial loan rate.** You may have signed up for a credit card offering an interest rate that was temptingly low but that was scheduled to jump much higher after an introductory period ended—typically three months.

■ **Interest rates in general have risen.** All of the company's customers are having their rates increased. In this case the issuer is required to have notified you of the rate increase. Unfortunately, many people don't bother to read these notices, assuming they are junk mail. Always read every piece of mail you receive from your credit-card company.

### STILL BAFFLED?

If you can't find any justification for the interest-rate increase in the issuer's literature, the increase may be due to factors related specifically to your account. In this case you do have a chance to fight back. Here's what to do:

Call the company's customer service number and ask the representative to explain why your rate was raised. You may find that the company reviewed your credit record and decided that you are a greater credit risk than when it issued your card (see "Keeping an Eye on Your Credit Rating," below). For example, if you have taken on a large amount of additional credit, or if you've been turned down for credit by another lender, your card issuer may have decided it has to raise your rate to protect itself.

If you feel that the increase was not justified, ask the card issuer to reconsider its decision. Sometimes the customer service agent you speak to is authorized to lower the interest rate for a longtime customer. If you use the card regularly and your payment record has been good, you may get your rate lowered immediately.

## Shop Around for a Better Rate

If you can't convince the credit-card company to reduce its new interest rate, you may consider looking for another card issuer that offers better rates. Major credit cards such as MasterCard and Visa are issued by banks, by savings and loans, and by credit unions, each of which is able to set its own credit-granting requirements.

When you transfer your credit-card balance to another card issuer, you would be smart to cancel your old, high-interest credit card. You will have to do this in writing, and some experts suggest that you also cut your card into pieces and return it in the envelope with your letter to the issuer.

**TAKE NOTE** *If your interest rate was just increased and you cancel your card before using it at the new rate, some state laws require issuers to let you pay off your closed account at the previous, lower interest rate. The notice you receive informing you of the impending rate increase will let you know if you have this right.*

## Keeping an Eye on Your Credit Rating

If you find out that your credit-card issuer raised your interest rate because of a review of your credit record, here are some steps to take:

■ **Get a written explanation of the credit-card issuer's decision**—but you need to make that request in writing within 60 days of the increase. Send a letter to the company at the address indicated on the back of your credit-card statement.

■ **Ask the credit agency for a copy of its report to your credit-card company.** (The card issuer should tell you which reporting agency it used, and the report should be sent free of charge.) If it contains any errors, you should note them on the form provided by the credit-reporting agency and send the information back. The agency must investigate your claim. If it can't verify the original information as correct within a reasonable time, it should delete that information from your credit report. If it does, it must send the corrected report to any creditor—including your credit-card issuer—that received it in the past six months.

■ **If you decide to close your credit-card account,** check your credit record again in about 90 days to make sure that it reflects the closure and that it shows that the account was closed at your request. Some credit-card issuers use what's known as a "soft" close, which allows you to reopen your account easily if you reconsider your decision. A soft close may not show up on your credit record, which will still indicate that your entire credit line with the card issuer is available. Having too much available credit can have an adverse effect on your ability to obtain a home mortgage, an auto loan, or even another credit card. If the credit agency still reports that your account is still open after three months, write the card issuer demanding that it notify the credit-reporting agency that the card account was closed at your request.

> *E*ven though you pay your credit-card bill
> in full every month, you are still being assessed interest and fees.

**Y**ou'd think any business would appreciate having a customer who pays bills in full and on time, wouldn't you? Well, think again. Your credit-card company doesn't make any money by simply letting you charge purchases, especially if you avoid finance charges by paying your bill in full every month. So more and more credit-card issuers are taking aggressive steps to increase the fees and charges they levy against the accounts of those who might otherwise be thought of as "good" customers (see "Keeping an Eye on Your Credit Rating," page 111).

### Finding a Better Deal

It is legal for credit-card companies to do this, provided that they give you advance notice and you have agreed to the charges. How do you agree to them? By using the card after being notified of the terms. (Needless to say, this is a good reason to read every piece of mail you get from your credit-card company.)

It's always a good idea to contact your current card issuer and ask it to change its terms to accommodate you as a good and reliable customer. But if it won't, or if what it offers still isn't what you want, it's time to look for another card company. One organization that can help you find a credit card that's more to your liking is Bankcard Holders of America. It compiles a list of banks that issue low-interest and low-fee credit cards. Write to it for information. Magazines such as *Money* and *Kiplinger's Personal Finance* also provide similar lists.

**Consumer Alert** *By using "convenience" checks you can write against your line of credit, you lose the right to get a charge back when you buy an item that's defective, as you would using your credit card. Plus, interest starts the day your check is presented and the fee charged to your account can be as much as 5 percent of the check amount.*

> *Y*our husband ran up thousands of dollars of debt
> on his credit card while gambling at a casino. Now the card issuer
> has a collection agency after you to pay the bill.

**I**f your name is not on your husband's credit card as a joint owner (and you don't live in a community property state, page 114), you don't have to make payments on your husband's charges, and you can take action to get the collection agency off your case. (If your name is on the card, of course, you will have to pay the charges.)

Write a letter to the collection agency (send it to them by certified mail, return receipt requested) demanding that it make no further attempts to contact you. Under the federal Fair Debt Collection Practices Act (FDCPA), a collection agency must stop contacting you about the debt once it has received this letter.

You may be able to take even stronger action. The collector may have actually violated the law simply by discussing your husband's indebtedness with you. Collectors are generally prohibited from having any contact with friends, neighbors, or even family members of a debtor except in order to locate him or her. Even then, they usually aren't allowed to contact you more than once.

The FDCPA gives you the right to file a lawsuit against a collection agency that violates the law. You must file your lawsuit within one year of the date of the collection agency's first contact with you. If your suit is successful, you can collect any actual damages you suffered, and the court may award up to $1,000 for each infraction of the law, as well as court costs and attorney fees.

Whether or not you file a lawsuit, if the agency continues to harass you, send a letter not only to your state attorney general but also to the Federal Trade Commission (FTC). The FTC has authority to enforce the FDCPA. In your letter you should state that the agency contacted you after you told it to stop. Enclose copies of your original letter and postal receipt. In recent years, the FTC has been aggressive in its investigation of debt-collection practices, and some debt collectors have been shut down as a result of the FTC's actions.

## WHEN THE FDCPA CAN'T HELP

The FDCPA applies to collection agencies and law firms collecting debts, but it *does not* apply to the creditor's own actions. So if the credit-card issuer's own collection department instead of a collection agency is contacting you, you cannot invoke the aid of the Fair Debt Collection Practices Act.

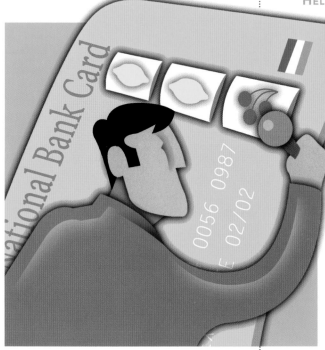

Many states have laws that place similar restrictions on creditors when they attempt to collect debts on their own. In this case, you should write to the consumer protection office of your state attorney general's office. Send a copy of the letter to the credit-card company. The attorney general's office can investigate the company's practices and will determine if it is in violation of state law. Depending on the state

in which you live, the company may be subject to fines, and you may also have the right to file a lawsuit in state court seeking damages from it based on the company's behavior.

## KNOW YOUR RIGHTS WHEN A DEBT COLLECTOR THREATENS YOU

You should also be aware that although debt collectors often threaten to garnish your wages or attach your property, they generally cannot act unless they first go to court and convince the judge to rule against you.

**TAKE NOTE** *The only exception is when your debt is secured—that is, when you pledge property as collateral against a debt or a loan you have. For example, a lender can repossess your car if you fail to make the payments on your auto loan. But it can't attach your wages to collect any other money you might owe without getting court authorization to do so.*

### HELPING HIM DEAL WITH THE DEBT

Just because you are not liable for your husband's debt doesn't mean you shouldn't take some steps to help him deal with the debt that he incurred and the gambling problem that caused it. Take the following steps:

- **Convince him** to cancel his credit cards if you can.
- **Cancel any joint accounts** to protect yourself from his debts and to help him control any future debts he may incur.

At one time, it was impossible for someone who lent money to a gambler to enforce his or her right to repayment in court. The courts held that since gambling was an illegal activity, it would be unfair to use the law to hold someone to a contract related to breaking the law. Today, however, some form of gambling is allowed in every state but Hawaii and Utah, and courts are more willing to find on behalf of a lender in the states that allow gambling. However, if the credit-card issuer threatens a lawsuit against your husband, don't assume that it will win its case. Get the help of a lawyer licensed in your state who can help you fight back. He may be able to…

- **Negotiate a settlement** with the credit-card company, allowing you to pay off some of the bill, or having the lender agree to waive interest and penalties.
- **Investigate** filing for bankruptcy. He can help you look into the pros and cons of such a move; it may be the best course to take. (For more on bankruptcy, see page 117.)

### GET HELP FOR THE GAMBLING PROBLEM

It may also be worthwhile to consider getting counseling for your husband's gambling addiction. Gamblers Anonymous and similar programs are offered in nearly every major city and many smaller communities as well. Check your telephone directory, or ask your physician about where to find one in your location. Your lawyer may also be able to help you find a program to combat an addiction to gambling.

### COMMUNITY PROPERTY: AN EXCEPTION

There is an important exception to laws that protect you from liability for debt on your husband's credit card. In what is known as a "community property state," the law makes spouses liable for each other's debts. The community property states, which offer you much less protection, are Arizona, California, Idaho, Louisiana, Nevada, New Mexico, Texas, Washington, and Wisconsin. Community property laws also apply in the Commonwealth of Puerto Rico. In these states you'd be wise to get a lawyer on your side.

---

*After your husband dies, you are denied a loan because you have no credit record in your own name.*

---

It's bad enough that you lost your husband; now you find that you are in a financial nightmare. Thankfully, the law is on your side.

The federal Equal Credit Opportunity Act (ECOA) makes it easier for women to get credit and it requires creditors to keep individual credit records. Even so, if you've been married a long time, your credit may have been reported only in your husband's name. Upon his death, you may be shocked to find out that a lifetime of careful spending and prompt bill paying have not been recorded in your name.

### SPEAK UP NOW

The time has come for you to act to establish your credit. You should:

- **Contact the credit-reporting agency** that the lender used in deciding to deny you credit. Under federal law, you must be given the name of this agency. This report is free as long as you ask for it within 60 days of being turned down.
- **Request a copy of your late husband's credit record as**

**well as your own.** Some credit agencies will give you this information when you tell them (in writing) that your husband died. Others may require that you send a copy of his death certificate. Examine both reports carefully. If you and your husband maintained a joint credit-card account, it may have been listed under his name alone, or it may show you as merely an authorized user. If so, your record may well show no credit in your name. You should have the credit-reporting agency amend the report and list you as having been a joint holder of the account.

■ **Write to the credit-reporting company** asking it to conduct an investigation that will correct the errors and omissions in your report. Ask them to send a copy of the corrected report to the lender who turned you down.

■ **Instruct them to show your name as "Betty Blow"** if your credit report now shows your name as "Mrs. Joe Blow." You should also contact any creditors who have listed you this way and insist that they make the same name change in their own records.

■ **Tell the lender about the problem.** You can expect to get a corrected credit report in about 30 days. Ask the lending institution to recon-sider your loan application when the new report is received by them.

## YOU'RE NOT DONE YET

Getting your credit record fixed at one agency doesn't mean it will be corrected at the other credit-reporting companies. Today, most lenders use one of three major credit bureaus, TransUnion, Experian, or Equifax.

You never know ahead of time which credit agency a lender may use. You must call all three and correct your reports with each one. Check back with each to make sure that your credit record is accurate. You may have to pay for a report from the other agencies. (Colorado, Vermont, and Georgia have laws that entitle you to one free report from each of these agencies once a year. Check with your state representative to see if your state has a similar law.)

**CONSUMER ALERT** *Federal law prohibits lenders from denying credit based solely on the borrower's age. Nor can they impose different terms for credit than they do on younger people with similar income, assets, and credit history. If you believe you've been turned down for credit simply because of your age, contact the Federal Trade Commission (FTC).*

---

## REASONS YOU CAN BE DENIED CREDIT

Under regulations created by the Federal Reserve Board, there are 18 legitimate reasons why a lender may decide to turn down your application for credit. They are:

- An incomplete credit application
- Not enough credit references
- An inability to verify credit references
- Temporary or irregular employment
- An inability to verify employment
- Insufficient length of employment
- Insufficient income
- An inability to verify income
- Too much outstanding debt or too many lines of credit
- Lack of adequate collateral
- Temporary residence
- Insufficient length of time residing in your current residence
- An inability to verify your residence
- No credit file
- Delinquencies on current debts
- Garnishment, attachment, repossession, or foreclosure
- Bankruptcy
- The lender grants credit to no one on the terms and conditions you request

*Your credit isn't very good, and now you've been contacted by a company that claims it can clean up your credit report for you.*

An unhealthy credit record can be a barrier to buying a house or a car, and in some cases it can even keep you from getting a job, so it's important to do whatever you can to improve your credit rating. But you would be wise to ignore the claims of any company that says it can wipe your credit record clean. These "credit repair" companies offer:

- Measures you can take yourself
- Tactics that are a pure waste of your money
- Strategies that can be downright illegal.

## YOU CAN DO IT YOURSELF

Some credit-repair companies will offer to get you a copy of your credit record and help you correct any errors contained there. And of course, you can expect to pay a fee for this service. The fact is that there is no need to pay anyone to help you with this because you can correct errors on your credit record yourself. Contact the credit bureaus directly to get copies of your credit reports, and make corrections or add explanatory statements yourself.

> **TAKE NOTE** *Experts estimate that at least one-third of all credit reports contain errors. It's a good idea to check your credit record periodically —once a year or so—and especially before making a major purchase such as a car or a house.*

Other companies take a more questionable approach. They obtain your credit report and then simply challenge all the negative information contained there, whether or not it's accurate. These companies rely on the requirement under the federal Fair Credit Reporting Act (FCRA) that the credit bureau must investigate the challenged information and either verify the facts or delete the information from your credit file. But the FCRA does not require credit bureaus to investi-

gate any claims that they believe are frivolous or irrelevant, and a letter that they receive that challenges every item in your credit report is almost certain to be considered frivolous. The money you pay to a company using this type of strategy (usually several hundred dollars or more) is simply wasted money.

## THE WRONG SIDE OF THE LAW

Remember that the advice given above applies to correcting errors or incomplete information on your credit report. If your report contains negative information that is accurate, then there isn't much that anyone, including a credit-repair company, can do to get those items off your report. Yet that is exactly what some credit-repair swindlers claim they can do. Their scheme involves what's known as credit identity-segregation. The company suggests that you create a new identity for yourself. It advises you to:

- Obtain a federal tax identification number and use this number in place of your Social Security number.
- Get a private post office box and use it as your mailing address.
- Change the way you use your name when applying for credit—for example, instead of "Joseph M. Blow" you should list your name differently, such as "J. Moe Blow."

According to the companies that run these identity segregation scams, you can put your credit problems behind you and obtain new credit by creating a new identity. But following the advice these companies provide is not only useless, it is illegal. Obtaining credit by fraudulently assuming a different identity is a crime—and as most convicts will tell you, getting credit from a prison cell is really difficult.

> **SMART MOVES**
>
> When dealing with a for-profit credit repair agency, always put it in writing! Under the federal Credit Repair Organizations Act, no agreement with an agency of this kind is binding unless it's in writing. Also, you have the right to cancel the agreement within three days.

## Go on the Attack

If a company offering one of these "surefire methods" for cleaning up your credit record approaches you, don't fall for its claims. Instead:

● Contact your state's consumer protection agency with information about the offer that you received.
● Call—and also send a letter to—the Federal Trade Commission, letting it know in detail about the potentially unscrupulous credit-cleanup company that contacted you.

## Looking for Useful Help?

You can get help overcoming debts by calling the Consumer Credit Counseling Service. CCCS has offices in every state and is a national, nonprofit organization dedicated to helping consumers negotiate debt-repayment plans. It also teaches budgeting and money-management.

---

### FILING FOR BANKRUPTCY

When debt gets out of control, filing for bankruptcy may seem like the only way out. For most debtors, the choice is between filing for either of the following:

**Chapter 7 bankruptcy.** Liquidates the debtor's property and uses proceeds to pay creditors. Debtors with few assets, mostly unsecured debts, and no regular source of income often use it.

**Chapter 13 bankruptcy.** Allows a debtor who has a regular source of income (such as wages from her job) to negotiate a three- to five-year repayment plan with her creditors, usually for an amount that's less than the total debt owed.

Filing for bankruptcy can solve many debt problems, but shouldn't be taken lightly. Bankruptcy stays on your credit record for 10 years, making it hard to get a credit card or a car loan, or to rent or buy a home. If you get credit, you may pay higher interest or a larger down payment.

■ **Not every debt can be wiped away** by bankruptcy. Bankruptcy doesn't excuse you from:

● Debts that come from your own willful or malicious misconduct

● Alimony or child support payments

● Federally insured student loans

● Local, state, or federal taxes (with a few exceptions)

● Criminal fines, penalties, or forfeitures

● Liability for injuries or deaths that you caused when you were driving while intoxicated

● Debts the court determines were incurred to defraud your creditors

■ **Bankruptcy will not help you avoid being evicted from your rented home or having your home loan foreclosed on.** While filing for bankruptcy calls a halt (in legal terms, an *automatic stay*) to collection, eviction, and foreclosure efforts, this is only temporary. Secured lenders such as your mortgage company and landlords can ask the court for relief from the automatic stay. Bankruptcy courts almost always grant these requests.

■ **Get professional help.** If your debt is large enough to make you think about filing for bankruptcy, get professional assistance. The Consumer Credit Counseling Service (CCCS) or a lawyer specializing in bankruptcy and credit problems can help you explore alternatives to bankruptcy or decide which chapter of the bankruptcy code to file under.

> *When you signed on with your stockbroker, you told her you were a conservative investor. You've lost a lot of money, and you think she's invested your money in stocks that were too risky.*

Whenever you buy stocks, you run the risk that your investment will decline in value rather than increase. If you are working with a reputable broker and a reputable firm, the broker will have asked you to complete a form that describes your tolerance for risk, along with other information. If your broker has recommended stocks that don't match this risk-tolerance profile, or has misrepresented stocks as being safer than they really are, you owe it to yourself to challenge her advice. How successful you will be in your challenge is by no means certain: not only is the degree of risk in a stock a matter of judgment, not fact, a stock price is also subject to unexpected events that neither you nor your broker can control. That said, it is possible to reclaim some or all of your losses.

### First, Talk It Out

Arrange a meeting with your broker and her branch manager and discuss your concerns with them. It may be that the stocks really do fit your investment profile but are merely going through a cyclical decline. Even the most successful ones sometimes decline temporarily in value.

Therefore, you should ask your broker to provide a written explanation for the reasons she recommended these particular stocks. Ask the manager to provide written confirmation of your broker's explanation of why these stocks were suitable for you, given your conservative tolerance for risk and other investment goals.

Begin keeping a log of your contacts with the brokerage about your concerns, listing the date and time of any meetings, follow-up phone calls, and the names and titles of persons you spoke to about your worries.

### Put It in Writing

If the broker won't give you a written explanation, it's time for you to act more formally. Write the broker and her manager a letter, recounting your concerns and reminding them that you have not received a written explanation for their investment advice. Give them a specific time period in which to act, and tell them the actions you want them to take, such as refunding your losses. This is an acknowledgment that the investment

that was made was one that your broker recommended and not one you made against her advice and that the investment was out of line with your stated goals and risk tolerance.

Don't be surprised if you get no response to your letter, or if the response you do get denies that your broker acted improperly. But don't give up. Send another letter to the president of the brokerage firm, repeating your demand for restitution and enclosing copies of your previous correspondence with your broker and her boss.

### Getting Regulators Involved

If there's still no response from your broker, or if the firm continues to insist that it acted properly, you can take further steps.

- **Contact your state securities commission's office** of consumer protection. You can get the name and address of this agency from the state capitol's general information telephone number. Be sure to ask for the name of the person who heads this agency, and address your complaint to him or her. Briefly describe the problem and the brokerage's responses, if any. Include copies of all your correspondence and copies of any supporting documents, such as your brokerage statements and investor profile. Expect the state agency to take several weeks to several months to investigate your claim and provide you with a response. In some cases, it may be able to convince the brokerage to restore your lost funds as a way of avoiding a long and detailed look at the firm's selling practices.
- **Send a copy of your complaint to the Securities and Exchange Commission** (SEC), Office of Investor Assistance and Education. While this office doesn't usually intervene on behalf of individual investors, it will notify the brokerage that it is the subject of a consumer complaint. If the brokerage already has a record of having several complaints, the SEC could launch its own investigation of the firm.
- **Consider finding an independent stock analyst** who will review the case and back up your claim that the investments your broker

made were indeed not in tune with your investment goals and risk tolerance.

## ARBITRATING YOUR DISPUTE

Your initial agreement with the brokerage firm almost certainly includes a provision that requires you to arbitrate any disputes that cannot be resolved informally. While arbitration is supposed to be less formal and less expensive than a lawsuit, the process does have strict rules that must be followed. In theory, you don't need a lawyer to represent you in arbitration, but you can be sure your broker will have at least one lawyer appearing on her side of the table. Having a lawyer experienced in handling securities arbitration working for you will greatly improve your chance of success.

Many lawyers who practice in this area will work on a contingency basis, taking their fee as a percentage of any money you recover from the brokerage. Be aware that unless your case involves a significant amount of money, it may be hard to find a lawyer willing to represent you.

Keep in mind that while you are waiting for your arbitration hearing, you, or your lawyer, are likely to be approached with a settlement offer from the broker's lawyer. Consider any settlement proposal carefully. It may be that accepting the offer will at least partially restore your losses without requiring you to take the chance of getting nothing at all from the arbitrator.

Your lawyer will be able help you evaluate an offer and to give advice about a particular arbitrator's record. If the arbitrator favors individual investors, you may be better off taking your chances in arbitration rather than settling. But remember that your lawyer can't make this decision for you. The ultimate responsibility, of course, will be yours.

**TAKE NOTE** *Arbitration in cases involving stockbrokers is generally binding, which means you can't pursue the matter in court if you don't like the outcome. And unlike judges, arbitrators don't have to provide you with an explanation for the decision they reach.*

## MAKING YOUR CASE

If you go to arbitration, you will get to tell your side of the story to the arbitrator. (If your claim is a large one, usually $10,000 or more, it's likely to be heard by a panel of arbitrators rather than a single arbitrator.) You will want to provide them with all of the evidence you have collected in support of your claim. How you act during the proceeding is very important:

- Be calm; don't allow yourself to be bullied by the broker's lawyers, who will be allowed to cross-examine you.
- Don't get drawn into shouting matches or personal attacks on your opponent.
- Answer the arbitrator's queries as straightforwardly as possible. If you don't know the answer to a question, say so.

The brokerage then gets to present its case, and you or your lawyer can cross-examine the witnesses it presents. Finally, each side in the dispute gets to make a closing argument. Then it is up to the arbitrator.

You can expect to receive a decision several weeks after the hearing takes place. Unless you have evidence that your opponent was guilty of perjury or other serious misconduct during the arbitration process (which is highly unlikely), the arbitrator's ruling is final.

## HOW TO PICK A FINANCIAL PLANNER

You've worked hard and saved some money. Now may be the time to find an expert to help you plan the best way to put that money to work for you. Ask business associates, friends, and family members for the names of financial planners. Your insurance agent, lawyer, or accountant may also have recommendations. When you interview a prospective planner, ask:

■ **For a brochure about himself and the firm** he works for, and documentation, including the Application for Investment Advisor Registration form (ADV) that he or the firm filed with either the federal Securities and Exchange Commission or the state securities commission. The ADV gives information about the planner's experience and training. Generally, you should expect your planner to have more than five years' experience.

■ **If he is a certified planner.** The certification will be designated by the letters *CFP, ChFC,* or *PFS* following his name. Certification means the planner has completed additional course-work and passed a series of examinations on subjects such as taxes and estate planning. Ask him where he received his professional certification—and follow up with a phone call to be sure that the certification is authentic.

■ **Your state's securities commission** to verify that the planner has not been the subject of any complaints with the state. Your state capitol's general information telephone exchange can give you the phone number of the agency.

■ **If the planner has a specialty.** Some planners work mostly with professionals, such as doctors or lawyers, for instance, or with two-income couples with children, or with clients nearing retirement age. You want a planner who can understand your particular financial situation.

■ **For the names and numbers of current clients** whom you can call for references. If he demurs, claiming that this information is confidential, remind him that clients can waive confidentiality. If he still doesn't cooperate, you may want to start looking for another candidate. Call the references and find out…

  ● How they like the planner

  ● How successful his efforts have been for them

  ● Whether they would recommend the planner to others.

Plus, it's not a bad idea to ask them if they're related to the planner in some way; a relative's opinion may not be objective.

■ **How the planner will get paid.** A fee-only planner puts your financial plan together for a one-time fee or for an hourly rate. A commission-based planner makes his money on the financial products and services he sells you. A hybrid planner may charge you a fee and earn commissions. Fee-only planners may cost more up front, but they have no vested interest in recommending a product with a higher commission over one that may actually be more beneficial to you. So, for most people, fee-only planners are probably the best bet, even though their fees can seem high—several thousand dollars or more.

■ **How you can get out of your relationship** with the planner if things don't work out as you hope. You should be able to end your association with a simple letter, and, obviously, you should expect to get a refund of any fees you've paid that remain unearned.

■ **How compatible you feel with the planner.** Does he answer your questions with candor? Is he tuned in to the kind of financial strategy you have in mind? Do you find yourself looking forward to your next session with him? If not, you better go back to the drawing board.

You put a "stop-loss" order on a stock.
The brokerage firm didn't honor it, and you have lost
thousands of dollars as a result.

This is a pretty straightforward situation. A "stop-loss" order requires the brokerage firm to sell a stock you own when its value falls to—or below—a specified price. If the firm didn't do so when the stock value fell, it owes you money. But you should find out why the stop-loss order was not implemented, because it could affect the way you deal with the situation.

## FIND OUT WHY

Ask your broker to find out why the stop-loss order wasn't honored properly, and demand to see the time-stamped ticket showing when your sale was carried out. Perhaps it was on a day when your stock's price was dropping rapidly, and the firm couldn't act in time to avoid additional losses. Say, for instance, that your stop-loss price was $12 and the stock was sold at $11.50. While you can ask your brokerage to pay the additional half-dollar per share into your account, the firm may refuse. Market conditions change rapidly, and if the firm tried in good faith to

honor your order, the loss will be yours to bear. If, though, you get no reasonable explanation for the firm's failure to sell, you have a more serious problem. You should, of course, still demand restitution, but in this case you may want to tell the state securities commission about your problem. It will investigate your complaint, and if you are having trouble getting satisfaction from the brokerage, it may be able to intervene.

## GETTING SATISFACTION

If the stock was *never* sold, and its value plummeted before you discovered the problem, you may be able to get your money back. Contact the Securities and Exchange Commission (SEC) with your complaint. Brokers who are the subject of several complaints can be investigated, fined, and ordered to comply with regulations governing the way they handle transactions for their customers. Individual brokers who have a pattern of unethical or illegal conduct may also have their licenses suspended or revoked.

An e-mail you received touted a hot new stock.
You invested, but instead of increasing in value, the stock's price
has dropped out of sight.

The Internet can be a source of valuable data—but it is also fertile ground for crooks and con artists to spread misinformation designed to separate consumers from their money. Whether you can recover anything from your costly misadventure on the Internet depends on your quick action—and a bit of luck.

One scam on the Internet that's become more and more prevalent involves so-called investment advice. Using chat rooms, message boards, and e-mail, rip-off artists are stealing billions of dollars from consumers annually. The most pernicious

racket used by these swindlers is the manipulation of the prices of little-known, thinly traded stocks by claiming to have inside information.

## THE "PUMP-AND-DUMP" SCAM

Internet services allow individuals to post messages using a screen name, and most services allow individuals to use more than one screen name. It's pretty easy for a few individuals to create the illusion that there's a great deal of sudden interest in a stock by using their multiple screen names to hype a stock, or stocks that they own. Sometimes the stocks aren't even properly registered with a securities exchange.

Typically, these individuals have purchased shares of the stock at a relatively low price. By claiming to have "advance knowledge" of a "big new contract" or "a major technology break-through," they create excitement about the stock among investors looking for a large, quick gain. These investors buy the stock and the price goes up. Then the original investors sell their shares, reaping the profit created by the excitement they created. Those who invested later watch the stock price drop back to its original levels, or in some cases to nothing, when the promised "big deal" or "breakthrough" fails to materialize.

### TRACKING DOWN THE SWINDLERS

If you fell for an offer to invest in a stock that's "ready for explosive growth" but that turns out to be a disaster, you should immediately make three important phone calls to the following:

■ **Your state's securities commission.** These agencies are taking a much more aggressive stance against Internet securities fraud. In a number of cases, investigators have been able to track down and take legal action against charlatans involved in fraudulent Internet stock promotions. If the securities commission's watchdogs succeed in finding your swindler, you might be able to get some of your money back from him.

■ **The Securities and Exchange Commission** (SEC). In some cases, the SEC has discovered that an Internet investment scam originated with a licensed broker. A broker may be personally liable for making false or misleading statements over the Internet (or at any time, for that matter). More importantly, her employer may also be liable for the misrepresentations, which could make it easier to recoup the losses you suffered. In other cases, the person touting the stock has been deemed an "agent" of the company, which means she is required to disclose her relationship with the company. Failing to do so can subject both the agent and the company to fines.

■ **Your Internet Service Provider** (ISP). Tell the provider about the swindle and ask it to try tracing the message's origination point. Some major ISPs will terminate the accounts of clients who are using e-mail to make unsubstantiated claims about financial investments. This won't help you get your money back, but terminating the account may save someone else from making the same mistake.

---

### PROTECTING YOURSELF FROM INTERNET INVESTMENT SCAMS

Here's what you can do to avoid becoming a victim of a cyberspace-investment rip-off:

■ **Don't assume that your ISP monitors** its investment chat rooms and bulletin boards. While most ISPs are good about responding to individual complaints, they usually don't have the personnel or expertise to take an active role in keeping crooks off their sites.

■ **Stay away from obscure stocks** that aren't traded on the major stock exchanges. These are the easiest to manipulate. Don't invest a penny before contacting your state securities commission to find out if an investment and the person offering it are properly registered.

■ **Do your own research,** or get expert advice. Most full-service and many discount brokerages can provide you with far more reliable information about a stock than the claims made by an unknown e-mailer or chat-room inhabitant.

You're not the first to be duped by a con artist using the cover of a church fellowship—or some other social organization—to work a financial scam. But you can fight back. Law enforcement and regulatory agencies take a dim view of those who perpetrate financial

crimes, and by reporting your experience and cooperating with investigators, you stand a chance of seeing the person who victimized you caught and brought to justice.

■ **Go at once to the police** and report your problem. Then canvass the congregation to see if anyone else has been victimized. The more information and documentation you can come up with, the better the chance that the police will be able to track the crook down and get

his bank accounts and other assets frozen until he can be tried and, if found guilty, ordered to make restitution.

■ **Call the consumer protection department** in your state attorney general's office for assistance. This agency can put fraud investigators to work to settle your case.

**TAKE NOTE** *The laws in many states make it a more serious crime to defraud a senior citizen; if you're a senior and you live in one of these states, the attorney general's office will probably take a more aggressive interest in investigating and settling your case.*

If the crook has left the state (and is tracked down through mail-forwarding orders, banking activity and so on), the attorney general's office may be able to coordinate efforts with its counterpart in the state where he's now operating. It may also be able to involve federal law enforcement agencies such as the FBI in the investigation. If the con man has been charged with a felony in your state, he can also be charged at the federal level for fleeing across state lines to avoid prosecution.

## GETTING YOUR MONEY BACK

Once the crook is caught, the authorities will launch a criminal action against him. Should that not result in restitution of your funds, you may want to hire an attorney to help you file a civil lawsuit against the culprit. Some lawyers will take on this kind of litigation on a contingency fee basis, but before they will agree to do so, they will want to investigate the case and determine if the con artist has sufficient assets to make it worthwhile for them to go to court for you.

## SCAMS IN THE MAIL AND FRAUD OVER THE INTERNET

The world of finance is full of pitfalls that can trap the unwary. Prominent among them are pyramid schemes that promise sky-high returns in a short period of time. The most notorious of these is known as the Ponzi scheme, named after Charles Ponzi, who originated the mail scam in the early part of the 20th century. In its original incarnation, Ponzi promised friends and neighbors that he could earn them a return of $75 for every $50 they invested and do it in a three-month period. His scheme was simple. Here's how it worked:

■ **Ponzi used the money given to him by later investors to pay the earlier ones.** It worked like a charm. Early investors got the promised returns and more investors rushed to climb on the gravy train. In just more than a year Ponzi defrauded his clients of more than $10 million—a lot of money today and even more in 1910. But the scam was destined to collapse under its own weight.

■ **To keep paying high returns in the short period promised,** Ponzi had to continually attract new money. Ultimately, he would have had to have every person on the planet participating as "investors"—at that point, he would have been forced to start looking for money from extraterrestrials. It never got that far, however, and U.S. Postal Inspectors were able to charge Ponzi with violating the laws against mail fraud.

■ **Scams in the 21st century are flourishing like toadstools.** Today, thanks to the Internet, Ponzi schemes, chain letters, and other pyramid scams often show up as e-mails touting big returns. You are promised that your mailbox will be flooded with thousands of dollars from those farther down the list.

All you have to do, the scammers insist, is...

● Add your name and address to a mailing list

● Send a few dollars to those already listed

● Forward the message to a number of other e-mail addresses.

Often the email sender will claim to be a lawyer who's given up her practice in order to make money using this Internet mailing list. "It's all perfectly legal," the e-mail assures you, and it may even refer to a statute that supposedly supports the scheme's legitimacy. *Don't fall for it.*

■ **Steps you can take to protect yourself if you are offered one of these cyber-scams.** Contact the customer service department at your Internet Service Provider (ISP), and describe the e-mail, with the sender's address and other relevant details. The ISP can investigate on its own as well as providing information to the FBI and other government agencies on the trail of Internet scams.

■ **If you get a scam letter in the mail,** you should immediately contact the USPS Inspectors. Call or visit your local post office to find out how to reach them.

You lent your brother-in-law the money
to buy a used car, but now he isn't making the payments
on the loan because the car needs repairs.

Your brother-in-law owes you the money, period. Keeping the used car running is his problem, not yours. So, since it's too late for you to reconsider getting financially involved with relatives, your problem now is to decide how hard you want to fight to get your money back from him—and how much family strife you are willing to stir up.

In family situations, taking an informal approach is always the best first step. Give your brother-in-law a call, and point out that he's late with his payments, and remind him of his obligation to repay you.

### FOLLOWING A PAPER TRAIL

If you made the loan just by writing a check with no agreement on paper, you can get him to repay you (see below). But if you put the loan agreement in writing, you have much more leverage over him. Ideally, such an agreement states:

- ✔ The amount of the loan
- ✔ The interest being charged
- ✔ The payment schedule
- ✔ A statement of his promise to repay the loan.

If he's experiencing financial problems (such as reduced pay because he can't get to work while his car is out of commission), you can offer to amend your original agreement, if you have one, either by lowering the monthly payments or perhaps by offering a moratorium of a month or two. Or, if you didn't write the document when the loan was first made, now's a good time to draw one up.

If your brother-in-law is agreeable, write him a letter outlining your agreement, and ask him to sign it as acknowledgment of your new understanding.

### SMART MOVES

Never lend money to anyone, including your relatives, without putting the loan agreement in writing—even if doing so makes you feel like a nitpicker.

### IT MAY NOT BE THAT EASY

If your brother-in-law won't agree, or if he still doesn't make the payments under your new agreement, you'll have to do some soul searching. Collecting money from a business or someone with whom you have no personal relationship is hard enough. Add the possibility of riling family members with a demand for payment and even threatening a court case, and the problem gets thornier.

If you decide to go ahead and try to collect the money (with or without a written loan agreement in hand), you should write your brother-in-law a *demand letter* (page 456). In your letter include…

- ● The date of any original agreement
- ● The date of any subsequent modification
- ● The amount of money in which your brother-in-law is in arrears.

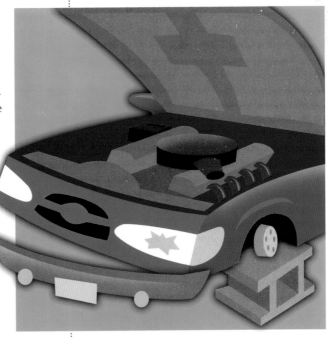

● The remedy you want, that is, getting his payments caught up. Better yet, ask for his immediate payment of the entire debt.

*Even if you win your case, it's still up to you to collect the money.*

Send the letter to him by certified mail, return receipt requested. In the letter, give him a reasonable time period in which to respond (10 business days is usually enough). If he still refuses to pay you, you will then have to decide if you want to take the matter to court.

### GOING TO COURT

If, for whatever reason, you don't have anything in writing, you can still pursue a court case. For example, your canceled check made out to your brother-in-law, along with testimony from your spouse, family members, or friends who knew about the loan, can help establish your case. Your demand letter will also strengthen your case.

Depending on the amount he owes you, small claims court may be your best bet. You can find out the maximum dollar amount that your small claims court has jurisdiction over by calling the clerk at the courthouse.

**TAKE NOTE** *If your claim is only slightly greater than the small-claims limit, you could still decide to seek a lesser figure that will let you file in small claims court. That way, you'll avoid the added expense and delays of filing for a hearing in a regular law court.*

In small claims court, a lot of decisions are based on the judge's ability to evaluate witnesses. Being truthful, avoiding personal attacks on your brother-in-law, and respectfully answering the judge's questions will help the court reach a decision that's favorable to you.

### IT'S NOT OVER YET

Even if you win your case, it's still up to you to collect the money from your brother-in-law. Ask the clerk of the court for the forms you will need to enforce your judgment. Generally, there are three sources from which you can collect money awarded to you by the court. You can...

● Turn to your brother-in-law's employer, who will withhold the money from his pay.
● Obtain judgment from his bank accounts.
● File your judgment as a lien taken out against his property.

The sheriff's department or other local law enforcement authorities will deliver your *writs*— the documents authorizing you to collect on your judgment—to the employer, the bank, and the office where county real estate records are kept. You must pay for this service, but the law lets you ask to be reimbursed by your brother-in-law for the cost of delivery. The clerk of the small claims court can provide you with the right form to file in order to make this request.

After all this, whether you get your money back or not, you will have learned a useful lesson: Be careful to whom you loan money.

**Your property tax assessment is thousands of dollars higher than the price you could get for your home.**

If your property has been overassessed, this is a fight you have a good chance of winning. Assessors can make mistakes, and the laws in every state give you the right to challenge them. Diligence and persistence on your part may well get your property tax lowered.

Your assessment is gauged by comparisons of the fair market value of your property with that of others in the community that are similar in size, age, and condition. You should get a notice of the assessed value of your home each year from the taxing authority. If your assessment increases dramatically, or if you think it's inaccurate or unfair, you should appeal it.

The assessment notice will usually provide the details for appealing the assessment; you have to send a letter stating that you intend to appeal the assessment within a specified time period, such as 30 days. Note: If you miss the cutoff date, you can lose the right to an appeal.

### What's Wrong With This Picture?

In order to get the assessed value of your property reduced, you'll have to show that the assessment is wrong. In some cases, this isn't very complicated. The assessment may state that…

- Your house has 2,000 square feet of living space when it has only 1,500. (Measure your rooms and send the data to the assessor.)
- The dimension of your 10,000-square-foot lot is listed as being 15,000 square feet. (Measure the lot and send that information to the assessor.)
- The finished area of your house has four bedrooms when it has only three. (Sign an affidavit stating the truth.)
- Your house is made of brick when it's actually frame. (Take photos to prove your claim.)

### Doing the Homework

If you find no specific errors in your assessment, you need to arm yourself with other evidence that your property has been overvalued. You can hire a professional appraiser to provide an independent appraisal, but you can also do your own research:

- Check with local real estate agencies for information about recent sales of similar properties in the community where you live.
- Look up data about comparable sales from property records at the county courthouse.
- Scan local newspapers, which print information about local real estate transactions.

**TAKE NOTE** *Don't take too long. After you've indicated your intent to appeal, your window for actually making the appeal is likely to be relatively narrow—usually less than 90 days. You won't get a hearing if the deadline expires.*

### The Appeals Process

For the most part, you don't need the help of a lawyer to challenge a property tax assessment. Nor do you need to hire one of the many companies that offers to reduce your property taxes for you, for a price, of course—often half the amount that you save in taxes.

Since the procedures for representing yourself are relatively straightforward, you can probably handle most stages of an appeal on your own. Following is a general overview of the process.

### The First Encounter

Different locales have different procedures for handling a dispute of this kind. For example, a specific day or days may be set aside for residents to appear at the town hall to air their grievances. In any case, the procedure for setting up a meeting is usually described on your tax bill. These sessions can be quite informal and easygoing, and you may be pleased with the results.

- **Do your research ahead of time** and take copies of evidence supporting your reasons for seeking a reduction for the assessor's review.
- **Be businesslike** and calm when making your case to the assessor. Remember that the assessor isn't responsible for tax rates, so merely complaining that property taxes are too high isn't going to be a very convincing argument for a reduction.

If the assessor agrees that your assessment was incorrect, ask her when you will get an amended assessment. If she won't lower your assessment, ask her how you can obtain the forms you will need to make a formal appeal.

## How to Deal With the Appeal

Your formal appeal will be heard by a local board of government officials. It may be called the Property Tax Equalization Board, the Board of Tax Review, or something similar. In this hearing, you will have the burden of proving that the assessment of your property is in error; the board will assume that the assessment is correct, so having viable evidence is essential.

- **Prepare for the hearing.** Find out how many board members will be in attendance, and be sure to have enough photocopies of documents—such as appraisals, comparable sales figures, and photographs—so that each board member can have one.
- **Present your evidence** and be prepared to answer questions from the members of the board about how you arrived at your figures. Be polite and answer those questions honestly. If you don't understand a question, don't hesitate to ask that it be rephrased.
- **Listen carefully as the assessor makes her case.** Before she begins, however, ask the board to have the assessor provide you with copies of any documents she's going to rely on in support of the assessment. (The assessor probably won't have the documents until the time of the hearing, meaning this will be your first chance to see them.)
- **Make notes about any state-ments you disagree with,** but be careful not to interrupt or make gestures or sighs of disapproval. You'll usually have the chance to rebut the assessor's statements or ask her questions about her testimony. For example, if the assessor testifies that she determined the value of your property by comparing sales of other houses in your neighborhood, you might ask her if she's aware that some of those houses are much newer than your own. (Newer houses are often more expensive because the construction costs are higher and the houses are more likely to include extra amenities.) Be polite, nonconfrontational, and brief—the board probably has a full schedule, and expects all involved to get to the point.

- **Wait for the notification from the board.** You'll get a letter, typically within several weeks. The exact time limit for reaching a decision varies. You may learn that…

  - You have won your case, and that the board is ordering your assessment reduced to the figure you requested in your appeal.
  - You have gotten a partial reduction in your assessment.
  - The board has found that the original assessment was justified.

## What to Do Next?

If you don't get what you want, you can appeal the board's decision. In some states, that means an appeal to a county board, while in others your next step is taking your appeal to court.

Be sure you understand the appeals process in your state. Some states require that you pay the taxes on your property—even though you dispute the assessment—or the court will not hear your appeal. In many states, skipping a step in the review process (going to court before you've appealed to a state appeals board) could mean having your appeal dismissed.

You haven't needed a lawyer so far, but getting legal help at this late stage is probably smart—especially if you have to go to court. The procedures are more formal and complicated than the steps you've already taken, and you'll be glad to have a professional on your side.

*Your property taxes have gone up considerably, but your Social Security hasn't kept pace and you are afraid you may lose your home.*

You are not alone. Recognizing that many citizens share your problems, every state in the union offers various exemptions and reductions in property taxes to homeowners in certain categories who need help. Among those who can often qualify for tax relief are…

- Disabled homeowners
- Senior citizens
- Disabled veterans
- Widows of veterans
- Low-income homeowners
- The blind.

On a more local level, many counties and cities also give further assistance to homeowners having trouble paying their property taxes. For example, some cities allow older citizens to work off a portion of their property tax by volunteering services to the city.

**TAKE NOTE** *The most important thing to remember about getting the exemptions you are legally entitled to receive is that you must ask for them and be persistent.*

## STRAIGHTFORWARD STEPS TO TAKE

It is a fairly simple matter to pursue the goal of getting these property tax exemptions.

- **Call your local tax authority** as soon as you receive your bill. Ask the person you speak with for information about specific property tax exemptions available in your state and town. Be sure to find out what forms you need to complete in order to obtain a specific exemption or reduction.
- **Complete the forms and return them** to the tax authority, along with any supporting documents that may be required, such as a doctor's statement of disability, a birth certificate, or income tax returns. Be sure to ask if photocopies of these documents are acceptable; if they are not, keep photocopies for your own records. The tax authority will review your application, and in the majority of cases it will notify you that you have been granted the exemption you seek.
- **Keep the notification in a safe place,** such as a fireproof file box or home safe. Note: You may be required to reapply after a stated period for some exemptions, such as those based on your income level or disability.

If you are refused the exemption you applied for, you should be notified of the reason as well as the procedures for appealing the tax authority's decision. Follow the instructions on filing an appeal carefully and take special care to meet the deadline.

## IF YOU NEED HELP

Is a law school located anywhere near you? If so, be aware that many law schools operate student clinics that can help you make your way through the appeals process.

You may also find that your state or local department of social services will assist you or direct you to free or low-cost sources of legal help available to the disabled and older residents.

axes are never welcome, and surely an unexpected tax delivers a double whammy. Local governments can assess residents to pay for a special benefit, such as building sidewalks at their curbs. But sometimes governments go overboard with these assessments, and this is where you can fight back.

You have to determine if the sewer system is a special improvement or a general one. If it is special, decide if your property should be included in the assessment.

■ **A special assessment may be illegal** if it is for something that provides a *general* benefit to the community, such as water lines in the city's main thoroughfares. Some courts have ruled that such an improvement must be paid for by general revenue bonds or out of the city's general tax fund.

■ **The local government may have overstepped its authority** if it has created a special assessment district in which the taxed residents will benefit only indirectly or not at all from the "improvement."

## TAKING THE OFFENSIVE

Your first opportunity to fight such an assessment will come after there's official notice of the improvement to be made. The notice will usually come by mail and will describe the benefit to the homeowner and the proposed assessment that will pay for it. It will also include information about the public hearing (date, time, and place), which you should attend and raise your objection.

State laws determine how much time is allowed between the notice and the hearing. If the law requires a 10-day notice and you receive only 9, a court could find that the local government had violated your right to notice and require it to start the process all over again.

Before the hearing, you will need to contact the hearing board to schedule your appearance. If many of your neighbors have objections, the time for your appearance may be limited, but you cannot be denied the opportunity to be heard.

To defeat the special assessment, you must show that the proposed benefit…

● Doesn't provide any community benefit. It helps a new business, but no one else.
● Doesn't provide special benefit to your property. The sewer system will benefit the new development near your farm, but it won't help you because you are on a septic system that won't be converted to the sewer system.
● Doesn't warrant being done. The improvement is unnecessary; the current system is perfectly adequate.
● Doesn't provide immediate benefit to you as a taxpayer. Too much of the cost of the improvement is being assessed against a few in the district (five property owners are being asked to pay the cost of an improvement that ultimately will benefit hundreds of homes).

## WHAT IF YOU DON'T CONVINCE THEM?

If your arguments don't prevail and the hearing board decides in favor of the special assessment, you can make an appeal in your state court system. As a rule, the courts respect official decisions, but they are not allowed to rubberstamp them. The court could rule against permitting a special assessment if it finds that the local government did any of the following:

● Acted in an arbitrary way
● Violated its own rules in creating the special assessment district
● Had been otherwise unreasonable in making its determination.

The court could order the city to dissolve the special assessment district and pay for the improvement out of its general fund or by issuing bonds. It could also require a reassessment if it finds that the amount being charged is more than necessary for the proposed improvement.

In cases of this kind, getting the court to decide in your favor won't be easy, but it has been done. However, a lawyer's help will be essential in pursuing your case, and that can be expensive. But if you and your neighbors are equally opposed to the assessment, joining forces with them can help lessen the cost of a lawsuit by spreading legal fees among a number of plaintiffs.

> *T*he IRS has audited your return and assessed additional taxes. The auditor is threatening to file a lien or seize your home if you don't pay up immediately.

Take this threat very seriously. The Internal Revenue Service can be a dangerous opponent, and it has enormous latitude in the actions it can take to collect overdue taxes. On the other hand, it cannot simply take your home away from you without going through a strictly regimented routine—which offers you various opportunities along the way to avoid or mitigate your losses. This is a somewhat complicated procedure, and you should consider getting legal help to guide you through it.

> *A Problem Resolution Officer (PRO) is empowered to cut through red tape and help solve taxpayers' problems.*

### FIRST STEPS FOR THE IRS

Before it can file a lien against your home, the IRS must first…

- Send you a bill for the taxes it claims you owe
- Send you a demand letter, giving you 10 days to pay the taxes owed or face action
- File a Notice of Federal Tax Lien in the property records of the county where you live.

### YOUR FIRST RESPONSE

A Federal Tax Lien can make it impossible for you to sell or refinance your home, so your first concern should be to ward off the threatened lien.

Immediately call the telephone number listed on the notice. Ask the IRS employee handling your case what steps you can take to avoid having the lien filed. It may be possible to propose a payment plan, or even to obtain what's known as an *Offer in Compromise*, allowing you to settle your tax bill for less than the full amount owed (page 135). If the IRS employee won't help, call your nearest IRS district office and ask for help from a Problem Resolution Officer (PRO). PROs are empowered to cut through red tape and help solve taxpayers' problems. Point out to the PRO that filing a lien against your property may do more harm than good, as it will keep you from refinancing your home to pay your tax bill.

If the PRO can't or won't help, ask to speak to his supervisor, who may be more willing to provide assistance.

### IF A LIEN IS FILED

If these tactics don't work and a lien is filed against your property, the IRS must notify you in writing of the filing within five business days. The written notice must tell you that you have the right to request a hearing within 30 days from the sixth day after the lien was filed. At this point, you have three options:

- **Pay the tax in full** and obtain a Satisfaction of Lien from the IRS within 30 days of making payment.
- **Request a partial discharge.** This works only if the IRS has filed liens against several assets. If it agrees to lift the lien on one of them, you may be able to sell it and satisfy your tax debt.
- **Ask for a hearing** to appeal the lien. Write a letter to the district director, referring to the lien notice you received and requesting a hearing. Enclose a copy of the notice and send your letter by certified mail, return receipt requested. When you get a hearing, one of your goals should be to explain to the hearing panel that there are other less severe ways in which the IRS can collect the taxes you owe. If you're convincing, the lien will be removed. (The record of the original filing will still remain part of your credit report, however.) Having an experienced tax attorney or an enrolled agent with you can help, because they have experience negotiating and know what evidence to present about other ways the IRS can collect from you.

### A LEVY IS WORSE THAN A LIEN

A lien serves as public notice of a debt owed to the IRS (and also marks the debt against your credit record). A levy involves actually seizing property you own and is a much more serious proposition. Most of the nearly 3 million levies the IRS issues each year are directed toward businesses and financial institutions, but a few thousand every year are issued against individual taxpayers. Typically these levies are for citizens' motor vehicles, boats, or business property. But just about any property you own, including your home, can have a levy against it.

Just as it had to send you a demand letter before filing a lien against your property, the IRS must provide you with a Notice of Intent to Levy before it can seize your home. Generally, this notice must be given at least 30 days before any seizure takes place, although in some cases that period may be shortened if the district director of the IRS decides that delaying seizure would jeopardize collection of the debt. The Notice of Intent must contain the following:

- An explanation of the tax debt you owe
- Alternatives
- An explanation of your right to an Appeals Office hearing before the seizure takes place.

**TAKE NOTE** *You have 30 days to file for an appeal. If you go to a hearing and lose, you can file a civil suit in U.S. district court or the Tax Court.*

## LAST CHANCE TO AVOID SEIZURE

Seizing a residence is a last resort for the IRS, but if you consistently fail to respond to its collection efforts, the IRS district director can authorize seizure. At this point you have one final chance to arrange a payment plan with the IRS that will allow you to keep your home.

If you still refuse to cooperate, the Internal Revenue Service will post a Notice of Seizure on your home, generally on your front door, and will deliver another copy to you, either in person or by certified mail.

The IRS cannot evict you, but it will publish a notice in the local newspapers announcing that on a given date your house will be auctioned, either by sealed bids or at public auction. Although the IRS wants to realize as much money as it can, it will set a minimum bid—which is often quite a bit less than what the property might bring on the open market, so the chances are good that your house will be sold.

The buyer of your property at auction cannot enter your home—yet. First, she has to bring an eviction suit against you in your state court, which the court will grant.

## ONE FINAL HOPE

So, it's come to this: Your house has been levied and auctioned off to the highest bidder, who has gone to court to evict you—but you still have one last hope. You can go to court and force the new owner to sell your house back to you. You have 180 days in which to redeem your home by paying him the full amount he paid at the auction plus 20 percent annual interest, calculated from the date of the sale.

In other words, even when all else has failed, you still have six months to scratch together the wherewithal to reclaim your house.

## IRS AUDIT SECRETS

Although it happens to only about 1 percent of all taxpayers in any one year, the chance still remains that one day you may find that most unwelcome piece of mail in your mailbox: an audit notice from the Internal Revenue Service. Over time, about half of all taxpayers will be audited at least once; the odds increase if…

- You're self-employed.

- You are a lawyer or a doctor or engage in another line of work where you're likely to be paid in cash.

- You take deductions that are disproportionate to your income.

Once you get the dreaded notice, there is no way to avoid the audit, but getting through the ordeal can be much less stressful if you remember the following:

■ **You are not required to provide information about any other tax year,** even if the auditor asks you for it. The audit notice indicates the tax year under examination.

- You may be required to provide information about items such as capital losses that you carried over from a previous year to the year under examination.

■ **Stay calm. Don't get emotional** or make personal attacks on the auditor. It's not her fault that (in your opinion) taxes are too high or that the government spends your money foolishly. Stick to the facts, answer the questions you are asked if you can, and *don't volunteer information* that may open a door to items that didn't concern the auditor in the first place.

■ **Consider carefully any offer by the auditor to make minor adjustments,** especially if she seems to be in a hurry and anxious to close your case. Giving up a little now can help you avoid a prolonged audit later.

■ **You have the right to ask for a supervisor's assistance** in moving matters along, if you and the auditor reach an impasse on certain points. And if the auditor is uncooperative, insulting, or accusatory, you have the right to request a different auditor.

■ **Provide relevant check stubs, receipts,** logs, and other papers that might be useful.

■ **You can have a tax professional represent you at your audit,** if you don't want to attend. Choose an experienced professional. He may not know the answers to all the auditor's questions, so he'll ask that they be put in writing. This delays the audit, which is something most auditors don't want to happen, since they are evaluated on how many cases they can close. Your auditor may decide not to pursue the matter and make an offer to settle, so she can get on to the next case.

Believe it or not, it's possible that the IRS may be willing to reduce an oversized tax bill to just pennies on the dollar. As part of its effort to be more "taxpayer friendly," the IRS is offering an increasing number of taxpayers saddled with big overdue balances a little-known option called an *Offer in Compromise* (OIC). Under an OIC arrangement, the IRS agrees to settle your account for less than the total tax due.

*The IRS is eager to get you back on the rolls as a taxpaying citizen.*

The OIC is definitely not a panacea for the average taxpayer dismayed by the amount of the April 15 tax bill. To qualify, you must convince the IRS that there is good reason to doubt either…

- That you actually owe the taxes
- That the IRS can collect the full amount from you, either now or in the future.

Practically speaking, the first of these is not a likely option. Before you ever get to the point where an OIC is a consideration, you will already have had a lot of communication with the IRS. It will have investigated your case and decided that, for instance, you have seriously underpaid your past taxes, or that you haven't filed and paid any taxes at all for several years. Chances are the IRS has got you dead to rights.

So how do you convince the IRS that you will not be able to pay all that you owe, now or in the future? While every OIC is evaluated individually, your chances of getting your tax bill reduced diminish if you have a high-paying job or the prospects of one, or if you own expensive personal property or real estate. On the other hand, you may get a larger amount taken off your tax bill…

- If you are older
- If you have few assets and limited job prospects
- If you have health problems.

The IRS is eager to get you back on the rolls as a taxpaying citizen; if you make a case that paying your back taxes will cripple you financially, the IRS may be willing to make a deal.

## MAKING A DEAL

The first step in submitting an Offer in Compromise is to complete and file IRS Form 656. If your offer is based on doubt that the IRS can ever collect all it's owed, you'll have to fill out at least one financial disclosure form, Form 433-A, *Collection Information Statement for Individuals.* If you're self-employed, Form 433-B, *Collection Information Statement for Businesses* must also be completed.

On Form 656, you'll list the taxes you owe, how much you propose to pay, and how you intend to pay it. You have three choices:

- You can pay the full amount you propose as a lump sum.
- You can make a down payment and propose periodic payments.
- You can propose periodic payments with no down payment.

You will also add a statement of your reason for making the offer (for example, "doubt as to the collectibility of the full amount of tax, penalty, and interest owed"). Sign the form and send it and the disclosure statements to the IRS.

## WHAT YOU NEED TO TELL THE IRS

The IRS will want documentation of the information on your disclosure statement. Be prepared to provide copies of the following:

- Income tax returns for the past two years
- Titles to vehicles you own
- Bank and brokerage statements
- Rent or mortgage receipts
- Deeds and mortgages
- Unpaid bills
- Reports from doctors on medical problems you may have.

After you've filled out the forms correctly, the IRS may take up to a year to review your offer and make a determination about accepting it.

**TAKE NOTE** *During this time, be sure to stay up to date on current taxes owed and with filing returns or extensions.*

## HOW MUCH IS ENOUGH?

There are no hard-and-fast rules for the amount you should propose to pay in your Offer in Compromise. IRS regulations prohibit only offers that are frivolous (for example, offering to pay $1 on a balance due of $100,000). It may be worthwhile to talk to a tax attorney about your situation before making an offer. In fact, some companies now specialize in making and managing OICs for their clients.

## IF YOUR OFFER IS REJECTED

Offers in Compromise may be rejected for several reasons, most often because the Internal Revenue Service believes that the amount of your offer is too low. If so, the IRS must tell you what it believes is an acceptable amount.

Don't give up if your OIC is initially rejected. Contact the person who signed the letter turning down your offer and try to convince her to reverse her decision. If that effort fails, you have the right to file a formal written appeal within 30 days of the date of the written rejection of your OIC. A separate division of the IRS hears appeals, and many offers that are rejected at first are either negotiated to more favorable terms for the taxpayer or accepted outright.

## IF YOUR OFFER IS ACCEPTED

Good things can happen when your OIC is accepted. For example, any recorded tax liens on your property must be removed within 30 days of the acceptance. That means your credit record will be cleared and your credit rating will improve dramatically. If you proposed making installment payments, interest accumulates only on the amount of the offer, not on the original amount you owed the IRS.

Under any accepted OIC, you will save a significant amount of money. For example, one taxpayer who owed the IRS more than $100,000 had his offer of a $5,000 payment accepted. Of course, you can't count on landing that big a deal, but be aware that in one recent year, the IRS accepted more than 25,000 OICs. It collected $290 million of more than $1.9 *billion* in overdue taxes, meaning that of the OICs accepted, the IRS wrote off around 85 percent of the taxes owed.

### HOW A LAWYER CAN HELP YOU WITH THE IRS

Getting professional legal help when faced with a threat of lien or levy from the IRS is always a good idea. By the time you reach this level of action by the IRS, having a trained and experienced expert on your side is almost a necessity to help you beat the IRS charges, or at least reach a compromise. An experienced lawyer can...

● Help you navigate the complexities of the IRS procedures.

● Make your meetings with IRS representatives go better. Hostile confrontations between you and the IRS never help your cause.

● Stay far more detached and rational in the face of the IRS claims than most people can.

The legal fees you pay can be lower than the penalties and interest you could owe—and they're also deductible from your tax return for the year in which you pay them.

*The IRS claims that your tax preparer
made an error in your return, and it is assessing you
additional taxes, penalties, and interest.*

You are not alone. The IRS sends out hundreds of thousands of automated adjustment notices to taxpayers each year claiming that they underpaid their taxes and requesting payment. The most common automated adjustment notice is Form CP-2000.

A number of studies have found that between one-quarter and one-half of these forms sent by the IRS are wrong, and the taxpayers who receive them don't really owe any additional taxes.

## IF THE IRS IS WRONG

Check with your tax preparer and ask her to review the CP-2000. If she convinces you the IRS has made an error, you should…

■ **Call the IRS** at the number listed on the CP-2000. Ask for a complete explanation of the reason for the adjustment. Tell the IRS representative why you believe the adjustment is mistaken, and tell him that you will send proof supporting your claim by mail. Ask him to cancel the additional bill—in IRS jargon, an *abatement* of the additional tax, interest, and penalties. It's not likely that you will get the issue settled with a single call, but it's important to respond quickly to any IRS communication asking you for more money.

■ **Write to the IRS within 60 days** of the date on the CP-2000, objecting to the additional assessment. Under federal law, failing to do so makes the adjustment final. There is no IRS form for doing this, so you will need to write a letter. The letter should contain…

● Your name, address, telephone number, and Social Security number (and your spouse's if you filed jointly).
● A brief statement of why you believe the CP-2000 is in error. For example, "The amount of compensation reported by my employer was incorrect. I received only $45,000, not $48,000 as reported on my W-2."

● A request that the tax, interest, and any penalties be abated.
● Copies of any documents that support your position, such as your corrected W-2 or a letter from your employer as well as a copy of the IRS notice you received.

**TAKE NOTE** *Don't send originals when communicating with the IRS; if they get lost, you'll have a harder time fighting later IRS claims.*

It is probable that the IRS will give you the abatement you request after reviewing your letter. If it doesn't, however, you should contact the Problem Resolution Officer (PRO) at the IRS district office for assistance.

## IF YOUR TAX PREPARER GOOFED

If your tax preparer made an error, you will still owe the additional tax. However, you should demand that she pay any ensuing penalties and interest, since you relied on her professional expertise to avoid problems with the IRS in the first place.

Many tax preparers have a policy of automatically paying penalties and interest that result from their errors or omissions. If yours doesn't, or if she claims that the error wasn't her fault (for example, because she claims you failed to provide her with a 1099 or the correct W-2), you can consider action to make her pay. But don't rush to judgment here: The preparer has to rely on the information you provide her, so if you did give her inaccurate information, or failed to provide the right forms, she's not liable.

On the other hand, if you're sure you provided her with complete and accurate material, write her a letter. Include copies of your original return, the CP-2000 you received, and any other correspondence you exchanged with the IRS. Insist that she reimburse you for the penalties and interest assessed by the IRS. Send the letter by certified mail, return receipt requested.

**SMART MOVES**

Before hiring a tax preparer, work out ahead of time how costly errors will be compensated and try to get it in writing.

### GETTING IT BACK

If your tax preparer continues to refuse to pay what your are owed—and you have come to the conclusion that the amount owed is worth the trouble—you may decide to sue. Depending on the amount in question, you can either file your suit in small-claims court or take your case to the regular state court system.

If the preparer is a lawyer or accountant, you can contact the appropriate licensing authorities with information about your problem. The licensing board will investigate your claim and may take disciplinary action against the tax preparer, not just for the initial failure to perform her duties in a professional manner but also for her failure to respond to your complaint.

## A TRUST WON'T HELP YOU AVOID INCOME TAX TODAY

A trust is a legal entity that holds and manages assets for your benefit or for your spouse, children, or an older adult in your family. Trusts can be useful in reducing estate taxes, the money your estate may owe the government when you die. Remember that what they do *not* do is protect you from paying current taxes. Protect yourself from trust scams by...

■ **Detecting a trust scam.** In recent years there has been an upsurge in the number of scam artists touting trusts as tax shelters. For an initial fee (usually several thousand dollars) and a monthly management fee (sometimes as much as $1,000), these con artists promise to create trusts for you that will provide a way to lower your income taxes while you are alive. Don't be taken in by these swindlers' claims. In reality, trusts offer very little in the way of protection from income taxes. Using one of these trusts could even expose you to criminal charges. You can tell that a trust offer is too good to be true if the promoter or his brochures make any of the following claims:

● You can assign your wages to the trust and not pay taxes on them.

● You get to keep control of the assets you place in the trust, while owing no taxes. The truth is, if you have "control and use" of the assets or the income those assets produce, you still owe taxes on them.

● You can make personal expenses deductible by funneling them through the trust.

● You can create trusts to confuse creditors and the Internal Revenue Service (IRS).

Furthermore, be particularly wary of anyone who is reluctant to have your accountant or tax lawyer review the trust proposal, claiming that the proposal is based on laws either too new or too sophisticated for them to understand.

■ **Saying "No" if someone offers you such phony or misleading propositions.** Then call your state attorney general's office of consumer protection or the IRS and report your encounter. Currently, the IRS has hundreds of agents who do nothing but investigate and prosecute promoters of these fraudulent trusts.

**U**nder federal law, both spouses are fully responsible for all statements on the return and for paying the taxes owed on a joint return. The Internal Revenue Service has the right to go after either spouse (whether they are married or were divorced during the tax year in question), and if the IRS decides you have more assets or are better able to pay than your husband, and if you signed the return, you may be on the line for the full amount.

However, if you innocently signed a return that understates income or overstates deductions and credits, you can be relieved of liability under what's known as the *innocent spouse rule.*

To convince the IRS that you shouldn't be responsible for paying the additional taxes, you will have to show…

- That all or part of the tax understatement was the result of your ex-spouse's actions
- That you did not know or had no reason to know about the understatement and that it would be unfair to hold you liable for your ex-spouse's actions.

So, how do you prove this to the IRS? Here are some examples: Your ex-husband kept two sets of books for his business and you weren't aware of that. Or perhaps he has been stashing money away that you didn't know about—and your lifestyle doesn't reflect the extra money. Yet another possibility is that he threatened to harm you if you didn't sign the return.

This information goes to the IRS on Form 8857: Request for Innocent Spouse Relief, which you can get at many public libraries, by calling (800) 829-1040, or by downloading it from the IRS Web site, www.irs.ustreas.gov.

**TAKE NOTE** *Different, more stringent rules apply for tax returns filed on or before June 22, 1998. If you filed your return before the cutoff date, ask the IRS what you have to prove in order to get innocent spouse status.*

When the IRS deals with your request, it may decide that you are an innocent spouse and relieve you of any need to pay the additional taxes owed. If it determines that you are only partially responsible for the underreporting, it may reduce the amount of its claim proportionately.

> **Y**ou can be relieved of liability under what's known as the "innocent spouse rule."

## SUING THE IRS

If the IRS refuses to grant you innocent spouse status, it will send you a denial notice. At that point, if you still feel that your proof of innocence is convincing, you can file a lawsuit against the IRS in Tax Court challenging the decision. You must file your suit within 90 days of the date of the denial notice. Once your suit is filed, the IRS is prohibited from taking any collection action against you until the case is heard and the court issues its ruling.

If the amount in question is not large, filing a case in Tax Court is inexpensive and relatively easy. You may be able to handle the case yourself. The Tax Court uses a *Small Case procedure* (also called the S-case procedure) for IRS claims of back taxes under $50,000 in any one year. But even if you decide to represent yourself in Tax Court, you should get the advice of a tax professional, such as a certified public accountant (CPA) or a tax lawyer, who can help you prepare your case and make sure that all the required forms have been completed correctly. If your case does not qualify as an S-case, you will definitely need to get legal help.

The Tax Court judge may issue her ruling right after hearing your case, but it's more likely that you will receive her decision by mail several weeks later. A drawback to the S-case procedure is that you have no right to appeal a decision that goes against you. If your case isn't an S-case, you can appeal the ruling. However, such an appeal is expensive and not all that likely to succeed.

## An Argument for Filing Separate Tax Returns

A tax professional can (should) advise you whether you save the most money in taxes by filing in joint name or filing separately. Most married couples, but not all, file their taxes jointly.

■ **Consider one often-overlooked argument for filing a separate return.** On a joint return each spouse is liable for the entire tax bill. For example, if your husband…

- Seriously underreports his income, or

- Takes a deduction that's disallowed by the IRS…

…you are just as liable for the tax as your husband is. Had you filed separately, he alone would be responsible for the tax and any interest and penalties that have accrued. Of course, making a decision to file separately for this reason could create a touchy domestic situation—but it may be a risk worth taking.

*You hire a woman who comes to clean your house four hours every week. She demands that you contribute to her Social Security and unemployment insurance accounts.*

Some years ago this matter set off a political firestorm, dubbed "Nannygate," when a political appointment was derailed because the nominee had not complied with the existing law governing Social Security (SS) payments to domestic employees. That event prompted new legislation with new guidelines.

> *If the IRS discovers that you didn't make the required payments, you could face serious penalties.*

In this case, it seems unlikely that you have to contribute to your housekeeper's accounts. However, you may have to in the future, and you should pay careful attention to the rather complex requirements of the law.

### When You Have to Pay

Federal law is very specific about when you have to contribute to the Social Security, Medicare, and unemployment insurance accounts of household workers, such as cleaners, cooks, and gardeners. Before you can make a decision about your housekeeper's request, you need to establish her status in terms of the law. Find out…

- If your housekeeper works for an agency that provides workers to a variety of households and businesses
- If she has any other clients besides you.

If the answer to either of the above questions is yes, then you are not the housekeeper's employer for tax withholding and reporting purposes. In the first case, she would be an employee of the agency. In the second, she is considered an independent contractor, who must pay her own taxes. (Because the housekeeper works for you only a few hours a week, the odds are good that she has other clients.)

## WHEN THE ANSWER IS NO

If the housekeeper is not working for an agency or anyone else, then you may need to contribute to her Social Security and Medicare, and perhaps to her unemployment insurance as well. Here are guidelines to follow:

- **She earns more than $1,100** from you in the calendar year. You must pay an additional 9 percent of the wages you pay her for your contribution to Social Security and Medicare. The housekeeper must contribute the same amount as her share of SS and Medicare, but some generous employers choose to pay that share, too, as a kind of fringe benefit. In that case, you would owe the government a total of 18 percent of her wages.

- **You pay her more than $1,000** in any calendar quarter. You must also make payments of federal unemployment tax. This is separate and in addition to the SS and Medicare tax.
- **She asks you to withhold income taxes** from her pay. This, again, is different from SS and unemployment insurance, and she has the right to request that you deal with it. Get the withholding schedule from the IRS by calling (800) 829-3676, figure the withholding amount, and file the form.

Recent changes in federal law allow you to include all these tax payments in your own quarterly estimated tax payments. Or you can handle it by increasing the amount your employer withholds from your own paycheck. If the amount withheld isn't enough to cover the housekeeper's tax payments as well as your own, you can be subject to penalties for underpayment of taxes.

## BEWARE THE EASY WAY OUT

Hiring household help can involve a lot of paperwork and added expense, and its hard to resist the temptation to ignore the legal requirements and pay your housekeeper "under the table." But if the IRS discovers that you didn't pay, you could face serious penalties.

You may think that you and your housekeeper have an understanding about keeping your payments a secret, but the IRS says it usually learns about failure to pay taxes for household workers from the workers themselves, when they apply for unemployment or Social Security payments.

## FORMS, FORMS, AND MORE FORMS

In addition to withholding the appropriate taxes, there is a daunting array of forms to fill out. Some of these forms must also be filed with the government. You will need…

■ **Form I-9,** *Employment Eligibility Verification.* Your housekeeper must complete this form to prove that she is either a U.S. citizen or an alien with legal permission to work in the United States. You can obtain this form from the Immigration and Naturalization Service (INS) by calling (800) 870-3676. This form isn't filed with the government, but you must have it in your records in case the INS comes calling.

■ **Form SS-4,** *Application for Employer Identification Number,* which you will use on forms you file with the IRS. You can get this form by calling the IRS at (800) 829-3676.

■ **Form W-4,** *Employer's Withholding Allowance Certificate.* You need this form only if the housekeeper wants you to withhold income taxes. Available from the IRS at the telephone number above, this form isn't filed, but it stays in your records.

■ **Form W-2,** *Wage and Tax Statement,* which you must complete and give to your housekeeper by January 31 of the year following any year you employed her. Call the IRS at the number above for this form.

■ **Form W-3,** *Transmittal of Income and Tax Statements.* You must send this form, along with Copy A of the W-2, to the Social Security Administration no later than February 28. It is available from the IRS.

■ **Schedule H,** *Household Employment Taxes,* which you must file with your own Form 1040 no later than April 15 (later if you receive an extension on time to file your return). Again, you can get this form from the IRS.

■ **State forms.** You may also have to pay into an unemployment insurance fund and workers' compensation account, and withhold state income taxes. Check with your state tax department for the forms and schedules you will need.

> **Y**ou've taken a deduction for your
> home office, but the IRS auditor wants to disallow it.

As more and more people join the already huge army of home-based workers, the question of what can be deducted as a business expense becomes urgent. Although the government liberalized the rules on home-office deductions in 1999, the Internal Revenue Service still looks very closely at tax returns that claim this deduction. To persuade the auditor that your claim is legitimate, you'll need to prove that what you're calling an office really is one.

### DOES YOUR HOME OFFICE QUALIFY?

You must meet one of the following conditions:

● It is the principal place where you conduct your business.
● You use the office to conduct meetings with clients and customers on a regular basis.
● You use the room you are calling an office to maintain records for your business and you have no other office. For example, if you run a

lawn-care business out of your home and use your office merely for record keeping and sending out bills to your clients, you are entitled to a deduction under the new rules.

---

*You can deduct an amount proportional to the square footage of your home that is dedicated exclusively to business use.*

---

In these cases, you can deduct an amount proportional to the square footage of your home that is dedicated *exclusively* to business use (you can't use the space for personal or family activities). For instance, if the house is 2,000 square feet and your office is 200 square feet, you can take a deduction equal to 10 percent of your mortgage or rent payment, plus a similar deduction for electricity and heat, and the entire cost of a dedicated business telephone line.

## HOW TO SUPPORT YOUR DEDUCTION

Tax experts recommend several ways to bolster your claim to a home-office deduction:

● Have a separate entrance to the home office.
● Have a separate telephone line installed into the home office, and list the number in the Yellow Pages.
● Keep a record of the time you spend in the office on business activities.
● Keep a diary of the customers and clients who meet with you at the office, and the date and times when those meetings take place.

## IF THE AUDITOR STILL SAYS NO

Don't give up if the auditor won't allow you the deduction or says you don't have enough evidence to prove it. You have several options to pursue in getting the original ruling overturned.

■ **File an appeal.** Generally, you have 30 days from the time you receive notice of the audit

results to ask for an administrative appeal. There's no special form for filing an administrative appeal, so you'll have to write a letter to the office indicated on the notice you get from the IRS (send it by certified mail, return receipt requested).

■ **Ask for a meeting with the auditor's supervisor.** You can call the IRS office and set up an appointment to make your case in person.

> **TAKE NOTE** *Keep in mind that getting a meeting with the supervisor does not extend the time for filing your written appeal.*

### FINDING A FRIENDLY VOICE

There is still another channel to explore within the Internal Revenue Service itself. You can call a Problem Resolution Officer (PRO), an IRS employee whose job is to help straighten out taxpayer problems that aren't resolved through normal administrative channels. Call the IRS toll-free at (800) 829-1040 and ask to be connected with the Problem Resolution Program. Be prepared to leave your name and a telephone number where you can be reached during the day. You should get a return call within a few days.

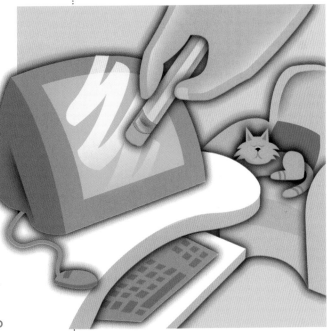

When the Problem Resolution Officer calls, explain your problem to him or her. The PRO will more than likely ask you to write a letter describing your problem with the deduction, and you should make it as thorough as possible. Make sure your letter includes the following:

● Your name, address, daytime telephone number, and Social Security number
● Copies of any notices you got from the IRS
● Copies of all previous correspondence between you and the IRS about the problem
● A statement of the problem and why you need the PRO's help
● A statement of the action you want taken.

The PRO will investigate your problem and may be able to convince the auditor handling your return to reconsider his decision based on the law and the evidence in your favor.

## WHEN THAT DOESN'T WORK

You can file a lawsuit against the Internal Revenue Service in Tax Court challenging the auditor's decision. You must file suit within 90 days of the date of the notice denying your appeal. Once your suit is filed, the IRS may not take any collection action against you until the case is heard and the court issues its ruling.

## THE MOST OVERLOOKED DEDUCTIONS

To reduce your tax bite, you want to take advantage of all the deductions that you can. These are the most common ones that taxpayers forget to list on their returns:

■ **Deductible interest on a home equity loan.** Interest that you pay on the first $100,000 of a home equity loan is fully deductible. Interest that you pay on a loan in excess of $100,000 can offset other investment income you received from dividends or interest.

■ **Charitable donations of household items.** If you regularly donate furniture, clothing, and other household goods to charities, you can deduct the value of your contributions by using IRS Form 8283. The form includes a range of fair market values for items commonly donated. Donate a couple of coats, a set of draperies, and a few appliances, and you could easily accumulate several hundred dollars in deductions.

■ **Self-employed deduction for health insurance.** Taxpayers who run their own businesses and buy health insurance can deduct 60 percent of the premiums they pay from their adjusted gross income. In the year 2000, if your health insurance premiums are $350 per month ($4,200 annually), you get a deduction of $2,520. (Future deductions are tied to inflation.)

■ **State income tax deductions.** If you pay state income tax for 2001 before the end of the year, instead of waiting until April 15, 2002, you can deduct that amount from your 2001 federal tax return.

■ **Parent or grandparent support.** As the population ages, more and more taxpayers may be eligible for this deduction. Generally, you can take it if you provide more than half of the parent's or grandparent's support (including medical expenses). The person you're claiming can't have more than $2,750 in reportable income, excluding Social Security. The total available deduction for you is currently $2,750. (Future deductions are tied to the inflation rate.)

■ **Excess Social Security taxes.** The government sets a maximum amount of earnings on which you pay Social Security taxes (in 2000, the maximum was approximately $74,000). If you work at two jobs, one of which pays $60,000 and the other $20,000, your employers between them deducted more for Social Security than the law requires you to pay.

**A**s company bookkeeper, you're aware that your employer has been withholding taxes from employee paychecks but isn't forwarding them to the government.

**Y**our boss is running a new business and is having financial difficulties. As owner, he may justify not forwarding the money deducted from his employees' paychecks by considering it a loan, one that he'll pay back as soon as his finances improve. If this pattern continues, he will be in big trouble with the government.

### GATHERING EVIDENCE

As a key employee with access to the money, you should gather evidence to protect yourself from future trouble with the IRS. You should write memos and make a log of conversations in which your employer told you not to pay company

employees' taxes to the IRS or refused to send out W-2 forms. Such documentation can help show that you were only acting on his orders and were not involved in the decision-making process. The IRS will go into action once it discovers that

taxes were withheld on the employees but not forwarded or that W-2 forms were not actually sent out. A revenue officer will call or visit, demanding full payment of all withheld taxes, along with penalties and interest. If your employer can't or won't make payment, he may be subject to criminal prosecution as well as being personally liable for a civil penalty equal to 100 percent of the taxes collected but not forwarded. The IRS can also seize the business, sell it, and use the proceeds to satisfy your employer's tax debt.

It is unlikely that you will be held personally liable for the unpaid taxes. But as someone who has had any involvement in preparing the company's tax returns or keeping the company's books, you would be wise to consult a lawyer. The IRS has been known to seek repayment from employees of such a company who were "responsible" persons because they signed company checks.

Using the notes and evidence you have kept about your employer's behavior, your lawyer can help you convince the IRS that you were only acting on the instructions of your employer.

### STAYING OUT OF TROUBLE YOURSELF

To ensure that you don't get dragged into personal difficulty with the IRS along with your employer, remind your employer in writing that he is legally obligated to give you a W-2 by January 31 each year. If he refuses, you can complete your return using the information from your paycheck stubs. If you don't have the stubs, you can estimate your pay and the amount you believe was withheld. Make sure you attach a note to your return stating that you did not receive a W-2 from your employer.

### WHEN IS AN IRS RETURN FRAUDULENT?

Willfully overstating or claiming false deductions or credits can be fraudulent, as can failing to report income. The IRS may find this by looking at bank deposits, by looking at bank transfers, and even by looking at the difference between the figures on the return and the lifestyle of the taxpayers—for example, reporting $20,000 in income while you live in a $500,000 house and make $4,000 mortgage payments each month.

■ **Most cases brought by the IRS are civil suits,** but a civil case can become a criminal one. Someone who is charged with and convicted of defrauding the IRS could be sent to federal prison.

■ **Failure to report a significant amount of income** raises the question of fraud, though what's significant will vary from case to case. It is rare for the IRS to cite fraud just because you were aggressive about taking certain deductions.

If the IRS contacts you because it claims you have filed a fraudulent return, you should get a tax lawyer immediately. Don't say a word to the IRS investigators without first consulting him. If you don't know who to hire, call your local bar association's referral service for the names of lawyers who handle IRS fraud cases.

---

*You learn that your neighbor, an IRS employee, has been discussing your tax returns with mutual friends.*

---

Paying taxes is a painful duty, but at least you have the right to expect it to be a private matter between you and the government. If you discover that your personal financial information has been fodder for conversation at a neighborhood cocktail party or backyard barbecue, not only should you be outraged, but also you should—and can—do something about it.

> *Your grounds for a suit lie in the invasion of your privacy.*

By law, your federal tax returns and the information they contain are confidential and can be disclosed only under specific circumstances. Still other federal laws limit which IRS employees may have access to your tax records. Even so, in one 13-month period the IRS identified more than 5,000 cases in which it suspected that its employees had intentionally accessed taxpayer information without authorization.

#### PUTTING YOUR COMPLAINT ON RECORD

If you discover that you've been victimized by a talkative IRS employee, you should immediately call the National Taxpayer Advocate's office at (877) 777-4778 (a toll-free number). You'll be given the number of the Taxpayer Advocate's office that is located in your state. This office operates independently of the district director and other IRS administrators and reports directly to Congress.

Explain your problem to the advocate. You may be asked to tell…

● The name of the IRS employee
● The names of those to whom he revealed your tax return information

● How you came to learn about the unauthorized disclosure.

The Taxpayer Advocate will investigate your complaint. She will interview the employee and his supervisor and may refer your complaint to the U.S. Attorney's office for prosecution. By talking about your tax return with others who aren't entitled to hear about it, your neighbor can be fined as much as $5,000 or sentenced to up to five years in a federal prison, or both. Even if no criminal charges are filed, your neighbor could be dismissed from his job for his lack of discretion.

If you don't get a helpful response from the Taxpayer Advocate, you can contact your state's U.S. Attorney yourself. You'll find the telephone number in the federal government listings of your telephone directory.

### FILING A LAWSUIT

The same laws that make it a crime for your neighbor to look at your tax returns or talk about them without authorization also give you the right to file a civil lawsuit against the employee and the U.S. government. Your grounds for a suit lie in the invasion of your privacy. Damages are pretty difficult to pin down. They depend on…

- ● How outrageously the IRS employee acted
- ● How widely the information was spread
- ● How much effect the disclosure had on your

business or professional reputation and ability to earn income, get loans, and so on.

You must file your suit in federal district court. This is a serious matter and not one to pursue without professional help. Talk to a lawyer who specializes in tax litigation. She can help you

evaluate your case, the chances for its success, and the damages you could be awarded. If necessary, contact the attorney referral service operated by your state or local bar association for the names of lawyers who can help. If you win your case, the government can be required to pay you reasonable attorney fees in addition to damages.

---

*You are due a refund on your income taxes.*
*Weeks have passed and you still don't have your check.*

---

If you file your return by the April 15 deadline and don't receive your refund by June 1, federal law entitles you to receive interest on the refund, unless the Internal Revenue Service has a legitimate reason for holding it back.

### TRACKING DOWN YOUR REFUND

The IRS has the right to withhold your refund if you owe child support payments or if you have not repaid a government loan. If neither of these applies to you and if you haven't received your tax refund from the IRS within 10 weeks of filing your return, you should take action.

## What to Do

First, check on the status of your refund by calling the special IRS Automated Refund Information (ARI) telephone number— (800) 829-4477. You will need to provide your Social Security number, your filing status (single, head of household, filing jointly), and the amount of the refund you are expecting to receive. Once the ARI representative has this information, he can give you a ballpark idea of when you will receive your refund check.

If you don't receive your refund in the promised time limit, write the IRS Center where you mailed your return. Include your name, address, Social Security number, and an explanation of your problem. Send your letter by certified mail, return receipt requested, and keep a copy of your correspondence for your files.

### Smart Moves

IRS workers have fewer returns to handle early in the year. The earlier you file your return in the tax season, the less time you'll have to wait to receive a refund.

If you still don't get your refund (or are dissatisfied with the response you receive), contact the Problem Resolution Officer (PRO) at the IRS Service Center where you mailed your return. The PRO will look into the matter and report back to you within five working days.

If you have been told that your refund is being withheld because of overdue child support or an unpaid government loan, the PRO will provide you with information about how to contest the withholding.

## The Final Step

If your claim to a refund is denied, or if six months go by without any action by the IRS, you can file suit in the federal district court with jurisdiction in your state, or in the U.S. Court of Federal Claims. In both courts the rules of procedure are complicated and must be followed carefully, or you risk having your claim dismissed on a technicality. A qualified lawyer's help is crucial in bringing a lawsuit in this case.

### Fine-tuning Your Withholding

Getting a big refund check from the IRS means that you either had too much withheld from your paycheck or you overpaid your estimated taxes during the previous year. Either way, you've given the government an interest-free loan of your money.

■ **Ask your employer for a new Form W-4** to avoid grossly overpaying your income tax in the future. You can take additional allowances on this form to reduce the amount of tax withheld from your paycheck.

■ **Be sure that the amount of estimated tax you pay equals the amount you actually owed** during the previous year, or at least 90 percent of the amount you will owe on the current year.

**E**ven the best tax preparers differ on what deductions are allowable and under what circumstances. If you've discovered that your accountant was more cautious than necessary and missed taking a legitimate deduction or credit that would have lowered your tax bill, you can still do something about it.

**TAKE NOTE** *Whether your tax preparer is cautious or aggressive in deciding what is a legitimate deduction, remember that you are the one who is legally responsible for the information included in your return.*

## GETTING IT BACK

Happily (and perhaps no surprise), the Internal Revenue Service (IRS) has a form just for this situation. Here is how to go about claiming a belated deduction or credit:

- **File IRS Form 1040X,** *Amended U.S. Individual Income Tax Return,* within three years of the

date when you filed the original return, or within two years of the date you paid your tax, whichever is later. For example, if you filed your return for 2001 on April 15, 2002, you have until April 14, 2005, to claim a refund using an amended return.

- **Consider hiring a professional tax preparer** or a tax accountant to help you. While you can complete and file the amended return on your own, a professional can be helpful, especially if the amount you want refunded is substantial, relative to your income. You will also need to attach any supporting documentation.

   - **Mail the completed and signed form** to the designated IRS center where you now file your tax returns. Send it by certified mail, return receipt requested. This way you'll have proof of mailing before the deadline as well as proof that the Internal Revenue Service received the form.

   The IRS will review your amended return, and if it agrees with your calculations, it will refund the amount you overpaid. If it disagrees, it must tell you…

   - The refund was refused
   - Why it was refused
   - How you can appeal.

   Remember that amending your federal income tax return may effect how much state and city income taxes you owe. Check with your state or city tax departments to find out how to amend those returns.

**TAXPAYER ALERT** *Filing an amended return to get a refund may increase the chance of having your tax return audited for the year in question. If the amount of money is relatively small, it may be better to let sleeping dogs lie.*

## FILING INCOME TAX RETURNS ELECTRONICALLY

For several years now, the IRS has made a major effort to promote its "e-file" paperless tax return. According to the IRS, making an e-file offers several benefits:

● With an e-file return you can expect to get a refund in about half the time it would take if you filed a traditional return.

● In many states, you can file your state income tax return along with your federal return using e-file.

● When the system was new, e-filers had to use a tax preparer authorized by the IRS. Now if you buy a tax-preparation program that is compatible with the IRS system, you may be able to e-file your tax return from your home computer.

● You can authorize the IRS to debit your bank account electronically for any additional taxes you owe—such as insufficient withholding or estimated tax payments—on a date you determine, as long as it is not later than April 15.

You can also file your return using a touch-tone telephone. You call the IRS district office and follow the answering-service menu to enter your Social Security number, adjusted gross income and taxes paid, and whether you want your overpayment refunded or credited to next year's taxes. In general, this "telefile" option is available only for taxpayers who have very simple returns. IRS publication 255 gives detailed information on who can use it.

For more information about filing your tax return electronically, go to the Internal Revenue Service Web site at www.irs.ustreas.gov.

BUYER BEWARE

> **Y**ou sent away for an herbal supplement that promised to cure your arthritis, but the product never arrived.

**S**hopping by mail is one of the conveniences of modern life, but it also has its drawbacks. Items ordered may not be what you expected, may take weeks and weeks to get there, or, worst of all, may never make it to your mailbox.

*If you really want the product, you can set a new deadline for the company to ship your order.*

## KNOW YOUR RIGHTS

Products you order by telephone, mail, fax, or Internet are covered by the Federal Trade Commission's *Mail or Telephone Order Rule:*

- The seller must meet its deadline if it promises or advertises a specific time period within which the product will be shipped, such as "allow eight weeks for shipping."
- Your order must be shipped within 30 days if *no* specific shipment period is listed.
- The seller must notify you of the delay if it can't meet the shipping deadline. It must give you a new delivery date and offer you the chance to cancel your order and receive a refund of any money you paid.
- The company must send the refund to you within one week of your cancellation.

## CONTACT THE COMPANY

First, try to fix the problem directly with the company. Call its customer service number if it has one. If it doesn't (and many small mail-order companies don't), write a letter to the address where you sent your order. Include all the information about your order: The date you placed it, the items ordered, and the method of payment.

If the company has missed the deadline for shipping and you want the order canceled, say so. If you really want the product, you can set a new deadline for the company, stressing you'll cancel the order if it is not met. Keep a copy of the letter for your files, in case you need to follow up.

## GO TO A HIGHER AUTHORITY

If you don't receive the product or the refund you requested, you can take other actions:

- **Report the company to the Better Business Bureau** where the firm is located. It may be able to convince the company to fulfill its obligations in order to keep its good record.
- **Write to your state's consumer protection office** and the consumer protection office in the state where the company is located. Some agencies are very aggressive in their investigations. Include a copy of any ad you responded to, your correspondence with the company, and any response you received. If you paid by check and the company cashed it, send a photocopy of the canceled check as well.
- **Contact the U.S. Postal Inspection Service** with the same information. Its address is available at your post office, or visit the Postal Service's Web site at www.usps.gov to find out how and where to file your complaint. The USPS can issue fines and obtain consent orders to help halt mail fraud.
- **Contact the FTC** (page 467). It has powers similar to the USPS and often coordinates investigations with the Postal Service.

**SMART MOVES**

Use a credit card when making a mail-order purchase. If the company fails to deliver your order, contact your credit-card company to dispute the charge. The credit-card company can cancel the charge if it confirms that your order was never shipped, or if the mail-order company refuses to cooperate in the credit-card company's investigation.

**C**ompanies send out thousands of unsolicited checks every month to entice consumers to buy a product or service. But beware: On the back of the check is the fine print stating that by endorsing and cashing the check, you authorize an automatic charge to your credit card or a change in your telephone service. Often the check will be enclosed in your credit-card statement; sometimes the company making the offer *is* your credit-card company.

Although it may seem deceptive, this practice is legal. Insurance companies, long-distance telephone service providers, and magazine publishers use unsolicited check offers, which can end up costing you money for products and services you neither want nor need.

## BE WARY

You can prevent inadvertently signing up for something by never cashing a check that you receive in the mail unless…

- You know where the check came from.
- You read the fine print on the back.
- You understand the offer and your obligations.
- You have the right to cancel the arrangement without penalty.
- The offer is for something you want or need.

## CANCELING THE MEMBERSHIP

You can take the following steps to get rid of the unwanted product or service and the charge:

- **Contact the customer service department** of the travel club and cancel your membership. Understand that as a condition of cancellation, you may have to pay back the amount of the check you cashed.
- **Call your credit-card company** and cancel your authorization of any future charges made by the club.

- **Write your state's consumer protection agency** to complain about the use of unsolicited checks as a marketing ploy. This regulatory agency compiles complaints from consumers and can propose legislation that would restrict or prohibit the use of this kind of advertising.

## GETTING OFF MAILING LISTS

Many companies that sell by mail rent the names of their customers to other mail-order merchants. This practice is legal, but the result for you can be a mailbox crammed with catalogs and sales offers. To reduce the amount of direct-mail advertising you receive:

■ **Contact the companies whose mail you don't want** and insist that they take you off their mailing lists. Most reputable companies will honor your request.

■ **Write companies that you *do* want to get mail from** and ask that they not share your name, address, or other information about you with any other mail-order company. Many companies have a box on their order forms that you can check to make this request. (Even if you aren't placing an order, you can avoid junk-mail overload by checking this box and mailing the form to the company.)

■ **Write the Direct Marketing Association** (DMA; page 467) and request that your name be removed from their member companies' mailing lists. Be patient—it will take several months before you see a reduction in unwanted mail. Moreover, when you next order by mail, you could trigger a new deluge of mailings. For this reason, some experts suggest making this request to the DMA on an annual basis.

*The telephone company keeps promising to install your telephone line "within the next few days," but three months have gone by and you're still without phone service.*

Waiting for promised service that never comes is maddening. But when the wait leaves you without a vital service, such as a working telephone, it's more than an inconvenience. Fortunately, there are steps you can take to remedy this situation.

### CALL THE PHONE COMPANY

First, give the telephone company one last chance to make good on its promise:

■ **Call the customer service office** and ask to speak to a supervisor. (Be sure to get her name.) Explain the situation, including your initial request for service, the date you were promised service, and your subsequent calls to schedule installation of the phone line. Ask the supervisor to give you a specific date when your line will be installed. Insist that the date be within a certain time period, such as by the end of the week.

■ **Call customer service again on the promised date** (from a neighbor's house or from your cell phone). Confirm that you are scheduled for installation service on that day. Ask the representative to provide you with a time frame for the service.

■ **Don't leave the house unattended.** Telephone installers have an unfortunate habit of showing up during the 15 minutes you spent running down to the corner store. Coming home to the installer's "Sorry I missed you" sticker on the door just means more delays in getting your service.

### IF THE INSTALLER IS A NO-SHOW

If you are still without phone service, call customer service once more and ask to speak to the supervisor who promised you installation. Insist that she obtain installation for you immediately.

If she can't or won't, take your complaint to your state's Public Utility Commission (PUC), the agency that handles consumer complaints about phone service. (Telephone companies are regulated almost exclusively at the state level.) You'll find the phone number in the state government listings of your telephone directory.

If the telephone line is a second or third line into your home, it may take some time before your complaint is handled. However, if this is your only phone line, some states will require the telephone company to provide you with a cellular or digital phone at no cost. The company also subsidizes the cost of using this "loaner" until your line is installed.

It's also a good idea to get in touch with the local media about your plight. Your newspaper's or television station's consumer reporter may be able to get the phone company to respond even more quickly than the PUC can.

**You answer an ad by calling the listed telephone number. You learn nothing of value from the five-minute call, but end up with a $35 charge on your telephone bill.**

This scam plays upon the little-known fact that some unscrupulous companies illegally bill their unsuspecting clients for information or services in addition to the actual telephone connection time of their call. Others illegally transfer the call you make to a toll-free number—area codes 800, 877, or 888, for example—to a toll exchange without your knowledge.

### DISPUTE THE CHARGE

As soon as you see the charge on your bill, call your telephone company and explain what happened. There is no question that switching your call from a toll-free number to one that charges a per-minute or per-call fee is *illegal.*

It is also illegal for a company to charge you for services or information that you have not agreed up front to pay for. (Did you read all the small print in the ad, which would have raised a red flag?) In most cases, the telephone company will remove the charges from your bill right away. If it doesn't agree to do so over the telephone, follow the instructions on your phone bill for disputing a charge. Keep copies of all your correspondence and be persistent.

### GO AFTER THE CROOKS

Write a letter to your state's Public Utility Commission (PUC) explaining what happened in detail, and enclose a copy of your telephone bill. Then send a copy of the letter to your telephone company. Although the PUC won't go to bat for you personally, it will notify the telephone company if it gets a number of complaints. You can also choose to write the Federal Communications Commission (FCC; page 467), which has the power to investigate the scammer and put it out of business.

> **CONSUMER ALERT** *Telephone scam businesses sell easy solutions to tough problems. You know you can't lose 20 pounds in two weeks, you can't solve credit problems with a phone call, and a stranger on a psychic line can't tell you your future. When offers are too good to be true, don't be conned.*

> # You can't sit down to dinner without being interrupted by telemarketers.

**M**any people find telemarketing calls more than annoying—indeed, a scourge—and now there's something you can do about them. The Federal Trade Commission (FTC; page 467) has established regulations to give consumers more control over telephone sales calls. Most important, telemarketers must stop calling you if you tell them you don't want any more calls. A company that calls after that is breaking the law, and owes you a $500 penalty.

## THE TELEPHONE SALES RULE

The FTC's *Telephone Sales Rule* clearly sets out consumers' rights when it comes to telemarketing. This rule applies to most businesses, but not to nonprofit organizations, companies conducting public opinion surveys, or political groups. The rule states that telemarketers…

- Cannot call before 8 A.M. or after 9 PM
- Must say at the start of the call that they are calling to sell you something

> *The FTC's Telephone Sales Rule clearly sets out consumers' rights when it comes to telemarketing.*

- Must tell you the name of the company they are calling for and identify the product or service they are selling

### SMART MOVES

You can cut back on the number of telemarketing calls you receive by writing the Direct Marketing Association (page 467) and asking to be taken off telemarketers' lists. This won't stop all calls, but you should notice a drop in sales calls within a few months of your request.

- Must tell you all the costs and conditions of an offer before taking any money or credit-card information
- Cannot make any false or misleading statements about an investment's earning potential, risk, or profitability, or about any service that the telemarketer is selling
- Must stop calling you when you ask them to place your name on the "do not call" list.

### ENFORCING "DO NOT CALL"

Here's what to do when you receive an unwanted telemarketing call:

- Get information about the telemarketer: his name, the name of the company he works for, and its mailing address. Also write down the time and date of the call.
- Ask to be put on the "do not call" list.

● Record the same information again (his name, the company, etc.) if you get a second call from the same telemarketing company.

Write to the FTC if a company violates the FTC's Telephone Sales Rule. Note the date and time that you informed the company to place you on its "do not call" list and the date and time of the follow-up call you received. Demand that the company pay you $500, the fine that is imposed by the rule. Send the letter by certified mail, return receipt requested, and be sure to keep a copy. If the company doesn't respond…

■ **Consider filing a small claims lawsuit** to collect the fine owed to you.
■ **Notify the Federal Communications Commission** (FCC; page 467) and your state's consumer protection agency in writing. These agencies can not only fine companies but can also obtain court orders against businesses that violate the law.

## TEN WARNING SIGNS OF A TELEMARKETING SCAM

Many telemarketers represent legitimate businesses, but some are simply trying to con the unwary. Stay away from telephone offers if the salesperson:

● Claims that you requested the call when you know you didn't.

● Acts as if you and he have spoken before when you know you haven't. This is a common ploy of "boiler room" callers offering questionable investments.

● Claims that he is calling to offer a "surefire" or "risk-free" investment opportunity. There's no such thing, and if there were, why would he be willing to share information about it with a total stranger?

● Claims that you've been "specially selected" to receive a product or service at a reduced price. In this case, "specially selected" usually means your number was the next one on his calling list.

● Asks for a credit-card number in order "to verify your eligibility" for a prize or a special offer. Never give your credit-card number to anyone you don't know.

● Tells you that you've won a prize but that you must attend a meeting in order to claim it. The meeting is going to be a high-pressure sales pitch designed to get you to spend money on items you probably don't want and almost certainly don't need.

● Refuses to send you any written material about the offer or the company he represents. A legitimate business will be happy to send written information about its products or services.

● Tells you that the offer is only available if you act immediately. Any reputable company will give you time to consider an offer.

● Offers to send someone to your home to pick up your payment. This ruse is often used by fraudulent charity solicitors, who claim to need the money immediately "in order to keep our doors open to the needy."

● Offers a deal that simply sounds too good to be true.

# Your telephone carrier has been changed without your authorization.

If this has happened to you, you are not alone. You are a victim of "slamming," the practice of changing a telephone customer's long-distance service provider without his or her express permission.

You may have unwittingly authorized changes in your telephone service. One tactic used to get consumers to "authorize" a change is to offer them a chance to participate in a sweepstakes or other contest. The consumer must fill out a form and sign it in order to enter the contest. Consumers eager to win an expensive prize often overlook the fine print on the entry form that authorizes the change.

Another technique used by slammers is to send a "gift check" through the mail. When you endorse the check and cash it, you "authorize" the changes in your telephone service.

## PHONE THE PHONE COMPANY

If you discover that you have been slammed, contact your local telephone company immediately. The company's customer service department will help you switch your service back to your original provider at no cost to you.

You should also ask the telephone company how you can block changes to your long-distance service and other services in the future. In nearly every state, telephone companies have free programs that require you to personally authorize any changes in your telephone service.

You should also report the slamming to your state's Public Utility Commission and attorney general and the Federal Communications Commission (FCC; page 467). The FCC has been particularly aggressive in penalizing companies that engage in slamming, with fines of as much as $500,000.

## PRECAUTIONS YOU CAN TAKE

Even with all of the protections against slamming available to consumers, the practice continues. Here's how to avoid having a recurring problem:

- Check your telephone bill each month for changes to your service, new names of service providers, and unfamiliar names of products and services.
- Examine your bill carefully for any monthly fees you did not authorize.
- Designate one person in your family to be responsible for any changes in services.
- Read the fine print on contest entries and checks you receive in the mail, and any other forms you are asked to sign.
- Notify your telephone company and the FCC of any problems or charges that continue to appear after you have been reconnected to your preferred service provider.

# Your telephone bill arrives, and it includes charges for services you didn't order.

Next to "slamming" (changing your long-distance carrier without authorization), "cramming," the term for adding charges for services you haven't requested, is one of the most common nuisances that telephone company customers face. These charges are easy to overlook because they're often included (whether by accident or design, depending on the telephone company) in a long list of legitimate taxes and fees, such as "Internet connectivity" and "emergency service provision." While you are required to pay for valid services, you don't have to pay for services such as caller identification or voice messaging unless you actually ordered them.

## GO TO THE SOURCE

If you think you've been crammed, first contact your telephone company:

- **Find out what the charges are for** and who authorized them. If the company can find no record of your authorization, ask that the charges be removed from your account.
- **Request a block on your account.** This will prevent unauthorized changes or additions to your service. Once the block is in place, you will have to ask the telephone company to remove it before you can add services or change your long-distance carrier.

## GET CONSUMER PROTECTION

Report this practice—in writing—to your state's Public Utility Commission (PUC) and attorney general's office, the Federal Communications Commission (FCC), and the Better Business Bureau. These agencies don't usually intervene on behalf of individuals, but your letter will help them develop a case against any company that

*Cramming—adding charges for services you haven't requested—is one of the most common nuisances to telephone company customers.*

engages in fraud or deceptive business practices. Some companies found guilty of cramming have been heavily fined and served with court orders prohibiting them from continuing their deceitful methods of doing business.

---

The Internet and e-mail have made communication more convenient than ever. Unfortunately, this hasn't gone unnoticed by crooks and con artists, who use bulk e-mail—known as *spam*—to reach millions of potential victims at extremely low cost. You should suspect an e-mail scam if you receive any of the following:

- **E-mail from an anonymous sender.** Several programs allow e-mail users to disguise their true identities. Always get the name, street address, and telephone number of anyone you're considering doing business with, no matter how you learn about them.

- **An e-mail offer that sounds too good to be true,** such as "the secret to making big money overnight," or "the longevity formula the government doesn't want you to know about."

- **An e-mail offer that requires your screen name and password.** Some e-mail scams claim that they need this information in order to send you a bargain or something free. They may even pretend to be from your Internet Service Provider (ISP). Never provide your password to anyone. Your ISP doesn't need it, and others could use it to access your e-mail account and charge merchandise at on-line retailers that have stored your credit-card information.

- **An e-mail that asks you to send money** to a post office box so the sender can "rush you the details of this incredible offer. Never send money to someone you don't know, even if they offer a "lifetime money-back guarantee." It's highly unlikely the sender will be around to send you your money back if you don't get what you're promised.

- **An e-mail offer that proclaims its honesty.** Be suspicious of statements like "government approved," or "This is not a scam." Government agencies don't approve e-mail offers, and legitimate companies' reputations generally speak for themselves. Anyone who feels the need to make a big deal about their honesty probably has something to hide.

**Y**ou answer an ad offering to clean your carpet for an attractive price. When the crew arrives, the supervisor refuses to do the job for the advertised price, insisting on an added fee for spotting.

**T**his is the old "bait-and-switch" tactic: Advertising one price, then trying to "switch" you to a more expensive purchase. The "bait" is the low price. Once it has hooked you, the company's employee tries to convince you that what you agreed to buy isn't a good product or service. He then tries to substitute another, more expensive one.

### SPEAK UP

If this happens to you, here are two important steps to take:

**SMART MOVES**

Check out a company's reputation before hiring it by contacting your local Better Business Bureau (BBB). If the BBB has a long record of unresolved complaints about the company, don't hire it. Remember: If a price sounds too good to be true, it probably is.

■ **Insist that the crew perform the service at the price you agreed on.** If they refuse, contact the company's office and demand to speak to the manager. Explain the situation and have her instruct her employees to honor the price you agreed to pay. If the manager won't comply, tell the crew to leave.

■ **Contact the Better Business Bureau** (BBB) to file a complaint against the company. The BBB can warn other consumers about the company's deceptive tactics. You can also notify the consumer protection division of your state attorney general's office of your problem. Include a copy of the ad you responded to and an account of the company's refusal to honor the advertised price. The consumer protection office can investigate your claim, and it may bring legal action against the company if it determines that the company's tactics violate state law.

### CAN YOU SUE?

In a case like this, your damages would be limited to the difference between the amount you agreed to pay the original company and the amount you ultimately paid another firm to perform the same work. While it may be possible to file a small claims suit against the company, you need to weigh the cost in time and energy against any amount you are likely to collect.

*You get a call asking for a donation to a charity that sounds familiar, and the solicitor offers to have a representative come right over to get your check.*

Not everything that sounds like a good cause really is. One popular scam involves telephone solicitations from an organization with a name that's similar to that of a nationally known charity. The caller thanks you

*Any reputable charity will send you information about its work and a pledge form, and give you time to consider your donation before you send it.*

for your previous support (even though you may never have given any) and tells you about an urgent need for funds. Of course, the charity will be happy to send someone over to pick up your donation so it can be put to use right away.

Don't fall for this. Any reputable charity will send you information about its work and a pledge form, and give you time to consider your donation before you send it.

### BEFORE YOU GIVE

Be sure to get information about any charity to which you are considering making a donation:

- **Get written information** about the charity's mission, a review of the projects it supports, and a list of its board of directors.
- **Find out where the charity gets its funding** and how much of the money it raises actually goes to charitable purposes. Some charities spend as much as 90 percent

of donations on administrative and marketing costs. That means only 10 cents of every dollar donated is actually dedicated to helping others.

- **Ask for the organization's IRS certification** as a nonprofit organization. A recognized non-profit will have what's known as 501(c)(3) status from the IRS and will be happy to provide a copy of its certificate.
- **Check with the office of your state's secretary of state** to find out if the charity is registered to do business within the state.
- **Contact the Better Business Bureau** and your state's consumer protection agency to see if there are any complaints on file about the charity.

While it may seem hard-hearted to be so cautious about contributing to what seems like a worthy cause, it's really soft-headed not to take precautions. After all, you want to be sure your donation goes to those who truly need it and not into the pocket of a con artist.

*The infomercial said it would help make you rich, but all you got for your money was a pitch for an "advanced course" and a booklet. You sent it back and you haven't received your refund.*

The product (or course or tape) can chop, dice, give you rock-hard abs, make you rich. You name it. Infomercials—program-length advertisements for everything from compact discs to self-improvement courses—have become almost as ubiquitous as sit-coms. They're a great source of revenue for broadcasters, but when they promise what they can't deliver, they can be a major headache.

Some get-rich-quick infomercials guarantee that you will learn the "secret steps" to making a fortune by buying the company's literature. Others ask you to attend a free seminar to learn these "secrets." The literature often turns out to be little more than instructions for placing ads in newspapers or magazines, and the seminars are just a sales pitch to lure you into investing in the company's products or services. In most cases, these programs offer a financial opportunity for the seller but not for you. According to consumer advocates, very few people who buy wealth-building programs from infomercials make any money at all.

## ORDER WITH CARE

If you still want to place an order, ask about the company's refund policy before you do. Some companies allow you only 10 days in which to examine the materials you receive. A 30-, 60-, or 90-day period is better. Be wary of outfits that have a one-year return period: They may count on your forgetting to return the materials, or they may plan to be out of business or operating under another name by then.

If you don't have a credit card, some companies will tell you that they can take your checking account information over the telephone and debit your account for the purchase price. *Don't give out your checking account and bank routing numbers over the phone.* The salesperson may be able to use this information to clean out your account or sell the information to criminals. Using your checking account also limits your ability to get a refund if there's a problem, since you won't have the protection that a credit card offers.

### GETTING YOUR REFUND

If you've met the company's requirements for returning the merchandise, expect a refund within 30 days.

■ If you ordered with a credit card, the credit should appear on your next statement or the one after that. If it doesn't, notify your credit-card issuer. Once they get involved, the company must comply or risk losing its ability to accept credit cards in the future.

■ **If you paid by check or money order** and have not received a refund within 30 days, contact the company again in writing and demand your money back. Include a copy of the shipping documents from when you returned the materials, and send your letter by certified mail, return receipt requested.

■ **If you get no response to this letter,** report the company to the Better Business Bureau in the community where it is located. You can also file a complaint with the U.S. Postal Inspection Service. Contact information is available at your local post office, or visit the Postal Service's Web site at www.usps.gov for information about how and where to file your complaint.

### SMART MOVES

Play it safe and contact the Better Business Bureau and your state's consumer protection agency to check out the company's record of complaints before you order anything. Remember that "experts" who provide product endorsements are often paid by the company they are endorsing. Testimonials might also be paid for by the advertiser and may not reflect the experiences of most customers.

Nearly every product on the market is covered by a warranty. In some cases, this is a written document provided by the manufacturer. But even when there's nothing in writing to set out your rights if a product turns out to be defective, the law often implies a warranty. Here is how warranties work and how they differ from one another:

### Written Warranties

● A *full warranty* obligates the manufacturer to repair a defective item. If a repair isn't possible, the manufacturer must give the customer the choice of a full refund or a replacement of the item at no cost. The only limit allowed on a full warranty is a time limit: For example, a full warranty might be for one year only (but if it is, it must say "Full One-Year Warranty" in the title of the document).

● A *limited warranty* is also made in writing, but it may require a purchaser to pay for some or all of the cost of repairs for a defective item, or it may cover only certain parts of the item. For instance, a limited warranty on a refrigerator may cover the compressor but not the interior light or icemaker. A limited warranty must be specific about what's covered, what's not, and what the purchaser will be required to pay for. Like a full warranty, limited warranties may also be for a specified period of time.

### Implied Warranties

● In most states, the law implies a *warranty of merchantability.* This means that a product you buy will do what it's intended to do: An air conditioner will cool the air, a television will pick up broadcast signals.

● The other kind of implied warranty is the *warranty of suitability for a particular purpose.* In this case, a product must do what the manufacturer claims it will do: For example, a coat labeled "waterproof" must repel water.

Implied warranties are created by state law, so the methods for enforcing them vary from state to state. You can get information about how to enforce an implied warranty from your state's office of consumer protection.

### Extended Warranties and Service Contracts

● Beware. Retailers often offer extended warranties (also known as service contracts) when you purchase items such as computers, vacuum cleaners, or other home appliances. These warranties can be expensive, and often they cover the same problems already covered by the manufacturer's warranty. In addition, they may exclude so many problems that they are virtually worthless. They may also require you to have the product maintained on a predetermined schedule or lose the protection they promise.

● Some service contracts require consumers to pay a deductible; others are offered by companies that spend more time disputing claims than paying them. Be cautious when it comes to buying a service contract. In many cases, the money you spend simply isn't worth it.

*Before your father died he asked to be cremated. The funeral home tells you that, under Environmental Protection Agency rules, you will have to pay $1,500 for a vault to inter his ashes.*

No state or federal law requires you to entomb ashes. Nor is there any law that says you must purchase a casket for the cremation or an urn to store the ashes. These are just some of the scams that have been perpetrated by greedy funeral directors in order to get more money from grieving family members at a vulnerable time.

### THE FEDS WILL BACK YOU UP

The Federal Trade Commission (FTC) has enacted a series of regulations to help consumers avoid paying for unnecessary or unreasonably expensive services offered by funeral-home operators. Ask the funeral director to show you the text of the law or regulation he's referring to. When he can't provide it, inform him that you will not pay for any items that are not required by law or permitted under the FTC's *Funeral Rule.*

If your father's body hasn't yet been moved to this funeral home, consider choosing a different one to handle your father's cremation—one that abides by the FTC rule. You may want to do this even if the body has already been transported to this funeral home. You will have to pay to have

the body moved again, but you can probably recover the cost in court or through the intervention of government agencies.

### REPORT THEM TO THE GOVERNMENT

Fraudulent funeral-home practices should be reported to the authorities. Here's how to do it:

- **File a complaint with your state's Bureau of Licenses.** This agency licenses funeral homes, and it may suspend or revoke a funeral home's license if there is a pattern of complaints against it.
- **Contact your state and local consumer protection agencies** and file a complaint. They may be able to intervene on your behalf and recover any additional costs you incurred as a result of the funeral home's misrepresentations. They may also be able to fine it for violating state consumer protection laws.
- **Notify the FTC** of the funeral home's prohibited conduct. The FTC has a variety of enforcement tools it can use to prevent the funeral home from engaging in deceptive conduct in the future.

*When you pick up your silk blouse from the dry cleaner, it's ruined. The cleaner says it's because the material was shoddy, and she's not to blame.*

Now you know what the saying "being taken to the cleaners" really means. Dry cleaning is a source of thousands of consumer complaints every year. In a case like this, you have a recourse. When you leave clothing with a dry cleaner, you create a type of contract called a *bailment,* in which you hand over personal property with the understanding that it will be returned later. Because the dry cleaner will make

money from this contract, the law requires her to use *reasonable care* in the way she treats your clothes. This means that she should use the kind of cleaning solutions and procedures that the average dry cleaner would use.

### GET IT TESTED

To settle the question of who's responsible for the damage to your blouse, ask the cleaner if she will agree to have the garment tested by a laboratory. For example, if she is a member of the International Fabricare Institute (a trade organization many dry cleaners belong to), she can send the blouse there for analysis. The lab results will show whether the problem is a result of the cleaner's mistake or because the fabric was defective. (Other test labs can also do similar tests.)

### IF THE DRY CLEANER IS AT FAULT

If the lab tests show that the dry cleaner's negligence caused the damage, ask her to reimburse you for the blouse. Keep in mind that she may offer you less than the price you paid. Legally, the cleaner is required to pay you only the blouse's actual value; if the garment is one you've had for some time, the offer could be for much less than the cost of a new blouse.

If she won't accept responsibility despite the test results—or if she won't agree to testing:

- **Write her a letter stating the problem,** the dates of conversations you had with her, and her responses to your request for compensation. Ask her to pay for replacing the blouse. If you have the receipt, enclose a copy (not the original). State a deadline by which you expect a response.
- **If you still don't get reimbursement,** file a complaint with the Better Business Bureau (BBB). Many businesses that belong to the BBB agree to take part in programs designed to mediate customer complaints. While the BBB

can't make the cleaner compensate you, it can note the company's refusal to correct the problem. Companies that fail to meet BBB standards can have their membership revoked.

> *Companies that fail to meet Better Business Bureau standards can have their membership revoked.*

### GO TO COURT

You can file a lawsuit in small-claims court, asking the court to order the dry cleaner to repay you for the lost value of the blouse. Sometimes merely filing the suit will be enough to prompt a local business owner to offer a reasonable settlement.

Dry cleaners and other businesses sometimes try to limit their liability by posting disclaimers in their stores or printing them on receipts. But if the disclaimer is one that a customer wouldn't be aware of—for example, if it's posted in small print on the rear wall of the store—a court would probably rule that the disclaimer isn't valid.

### WHEN THE FABRIC IS AT FAULT

If the lab tests show that the problem was in the fabric or the way the blouse was manufactured, your claim will be against the company that made it. Try the following:

- **Return the blouse to the store** and take along a copy of the lab results. The retailer may be willing to replace the blouse or refund your money on the spot.
- **Contact the manufacturer directly** if the retailer can't help you. (The retailer should be able to provide the address and phone number.) Explain your problem and ask how to return the blouse and get a refund. If you return the blouse by mail, get proof of delivery, either by sending the blouse through a private shipping company or by return-receipt service from the post office.
- **Get in touch with the Federal Trade Commission** (FTC) if the manufacturer

won't cooperate or denies liability. Recently the FTC fined a major clothing manufacturer $300,000 when its investigation showed that the company's clothes were damaged or destroyed even when cleaned according to the care directions on the label.

## YOUR LAST RESORT

While it may also be possible to file a small claims lawsuit against the manufacturer, collecting your judgment could be a problem. This is true especially if the manufacturer's place of business is located in a different state.

## THE SMART WAY TO COMPLAIN

When a business doesn't deliver what it promises, the odds of getting the problem resolved in your favor are greatly improved when you do the following:

■ **Know your legal rights.** In addition to the information in this book, you will find a wealth of information about consumer rights and remedies in pamphlets provided by your local or state bar association. It's also available on Web sites maintained by various government agencies, and at your local library, where you'll find copies of your state statutes and local ordinances.

■ **Act promptly.** The longer you delay, the less likely you are to get the solution you want.

■ **Talk to the right person.** Trying to solve a problem at the local furniture store by talking to an office clerk won't be as effective as speaking directly to the customer service manager or the store manager.

■ **Have a solution in mind.** Merchants aren't mind readers. If you want a refund instead of a replacement, say so. Most reputable merchants want to keep customers satisfied. If the remedy you propose is reasonable, chances are they will agree to it.

■ **Be firm, but don't get personal.** Calling the company's employees derogatory names or making threats is one of the fastest ways to put an end to what might have been an easy negotiation.

■ **Document everything.** Write down the names of the people you talk to, their titles, and their responses. Keep copies of bills, warranties, and any correspondence you have had about your problem.

■ **Be persistent.** If you can't get a satisfactory response right away, being persistent can pay off. If the person you're speaking to won't budge, ask to speak to her supervisor.

■ **Put it in writing.** If you can't appeal in person or over the phone, or these appeals haven't worked, writing a clear, concise letter and sending it to the owner or president of the business could get your problem resolved. (For an example of an effective letter of complaint, see page 455).

■ **Get help.** Contacting consumer protection agencies, federal agencies such as the Federal Trade Commission or the Food and Drug Administration, and even enlisting the media may help bring an end to an intractable problem.

■ **Consider the courts.** If the problem is serious and the amount at stake is worth it, filing a lawsuit may be your best last resort. Getting a lawyer's advice, even if you're planning to go the small claims route, can help you weigh the pros and cons of a courtroom battle.

> **Y**ou want to join a health club. The membership contract limits you to "nonpeak" hours, which are the same hours you work. The club's salesman says you'll be allowed to use the club at any time.

**A** membership in a health club may help you master midriff bulge, but it can also give you a headache. Health-club memberships and the techniques used to sell them are common complaints. The salespeople often tend to gloss over contract restrictions and fees and want to hurry you into signing up. But there are ways to avoid a problem with the contract.

### BEFORE YOU SIGN ON THE DOTTED LINE

When you visit a health club for the first time…

- **Time your visit carefully.** Go at the time of day you will most likely use the facility. A club that's nearly empty when you visit at midday could be packed with clients after work, when you plan to work out.
- **Announce that you are only looking.** Tell the salesperson that you will not sign a contract during this visit. Consumer protection experts suggest that you visit at least three clubs before you decide on one to join.
- **Ask about add-ons** to the basic membership—initiation fees, fees for exercise classes, and locker-room charges that may not be disclosed in the club's advertising.

### EXAMINE THE CONTRACT

Once you find a club, look carefully at the contract. Never sign a contract under a salesperson's pressure. Claims that "this offer is good only if you sign up today" or assurances that "this is all just legalese for what we discussed" are a red flag. A reputable health club will let you take a copy of the contract with you so you can review it or have a lawyer look at it. Many health-club contracts contain several pages of fine print that may…

- Limit your visits to the club
- Set time and day-of-the-week restrictions
- Attempt to limit the club's liability if you are injured on site

- Require you to waive your right to file a lawsuit if you and the club disagree about any of the contract's provisions.

> **M**ake sure what the salesperson tells you is there in black and white in the contract.

Ask about cancellation provisions. Can you cancel your membership and receive a refund if you move away or become ill? Make sure that anything the salesperson tells you is there in black and white in the contract.

### GETTING OUT OF THE CONTRACT

Even if you've already signed on, you may be able to get out of the contract. Check with your state's consumer protection office for information about what laws, if any, govern health-club contracts in your state. In

some states, if you sign a health-club contract and change your mind, you can cancel it within three business days of the day you signed it.

Even in states with no special laws about health-club contracts, there may be other laws that will allow you to cancel your contract:

■ **If you can show that you signed the contract as a result of fraud or because you were under duress,** a court might rule that the contract is void, and any money you paid would have to be refunded to you.

■ **If the contract is full of legalese,** a court could void it. In some states consumer contracts must by law be written in plain English by law. You'll need a lawyer for this. Check with your state bar association for referrals to lawyers who handle consumer cases.

Finally, don't forget the power of the media. Many newspapers have consumer reporters who may be able to get you out of your contract and get you a refund. Local television and radio stations may also be interested in your story.

## THE "RENT-TO-OWN" RACKET

It sounds like such a good deal. No credit, bad credit? Need a television, a washer or dryer, or a great stereo? Then come on down to your local rent-to-own store. Just make a low weekly payment for 18 months or so, and the appliance is yours! There's not even a credit check required. And if you want to stop making payments, simply return the item to the store.

■ **This "good deal" is akin to highway robbery.** Take the example of a typical rent-to-own contract for a color television set. You pay about $15 a week. Make the payments every week for the term of your contract (in most cases, 78 weeks), and at the end of the term you will have paid $1,170 for a TV that would have cost you less than $250 at most retail stores!

■ **Another problem is what those in the business call "no long-term obligation."** What this means is that if you miss a payment, the store will come and reclaim the television set. Any money you've already paid is lost. Say you've paid $15 a week for 50 weeks; you will have paid $750—three times the retail price of the television, but you'll have no TV to show for it.

■ **Only a few states require rent-to-own stores to disclose facts** about the items you rent and the total you'll pay before you own the item. In many states, the law doesn't even require the store to tell you if the item you're renting is new or used. You could end up renting-to-own an item that's already seen a lot of use by another customer.

What's a consumer to do? Putting $15 a week in a bank account will let you buy a brand-new, manufacturer-warranted $250 television set in about four months. While it's tough to defer gratification, sometimes doing so is the only sensible move.

As the saying goes, you can never be too rich or too thin. Consumers spend billions of dollars every year on products, programs, and machines that promise to help them lose weight. Companies touting these products makes all kinds of claims:

- **Claim:** "This 2,000-year-old secret is the natural way to lose weight without dieting!" *Reality check:* If this has been around for so long, how in the world did it manage to remain a secret from the medical profession but not from a weight-loss counselor with little or no medical training?
- **Claim:** "Eat whatever you want, never exercise, and lose weight even while you sleep!" *Reality check:* The experts agree: Short of surgery, the only way for most people to lose weight is to eat less and exercise more.
- **Claim:** "So new and revolutionary that your doctor probably hasn't even heard of it!" *Reality check:* A truly effective "revolutionary" product will be well known in the medical profession and documented in medical journals, not advertised in the back of a magazine or on the bulletin board of a health club.

### GETTING OUT OF THIS TRAP

If you've fallen prey to a bogus weight-loss program or purchased any other fraudulent health-care product, here are some steps you can take to get your money back:

- **Ask for a refund** from the company that sold you the program. But be warned that getting your money back may not be easy. Companies running weight-loss scams often claim that the reason the program didn't work is because the customer didn't follow instructions.
- **Complain to your state's consumer protection agency.** (Their number is listed in the state government section of your telephone directory.) This agency can often negotiate with companies suspected of fraud to get refunds for customers. The consumer protection agency can also prohibit the company from continuing to sell useless products.
- **Contact the Food and Drug Administration** (FDA; page 467). The FDA can investigate companies selling dangerous or useless products. Investigations may include sending warning letters, requiring product testing, or banning the products from sale in the U.S.

You'll naturally be surprised and angry to hear the salesman expects a cancellation fee, but don't fall for his claim—he's full of hot air. Under both federal and state law, you have the right to cancel your purchase—and get a refund of any money paid—when you buy items that cost more than $25 from a door-to-door salesman or when you make your purchase somewhere other than the seller's normal place of business. The only exceptions to the rule are for arts and crafts you purchase at a fair or when you buy a car, truck, camper, or van from a dealer who has a permanent place of business but is conducting sales off-premises.

According to a Federal Trade Commission (FTC) rule, called *Cooling-Off Period for Sales Made at Home or at Certain Other Locations*...

● Sellers must provide buyers notice of their right to cancel the sale within three business days and receive a full refund.
● Sellers must provide two copies of an actual cancellation form.
● Sellers are not allowed to charge a cancellation fee.

**TAKE NOTE** *If the sale was made in a language other than English, you should receive the cancellation information in that language.*

### CANCELING THE SALE

If you want out of the contract, first tell the salesman you are canceling the sale as permitted by federal law. Mail the cancellation form that the salesman provided to the company's address.

Send it certified mail, return receipt requested.

If the salesman didn't give you a cancellation form, or you can't find it, write a letter to the company stating that you are canceling the contract as permitted under the FTC's Cooling-Off Rule. This should also be sent certified mail, return receipt requested.

Remember that you must act within three business days of the day you signed the contract or agreed to make the purchase. However, the three-day period doesn't begin until you receive notice of your right to cancel. If you didn't get the notice, the clock hasn't started ticking yet. Still, it's best not to delay any longer than necessary.

### GETTING YOUR MONEY BACK

After you cancel the sale, the company should send you its copy of the contract you signed and return any money you paid or credit your credit card within 10 business days. If it doesn't, proceed as follows:

■ **Contact the credit-card issuer** (if you paid by credit card) to dispute the charge.
■ **Notify the Better Business Bureau,** which can warn other consumers about the company's illegal business practices.
■ **Contact the consumer protection division** of your state attorney general's office. State laws usually parallel the FTC rule, and the agency can sue the company to get your payment refunded and can fine the company.
■ **File a complaint with the FTC,** which can take action against the company. The FTC has been successful in obtaining refunds for customers as well as entering into *consent orders* with companies that violate the FTC rule. Under a consent order, the company agrees not to engage in future violations of the rule or it will face additional fines and penalties.

You're not alone: in 1999, consumers lost more than $3 billion to Internet fraud, according to the National Consumer League. The majority of problems by far occurred with on-line auctions. Consumers either didn't get the item they ordered, or found when it arrived that it wasn't as described by the seller.

## CONTACT THE SELLER

If you experience either of these problems, your first step is to contact the seller. Packages can go astray; if you haven't received the item, it may have been misdelivered or could be sitting in a shipping company's warehouse.

Similarly, if you aren't satisfied with the item because it's not as it was described, let the seller know. Most sellers are honest, and if you have a legitimate complaint, the seller may be willing to accept a return of the item and refund your payment. (Be sure to keep copies of all e-mail and any other correspondence between you and the seller about the item.)

## NOTIFY THE AUCTION SITE

If you and the seller can't resolve the problem directly, try the following:

- **Complain to the on-line auction site,** and provide it with copies of your communication with the seller.
- **Use a dispute resolution service** if the on-line auction site offers it. These services are designed to help customers who have problems with sellers, and may be able to help you obtain a full or partial refund from the seller.
- **Take advantage of the auction site's insurance program.** For example, eBay will reimburse purchasers up to $200, minus a $25 deductible, when they pay for an item and don't receive it, or receive an item that doesn't match its description.

In most cases, these actions will bring a satisfactory resolution to your problem, and you'll be able to bid on-line with more confidence.

## IF IT'S FRAUD

If you think that you've been the victim of fraud, contact the auction Web site's security staff. They can investigate your problem. If they find that the seller operated dishonestly, they can cancel the seller's account and refer your complaint to federal law enforcement authorities.

You should also consider filing a complaint with the Federal Trade Commission (FTC). The easiest way to do this is to fill out a complaint form on-line; visit their Web site at www.ftc.gov for instructions.

## PROTECT YOURSELF IN THE FUTURE

If you want to continue to make purchases on the Web, there are several steps you can take before you buy to protect yourself and minimize the chance that you'll be the victim of one of the many con artists lurking on-line:

- Stick to established on-line services, such as amazon.com or eBay. Remember that Web sites come and go, and not all auction sites offer buyers the protection that is available at the major sites.
- Investigate the site's buyer protection policies. Does the site offer insurance, dispute resolution services, and a way for buyers to rate a seller's reliability?
- Check the seller's reputation with other on-line buyers. Does he deliver promptly? Are the products the seller delivers of the quality described on-line?
- Pay with a credit card, so you can contest the charge if you don't get what you ordered.
- Consider an escrow service to hold your payment for more expensive items.

## ON-LINE ESCROW SERVICES

Using an escrow service can protect you from a big financial loss when you're buying items that exceed the maximum insurance coverage offered by an auction Web site. Here's how escrow services work:

- You set up an account with an escrow service, such as i-Escrow.com.

- You and the seller must agree to use the escrow service and agree on a price for the item being purchased.

- As the buyer, you deposit the purchase price into the escrow account.

- The escrow service notifies the seller that the money has been deposited, and the seller then ships the item to you.

- When you receive the item, you inspect it to make sure that it's what you expected.

- If you are satisfied with the item, after a predetermined period the money is released from the escrow account to the seller.

- If you aren't satisfied with the item, you notify the escrow service and return the item to the seller within an agreed-upon period, such as five business days.

- Once the seller gets the item back, the money in the escrow account is returned to you, usually minus the escrow service's fee for handling the transaction.

# A moving company charges you extra money to transport your furniture and household goods to your new home.

You may not get much help from the government here, but don't despair. You can help yourself.

The federal Department of Transportation, which oversees the interstate moving industry, assumes that the consumer disputing extra moving charges will seek arbitration or file a lawsuit. States vary widely in the policing of local movers: Some are avidly pro-consumer, while others seem content to let the industry police itself.

In general, movers are required by law to deliver your goods and furniture to your new home on time. But cost is another matter, with estimates either nonbinding or binding.

## NONBINDING VS. BINDING

What you do on your own behalf depends on the agreement you have with the mover.

- **A nonbinding estimate** is based on the mover's "guestimate" of the actual weight of your shipment, which is difficult to know beforehand. If the weight is higher than the estimate, you must pay the extra cost. (In some cases, you may end up paying less than you expected, but it is much more likely that you'll be paying more.)
  - If the actual amount due is no more than 110 percent of the estimate, regulations require you to make full payment at the time of delivery.
  - If the amount due is more than 110 percent, you must pay the estimated amount, and then pay the excess within 30 days.
- **A binding estimate,** which guarantees that the moving cost won't exceed a certain amount, is something you have to ask for.

Most reputable moving companies are likely to oblige you, but don't expect them to tell you that binding estimates are an option. If you're intent on getting a binding estimate and the mover refuses to cooperate, scout around for a company that will.

## REFUSAL TO UNLOAD

If you have a *binding estimate* in writing from the moving company, point this out to the driver of the truck. If he refuses to unload your goods, you should immediately call the moving company's office (if it is a small outfit) or its customer service department (if it is a large firm). The driver should be told to unload the shipment immediately.

If you have a *nonbinding estimate,* you may have to pay the extra 10 percent.

If the driver still refuses to unload your shipment, you have a choice to make: to pay the additional amount, or to refuse.

- ■ **If you agree to pay the extra money,** be sure to get a written receipt signed by the driver.
- ■ **If you refuse,** the driver will most likely take your goods to a local warehouse or storage

unit, where they will be stored until the matter in dispute can be resolved.

## PUT IT IN WRITING

If you paid the additional amount but feel that the charge was excessive, contact the moving company immediately. Write a letter outlining the reasons why you think that the cost of the move was too high. In your letter…

- ● Request a refund of the excess amount.
- ● Specify a reasonable deadline by which you expect the mover to respond, such as within 30 days.
- ● Include copies of any supporting documents such as the bill of lading and the estimate you received.

Send the letter via certified mail, return receipt requested. If the mover is affiliated with a large moving company, send a copy of everything to the customer service department at its headquarters. Keep a written record of all your conversations and correspondence (in case you have to appeal to a state or federal agency; see below).

If your goods were put in storage, follow the same steps as above, and offer to pay…

- ● The original amount due
- ● Any excess charge you think is reasonable.

## YOUR LAST RESORT

If you are still unable to convince the mover to deliver your goods, you should contact your state transportation department or, if your move was across state lines, the federal Department of Transportation. You may also want to contact the consumer protection division of your state attorney general's office. Provide each of these with copies of all correspondence and documents, as well as a log of all telephone calls between you and the mover and the nature of those conversations.

If your mover belongs to a national or state transport association, contact these organizations as well. One of these groups may be able to help you resolve your dispute.

If all else fails, you may need to file a lawsuit against the mover to regain your money or to have your goods released from storage. You may also be able to get your local prosecuting attorney to file criminal charges against the moving company for theft if it continues to keep your goods.

Don't think you're fighting a losing battle: It's one you may well win. In one recent case, the owner of a moving company was convicted of unlawfully refusing to deliver goods to a customer. He was fined and was also ordered to pay restitution and to perform community service.

---

## HOW TO CHECK THE INTEGRITY OF A MOVER

Moving is a stressful experience at best; having to deal with a troublesome or unethical moving company only makes the situation worse. To avoid problems on moving day, it pays to do some research before hiring a mover. Recommendations from friends, relatives, and business associates are a good place to start. It is also advisable to interview several moving companies, since rates among movers vary. Here are some questions to ask.

■ **Does the mover carry liability insurance and workers' compensation insurance?** Some movers try to cut expenses by skimping on these kinds of coverage. If the mover damages your home (either the one you are leaving or the one you are moving to), liability insurance will help cover the cost of repairs. Workers' compensation insurance will help pay for any injuries suffered by the mover's employees during the course of your move. In many states, you can verify this information with the transportation department.

■ **Does the firm use its own employees, or does it hire day laborers?** Employees are more likely to be properly trained in moving techniques, which can limit damage to your furniture and goods. Day laborers may not have the same level of knowledge or experience. In addition, day laborers may not be as honest as a company's regular employees. "Here today and gone tomorrow," day laborers may be more inclined to help themselves to some of your property as a supplement to their day's wages.

■ **How long has the mover been in business?** Some experts suggest that you check last year's telephone directory to see if the moving company was in business the previous year. If not, you may want to investigate further: Movers who have lost their license to operate, been sued, or been the subject of many consumer complaints can simply go out of business and then reopen under another name.

■ **Will the mover give you the names of previous customers?** Most reputable movers will be happy to give references, but be sure to check them out carefully. Some less scrupulous companies have been known to hand out the names of personal friends and family members as references in order to ensure glowing recommendations.

■ **Does the mover belong to any local or national trade groups, such as your state's transport association or the American Moving & Storage Association?** These organizations require members to follow a Code of Ethics, and movers who don't can have their memberships canceled.

*Beware of movers who provide extremely low estimates. This is known as* lowballing, *and since most estimates are nonbinding, you could find yourself paying a lot more than you expected.*

*Your discover that your elderly aunt has been spending large sums of money on seances and fortunetellers.*

Whenever you deal with astrologers, card readers, psychics, and other "spiritual advisers," the potential for being taken advantage of is great. While many of these guides and advisers take an honest interest in trying to help their clients, there are plenty of con artists ready to prey on the forlorn and the gullible. Providing "contact" with a dead spouse or a deceased parent or child is one commonly used method of separating a lonely woman from her money. So is discovering a "curse" that can only be removed by providing the spiritualist with a large sum of cash.

These phony advisers are dangerous, and not just to their victims' bank accounts. They may also keep a troubled person from seeking medical help or psychological counseling. Fortunately, the law in most states takes a dim view of this type of fraud, especially when it targets the elderly.

## CALL THE POLICE

Contact your local police department with your concerns. You should be prepared to provide the authorities with the following:

- **The name of the "spiritual adviser,"** as well as her address and any other identifying information, such as a physical description. It's important to do this as quickly as possible, since many of these scam artists change their name, appearance, and locale often, especially when they suspect that law enforcement officials may be on to them.
- **A statement from your aunt** about her meetings with the adviser. This could be embarrassing for her. Many older people are reluctant to admit they've been taken advantage of by a con artist. Ask the police if there's a victim's advocate who can assist your aunt in making her statement.
- **Evidence of any payments** your aunt made, such as canceled checks, bank withdrawal slips, or credit-card statements.

The police will investigate your aunt's situation and can bring a

variety of criminal charges against the crooked adviser, including theft by deception and fraud. If convicted, the adviser could be ordered to make restitution to your aunt as part of her sentence.

## SCAMS FROM THE SPIRIT WORLD

A dishonest spiritual adviser or medium is an expert, all right—at defrauding her unsuspecting victims, not foreseeing the future. Here are some of her methods.

**A "spiritual adviser" may...**

● Gain her victim's trust, perhaps by offering a "free reading" when she notes that the victim is "troubled" or "looking for answers." (Why else would she be there?) The adviser offers some vague information that the victim interprets as being proof of the adviser's powers.

● Glean personal information from the victim. If the adviser is clever, she can then rephrase what she's learned to make it sound as if she has some special insight into the situation.

● Ask for a small payment, such as $20, to pay for a potion or for a "blessed candle" to help chase away the evil spirits causing the victim's problems.

● Say that she underestimated the power of the evil spirits. Although the victim has made the first payment, the problem hasn't subsided. This isn't because of the adviser's lack of powers. Stronger spells are needed, and stronger spells are more expensive. The cycle repeats itself until the victim wises up and quits paying, or—in too many cases—when she's run out of money.

**A "medium" may...**

● Offer to be a contact between the victim and a deceased relative or friend, but only after meeting the victim and cleverly obtaining information about her personal history, financial status, and level of gullibility.

● "Make contact" at the seance with the deceased and provide some statement designed to soothe the troubled mind of the victim, either about the dead person's afterlife or about some unresolved conflict that existed between the deceased and the victim. Sometimes, this takes place at a single seance. More often, multiple seances are held, all at additional cost.

● Add another twist to the scam. Through the medium, the deceased will instruct the victim to withdraw money from a bank account and send it to "an old friend who's in trouble." Eager to please, the victim goes along with the request, never questioning that the "old friend" is someone she's never heard of, living at an unfamiliar address. In fact, this person is an associate or family member of the medium.

*You make a reservation at a three-star hotel downtown. When you arrive, you're told that no room is available. The desk clerk offers to get you a room at a budget motel near the airport.*

Like airlines, many hotels *overbook*, taking reservations for more rooms than they have available. Hotels justify the practice as a protection against no-shows—travelers who make reservations but never show up, leaving the booked rooms unoccupied. Nevertheless, hotel overbooking is generally against the law. In some states, a hotel guilty of intentionally overbooking can even be fined.

---

*The hotel should find you a comparable room at a similar hotel and pay any additional expenses.*

---

Still, that's little comfort to the weary traveler with reservations who's being denied a room. It's knowing what to do when the desk clerk says "Sorry, full up" that can make or break a trip.

### YOUR LEGAL RIGHTS

Your right to a room depends on the kind of reservation you made. If you have a *guaranteed* reservation—that is, you reserved the room with a credit card or put down a deposit—the hotel is obligated to hold a room for you all night, even if you don't arrive until after midnight. Your part of the bargain is that if you don't show up or cancel your reservation by a specified time, the hotel generally has the right to charge you for one night's stay. Some resort hotels that require a minimum stay may charge you for the full period of your reservation if you fail to cancel or show up; be sure to check the hotel's specific policies at the time you make your reservation.

Legally, a hotel that fails to honor a guaranteed reservation is required to put you in the same position you would have been in if a room had been available. This means that the hotel should find you a comparable room at a similar hotel and pay any additional expenses, such as taxi fare to the new hotel and telephone calls to inform your family or employer of your actual location. Hotels that will accept credit cards to guarantee reservations must provide these services or risk breaching their agreement with the credit-card company as well.

Don't confuse a guaranteed reservation with one that's merely *confirmed* (made without a credit card or deposit). A hotel is only obligated to honor a confirmed reservation if you arrived by a specified time. If you come later than that, you may find that your reservation has been canceled. In this case, the hotel would have no further obligation to provide you with a room. (If you know you're going to be late, you can avoid this problem by calling and guaranteeing the reservation before the cutoff time.)

### INSIST ON A ROOM

If you've arrived on time for a confirmed reservation, or if you had a guaranteed reservation. . .

- Demand that the hotel either honor your reservation or provide you with a comparable room at a similar hotel.
- Don't leave the desk until an acceptable room has been arranged.
- Ask to speak to the manager if the desk clerk refuses to help you.

As with any consumer problem, be sure to get the names and titles of those you deal with.

As frustrating as the situation may be, don't threaten the clerk or any other member of the hotel staff. A hotel can legitimately refuse a room to a customer who acts violently or otherwise disturbs the peace and quiet of other guests.

It's entirely likely that you will be relocated. In some cases, a vacant room may almost magically appear; more often, a room will be found for you at a nearby hotel. If the hotel you are transferred to is more expensive, you should be compensated for the extra expense. If it's a hotel that's less expensive or priced about the same, the hotel that failed to honor your reservation should pick up the entire cost of your lodging there.

### CALL OR WRITE A LETTER

If you remain unhappy with the hotel's handling of the situation, take the following steps:

- **Notify your credit-card company of the problem** if you used a credit card to guarantee the room. Denying you a guaranteed room may violate the hotel's agreement with the credit-card company, and you may be entitled to a refund of the room's cost as well as a free room elsewhere.
- **Complain to the parent company if the hotel is part of a chain.** This can be especially effective if you are a member of the chain's frequent-traveler program. Enrollment in these programs is free, and being able to point to your membership and loyalty to the hotel chain could bring you some compensation, most likely in the form of coupons to use for discounts on future stays.
- **Contact the owner if the hotel operates independently.** You may be able to do this in person or by telephone while you are in the area, but if you can't make contact until you return home, it's best to write a letter. Again,

outline the problem you encountered, state why you were dissatisfied with the response, and propose a solution, such as compensation in the form of money or discounts.

### YOUR LAST RESORT

It is possible to sue a hotel for failing to honor your reservation, but it's not always practical. Why? Because you may have to sue the hotel in the community in which it's located. If that's far from your home, the limited amount of damages you can recover (plus the inconvenience of traveling back to the hotel's locale) may make it economically unreasonable to go to court.

It may be worthwhile to contact the office of consumer protection in the hotel's home state. A record of complaints can prompt the state attorney general to bring a lawsuit on behalf of you and others with similar problems. If the state law provides for a fine, the attorney general may have additional ammunition to use against the hotel.

---

*T*he deluxe cabin you reserved at an
expensive dude ranch turns out to be a run-down dump.

---

The brochure promised an authentic western experience in top-of-the-line accommodations, but when you get to your cabin you find a torn bedspread, peeling linoleum, and a dripping faucet. What can you do?

### REQUEST A DIFFERENT CABIN

When you arrive at the ranch, take a good look at the condition of the main building and the resort's other facilities. This will give you some idea of how well the guest cabins are maintained. Before checking in or handing over your credit card, ask the desk clerk to show you the cabin you've been assigned.

If you don't like it, request a different one immediately. If the clerk refuses, ask to speak to the manager or owner. Explain why the cabin you were offered is unacceptable, and ask again to be given other accommodations.

You may be told that another cabin is not available right away. Ask when one will be ready, and politely insist that you be moved to it as soon

as possible. If you do this in a public area, such as the lobby or check-in desk, you may get better results. It's more potentially embarrassing for the ranch when customers complain in plain view of some of the other guests.

If no other cabins are available, there are still several other options for you to pursue:

- Leave and find new accommodations (not always easy in a remote location). If you leave, you may have to go to court to get any of your advance fees or deposits returned.
- Stay and ask for a rate reduction.
- If you're refused, stay at the agreed rate and document a claim against the ranch. (Having your camera or video recorder along will help.) Note differences between what you received and what was promised in the ranch's advertising brochures, magazine ads, or on its Web site. Your case for a refund will be stronger if you can show that the problem endangered your safety or health (such as windows or

doors that didn't lock, or a toilet that didn't flush properly) rather than merely offended your aesthetics (the bedspread was ugly or the view wasn't what you were promised).

### PUT IT IN WRITING

When you get home, write to the ranch's owner. Be sure to state the problem clearly, explain why you believe you're entitled to compensation, describe the compensation you want, and set a time limit for a response from the ranch.

If you honestly believe that the ranch's advertising was deceptive, you can contact the consumer protection division of the state attorney general's office in the state where the ranch is located. If the ranch is a member of the Better Business Bureau or a trade association, such as the Dude Ranchers' Association, you can write a letter to them with your complaint.

### YOUR LAST RESORT

If all else fails, you can file a lawsuit against the dude ranch, although it may be hard to establish jurisdiction over the ranch in the community where you live. However, state laws may allow you to sue locally because the ranch conducted business in your state by advertising or soliciting customers there.

Dude-ranch vacations can cost thousands of dollars a week, so it may be worth talking to a lawyer if your vacation wasn't what you were led to believe it would be.

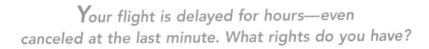

## Your flight is delayed for hours—even canceled at the last minute. What rights do you have?

Sitting on an airplane that's going nowhere or waiting for the next scheduled flight when the original flight has been canceled is very frustrating—and it's happening more all the time. For example, an airline supervisor may see two half-booked flights in a row and decide, without telling passengers, that the company can fly one plane with a full load more economically. And bad weather, mechanical problems, or delays assembling flight crews can also cause havoc. Even after you've reached the destination airport, your arrival can be stalled if there's no gate available for your plane to dock.

### FIND OUT WHAT'S GOING ON

Your options are limited but worth pursuing. First, ask the gate supervisor at check-in or the senior flight attendant the reason for the delay, and write down his name. In many cases when a departure from the gate is delayed, the airline will board the flight and want you to stay on the plane. (Reassembling passengers who have scattered throughout an airport only causes further delays once the flight is cleared for takeoff.)

If it appears that the delay will be long—for example, if you're waiting for an airplane part that has to be flown in—ask the senior flight attendant to ask the captain or ground crew if you can get off the plane. If the answer is no, you have done as much as you can for now. Don't try to take matters into your own hands, and above all don't become abusive or threatening with the flight attendants. Not only could doing so add to the delay, but federal law makes it a felony to interfere with a flight attendant during the performance of his duties.

If your arrival is delayed because there are no available gates, all you can do is sit tight. Your plane may be only a hop, skip, and a jump from the terminal, but concerns for passenger safety mean that the airline will not allow you to deplane until your plane is at a gate.

### REQUEST COMPENSATION

If you're on a domestic flight, once you reach your destination, you can take the following steps to be compensated for the delay:

■ **Get a copy of the airline's Contract of Carriage** (available at their customer service desk and ticket counters), a document that tells you what remedies are available to delayed passengers. This varies from airline to airline. If the delay kept you from making the last connecting flight to your destination that day, under one airline's Contract of Carriage you may be entitled to receive a free hotel room, meals, phone calls, and assistance in getting on the first available flight the following day. In the same situation, another airline's Contract of Carriage may provide nothing.

■ **Ask to speak to a supervisor** at the airline's customer service desk or ticket counter, and note the supervisor's name and title. Tell her your complaint and ask what she will do to compensate you for the delay and inconvenience. Even though an airline's official Contract of Carriage may be less than generous, some carriers will provide compensation as a goodwill gesture. If you are a frequent flier on the airline, be sure to point this out. Airlines know that it's more cost effective to keep their regular customers happy than to attract new ones.

■ **Know what you want.** Are hotel accommodations and meal vouchers sufficient compensation, or has the delay caused you so much inconvenience that you feel entitled to a free round-trip ticket too? Keep in mind, though, that the amount of compensation you will receive—at least immediately—isn't really up to you. The airline is required to act only within the terms of its Contract of Carriage.

■ **Write the president of the airline** if you are still dissatisfied with your treatment. Describe the problem, the responses you received from airline employees (along with their names and titles), and the compensation you expect. Keep the letter brief, direct, and professional; a one-or two-page letter that calmly sets out the events and a proposed remedy is most likely to get a positive response.

In order to decide whether to file a lawsuit, try to weigh the amount of damages you may be able to recover against the time and expense of going to court. Keep in mind that a court will likely decide in favor of the airline unless it willfully failed to live up to its Contract of Carriage. However, if the airline's actions were a result of its own failure to act in a reasonable way (such as by neglecting to have a crew assembled at takeoff time to fly the plane), your case has a much greater chance of success.

Unless your provable damages are large, you may want to pursue a small-claims court action against the airline.

### ON INTERNATIONAL FLIGHTS

Regulations governing flights to or from countries other than the United States are contained in a 1929 treaty known as the Warsaw Convention and generally give airlines much greater protection against the claims of delayed passengers.

While all of the preceding advice regarding delays and cancellations applies to disputes about an international flight, an airline may try to avoid any liability by claiming protection under the Warsaw Convention's provisions.

### YOUR LAST RESORT

If the airline refuses to compensate you, or if you remain unhappy with its offer, you can hire a lawyer and file a lawsuit against the airline carrier. Remember, though, that if you accept any compensation you may be required to release the airline from further liability as a condition of receiving the compensation.

---

## THE ABCs OF OVERBOOKING

Airlines are allowed to overbook—to sell more seats than they actually have. They do this because experience shows that not everyone who reserves a seat will actually appear to claim it.

■ **Gate attendants will first ask for volunteers** who are willing to take a later flight. To encourage volunteers, the airline will usually offer an incentive, such as a discount voucher, a free round-trip domestic ticket, or first-class seating on the later flight. This kind of compensation can be a good deal if you aren't in a hurry. In fact, some air travelers volunteer at check-in, even before it's announced that the flight is overbooked.

■ **If there aren't enough volunteers,** the airline must begin bumping passengers, or leaving them behind involuntarily. Typically, the last passengers to check in get bumped first. In most cases bumped passengers are entitled to compensation depending on how long it takes to get to their destination. The exceptions are if the airline can get you there within one hour of your original arrival time, or if the plane you were to travel on seats fewer than 60 passengers. Some other exceptions may also apply, so ask your travel agent or the airline's customer service personnel to provide you with a copy of the airline's specific policies.

In other cases, compensation is set by federal law. On domestic flights, an arrival delay of. . .

● More than one hour but less than two hours entitles you to the value of your ticket for that flight segment, up to a maximum of $200.

● More than two hours entitles you to twice the value of that part of your ticket up to $400.

On international flights, if your arrival is delayed by...

● From one to four hours, you will receive up to $200.

● More than four hours, the airline will pay you a maximum of $400.

These figures apply only to flights within or departing from the U.S. Other countries have their own rules for passengers bumped from flights originating from or operating within their borders. Ask your travel agent or airline personnel what compensation you may be entitled to.

Finally, federal law gives a passenger the right to refuse the compensation the airline offers and recover damages in a lawsuit. But in most cases, a lawsuit can cost more than the damages you could recover. Think carefully before rejecting the airline's offer.

Problems with lost, delayed, or damaged baggage are the number-one passenger complaint against airlines. If your suitcase is dented by careless baggage handlers, it can be hard to get compensation because airlines go to great lengths to disclaim responsibility for damage. Fortunately, though, when it comes to lost or delayed baggage, your rights are protected both by federal law and by the Warsaw Convention.

## FILE A CLAIM

To improve the odds of your luggage arriving when you do, insist that it be tagged with the proper flight and destination information before you leave the counter. Sometimes ticket agents

will staple the claim check to your ticket jacket before tagging your luggage, only to confuse your bag's destination with another passenger's.

If your bag does go astray, file a report with the airline's baggage claims representative. (The baggage office is normally located near the carousel where bags arrive.) You will be given a form to fill out, describing the bag and its contents. Be as accurate as possible, as it will be the basis for compensation if your bag is lost forever.

Keep a copy of the form for your records. If there is no airline employee available to take your claim (this can happen if your flight arrives late in the evening or at a small airport), get the airline's baggage service phone number from an airline representative and immediately report the problem. Be sure to get the name and title of the person you speak to on the phone.

If and when your bag is found, ask the airline to deliver it to you where you're staying, or to your home address; there should be no charge. Happily, most luggage shows up in a relatively short time, usually because it was placed on a later flight. But if yours doesn't, you will have to take further action to be compensated.

## GET REIMBURSED

If your bag is delayed for more than a few hours…

- **Ask an airline representative if the company will reimburse you for expenses** you incur while it is missing. Some airlines will provide a toiletries kit. Others will require you to purchase items you need and then seek reimbursement.
- **Have receipts of any purchases you've made.** The airline will scrutinize your claim closely before making a payment. If you are attending a formal dinner party on the evening of your arrival and your tuxedo was in the missing bag, the airline may agree to pay for the cost of a rented tuxedo. However, claims for nonessential items, such as swimwear, will probably be denied.

In about 1 percent of cases, a bag is truly lost. If this happens to you, you will need to submit a follow-up claim. This typically requires filling out yet another form, although some airlines will use the information from your original claim. Once again, be as thorough as possible in describing the lost bag and its contents. In a few cases, this information will help the airline locate your bag, but it's more likely that it will be used by the airline to determine its value and the amount it will pay you for the lost luggage.

You should receive a check from the airline within about six to eight weeks of filing your claim. If you disagree with the value placed on your claim, don't cash the check. Examine it closely: There is probably a provision on the back stating that by endorsing the check, you are accepting it as final payment of your claim.) If there's good reason to seek a bigger payment from the airline, contact the carrier's claims department with additional information supporting your request for more money. This sometimes will prompt the airline to increase its offer.

If you remain dissatisfied with the airline's conduct or its offer of compensation, you can file a complaint with the federal Department of Transportation. (Visit their Web site at www.dot.gov for more information about con-

sumer questions and complaints.) While the DOT doesn't intervene on behalf of individual airline passengers, it does use these consumer complaints to recommend changes in federal laws and regulations that govern airline carriers.

## YOUR LAST RESORT

Under certain circumstances, however, you can recover more than the limited amounts provided for by law and the airline's own policies. For example, an airline that fails to follow its own procedures and policies for handling baggage—such as by not trying to locate a missing bag or by misleading a passenger about the bag's whereabouts—could be found liable for additional damages.

Proving your case could be difficult, however, because you need access to evidence about the airline's procedures and supporting testimony from airline employees. Talk to a lawyer to determine whether your case is financially worth pursuing in the court system.

### SMART MOVES

Never check baggage with items you can't do without. This includes cameras, jewelry, cash or negotiable securities, your passport, eyeglasses, prescription medicines, and anything of great sentimental value. You should also carry on all glass items and containers that, if broken, can damage your bag's contents.

### COMPENSATION FOR LOST BAGGAGE

Airlines are allowed to limit their liability for lost baggage:

- **On domestic flights,** federal regulations limit liability to $2,500 per passenger. You can also purchase luggage insurance, generally up to a maximum of about $5,000.

- **On international flights,** the Warsaw Convention limits liability to about $9 per pound, up to a maximum of $640 per checked bag. If your bag was weighed, compensation is based on the bag's actual weight; if it wasn't weighed, the rules assume that a checked bag weighs approximately 70 pounds.

Airlines generally compensate you for the *depreciated value* of your property, not the replacement cost. So while it may cost you $300 to replace a suit that was lost, the airline will offer a lesser amount, reasoning that you had already used up some of the suit's value. If the items in your luggage were new, or if you dispute the amount offered, you will probably have to provide receipts to show when they were purchased and the amount you paid for them.

Taking a cruise should be a relaxing and enjoyable voyage. But when a cruise line fails to provide the accommodations it promised a disabled traveler, it not only spoils the fun—it may also be against the law.

### REQUEST A CHANGE

Your first step is to refuse to move into an inadequate cabin until you speak to ship personnel. Request that you be reassigned to a cabin that has the facilities you need. For example, if you use a wheelchair, ask for a cabin that is wheelchair *dedicated* (has no thresholds at doorways), not one that is merely wheelchair *accessible*.

---

*Cruise lines prefer to avoid negative publicity, especially about matters as sensitive as their treatment of disabled passengers.*

---

If the ship's personnel claim that they cannot reassign you, insist on speaking to the ship's purser or even the captain. It may be possible for other passengers to be moved in order to provide you with the cabin you were promised.

### DOCUMENT THE PROBLEMS

If the ship's personnel still refuse to help, start documenting your complaint immediately:

- Write down the names and titles of everyone you speak to.
- Take photographs of the obstacles you encounter in your cabin, such as a lack of grab bars, the presence of high door sills, or a bath entry that's too narrow for your wheelchair.
- Keep an eye out for, and photograph, other obstructions that make it difficult for you to have full access to the ship's facilities. Under the 1990 federal Americans with Disabilities Act (ADA), cruise ships must provide disabled passengers with access to the ship's public areas. You're more likely to encounter access problems on older ships that have been retrofitted to make them more accessible; in some cases, the attempt to remove barriers may be only partially successful. Newer ships are designed to be ADA compliant. However, if your cruise originates and ends in countries other than the United States and never enters an American port, the ADA may not apply.

### GET REIMBURSEMENT

Write to the cruise line's customer service office when you return home, and describe your experience. Include details about your exchanges with crew members. Enclose a copy of your travel documents and copies of the photographs you took.

Decide what to ask for:

- If you were completely unable to take advantage of the ship's facilities, you may want all of your money back.
- If you were able to use some of the ship's facilities, you might consider asking for the difference in value between what you were promised and what you received.

Determining this amount can be tricky, but it's best to err on the side of asking for a larger refund than a smaller one; the cruise line is almost certainly going to offer less than you request. In fact, while some cruise lines may refund some or all of your fare, it's more likely that you will be offered free or reduced-cost passage on another cruise.

### SEEK OUTSIDE HELP

If you're not satisfied with the cruise line's response, consider contacting a national travel magazine that offers troubleshooter services. This can be a very effective tactic, because cruise lines prefer to avoid negative publicity, especially about matters as sensitive as their treatment of disabled passengers.

The magazine's staff, or the threat of an upcoming article showing the line in an unflattering light, may convince the cruise line to increase the compensation it is offering you.

You may also want to file a complaint against the cruise line for violating the ADA. Contact the federal Department of Transportation (DOT) or the Department of Justice. The DOT doesn't intervene in individual cases, but uses these complaints as guidelines when they recommend changes in federal legislation and regulations.

### YOUR LAST RESORT

If the cruise line's offer is unacceptable, you may be able to mediate. Mediation is usually less expensive and faster than a lawsuit.

The cruise line may not agree to mediation, in which case a lawsuit may be your last, best option. A lawsuit will be based on breach of contract: the cruise line promised you something, then failed to provide it. You can use small-claims court if the damages you seek are less than the court's jurisdictional limits. (Some claims against cruise lines are subject to maritime law—but that means bringing suit in an admiralty court!)

Contact a lawyer experienced in transportation law to help you decide what claims to bring against the cruise line and where to bring them.

> **Y**ou get a telephone call offering
> a free Caribbean cruise, but the caller asks for your
> credit-card number to confirm your identity.

**T**his is one of the most common of travel scams, designed solely to separate you from your money. An offer like this is almost guaranteed to be phony. Cruise lines don't ordinarily give away trips, and if they did, they wouldn't require your credit-card number.

### HANG UP

In this case, fighting back and winning is as easy as hanging up the telephone. Never give a credit-card number or any other personal information, including social security number or PIN (personal identification number) for your ATM card, to someone who calls you. Identity thieves can use this information to obtain credit in your name, and in some cases they can even access your bank accounts.

After hanging up the phone, use your telephone's last-call-return feature. By dialing *69, you'll usually hear the number from which the call was placed. Some callers can block their number from being traced with this feature, but it's very unlikely that any legitimate company would do so. If you get the number, write it down and notify the consumer protection office of your state attorney general's office. It may have reports from other consumers who received similar offers. The attorney general may be able to locate the whereabouts of such callers and bring criminal charges against them and their employers.

*You book a cruise with a stop at St. Thomas so you can see your relatives there. But after you depart, the captain announces that another port is being substituted.*

Cruise lines give themselves wide latitude in making changes to the scheduled itinerary. This is because weather conditions at sea can change quickly, and ships' captains must have the ability to avoid storms that could damage the ship and injure passengers and crew. Your ticket and contract with the cruise line probably limits its liability if a port of call is substituted for another or even skipped entirely.

## ASK FOR A REFUND

Find out what the captain's reasons are for making the change. Keep in mind that while the cruise line can attempt to limit its liability, it may not be able to do so in all cases. For example, while an imminent hurricane warning may permit the captain to divert from a scheduled port of call, simply deciding that there aren't enough passengers interested in that port's shore excursions won't let the cruise line off the hook.

Read the terms and conditions of the cruise—they're part of your ticket packet. They will probably include a provision that allows the cruise line to make destination changes even after the ship has departed from its home port.

Even if the change is one that's permitted by law and your contract with the cruise line, you may still be entitled to some compensation if the change significantly lessened the value of the trip. Ask the ship's purser for a refund of some of your cruise's cost, perhaps in the form of shipboard credits to use in the health club, beauty salon, or casino. Explain why the stop was important to you, and you may receive a sympathetic response. Cruise lines spend millions of dollars on advertising, and they know that a dissatisfied customer will tell friends and family about problems he or she encountered. Be pleasant but persistent.

## FOLLOW UP IN WRITING

If you can't get financial credit or other compensation for the missed port of call while on board, write to the cruise line's president when you get home. (Cruise personnel can give you the name and address.) In your letter…

● Describe the problem and the steps you took on board to obtain compensation for the itinerary change. Include the names and titles of ship personnel you spoke to and how they responded to your request.
● Explain why the change in ports diminished the value of your cruise.
● State the response you expect, such as a partial refund or credit toward a cruise in the future. Be realistic; missing one day in port on a 10-day cruise is no reason to expect a full refund of your fare, because you had the benefit of the other ports and the ship's facilities for the other days of your trip.
● Ask for a response by a certain date, such as within 30 days. Be sure to keep a copy of this letter for your files.

If you don't get a response to your first letter, consider sending a second, more strongly worded one. Remind the president of your earlier letter, and enclose a copy of it. Politely demand that the cruise line provide you with the compensation you requested in your first letter.

Sending a copy of your letter to the consumer advocate at a national travel magazine or to the travel editor of your local newspaper may also spur the cruise line to action, since bad publicity is something most cruise lines want to avoid.

## YOUR LAST RESORT

It's possible, but difficult, to bring a lawsuit against a cruise line. Most cruise-line tickets include a provision requiring that any lawsuit brought against the company be filed in a specific court, which may be located some distance from your home. Although in a few cases this choice of forum provision has been successfully challenged, in most cases the courts have required consumers to bring their suits in the court that is chosen by the cruise line.

Try to evaluate the potential for being awarded damages (as well as how much compensation you might win) in light of the time, energy, and money that bringing such a lawsuit will involve.

*You book your dream vacation, only to discover that the tour company you used has gone out of business.*

Using a tour operator to plan your vacation can make travel arrangements a snap. But if the operator goes out of business after you've paid for your trip but before you take it, it can cause heartache and financial troubles.

## GETTING YOUR MONEY BACK

The steps you can take to get a refund depend on the answers to several questions:

■ **Did you pay by credit card?** If so, you may be able to get a charge-back, which means that any payment you made will be credited to your account. First call, then write, the card provider and request a charge-back; most credit-card companies allow charge-backs within 60 days of the date of the purchase. (Check with your card provider for specific details about this policy.) You'll find the address to write to, along with the information to include in it, on your card statement or by calling the card's toll-free number.

■ **Was the tour company a member of a trade association that provides a consumer protection plan?** If it was, contact the association for information about filing a claim. The two largest trade organizations for tour operators are the U.S. Tour Operators Association (USTOA) and the National Tour Organization (NTO). These organizations offer consumer protection programs designed to help repay consumers when an operator goes out of business or otherwise fails to provide you with promised services.

■ **Did the tour company put deposits in an escrow account?** If it did, money paid to the tour operator may be isolated from creditors' claims. Contact the financial institution where the account is located and file a claim for the return of your money. (If you don't know the answer to this question, the trade organization that the company belonged to can tell you how to reach it.)

■ **Did the tour company have a performance bond?** A bond serves to protect consumers in the event that the company goes bankrupt. If you don't know, contact your state attorney general's office for assistance.

## YOUR LAST RESORT

If the answer to each of these questions is no, your last resort is to file a claim in bankruptcy court. You will be provided with notice from the bankruptcy court and a claim form to fill out and return to the court. Be forewarned that, because bankruptcy courts are backed up and cases are complex, getting your money can take months or even years. In the end, you may get back little or nothing because there's probably a long line of creditors ahead of you. Still, filing a claim in bankruptcy court requires nothing beyond completing the form, so it's worth the initial effort.

**TRAVEL ALERT** *Don't select a tour company if it won't take credit cards for payment. Fly-by-night tour operators who accept only checks or cash for payment may close their doors without providing any services. You could be left with no hope of getting your money back.*

*On a bus trip to your granddaughter's wedding, the driver falls asleep at the wheel and crashes the bus. Because of the accident, you miss the ceremony.*

Not only are you cramped from the long ride and shaken up by the bus accident, but you are also angry because you have missed an important family celebration.

Interstate bus companies are legally required to use extreme care in transporting their passengers. Like airlines, they often have Contracts of Carriage (page 181), which they use to limit their liability when something goes wrong. In this particular case, the bus company clearly breached the contract that your ticket represents.

### SEEK COMPENSATION

If you were not injured in the accident, the bus company should at the least refund your fare and arrange alternative transportation for you. If you are injured, the bus company is also responsible for your medical expenses and pain and suffering.

Even if you have no obvious injuries, an insurance claims adjuster for the bus company will probably contact you. This is because some injuries don't become apparent until days or even weeks after an accident takes place.

In addition, you may be able to seek compensation from the bus company for the emotional suffering that you experienced as a result of missing your granddaughter's wedding. Not all courts allow passengers to collect for this kind of claim, though, because it's difficult to set a monetary value on emotional suffering.

Don't let the insurance adjuster pressure you into agreeing to a settlement of your claim until you've had the bus company's offer reviewed by a lawyer. Many lawyers provide a free initial consultation for cases of this kind. Check with your local bar association for a referral.

## PLANNING A TRIP BEYOND U.S. BORDERS

For a driving trip north or south of the United States border, you'll need more documentation for your car than you normally stash in your glove compartment.

■ **If you are headed to Canada,** your own automobile insurance is probably valid as long as you have liability coverage in excess of $200,000 Canadian (about $150,000 U.S.). Be sure to have proof of car ownership or rental papers available for inspection at the border.

■ **If you're driving to Mexico,** there are additional requirements. Most U.S. insurance policies exclude coverage in that country, so you'll need to buy special insurance from an agency at the border crossing. (AAA members can obtain this insurance at their local AAA office.)

■ **If you're taking your car more than a few miles into Mexico,** you will also need to make a refundable credit-card deposit. This is to deter visitors from driving cars into the country and selling them. The amount of the deposit depends on the type and year of your car, but it can be as much as $800. Bring your original registration papers along with a photocopy of them, and don't forget to get the deposit returned when you return to the United States.

■ **If you're driving a company car or one that belongs to a friend,** you will also need a notarized statement from the owner authorizing you to drive the vehicle. Most rental car companies in cities near U.S. borders prohibit renters from taking cars into Canada or Mexico. Check the terms of your agreement before attempting to cross the border.

■ **Whether you're driving to Canada or Mexico,** don't forget to take along your driver's license and your passport or a certified copy of your birth certificate. If you're staying in Mexico for more than three days, you will also need to get a Mexico Tourist Card, which is available at border crossings at no charge.

If you're planning a trip out of the United States, it's important to know that most health insurance policies won't cover treatment for illnesses or injuries you suffer while abroad. Before leaving on your vacation or business trip, do the following:

■ **Check the terms of your policy** to see if it includes coverage for treatment or hospitalization while you are out of the country.

● If it doesn't, contact your insurance agent to see if the company can provide an endorsement, or rider, to provide coverage while you are abroad.

● If it won't, contact your travel agent about purchasing a travel insurance policy that includes coverage for medical treatment for accidents and illnesses. Many of these travel insurance policies provide only limited coverage, and some require that you actually be hospitalized before paying benefits. Compare the benefits and costs of several policies before making your choice.

■ **Consider purchasing medical evacuation insurance** if you're traveling to a part of the world where medical care is scarce. These policies will cover the cost of transportation to adequate medical facilities, and may even pay for the cost of bringing you back to the United States. Again, coverage and costs vary; review policies from several companies before choosing one.

*You've signed a contract to buy a beauty of a classic car, but when you try to pay, the owner says she has changed her mind.*

There's still a chance you can park a classic in your garage. In most cases, the law doesn't require a seller who changes her mind about a contract to follow through on her promise. Instead, it allows an injured party...

- To sue for damages
- To ask the court to order *specific performance,* a rare judgment that requires the seller to complete the deal when the subject of the contract is so special or unique that there's no adequate way to compensate for the injury.

## APPLY SOME PRESSURE

Before going to court, you can put some pressure on the owner. Here's what to do:

■ **Write to the car's owner** and remind her of her obligation to live up to the contract. Give her a deadline by which you expect her to deliver the car and accept your payment. Send this letter by certified mail, return receipt requested. Keep your contract and correspondence on file as proof of your efforts.

■ **Hire a lawyer and get him to write a letter** to the seller if you fail to convince her to honor your contract. Because classic cars are usually expensive, your dispute may not fall within the dollar limits of small-claims court. Your lawyer can, however, send another letter to the seller. If you are fortunate, a lawyer's letter showing that you are serious about your claim may be enough to convince the seller to complete the sale.

## YOUR LAST RESORT

Should the seller refuse to budge, you will probably have to file a lawsuit to get her to part with the car. Before you sue, however, be aware that the court won't order a specific performance without good cause. You must show that there is no other reasonable substitute for this particular car. You may need to provide the testimony of automotive experts or other car collectors to support your claim. If the court finds that money damages won't be enough to correct the seller's wrong, it will order that the car be delivered to you in return for the agreed-on price.

## PICKING UP YOUR NEW CAR

Whether it's brand new or preowned, an automobile is a major purchase, and it's up to you to see that every *i* is dotted and *t* crossed before you take possession.

■ **Never take a car off the dealer's lot until all the paperwork on the sale is completed and signed** by you and the dealership's *authorized* representative. Read contracts and loan agreements carefully and double-check the figures. Then be sure that you have copies of everything that you and the dealer signed, and keep your copies in a safe place.

■ **Be persistent if the dealer's authorized person is unavailable or refuses to cooperate.** Ask for the return of any checks you have written to the dealership as well as the keys to any vehicle you are trading in as part of the deal. If the dealer claims that he "can't find" your deposit check, tell him to call you as soon as it turns up, then get up to leave. Being willing to walk away often encourages the dealer to then take another look and (surprise!) find your deposit check. If the check isn't produced, immediately call your bank to stop payment on it.

> **Y**ou took the salesman's word and drove your
> new car home before the manager signed your sales contract.
> Now you find that the terms of the deal have changed.

**O**f course you're anxious to get on the road in your brand-new car, but driving your car off the dealer's lot before all the paperwork has been completed and signed is an invitation to trouble. The door is open for a less-than-honest dealer to suddenly discover that...

- Your down payment isn't big enough.
- The value of your trade-in is less than you previously agreed to.
- The sales manager can no longer approve the sales price.
- The loan company can't provide financing at the rate you were promised.

There's a reason dealerships sometimes engage in this tactic: They hope you will be delighted with your new vehicle and will readily agree to last-minute changes in your deal—even paying a little more to keep your car.

If you disagree with the dealer's revised terms, the obvious solution is to return the car. But this can still be costly. If you return a vehicle you don't own, be prepared to pay a "rental fee" for the time the car was in your possession. Your purchase agreement probably includes a provision stating that if the deal falls through, you must pay the dealership a daily fee plus a mileage fee for the time you had the car. These charges can be as much as $100 per day plus 25 cents per mile. Suppose you take the car home on Friday and drive it 200 miles; then on Monday, the dealer calls to tell you that the deal didn't go through. Your weekend of driving could end up costing you as much as $350.

## COMPLAINTS, COMPLAINTS

If you find yourself in this position, here's what you can do:

- **Call the automobile-dealer licensing authority**—the author-

ity is empowered to investigate consumer complaints and to suspend or revoke the license of a dealer with a history of shady practices—and complain. (Every state has one; you'll find the phone number listed in the state government section of your telephone directory.) When you call, be specific about your experience.

- **File a report with the Better Business Bureau** to warn other consumers about the problems you encountered.

- **Write to the president of the car company** and describe your experience with the dealer. Automobile manufacturers want to protect their reputations. If a manufacturer receives a significant number of customer complaints, it can take action and even cancel the franchise of a dealership that consistently engages in unethical behavior. Your complaint alone probably won't cause the dealer to lose his franchise, but chances are you are not the only customer who has been mistreated.

## TOP FIVE TIPS FOR SAVING MONEY WHEN YOU BUY A CAR

■ **Have a price firmly in mind** *before* you begin talking to a salesperson. You can obtain good information about vehicle prices, rebates, and dealer hold backs (a manufacturer's credit that cuts the dealer's cost) from *Consumer Reports* magazine, the American Automobile Association, and Edmunds Publishing. Edmunds publishes a number of automobile price guides and offers regularly updated information at its Internet Web site: www.edmunds.com.

■ **Avoid answering questions such as "What kind of monthly payment are you looking for?"** when you talk with salespeople. Your answer may be a tip-off to a savvy salesperson that you might be talked into leasing, because it's the monthly payment that seems most important to you. Focus on the selling price of the car.

■ **Get financing information from your bank or credit union before you begin shopping,** and don't talk about dealer financing until you have settled on a price. Then you can compare the dealer's lending rates and terms with those of your own financial institution.

■ **Don't discuss a trade-in or give the salesperson the keys to your present car** until you have agreed on a price for a new one. Hanging on to your car keys is a method some dealers use to keep you at the dealership and wear down your resistance.

■ **Get up and walk out if you feel pressured** or if you can't get the dealer to make a reasonable offer. The salesperson may just suddenly come up with the deal you want after all, especially if losing the sale means that she will miss her monthly quota. And if the sales staff can't make an acceptable offer, there are other dealers who do want to do business with you. Shopping around is always a good idea.

**Y**our new vehicle has been on order from the factory for six months. The dealership can't give you a delivery date and refuses to refund your deposit.

**Y**ou are willing to wait a few weeks for your new car to arrive, but how long is too long to go on waiting? Your purchase order should specify a delivery date. The manufacturer's failure to deliver the car by this date is a breach of your sales contract.

If the breach of contract is serious, *you have the right to cancel the contract.* While missing the delivery date by a week may not be enough to convince a court to let you out of your sales agreement entirely, a dealer's failure to make the delivery for several months probably will allow you to void the sales contract and have your deposit returned to you by the dealership.

### DON'T WAIT; ACT

Your goal is to have your new car as quickly as possible. When a reasonable waiting period has passed and your car is still not available, you may want to cancel your contract. The first step is to get in touch with the dealership's sales manager and tell her that you want to cancel your order because the delivery date has passed. If your deposit isn't refunded, go higher up. Ask to speak to the owner or president of the dealership, explain the situation, and tell the owner that you want to cancel the contract. You should have a copy of your agreement in hand so that you can point out the missed delivery date.

*It's a good idea to record the dates and content of all your conversations with the dealership in case problems arise later.*

- **Put things in writing** if the dealer refuses to honor your requests. Compose a demand letter, insisting that the contract be voided and your money returned. (Make your demands specific, but keep the tone of your letter calm and businesslike.) Send your demand letter to the dealership by certified mail, return receipt requested, and begin a file of all contracts, correspondence, and receipts.
- **Call the Better Business Bureau** in your area. The bureau can mediate disputes between its member companies and their dissatisfied consumers. It may be able to take action on your behalf.
- **Contact your state or local consumer protection agency** as well. Consumer protection officials may be able to intercede in the matter and persuade the dealership to cancel your order and return your deposit money.
- **Send a copy of your demand letter to the automobile-dealer licensing authority** in your state (page 193), and be sure to include a copy of your car contract and copies of any other correspondence that you have had with the automobile dealership.

If you still don't get a satisfactory response, it may be time to talk to a lawyer. Explain your problem and ask the lawyer to write a letter to the dealership on your behalf. His letter may have the impact on the dealer that you want.

## YOUR LAST RESORT

If all of your other efforts have failed, you may have to file a lawsuit against the dealership to recover your deposit and cancel the deal. If the amount is relatively small, you can—depending on the legal system in your state—bring your suit to small-claims court. But if the deposit is large, your claim could fall outside the small-claims court's jurisdiction.

You will probably need a lawyer's help to pursue your case in your state trial-court system. The dealership will have legal representation; having a lawyer on your side helps level the playing field. Remember that filing suit doesn't necessarily mean your case will end up going to trial. It's possible that the dealership will be persuaded to settle once it is clear that you are willing to take the matter to court and fight for your rights.

*Your brand-new car spends more time in the dealer's service department than in your garage, and the problems just won't go away.*

You expect a new car to run sweetly, but you can sometimes get a sour deal. Fortunately, laws in every state protect consumers who purchase cars with serious defects that can't be fixed or that reoccur. These "lemon laws" vary from state to state, but generally they give a new-car buyer the possibility of obtaining a refund or a replacement vehicle if...

- The car has been in the shop for the same repair four or more times in a specified period (12 months in some states, 18 in others).
- The car has been out of service for 30 days or more during a specified period (again, it's usually for 12 or 18 months).

To take advantage of lemon laws, however, you must give the manufacturer reasonable opportunity to fix the car. And typically you will have to take several other steps before you can seek legal protection.

**TAKE NOTE** *You need to document each visit for repairs in order to show that you've reached the number of repairs required to be covered under lemon-law protection.*

## STEPS TO FIX A LEMON

Once you realize that your car has a recurring problem or when the repair time begins to mount up, you will then be ready to take action:

- **Write to the service department manager at the dealership** where you had your car repaired. Clearly explain the problem you've experienced (the engine continues to overheat despite your repair attempts, for example). Include copies of all warranty service orders you've received from the dealership.
- **Get a new work order** every time you take your car in for service, and keep your copies. Don't let the service manager convince you that the problem is on a previous order so you don't need a new one.
- **Save all receipts for any outside work** done if your car breaks down while you're away from home and you have it repaired by someone other than your dealer.

- **Contact the manufacturer's area representative** if the dealership can't fix the problem. You can get the representative's address and telephone number from the dealer, or it may be in your owner's manual. After you talk to the representative, be sure to follow up with a letter and include copies of your correspondence, work orders, and a log of your conversations with service department personnel.
- **Contact the manufacturer's home office** if the area representative can't get the problem solved. The procedure for this is described in your owner's manual. The manufacturer may want you to submit to arbitration, but be aware that some automobile-makers arbitration programs restrict your right to appeal a decision that goes against you. Carefully check the terms of your warranty and the arbitration agreement to be sure you aren't limiting your right to proceed with an appeal.

### INVOKING THE LEMON LAW

While the exact procedures for using lemon laws vary from state to state, generally you must follow these steps:

- Send the manufacturer another letter (by certified mail, return receipt requested) telling the company that you are invoking the state's lemon laws and requesting a refund or a replacement vehicle.
- Give the manufacturer one last chance to fix the car you bought.
- Submit your claim to a free, state-run arbitration program if such a program is available, or
- File a lawsuit in state court.

If you win your suit, you can expect to receive a refund of the price you paid for the car (minus a deduction for your use of the vehicle) as well as a refund of taxes, finance charges you paid to obtain your car loan, and the license and registration fees for the car. You may also be able to choose between a refund or a new vehicle from the manufacturer.

*The dealer swore that your used car was in excellent condition. Six months and thousands of dollars in repair bills later, you learn that the car had been in a major collision.*

**B**uying a car "as is" doesn't mean you can be duped into buying a damaged car. In most states, a licensed dealer must disclose in writing if a car was seriously damaged in an accident, was swamped by a flood, salvaged, or rebuilt. Failing to disclose these problems can have serious consequences, and the deceptive dealer can be prosecuted for fraud.

## WHEN THERE'S A PROBLEM

When you discover a major, undisclosed problem with a used car, get your mechanic to provide a written report on the car's condition, including an explanation of how he determined that the car was previously damaged. Take this report, along with the car and repair bills, to the dealer. Insist that you be allowed to return the car and have your purchase price and the repair costs refunded.

- **If the dealer won't agree,** you should immediately get in touch with your local district attorney or the state attorney general's consumer protection division. You will also want to contact your state's automobile-dealer licensing authority. Provide the division and licensing authority with…

✔ A copy of your contract
✔ A copy of the title to the car (if you have it)
✔ A copy of the report from your mechanic.

It's important that you assist government agencies as they investigate your problem. You may need to make your car available to them for an additional inspection, and you may be asked to file affidavits or to testify against the dealer in court.

- **If your claim is found to be valid,** the dealer can be required to refund your money and can also face civil penalties. It's possible that criminal charges may be filed against the dealership and any employees who participated in the fraud. If convicted, the employees could get jail time, although it's more likely that a fine, probation, and the forfeiture of the salesperson's business license will be the outcome.

### SMART MOVES

Always have a used car inspected by a qualified, independent mechanic. Get a written report on its condition and an estimate of the costs of needed repairs. If the dealer won't let you have the car inspected, take your business elsewhere.

> ## Leasing your car seemed to be a good idea. Now you hear that dealers charge for "excess wear and tear" at the end of the lease.

When you lease, you rent a new car for two or three years, then return it to the dealer. Up-front costs are generally lower than a down payment, and monthly payments can be lower, too. This arrangement is enticing, but it is by no means problem-free.

● Lease agreements usually give the leasing company the right to charge customers for "excess wear and tear" on the car at the end of the contract. Unfortunately, what seems like normal wear and tear to you may be "excessive" in the eyes of the dealer. In some cases, an unethical dealer may decide that the original deal was not as profitable as he thought, so he tries to make up a little of his "losses" at the end of the lease.

---

## Unfortunately, what seems like normal wear and tear to you may be "excessive" in the eyes of the dealer.

---

● Most leases limit the number of miles you are permitted to drive the car. A few years ago, the average allowance for a leased car was 15,000 miles per year; today it's more likely to be 12,000 miles. If you exceed the mileage allowance in your contract, you will face a charge for each additional mile you drive, sometimes adding up to as much as 25 cents per mile. Should you drive just 4,000 extra miles over the course of a three-year lease, you may find yourself paying an additional $1,000 to the company when you return the car. (Some lessors will now offer you the option of purchasing extra mileage up front when you take out the lease.)

### BEFORE YOU RETURN THE CAR

When your lease term is nearing its end, take the car to a mechanic you trust; ask for a top-to-bottom inspection, and keep the report on file.

■ **If problems are found with the car,** ask the mechanic if he thinks the problems are normally associated with the age of the car and the miles it has been driven.

■ **If the mechanic says that there is excess wear to any item,** get a written estimate for having that item replaced or repaired. You may choose to have the problem fixed before returning the car, or you may decide to return the car in its current condition.

■ **If you decide to return the car without repairs,** the written estimate you get will give you a dollar amount to compare with any repair claim made by the leasing company.

**TAKE NOTE** *Even if your mechanic determines that there is no excess wear or tear to the car, you should get a written statement of his opinion. This will give you ammunition in dealing with the lessor, should you need it.*

On the day you return the car to the dealer, take photographs or make a videotape of the car inside and out so that you'll have visual proof that there was no excess wear and tear to the car's exterior or interior when you turned it in.

### WHEN YOU RETURN THE CAR

Don't wait until the last minute to drop the car off at the dealership and go on your way. It's a good idea to return a leased car a few weeks before the end of the lease term. Take a copy of your mechanic's report when you go and...

■ **Ask that the dealer have a qualified employee inspect the car** and note any evidence of excess wear and tear *before you leave the lot.* Have the employee put the car up on a lift to inspect its brakes and undercarriage.

■ **If your request is refused, get a written statement that waives any claims of excess wear and tear** from the dealer's leasing manager or someone with the authority to bind the dealership. Get the agent to authorize the return of any refundable security deposit.

You may not get the dealership to give you a waiver statement, but it never hurts to ask, and a dealership that wants your future business will usually make an effort to accommodate you.

## In Excess

If the dealer says that the car shows excess wear and tear...

- Ask the dealer to provide you with a written list of the items in question and the estimated cost of repairs done by the dealership.
- Compare the dealer's list with that provided by your mechanic.

If the dealer has listed items that your mechanic said were in normal condition, point these items out to the dealer. If the dealer and your mechanic agree about an item and you decided not to fix it before returning the car, check the dealer's price against your mechanic's estimate. If the prices are similar, you may want to have the dealer do the repairs. But if the dealer's price is significantly

*It's a good idea to return a leased car a few weeks before the actual end of the lease term.*

higher than your mechanic's, offer to have the repairs made and return the car to the dealer before the lease term expires. (You can't do this unless you return the car early.) The dealer may simply decide to take your mechanic's estimate and reduce the amount of money charged for repairs.

## Final Steps

When you have turned the car in at the end of the lease, get the dealer or leasing company to provide you with a written release stating that the car was returned and accepted and that you have no further liability for any charges associated with the lease. Make sure this document is signed by the leasing company's manager or owner so that

there won't be any opportunity for the company to claim that the release was given by someone not authorized to provide it.

The dealer or leasing company is obligated to refund any security deposit to you within 30 days of your having returned the vehicle. If you don't receive your money, you should write a letter to the dealership reminding it of this obligation. Clearly indicate that the payment must be made to you within 10 business days. Enclose a copy of the dealer's release, and send your letter by certified mail, return receipt requested.

- **If the security deposit isn't forthcoming,** contact your state automobile-dealer licensing board and the consumer protection division of the state attorney general's office (listed in the government pages of the phone book). They may get the dealer to return your deposit.
- **If all else fails,** consider filing a lawsuit against the dealer in small-claims court to recover your security deposit.

**Consumer Alert** *Most leases require that you return the car with matching tires. If you've replaced a tire or two, the dealer will usually insist on charging you full price for an expensive matched set. In this case, buy a set at a discount store before returning the car.*

## SHOULD YOU BUY OR LEASE YOUR NEW CAR?

The answer depends on your financial situation, but experts tend to agree that most consumers are better off buying than leasing a vehicle. Although the payments you make to buy the car are typically somewhat higher than lease payments, keep in mind that at the end of your car loan, you will own a vehicle that's probably still worth several thousand dollars or more. At the end of a lease, however, you will give the car back and have nothing to show for it. In addition, lemon laws that protect you when you buy a car don't always apply when you lease one. Only about half the states extend their lemon laws to leased vehicles.

So when does it make sense to lease instead of buy? A lease could be a good deal if:

■ **You work in a business such as real estate that requires you to transport clients.** A lease may allow you to drive a more impressive car than you could afford to buy.

■ **The lease period is *shorter* than the manufacturer's warranty on the car.** But be wary if the warranty runs out before the lease. Making a major repair to a car you're about to return to the leasing company can be a pocketbook-draining (and stomach-churning) experience.

■ **You are leasing primarily for business use and can take advantage of the tax deduction** allowed by the IRS. Don't rely on a salesperson's assurances that your leasing cost will be tax deductible. Consult with your tax adviser or the IRS about your specific situation before you sign the lease agreement in this instance.

**Y**ou sold your old car to a neighbor, who made a down payment and promised the balance a week later. She wrecked the car, and now she won't pay.

**F**inancing a used car for a private buyer generally isn't a good idea. Even if you're selling to a friend, it's best to get paid in full before turning the car over. Though the situation described here seems like a disaster, it's still possible to fight back and get your money.

### GETTING YOUR DUE

The fact that the car is wrecked has no bearing on the buyer's obligation to pay you for it. Since the buyer is a neighbor, taking an informal approach is probably the best first step. Give her a call and point out that you expect her to pay the balance due on the car that she bought.

If your neighbor still refuses to make the final payment on the car she bought from you, your next step is to send her a demand letter (page 195). Your letter should include...

● The date of your original agreement
● The amount she still owes for the car
● The remedy you want (immediate payment of the entire amount she owes).

Send the letter by certified mail, return receipt requested. Give your neighbor a reasonable time to respond. (Ten business days is usually enough.) If she still refuses to pay, you must decide if you want to take the matter to court. Depending on the amount you're owed, small-claims court may be your best bet. Call the clerk at the courthouse to find out the maximum amount your small claims-court would handle.

### YOU HAVE TO COLLECT YOUR MONEY

Once you've won your case, it's then up to you to collect your money. Ask the clerk of the court for the forms you need to enforce the court's award. Generally, you have three sources you can look to in order to get paid. You can seek payment from the buyer's employer, who will withhold the money from her pay; obtain your judgment out of her bank accounts; or file your judgment as a lien against her personal property.

The local law enforcement authorities will deliver *writs* (court orders) on your behalf. You must pay for delivery, but the law lets you ask to be reimbursed by the buyer for the added expense. The clerk of small-claims court can send you the form you need for this request.

### PROTECT YOURSELF IN THE FUTURE

When you sell a car, create a bill of sale. Under a law known as the *Statute of Frauds,* any sale in which the buyer will pay more than $500 must be documented in writing in order for the court to enforce the agreement. You can get blank bills of sale at most office-supply stores. One copy should go to the buyer; keep another for your files. The bill of sale should show...

✔ The names, addresses, and telephone numbers of both buyer and seller
✔ The date of the sale
✔ The year, make, and model of the car
✔ The car's VIN, or Vehicle Identification Number (you'll usually find it stamped on a metal plate on the car's dashboard)
✔ The car's odometer reading
✔ The amount of money paid for the car and the method of payment.

You must also put your loan agreement in writing. The agreement should set out...

✔ The amount of the loan
✔ The interest being charged
✔ The payment schedule
✔ The borrower's promise to repay the loan.

---

## You missed a few payments on your car loan. This morning, the repossession company towed the car away.

Waking up to find your driveway empty is not a good way to start the day. When you bought your car on credit, you gave the lender what's known as a *security agreement* for the vehicle you financed. This means the car is collateral for the loan. If you *default,* or fail to make payments, the lender has the right to repossess the car and sell it to another buyer in order to recover dealer losses. On the theory that telling someone his vehicle is about to be repossessed could encourage him to hide the car, in most states the lender can take your car without providing you with advance notice.

### THE RIGHT OF REDEMPTION

Before the lender can sell your car to another buyer, it must give you the *right of redemption.* Some auto-financing contracts allow you to redeem the car by bringing your payments up to date and by reimbursing the lender for repossession costs, storage fees, and other reasonable expenses. More commonly, loan contracts contain what's known as an *acceleration clause:* This clause requires you to pay the entire amount owed (not just back payments), plus the lender's repossession expenses before you can get your car back.

### WHEN YOUR CAR IS REPOSSESSED

Contact the lender immediately after you discover that the car has been towed to see if you can have it returned. Even if your loan documents contain an acceleration clause, you may be able to convince the lender to modify the original agreement in your favor.

■ **If the lender agrees,** be prepared to pay the back payments and the reasonable costs of repossession in cash or with a certified check.
■ **If other lenders refuse to help you with a loan to get caught up** on your car payments, consider asking for a personal loan from your friends or your family members.

## How the Law Protects Used-Car Buyers

Look for protection from the Federal Trade Commission's Used Car Rule, the federal Odometer Anti-Tampering Law, and state laws on unfair and deceptive business practices.

### The Used-Car Rule

Anyone who sells more than six used cars in any 12-month period is a dealer and is required to post a "Buyers Guide" on the side window of cars for sale. This Buyers Guide must state:

● That the buyer is entitled to get all the seller's promises in writing

● Whether the car is covered by a warranty and, if so, how long it is for and the systems it covers as well as whether the buyer will be expected to bear any costs for parts or labor

● Whether the car is being sold "as is" with no written or implied warranties

● That the buyer should remember to ask the seller to allow an independent mechanic to inspect the car before purchase

● A list of major defects that can occur in used cars generally

● The name, address, and telephone number of the dealer and the name of the company person to contact with complaints

● Information provided on the Buyers Guide becomes a part of your sales agreement and takes precedence in case of contradictions between the guide and a term of the contract; dealers who fail to provide a Buyers Guide can be charged with violating federal law.

### The Odometer Anti-Tampering Law

This law requires anyone selling a used car, including a private party, to provide the buyer with a signed odometer statement on request. This statement must disclose…

● The odometer reading at the time of the sale

● Whether the reading is accurate or is inaccurate (because the odometer was replaced or because the mileage exceeds the maximum that the odometer will show), or

● If the seller cannot say whether or not the mileage is accurate.

Refusing to provide an odometer statement or making a false statement is a violation of federal law. You may be able to detect a false reading if the numbers are misaligned, the cable has been tampered with, or if the vehicle wear is excessive when compared to the reading. Violators are subject to fine or imprisonment, or both.

### Unfair and Deceptive Practices

Every state has laws prohibiting business practices that are immoral, unethical, or corrupt or that substantially injure consumers. In plain English, such practices would include:

● Failing to disclose dangerous defects

● Failing to tell a buyer that the vehicle had been advertised at a lower price

● Failing to disclose that the vehicle has received unusual use (as a taxi or delivery vehicle)

● Failing to tell the buyer that parts or service for the vehicle are not readily available

● Misrepresenting the car or its parts, such as saying the transmission is new when it is not.

If you have a claim under your state's unfair business practice laws, call a lawyer immediately. Time limits known as *statutes of limitation* apply to bringing claims under these laws. In some states, winning your case may entitle you to double or triple the amount of any actual damages you incurred and to receive reimbursement of court costs and attorney fees.

Ne fine day the mail carrier drops the usual avalanche of catalogs, your utility bill—and a speeding ticket. How can this happen? To deter speeding (and according to some critics, to increase local revenues at a relatively low cost), some cities now use cameras posted along roads to catch speeding drivers.

> *Y*ou have the right
> to contest a photo ticket,
> just as you do
> for any traffic ticket
> you receive.

Although the technology varies somewhat, generally the police park a car or van on a street. The vehicle is equipped with a radar-activated camera. Any car exceeding the speed limit is detected by the radar, which triggers the camera to photograph the vehicle and its license plate. When the picture is developed, the license plate number is matched with motor vehicle records. A ticket and a copy of the photograph are then mailed to the vehicle owner at the address listed in the records.

Take heart. You have the right to contest a photo ticket, just as you do for any traffic ticket you receive from an officer.

## DEFENSES YOU CAN USE

If you decide to fight a speeding ticket based on "photo radar," here are some defenses you can raise:

- **The vehicle identified in the photo isn't yours.** A dirty or obscured license plate could be mistakenly identified by law enforcement authorities.
- **The person driving your vehicle isn't you.** You are not liable for a speeding ticket just because your car was speeding. If you lent

your car to a friend or a family member, you should ask to have the ticket issued in your name dismissed.

- **The photo shows more than one vehicle.** If your car was traveling in a closely spaced group of vehicles, the radar may have picked up the speed of another car. If so, ask to have the ticket dismissed.
- **The ticket contains incorrect information.** For example, the ticket might show that you are being charged under a statute number that covers an offense other than speeding.
- **There was no warning sign telling you that photo radar was in use.** Some communities have laws requiring the police to post a warning sign some distance ahead of where the photo-radar vehicle is stationed. But be sure to check local statutes before trying this defense, and be sure there really wasn't any warning sign.

**TAKE NOTE** *Do your homework by researching the state motor-vehicle code. You can find the code included in the collected state statutes that are available at most public libraries, the county courthouse, and most law school libraries. Check*

*with a librarian or courthouse official to be sure you have the most current volume.*

## HOW TO FIGHT A TICKET

Whether your ticket comes to you through the mail or whether it is issued to you by a law-enforcement officer, you should...

- **Look at the ticket for the date by which you must either pay your fine** (which amounts to a guilty plea), appear in court, or request a court date. Don't miss this deadline or you will limit your ability to contest the ticket at a later time.
- **Decide if you want to fight the ticket.** You generally have a choice of pleading "not guilty" or "guilty with an explanation." Pleading not guilty is a right guaranteed by the U.S. Constitution, and you can plead not guilty even if you know you actually did the deed that you've been accused of doing. Pleading guilty with an explanation may be worthwhile if you have a reasonable excuse for the violation. For example, if your speedometer was defective, you can explain this to the court and provide proof, such as a mechanic's statement that the speedometer of your car was miscalibrated and that it has since been repaired. The charge against you or the fine may be reduced.
- **File your plea, following the instructions on the ticket.** Depending on where you live, you may be able to do this...
  - In person by appearing in traffic court
  - By certified mail
  - By going to the local traffic-court clerk and requesting a trial date.

When requesting a trial date, you may be required to post bail—usually equal to the amount of the fine. The bail amount will be returned to you when (and if) you win your case.

Being on the receiving end of a ticket of any kind is no fun, but the good news here is that by being well prepared to defend yourself and being willing to assert your rights, you stand a good chance of winning your case.

Taking the time to understand the law and to make the law work for you could help you to keep your driving record clean.

---

*Your fender was crunched and your windshield cracked when a tree limb fell on your car. Your insurance company insists that you use one of its "preferred" shops for the repairs.*

---

The trouble is, that the "preferred" shop isn't known for doing high-quality work. Do you have to use the services of a preferred shop in order to collect on your auto insurance?

Under the terms of your insurance policy's collision and comprehensive coverage, you have the right to have your car restored to the condition it was in *before* it was damaged. The insurance company is required to reimburse the cost of all necessary repairs done, minus the amount of your insurance deductible.

But some insurers pressure their policyholders to use repair shops that have special relationships with the insurance company. Unfortunately, some of these shops may not use the best-quality replacement parts. They may cut corners on parts or labor. But because they will do the work for the price offered by the insurer, they tend to get a lot of business from the insurer's clients.

Using lower-quality replacement parts can...

- Diminish the resale value of your car.
- Cause future repair problems—most experts agree that parts made by a manufacturer other than the original one often don't fit the car as well. Poorly fitted parts can contribute to water leaks and affect the integrity of the car's structure. Studies have shown that these parts also rust more easily.
- Endanger you and your family—for example, a low-quality replacement bumper could collapse more quickly in a collision, contributing to or causing injuries that wouldn't have occurred with the original bumper.

## PROTECT YOUR INVESTMENT

Begin by checking the terms of your automobile insurance policy. Most policies will allow you to choose your own repair facility, but a few may limit your choice to those repair shops on the insurer's approved list.

If there is a restriction in your policy, take your car (if it can be driven) to several of the shops on your insurer's list. If your car is too badly damaged to drive, call the shops. Be sure to ask the following questions before any work is done:

● Will you use original-equipment manufacturer parts or after-market parts to make the repairs? Original-equipment manufacturer parts, also called OEM parts, are made by the company that built your vehicle. After-market parts may look the same, but they often fail to meet the OEM standards since they're usually made by companies without access to the manufacturer's specifications. After-market parts are generally cheaper, and many insurers encourage repair shops to use them in order to save money.

● Will you notify me and the insurer if additional accident-related repairs that aren't covered by the adjuster's evaluation are necessary? Some insurance companies have been found guilty of forcing repair shops to remain silent about hidden problems or else lose their lucrative stream of "preferred shop" business.

● Will you agree to put your promises in writing and give me a copy of the document? If the shop refuses to cooperate, look elsewhere.

You may be unable to find an auto-repair shop on the insurer's approved list that satisfies you. Contact the claims adjuster and explain your problem. If you aren't restricted by the terms of your policy to repair shops on the company's list (and very few policies will have this requirement), take your vehicle or have it towed to the repair facility of your choice.

## TAKING CARE OF ADDED PROBLEMS

There may be some damage from the accident that wasn't seen by the claims adjuster during his original inspection of your vehicle.

■ **When additional damage is found:** Get in touch with the claims adjuster and insist that someone from the insurance company contact the repair shop and authorize the needed repairs. An adjuster may need to visit the repair shop and conduct another inspection before the added costs are authorized.

■ **When the adjuster won't okay the added work:** Contact his supervisor. Then get the repair shop to prepare a written detailed statement describing all of the overlooked damage.

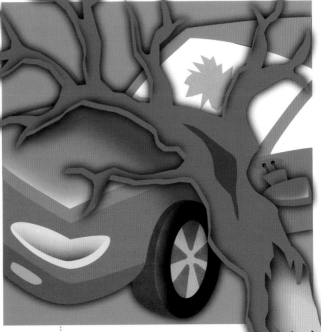

■ **When the added repairs are approved:** Get the repair shop's written assurances that it will use OEM parts, even when the insurance company approves the additional work. You also need to review the repair shop's written warranty on parts and labor before you authorize any work being done on your car.

The insurance company may still balk at paying for more repairs, or it may insist that you use less costly parts. If so, contact your state's Department of Insurance (listed under government agencies in the phone book). This agency can investigate the company's practices. If it finds your insurer has violated state law, it can order the company to change the way it handles claims.

You may also want to contact a private attorney. In recent years, a number of successful lawsuits have been brought against insurance companies for "steering" policyholders to repair shops that use inferior auto parts or fail to perform necessary work in order to save money on behalf of insurance companies. A number of class-action lawsuits brought on the behalf of thousands of policyholders have actually resulted in multimillion-dollar verdicts against some of the nation's biggest auto insurance companies.

## BEWARE OF "SETTLING ON THE SPOT"

You're driving down Main Street when a car suddenly backs out of a parking space and puts a deep crease in the door of your car. You and the other driver hop out to inspect the damage. Reaching for his checkbook, he offers to pay you $500…"if we can just keep this to ourselves."

Don't fall for this on-the-spot offer. It can be tempting to take the money and avoid all the hassles of police reports and insurance claims, but most states will require you to report accidents whenever…

- There are personal injuries

- Property damage exceeds a certain limit, such as $200

- Drugs or alcohol may be involved; if you suspect this or if the other driver appears intoxicated, call the local police immediately.

Unless you are an experienced mechanic, you probably can't evaluate the full damage on the spot. It may initially appear that the problem is only cosmetic. Later you could find out that the damage is more serious and the other driver's offer was not nearly enough to cover your repair costs. Getting him to pay the extra amount won't be easy, however, if you've taken his check.

Worse, the check you accept on the spot may not be good. If the check comes back marked "insufficient funds," you'll have to file suit to collect on it.

All in all, it's best to resist the temptation to "settle on the spot." Get the other driver's name, address, telephone number, and insurance information, and contact the police.

If you have collision insurance, your insurance policy may require you to notify your insurer of all accidents involving damage to your car. Should you fail to notify the insurance company, your insurer may try to deny any later claims from different accidents by saying the new damage was really caused by the previous unreported accident.

It's a sign of our computer-linked times. A growing number of rental-car companies now screen driving records in an effort to reduce their financial liability when a driver is involved in an accident. By entering your driver's license number into a special computer program, the

---

*If your driving record is spotty, check beforehand to see if the rental company screens driving records.*

---

car-rental agent can access your record with your state's Department of Motor Vehicles (DMV). The program doesn't link directly to the DMV but to a company that compiles driver's-license data from the states. Generally, rental-car companies that screen potential clients will refuse to rent a car to anyone who...

- Has been convicted of driving under the influence (DUI), driving while intoxicated (DWI), or driving while alcohol-impaired (DWAI) within the past three years. A few companies won't rent to you if you were convicted of any of the above in the past five years.
- Has three or more moving violations within the past two years.
- Has been the cause of an accident that resulted in injury or death within the past three or four years, or two or more noninjury accidents in the same period.
- Has had a driver's license suspended or revoked within the past five years.
- Has been convicted of driving without having the legally required insurance coverage.

## DO YOU HAVE OTHER OPTIONS?

If your driving record is spotty, check beforehand to see if the rental company screens driving records. Ask what criteria it uses to reject customers. You can always call other rental companies. Since not all companies do this kind of screening, you may find one that won't investigate your driving record before renting to you.

**TAKE NOTE** *Companies that don't screen driving records may ask you to sign a sworn statement that your driving record meets their criteria (no recent accidents or alcohol-related driving offenses). If you make a false statement and have an accident, the rental company could use your statement against you and seek reimbursement for any liability it incurs.*

## IF YOU'RE REJECTED UNJUSTLY

It's possible that you could be denied a rental car due to inaccurate records in the company's computer software or because you were involved in an accident that wasn't your fault. Get a copy

of your driving record from your state's DMV (for a small fee) and provide the information directly to the rental-car company. Then ask that your name be taken off its list of unacceptable drivers. You can get information about where to send your request by asking the rental-car company's office manager or by calling the parent company's toll-free number.

## LICENSE REQUIREMENTS FOR YOUNG AND OLD DRIVERS

Young drivers, especially those under 18, are likely to be involved in more auto accidents than more mature drivers. Beginning drivers lack the skills that come with experience and tend to exercise poorer judgment. As a result, nearly two-thirds of the states have changed their driver's licensing requirements for young people. Although the exact requirements differ somewhat, in most states the new laws set out a three-step process:

● A minimum supervised learning period beginning at age 16 (15 in some states) is required. The young driver's parents or legal guardian must certify that the new driver has received from 30 to 50 hours of supervised training over a six-month period.

● An intermediate period lasting until age 18 is required. The teen driver's nighttime driving is restricted, and a limit is set on the number of teen passengers allowed in the car.

● A full-privilege license is issued only after the teen driver has successfully completed the learning and intermediate periods.

Having an accident or more than one ticket may subject the young driver to additional training requirements. Many licensing laws aimed at beginning drivers also impose lower limits for a DUI (driving under the influence) conviction. Several states have enacted "zero-tolerance" laws for underage drivers: if any alcohol is detected in the young driver's blood, his license may be suspended, and a lengthy waiting period may be imposed before he can reapply for a license.

At the other end of the spectrum, drivers older than 65 also are involved in proportionally more accidents than motorists in their prime. Vision and health problems, along with slower reflexes, contribute to many of these accidents.

In a few states, the law prohibits the licensing authority from treating drivers differently solely on the basis of age. But a growing number of states are modifying their renewal procedures to help ensure that older drivers don't present a danger to themselves or others. In some states, renewal periods for 65+ drivers are shorter than for younger drivers, and eye tests may be required more often. When an older driver has a history of accidents or violations, the licensing agency may require physical or mental examinations, a physician's report, or a retake of the full driving test before renewing a license.

The licensing agency can also renew the older driver's license subject to conditions, such as:

● Restricting the time of day when the driver can operate her vehicle (for example, during daylight hours).

● Restricting where the driver can operate a vehicle (such as on city streets and for trips necessary to obtain medical care and treatment).

● Requiring additional mirrors to assist the driver in backing and turning.

Generally, the additional restrictions kick in at age 65, although in a few states these laws apply after the driver turns 70 or 75. Contact your state's driver's licensing authority for information about the specific age-related driving laws in your state.

> **Y**ou got a parking ticket even though the parking meter wouldn't take your money and you left a note on the meter indicating that it was broken.

**A**lthough parking meters today are more reliable than they were just a few years ago, they can still break down and can sometimes run fast so that you don't get all the time you paid for.

### FIGHTING THE TICKET

Knowing that every parking meter has a serial number is the key to your plan of attack when you fight back. Here's what to do:

- **Check the parking ticket to see that the meter number is recorded there.** If it isn't, you probably won't have to pay the ticket at all, *since the ticket itself is defective.*
- **Write down the meter's number as well as its location,** plus the date and the time you

parked there. Compare the information to what's written on the ticket.

- **Read the instructions on the ticket about how to plead not guilty.** The procedure for contesting a parking ticket varies from place to place; in some cities, you can plead not guilty by mail, while in others you must appear in court in person. If you can't find the instructions for pleading not guilty, or you don't understand them, call the parking bureau's telephone number, which is usually listed on the ticket, and ask for instructions on the correct procedure.

Meters are routinely emptied and a defective meter should be spotted at the time that the meter reader checks it. The parking bureau keeps records of the meters that are defective or in need of repair. It is likely that the bureau's records will show that the meter you were ticketed for was repaired *after* your ticket was issued, and in most cases the ticket will be voided. With the information you've gathered, you should have little trouble beating this ticket.

**DRIVER ALERT** *Never ignore a parking ticket; your costs may double after a specified period of time. Ignore a few tickets and you may not be able to renew your automobile registration. Worse, your car could be "booted." A boot is an immobilizing device placed on one of your car's tires. You'll have to pay all the fines plus a fee to have the boot removed before you can drive again.*

## SECRET WARRANTIES: GET YOUR CAR FIXED FOR FREE

Whenever you hear about a recall, you know that some very important people are very unhappy. Automobile manufacturers dread being forced to recall their vehicles. Recalls are expensive, and the publicity never enhances the manufacturer's reputation for quality.

■ **Manufacturers like to avoid publicly advertised recalls.** Thus some of them will agree to fix widespread problems without charge—when customers complain. But the offer isn't publicized, and you may not know the free repairs are available. If you don't complain, the service departments of some dealers won't tell you about the "secret warranty." They'll simply charge you full price for repairing the problem.

■ **Be sure to speak up** whenever you have a car problem that you believe should be covered by your warranty or that you know is common in models such as yours. Ask if the manufacturer covers the repair. The dealer's service department may be authorized to take care of the problem at no cost to you.

■ **If the problem affects your car's safety,** you may also want to notify your state attorney general's office or call the National Highway Transportation Safety Commission's safety hotline at (202) 366-0123. When these authorities determine that a problem is widespread, they can take steps to force the manufacturer to recall the vehicle. Your call could help make the roads a little safer for you and everyone else.

---

# Your car is badly scratched at the local car wash and the operator refuses to pay for the repairs.

A damaged paint finish is more than irritating; it can be costly and time-consuming to repair. But your case for compensation depends on a couple of legal concepts. One is the ability of the operator to *disclaim* the car wash's responsibility, and the other concerns whether or not the car-wash operator or her employees were *negligent.*

■ **Disclaiming responsibility**—dry cleaners and car washes commonly try to disclaim, or deny, responsibility for damage they do to the property of customers. You may notice that the operator has posted a sign at the entrance to the car wash, stating that it isn't responsible for damage to antennas, wipers, pinstripes, or other exterior trim. The reason for this disclaimer is simple: Washing a car using machinery (as opposed to the hose-and-bucket method) can cause unintentional damage to some car parts.

■ **Negligence**—if the damage was the result of the negligence of the car-wash operator or one of her employees, it's not likely that the operator can disclaim responsibility, *even if a sign is posted.* For example, if a tire-cleaning product comes in contact with paint and mars the car's finish, it is due to negligence.

### SMART MOVES

Keep a notepad, a pen, and an inexpensive camera—the disposable ones work fine—in your car's glove compartment so you can take notes and photographs if you're in an accident or if your car is damaged at a car wash or a repair shop.

> ### As soon as your car comes out of a car wash, give it a close inspection.

## TAKE ACTION ON THE SPOT

As soon as your car comes out of a car wash, give it a close inspection. If you notice damage that goes beyond the norm—small scratches caused by the car wash's brushes are to be expected—talk to the manager or owner immediately and point out the problem. Be sure to get her name and title. (You may also want the names and addresses of any witnesses to this conversation.) The manager will do one of three things:

- **Make a settlement offer on the spot** (the least likely option). Accepting her offer will put an end to the matter, but don't take an offer that is so low it won't cover the cost of repairs.
- **Require you to file a damage claim.** If you are asked to file a damage claim, get the appropriate form from the car-wash operator or get the name of the car wash's insurance company and agent. Contact the agent, who can arrange an inspection by a claims adjuster. (If the damage is serious, you might want to get a second estimate.) If you decide to accept the insurer's offer, be prepared to sign a release relinquishing any further claims arising out of your visit to the car wash.
- **Deny responsibility.** Your next step is to build your case and send it to the car-wash owner.
  - Take a photograph of the damage. It helps to have a "before" photo for comparison.
  - Get a repair estimate. If you can, get more than one, so you can show that what you paid or are asking the car wash to pay is fair.
  - Write a letter to the car-wash owner (sent by certified mail, return receipt requested). Explain the problem, include a paragraph asking the owner to reimburse you, and set a deadline for a response. Keep your letter polite, businesslike, and short. Enclose copies of the estimate(s) and a copy of the photo.

## IF YOU GET LITTLE OR NO RESPONSE

Should you get an unacceptable response or no response at all, write a second letter to the owner. Again, send it by certified mail, return receipt requested, and be sure to keep a copy for your records. In this letter, you may want to state that you intend to take appropriate legal action if your claim isn't satisfied. Be sure to set another deadline for the car-wash owner's response.

If the car-wash owner still denies responsibility, you may proceed to file a lawsuit in small claims court (page 192). If your state doesn't have a small-claims process, you'll want to carefully consider the costs of a trial-court lawsuit before deciding to sue. Your case will be helped if you have witnesses who can testify about your conversation with the car wash's employees.

## COMMON AUTO-REPAIR SCAMS

Unless you are comfortable with car grease on your hands, chances are you could fall victim to a repair shop that tries to talk you into doing phony repairs to your car. Here are some common repair-shop scams and how to avoid them:

■ **Front-end fraud**—the mechanic puts your car on the lift and grabs a front tire. "See that wobble?" the mechanic asks. "You're going to need new ball joints along with your front-end alignment." Take the car to another mechanic for a second opinion; some wear and tear to ball joints is acceptable, as long as it falls within the manufacturer's allowances.

■ **Battery blowup**—while looking under the hood, the mechanic points out corrosion on your battery and suggests that you need to replace the battery before it gives out. Modern batteries rarely fail without some warning. Take your car to another mechanic and ask him to test it and to clean the terminals and cables.

■ **Shock-absorber scam**—the gas station attendant pushes down on a corner of your car. "Look at that bounce," he says. "Your shock absorbers need to be replaced." Actually, it's normal for a car to bounce when you push down on its corners. If you're concerned, get a second opinion from a reputable repair shop.

■ **Transmission trouble**—the mechanic changing your car's transmission fluid brings you a container. "Those metal shavings mean your transmission's ready to go," he tells you. "We can rebuild it for $3,000." Even if there are metal shavings, some will occur even in a well-maintained and perfectly fine transmission. Have him replace the fluid, and get a second and even a third opinion before agreeing to a major transmission repair.

**To find a trustworthy mechanic,** follow the recommendations of friends, family, neighbors, and business associates who are happy with their mechanics. You can also check to see if the repair shop participates in the American Automobile Association's Approved Auto Repair Program. Member shops must meet the AAA's standards.

# You hit a pothole, causing damage to a tire and wheel. You want the city to pay for the repairs, but your friends tell you not to bother.

Traffic was heavy one day when you were driving, and you couldn't avoid hitting the yawning hole in the street. Because of the legal, if annoying, concept known as *sovereign immunity,* governments often don't have to take responsibility for their negligent acts. Increasingly, however, cities, states, and even the federal government are allowing private citizens to seek compensation when they are injured or suffer property damage as a result of government action (or, in this case, inaction).

## TAKING ON THE GOVERNMENT

Here's what you will need to do to fight back:

● Note the day and time when you hit the pothole as well as its exact location.
● Take a photograph of the pothole if you have a disposable camera handy.
● Find out which government agency is in charge of maintaining the road where the pothole is located. Call the city's transportation or streets department and ask. (Even if the street

runs through a city, it may be the responsibility of the state or county highway department.)

> **B**y showing that you're serious about the matter, you may encourage the city to settle without the need for a courtroom battle.

● Ask for a damage claim form from the appropriate agency. Complete the form and include all required information, such as location, date and time, and an estimate or repair bill for the work needed on your car.

**TAKE NOTE** *It is important for you to act quickly, because the law usually gives you a very short time to file your claim for damages against a municipality or state agency.*

If the agency denies responsibility for whatever reason, get in touch with a lawyer who can confirm or rebut the department's claim. As a rule, you must prove that:

● The department had knowledge of the hole and failed to fix it (there is a detailed history of previous reports and claims).
● The hole remained unrepaired for too long. (The amount of time given depends on the city or town; some allow 48 hours for repair.)

Proving your claim can be difficult, but it's not impossible. You can interview area residents and get their sworn testimony. What's more, the agency's records are public and may provide evidence about when it was informed of the pothole and whether it acted quickly enough to repair it. By showing that you're serious about the matter, you may encourage the city to settle without the need for a courtroom battle.

> **Y**ou're traveling out of state when a gas-station attendant spots a leaking head gasket that he claims must be replaced immediately. Back home, your mechanic tells you the repair was unnecessary.

**W**hile most auto-repair businesses are honestly run, there are some bad apples in the barrel. These dishonest service stations often trick out-of-state drivers into expensive and unneeded "emergency" repairs. Their theory is that even if you discover their unethical and illegal behavior, you won't take the time to seek reimbursement once you're in your home state. Don't be put off by their tactics.

### STAGE A COUNTERATTACK

As soon as you discover that an automobile repair was unnecessary, you should...

■ **Write to the service station operator** and insist on a refund for the unnecessary repair. Send along any evidence you have in support of your claim, such as a copy of a letter from your own mechanic that supports your claim. The opinion of another mechanic will help strengthen your case against the bad shop.

■ **Contest the charge with your credit-card issuer** if you paid for the repair with a credit card. The issuer will investigate your claim and, depending on what it uncovers during the claim search, it may decide to cancel the repair charge.

■ **Send a copy of your letter to the Better Business Bureau** (BBB) in the city where the service station is located. The BBB can investigate, and if the service station is a BBB member, the bureau may be able to persuade the station operator to settle the matter by reimbursing you for some or all of your costs.

■ **Contact the consumer protection division of the attorney general's office** in the state where the station is located. You can get the telephone number and address from long-distance information or by calling the state capitol's general information number. Find out the steps for filing a formal written complaint. This agency can investigate your claim and may be able to take action against the service station operator. In some states, the consumer protection agency can:

● Obtain reimbursement from the business and forward that money to you.

● Use the threat of criminal prosecution to convince the service station operator to make things right for you.

■ **If the service station belongs to a national or regional chain,** contact the home office.

Pressure from the company's headquarters can be persuasive, since reputable businesses don't want their image tarnished by dishonest franchise owners, and local businesses don't want to lose the benefit of their affiliation.

■ **Use the media.** Contact newspapers and radio and television stations in the area where the service station is located. They can often put pressure on an unethical business owner, especially if they learn of other complaints.

> **Y**ou were stopped at a traffic light when your car was struck from behind. Naturally, the driver of the other car has no liability insurance.

**G**etting hit is bad enough. Getting hit by an uninsured driver is infuriating. Even though the law in nearly every state requires drivers to carry liability insurance, it's an unhappy fact that millions of people on the road today are "going naked," or driving without insurance coverage. While it would be far easier if the driver who hit you was insured, there are ways to receive compensation for the damage and any injuries you suffered. So don't give up the fight yet.

### CALL YOUR OWN INSURER

If you have *collision* insurance coverage as a part of your auto-insurance policy, your own insurance company will pay for the necessary repairs to your vehicle, minus your deductible. Collision insurance isn't based on fault, but the insurer will probably want to reserve the right to obtain reimbursement from the other driver for what-ever payment you receive.

Your own automobile-insurance policy may also include *uninsured or underinsured motorist* coverage. This coverage is specifically designed to pay your losses for any bodily injury that you, your family members, or others in your car suffer in an accident with a motorist who has little or no liability coverage. It also covers you in the event that you are the victim of a hit-and-run accident.

Keep in mind that this coverage applies only when the other driver is at fault. That is, the other driver must be liable to you for damages in order for your own insurer to pay off underinsured or uninsured motorist coverage. If the accident was your fault, then you won't get any benefits.

Your total benefits are limited by the amount of coverage you purchased. For example, if you bought *25/50 coverage,* the maximum your insurer will pay for any individual injured is $25,000, and the total it will pay for everyone injured is capped

at $50,000. In some states, if the accident was partially your fault, your coverage may be reduced by an amount equal to your contribution to the accident. If your insurer determines that you are 50 percent at fault, for example, you will receive half of your covered costs up to your dollar limit.

### GOING AFTER THE OTHER DRIVER

Insurance is great— if you have it. But as motor vehicles age and decline in value, many owners drop their collision coverage to save money on premiums. You may have opted for a high deductible in order to reduce payments on the policy. Because underinsured- and uninsured-motorist coverage is usually an optional part of auto-insurance policies, you may have decided not to buy it. Without coverage, you have to look at other options for getting compensation.

Small-claims court may be your best option, depending on the amount of your claim. In some states, the maximum amount for which you can sue in small-claims court has increased over the years, and many states now have limits of several thousand dollars or more. Small-claims court procedures are simplified to make it easier to bring a case without a lawyer; in fact, many small-claims courts discourage or prohibit lawyers from appearing.

If your claim exceeds the small-claims limit, you have several choices:

- **Reduce the amount of your claim** so that it falls within the small-claims court limit. This can be a smart move if the amount you're seeking isn't much greater than the small-claims court maximum.
- **Pursue your claim in the regular trial court** in your state. You can proceed without a lawyer, but be warned that procedures are

---

**SMART MOVES**

Visit the small-claims court days before your own case comes up for a hearing. Watching the action will help you understand the procedures and the judge's personality. On the day of your hearing, get to court early. That way you'll have time to collect your thoughts and steady your nerves—and be able to avoid costly mistakes.

more stringent, and the risk of having your claim dismissed for procedural mistakes is far greater than it is in small-claims court; a good lawyer can protect you against legal pitfalls.

- **Ask a lawyer to advise you without representing you in court.** Some lawyers will help you fill out forms and assist in pretrial preparation without actually appearing in court on your behalf. Expect to pay a lawyer an hourly fee for this service.

- **Hire a lawyer for a percentage** of the amount you recover. Because the negligent driver was uninsured, a lawyer will want to look at the possibility of actually collecting enough money to make the case worth his time. If the amount of your damages isn't large, or if it appears that the other driver has few assets with which to pay a judgment, you may find yourself being turned down by most personal-injury lawyers.

to your demand letter or because she offered to settle for less than the amount you believe is fair. Contact the small-claims court administrator at your local courthouse for the necessary forms to begin your case.

## BEFORE YOU GO TO COURT

If you decide to go after the other driver on your own, you'll need to give the other driver formal notice of your claim and an opportunity to pay up without going to court. Write a demand letter to the driver who caused the accident (page 456). In your letter, be sure to clearly set out these points:

- When the accident happened
- Why you consider her responsible
- What auto damages and personal injuries you have suffered
- What medical treatments you have received and their total cost
- What income you have lost, if any, because of the accident
- What other damages, such as mental anguish and suffering that you suffered
- What compensation you are seeking.

Finally, give the other driver a deadline by which to respond to you—no more than 30 days from the date of your letter. Send your letter by certified mail, return receipt requested.

## GOING TO SMALL-CLAIMS COURT

You may decide to take your case to small-claims court because the other driver never responded

**TAKE NOTE** *Ask the clerk if there is a Small Claims Adviser available in your county. An adviser can help you understand and use the small-claims process more efficiently. In court systems that make advisers available, their services are free.*

- **File a complaint**—a document that names the person against whom you're bringing your lawsuit and the basis for the suit. A copy of the complaint must be delivered to, or *served on*, the other driver (the *defendant*), together with a *summons* that orders the defendant to appear in court on a specified date. You can't serve the complaint and summons yourself; someone who has no interest in the case, such as a process server, must deliver it.

- **Get organized** before you go to court. Small claims proceedings are generally brief, and you will have only a short period of time in which to make your case to the judge.
  - Have all the documentation of your claim ready in a file for the judge to review.
  - Group your documents according to content. For example, have all your medical records and medical bills together and organized by date. Photographs of the accident

scene, the damage to your car, and any photos of your injuries should be together. Copies of statements by witnesses and police reports should also be in the file.

● Place three copies of everything in the file—one for the judge, one for you, and one for the defendant to review.

■ **Prepare a *brief statement*** to give when your case is called, and stick to the facts. In your statement, tell the judge where and when the accident happened, how it occurred, the damages you suffered, and the amount that you want the court to award you in compensation. You can ask the court to include your court costs in your award.

---

*P*repare a brief statement
to give when your
case is called, and stick
to the facts.

---

■ **Answer the judge's questions** in straightforward language. Don't try to "talk like a lawyer." Be polite and as calm as possible, but remember that even experienced trial lawyers often have "butterflies" when they appear in court. If you don't understand a question the judge asks you, ask him to rephrase it.

■ **Control yourself.** After you present your case, your opponent will have a chance to speak. She may make statements that amuse, anger, or even outrage you, but suppress your urge to defend yourself or show irritation or other emotions. Shaking your head in disagreement, interrupting, laughing, or muttering won't help your case, and may actually hurt it.

When the defendant is finished speaking, you may have an opportunity to respond to specific

statements she made. Again, be businesslike and respectful, and never make personal attacks against the defendant. You may be tempted to call your opponent a "bald-faced liar," but restrain the impulse. The court will be more inclined to listen to your side if you calmly point out why the accident couldn't have taken place the way the defendant described it.

In some small-claims courts, the judge will announce his decision immediately; in others, he will hand down his judgment after deliberating. If he finds in your favor, he may decide to award you the full amount of your claim, or he may reduce it. Generally, you can't appeal a small-claims court verdict in your favor, even if the award is for less than you think is adequate.

### COLLECTING YOUR JUDGMENT

It's up to you to collect any money you win. Losers in small-claims court are seldom eager to pay up. First write the defendant a letter referring to the judge's decision and giving her a deadline by which to make payment. Send the letter to her by certified mail, return receipt requested.

If your letter doesn't do the trick, you have several collection options, each of which involves getting forms called *writs* from the court:

● Have a writ delivered to the defendant's employer, who can *garnish,* or withhold, the money from her wages.
● Have a writ delivered to her bank ordering the money to be withdrawn from her account (for which you must have the number).
● File your judgment as a lien against her real estate or personal property, such as a car, stocks, or bonds.

The sheriff's department or other local law enforcement authorities will deliver writs on your behalf. You must pay for this service, but the law lets you ask for reimbursement from the defendant. The court clerk also has the form you need to file with the court to request reimbursement.

If you are involved in an automobile accident, there are some important rules to follow in order to protect yourself from potential problems:

- **Stay at the scene of the accident.** The penalties for hit-and-run accidents can be serious.

- **Get yourself and your vehicle out of traffic** if you are in a heavily traveled area and the car can be moved. Avoid any risk of further damage or injury to yourself or other drivers.

- **Get medical assistance for anyone who has been injured.** Don't try to move the victim yourself, especially if he is unconscious or complains of neck or back pain. Provide whatever first aid you can, especially to stop serious bleeding, and wait for emergency medical personnel to arrive on the scene.

- **Never make any statements to anyone** that could later be construed as accepting responsibility for the accident. Even if you think the accident was your fault, there may be circumstances you aren't aware of that make the other driver liable. Comments as simple as "sorry about that" to the other driver or "I never saw her coming" to a bystander can severely hamper your insurer's ability to defend you if others involved in the accident decide to sue.

Get the following information as soon as you are out of harm's way:

- The driver's name, address, license number, and state where the license was issued

- The owner's name, address, and telephone number if the driver doesn't own the vehicle

- The driver's automobile-insurance company, policy number, and his insurance company's telephone number and address

- The year, make, and model of all other cars involved in the accident

- The names, addresses, and telephone numbers of passengers and witnesses

- The name and badge number of any law enforcement officer on the scene, and the location of the police station where you can obtain a copy of the officer's accident report.

*You were injured on your commuter train. The railroad has offered a quick settlement, but they want you to sign a release you don't understand.*

Put on the brakes. While the railroad's quick action may seem admirable, it's possible that a swift settlement is really designed to limit the railroad company's liability for any of your injuries. By signing that release, you could be giving up compensation for injuries you may not be aware of yet. Before you ever sign a release after any accident, get good professional advice:

- Have a thorough medical examination by a doctor of your own choice.
- Get the advice of a lawyer to determine whether the offer is for enough to compensate you adequately. While you don't need to have a lawyer's help, especially in the early stages of a personal injury claim, it's a good idea to talk to a professional before you sign anything.

## MEDICAL EVALUATION

Don't assume you're okay just because you feel fine (or at least are not in severe pain) immediately after an accident. Some injuries don't show up right away. Soft-tissue injuries to muscles and tendons may not appear for days after an accident. Emotional and psychological injuries may take some time to become apparent. So whenever you are in an accident…

---

*If you suffer a permanent disability, be sure you have a written statement from your doctor fully explaining your condition and describing your limitations.*

---

- **Get medical attention immediately.** If you don't seek treatment and your condition worsens, you could be found partially liable for your resulting medical costs.
- **Don't wait for the other party** to offer to provide medical treatment for you. Use your own medical insurance if necessary to have an exam and begin any necessary treatment. You should be repaid for these costs as part of any settlement or verdict.
- **Get a second opinion** if you question your physician's evaluation or treatment plan. Some doctors don't like personal injury cases and may suggest that you just "buck up and get on with your life." A second opinion won't hurt, and it should be paid for in your insurance settlement or verdict.
- **Be absolutely sure that you feel completely recovered** before agreeing that you don't need further treatment. If you disagree when your doctor says you don't need more care, get a second medical opinion.

**INJURY ALERT** *At some point in the process of settling your claim, you may be asked by the railroad's insurer to submit to an exam by an Independent Medical Examiner (IME). This exam is designed to help the insurer minimize or deny your claim. The IME doctor isn't really independent, but works for the railroad's insurer. Be on your guard. The IME may record in his files something you say that seems to contradict earlier statements to the adjuster or to others investigating the accident. Talk to your lawyer before seeing an IME.*

If you suffer a permanent disability, be sure you have a *written* statement from your doctor fully explaining your condition and describing your limitations. Your doctor's statement should also describe any accommodations or changes your employer may need to provide to help you continue working.

## DEALING WITH ADJUSTERS

When you make a claim, it's assigned to a claims adjuster for the railroad's insurer. The adjuster's job is to investigate your claim and determine the amount of compensation the company will pay. When you are contacted by the adjuster…

- **Don't sign anything.** Get the claims adjuster's name and telephone number. Thank her for the quick response, but tell her that you won't sign a document you don't understand without independent advice.
- **Don't be persuaded** by the adjuster's oral statements that "this is just a standard form" or "we'll consider paying more later."
- **Don't be bullied** if the adjuster asserts that your claim won't be paid because of your "failure to cooperate." But make a note of any such comments the adjuster makes.

If you feel pressured to sign, you are probably dealing with an insurer that wants to settle your case quickly and cheaply. Chances are, you aren't qualified to evaluate what your own claim is worth. It's a complicated task even for a seasoned professional. Keep in mind that the railroad—like airlines and bus companies—is a *common carrier*, and by law it is obligated to use great care in transporting its passengers. If you later discover that the accident was due to some serious breach of this legal obligation (for example, if the accident was due to the engineer's being drunk), you may be entitled to more damages than you thought. A good personal-injury lawyer can help balance the power between you and an insurer that handles thousands of claims, employs dozens of adjusters, and has an army of lawyers trying to minimize how much money you get.

## HIRING A PERSONAL-INJURY LAWYER

Open the phone book, and it may seem that there are as many personal-injury attorneys as stars in the sky. Don't assume that all lawyers who take personal injury cases are equally qualified. And don't equate the size of a lawyer's advertisement with the quality of his work. How do you find the right personal-injury lawyer? Ask friends, business associates, and neighbors for recommendations. Your state or local bar association's referral service can provide the names of several lawyers for you to interview. If you have a family lawyer, she may be able to handle the case or refer you to a personal-injury attorney she knows and respects. As you talk to the attorneys, you should ask…

● How long have you been in law practice, and how long have you been practicing personal-injury law? You want an experienced personal-injury lawyer.
● How much of your practice is devoted to handling personal-injury cases? It's a case of the more the better for your interests.
● How much of your work is on behalf of individuals (plaintiffs) and how much on behalf of insurance companies? Some personal-injury lawyers represent plaintiffs in some cases and defendants in others. You'll want to hire one who spends most or all of his time representing plaintiffs.
● How will you communicate with me about the progress of my case? Your lawyer should provide you with copies of all important correspondence and keep you regularly informed about court filings and hearings.
● Will you handle the case yourself, or will I be working with one of your associates? Some lawyers are known as rainmakers. They bring business into their firm and then hand off the day-to-day work to other, sometimes less-experienced lawyers. If you'll be dealing primarily with another attorney or a paralegal, you should also talk to that person before signing on as a client.
● How will you be paid? Most personal-injury lawyers will work on a contingency fee basis, which means that they receive a percentage of any settlement or verdict they win for you. Many lawyers ask for one third of the total, but this is negotiable. You might offer to pay…
   —20 percent of the total if the case is settled without filing a lawsuit
   —25 percent if the case is settled after filing suit but before trial begins
   —33 percent of any amount of money that is awarded by the court
● What costs will I be responsible for? Most personal injury lawyers will advance expenses and then deduct them from the money you receive in your court judgement. Make sure that expenses are deducted *before* the attorney takes his percentage of the judgement, so you'll get more money in the end.

Never feel pressured to sign a retainer agreement with a lawyer. Take some time to consider the way your personality meshes with the attorneys you interviewed. Some attorneys are aggressive and confrontational; some are more inclined toward quiet negotiations. Either strategy can be effective, but in any case, it's a good idea to have an attorney whom you can trust and work with comfortably.

## IF YOU GO IT ALONE
Not everyone wants to use a lawyer when the claim isn't very big.

If you decide to deal with the railroad-carrier company and its insurer on your own, you can protect yourself against accepting a settlement that's too low by following these steps:

■ **Keep good records.** Start a journal of your daily activities and record the pain you experience. Log all conversations you have with the insurance company's representatives, noting the time, date, and substance of each conversation. Keep a separate file for all medical records and expenses related to the accident.
■ **Be wary about making statements.** The insurance company's adjuster may call or visit you and ask to make tape recordings of these conversations. This tactic is designed to trick or trap you into making inconsistent statements that can be used to deny or minimize your claim. If you can't settle your claim and must go to court, there will be written questions for you to answer under oath (interrogatories) as well as sworn answers to oral questions (depositions). Don't submit to any recorded statements before then.
■ **Get the insurer's top offer,** but keep in mind that there may still be room for negotiation on the settlement. For example, if you tell the insurance company that you are thinking about having a lawyer review the offer, you may find the adjuster will substantially raise the amount he offers you. You don't have to accept the larger amount on the spot. You can still have a lawyer review the higher offer. If your lawyer thinks he can get you even more, offer him a fee based on any money in excess of what you've already been offered. This way, you'll keep the full amount you were able to negotiate for yourself and then pay attorney's fees only on any additional money your lawyer can obtain for you.

*O*n the way home from a party at your house, one of your guests was arrested for DUI. Now he wants to sue you for serving him beer.

If only everybody would take the blame for their own bad behavior. Legally, however, the host of a party held in her home has a duty to act reasonably when serving alcohol to her guests. Some courts have held party hosts liable when a third party was injured in an accident with a drunken driver. If you encouraged your guest to drink and did nothing to stop him from driving away while he was inebriated, then you might be in danger of a lawsuit brought by other injured motorists or pedestrians. But in this situation, it's unlikely that your guest can collect any damages from you. To some extent, the law still holds people responsible for their actions.

### IF A GUEST THREATENS TO SUE

It's possible your party guest will get no further than complaining that his DUI (driving under the influence) was *your* fault. But by talking to an experienced attorney, he'll quickly discover that he has no real *cause of action,* the legal term for a case against you. On the other hand, your guest could find an inexperienced lawyer or one who is willing to write a letter on his behalf in hopes of bluffing you into offering some compensation. If he persists in his claim, call your homeowner's insurance company immediately.

Under the liability portion of your home-owner's insurance policy, your insurer has a legal obligation to defend you against claims made by others. Your insurer must provide this defense at its own expense—even if the guest's claim is fraudulent, false, or groundless.

Your insurer's legal department will contact the guest's lawyer or the guest directly if he has no legal counsel. It will tell the insurer or the guest that the claim made against you has been reviewed and found to be without merit. This should be enough to put an end to the matter.

If your guest won't give up, he'll have to deal with your insurer, so…

- Be ready to cooperate fully with your insurance company.
- Don't get involved personally. And don't discuss anything related to the claim with the guest once the matter has been handed over to your insurer's claims department.

Can you simply ignore the guest's claim? That's never a good idea. If the case should get to court, failing to defend yourself could result in a *default judgment* against you. A default judgment occurs when the defendant (you, in this case) in a legal action doesn't appear in court to contest the charges. Default judgments can be undone, but the process is even more expensive and time-consuming than fighting back in the first place.

**TAKE NOTE** *Homeowners' insurance policies exclude coverage for business activities being conducted at your home. So if your guest was an employee, client, or other business associate, your insurer may be able to avoid having to defend you. If you have business meetings or other business-related events in your home, it's essential that you have business liability insurance.*

Contact your insurer for more information on your responsibilities as a host (for a similar scenario, see page 56). While it's unlikely you can be held liable for the guest's DUI costs and fines, you need to be aware of a host's legal duties, to avoid possibly having to defend yourself in court.

*Without your knowledge, a neighbor's child
came into your backyard and then fell off your children's swing set.
His parents are demanding that you pay the medical bills.*

In law, like sand-lot ball, kids have different rules than adults. Accidents involving children are always cause for concern because children aren't considered capable of always making rational decisions in the same way that adults are, and therefore are not held accountable. An adult who entered your yard without your permission would be considered a trespasser; a young child who does the same thing might not—especially if you maintain what's known as an attractive nuisance.

An attractive nuisance is an object or condition on your property that both attracts children and poses a potential hazard to them. Swimming pools, trampolines, and playground equipment could all be considered attractive nuisances. Of course, it's impossible to make the world completely safe for children, but the law does require owners of attractive nuisances to take appropriate steps to minimize the risk of injury.

## DON'T TAKE THE BLAME

If your neighbors claim that the accident was your fault, don't make statements that could be taken as admissions of liability. Instead, report the claim to your homeowner's insurance company immediately. In deciding whether your neighbors have a claim based on an attractive nuisance, your insurer will look at several factors (the same ones a court will consider if a lawsuit is filed):

> *It's impossible to make the world completely safe for children, but the law does require owners of attractive nuisances to take appropriate steps to minimize the risk of injury.*

- **How old was the child?** A four- or five-year-old is unlikely to understand the risk of unsupervised play on the swing set or to know that entering your yard without your permission is wrong. (The court may consider the actions of the child's parents in determining your negligence, but it's unwise to rely on this as your defense.) An older child, on the other hand, is presumed to have greater skills in understanding, and his parents are less likely to be entitled to compensation. Most states refuse to apply the doctrine of attractive nuisance to children in their teens, and they will likely look at claims involving children approaching their teens on a case-by-case basis.
- **Was the child attracted** by something you put in your yard or by some natural feature? A swing set is more likely to be considered an attractive nuisance than a stream; a trampoline is more likely to be one than is your old oak tree.
- **Did you have prior knowledge** that children might come on the property without your permission? For example, if you've had kids playing in your yard before and

you haven't been able to keep them out, a court could hold that you had an obligation to take stronger measures.

■ **How reasonable were your efforts** to keep children out of your yard? If your yard is unfenced or you keep your gate open and unlocked, your potential for liability is much greater. But if you have a high fence that could be expected to keep small children out, your potential for liability will usually be less.

It's human nature to feel a degree of guilt whenever a child is hurt, and you may be tempted to agree with your neighbors' claim. After all, you have insurance, right? But while you probably feel some moral responsibility for the child's suffering, the law in your state may limit your legal accountability. Remember, too, that you have an obligation to cooperate with your insurer in defending yourself against your neighbors' claim. Failing to cooperate could cause the cancellation of your insurance policy. Refer all claims to your insurance company's claims department. And you should try not to discuss the accident with the neighbors or anyone else until a settlement has been concluded.

## How Damage Awards Are Calculated

In calculating the amount of compensation you may be entitled to as the result of a personal injury claim, insurance companies use a formula based on years of experience with similar claims. Generally, when you're injured by someone's actions, you are entitled to payment...

- For medical treatment and related expenses, such as medications and therapy
- For lost wages during the time you miss work
- For physical pain and suffering
- To compensate you for any permanent disfigurement or disability
- For lost opportunities to engage in social, family, and educational activities
- For emotional damages.

The way in which insurance adjusters arrive at a total figure to offer for all of the above depends on several factors. Generally you will be offered more money depending on...

- How serious your injuries are
- How much time you need to recover fully from your injuries
- How painful the injuries you suffer are
- How obvious the injuries are
- How disfiguring the injuries are.

> *The housekeeper you hired to clean your home tripped on a rug in your hallway and broke her leg. Now she claims that you should pay her medical bills and pay for her lost income.*

Your parents taught you to show concern when someone is hurt in your home. It's a good-hearted impulse, but it can cause you serious trouble. Even saying "sorry" can have unintended consequences if the injured person wants to sue. Whether or not you are going to be liable for your housekeeper's injuries will depend on several factors. But it's essential to contact your homeowner's insurance company as soon as possible after the worker is injured. Before agreeing to pay, your insurance company is going to ask a few questions. For example:

## SMART MOVES

Before hiring people to work at your house, make sure they have their own insurance coverage. Ask them to give you a copy of their policy's declarations page, then call the company to make sure the policy is still in effect. Some workers pay for insurance, obtain a policy, then cancel it to save money.

homes, she may be responsible for providing her own insurance coverage.

- Does the housekeeper use her own supplies and equipment to clean your house? If so, it's more likely that she should have her own insurance coverage.

If the answer to any of these questions is yes, then it's likely that you aren't responsible for paying the housekeeper's medical bills and reimbursing her for lost income. Either she is an employee of the service that sent her to your home, or she is an independent contractor and should have her own insurance coverage.

*It's essential to contact your homeowner's insurance company as soon as possible after the worker is injured.*

- Does the housekeeper work for an agency that serves a variety of households and businesses? If she does, then it's likely that the agency is responsible for her workers compensation coverage.
- Does she work exclusively for you, or does she have a number of clients? If she advertises her services and cleans a number of

*Your skiing trip was ruined when you were struck by a ski lift and injured. The resort claims that it isn't responsible because of the disclaimer printed on your lift ticket.*

By their nature some activities, such as skiing, are more dangerous than others. No matter how experienced the skier, injuries can occur, and the injured parties often look for someone else to blame. As a result, most ski resorts print notices on their lift tickets that claim to release

them from any liability. When you buy your lift ticket, you enter into a contract with the ski-resort operator, and the ski resort's notice becomes a term of that contract. And if you fall on the slope and injure yourself, the resort isn't responsible. The courts will find that you assumed the risk of injury when you purchased the ticket, because it's common knowledge that there's a relatively high risk of getting hurt while skiing.

But even with a printed notice, you can't be forced to release a business from *liability for its own negligence.* If your injury was the result of the carelessness of the resort or one of its employees, the resort may still be required to compensate you. And if the notice is inadequate (the resort's disclaimer was printed in type so small that you couldn't reasonably be expected to read it without a magnifying glass), then the resort's attempt to escape paying you compensation may also fail.

## FIRST AID AND FILING CLAIMS

When you're injured, you must take care of yourself medically and legally.

■ **Get immediate medical treatment,** even if you have to pay for it yourself. Failing to get treatment can be a form of *contributory negligence* or *comparative negligence.* In legal terms, this occurs when you fail to take reasonable and prudent steps to protect against further injury or damage. For example, suppose the ski lift struck you in the back of the head. Despite experiencing blurred vision along with severe head pain, you decided not to go to the doctor. Then your condition worsened and required surgery to relieve a blood clot. Your failure to get immediate treatment that might have prevented the clot could be considered contributory or comparative negligence. Depending on how the negligence is categorized, and the laws in the state where the accident took place, you could be barred from any recovery, or the amount of your compensation might be reduced by the percentage of your injury that the court attributed to negligence.

■ **File a claim with the ski resort.** Send the resort a demand letter (by certified mail, return receipt requested), and clearly state…
- The time and date of your accident
- The way the accident happened
- Why the ski resort is responsible: For example, the lift operator was talking and failed to see that the lift chair was out of control
- The nature of your injuries
- The kind of treatments you've had and the medical expenses you've incurred
- What income you lost, if any
- What other damages you suffered, such as

the cost of lodging that you couldn't use because you were hospitalized
- The total compensation you want the resort to pay. (This amount can be greater than the monetary damages you've outlined in order to cover your pain and suffering and any other non-economic damage.)
- A deadline by which you expect the resort to respond to your claim, such as within 30 days.

The first response to your demand letter will probably be a telephone call from an adjuster employed by the resort's insurance company. The insurance adjuster's job is to investigate your claim and decide what compensation, if any, to offer. Be sure to get the adjuster's name and title, as well as her telephone and fax numbers, and her email address.

## PLAYING THE NEGOTIATION GAME

Negotiating a personal-injury settlement can be like a game with its own rules and protocol. You have to know how the game is played to win the compensation you deserve. It can be nerve-wracking, so be prepared.

But if you want to be fairly and adequately compensated for your injury, remember that you have a good deal of control over how the game is played. You can blink and accept the insurer's offer at any point. A lot depends on your situation and your tolerance for negotiation.

- **The adjuster's first move:** No matter how reasonable the claim in your demand letter, it's almost certain that the adjuster will assert that you're asking for more money than you're entitled to receive. She may suggest that the resort isn't liable, or that the amount and type of medical treatment you received cost more than your injury required.
- **Your first move:** Point out to the adjuster all the evidence that supports the dollar amount you proposed as a settlement. If the adjuster says you've been to the doctor too often, politely ask her to describe her medical training and where she received it. If she tells you the resort isn't liable for the lift operator's actions, remind her that employers are legally responsible when their employees' negligence causes injury to others. If you have carefully gathered your facts, you can't be bullied into backing down.
- **The adjuster's second move:** The next step for the adjuster will usually be to make you an initial settlement offer—almost always a lower figure than the one you requested. A low

monetary offer allows the adjuster to test your commitment to the figure you have proposed.
- **Your second move:** You have no obligation to accept the first settlement offer you receive. Remember that claims adjusters don't get their raises, bonuses, and promotions for being generous with the company's money. But if the adjuster's settlement offer is close to your demand, you may want to consider it carefully. Is the difference in the amounts worth the time and energy you'll spend on any further wrangling? You don't have to respond immediately; take your time and tell the adjuster that you'll get back to her.

> *If your injury was the result of the carelessness of the resort or one of its employees, the resort may still be required to compensate you.*

- **Next moves:** At this point, the adjuster may make you a second offer that's higher than her first one. If her offer is closer to your demand, you can make a counteroffer. Suggest a figure that's a little less than your original claim. But if the adjuster's second offer is still too low, thank the adjuster for her time and tell her you want some time to consider your options.
- Write the adjuster a letter responding to the reasons she gave for her offer. Explain why the amount isn't enough money to compensate you adequately. If you're willing to put your counteroffer in writing, include it in your letter and give the adjuster a deadline of a few days by which to respond.
- If you aren't too far apart on the dollar value at this point, it's likely that the adjuster will agree to your counteroffer or propose a figure that's closer to your offer. Again, deciding whether to accept her offer depends on factors such as your tolerance for continuing the negotiations and your willingness to risk going into court and receiving less than has already been offered.

As you negotiate with the ski-resort's insurance adjuster, remember that time could be your best ally. A claims adjuster usually has dozens of files to work on at once. Getting your claim paid and your case file closed may seem very attractive to her. When the offers have gone back and forth several times, one more counter-offer may be all that it takes to get the adjuster to agree to a settlement on your terms.

> **A** *claims adjuster usually has dozens of files to work on at once. Getting your claim paid and your case file closed may seem very attractive to her.*

### NAVIGATING THE END GAME

Once you've both agreed orally to a settlement figure, the adjuster can tell you how soon she can send the documents you need to sign to formally close your case. At this point, you should write to the adjuster, confirming the figure you agreed on and restating that time period in which you expect to receive the settlement agreement and the release. As with all financial correspondence, it's a good idea to send your confirmation letter to the adjuster by certified mail, return receipt requested, and keep a copy of it for your files.

When you receive the settlement papers, you should…

- Review the documents carefully. Be sure that they accurately reflect the agreement that you made with the adjuster.
- Not sign any agreements or releases until you are *completely* satisfied with the terms
- Not make changes or deletions in the agreement yourself, since this will delay getting your payment and could lead the adjuster to void the agreement entirely
- Consult with a lawyer before you sign anything that you don't completely understand.

If everything is as promised, you will sign the agreement and release, keeping copies for your files, and return the originals to the adjuster. Once she has your signed documents, you can expect to receive your payment within a relatively short period, usually no more than a few weeks.

---

## LAWS THAT PROTECT THE INJURED

In recent years, the federal government and a number of states have enacted laws that protect injured and disabled citizens in the workplace. Two of these acts that can make life after an accident a lot easier for the victims are:

- **Americans with Disabilities Act.** If you're permanently disabled as a result of an accident, you are probably entitled to the protection of the Americans with Disabilities Act (ADA). Under this federal law, your employer must make reasonable efforts to accommodate your disability (a wheelchair-accessible office, for example). If you change jobs or start looking for a job after being disabled, a potential employer is prohibited from asking you about your disability until after making a job offer. Your lawyer can provide detailed information about how to use this law to protect you from discrimination because of your disability.

- **Family and Medical Leave Act.** If you work for a company covered by the federal Family and Medical Leave Act (private companies with 50 or more employees, or public agencies), you have the right to take up to three months of unpaid leave to recover from your injuries. Your employer cannot terminate you during this time period, and when you return to work, the employer must provide you with the same job you held before you took the leave or an equivalent position. State laws may give you the same or similar rights if the federal law doesn't cover you.

f this accident had happened 100 years ago, you'd be out of luck (page 231). Today when you are injured by a product, such as a weed trimmer, the rule of strict liability entitles you to be compensated—provided the injury isn't due to your misuse of the product (using the weed trimmer to strip paint from a wall) or substantial alteration of the product (replacing the nylon trimming thread with steel wire, for example).

## THE STEPS TO COMPENSATION

There is a straightforward path to consumer satisfaction for you to follow:

- **Keep the product.** This is the first and most important step in pursuing your claim. The manufacturer will almost certainly want to examine it and has a right to do so.
- **Contact the store** where you purchased the weed trimmer. Once the seller knows about your claim, it will contact the manufacturer. (The retailer may be held liable if the danger or defect is due to some problem with storage, alterations, or assembly.)
- **Proceed directly against the manufacturer** if you can't bring a claim against the seller. The manufacturer's name and address may be on the product or on the packaging, but if you can't locate it, ask for help at your local library. There are national and international directories of manufacturers that your librarian can research. And of course, you can look for the manufacturer's web site on the Internet.
- **Write to the seller,** the manufacturer, or both to make your claim. In your letter, you'll want to include…
  - The date, time of day, and location of the accident
  - A description of the product, including model and serial numbers if available
  - A request that the company contact you for additional information
  - Your name and the address—the place where you want the company to send correspondence regarding your claim. While you don't need to include your telephone number, you'll speed the settlement process by conducting most of your negotiations over the phone. Feel free to tell the company if there

are certain times of day that you do or don't want to be called and if you prefer to be called at work rather than at your home.

Send your letter by certified mail, return receipt requested. At this point, you don't have to make any specific claim for damages or describe the injuries you suffered when the weed trimmer malfunctioned. That will come later, once you've

> *One way to interest a lawyer in your case is to ask about filing a class-action lawsuit.*

had a chance to evaluate your injuries and other damages. Your only task now is to make the company aware of the problem and let them know that you intend to pursue the matter.

In most cases, you will find yourself negotiating with a claims adjuster from the company's insurance company (page 227). But what do you do if you are unable to come to an agreement with the company's insurer about your damages?

## THE INS AND OUTS OF GOING TO COURT

Product liability lawsuits can be complicated and expensive, so…

- Expert witnesses may be necessary to determine just what contributed to the defect in the product that caused your injury.
- Pretrial investigation, known as the *discovery process,* can be time-consuming and costly.
- You may need to obtain copies of company documents, test procedures and results, and internal memos and other papers related to the way the weed trimmer was designed, manufactured, and shipped.

Getting the help of an experienced product-liability lawyer is almost a necessity. But unless the damages you suffered are large enough to make it worthwhile for a lawyer to take your case, there's a good chance you won't find a lawyer willing to represent you. You might want to file suit in small-claims court (page 217), but in some jurisdictions, the company being sued is allowed to move the trial into the state's regular court system, where the procedures are more complicated and lawyers are used. Despite the laws that are supposed to protect consumers, you may feel like David facing Goliath when you go against large and powerful companies. Just getting your day in court can seem like an impossible task.

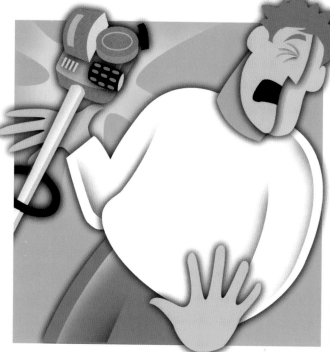

## CLASS ACTION LAWSUITS

One way to interest a lawyer in your case is to ask about filing a class-action lawsuit. Not every personal-injury attorney handles class-action cases, but most can recommend a lawyer or law firm that does. Your local or state bar association can also provide names of attorneys who may be able to help you. Lawyers like class-action lawsuits because of the opportunity to earn much larger fees. The pressure and expense of defending a class-action suit often encourages companies to settle without going to trial.

In a class-action suit, the court permits one or more plaintiffs to represent a group who have suffered similar injuries at the hands of the defendant. Once the court determines that a large enough group of potential claimants exists and that it wouldn't be practical for all of the cases to be heard separately, it can certify the action on behalf of the class. To obtain class-action certification, you must show…

- That a group of potential claimants exists (persons who bought weed trimmers from the company and suffered injuries)
  - That the claimants all have substantially similar claims (they may have been injured by a defect in the weed trimmer's design that caused it to backfire)
  - That it would be a burden on the courts to have each claimant file suit individually (thousands of similar weed trimmers were sold by the manufacturer).

You've probably seen notices about class-action suits on television and in your local newspaper. These advertisements are placed by the attorney or law firm representing the class. The advertisements give potential class members notice of the pending litigation and offer those who want to pursue their claims separately the opportunity to opt out of the class.

Once the class has been certified, the defendant may agree to a settlement out of court, or the case can go on to trial. All the members of the class—except those who chose to pursue their cases alone—are then bound by the results of the class-action litigation.

**CONSUMER ALERT** *If you bought the weed trimmer secondhand—at a yard sale, for instance, or you purchased it from a neighbor—the person who sold it to you won't be liable unless he did something to the trimmer that made it dangerous. Strict liability applies only to those who are regularly involved in selling a product.*

At the beginning of the 20th century, the law made it very difficult for individuals to get compensation when a product was unsafe or poorly manufactured. Back then, courts applied the *doctrine of privity* to limit consumers' rights. Under this doctrine, there had to be a direct relationship between the injured person and the person alleged to have caused the injury. Say that you went down to the general store and bought a wagon made by Wagonmakers Co., and then the wagon's wheels fell off and you were hurt. You couldn't sue the manufacturer, because you hadn't dealt with it directly. Since the general store didn't make the wagon, you couldn't sue it either. Over time, however, courts began to see that the doctrine of privity created an unfair result, especially as manufactured goods became more complicated and dangerous.

Today, product liability law allows consumers injured by unreasonably dangerous or defective products to seek damages from everyone in the distribution chain. Generally, this includes…

- The original manufacturer
- Wholesalers and distributors
- Assemblers and repair people
- Suppliers of component parts
- Testing laboratories that examined the product in question
- Retailers

### When Can You Make a Claim?

A product can be unreasonably dangerous for several reasons:

- An unreasonably dangerous defect in product design so that it fails to operate properly even when manufactured according to specifications
- A dangerous defect because of improper procedures in the manufacturing process
- A dangerous defect because the product was mishandled in shipping or storage.

Your claim can be based on negligence, on breach of warranty, or on strict liability:

- **Negligence.** To file a product-liability claim based on negligence, you must show that the manufacturer…

  - Owed a duty to you as a consumer (to make a safe product)
  - Breached its duty (for example, by utilizing a faulty design)
  - Caused you to be injured as a result of that breach of duty.

- **Breach of warranty.** Today the law in nearly every state provides for an *implied warranty of merchantability*. This means that when a product is sold, it is safe when used for its intended purpose. A defective product that causes injuries when used in the correct manner has breached this implied warranty. If you followed the directions when you started the weed trimmer, the manufacturer and seller can be responsible for compensating you for your injuries and other damages.

- **Strict liability.** In most states, the law now imposes *strict liability* on those who regularly put products into the stream of commerce. Under the theory of strict liability, the manufacturer or seller of a defective or unexpectedly dangerous product can be held liable for damages— without your having to prove that they were actually negligent.

**Your** two-year-old daughter choked on a small toy. The toy company says it isn't responsible, because the toy came in a package with the warning "Not for children under age 3."

Thanks to quick emergency treatment, your child's accident wasn't fatal—but it could have been. And you are understandably angry with the company that made such a dangerous toy.

In fact, the law recognizes what is known as a *duty to warn* that requires manufacturers, distributors, and sellers to notify customers of potential dangers that can arise when a product is used. Companies often try to limit their liability for dangerous products by placing disclaimers on the products' packaging. Federal and state regulators also work hard to ensure that companies making products aimed at children exercise extreme care in labeling their products with warnings that specify suitability for particular age groups.

### GET A LAWYER

This is not the kind of claim you should attempt to handle yourself. For you to remain calm and businesslike after your child has been injured is difficult, and you don't want your claim dismissed or minimized because of your emotional reactions. Get in touch with an attorney who has experience handling personal-injury and product-liability claims. An experienced lawyer knows how to contact the toy company who manufac-

tured the toy and present your claim to them in a professional manner. She will handle your case on a contingency fee basis, especially if your child's injury was a serious one.

### GET THE GOVERNMENT ON THE CASE

The U.S. Consumer Product Safety Commission (CPSC) is authorized to protect consumers from dangerous products in hundreds of categories and is very aggressive in investigating complaints about toys, bicycles, and other products marketed to and for children. With information from you, the CPSC will investigate your complaint, and the company that manufactured the toy could be ordered to recall it. Companies that fail to cooperate with the CPSC can be subject to fines and the CPSC can also obtain injunctions forcing the company to stop selling its products.

**CONSUMER ALERT** *Not every company takes its duty to warn customers as seriously as it should. Warning labels on packages may not be conspicuous (for example, when the warning is placed on the bottom of the package) or may not be legible (as when the color of ink or the small size of the type makes the label difficult to read).*

**Your** friend drove you to the grocery store. She caused an accident and you were injured. Now she says she was just doing you a favor and you can't expect her to pay your medical bills.

Your friend is a nice person. You like her. So, naturally, you're torn between loyalty to your friend and your own need to be reimbursed for medical examinations and treatment costs, which were, after all, due to the accident that she caused. But fair's fair, and you did not cause either the accident or your injuries.

There was a time when *automobile guest statutes* made it very difficult for a nonpaying passenger to collect for injuries suffered in a car driven by someone else. But in many states, these laws have been repealed or declared unconstitutional. Today drivers are usually held to owe nonpaying guests in their car a duty of *ordinary care.*

Courts have found drivers liable for their passengers' injuries when the drivers have done something that increased the hazard of traveling by car. For example, drivers have been found liable when they were involved in an accident as a result of…

- Driving onto sidewalks or curbs
- Crossing the center yellow line into oncoming traffic
- Failing to signal turns
- Failing to stop at a red light or stop sign
- Driving in excess of the speed limit
- Driving while alcohol- or drug-impaired.

If you believe that your friend was guilty of any of the incidents described above and that your injuries resulted from her negligence, you probably do have a valid claim against her.

If another driver was involved in the accident, you should file a claim against his insurer. But your friend should also provide you with the name and address of her automobile insurance company. If she won't cooperate, you will need to contact her by mail. In this notification letter, you will need to…

■ **Set out the bare details of the accident,** including the date, time, and location of the accident. ("On May 1, 2000, at approximately 3:15 P.M., while I was a passenger in your car, you and Joe Blow were involved in an automobile accident at the corner of Fifth and Swift Streets in Littletown.")

■ **Request that your friend provide** you with the name of her insurance carrier and that she also forward a copy of your notification letter to her insurer.

Send your signed letter to your friend by certified mail, return receipt requested. Find out the name of your friend's insurer and send it a copy of the letter. Then wait for the company's claims department to contact you. When the adjuster calls, you'll

want to be ready to negotiate the dollar amount of your claim (page 224).

If, in fact, the accident wasn't your friend's fault (if, for example, she had stopped at a light and her car was struck from behind), she probably won't have any liability for your bills.

> **C**ourts have found drivers liable for their passengers' injuries when the drivers have done something that increased the hazard of traveling by car.

Don't assume that she is blameless, however. Circumstances surrounding an accident can color perspectives. It's better to file your claim and have it turned down by your friend's insurance company than to miss the opportunity to collect for your injuries from the responsible party.

## WHEN A PERSONAL-INJURY LAWYER CAN HELP

When injuries shake you up or confine you to bed after an accident, you may not have the energy or the focus to do full battle for compensation. That's when a personal-injury lawyer proves his worth. A good personal-injury lawyer can do the following:

- **Investigate the accident** right away. Many personal-injury lawyers and law firms employ private investigators to do the legwork. The private investigator can take photographs of the accident location, the vehicles involved, and any damaged property, as well as gather any other visual evidence that might change before your case goes to court. (A classic example of altered evidence is a stop sign, hidden by a tree branch at the time of the accident; the sign shows clearly after the city later prunes the surrounding foliage. A dated photo proves the sign was obscured when the cars crashed. )

- **Check to see that the official accident report** is filled out, and be sure that the information in it is accurate. If the information is wrong, your lawyer can ask to have the report corrected or to have missing material included. The insurance companies and the court (if your case ends up there) will use this report, so it's important that it be correct and complete.

- **Locate and interview witnesses** to the accident. If there were witnesses whom you didn't identify at the scene of the accident, your lawyer can hire an investigator to track them down or place advertisements in local papers to help find them.

  You have—or your lawyer has—two responsibilities with witnesses:
  ● To record their observations of the accident and collect any diagrams of the action or notes they can provide as soon after the event as possible. Memories fade over time.

  ● To stay in contact with them so that they will be available when they are needed to testify. Using an attorney as the witness liaison allows you to stay aloof from them. If you talk to witnesses too often, the relationship could taint their testimony.

- **Report to your insurance company.** If you have collision insurance, your insurer should be able to make a settlement to repair your vehicle or provide you with a new one. If the company's claim department drags its feet, your lawyer can encourage it to act more quickly.

- **Deal with insurance-company adjusters.** It's often a good idea to let your lawyer handle these people, especially if there are questions about who was really responsible for the accident. Adjusters may want to tape-record their conversations with you. By asking questions in a particular way, they may be able to trap you into giving answers that will allow them to deny your claim or settle it for a lesser amount. Your lawyer can help you avoid the pitfalls of negotiating with adjusters.

If you decide to hire a lawyer early on, you or someone in your family should keep track of the actions she takes on your behalf. Be sure to cooperate with your attorney as much as possible. You may be required to give a deposition and to answer written questions called *interrogatories*. Be prepared to attend settlement conferences as well as the trial if the matter can't be settled out of court. Finally, remember that your lawyer works for you. Listen to her recommendations on strategy, tactics, and settlement. But also remember that you make the ultimate decisions on when to settle, for how much, and whether to proceed to trial.

**Y**ou find out that the source of your chronic pain
is a clamp left behind from a surgery done several years ago.
The surgeon says it's too late for you to file a claim.

**O**ver time, memories fade, witnesses move away or die, and proving a case becomes more and more difficult. In every state, the law imposes a *statute of limitations* on your ability to file a personal-injury or medical-malpractice lawsuit. These statutes require you to file your suit within a certain time period after you're injured. There are some good reasons for this requirement. For a would-be defendant in a lawsuit, having the threat of legal action hanging over his head indefinitely is unfair.

But sometimes an injury doesn't become apparent for years. This is often the case…

- When the injury was caused by exposure to chemicals or radiation and the effects appear long after the initial exposure
- When your injury is the result of a medical procedure that you underwent while you were under anesthesia.

*If the local statute of limitations allows you to file suit, you should act quickly.*

In these cases, the law in most states allows you to file your lawsuit within a specified period after you discover the injury. Generally, you have a year after you learn of the injury to start a legal proceeding. You can find out what your state's statute of limitations on cases like yours is by visiting your local courthouse's law library or by contacting a lawyer.

**TAKE NOTE** *The law that applies will be the one in the state where the injury took place, no matter where you live now.*

If the local statute of limitations allows you to file suit, you should act quickly. You will need a lawyer to bring your claim; most medical malpractice insurers aggressively defend their policyholders. If the doctor is uninsured, it can be daunting to deal with him yourself and track down his assets for payment. Medical-malpractice cases are tough to win, but with an experienced malpractice attorney's help, you stand a much better chance of settling your claim to your satisfaction than if you try to go it alone.

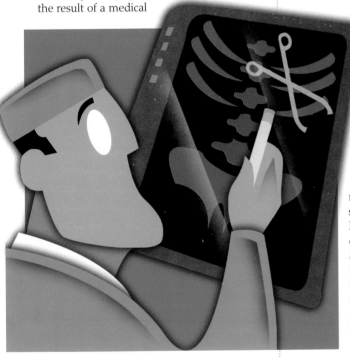

> **W**hile crossing the street, you were hit by
> a car. At the hospital, a lawyer you don't know comes into
> your room and offers to help you file suit.

**Y**ou've heard about "ambulance chasers," or those lawyers who hound accident victims when they are most vulnerable. The truth is that most lawyers abide by the rules that prohibit them from soliciting clients under adverse circumstances. But there's always a bad

> *S*hould you be harassed
> by an "ambulance chaser,"
> you can file a complaint
> with your state's attorney
> disciplinary committee.

apple in every barrel. How do less-than-ethical attorneys know when there's been an accident and where to find the victims? These lawyers listen to police scanners, and they or one of their employees may show up at the scene of the accident even before the police arrive. Or they may have a contact in the hospital emergency room who alerts them about recent accident victims.

Lawyers who contact you this way are probably not people you will want to deal with. They rarely have their clients' best interests at heart but instead are looking to arrange a quick settlement and a quick pay day for themselves. They often fail to investigate their cases carefully and may overlook potential compensation you would be entitled to receive.

If you are ever contacted by a lawyer you don't know shortly after being in an accident, or by someone working for one of these lawyers, refuse their services. Instead, get the advice and assistance of a lawyer whom you select and can trust.

Should you be harassed by an "ambulance chaser," you can file a complaint with your state's attorney disciplinary committee. In some states, this agency is operated by the court system; in others, the state bar association runs it. Your local court clerk can provide you with information about where and how to file a complaint about attorney misconduct. You can also find the information in your state's statute books at most public libraries.

If the state disciplinary committee finds that the lawyer who contacted you violated any of the rules of professional responsibility, it can take a variety of actions against that lawyer, including suspending him from the practice of law or even ordering that he be disbarred.

> **Y**our car was struck by a snowplow operated by
> the highway department. You are injured, but your friends all say
> you haven't got a prayer of collecting the damages.

**W**ho says you can't fight city hall? Although the doctrine of *sovereign immunity* once banned any legal claims against the government, the modern approach gives private citizens the right to seek compensation from the government when it causes them harm. If you're injured on government property, or if a government employee is involved in an accident with you, there are special procedures you must follow in order to receive compensation. Be warned that the government gets to make the rules about how and when you file your claim. And each level of government—state, county, and local—may have its own set of rules.

## WHO'S RESPONSIBLE?

Your first step is to determine which government entity is responsible. Was the snowplow operated by the city, county, or state highway department? Ideally, you should have received this information at the time of the accident, but if you didn't, contact the police for a copy of your accident report.

*The laws that require government entities to take responsibility for damages usually don't require them to do so without a fight.*

■ **Act quickly.** Most government units place fairly short time limits on filing a formal written claim—sometimes as short as 30 days from the date of the accident. To find out the filing deadline in your case, call the city or county attorney's office or the state attorney general's office if your claim is against a state department. By law, officials must tell you the deadline. Be sure to get the name and title of the person you speak to, in case the government later claims that you filed too late.

■ **Ask the government agency for a claims form.** In a few states, no forms are used, so you have to make a claim without one. Generally, your claim must include the following:

● Your name, address, and telephone number. If you're filing on behalf of yourself and your minor child or children, include their names and a statement that you are acting on their behalf as their parent and legal guardian.

● A short description of the date, time, and location of the accident and a brief statement of why you believe that the government is liable. For example, "The snowplow operated by James Stevenson, a state employee, made a left turn without signaling and struck the side of my car."

● A description of the injuries and the property damage that you suffered as a result.

● A claim for compensation—in the short time allowed for filing,

you may not have completed your medical treatment, so it can be hard to figure how much money to ask for. Most experts suggest setting the amount of your claim relatively high. As negotiations with the government progress, the amount of the claim will likely change anyway.

● The date of your claim and your signature.

## HOW TO FILE YOUR CLAIM

You may want to consult a lawyer to make sure that you've addressed your claim to the appropriate place and included all the information required by law. In most cases, you should file your claim directly with the agency involved in the accident. But in some states, you must file your claim with the city or county attorney if the agency operated at that level. If the accident involved a state employee, you may have to file with a Department of Claims or the state attorney general's office.

**TAKE NOTE** *If you don't want to hire a lawyer but aren't absolutely certain which agency to file with, file your claim with all of them. This way, you don't risk missing the deadline by filing with the wrong agency. Once it becomes clear exactly which agency is involved, you can withdraw or drop your case against the others.*

Mail or deliver two copies of your claim to each government agency. If you use the post office, send the claim by certified mail, return

receipt requested. Ask the agencies to return one of the copies marked with the date and time it received your claim. If you deliver the claim in person, the clerk should stamp the copies with the time and date, then return a copy to you.

## WHAT HAPPENS NEXT

In the majority of cases, the government's first response will be a letter denying liability for the damages you suffered. Don't be too alarmed. The laws that require government entities to take responsibility for damages usually don't require them to do so without a fight. Once your claim is denied, you have the right to bring a lawsuit against the government. Filing a lawsuit is the event that will finally trigger the negotiation process.

After you file your suit, you will most likely receive a call from a claims adjuster. Like an adjuster from a private insurance company, this person's job is to investigate your claim and decide what compensation to offer. Like any claims adjuster, her task includes figuring out ways to get you to accept the smallest amount of money possible. Fighting back and winning involves being aware of adjusters' tricks and tactics, being prepared and organized, and knowing what you want.

## DEALING WITH THE ADJUSTER

No matter what amount you claim, the adjuster will tell you that you're asking for more than you're entitled to receive. She may suggest that the government isn't liable or that the amount and type of your medical treatment was excessive. She may tell you that in order to avoid long and drawn-out negotiation (and because she's such a good person), she's willing to settle your claim without having to "get the lawyers involved." Then she'll propose a very low payment, mainly to see how much research you've done about your claim and if you're desperate enough to take a quick settlement.

■ **Tell her thanks, but no thanks.** Point out all the evidence that you accumulated in support

### SMART MOVES

Experienced personal-injury lawyers recommend that you immediately begin a daily diary of all health problems that occur after an accident, and log in all treatments and expenses. As you recover, it's likely that you will forget just how much pain you experienced immediately following the accident. Writing down your experiences as they happen is important to the eventual outcome of your claim.

of the figure you proposed. If she claims that you've been to the doctor too many times, tell her (if it's true) that you may not be finished with medical treatment yet. If she questions the agency's liability, refer her to the accident report that named the snow-plow driver as the party responsible for the accident. Be calm and don't let the adjuster manipulate you into making any statement indicating that you're willing to settle for a pittance instead of the full amount your claim is worth.

■ **Make a counteroffer.** The adjuster may make a second, higher offer. If this offer seems reasonable but is still less than fair, it's time to make a counteroffer. The adjuster may be able to agree to the dollar amount you suggest, or she may need to discuss it with a supervisor before approving it. Most adjusters have limits set in advance on the amount of money that they can offer to settle a claim.

■ **Think it over.** If the second offer isn't much better than the first, tell the adjuster you want some time to think it over. Then write the adjuster a letter. Point out why her justifications for the low offer are inadequate. Restate the original amount of your claim, and give her a date by which to reply to your letter, such as within 30 days. Send the letter certified mail, return receipt requested, and save a copy for your files. If your reasons are sound and well documented, your letter may convince the adjuster to meet your demand or to raise her own offer.

## SETTLEMENT DOCUMENTS

Provided your claim is reasonable, it's extremely unlikely that you will actually have to go to court to collect from the government. By negotiating with the adjuster, you will ultimately arrive at a figure that you and the government can live with. After you agree orally to a settlement figure, write a letter to the adjuster, confirming the figure and requesting the written settlement agreement and any necessary releases within a specified period. The adjuster has probably told you how soon she can send the forms, and you should restate this time period in your letter. Send your confirmation letter by certified mail, return receipt requested.

When you receive the settlement documents, review them carefully to be sure that they accurately reflect the agreement you made. For example, if you agreed to a lump-sum payment but the written agreement offers installment payments, the document must be corrected by the adjuster (if you make any changes or dele-tions yourself, you will cause time-consuming bureaucratic problems) before you sign off. Don't sign your name on any agreements or releases until you are completely satisfied with the terms.

When you are satisfied, sign the agreement and release, keep copies for your files, and return the original documents to the adjuster. Once the papers are in the adjuster's office, you can expect to receive your payment in a relatively short time period, usually no more than several weeks.

*At a Little League game, your 10-year-old son was injured when a teammate threw a bat at him. League officials claim they can't be held responsible because you signed a waiver of liability.*

Kids will be kids, but that doesn't mean your child should be harmed by an angry teammate. When you enroll your child in most recreational activities, you are generally required to sign a release that relieves the organizers of the activity from liability in the event that your child is injured. But even when you sign

*Ten-year-old ballplayers aren't held to the same level of responsibility for their actions as are older players.*

a release, you are usually only excusing the organizers from having to pay for injuries your child may suffer during ordinary play. So if your son broke his ankle sliding into second base, you probably would have no claim for the injury.

In this case, however, your son was the victim of behavior that isn't a normal part of playing little-league baseball. Throwing a bat can constitute reckless or intentional behavior that shows a disregard for the safety of other players.

Of course, 10-year-old ballplayers aren't held to the same level of responsibility for their actions as are older players. But it's possible that a court will find the league responsible for failing to adequately supervise its players. For example, suppose the player who threw his bat at your son had done the same thing on several earlier occasions. The league may have had an obligation to suspend or even to expel this misbehaving player from the league. If it didn't take action earlier on, then the league may be guilty of endangering your child.

### THE FACTS OF YOUR CASE

Court decisions can vary widely even in the same state, depending on the exact facts of each case. So talking to a lawyer who practices personal-injury law is probably your best course of action. A personal-injury lawyer can help you determine who may be responsible (the player, his parents, the team manager, the league, or any combination of these people) and also tell you what kind of damages you and your child are entitled to receive. An experienced lawyer can also review the release you signed before enrolling your son in the league and determine what effect the release could have on the league's liability.

In some states, you can file a lawsuit on your own behalf as well as on behalf of your child. Whether this kind of suit is permitted and what its chances of success will be depend on your state laws and previous court decisions in the jurisdiction where you live. Be sure to get specific legal advice before beginning to fight back.

*At the grocery store, you slipped on a wet spot on the floor of the produce department and fell, hurting your back. The store's management refuses to pay your medical bills.*

Most of us don't think of the vegetable section of a grocery store as a danger zone. But next to automobile accidents, *premises liability* cases are the most common sort of accidents reported. Commonly known as *slip-and-fall cases,* these accidents most often happen in supermarkets and drugstores. They also occur when someone trips on a city sidewalk or has a fall in just about any commercial building.

When you enter a store or other commercial building to shop or conduct business, you are what the law calls an *invitee.* While you're on the premises, the owner or operator of the business has a duty to protect you from dangers he knows about. He also has a duty to protect you from dangerous situations he ought to discover through reasonable care. A business's customers have a right to expect that they will be safe from reasonably foreseeable injury while in the store.

### CLEANUP ON AISLE THREE

As the injured party, the law places the burden of proof on you, and proving a slip-and-fall case isn't always easy. To convince a court of the store's responsibility in your case, you'll need to show that the owner or operator of the store had *actual or constructive knowledge* of the wet floor in the produce department. This means that…

- The wet floor was the result of the actions of the store's operator or of the store's employees (the employees had spilled the water themselves).
- The store had actual knowledge or notice of the dangerous condition (someone reported the spill to store personnel, or an employee noticed it).
- The condition had existed for so long that the store should have known about it and should have taken steps to remedy it (the floor had been wet for hours, but no employees or managers had

inspected the situation and mopped up or cordoned off the area containing the spill).

Courts often find that a spill wasn't on the floor long enough for the store to have discovered and fixed the problem. But testimony from other customers and from store personnel—that the spill was a recurring problem, for example, or that it had been noted some time before your fall and nothing had been done—can help you win your case. Courts have ruled that actual or constructive knowledge isn't always required when an unreasonably dangerous condition is either continuous (that display case always leaks) or reasonably foreseeable (piling those strawberries up too high made it likely that some of them would fall on the floor and get crushed underfoot).

### THE STORE FIGHTS BACK

Defendants in slip-and-fall cases almost always raise the question of your contributory or comparative negligence as part of their defense. In essence, the store argues that you should have seen the wet spot and avoided it.

But there are a couple of situations that may have prevented you from seeing the dangerous wet spot on the floor:

> **W**hile you're on the premises, the owner or operator of the business has a duty to protect you from dangers he knows about.

• Stores often create attractive displays and stage promotions designed to catch your attention. If the store was encouraging you to admire its handsome mound of strawberries or offering samples of its products to its customers, it can't then argue that you should have kept your eyes glued to the floor.

• If the lighting was poor or the design on the floor made it difficult to tell a wet spot from a dry one, the store's attempt to shift the blame to you is unlikely to be very successful.

Some stores have tried to argue that because their store is self-service, the injured customer created the problem himself. For example, if a shopper takes watermelons out of an ice-filled display case, he may spill water and ice on the floor around the display. If he slips on the ice, the store claims that the customer caused the spill and the business is not responsible for any injuries. But courts have ruled that when a store offers self-service to its customers, it isn't just for the shoppers' convenience. The store benefits because it doesn't have to hire as many clerks and other employees to help the customers. So this kind of "you did it to yourself" argument isn't usually successful.

## GETTING YOUR DUE

To win your slip-and-fall case, you must act quickly. Witnesses should be interviewed and photos taken. If you're in a great deal of physical pain, taking action yourself may be impossible. Enlist the help of friends or family members who may be able to help. Call your lawyer; he may know an investigator who'll take on the job.

While everyone has heard about big awards in slip-and-fall cases, most claims are settled for far less than the awards trumpeted on the evening news. In fact, many giant-size awards are reduced on appeal or by negotiations that take place while an appeal is pending. Injured parties need money. Big businesses and their insurers can often convince a winning plaintiff to accept less than the full amount of a jury award by talking about lengthy appeals and the likelihood that the verdict will be overturned or a new trial ordered.

> **Y**ou read an article about doctors in the local newspaper. A former patient of yours is quoted as calling you a "quack."

Hateful words can hurt more than your feelings. The First Amendment doesn't give someone the automatic right to use words that are aimed to wreck your reputation and career. When someone makes an untrue and derogatory statement about you and holds you up to ridicule, contempt, hatred, or abuse, she may be guilty of *defamation.*

• Defamation that's spoken is called *slander.*
• Defamation made in writing is *libel.*

In most states the distinction between slander and libel isn't as significant as it once was. In law, defamation is a *tort*—a civil wrong committed by one person against another—and can be the basis for a lawsuit. Sound simple? Before you rush into court to sue your former patient, there are some important facts you should know.

## THE ELEMENTS OF DEFAMATION

If defamation claims were easy, the courts would be hearing them every day, all day. But there are limits on your ability to prove that you were defamed. In order to proceed with a defamation lawsuit, you must first ask some questions about your former patient's statement:

■ **Was the statement communicated to someone other than yourself?** If your former patient insulted you in a private conversation between the two of you, no defamation has taken place. But if, as here, she's quoted calling you a quack in a public forum, or if she told your neighbors and other patients that you're a quack, then the first element of defamation has been met.

■ **Were you identified as the person about whom the statement was made?** If the article didn't name you specifically or if the statement was something like "All doctors are quacks," your defamation claim is probably not strong. However, if the article didn't use your name but identified you by the nature of your practice, and if you are the only doctor practicing your specialty in the area, then a court might decide that this identification was enough to defame you.

■ **Was the statement really injurious?** Calling you a quack probably is, because it can directly affect your ability to earn a living. In fact, if you noticed a rash of cancellations by other patients or a sudden drop in referrals after the article appeared, you have solid evidence that you have been damaged by your former patient's remarks.

■ **Was the statement untrue?** If you've been stripped of your license to practice or have been the subject of a multitude of malpractice suits, a court may decide that there was enough truth to the former patient's statement to deny your claim of defamation.

■ **Was the former patient's statement privileged in any way?** For example, if your former patient is a member of the state legislature and she made her comments there in the discussion of pending legislation about regulating doctors, you may not be able to bring a case against her, no matter how harmful or untrue her statement was. The law extends special protection to lawmakers and other government officials when they make otherwise defamatory statements in the course of conducting official government business.

■ **Are you a public figure?** If you're often in the public limelight, the law generally makes it harder (although not impossible) for you to receive damages when someone makes a defamatory comment about you. To succeed, you must prove that the statement was made with actual malice. *Actual malice* is defined as making the statement with knowledge that it isn't true or with reckless disregard as to its truth or falsehood.

## WHAT ABOUT THE NEWSPAPER?

Because it printed your ex-patient's comment about you, the newspaper could also be held liable for defamation. The paper may be liable under what's known as *republication:* the former patient defamed you by making the statement to a reporter, and the reporter and the newspaper defamed you by republishing the statement to the periodical's readers.

## HOW TO RECLAIM YOUR REPUTATION

You can demand a retraction from the former patient and the newspaper. If the retraction is given the same prominence in the paper as the original statement, this will go a long way toward reducing the amount of damage you've suffered. But it won't undo the damage entirely.

If the newspaper and your former patient refuse to take back the damaging remarks, you may want to file suit against the newspaper, the reporter, and the former patient. If you win, you can be awarded damages from all of them for injuring your good reputation in the community. Damages could include compensation for…

- Actual and presumed financial losses
- Emotional distress and suffering caused by the defamation
- Physical illness and suffering caused by the defamation
- Punitive damages, if the jury decides that the defendants acted with malice.

Defamation awards can be large. In a recent case, a jury awarded a Colorado couple more than $10 million dollars after they were falsely and unfairly accused of anti-Semitism at a press conference conducted (ironically) by officials of an antidefamation group.

It isn't always easy to make a defamation case stick, so good legal assistance is essential. Check with your state or local bar association for the names of lawyers in your area who have experience handling defamation cases.

INSURANCE TANGLES

**You file an insurance claim, but the claims agent says your policy has lapsed because your premium wasn't paid. Your bank statement shows your check was received before payment was due.**

In a situation like this, the best-case scenario is that the problem is the result of a mix-up and can be easily corrected. The worst-case scenario is that your agent has diverted the payment for his own use. Here's how to find out whether it's an innocent mistake or whether it's outright theft, and what you can do about it.

### CONTACT YOUR INSURANCE REPRESENTATIVES

First, call your agent about the problem. It may be that your payment was incorrectly credited to another policyholder's account. If this is the case, your agent needs to contact the insurance company and have your policy reinstated. Be sure that he informs the insurance company that your payment was made in time to keep your policy in force, and ask him for a copy of any written communication he has with the insurer.

If the agent drags his feet about helping you, take it upon yourself to get in touch with the insurer's home office. Write to the customer relations department at the address shown on your policy. Your letter—sent by certified mail, return receipt requested—should state the following:

- You have had a claim denied, supposedly due to a lapse in your policy.
- You paid the premium to your agent before the policy would have lapsed for nonpayment (enclose a copy of the front and reverse side of your canceled check).
- Your agent has not cooperated in getting your policy reinstated and your claim paid.
- You expect to have the matter settled in your favor within a specified period of time (10 business days is plenty in most cases).
- You reserve the right to take further action if your policy isn't reinstated and your claim paid by the deadline you've assigned.

This is likely to get results. An insurance agent who is authorized to accept premium payments is acting on behalf of the parent-insurance company. The insurance company probably does not want trouble with the state over the mistake—honest or otherwise—of its agent.

**If the insurance company balks at your demand...or if it simply ignores...[it], it's time to get your state—insurance department involved.**

### CALL THE INSURANCE COPS

If the insurance company balks at your demand for acknowledging your payment and paying your claim, or if it simply ignores the demand, it's time to get your state-insurance department involved. (You'll find the telephone number for the state department in the state government listings of your telephone directory.)

Ask to speak to someone in the consumer-protection division, then give him a brief account of your problem. Find out how to file your claim in writing. The department may have a form for you to complete, or it may simply ask for a letter and copies of correspondence and documents that support your complaint.

The state-insurance department will investigate your claim and then will order the insurance company to reinstate your policy and pay your claim, or else face penalties. These penalties could include fines or possibly having their operating license suspended or revoked.

The state-insurance department will also look into the ethics of your local agent's actions. If the department decides that the local agent has misappropriated your insurance payment, it can suspend or revoke his license to practice and, in some cases, even recommend that the individual agent be criminally prosecuted.

> *Your health-insurance application was rejected because the insurer says it has information proving that you have a preexisting heart condition. You know that you don't have a heart problem.*

Insurance companies may appear to know more about you than you know about yourself. When you apply for health, disability, or life insurance, you're almost always required to have a medical exam, with the results being forwarded to the Medical Information Bureau (MIB), a storehouse of health-related information kept on millions of insurance applicants. These files record not only medical problems but also family history of diseases, the results of lab tests, suicide attempts, and psychological disorders. That's not all—they also have information on risky hobbies you may engage in, such as playing rugby or flying experimental aircraft; any occupational hazards you may be exposed to; and also your driving record.

The problem is that, like credit records, MIB's files can often be inaccurate. Sometimes a doctor enters a wrong code in an MIB file, or the MIB can't read a code, or your record is confused with someone else's, resulting in you being improperly denied.

## SMART MOVES

If you're planning to buy life, health, or disability insurance, examine your Medical Information Bureau (MIB) file before you apply. Getting an advance copy will cost you $8, but knowing what's in your file can save you time and trouble later.

## CHALLENGE IT

Here are the steps to disputing the rejection:

■ **Contact the insurer** and ask if the decision to deny you coverage—or to charge higher rates—was influenced by information contained in your MIB file. The same law that covers credit reports requires insurers to give you this information.

■ **Get a copy of your MIB file.** If you have been denied coverage on the basis of your MIB file, you have a right to a free copy so you can review it. Call the MIB at (617) 426-3660 and ask how to obtain your file.

■ **Challenge the report** if you believe that it is incorrect. Call the MIB and point out any inaccuracies in your file. Your call will set the following investigation in motion:
● The MIB will contact the insurer that submitted the information.
● The insurer is then required to check with the physician who provided the information.
● The insurer must also make reasonable efforts to contact the doctors that you suggest. They can support your challenge.
● If the report is wrong, it will be deleted from your file.

■ **Request a reexamination** by the insurer that turned you down, if after everything you've done, they still dispute your challenge.

■ **Add a statement to your insurance file** that disputes the findings if nothing you do convinces the insurer to change the report.

## MEDICAL SAVINGS ACCOUNTS

In the late 1990s, Congress passed legislation that enables at least some Americans to pay for health care with tax-free savings. Medical Savings Accounts (MSA) are available to people who are self-employed and to those who work for a company that has 50 or fewer employees and offers no health-care coverage for its employees. If you are young, relatively healthy, and can afford it, an MSA can be worth investigating. In a nutshell, with an MSA you'll find the following:

■ **You purchase a private health-insurance policy** with a large deductible (the amount you have to pay before the insurer has to begin making payments). You also must make some co-payments (contributions toward expenses after your deductible is met). But the total you must pay out of pocket each year is capped. Individuals can pay no more than $3,000, while a family's contribution is capped at $5,500. Figures are periodically adjusted for inflation.

■ **You open an MSA savings account,** which must be held by a bank, insurance company, or other custodian. The money you can deposit each year is limited: up to 65 percent of the deductible for an individual, up to 75 percent of the deductible for a family. The money in the account earns tax-free interest. When you turn 65, the only money you have to pay taxes on is the excess amount you deposited and the interest earned over time. As a senior citizen, your tax rate will be lower and the tax bite won't be so large.

■ **You write a check on your MSA account** when you need to pay for medical treatment. Any money that's left at the end of the year is yours to keep, and taxes are deferred until you are age 65, or until you withdraw the money for a nonmedical purpose.

MSAs are not suitable for those people who have health problems, nor are they suitable for those who may have nonmedical emergencies that they can't pay for with other funds, because there are penalties in addition to the taxes you pay for withdrawing the money before you reach the age of 65. Talk to your insurance agent or contact your state-department of insurance for information about those insurers that offer MSAs to residents of your state.

*When you receive your health-insurance policy, you notice that the agent has changed some of the answers on your health questionnaire.*

Insurance agents get commissions for selling policies, so it's in their financial interest to make a sale. With this in mind, some unethical agents will "cleansheet" an application—meaning that they minimize an applicant's health problems, or perhaps even falsify answers on the application in order to get the insurer to approve it. Unfortunately, you could be left dangling if the insurer later discovers that the answers on the application were untrue; it can deny your claims.

### REPORT THE PROBLEM

Don't accept the agent's assurances that "everybody does that" or "answering that question isn't important." In fact, at this point you're probably better off having no contact with the agent at all. Instead, take the following steps:

■ **Write to the insurance company** as soon as you discover the problem, and describe the error. (Their address should be listed on the policy.) Ask that they give you, in writing, a statement that they have received the corrected application information and that your policy will continue to be in effect.

- **Contact your state department of insurance** and report the insurance agent's actions. The insurance department licenses agents, and if it finds that your agent has falsified applications, it can revoke her license to do business. It may also be able to fine the agent for violating state-insurance regulations.

### THE TRUTH ABOUT INSURANCE

Whether you will be accepted for coverage and what your insurance rates will be are determined by the answers you put on the insurer's detailed health questionnaire. If you or someone in your family whom you want to cover has recently had cancer, heart disease, or other serious illnesses, you may have a hard time getting health insur-

ance, or the cost of the insurance coverage may be so high that it's not affordable.

---

*Insurance agents get commissions for selling policies, so it's in their financial interest to make a sale.*

---

If the insurance company turns down your request to amend the policy, you'll have to look elsewhere for a new legitimate policy. Unfortunately, you may find that your new policy comes with higher payment rates or limited benefits, but at least you won't be denied insurance coverage when those big medical bills start to roll in.

---

*Your health-insurance rates keep going up and up, and you just received notice of another rate hike. You wonder if there's anything you can do.*

---

Although it may seem that insurance companies raise rates with abandon, in fact a rate hike requires the approval of the state department of insurance. In recent years, some insurers have tried to raise rates without getting approval first. If they're caught, they may claim that the rate increase was a mistake or was made because policy holders needed to be notified of the increase by a certain date—after the increase.

Neither argument holds much water, especially when it's discovered that some of these increases remain in place even after the state denies or reduces them. State-insurance regulators have issued hundreds of thousands of dollars in fines against companies

that raised rates without permission. In addition, insurers who failed to obtain the state's consent to rate increases have often been ordered to refund the excess amount to their customers.

### SMART MOVES

You can learn about the latest lawsuits, major state insurance department complaints, and investigations into insurance-company practices from around the country on the Internet at www.insure.com.

#### INVESTIGATE HEALTH-INSURANCE HIKES

When your insurance rates go up, you can find out if the rate hike was authorized by doing the following things:

- **Contact your insurance agent** or your insurance company's customer-service department and ask for verification that the rate increase has been authorized.
- **Call or write your state department** of insurance and ask it to verify that the higher

rate was approved. The department of insurance may take a few days to give you a response. In the interim, make the higher payment in order to keep your coverage in place. If the rate hike wasn't approved, you should be able to get a refund. If the hike was approved, you'll have to pay the higher rate from now on in order to maintain your policy.

**TAKE NOTE** *Applying for an increase isn't the same as having it approved. If you're told that the application for an insurance rate increase was made on a particular date, ask for the date it was passed. If the rate hike was approved, there isn't much you can do about it. But you can, however, start shopping for less expensive protection.*

## YOUR LAST RESORT

If you discover that your insurance company has raised its rates without getting the required approval from the state department of insurance, consider filing a lawsuit against the insurer. Talk to a lawyer who has experience in handling cases against insurance companies.

It may be possible to file a federal class-action suit on behalf of insurance policy holders in other states as well as yours. (Companies that violate regulations in one state are often found to have violated them elsewhere.)

If the company has misrepresented its authorization to raise payment rates, it could be liable for damages in addition to having to refund any extra money it collected from its policyholders.

## HOW TO REDUCE YOUR INSURANCE PREMIUMS

While insurance rates continue to increase, there are steps you can take to cut the cost of your insurance protection. To lower your premiums…

■ **Increase your deductibles**—raising the amount you pay before the insurer starts to kick in can be a great way to reduce your overall insurance cost. For example, upping your health-insurance deductible from $250 to $1,000 can mean a savings of 20 percent or more on your premium. It may be worth it if you are in good health, or have an accident-free history.

■ **Take advantage of "good behavior" discounts**—if you reduce the risk to the insurer, the insurer will often reduce the cost to you. To lower your premium with your auto insurer…

- Install antitheft devices, such as alarms and ignition cutoffs.

- Install a "lowjack" transmitter that helps police track your car if it is stolen.

- Send your children to driving school, or enroll in a defensive-driving course.

- Encourage your teenagers to get good grades to become eligible for insurance discounts.

To reduce your home-owners insurance premium…

- Add deadbolt locks and burglar alarms to your home.

- Modify landscaping to minimize places where burglars or intruders could hide.

To get a reduction in health- and life-insurance rates…

- Stop smoking.

- Look into wellness programs that your insurance company may sponsor.

■ **Shop around**—insurance rates can vary dramatically from one insurer to the next. The same policy that company A offers can cost as much as 15 percent less at company B. If you're happy with your current insurer except for the cost, let your agent know that you got a lower quote elsewhere. He may be able to offer you a similar discount.

■ **Give your business to one company**—if you have your homeowner's and auto insurance with the same company, you are usually eligible for a discount on both policies.

Not all insurance companies are as solid as you might like to think. According to Standard & Poor's, a company that rates insurers, 35 companies providing coverage to millions of Americans became insolvent in 1999, and that number is expected to rise in the coming years. In most cases, insurance companies fail because they don't charge high enough premiums to cover the expenses involved in paying their customers' claims. Happily, in most states the law provides you with financial protection when an insurer goes broke.

## WHO PAYS THE BILLS?

In most states, if your insurance company is unable to pay claims, payment is taken over by the state insurance department. Claims are paid from *guaranty funds,* fees paid by all licensed insurers operating within a state. These funds are similar to insurance for bank customers—they protect consumers when an insurer goes bankrupt or goes out of business.

If an insurance company is failing, most states require that it send its customers written notice of its insolvency. It must also tell you the following:

- When your coverage will end
- How your outstanding claims will be paid
- When the state-guaranty fund will take over the payment of your claims
- How to contact the state-guaranty fund with questions about your coverage. .

At about the same time, your state insurance department will write you to confirm that it is taking over the claims process.

## FULL OR PARTIAL PAYMENT?

Most state-guaranty funds are able to pay the full amount that would have been covered by your insurer. In a few states, however, these funds may be insufficient to pay very large medical bills. If this is your situation, you should be notified early.

Keep in mind that health insurance doesn't relieve you of the primary responsibility for your medical bills. You may end up having to pay a greater portion of the medical bills out of your own pocket. Sometimes, though, health-care providers will agree to accept the state's payment as payment in full. Contact your providers' billing departments and ask if they can negotiate such an arrangement.

## KEEP YOUR DOCTORS INFORMED

There can be delays in getting payment as the state insurance department takes over claims administration from your insurer. In the meantime, you will probably continue to receive bills from your health-care providers, with reminders to pay, which will become increasingly insistent. When that happens, here's what to do:

- **Contact the health-care providers** who haven't been paid and let them know about the insurance company's failure. Most doctors, clinics, and hospitals will be patient once they learn about the problem, as long as you keep them informed and don't simply ignore the bills they send out.
- **Consider paying at least a token amount** on outstanding bills as you receive them. Some experts suggest doing this to show that you are acting in good faith. This may make the health-care provider take a less strident tone in its collection letters and invoices.
- **Make all payments by check or money order,** and keep good records of the date and amount you paid. When the state reimburses a doctor or hospital that you've already paid, you should receive a refund. Sometimes a health-care provider can be as slow to refund your money as the state was to pay the claim. You can speed this process by presenting your payment record along with the notice of payment the state will send you.

## STAY IN TOUCH WITH THE STATE

The state insurance department will pay claims it is aware of as long as they were made while your coverage was still in effect. But claim forms sometimes go astray, and a claim you submitted to your insurance company may not make it into your file with the guaranty fund's claims representatives. It's a good idea to give the guaranty fund copies of all of the unpaid claims that you had filed prior to the time your insurer failed.

If you continue to get collection letters or calls from the unpaid providers, write a letter asking the state insurance department to contact them about your situation. This may ease their minds about receiving payment.

### FIND NEW COVERAGE

Although you probably don't have to worry about having your outstanding bills paid, you will need to find a new insurer to cover you in the future.

Talk to the guaranty association's representative: he or she may have a list of insurance companies that are willing to work with the customers who are left without coverage.

Keep in mind, however, that you may not find the same level of coverage at the same price as before. Insurers are allowed to set their own rates for the policies they offer, and they may sometimes exclude certain preexisting conditions or limit the benefits they pay for them.

---

## INSURANCE SCAMS

Not every company on the Internet is what it appears to be, and that's true of some insurance companies as well.

■ **Beware of a professional-looking Web site that offers rock-bottom insurance rates**—far lower than those you can obtain elsewhere.

■ **Some companies selling insurance in cyberspace may not be licensed in your state,** so if the company fails, your state department of insurance can't protect you. Others may operate outside the United States, where federal laws can't reach them.

■ **Other companies may be outright crooked** and will take your money and run, shutting down their Web sites and opening others with a different name.

*Always check with your state department of insurance to confirm that a company is licensed to do business in your state before signing on and sending any of your money to an Internet insurance company.*

---

*You bought disability insurance to protect you if you were unable to work. Now that you need it, the insurer claims that you aren't disabled and refuses to pay the benefits.*

---

Fraudulent claims for disability insurance are becoming epidemic in this country, making insurers increasingly cautious about paying disability claims. And if your insurer is suffering financial difficulties of its own, it may delay or deny claims that it once would have paid without question. Although most disability insurers pay legitimate claims as promised, and they deny only those that don't meet the terms set out in the insurance policy, there's always the chance that

you're being taken advantage of by one of the insurance industry's bad apples.

### FILE AGAIN

If you receive a denial-of-benefits letter for your claim from the insurer, you can do the following:

■ **Contact your insurance company** and ask for a detailed explanation of the reasons it used to refuse to pay your claim.

- **Obtain another form** if your claim was denied because you didn't complete the the first one properly.
- **Ask your doctor for help in filling out the new form.** Some companies slant questions on the claims form in a way that's designed to get you to minimize a disability. Having your doctor's help in completing the form can reduce the chance of your being denied again. Be sure to make copies for your files.

**TAKE NOTE** *Advise your doctor of the work you do and the psychological and physical requirements involved. This way, he won't unintentionally increase the chances that your benefits will continue to be denied.*

## CALL IN THE STATE WATCHDOGS

If the insurer reconsiders your claim and still refuses to pay, it's time to enlist outside aid. First, understand that taking on an insurance company alone is probably not a good idea. Instead, get in touch with your state insurance regulators immediately and let them know all about the insurer's actions. In some states, the state insurance department can take legal action against an insurer that fails to pay legitimate claims.

## HIRE A LAWYER

While there may be some expense, you should also contact an attorney to help you deal with the company. She will want to see the following:

- ✔ Your disability policy
- ✔ Your doctor's reports
- ✔ Claims forms that you have completed
- ✔ Correspondence between you and the insurance company about how to settle your claim.

If after reviewing the material you provide, the lawyer determines that the company's denial of benefits is unjustified, she may be able to resolve the problem for you by writing a letter to the firm pointing out its mistake.

Insurance companies have been known to deny benefits they should have paid, in the hope that the policyholder would not spend the time and money to pursue the matter in court. By hiring an attorney, you will show the insurer that you mean business and won't accept its improper denial of your benefits.

Once you hire an attorney, the insurance company may contact you with an offer to settle your claim for a lump sum. Refer all such offers to your lawyer. The company's settlement offer may seem generous at first, but it could actually be far less than you are entitled to receive over the full term of your disability. A lawyer experienced in dealing with insurance companies can help you accurately evaluate the company's offer.

## Go to Court

If you still can't get satisfaction on your claim, talk to your lawyer about the possibility of filing a lawsuit against your insurer. In most cases, if the chance for success is good and potential damages are large enough, your lawyer will agree to take your case on a contingency basis, accepting a portion of the money you receive as payment.

Be sure to ask about having the insurance company pay for your legal fees in the event that you win your case, but be aware that some courts are reluctant to do so if the insurer can make a reasonable case for rejecting your claim.

However, if your insurance company is found to have acted in bad faith, getting your legal fees reimbursed is much more likely.

### PICKING A DISABILITY INSURANCE POLICY

Disability insurance is designed to replace some or all of your income when you are seriously injured or suffer a major illness and are unable to work. But policies vary widely in what they cover, how much they pay, and the length of time for which they provide benefits. A good disability insurance policy...

■ **Offers an elimination period of 90 to 120 days**—the elimination period is the time you have to wait after you are disabled before benefits begin. You can save a lot of money on premiums by choosing a policy that isn't required to begin paying immediately. Put the savings in an interest-bearing bank account to help pay for the early period of your disability.

■ **Covers 60 percent of your gross income**—disability benefits are tax-free when you pay for your own policy, so you don't have to buy coverage for income that would otherwise be going to Uncle Sam. Nor do you need to pay those increased premiums.

■ **Covers partial disability**—this would apply if you are able to perform some of your usual work but not all of it. Your policy should help make up the difference in income.

■ **Covers you when you can't work at your own occupation**—otherwise, if you're able to work at *any* job, no matter how unrelated to your occupation, you could be denied benefits.

■ **Provides *predisability inflation protection***—this gives you the option of increasing your coverage every year for a stated time period, for a small increase in premiums. If you don't want the higher coverage, you don't have to pay for it.

■ **Covers you only until retirement age**—once you reach retirement age, you won't have any lost wages to worry about replacing. This policy will be much less expensive than one that promises to pay benefits for life.

■ **Offers waiver of premium,** which means you don't have to continue paying on your policy during the time you are receiving benefits.

> *Y*our elderly mother, who suffers from mental lapses, recently bought a life-insurance policy she doesn't need from a company she saw on television.

The law in every state requires that a person have the *capacity* to enter into a contract in order for it to be enforceable. Capacity means being of sound mind: able to know what you are doing and the consequences of your actions. While it's possible that your mother's mental state doesn't mean she's incapable of handling certain day-to-day matters, if she doesn't remember buying the policy or why she bought it, you probably have a good case for canceling her purchase.

## ACT QUICKLY

Most insurance policies provide what's known as a *free look*. After you purchase the policy, you have a specified period—usually between 10 and 30 days—in which to review the policy. If you choose to return it within that period, any premiums you paid must be refunded. If your mother's policy is still in the free-look period, getting the policy canceled shouldn't be all that difficult. Simply have your mother write the word "canceled" and the date across the declarations page, and return the policy to the company by certified mail, return receipt requested.

### BEYOND THE "FREE LOOK"

If you're past the no-questions-asked time period provided by the free look, you will next need to take the following actions:

- **Call the insurer** and explain the situation. There's probably a toll-free customer service number on the policy or the materials that came with it. Be sure to record the name of the representative, as well as the date and time of the conversation and what was said.
- **Ask that the insurance policy be canceled** and that the company refund any unearned premium to your mother.
- **Put your request in writing** and return the policy to the insurer if a phone call is not enough. Be sure to keep a copy of your correspondence for your files.

### NOTIFY THE STATE

If the insurer your mother bought the policy from refuses to cancel it, you may want to take stronger measures. Contact your state department of insurance (listed in the phone book's government listings in the white pages) and register your complaint.

The department can review the company's advertising and marketing

---

### SMART MOVES

If you have an elderly parent whose mental state makes it impossible for her to handle her finances or to care for herself in other ways, consider having yourself or someone else appointed by the court as durable power of attorney in order to manage her finances and major life decisions.

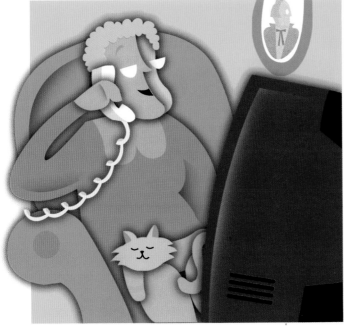

practices. If it finds that the company should have known about your mother's condition—for example, if her application was incomplete or filled out in a way that would indicate that she was confused—it could require the insurance company to cancel her policy and refund the premiums.

## INSURANCE YOU *DON'T* NEED

Some insurance policies are simply a bad buy, either because they are too expensive for the amount of coverage they offer or because they pay off only under very limited conditions, or both. Avoid spending your money on the following:

- **Credit life-insurance policies** offered by a bank or other lender. These policies offer what is known as decreasing term insurance: The total amount the policy will pay decreases along with the amount you owe. If you die with only one payment left, that's all the policy will pay. You can almost always buy regular term-life insurance that pays a specified benefit for less than you would pay for credit-life insurance.

- **Disability or unemployment policies** that offer to make your minimum monthly credit-card payments if you are injured or lose your job. Making the minimum payment will almost guarantee that your balance will never be paid off; in fact, with some credit cards, it may actually increase. And the insurance is expensive in relation to the coverage—typically about $1 per month for every $100 you owe.

- **Dread-disease policies** that provide benefits only if you suffer from a specified illness, such as cancer. Generally, these policies offer limited benefits in relation to the premium you pay. A regular, comprehensive health-insurance policy is always a far better value, because it covers more health problems and provides a greater benefit.

- **Hospital-expense policies** that pay a specified amount for each day you are hospitalized. Typically, these policies pay far less in benefits (for example, $100 per day when you are hospitalized for treatment) than the actual cost of a hospital stay, and they will likely cost too much for the coverage you get.

- **Air-travel insurance,** particularly the policies sold at airport kiosks pay your beneficiary if you die or are seriously injured or disabled as a result of a plane crash. But they cost too much for the benefits they pay, especially when you consider that commercial-air travel is one of the safest methods of travel.

    You may receive additional travel insurance free of charge when you charge your tickets to certain credit cards. Check the terms of your credit-card agreement to see if this coverage is offered by your company.

- **Burial-insurance policies** advertised on television and aimed at the elderly or those who can't obtain coverage elsewhere—these commercials try to convince older people that they will be brought to the brink of financial ruin by funeral expenses. Coverage is limited, and with many of these policies, if you die within two years of signing up, your beneficiary will receive only the return of any premiums you paid.

- **Pet-health insurance**—this is a recent addition to the ranks of unnecessary insurance. Most policies cost about $100 per year and offer limited benefits. For example, most of these policies won't cover regular office visits, exclude preexisting conditions, and place a relatively low maximum on the amount they will pay for surgery.

*Your son has a terminal illness,
and he's being urged to cash in his life insurance
for a fraction of its face value.*

With the onset of the AIDS crisis in the 1980s, a new business arose called the *viatical settlement* industry (from the Latin word *viaticum,* meaning "last rites"). It consists of companies that buy life-insurance policies from the terminally ill. Final-stage cancer patients and those suffering from full-blown AIDS are most often targeted by these companies.

These companies make money by buying policies at less than their face value. Generally, the shorter the life expectancy, the more a viatical company will offer for a policy. For example, someone who has been told they have less than a year to live may be able to receive $80,000 on a $100,000 policy, while someone with a three-year life expectancy may receive only $60,000 for a policy with the same face value. The dying person gets often desperately needed money to pay for medical care and other expenses while they are alive. The viatical company collects the policy's proceeds when the person dies.

Unfortunately, not all the companies offering viatical settlements are on the up-and-up. For instance, some offer to pay for the policy over a period of months. When the policyholder dies, they fail to complete the agreed-upon payments.

## LOOK INTO THE OFFER

If your son is considering a viatical settlement, you can help him by taking the following steps:

- **Investigate the legitimacy of the company** making him an offer for his policy. Contact the National Viatical Association at (800) 741-9465 and the Viatical Association of America at (800) 842-9811 to see if the company is a member of either organization.
- **Shop around.** Don't take the first offer you receive. Ask the organizations above to send

you a list of their members. Contact several and fill out the applications they send you. Offers can vary from company to company by thousands of dollars for the same policy.

---

*Find out if your
son's life insurance
policy contains a
"living benefit" provision.*

---

- **Contact your state Medicaid agency** if your son is receiving Medicaid and ask if the payment he will receive will disqualify him from further government benefits. Be sure to have them evaluate your son's continued eligibility before he sells his policy.

## EXPLORE OTHER OPTIONS

Find out if your son's life-insurance policy contains a "living benefit" provision. Today many insurers offer to let you withdraw a portion of your policy's face value if you develop a serious illness, such as AIDS, Alzheimer's disease, or terminal cancer. Some allow you to take out monthly payments for nursing-home or hospice care. Benefits are tax-free. There's less hassle, and his beneficiaries will receive any remaining benefits when he passes away.

While living benefits are more common in policies written in the past decade, some companies added this provision to older policies, often at no additional premium. As a result, many people who are eligible for living benefits aren't even aware of it. Help your son check his policy or contact his insurer for more information.

> **Y**our husband told you that he had life insurance.
> But now that he's dead, you can't find the policy anywhere.

In days gone by, many people had the same insurance agent for their entire adult lives. But today a vast population of people move around from town to town, or state to state, and insurance agents often change companies. The result is that if an insurance policy is lost or misplaced, it can be difficult to verify its existence, especially when the person who purchased it is now deceased. Still, there are steps you can take to track down a policy, even when you don't know which company wrote it.

### START THE SEARCH

Look through your husband's checkbook and canceled checks for names that could be those of an insurance company or insurance agency, especially if the checks were written regularly. If you find what may have been payments made for a life-insurance policy…

- **Call the company** the checks were written to and ask if your husband purchased a policy.
  - If the person you speak to confirms that there is a policy, request a claim form.
  - If there is no record of the policy, request the insurer's home-office address. The person you speak to may not have all the company's records available, especially if she works for an agency or the insurer's branch office.
- **Write to the insurer,** enclosing copies of the checks you think may have been written to pay the policy's premiums. In most cases, writing to the home office will be more effective than calling, because the employee investigating a written request will be under less time pressure than a telephone representative who may be evaluated on the number of calls she handles each hour.

If the insurer reports no record of an insurance policy in your husband's name, *don't* give up.

### ENLIST YOUR LAWYER

If you are using an attorney to help probate your husband's estate, ask him to investigate. Your attorney has a fiduciary responsibility to look for possible assets. He can contact the home offices of many insurers to find out if there's a policy in effect. To reduce the expense to the estate, ask him to use a paralegal for this, or, better yet, a service that will do the search for a modest fee.

### DO IT YOURSELF

You can save money by doing this search yourself. This may be time-consuming: in some states, dozens of companies are authorized to sell life insurance. But there's no time limit on filing a claim for life insurance benefits. As long as the policy was in force and the company remains in business, you can file your claim at any time after your husband's death. Try the following:

- **Contact your state department of insurance** for the names and addresses of companies licensed to sell life insurance in your state. Some states now make this information available on their Web site or will mail it to you free of charge if you call and request it. If you lived in another state when your husband bought the policy, you can get the list from that state's department of insurance.
- **Write to each insurer's home-office** address, and direct your letter to the lost- or missing-policies department. Include your husband's full name, date and place of birth, and Social Security number. The personnel will investigate and let you know if a policy was in force at the time of your husband's death, and will provide information about filing a claim.
- **Hire a company that will contact life-insurance companies** on your behalf. Your state department of insurance or an insurance agent will have information about companies that can help you track down a missing policy.

**TAKE NOTE** *Make sure that a company that offers to search on your behalf sends the information from the insurer directly to you, not to its home office. Keeping records private prevents an unscrupulous company from obtaining information about money you may be owed, and then trying to charge you a higher-than-normal fee.*

- **Contact the American Council of Life Insurance (ACLI)**. While it doesn't represent every life-insurance company, the ACLI can contact members about a claim for a missing policy on your behalf. This service is free.

> *Your agent persuaded you to trade in your life-insurance policy and buy a new one that he claimed was "a better fit." Now you find that you have less cash value and lower coverage than before.*

Trading in one life-insurance policy for another is rarely a good idea for the policyholder. Nonetheless, it's often recommended by insurance agents, because when you make the trade, your agent earns a new commission. This is known in the insurance industry as "churning," or unnecessarily replacing one policy with another one.

That second commission and any administrative expenses will come out of your policy's cash value. You'll end up with less cash value than when you started, and your policy has to earn more in interest or dividends just to put you back where you were before the switch was made, which could take years.

### STOP THE CHURNING

If your agent has tried this tactic on you…

- **Write to the president** of the insurance company your agent represents.
  - Describe how your policy was churned.
  - Insist that your original policy be reinstated.
  - Demand that any funds taken to pay for the new policy be restored to your policy.

Send the letter by certified mail, return receipt requested, and be sure to keep a copy for your records. In most cases, your letter will be enough to put things right.

### BRING IN THE STATE

If the insurance company doesn't agree that your policy has been churned, or if it refuses to credit your old policy, contact your state insurance department. Be prepared to provide the regulators with copies of…

✔ Your old and new policies
✔ Any documents that the insurance agent used to convince you to make the change
✔ Your letters to the agent or to the insurance company
✔ The replies you received.

The insurance regulators will investigate your claim and in some cases can order the insurer and the agent to cease and desist churning clients' policies. They may also be able to order the company to reinstate your previous policy.

### A CLASS-ACTION SUIT

In recent years, a number of class-action lawsuits have been filed against insurance companies in this country that either encouraged or failed to discourage their agents from churning cash-value life insurance policies.

In a class-action suit, some victims are named to represent a larger group of similarly affected policyholders. Lawyers who take on class-action suits usually do so on a contingency basis, taking a portion of any settlement or judgment that they win for their clients.

Consult an attorney with experience in insurance litigation to determine if filing suit is an option in your case. Write or call your state bar association's referral service. It can provide you with the names of attorneys in your state who are experienced in this area of the law.

## TERM- OR CASH-VALUE LIFE INSURANCE?

For years, there's been controversy over what type of life insurance is best: term life or cash-value life. Here's the lowdown on both, along with a description—and an evaluation—of the most common types of cash-value insurance.

**Term-life insurance** insures your life for a specified period of time and provides a specific benefit. So if you buy a $100,000 ten-year term-life policy, and then you die during that ten-year period, your beneficiaries get $100,000. Term life can be renewed and usually costs less than other types of life insurance, and the money you save can be put into stocks, bonds, and mutual funds.

**Cash-value life insurance** serves as an investment plan. Most experts agree that you can usually do much better investing on your own instead of through a cash-value policy. The following are some of the most popular life-insurance policies:

■ **Whole-life insurance**—some of your premium goes to buy insurance coverage; the rest goes to the savings portion of your plan. If you make premium payments until your death, your beneficiaries get the face value of the policy.

  ● Premiums on whole-life policies never change.

  ● Your total premium is divided between insurance coverage and the savings portion of your policy. The insurance company doesn't have to tell you how much interest you're being paid on the savings portion of your policy.

  ● The premium is high when you compare it with how much coverage you get and the minimal increase in cash value during the policy's early years. (These premiums pay a salesman's commission and administrative costs.)

  ● You need to pay premiums for a decade or more before any significant cash value accumulates. But most people fail to keep their policies for that long.

  ● You end up paying up to five times as much as you would have paid for term-life insurance during the same period, and you get much less back in cash value than you might have if you'd invested the same amount of money yourself.

■ **Universal-life insurance** is similar to whole life. The major difference is that you get a clear description of what part of your premium buys your insurance coverage and what portion goes toward savings.

  ● Most of these policies tell you how much interest you're earning on the savings portion. Interest varies with market conditions but is guaranteed to remain above a preset rate.

  ● The cash value of your policy accumulates more quickly than with whole life.

  ● With some universal-life policies, your beneficiaries can receive not only the face value of the policy but also the accumulated cash value. These policies are even more expensive.

  ● If you decide to cash in your policy, you're typically hit with what are known as "surrender charges." These can be substantial, and many policyholders find themselves receiving far less than they thought they would when they cash in their policies.

■ **Variable-life insurance** lets you choose how the savings part of the premium is invested.

  ● Typically, you can invest this money in stocks, bonds, mutual funds, or some combination of all of these. Your policy's return is based on the return your investments make.

  ● The insurer deducts part of each payment to pay for coverage, commissions, and expenses. As a result, the cash value and death benefit can vary from month to month.

**M**ost insurance companies try to settle claims quickly and fairly, but in some cases, getting your claim paid can be a hassle. That's because some insurers try to save money by delaying payment or by offering a sum that's less than they are obligated to pay. In fact, at some insurance companies, claims adjusters are evaluated for promotions and advancement on the basis of how little they get policyholders to accept, not on how fairly they handle their claims.

## EXAMINE YOUR COVERAGE

Before you assume that your insurance company is not dealing fairly with you, however, find out what's covered by the terms of your policy.

- **Full replacement-value coverage** means that your insurer has to pay what it would cost to buy a new item to replace one that you lost. If your three-year-old television set is stolen, and it would cost $500 to buy a new one of the same size and quality, you would receive that amount in cash or a television of that value.
- **Actual cash-value coverage** means that the insurer has to pay only the item's original cost *minus* the depreciation, which is based on its age. For that same television set, the insurer may offer you only $200, since that's what insurance-industry formulas determine would be the actual cash value of your television set.

Similarly, most policies place limits on the amount they will pay for certain types of losses. Stamp collections, coins, silverware, jewelry, and furs are usually covered only up to a specified amount, unless you purchase additional insurance for them. For example, many insurance policies will pay no more than $1,000 for jewelry, no matter what its actual value may be.

## TALK TO THE ADJUSTERS

To convince the insurance company that its offer is less than adequate, you'll have to do some research. For example, the adjuster handling your claim may think that the stereo you lost can be replaced with one that you know is inferior. Having warranty information for the stolen item, a product description, or a receipt detailing the system's features will be a big help in establishing a replacement value.

If you don't have that information available, ask the store that sold you the original equipment to help you reconstruct it.

*M*ost policies place limits on the amount they will pay for certain types of losses.

If you get nowhere with a telephone-claims adjuster, ask to speak to a supervisor. Telephone-claims adjusters are typically the low man on the claims-department totem pole and are usually assigned cases the insurance company expects to settle easily and inexpensively. In fact, most telephone adjusters have a limit placed on the amount they can offer to settle a claim. The adjuster's supervisor can review your information and, in many cases, raise the offer immediately.

## HIRE A PUBLIC ADJUSTER

If you and the insurance company remain far apart on assessing your claim, and if the total amount you think you are owed is a large one, consider hiring a public adjuster. These adjusters are usually former insurance-company employees with years of experience in claims procedures. Public adjusters know the "ins" and "outs" of getting the maximum amount for claims and can often be persuasive in convincing the insurance company to increase its offer to one that's fair.

Public adjusters usually are paid a percentage of the claims they obtain for their clients, so they have an incentive to work hard on your behalf. But not all adjusters charge the same percentage, so it pays to shop around. To find a good and affordable public adjuster, you should…

- Check the Yellow Pages of your telephone directory under Insurance Claim Services.
- Talk to several adjusters before making a decision on the one to hire.

● Ask the adjusters about their level of experience, payment structure, and past dealings with your insurer.

● Obtain references from past clients and check them carefully.

● Contact the Better Business Bureau to investigate any history of complaints against the adjusters to see if they were resolved.

Not every state requires public adjusters to be licensed. Ask the bureau of licenses in your state about its policy and if the adjuster you are considering is in good standing with the bureau.

## SETTLING TOO SOON

It's possible that your insurance company will raise its offer in the face of the evidence that you gather in support of your claim, although it still may not be adequate compensation.

**TAKE NOTE** *Don't be tempted to accept a higher offer and plan to pursue more money later. When you accept settlement, you are accepting the insurance company's estimate of your loss. The check you receive or the documents that accompany it may say that by cashing or depositing the check you waive your right to further payment.*

## CALL THE INSURANCE COPS

If despite your best efforts, you are unable to get adequate compensation for your losses, contact your state department of insurance. In some states, the agency that regulates insurance companies takes a very aggressive approach to investigating consumer complaints about claims-handling procedures, especially if it's aware of similar complaints against a specific company. Companies that fail to handle claims in a fair and timely manner can have their license suspended or revoked. You may find that a state investigation will trigger a more generous settlement offer.

## YOUR LAST RESORT

When all else fails, it's time to consider going to the courts. Some insurance companies will refuse to pay legitimate claims or refuse to pay them fairly, counting on the fact that the consumer needs money quickly and will settle for less, or won't have the time, money, or inclination to fight back. Insurance companies that refuse to deal honestly and fairly with their customers have often been found to have acted in *bad faith*. Bad-faith dealing occurs when an insurer…

● Refuses to pay claims without justification

● Delays making claims payments unnecessarily

● Deceives a policyholder about coverage limits or exclusions

● Exercises unfair advantage in pressuring a policyholder into an unjust settlement.

A successful lawsuit charging an insurance company with bad faith cannot only mean having your claim paid, but also result in the company being subjected to punitive damages—damages designed to punish the company for its bad behavior and deter it from future misconduct. Punitive damages aren't directly related to the actual money damages you might suffer, and they can be substantial. (In one case, an insurance company found guilty of "lowballing" a claims estimate was ordered to pay more than $7 million in punitive damages.) The company could also be required to pay your legal fees and court costs.

Proving bad faith isn't easy, and laws regarding who can bring a bad-faith lawsuit vary from state to state. Look for an attorney with a history of handling bad-faith claims successfully, and consult her about your chance of success. Taking on an insurer has been done successfully by those who knew how and when to fight back and win.

Homeowner's insurance provides two important kinds of protection: liability coverage to protect you against the claims of people who are injured on your property, and casualty coverage to help compensate you for damage to the house and your personal property. Depending on the type of home you own and the kind of coverage you need, as well as what an insurer will sell you, in most states there are seven different types of policies to choose from.

- **HO-1** is the most basic policy for single-family homes. It covers damage to the home and personal property from fire, lightning, windstorms, hail, explosions, riots, smoke, theft, vandalism, broken glass, and volcanoes, as well as damage to the structure caused by automobile and aircraft collisions.

- **HO-2** provides broader coverage than the HO-1 form. It protects against everything listed above as well as damage caused by the weight of snow, ice, or sleet; electrical power surges; heating, air-conditioning, and plumbing failure; appliance malfunctions, leaking, or freezing; building collapse; and falling objects.

- **HO-3** is also known as the *special-form* or *all-risk* policy. It provides protection against everything included in the HO-1 and HO-2 forms but it also goes much further, protecting against damage from everything with the exception of nuclear accidents, war, and earthquakes.

- **HO-4** is renter's insurance. It covers only a tenant's personal property, with no coverage for structural damage.

- **HO-5** is often referred to as *comprehensive coverage*. It provides all the coverage of an HO-3 policy but also provides greater coverage for personal property. This policy is the most complete (and most expensive) insurance policy that the owner of a single-family home can buy.

- **HO-6** provides coverage for condominium owners. It protects the condo's interior space and personal property in the condominium. Common areas and the building itself should be covered by a separate policy purchased by the condominium association. Individual condominium owners pay a prorated portion of that coverage as part of their association fees or maintenance assessment.

- **HO-8** is a policy designed specifically for older homes. It provides insurance from the perils named in the HO-1 policy and imposes a further limitation by insuring the home for its market value, not replacement value. For example, an older home may have a resale value of $60,000, but the cost of rebuilding the home might be $90,000. The HO-8 policy would provide only coverage up to the lower figure.

*Many of these policies offer very low limits of liability coverage. Sometimes the limits are as low as $25,000 per incident. In today's world, that's not enough coverage. Purchase as much liability insurance as you can reasonably afford. Most insurers can provide up to $300,000 of coverage through your home-owner's policy.*

- **Umbrella insurance** can provide liability protection of $1 million or more. Umbrella insurance policies are a smart purchase if you have a lot of assets that make you a potential target for a lawsuit, or if you have property that could contribute to the injury of another (such as a swimming pool or a hot tub). Both increased liability coverage in your homeowner's policy and umbrella insurance are relatively inexpensive.

> *Y*our insurance company refuses to fix your home's roof after it's been damaged by a hailstorm. It claims that your premium was late and your coverage was canceled.

In most cases, an insurer isn't allowed to cancel your homeowner's policy without giving you a written warning *and* a grace period in which to pay your premium and keep your coverage in force. However, it does pay off to pay your bills on time—the penalty for slow payment of your insurance premiums can mean that you could face paying for expensive damages that you thought you were protected from.

## First, Look at Your Records

If the above scenario happens to you, you first need to determine if your premium actually was paid on time.

- **If your homeowner's insurance is paid by a mortgage lender:** If you have a mortgage on your home, chances are your homeowner's insurance is paid out of an escrow account by the bank that holds it or the company that services it. With an escrow account, the lender collects a portion of the amount you owe for taxes and insurance each month, in addition to your payment of interest and principal.

  Take a look at the statement you receive from your lender. It should show the date on which your insurance premium was paid. Send a copy of this statement to your insurer, along with a letter demanding that it reinstate your coverage and pay for the damages as provided for in the policy.

- **If you pay your insurance premium yourself, you'll need to do some research**—if you own your home outright, or if you pay your insurance premium on your own, review your checking account to see when you wrote the check for your premium payment and whether it was paid by your bank. If it was, send a copy of the front and back of the canceled check to your insurer, along with the letter described above. That should solve the problem.

## When Insurers Cheat

If the check you sent was never deposited by your insurer, you could have more serious problems. The insurance company may not have deposited your check due to a simple error, or it may have been a calculated move. If, for example, your pay-

ment arrived at about the same time as the hail storm hit your community, the insurer may have decided to "lose" your payment as a way of limiting its losses, especially if it insures a number of properties in the area.

Whether this is the case or you are late in paying the bill, you are still protected by law. In most cases, your policy cannot be canceled without warning, even when you miss the payment due date for your premium. Instead, the law in most states requires the company to send you a notice of nonpayment and to provide a date by which you must send your payment in order to keep your coverage. And most policies contain a "grace period"—usually 30 days—during which the company agrees not to cancel your policy. So if you didn't get the notice required by law, or if the company broke its contract with you by failing to accept payment during the grace period, you will be able to collect on your claim.

## Where to Get Help

Your state department of insurance is the first place to turn to if you believe your policy was canceled without justification. Be ready to provide the department with the following:

- ✔ A copy of your policy
- ✔ Proof of payment (the statement from your mortgage company or your own canceled check—photocopy the front and back of it)
- ✔ Copies of any correspondence you've had with the insurance company about the payment problem
- ✔ The names and titles of anyone you spoke to on the telephone about the rejected claim
- ✔ A brief summary of what was said.

The department will investigate and may bring pressure to bear on the company to reinstate your policy and pay your claim, especially if it suspects that the insurer was acting to limit its liability.

## Go to Court

If you suspect that your insurer is simply refusing to pay your claim without justification, you may want to consult a lawyer about bringing a lawsuit, charging it with acting in bad faith, and engaging in deceptive and unfair practices. If your lawsuit is successful, the insurance company will have to pay your claim and could have to pay punitive damages to deter it from future bad-faith dealing with its policyholders. Contact your state or local bar association's attorney referral service for the names of lawyers who can review your case and help you evaluate the odds of success.

## FLOOD INSURANCE

Flooding caused by a broken pipe in your home is usually covered by your homeowner's-insurance policy, but flooding caused by a dam breaking, a stream overflowing, or other natural causes is not. To protect against natural flooding, you need to purchase a flood-insurance policy. These policies are available only to communities that are prone to natural flooding, and only when flood-management programs have been put in place.

Although you buy flood insurance from private insurers, the policies are administered by the federal government through the Federal Emergency Management Agency (FEMA). For specific information about the national flood-insurance program, call (800) 638-6620. Request publication FIA-2, *Answers to Questions About the National Flood Insurance Program*.

*After 20 years, your auto-insurance company tells you that it won't renew your policy.*

When it comes to auto insurance, there is no guarantee that your policy will be renewed. In most states, the insurer isn't even required to tell you why it's not renewing it. It may be because the company has decided to stop issuing auto insurance in your state, perhaps because new state restrictions make it less profitable. More likely, it's because you have...

- Filed a few claims
- Been ticketed for exceeding the speed limit or charged with some other violation of traffic laws
- Been involved in one or more automobile accidents.

As a result, a company can refuse to renew your coverage, provided that it meets a few conditions.

### THE NONRENEWAL NOTICE

Generally, state laws require an insurer to notify you in writing that it will not renew your policy. An oral statement or failure to send a renewal statement isn't good enough.

### SMART MOVES

If you plan to live abroad for a year or more, storing your car on blocks, talk to your auto insurer about maintaining a minimal amount of liability coverage on the vehicle. Otherwise, you may have a hard time getting good, affordable auto insurance when you return and put the car back on the road.

The insurer must notify you before your current policy expires—in most states, at least 30 days before your renewal date. This is to ensure that you have adequate time to shop for and purchase insurance from another company.

## POSSIBLE ACTIONS

There are several avenues to pursue to try to get your policy renewed.

- **Call your insurance agent** as soon as you receive a cancellation notice. In some cases, agents have been able to intervene on behalf of their customers—especially long-time ones—and have their policies renewed. To accomplish this, you'll need a reputable agent, a good driving record, and a company that's willing to reconsider its nonrenewal decision.
- **Review the company's statement carefully** if you live in a state where the insurer must notify you of the reason for nonrenewal. Insurance companies are generally careful with their record keeping, but they can make mistakes, and your company may have mistakenly credited someone else's accident or ticket to your driving record.
- **Find out if it's your child's fault.** Your child may have been ticketed or involved in accidents while he was driving your car and was covered by your policy. If he has moved out on his own, you may be able to convince the company to renew your policy.

## IS IT ILLEGAL DISCRIMINATION?

Like some mortgage lenders, some insurers have been known to engage in the practice of *redlining*, or refusing to write policies for residents of some areas of a community or offering only policies that are more expensive and provide far less coverage. But many states prohibit auto insurers from discrimination based on sex, race, national origin, or age. If you believe that the company's decision not to renew your policy is due to one of these factors, or redlining in conjunction with any of them, contact your state department of insurance with your suspicions. You should also contact your state's civil-rights commission, which can investigate the company's underwriting practices for evidence of illegal discrimination.

## GET NEW COVERAGE

Investigations by government agencies take time, and you will need to find another insurer to cover your car before the government may be able to take any action. If your driving record is good, it may not be difficult to find another company willing to provide coverage similar to that offered by your previous insurer, and at a similar rate.

But it can be a tricky proposition if your driving record is less than spotless. You may have a hard time convincing another insurer to take you on at all, even at a much higher premium. Yet the law in nearly every state makes it illegal to drive your car without liability coverage.

If you can't get insurance directly from an insurance company, every state provides a way to get coverage under *a shared-market program.* These programs require licensed insurers to take on otherwise uninsurable drivers. Generally, these programs fall into one of three categories:

- **Reinsurance plans** involve an organization that provides insurance to insurance companies. Essentially, insurers transfer their risk to the reinsurer on a number of policies. No one can be refused a policy in a state that offers a reinsurance plan.
- **Assigned-risk plans** require insurance companies to provide insurance to drivers who can't obtain it through traditional channels. Companies are "assigned" customers by the state in proportion to the total traditional auto insurance they write. For example, a company that covers 5 percent of a state's drivers has to provide assigned-risk coverage to 5 percent of those who are uninsurable.
- **Joint-underwriting plans** involve a special insurance company, called a joint underwriting association, or JUA, that's financed by all the insurers doing business in the state. These companies then share proportionally in the losses and profits of the JUA.

Unfortunately, no matter which variation on the shared-market program your state offers, you will end up paying far more for coverage than you would for a traditional policy. After a few years, however, if you have improved your driving record, you will have the opportunity to obtain a policy directly from an insurer.

**TAKE NOTE** *Don't try to take your chances and continue driving without auto insurance. Many states now have direct links to insurers that allow them to determine if you are covered, and nearly every state requires that you have an insurance card or other proof of financial responsibility while driving. If you're stopped for a minor violation or are involved in an accident that isn't your fault, you can be penalized severely for driving without insurance, including having your license suspended or revoked.*

The most important reason to have automobile insurance is basic liability coverage—to protect yourself from automobile-accident claims made against you. There are other protections as well. Here's what you'll find in the typical auto-insurance policy:

- **Bodily-injury coverage** protects you from claims that your driving caused physical injury to others. It also shields you from claims when your family members or others drive your car with your permission.

  *Do you need it?* In most states, this coverage is required by law, although the minimum mandatory coverage is almost always far too low. For example, in many states you are required to purchase insurance that pays a maximum of $25,000 to any person injured in an accident you cause, up to a total of $50,000 for everyone injured in the accident. Most experts recommend a minimum of $100,000 per person and $300,000 per accident.

- **Property-damage coverage** pays claims for damage you cause to the property of others.

  *Do you need it?* This is usually required by state law, but the minimum requirement is generally low: around $10,000 in most states. Consider boosting your coverage; higher limits usually add only a small increase to your premium.

- **Collision coverage** pays for damage to your car due to a collision or accident, regardless of who is at fault. Even if the other driver is liable, her insurer may stall on paying your claim. With collision coverage, you get your car fixed without undue delay. Your insurer will probably look to the other driver or her insurance company for reimbursement.

  *Do you need it?* If you own a new car, you'll want this coverage to speed along the repair or replacement of your vehicle. But the value of collision insurance declines as your car ages. That's because your insurer will pay based on your car's depreciated value. Some experts recommend dropping this coverage when your car is more than five years old, since the money you'll get for damages won't be enough to make the premium worth paying.

- **Comprehensive coverage** protects against theft, vandalism, and other damage to your car, and in some cases it covers the loss of your personal property when it is damaged or destroyed by fire or lightning. It rarely pays for personal property stolen from your vehicle, such as purses, laptop computers, and portable telephones.

  *Do you need it?* You may want this coverage for a new car, but, as with collision insurance, the older your car, the less useful—and relatively more expensive—this coverage becomes.

- **Uninsured- and underinsured-motorist coverage** protects you from drivers who are uninsured or have too little insurance. Instead of suing the driver, you file a claim with your own insurance company.

  *Do you need it?* In many states, you receive this coverage automatically, although you may be able to opt out of it.

- **Medical-payments coverage** protects you and other passengers in your car, paying medical bills and even funeral expenses. It also provides coverage if you're injured by a car while walking, or while riding in someone else's vehicle. In no-fault states, medical payments coverage is usually referred to as personal-injury protection (PIP), and in addition to medical and funeral expenses, it may also pay for wages lost while you recuperate from your injuries.

  *Do you need it?* Many states require this coverage. However, if yours does not, and you already have good health and disability insurance in your household policy, you may not need to purchase medical payments coverage.

**You** rented a car for a weekend getaway to the beach. After you returned the car, you discovered that you were charged $12 a day for insurance you didn't request.

If you have an accident in a car you rented, even if it isn't your fault, most standard rental car agreements make you liable for the full value of the car. To protect themselves, drivers sometimes purchase what's called a collision-damage waiver, or CDW coverage. This insurance is expensive, however, and in many cases it's

**You** may already be covered by your own auto-insurance policy or your credit card.

actually unnecessary. You may already be covered by your own auto-insurance policy or your credit card. Whether you are or aren't, you're supposed to be offered the option to accept or decline the rental company's CDW coverage. Sometimes the combination of an eager clerk and an inexperienced renter can add up to coverage you don't want or need.

### CONTACT THE RENTAL-CAR COMPANY

If this was your experience, you have a good chance of solving the problem by taking the following steps:

■ **Examine the agreement** you signed when you rented the car. It should contain a section offering a variety of insurance coverages and a space for you to initial to either accept or decline the coverage.
■ **Call the rental-car company's** customer service if you did not initial the box accepting the CDW coverage. Explain your situation and request a refund of the unauthorized charges. Be sure to get the name and the title of the

person you speak to, just in case you need to talk to them again.
■ **Write to the rental-car company** if a phone call isn't sufficient. Enclose a copy of the rental agreement, and in the accompanying letter, state the following:
  ● You did not request the CDW insurance.
  ● The rental agreement doesn't contain your initials authorizing the company to charge you for the insurance coverage.
  ● You want the total amount you were charged for CDW insurance credited to the credit card you used to rent the car.
■ **Contact the credit-card issuer** if you don't get satisfaction, and report the fact that you are disputing the amount of the charge made to your account. While the card issuer investigates, you aren't required to pay the disputed amount, and you can't be reported as delinquent to credit-reporting agencies. Once the credit-card company has clear evidence that you didn't authorize the charge, it will credit the amount to your account.

*You purchased a legal-insurance policy through the mail, but the lawyer assigned to you won't take your calls any more.*

Legal-insurance policies and prepaid legal-service plans have become popular over the past several decades. These plans typically provide a set menu of benefits, such as a simple will each year, the review of documents, telephone advice, and in-office consultations. Most plans also promise that purchasers will receive a discount from the lawyer's usual rates on other legal services, such as filing a lawsuit or creating a trust. Premiums for these plans are relatively low, usually around $10 to $15 per month. With many lawyers charging $100 or more just to write a will, the cost of these plans is very attractive.

While it's possible to get good-quality legal services through a legal-service plan, not every plan takes the same care in selecting its attorneys. Some lawyers sign on for the plans as a way to build their business, only to discover that the money they earn from the plan isn't enough to cover the expenses required to handle clients' problems. Their solution may be to drop the plan's clients.

### NOTIFY THE PLAN ADMINISTRATOR

If this happens to you, take your complaint to the plan administrator. (Look for the plan's toll-free phone number on your membership card or the enrollment materials.) Ask the representative to contact the lawyer and insist that he return your call. Most plans require the attorneys working with them to return client calls within a specified time period, such as 24 hours, or one business day. The plan representative can remind the lawyer of this contractual duty.

**TAKE NOTE** *Don't tell the customer-service represen-tative the details of your legal problem. If you should discuss these problems with the representative, you could lose the protection of the attorney-client privilege.*

If the attorney still doesn't return your call or if he refuses to assist you with a legal matter covered by your plan, take these steps:

- **Notify the plan administrator** and ask to be transferred to another attorney who practices in your community.
- **Schedule an appointment** with the new lawyer assigned to you, so that you can discuss your problem.
- **Follow up with a letter** to the plan adminis-trator. In it, be sure to include…
  - The name of the lawyer who refused to return your calls
  - The attempts made by you and the plan representative to contact the attorney
  - The fact that you ultimately had to be reassigned to another lawyer.

Lawyers who fail to provide services as promised can be removed from the plan's panel.

## GET GOVERNMENT HELP

If you feel that additional measures need to be taken against your original lawyer, consider filing a complaint with the state attorney disciplinary committee. The committee can investigate, and if it finds that the lawyer's actions violated the rules of professional responsibility, it can issue a punishment, probably in the form of a reprimand. However, if there is a history of complaints against the lawyer, or if she fails to cooperate in the investigation, more serious action could be taken, such as a public censure or suspension.

If you are dissatisfied with the way the plan administrator handled your problem, you may be able to file a complaint with your state department of insurance. However, some plans are not subject to oversight by insurance regulators. Contact the insurance department to find out if the plan is regulated and to obtain instructions on filing a complaint.

If the insurance department doesn't regulate the plan, you'll need to file your complaint with the attorney disciplinary committee. In some states, this is an arm of the state bar association, while in others the plan is run by the state courts. You should call your local courthouse for infor-mation about where to file your complaint.

> **Y**our mother suffered a stroke and isn't expected to recover, but the doctors and hospital refuse to turn off her life-support systems.

**M**odern technology makes it possible to keep breathing and heart function going even when brain activity has ceased. Without clear evidence that a person wouldn't want these life-sustaining measures, doctors and hospitals are often reluctant to remove them, preferring to use whatever methods are available to keep alive even those with no hope of recovery.

*The effects of a durable power of attorney for health care are more far reaching than those of a living will, because they give another person the power to make decisions about your care even when you are not terminally ill or injured.*

## MEDICAL DIRECTIVES

If your mother is like a growing number of Americans, she may have already prepared what are known as *advance medical directives*. These are documents that inform doctors and other health-care personnel about your wishes if certain medical conditions occur and you can't communicate. Generally, these documents include...

■ **A living will.** This document tells others about your desire for or refusal of certain medical treatments if you should suffer a terminal illness or injury. Without it, medical professionals may decide that they are legally obligated to continue life-prolonging procedures.
■ **A durable power of attorney for health care.** Sometimes referred to by its initials, DPOAHC, this document is also called a *health care proxy*. It gives a spouse, family member, friend, or someone else you trust the authority to make decisions about your medical treatment on your behalf. The effects

of a durable power of attorney for health care are more far reaching than those of a living will, because they give another person the power to make decisions about your care even when you are not terminally ill or injured. You must be unable to communicate your wishes in order for the other person to make these decisions for you. So if you are unconscious after an accident but your injuries are not potentially life threatening, the person named in your power of attorney (called your *attorney in fact*) can consent or refuse to consent to surgery or other treatment on your behalf.

## SEARCH FOR DOCUMENTS

First, try to find out if your mother completed a living will or a durable power of attorney for her health care. Some people who complete these documents neglect to make them available to those providing medical treatment. And in the case of an accident or medical emergency, the patient may be taken to a hospital or treated by doctors not aware that such documents exist. To track down these documents...

■ **Ask your mother's primary care doctor** if she has a copy of your mother's advance medical directives. If she does, she can provide them to the doctors caring for your mother. Those doctors should respect your mother's written wishes regarding life-support systems.
■ **Look through her files at home** to see if a copy of the durable power of attorney exists.
■ **Check other sources** she may have entrusted with information about her desires, such as...
  ✔ Her attorney
  ✔ Specialists who may have treated her for specific medical problems
  ✔ Hospitals, clinics, or other facilities where she may have received treatment
  ✔ A nursing home or assisted-living facility where she resided
  ✔ Her husband, children, or friends she may have provided with a copy.

If you locate your mother's living will or durable power of attorney, give a copy to the medical personnel treating her. If the document is a living will, the doctors can consider its provisions and decide if turning off her life-support systems would be in agreement with your mother's wishes. If she created a durable power of attorney for health care, they can contact the person named by your mother and have him advise them about the course of action to take.

## WHEN THERE AREN'T ANY DOCUMENTS

Even if you are unable to locate a living will or durable power of attorney, you may be able to convince doctors to remove your mother's life-support systems. To do so, you'll need to provide what the U.S. Supreme Court calls *clear and convincing evidence* of her desire to have life support ended when all hope of recovery is gone.

In one case, for example, a man suffered a serious stroke and could not swallow. His wife asked to have his feeding tube removed. She based her request on conversations she'd had with him before his illness, in which he stated that he didn't want to experience a lengthy hospitalization when there was no chance for him to recover. Her husband had also had similar conversations with other family members. Although the hospital initially refused to remove his feeding tube, it ultimately did so when a state court ruled that these conversations provided enough evidence to allow for the removal of the tube.

There are several options before you have to go to court, however, including the following:

- **Talk to the hospital's patients' representative.** She can work to mediate the dispute between you and the hospital personnel. Patients' representatives have often been successful in convincing doctors to reconsider their refusal to terminate life support.
- **Contact the hospital's ethics committee** and ask it to justify the refusal to take your mother off life support. Some hospitals won't take what they consider "premature" actions if there is *any* possibility of recovery, no matter how remote. Others have established time limits and won't act until these limits have passed. The hospital may be getting mixed signals about your mother's wishes. If, for example, your father insists that your mother would want care to continue, it may not have the clear and convincing evidence that the law requires. Without this evidence, the hospital could face a lawsuit from dissenting family members if it terminates life support.
- **Ask about surrogate decision-making.** Some hospitals and doctors are willing to consider allowing a close family member to make decisions based on what he or she believes the patient would have wanted done, even without clear and convincing evidence. The patient's outlook on continued life support could be arrived at by looking at her comments and decisions about doctors and medical care, at her religious beliefs, even at her lifestyle. For example, if your mother was very active until she suffered her stroke, how might she have felt about being incapacitated and unable to bathe, dress, or feed herself without assistance? Determining the answers to these questions may convince the hospital that continuing life support would be the opposite of your mother's wishes.

**TAKE NOTE** *If you suspect that the hospital's actions are motivated by the payment it's receiving for care, contact a lawyer immediately. Believe it or not, some state courts have actually made families who asked for life support to end— but whose wishes weren't honored—liable for the cost of the very care that they opposed.*

## GET OUTSIDE HELP

If working directly with the doctors and hospital doesn't resolve the problem, you may need to turn to outside sources for assistance. One national nonprofit organization, Choice In Dying, can provide you with specific information about steps you can take based on state statutes and court decisions. You can contact Choice In Dying by calling (800) 989-9455 or by visiting its Web site: www.choices.org.

Your state's department of aging or elder-care services may also be able to help by providing the hospital and doctors with clarification about state laws that will allow them to terminate life-support systems for your mother. Talk to the patients' representative about how to contact the appropriate agency in your state, or check the state government telephone listings.

Finally, consider filing a complaint with the state's medical and hospital regulators. In some states, doctors who have failed to follow patients' advance directives have been disciplined.

## GO TO COURT

When all other efforts have failed, you may need to file a lawsuit to force the hospital and doctors to take action. The organization called Choice In Dying (see telephone number above) can refer you to an attorney who will help you seek the court order you'll need. Your local or state bar association's referral service can also help you find a lawyer experienced in this area.

In some states, hospitals and doctors that fail to honor a patient's advance directives have been charged with civil battery, which is called the tort of unlawful touching or applying force to another. In one case, a court in Michigan found that a hospital was guilty of battery, or the unlawful striking or physical assault of a person, when it misrepresented procedures it performed that directly contradicted the patient's health-care power of attorney. The family of the patient was awarded some $16 million in damages, although this amount was reduced and the parties ultimately settled for an undisclosed amount. Not every state permits damage awards in these cases, however; a lawyer can help you determine if a lawsuit seeking damages is worth pursuing.

## MEDICAL CARE IN EXTREME SITUATIONS

When someone close to you has a life-threatening illness or a physical condition that requires drastic measures, you should know what treatment that person would want—or not want. Some people want limited medical efforts; others want extensive treatment. Here are both sides:

■ **Making a living will.** Living-will laws vary from state to state. Many states have specific living-will forms. Some provide checklists of health-care treatments that you can choose to receive or decline, while others merely allow you to decline "life-sustaining" procedures if you suffer from an incurable or irreversible condition that will cause your death. When creating a living will, you should ask yourself how you feel about receiving...

● Heart and lung resuscitation, including the use of cardio-pulmonary resuscitation (CPR), drugs, or machines

● Kidney dialysis, chemotherapy, or radiation treatment

● Antibiotics or other medications

● Surgery or other invasive procedures, such as the insertion of a breathing tube

● Artificial respiration

● Artificial hydration and nutrition (water and food delivered through a gastric tube).

In states that don't set out specific procedures for you to accept or refuse, you can create what's often called a *letter of instruction*, which you can attach to your living will. By doing so, you will give your doctors, medical personnel, and loved ones a much clearer indication of your wishes concerning life support.

■ **Exercising the right to aggressive treatment.** In some cases, doctors and hospitals may want to turn off life-support systems before the patient or his family members would wish. For example, you may not want to terminate your dying husband's life support because of his religious beliefs. You may also want the hospital or your husband's doctors to continue certain types of treatment, such as chemotherapy, long after the doctors believe such treatment is warranted.

There are few court decisions that have addressed this issue, but those that have generally give a deference to a spouse's or other family member's wishes to continue treatment against medical advice. If your situation requires you to oppose a hospital's or doctor's request to discontinue life support, notify the patients' representative and hospital ethics committee.

Ultimately, you may also need the help of a lawyer who is experienced in handling this type of case. In a few situations, medical facilities have actually sought a court order allowing them to terminate life support when the patient's family objected.

Being hospitalized is almost always a stressful experience, but it shouldn't be made worse by hospital staff members who don't treat patients with consideration and respect. However, hospital workers are only human, and sometimes they are unaware of how patients react to their personalities or the way they do their jobs.

### YOUR UNWRITTEN RIGHTS

When hospitalized, you have a right to expect that hospital personnel, including nurses, nursing assistants, laboratory workers, and orderlies…

- Will respect your wishes in regard to the amount of information you receive about your medical condition
- Will respect your privacy
- Will treat your personal property with care
- Will listen and respond appropriately to your concerns about the care you are receiving.

### THE HOSPITAL HIERARCHY

In a hospital, there are several levels of staff for you to talk to about getting a remedy to your problem. As always when making a complaint, be sure to document the name and title of the person you talk to, the date of your discussion, and the outcome of the conversation. Try the following:

- **Speak directly to the person** you're having difficulty with and let her know what behavior you object to. For example, if the nurse's aide who gives you a sponge bath doesn't pull the

---

**SMART MOVES**

Ask your spouse, another family member, or a friend to act on your behalf in the hospital. When you're in pain and weakened from an illness or surgery, following up on complaints about the way you're being treated can be an exhausting experience and may even slow your recovery.

---

curtain around your bed, complain directly to her. You may be able to end the unacceptable treatment with a simple, direct comment.

- **If the problem persists, tell your doctor about it.** He may be able to deal with the matter by talking to the employee or her supervisor; his concerns are likely to be given more weight than those you express yourself.
- **If that doesn't work, ask to speak to the employee's floor supervisor.** Explain your problem and propose a solution, such as having a different employee provide the services you need.
- **If the problem doesn't clear up, contact the hospital's patients' advocate** (sometimes called the *patients' representative* or *ombudsman*). The patients' advocate can often

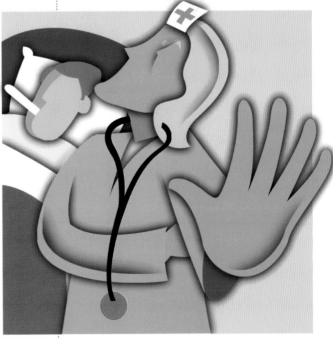

approach the offending employee or the employee's immediate supervisor and work out a viable solution to your problem.

■ **If things don't improve, complain to higher authorities** within the hospital. For example, if the problem is a nurse who loudly discusses your medical condition in the hallway when you've asked him not to, and the floor supervisor or head nurse hasn't interceded, get in touch with the hospital's nursing supervisor.

■ **If all else fails, notify the hospital's chief administrator** about the problem. You can get his phone number from the hospital operator, or look for it in the handbook you may have received when you were admitted. The administrator can investigate your claim, and if he finds that your complaint is warranted, he can take action on your behalf. If the problem is a serious one, he may bring disciplinary action against the offending worker, including suspension or even discharge.

Finally, remember that you don't have to stay in a hospital where you're unhappy with the treatment that you receive. Talk to your doctor about transferring to another hospital, or continuing your recovery at home with appropriate nursing care. (Before pursuing this last option,

be sure to talk to your insurance company about getting your home-health care covered under your plan as a medical necessity.)

## NOTIFY THE STATE

If your problem is a serious one and you remain unhappy with the way it was handled, you may want to contact the appropriate state regulatory agencies with your complaint.

For example, if you had a problem with a nurse that remained unresolved, contact the state board of nursing. Complaints about sanitation, meals, or other hospital-related issues can be referred to the hospital board. As always when making a complaint, be sure to spell out as much specific information as possible, including:

✔ Your name, address, and telephone number
✔ The names and titles of the hospital personnel with whom you had difficulty
✔ An account of your attempts to handle the problem through hospital channels
✔ The names and titles of anyone you spoke to about your problem and why their response wasn't satisfactory
✔ The names of others who witnessed the offensive behavior or other patients who shared similar experiences.

---

## You want to leave the hospital, but your doctor insists that you stay.

---

**H**ospitals aren't prisons, and you can't be forced to stay in the hospital against your will, no matter what your doctor or other health-care provider may want you to do. While

> *You are under no legal obligation to sign anything in order to leave the hospital.*

it's usually wise to follow your doctor's recommendations about treatment, including the length of your hospitalization, in some cases you may

feel that you will be better off continuing your recovery at home or in another hospital. If you strongly feel, for example, that the care you're getting is inadequate and your needs would be better met elsewhere, you may reasonably want to leave the hospital.

## DISCHARGE AGAINST MEDICAL ADVICE

In a situation where your doctor is reluctant to let you leave the hospital, you are entitled to what's known as a *discharge against medical advice.* If you insist on leaving, you will probably be presented with a form called an Unauthorized Discharge Release or an Against Medical Advice Release. Basically, this form will state that...

- You are leaving the hospital against the advice of doctors and hospital personnel
- The doctor and hospital will bear no responsibility for any decline in your condition
- You release the doctor, hospital, and hospital personnel from liability and agree not to sue them for health complications or deterioration.

You may be told that you cannot leave the hospital unless and until you sign this form. *Don't believe that for a minute.* You are under no legal obligation to sign anything in order to leave the hospital. In fact, any attempt by hospital personnel to keep you from leaving could be considered false imprisonment and could subject the hospital and the individuals involved to a civil lawsuit.

## INSURANCE ISSUES

The hospital staff or your doctor may tell you that if you leave the hospital against medical advice or refuse to sign the hospital's release form, your insurance company won't pay for the treatment you received. If this happens…

- **Call your lawyer** for advice about this possibility. She may advise you that the claim is false, or she may suggest that you make changes to the hospital's release form. For example, you can cross out any provisions that release the hospital from liability and can include a paragraph explaining why you're leaving the hospital.
- **Contact your insurance company** to explain the problems you encountered. Send your letter by registered mail with a return receipt requested.
- **Write to your doctor,** hospital administrators, and your state department of health to describe the conditions you encountered that led you to believe that prolonging your hospital stay was not in your best interest. Keep a copy of the letter to file.

*Your insurer says it's time for you to leave the hospital, but you and your doctor would like to extend your stay for a few more days.*

In an effort to save money, insurers want patients in and out of the hospital as quickly as possible. Many insurers now place standard limits on hospital stays for certain procedures and treatments. In most cases, these limits are determined by what's known as a *utilization review service,* which is run by insurance companies. The review service decides if you can go to the hospital in the first place, and how long you can stay once you're there. But not every case goes by the book, and complications from surgery or a weaker-than-normal physical condition may require a longer hospital stay than that approved.

## ENLIST HELP FROM THE HOSPITAL

If your insurer insists that you end your hospitalization before you or your doctor believes you should leave the facility…

- **Get your doctor's help immediately.** Ask her or her office to contact your health-insurance company and explain why extending your stay is medically necessary.
- **Ask the hospital's patients' representative** to intervene on your behalf. With your doctor's support, the patients' representative may convince your insurer that releasing you will

present a danger to your health and slow your recovery.

■ **Request that a family member be your advocate.** Your spouse may be the most effective voice in convincing the insurer to approve a longer stay in the hospital.

## FILE AN APPEAL

In many states, you and your doctor have the right to file a formal appeal with the utilization review service. Generally, you must file your appeal as soon as you are informed of the decision to deny payment for any additional hospital time. The review service must consider your appeal and give its decision quickly, usually within two days. While your appeal is being considered by the hospital, you should be allowed to remain in the facility while you're waiting for the decision.

If your appeal is rejected, you may decide to extend your hospital stay anyway, but you will then be financially liable for the additional charges incurred. Unfortunately, with hospitalization now costing several thousand dollars a day, that's simply not possible for most people. In most cases, you'll have to abide by the insurer's decision to terminate your hospital stay.

## LAST RESORT

If your release does turn out to be premature and your health suffers as a result, you may be able to bring a lawsuit against those responsible for forcing you out of the hospital.

The responsible parties could include the utilization review service, your insurance company, and the hospital. If your doctor didn't insist on the longer stay or if she failed to help you appeal the decision, she could also be liable if your condition worsens due to the early release.

Consult a lawyer with experience in this area to decide, with his help, whether to sue, from whom to seek damages, and how much to request. Lawyers who handle this type of case usually work on a contingent-fee basis, which means that they take a percentage of any settlement they obtain on your behalf. What percentage your lawyer will receive is a matter to be negotiated between you, but it is typically a quarter to a third of the total.

---

*A*fter your surgery, you receive the hospital's bill but you don't understand a good portion of the charges.

---

Some hospital bills can almost be enough to cause a medical setback, either because they're incorrect or because they're indecipherable. Studies show that many hospital bills list charges for services that weren't provided, and one study concluded that more than 90 percent of the hospital bills reviewed contained errors, the vast majority of which were to the hospital's benefit. Even if your insurer is covering the cost of your medical treatment and paying the hospital directly, you should receive copies of the hospital's bills and check them out for yourself.

While it may be tempting simply to throw them away or file them without taking a glance, it pays to understand charges for which you and

---

*Don't pay any amount of a bill that's in dispute until you have a complete explanation of the charges...*

---

your insurance company have been billed. Even if the insurance company is paying, you may have deductibles, copayments, and charges that aren't covered. Unnecessary charges can also lead to higher rates and reduced coverage by insurers.

## INFORMATION PLEASE

Take a look at the bills you've received. If there are charges that you don't understand or that you question, call the patient-billing representative (the phone number should be on the bills). If you have many questions, it may be easier to go to the billing office than to try to tackle them all on the phone. Then do the following:

- **Ask for explanations.** Many hospitals use billing codes for procedures, and sometimes these codes aren't adequately explained. If this is the case, ask the representative to go through each item of the bill you don't understand and explain it to you.
- **Contest incorrect charges.** If you didn't receive a treatment or service for which you were billed, inform the representative. For instance, you may find a charge for blood transfusions when you weren't given any blood during your stay, or you may be billed for a private room when you had a semiprivate one. It's unlikely that you'll have these charges removed immediately, but the billing representative can investigate the matter further and revise your bill later.

- **Watch for math "mistakes."** A procedure that should have cost you $400 might be listed on your bill as $4,000. Question any cost that shows up on your bill that seems out of line with what you were told to expect before you entered the hospital.
- **Look for duplicate billing** for the same procedure. You may find that you were charged for two or three blood "sticks" when you had blood drawn only once, for example. Ask the representative to remove any duplicate charge from your bill.

## REGISTER YOUR COMPLAINTS

If you suspect that you have been overcharged and you can't get the matter resolved by talking to the hospital's billing representative, then try the following:

- **Alert your health insurer.** Insurance companies typically take claims of overbilling seriously, because they're footing the bill. Your insurance company can investigate, and if it agrees with your conclusions, it can refuse to pay for unwarranted procedures. Your insurer's financial clout may get the results you want.
- **Notify your state's hospital regulator** if you believe that the hospital's billing practices are unethical or fraudulent. (This is usually a division of the health department, but in some states it may be a separate agency.) The hospital regulator can look into the matter, and if it finds a pattern of deliberate overbilling, it can refer the alleged misconduct to the state attorney's office for possible prosecution.

## YOUR LAST RESORT

If there is a copayment, don't pay any amount of a bill that's in dispute until you have a complete explanation of the charges, because deductibles, copayments, or other charges may not be covered. The hospital may institute collection proceedings against you. If the hospital or its collectors threaten a lawsuit, call a lawyer immediately. At that point, all phone calls and letters about the bill should go directly to your lawyer. Your lawyer will advise you on your possible responses to the hospital's collection efforts. She may suggest waiting out the hospital, proposing a settlement, or filing your own lawsuit against the hospital.

**You applied for Social Security disability benefits, but your application was turned down.**

Trying to get disability benefits from the federal government can be a daunting task. The Social Security disability insurance program is designed to help those who are unable to work due to a serious mental or physical condition, but rules for determining who is eligible to receive these benefits are strict.

## SOCIAL SECURITY CREDITS

To qualify for Social Security disability payments, you must have a recent work history. The formula for qualifying is based on your age at the time you file your application and the number of work credits you have earned. Credits are earned for each quarter in which you work and earn more than a specified amount of money (in 2000, that amount was $780). These are the rules:

- If you are older than age 31, you need at least 20 work credits earned within the last 10 years, and 2 additional credits for each 2 years of age over 42 up to age 62.
- If you are between the ages of 24 and 31, you need credit for working half the time between turning 21 and becoming disabled. This means that if you become disabled at age 30, you need 18 credits (two quarters of work for each of nine years) in order to qualify.
- If you are younger than 24, you need at least 6 credits in the 3 years before being disabled.

## ARE YOU DISABLED?

If you have earned enough work credits to be eligible, you must then undergo a five-step evaluation process, conducted by what's called the Disability Determination Services Office. This process requires answering these questions:

- **Are you working?** If you are and your earnings average $700 or more per month, you generally can't be considered disabled.
- **Is your condition severe?** Your disability must interfere with basic work-related activities in order for your claim to be considered.
- **Is your condition on Social Security's list of disabling impairments?** The Social Security Administration maintains a list of impairments for each of the major body systems. These impairments are considered so

severe that they automatically qualify you for disability benefits. If your condition isn't on the list, it decides if your impairment is equal in severity to one on the list. If so, you qualify for benefits. If not, go to the next question.

> *Your disability must interfere with basic work-related activities in order for your claim to be considered.*

- **Can you do the work you did before you became impaired?** The Disability Determination Services Office will look at your case and decide if your impairment interferes with your ability to do the work you did over the last 15 years. If the injury doesn't interfere, your claim will be denied. If it does, then there's another question to be answered.
- **Can you do *any other* kind of work?** The Disability Determination Services Office evaluates your age, education, past work experience, and transferable skills (those you used at your previous job that could be used in another type of work). It then reviews the job demands of different occupations, based on information provided by the Department of Labor. If it decides that you can do *any* other kind of work, your claim will be denied. The criteria aren't as stringently applied to older applicants as to younger ones.

## IF YOU ARE TURNED DOWN

If you are denied benefits, you can appeal the decision by doing the following:

- **Step 1: Request reconsideration.** The first move is a *request for reconsideration,* which you must file within 60 days of being denied disability benefits. A Social Security representative who was not involved in the first review will examine the record of the original determination and the evidence you submitted to support your claim. The representative will also look at any new evidence you submit, such as additional doctors' statements. If the representative upholds the original finding denying you benefits, go to the next step.

■ **Step 2: Ask for a hearing.** You can request a hearing before an administrative law judge (also called an ALJ) within 60 days of the reconsideration decision. The ALJ must not have had any involvement with the prior decisions in your case. You may bring witnesses to this hearing, and you are allowed to review the information already in your file as well as to introduce new documentation in support of your claim.

You may have a lawyer or some other representative, such as a family member, friend, or paid advocate, help you during the proceeding. The advocate isn't allowed to charge you or to collect a fee from you for his services without advance approval of the Social Security Administration. You can get a list of groups that can help you get representation from your local Social Security office. Your chosen advocate may even appear on your behalf, but you should be present so that you may be consulted during the hearing and the judge may see you for herself.

The ALJ will make a decision based on her review of the evidence in your file and the new information you present at the hearing. You will receive the decision in the mail; if you had a representative appear with you, that person will also receive a copy of the decision. If the decision reaffirms the earlier denial of benefits, you'll receive information about how to proceed further with your appeal.

**TAKE NOTE** *Although most ALJ hearings are held within 75 miles of the applicant's home, in some cases the hearing takes place farther away. If so, you may be entitled to payment for some of your travel costs. The price of a bus or*

*train ticket or reimbursement for the expense of driving your car are usually covered. If you need to stay overnight, you may also be reimbursed for the cost of lodging, meals, and taxis to and from the hearing site. If you can't pay for these expenses up front, the ALJ can authorize an advance payment for you. You must first show that without the advance, you won't be able to attend the hearing.*

### SMART MOVES

Keep careful records of your working life—pay stubs, tax forms, copies of income tax returns. Such records, which are necessary for filing your annual income taxes, also establish a full history of your employment should you ever need to file for disability benefits.

■ **Step 3: Going to the Appeals Council.** If the ALJ decides against you, your next step is to ask for review by the Social Security Appeals Council. Make the request within 60 days of the ALJ's decision. The council meets in Falls Church, Virginia, and considers the written record of your case. After review, it can either overrule the ALJ's decision and grant you disability benefits, or return the case to the ALJ with instructions for further review. The appeals council doesn't take on every case that's sent to it. Recently, there's been a growing backlog of cases that are waiting to be heard. Some cases have been pending for more than a year. If you win your case, however, you will be entitled to receive back benefits.

■ **Step 4: Consider filing a lawsuit.** If your Appeals Council ruling is unfavorable, your next option is to take your claim to federal district court. The time limit for bringing suit in federal court is 60 days from the day you receive the Appeals Council's decision.

Filing a lawsuit to contest a denial of Social Security disability benefits is your last resort, and one that must be considered very carefully. Only a small percentage of cases heard in federal court result in a reversal of earlier decisions. This is because courts give deference to the decisions made by the Social Security Administration and its hearings officers and the ALJs who hear the cases.

Consult a lawyer experienced in federal court proceedings about your chances for success before committing to a lawsuit.

> **You make an appointment with a new doctor, but when he discovers your religion, he refuses to treat you.**

As surprising as it may seem, doctors have no legal obligation to treat anyone, except in an emergency room. A doctor in private practice can refuse to accept a new patient for any number of reasons, except for those that are prohibited by local, state, or federal antidiscrimination laws. Generally, this means that you cannot be refused treatment because of race, national origin, gender, or religion. In addition, in some states and communities, you cannot be denied treatment because of your sexual orientation or gender-identity issues.

### CLARIFY THE SITUATION

Be sure you understand the reason that the doctor is refusing to accept you as a patient, and record any statements he makes about his refusal. A comment such as "We can't accept Muslim patients without offending

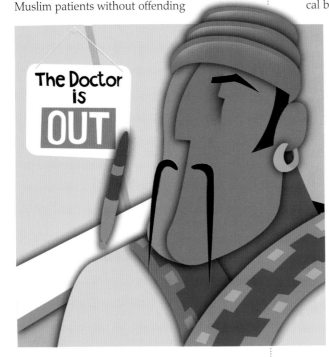

our other patients" is clear evidence of prejudice and illegal discrimination. But more subtle statements of prejudice may also be useful to note. For example, saying "you'll be much more comfortable with Dr. El Fayad" could also suggest that the reason for refusing you was illegal.

If you believe that you are being denied treatment illegally, do the following:

> **As surprising as it may seem, doctors have no legal obligation to treat anyone, except in an emergency room.**

- **Contact your state's board of medical examiners** and voice your complaint to them. Although this group typically reviews doctors' medical decisions and their fitness to practice, they are also charged with preventing unethical behavior. Discrimination that is based on religion or another prohibited classification violates your doctor's ethical responsibility.
- **Call your state's civil rights commission.** It can investigate your complaint and may be able to bring legal action against the doctor for violating state laws prohibiting discrimination against medical patients.
- **Get in touch with the U.S. Department of Justice** and ask it to look into the doctor's potentially unethical behavior. If it determines that the doctor has violated federal antidiscrimination laws, it may be able to file suit against him or even bring criminal charges.

### CONSIDER A LAWSUIT

Finally, consult a civil rights lawyer. A person who suffers illegal discrimination has the right in this country to file a private lawsuit and collect damages from the offending party.

A lawyer can help you to evaluate your particular situation and explain what will be required of you if you go to court. A lawyer can also help you to decide on the merits of your case and the likely legal fees involved in taking it to court.

## A Doctor's Duty of Care

A doctor's legal obligations toward a patient have been summed up in what are known as the standards of care that a physician must meet. These are...

■ **The doctor's obligation to obtain informed consent before treating a patient.** This does not require a doctor to obtain consent in writing, although written consent is legally required before surgery or another invasive procedure is performed (see "The Elements of Informed Consent," page 286), nor does it require him to set out the remote possibilities of harm that could result from the proposed treatment. It *does* require him to be sure that the patient understands the nature of the procedure being proposed and the likely risks involved. Failing to obtain proper informed consent before a procedure could be the basis for a lawsuit, and it might even lead to criminal charges of assault and battery against the doctor.

■ **The doctor's obligation to use reasonable skill and care in accordance with accepted medical practice.** This sounds pretty straightforward, but it can be very difficult to define. What's "reasonable" in one case may be unreasonable in another, and what's "accepted medical practice" in one place may be unacceptable elsewhere. Proving that a doctor has violated either standard is very difficult in court.

■ **The doctor's obligation to supervise others to whom he delegates a patient's care.** Nurses, therapists, and others who provide daily care for a patient are often held to be under the doctor's supervision, even if they aren't actually employed by him. A doctor has the legal duty to oversee their actions and to prevent them from causing harm to the patient.

■ **The doctor's obligation not to abandon a patient.** Doctors aren't under any legal obligation to accept a patient, but once they do, they are required to continue providing care until the patient no longer needs treatment, voluntarily terminates treatment, or until the doctor notifies the patient that he will not continue treatment and gives the patient adequate time to find another doctor.

Failing to meet any of these standards of care can be the basis for legal action against a doctor.

## You've asked your doctor to let you look at your medical records, but she refuses.

Getting access to your own medical records can be a lot harder than you might expect. That's because only about half of the states have laws that give patients the right to get possession of or even look at their medical records. A small number of other states give doctors, hospitals, and other medical facilities the option of providing the patient with a summary of his or her records at their discretion.

Why is it so difficult to convince health-care personnel to release your records to you?

Doctors may not want you to see comments they have made about you or to discover that they've discussed your case with other medical personnel. They may have made a diagnosis of serious illness that they think will cause you more harm than good if you know about it. Or in some cases, it may be that the records themselves are embarrassingly skimpy and incomplete.

Whatever the case, remember that while not every state specifically authorizes you to see your medical records, no state prohibits it.

## GETTING YOUR RECORDS RELEASED

First, attempt to work things out informally with your doctor, especially if you would like to maintain a good relationship with her. Try these steps:

■ **Explain why it's important to you** to have your records, and ask her to arrange a time when you can pick them up or review them. Tell her that you're willing to pay the reasonable cost of photocopying if that's an obstacle.

■ **Ask to see legal support for her denial.** Request that she show you a reference to the law that she thinks supports her claim. You'll discover that she won't be able to, because no such state laws exist.

■ **Check your state statutes** to see if there are any specific laws that give you the right to access your medical records. You'll find the state statute books at public libraries, law school libraries, and your county courthouse.
  ● If such laws are in your state, copy them.
  ● Write to the doctor asking her to furnish you with your records as provided for by law, and include a copy of the statutes that authorize patients' access to their own records.

■ **Put your request in writing** even if there is no state law that is in your favor. Putting the request in writing will provide evidence if legal action is required later. In your letter:

● Ask the doctor to give you her reasons for denying your request.
● Ask her to respond to your letter within a specified period of time.
● Include your name, address, and daytime telephone number.
● Send your letter by certified mail, return receipt requested.

■ **Find a new doctor.** If your doctor still refuses to release your medical records, or fails to respond to your request, you may decide to change doctors. Be sure to select a physician who's willing to let you see your records, and have him request that your former doctor send them to his office. You'll have to sign a form that authorizes their release. When he receives your records, you can review them.

## YOUR LAST RESORT

Ultimately, you may need to go to court in an effort to obtain an order requiring your doctor to give you access to your records. Your chances of success will depend to some extent on how serious your need is for getting possession of them. Ask a lawyer to review your problem and advise you about the best course of action. But unless your request is clearly frivolous, your chances of success should be good.

---

*Y*our doctor's behavior has grown increasingly erratic, and you're concerned that he may be abusing drugs or alcohol.

---

Doctors are under an enormous amount of stress on a daily basis. Like everyone else, some doctors handle pressure well and may even thrive on it. Other doctors are overwhelmed by the demands of medical practice and may turn to alcohol, illegal drugs, or prescription medications to help them make it through their stressful days.

According to one estimate, as many as 50,000 physicians in this country may be practicing under the influence of a drug dependency. This problem not only endangers the doctor's health but it can also cloud his judgment and, worst of all, diminish his professional skills.

## SUBSTANCE ABUSE WARNING SIGNS

Be on the lookout for the following symptoms of a drug or alcohol dependence:

● Physical deterioration
● Change in dress from neat and professional to extremely casual or sloppy
● Red eyes
● Smell of alcohol
● Inability to keep appointments and other attendance problems
● New cynicism, anger, antagonism, or sarcasm toward coworkers or their patients, or toward life's routine problems and pressures.

## TALK TO YOUR DOCTOR

If you feel comfortable doing so, talk to your doctor about the concerns you have. It may be that the doctor's behavior isn't related to alcohol or drug abuse, but is due to a lack of sleep or the burdens of his work schedule. In any case, he needs to know that you've seen a change in his behavior and that you're concerned about the effect it may have on the care he gives you.

## ENLIST THE MEDICAL EXAMINERS

If you can't approach your doctor, or if he denies that there's a problem but his erratic behavior continues, notify your state Board of Medical Examiners or Board of Healing Arts. In most states, you can contact this office by telephone, and you may be able to remain anonymous.

The problem of drug and alcohol abuse by doctors is well recognized, and states have now created intervention programs designed to help affected physicians recognize their problem and get treatment. Today all 50 states and the District of Columbia have established programs designed to help doctors overcome drug or alcohol problems. Upon investigation, the medical board may refer the doctor to one of these programs.

If he fails to complete an appropriate treatment, or if a relapse occurs, the medical board may notify the licensing board, which can take disciplinary action against a doctor who continues to practice under the influence of drugs or alcohol. His license to practice may be suspended or revoked in serious cases, especially when patients have actually been harmed as a result. Hospitals may also suspend the privileges of doctors who fail to obtain treatment for substance abuse.

**TAKE NOTE** *If you aren't certain that your doctor's problems or behavioral changes are drug related, talk to an attorney about your potential liability if you tell others about your concerns. If you speak out publicly and the doctor isn't involved in substance abuse, you could find yourself the defendant in a defamation claim.*

---

### MAKING A COMPLAINT ABOUT YOUR DOCTOR

If you have a problem with your doctor that you can't resolve face-to-face, you can make a formal written complaint. Contact your state Board of Medical Examiners or Board of Healing Arts for how to file a complaint. Some supervisory boards may ask you to write a letter, while others have a form for you to fill out. Either way, the regulators will want to know the following:

- The name of the doctor

- The complaint or concern you are writing about (for example, your doctor has charged you for hospital visits that did not occur)

- Any specific evidence you have to support your complaint (such as copies of your hospital bills and the doctor's bills)

- The days and times your problems with the doctor occurred

- The statements of any witnesses that support your complaint (such as a family member who was at the hospital with you at the times the doctor claims to have visited)

- Copies of any other documents related to your complaint (such as correspondence you've had with the doctor questioning billing)

- Your name, address, and your daytime telephone number.

You may be contacted by the board for additional information and could even be asked to testify at a hearing. If the board finds that your doctor has violated his ethical obligations or has violated the rules governing the practice of medicine in your state, the board can take several disciplinary actions against him, ranging from giving him a private reprimand to suspending or even terminating his license to practice medicine.

> *T*ragically, your doctor failed to diagnose
> your husband's cancer until it had already become inoperable.

The term *medical malpractice* usually calls to mind a botched operation or a patient being given the wrong medication. But the leading cause of malpractice complaints is the misdiagnosis of medical conditions, and the disorder that is most often misdiagnosed is cancer.

> *T*he leading cause of malpractice complaints is the misdiagnosis of medical conditions.

### CREATE A PAPER TRAIL

Once you've learned that your husband's doctor failed to properly diagnose his condition as cancer, proceed as follows:

- **Begin documenting your case.** If possible, create a log that indicates…
  - When your husband first sought help from the doctor
  - The doctor's comments, and the treatments and medications he prescribed
  - Additional doctor's visits and his responses to your husband's health concerns
  - Any other information you think is relevant to your husband's misdiagnosis.
- **Get your husband's records from the doctor.** (See page 281 for more information about what to do if your doctor refuses to relinquish medical records.)

### GO TO COURT

Consider contacting a medical malpractice lawyer. But be aware that, contrary to what many people think, winning a malpractice case isn't easy, nor is it likely to result in a big award of damages. Statistics show that doctors are acquitted in about three out of four malpractice cases. Of the ones they do lose, the average verdict is roughly $450,000. That may sound like a lot of money, but remember that your lawyer's fee will be up to a third of that. And laws in many states now place stringent limits on the money you can collect for noneconomic damages, such as your husband's

pain and suffering. Depending on the side you're on, these limits protect doctors from unscrupulous patients seeking a pot of gold for minor medical mistakes, or they prevent injured parties from getting adequate compensation for their years of pain and suffering.

To decide if you have a claim of malpractice worth pursuing, you and your lawyer need to ask yourselves these four questions:

- **Did the doctor owe your husband a duty of care?** (See A Doctor's Duty of Care, page 281.) A doctor you meet at a cocktail party who listens to your complaint about a sinus problem may not owe you any duty. But a doctor you visit in his office, who agrees to provide treatment and orders tests or other procedures, takes on a responsibility to provide you with adequate professional care.
- **Did the doctor provide inadequate care?** Once the doctor has taken on a duty of care, he's required to provide it in a way that should reasonably be expected from a member of the medical community. A mistake that results from the doctor's lack of knowledge, experience, or skill, or the failure to use reasonable judgment can be considered malpractice.
- **Was your husband harmed?** There has to be actual physical injury or damage to the patient's health in order for a malpractice claim to succeed.
- **Did the doctor's actions or inactions cause your husband's harm?** You must show that there is a direct link between the doctor's negligence in failing to diagnose the cancer and the harm your husband suffered.

### SHOULD YOU CONSIDER ARBITRATION?

Because malpractice lawsuits are complicated and time-consuming, you may consider arbitration. Some doctors and hospitals involved in potential malpractice claims will suggest arbitration in order to avoid the possibility of a large jury award based on sympathy for the plaintiff. Some plaintiffs' attorneys may also recommend arbitration to their clients to speed the process and get the doctor's malpractice payment to them more quickly.

In arbitration, your claim is usually heard by a panel of three arbitrators: one chosen by the doctor, one chosen by you, and one chosen by two arbitrators who are neutral and disinterested in the case. Evidence is presented to the arbitration panel by you and by the doctor. If the panel finds in your favor, it sets the amount of compensation you will receive. Only under extreme and rare circumstances can you appeal the arbitration panel's decision.

The decision to seek arbitration instead of suing in court is one that must be made on a case-by-case basis. The inability to appeal a decision that goes against you can be a major drawback to the arbitration process. Talk to your attorney before agreeing to the doctor's suggestion to submit your case to arbitration.

## NOTIFY THE STATE MEDICAL BOARD

In addition to filing suit against your husband's doctor or seeking arbitration, you may want to contact the state medical board to let the board know about the doctor's failure to provide you with adequate care.

The medical board can take action independent of the private lawsuit you file. The board can investigate your claim and discipline the doctor if it finds that your complaint is legitimate.

---

*Your doctor neglected to tell you about a possible complication from surgery. You had the operation, and now you feel worse than before.*

---

Whenever you have any medical treatment or procedure, the law requires you to give your *informed consent* to it. In many cases, this consent isn't in writing. For example, when your doctor gives you a flu shot, you aren't likely to have to sign a form allowing the doctor to administer it.

But when a procedure is serious, or when there's the possibility of significant risks associated with treatment, most doctors, hospitals, and other medical professionals won't proceed until you sign a form stating that you've been informed of the risks related to it. Failing to obtain your informed consent before treatment can make your doctor legally liable if you are injured as a result of her actions.

### WAS YOUR CONSENT VALID?

Even if you signed a consent form, your consent to the procedure may not have been valid. That would be the case if you signed the form under duress—because your doctor pressured you to sign it—or if the consent form failed to reveal a possible complication that your doctor knew or should have known about. Under these circumstances, you may have a legitimate negligence claim against your doctor.

Depending on your relationship with your doctor, you may want to approach him directly about the problem. But because of rules established by medical malpractice insurance companies, it's unlikely your doctor will acknowledge any wrongdoing in obtaining your consent.

### FILE A MEDICAL MALPRACTICE LAWSUIT

You will probably have to make a formal demand for compensation for the injuries you suffered. This is not usually something you should handle on your own. Instead, contact a personal-injury attorney who handles medical malpractice cases on a regular basis. An experienced lawyer can help you through the legal process.

## THE ELEMENTS OF INFORMED CONSENT

*Informed consent* means giving your doctor permission to perform a medical procedure after being notified of its benefits and risks. Before signing a consent form, you should…

- Know and understand the condition for which you are being treated

- Know the risks and benefits of the treatment your doctor proposes

- Be aware of alternative treatments that may be available, and the risks and benefits associated with them

- Be informed about the risks associated with refusing any treatment for the condition

- Be given the doctor's estimate of how likely it is that the treatment will be successful

- Receive an estimate of the time it will take to recuperate after treatment

- Be informed as to who will actually provide the treatment and what his qualifications are for doing so

- Get an estimate of all the costs associated with the procedure, including operating room costs, fees for attendants' services, and prescriptions

- Believe that the proposed treatment's benefits outweigh its risks

- Understand everything on the consent form

- Willingly give your consent to the procedure, and you must sign the consent form without undue pressure or influence.

## You discover that your teenage daughter has received medical treatment without your consent.

While the law gives parents the right to make decisions about the medical care and treatment for their children, this right isn't absolute. Depending on your daughter's age and the nature of the treatment she received, she may not have needed to tell you in advance or obtain your consent.

For example, if your daughter is older than the age of 14, the law in some states considers her a "mature minor," able to give her own informed consent for certain medical procedures. These may include tests for sexually transmitted diseases or pregnancy, prenatal care, or treatment for alcohol or drug abuse. She also may not legally need your notification or your consent to obtain contraceptive devices or birth control pills.

### LOOK INTO YOUR LAWS

Your first step is to check the law in your state and find out if the treatment your daughter received was one that she's legally permitted to have without your knowledge or consent. If it is, you'll have little recourse against the doctor or other medical personnel who treated her.

Your daughter, however, may have a grievance against them for violating her right to medical privacy if they disclosed the treatment to you, even inadvertently.

### TALK TO THE DOCTOR

If the treatment was one that you should have been made aware of beforehand, contact the doctor immediately and insist that she give you a full account of the problem, the diagnosis, and information about any prescriptions or other treatments she provided to your daughter.

If the doctor refuses to cooperate, contact the state medical board and file a complaint. The board will investigate your claim and can, if warranted, impose a variety of sanctions against the doctor.

## SEEK LEGAL HELP

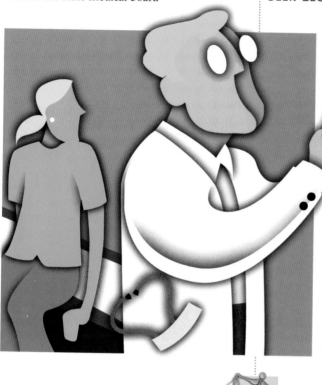

If the treatment she received harmed or injured your daughter, get in touch with a medical malpractice attorney. Your daughter's doctor may be liable for the cost of the care and treatment necessary to restore your daughter's health as well as compensation for the pain and suffering that she may have experienced as a result of the doctor's negligence.

You may also want to talk to your local prosecutor about this situation. As a minor, your daughter's consent to treatment may have been invalid, and the doctor may actually be guilty of committing battery against her, even if she suffered no real harm. The prosecutor's office can evaluate the case to determine if the doctor could be subject to criminal charges.

---

*You buy a new over-the-counter antihistamine, but when you open the package, you notice that one of the seals looks as if it has been tampered with.*

---

Since a rash of product-tampering problems that occurred in the 1980s, manufacturers of over-the-counter medications have gone to great lengths to improve packaging in order to make their products safe. Still, incidents of product tampering do occur, and it's always smart to closely examine over-the-counter medicines to be sure that all of the safety seals are secure.

## SAFETY MEASURES

If you use a product that you believe has been tampered with, and you have an unexpected reaction to the product, do the following:

- **Get immediate medical attention.** Call your doctor, a poison control center, or the emergency phone number 911 immediately.
- **Contact the Food and Drug Administration.** In an emergency situation, such as this, you can call the Food and Drug Administration 24 hours a day at (888) 463-6332 to report a concern. Be ready to provide…
  - Your name, address, and telephone number, and the names, addresses, and telephone numbers of anyone else who was affected
  - The name of the doctor who treated you and the hospital where you were treated

● A complete description of the product, including codes or other identifying marks on the package label or on the container

● The name and address of the store where you purchased the product

● The approximate date of purchase.

■ **Alert the store** where you bought the product; tell them it may have been tampered with.

■ **Notify the manufacturer** or distributor of the product. Most over-the-counter medications now have the number for contacting the manufacturer on the label, and in most cases this call is toll-free.

**CONSUMER ALERT** *Don't use any over-the-counter medication that isn't in a factory-sealed package when you purchase it.*

## GET LEGAL HELP

If you've been injured by a medicine that's been tampered with, it's a good idea to talk to an attorney about the problem. A lawyer can look into your circumstances and suggest a course of action against the manufacturer, distributor, or the retailer for failing to ensure that the product made it from the factory to consumers in its unadulterated form.

You and your lawyer may decide to file a *class-action* lawsuit, in which one or more plaintiffs represent a group of plaintiffs who have suffered similar injuries. The pressure and expense of having to defend themselves in a well-publicized class-action suit often encourages these companies to settle with all of the plaintiffs without ever going to trial.

---

### REPORTING PROBLEMS WITH A MEDICAL PRODUCT

If you or a family member experiences or witnesses a serious adverse reaction to a medical product, the Food and Drug Administration (FDA) wants to know about it. The FDA defines a serious reaction as one that is caused, or is suspected to have been caused, by a medical product and that resulted in...

● Death

● A life-threatening situation

● Admission to a hospital

● A longer-than-expected hospital stay

● A birth defect

● Permanent disability

● The necessity for medical care to prevent permanent physical damage.

Among the medical products that the FDA regulates are prescription and over-the-counter medications, blood products, special nutritional products such as dietary supplements and baby formulas, and medical devices such as pacemakers, heart valves, and hearing aids.

To report a problem, contact the FDA's MedWatch program at (800) 332-1088 and ask that a reporting form be mailed to you. Although you can complete this form yourself, the FDA suggests having a medical professional help you.

Be aware that health-care professionals are not required to file reports on suspected medical products. The FDA urges consumers to file their own reports if their doctor chooses not to report a problem you have had with any medications.

*That new makeup foundation you bought doesn't give your skin a healthy glow; it makes it break out in a rash. When you call the manufacturer, the company refuses to accept responsibility.*

Cosmetics is big, big business. While the federal government regulates the manufacture of cosmetics, it isn't as stringent a watchdog over cosmetics sales as it is over prescription drugs or over-the-counter medications. Before getting the government involved, there are some steps you can take on your own to try to get compensation for medical bills and related expenses you may have incurred as a result of using a company's beauty products.

## DOCUMENT YOUR PROBLEM

As in every situation where you have a complaint, keeping careful records of the problem makes it much more likely that you'll fight back successfully. You should…

- **Keep your store receipt** and the unused portion of the product, along with any packaging. This will give you proof of purchase.
- **Take photographs of the rash** or other problems the cosmetics caused. Cameras that record the date and time on the photo can help provide additional proof that the rash occurred *after* you bought the company's cosmetic product.
- **Get a statement from your doctor** that contains his diagnosis of the problem and its relationship to the cosmetics you purchased. The doctor should also include a description of the treatment he ordered and his prognosis for your recovery (for example, if your skin will require continuing treatment or if there is permanent scarring).
- **Collect all the bills** for treatment, prescriptions, bandages, or other items related to the rash. Photocopy and file all of them.
- **Mail copies of all the documentation** you have to the company's president. (You can obtain this address from the company's customer service department, from business directories available at the public library, or from the Internet.) Be sure to keep the originals for your files. Include a letter that sets out your case, stating…
  - That you used the company's product as directed by the product label, and then broke out in a rash that required medical treatment

  - The amount of money that you've spent on treatments for the problem
  - Information about any other losses, such as lost wages due to time spent at the doctor's office and away from your work as well as the pain and suffering you've experienced that resulted from using the product
  - A proposed solution to the problem, such as a cash settlement to cover all of the damages you suffered—some experts suggest that you calculate all of your actual costs, and then multiply that figure by three to arrive at a reasonable settlement offer
  - A deadline by which you expect the company to respond, such as 10 business days from the date of your letter. Send the letter to the manufacturer by certified mail, return receipt requested, so the company won't be able to claim that it was never received.

## DEALING WITH THE COMPANY'S INSURER

In some cases, you may hear directly from the company president or his representative, but you may also be contacted by a claims adjuster from the company's insurance company. Be sure to get the name, address, and telephone number of the claims adjuster or anyone else you talk to as well as that of the insurance company.

The insurer may make a settlement offer based on the documentation you provided, or it may deny any liability for the problem. In either event, don't assume that the case is closed. If the insurer offers less than you believe your claim is worth or if it denies liability, restate the reasons that you believe your claim is warranted, and ask the adjuster to reconsider.

## FILE A LAWSUIT

If the company or its insurer remains unwilling to cooperate, consider filing a lawsuit to collect for the injuries you suffered. Depending on the amount you're seeking, small-claims court could be an option, but if the amount is above the limits for small-claims suits in your state, you may want to pursue the matter in the regular civil court system. It's worthwhile to at least meet with a personal-injury attorney who can help you evaluate your claim, determine which court to use, and provide you with other assistance. For example, the lawyer may be able to write a letter on your behalf to convince the company to settle without the necessity of a lawsuit. Simply knowing that you are serious enough to get legal help may be enough to turn the tide in your favor.

## Contact the FDA

Cosmetics made and sold in this country are regulated by the Federal Food and Drug Administration (FDA). Contact this agency with your problem by calling (888) 463-6332 or by visiting its Web site: www.fda.gov. The FDA can investigate the situation and may discover that the manufacturer of the makeup you used is in violation of rules designed to protect customers from harmful products. For example, the cosmetics manufacturer may have failed to list all of the product ingredients as required by law. If you know that you're allergic to an ingredient but it was omitted from the product's label, the FDA may be able to take action against the manufacturer. Or it may determine that the product was somehow contaminated in the manufacturing process, prompting a recall or the seizure and destruction of the harmful product.

### ONLINE PHARMACY CAUTIONS

With the expansion of the Internet has come an accompanying growth in the number of businesses that sell prescription drugs on line. While most of these companies are legitimate, others may not be entirely on the up-and-up, and some are run by crooks. Before having a prescription filled over the Internet, look into the following:

■ **Is the Web site connected to a "bricks and mortar" pharmacy in the United States?** If so, there's probably nothing to worry about. The company may even have a pharmacy in your neighborhood, and you can save shipping charges by picking up your prescription there.

■ **Is the online pharmacy's office located in the U.S.?** Pharmacies outside U.S. borders aren't always subject to the same level of government regulation as those located in this country.

■ **Does the pharmacy tout miracle cures or alternative medicines?** You may be visiting the site of a con artist who is more interested in selling you costly but worthless products than in being sure your prescription is filled accurately.

■ **Does the pharmacy offer drugs "prescribed" by a doctor you've never seen?** Some Web sites have you fill out a questionnaire that's supposedly reviewed by a physician, who then prescribes medication that the Internet pharmacy provides. These "interviews" are often superficial and are never as good as an in-person examination by a doctor. Some can be downright dangerous because they fail to ask about other medications or supplements you take that could interact with the prescription and cause serious complications or even death.

If you suspect that you're dealing with a fraudulent online pharmacy, or if you want to report misleading promotions of any medicine, visit the Food and Drug Administration's Web site at www.fda.gov, or call (888) 463-6332.

> **Y**our father's nursing home has stopped giving him physical therapy, claiming that Medicare won't pay for it anymore.

**T**he good news is that Medicare will pay for "skilled rehabilitation services" that your father receives while residing in a nursing home that's designated a skilled nursing facility (SNF). These include the services of occupational therapists, speech pathologists, and physical therapists. The less-good news is that Medicare imposes strict limits on how many sessions it will cover.

## WHAT MEDICARE PROVIDES

Medicare will pay 100 percent of the cost for the first 20 days of his physical therapy. After that, it pays a portion of the therapy cost for another 80 days, minus a daily deductible (in 2000, that deductible was $96).

Under current Medicare law, your father is entitled to these 100 days of physical therapy in an SNF every *benefit period.* A benefit period begins the day a patient covered by Medicare is first hospitalized or enters an SNF. It ends after the beneficiary has been out of the hospital or nursing facility for 60 consecutive days. A new period begins if the beneficiary is readmitted to care after the 60-day period has passed. If your father has already had 100 days of physical therapy in this benefit period, then Medicare will no longer pay for it, and the nursing facility is no longer required to provide therapy for him.

## WHEN IT'S THE NURSING HOME'S DECISION

In some cases, nursing-home administrators have informed patients or their families that the home will stop providing these therapeutic services because the patient has reached a plateau, or isn't improving. But Medicare *requires* nursing homes to provide these services in order to "attain or maintain the highest physical, mental, and psychosocial well-being of each resident." According to the Health Care Finance Administration (HCFA), the agency that enforces Medicare laws, maintaining this well-being doesn't require

improvement. It means that the home must continue to provide the services in order to help keep your father's health and well-being from declining and to help preserve his current capabilities.

If your father's nursing home tells you that it intends to end his physical therapy for this reason, do the following:

- **Ask for a written explanation** for the decision from the nursing-home administrator.
- **Refer the administrator to the Code of Federal Regulations (CFR).** Tell her that the CFR prohibits terminating your father's physical therapy simply because he isn't improving.
- **Ask your father's doctor to write** the nursing home confirming that your father requires continued "skilled rehabilitation services."

If the home still refuses to continue therapy...

- **Demand that it provide you with a "Notice of Noncoverage."** Federal law requires the nursing home to give you this notice on request. Insist that the facility continue providing therapy for your father.

■ **Check the box on the notice** requesting that the bill for your father's continuing therapy be submitted to the Medicare *intermediary* in order to obtain a Medicare coverage decision. An intermediary is an insurance company that's responsible for handling Medicare claims within a particular state. The nursing home is not allowed to bill your father for the therapy treatment while the Medicare-coverage decision is being made.

## YOUR RIGHTS IN A NURSING HOME

Federal law provides residents of nursing homes with certain specific rights, and state laws may mandate additional rights as well. Among your rights when you enter a nursing home are…

■ **The right to information about fees** you will pay and services you will receive—you are entitled to receive this information in writing before you sign your nursing home contract.

■ **The right to privacy.** You have the right to have your medical records treated confidentially, and you also have the right to privacy in communicating with visitors in person, by mail, or by telephone.

■ **The right to self-determination, dignity, and quality of life.** You are entitled to be treated with respect by nursing home staff and to interact with others within and outside of the nursing home. You also have the right to make your own choices about the activities and programs you participate in and to make your own decisions about the health care you receive in light of your own interests and abilities.

■ **The right of access.** This means that you have the right to be visited by your attorney, government representatives, the state's long-term-care ombudsman, and others who may be advocates for you against the facility. With your permission, your lawyer and the state ombudsman have the right to examine your records at the nursing home.

■ **Visiting rights.** You have the right to have visitors at any reasonable time. You *also* have the right to *refuse* visitors.

■ **The right to financial control.** That means being allowed to handle your own finances and to receive information from the nursing home that describes the steps it takes to protect your personal funds.

■ **The right to participate in family and resident groups.** You have the right to meet with family members and other residents to discuss problems and work with them to bring these issues to the attention of nursing home administrators. The home must provide a meeting space and designate an employee to respond to written requests or complaints that result from family or resident meetings.

You are entitled to a written copy of all your legal rights when you enter the nursing home as well as copies of any changes that may take place because of new or revised laws. You should also receive information about your right to make a complaint to the state about neglect or abuse. If you don't receive this copy of your rights when you enter the home, ask for it. If you still don't get it, contact the state nursing-home regulators immediately.

**M**aking the decision to place a loved one in a nursing home is always difficult. But discovering that a nursing home isn't a good one after you've already signed the contract can be downright heartbreaking. There are several ways to address this problem.

Nursing homes in this country are regulated at both the state and federal levels and are subject to regular inspections—on an annual basis at least. Nursing homes that fail to meet the operating standards set by law are subject to a variety of penalties, including fines, loss of Medicaid funds, on-site management by state officials, even closure, with the facility's residents moved to other nursing homes.

## NURSING HOME GRIEVANCES

Federal regulations require nursing homes to maintain a formal grievance procedure to deal with complaints made by residents. You and your wife should have received a copy of the document explaining this procedure when she was admitted to the nursing home. The grievance procedure document should provide…

- The name or title of the person responsible for receiving resident complaints
- Contact information for that person
- A description of how complaints are investigated and responded to
- Kinds of corrective actions taken when the investigation of your complaint is concluded.

Nursing homes are required to respond immediately to residents' grievances.

## COMPLAIN TO THE NURSING HOME

Contact the official named in the grievance procedure document and let him know about the problems you and your wife have observed. Be specific. If meals are late, security is lax, sanitation is shoddy, or promised services aren't being

delivered, say so. Give examples to the official and provide the names of any nursing-home workers who haven't fulfilled their obligations.

Give the official time to investigate and take action to correct the problem. Most nursing homes are eager to avoid the hassles of state or federal investigations and will do their best to make things right for residents without the need for outside intervention.

## GET OUTSIDE HELP

If the problems with your wife's care persist, or if you are dissatisfied with the response you receive, you should take the following remedial steps:

- **Notify the state ombudsman.** By law, every state must have a long-term care ombudsman to serve as an advocate for residents of nursing homes and other long-term, health-care facilities. Tell the ombudsman about the problem and the response—if any—that you received when you made your complaint to the nursing home. The ombudsman can look into the matter, and if she finds in your favor,

## HOW TO CHOOSE A NURSING HOME

If you are looking for a nursing home for yourself or a loved one, it's a good idea to get information on and tour several before making a selection. Here's what to consider when choosing a nursing home:

■ **Is the nursing home state licensed?** Being licensed means that the nursing home meets minimum standards for building safety, sanitation, maintenance, and housekeeping.

■ **Is the nursing home Medicare or Medicaid certified?** Obtaining certification means that the nursing home agrees to certain additional conditions, such as providing a specified number of beds for patients enrolled in those programs and accepting the rate paid by those programs for enrolled residents, even if that's less than the regular daily rate.

■ **What are the physical facilities like?** Examine the buildings and the grounds, not just for how attractive and livable they appear to be but also for how safe they are. An old building, no matter how charming, may not have the latest in sprinklers and alarms or may require residents on upper floors to use stairs or fire escapes in case of an emergency.

■ **What are the individual living quarters like?** Are the rooms sufficiently spacious and clean? Are the furnishings in good repair? Is there natural light available? Are there grab bars in the bathroom? Are floor coverings made of nonslip materials? Is there space for personal belongings and adequate closet space?

■ **What are the employees like?** Administrators and admissions representatives should be neatly dressed and courteous and should honor appointments you've made to meet with them. They should answer your questions completely and explain all of the nursing home's policies and procedures thoroughly. You should tour the home and pay attention to the way personnel deal with the home's residents. Is interaction friendly and warm, or do staff members ignore residents or speak harshly to them? Ask about employee turnover; a high turnover rate may mean problems in the nursing home.

■ **What medical care is offered?** Is there a doctor on the premises around the clock, or on call? Check into whether the home has physical and occupational therapists, dietitians, and pharmacists on staff. Are nursing services provided by registered nurses, or is the facility staffed with nurses that have less formal training and education? Are alternative therapies, such as chiropractic treatment, available?

■ **What recreational and social activities are offered?** Does the home have a full-time activities director? What are the limitations on visiting hours, number of visitors at a given time, and ages of visitors (will your young grandchildren be allowed to visit you)? Is there a place to meet with visitors other than the residents' rooms? Are there regularly scheduled trips, programs, and educational activities?

■ **How's the food?** Are kitchen and dining facilities clean and well maintained? Do residents have a choice of meals, and are special dietary needs met? Is the food visually appealing, nutritious, varied, and palatable? Are residents required to take meals as a group, or can they have meals served in their rooms? Are snacks available around the clock?

she can contact the nursing home on your behalf to try to find a solution.

■ **Contact the state nursing-home regulators.** The state nursing-home board is legally required to establish procedures for investigating resident complaints, and to provide for

*By law, every state must have a long-term-care ombudsman to serve as an advocate for residents of nursing homes and other long-term health-care facilities.*

corrective plans and legal sanctions when they are warranted. While most state actions begin after a scheduled inspection uncovers problems in the nursing home, individual complaints can also lead to the state stepping in to order necessary changes.

■ **Call other state agencies that can help.** If the problem involves the quality of medical care your wife is receiving, you can make a complaint about individual nurses or nurses

aides to the appropriate regulatory board. If your complaint is about sanitation in living quarters or kitchen facilities, contact the Board of Health. Your state's civil-rights commission can launch its own investigation if you believe that your wife is being discriminated against illegally on the basis of her race, national origin, or religious beliefs.

■ **Talk to your local prosecutor.** If the situation your wife is experiencing in the nursing home is severe enough to constitute neglect or abuse, those responsible could be charged with violating state criminal statutes.

## CALL A LAWYER

Depending on what your wife's experience has been, you may be able to file a civil lawsuit against the nursing home for negligence or for breaching the terms of the contract you signed when she was admitted. In some states, you may also be able to sue based on the nursing home's violation of state regulations. In these cases, the damages you can collect are usually limited by law. Consult a lawyer with experience dealing with nursing-home resident complaints. The National Academy of Elder Law Attorneys can provide you with the names of attorneys in your community who specialize in this area. The American Association of Retired People (AARP) may also help you find a qualified lawyer.

---

*You need an operation, which you want to have performed in the hospital. But Medicare will allow you to have it done only at an outpatient facility.*

When Medicare is paying the bills, decisions about which types of surgery are performed in a hospital and which are performed at a clinic or in your doctor's office are made by a *peer review organization,* or PRO. This is a group of doctors who determine the medical necessity of health care performed under Medicare coverage. Increasingly, the Health Care Finance Administration (HCFA), the federal government agency responsible for administering health care, relies on these PROs for guidance in controlling the cost of medical care.

### ASK FOR RECONSIDERATION

If the above scenario happens to you, the PRO will notify you in writing that your request for inpatient hospital care has been denied. You can then file a request for reconsideration by doing one of the following:

● Writing to the PRO at the address on the notice you received
● Visiting your local Social Security office to ask for advice and help, or writing a letter to the Social Security Administration

● Contacting the Railroad Retirement Board if your Medicare coverage is provided through this agency.

Don't delay in making your request. By law, you must ask for reconsideration within 60 days from the day you received written notice of the PRO's denial. (The law assumes that you received the notice 5 days after the date on the letter.) If you are unable to meet the deadline, you can file a request for an extension with the Social Security office or the Railroad Retirement Board, but not directly with the PRO. Under certain circumstances, you may be excused for filing your request after the deadline. These circumstances include a death in the family, a serious illness experienced by you or a family member, or for a misunderstanding of the PRO notice.

When you file your request, you have the right to ask for an "expedited

reconsideration." (Deadlines for handling requests for an expedited decision vary depending on circumstances.) If you do, the PRO must consider your request and make its decision within 30 calendar days of receiving your letter. Your request for reconsideration should include…

● The PRO's initial notice of noncoverage
● A letter written by your doctor indicating that having your surgery performed in the hospital is a medical necessity
● Any medical literature, such as articles published in respected medical journals, and reviews that will help support your position that the PRO's insistence on out-patient surgery is an unwise or unsafe procedure for you (your doctor should be able to provide you with this material).

The PRO will send you a reconsideration notice informing you of its decision, the reasons for its decision, and the effect the decision will have on the benefits Medicare will pay. It must also give you a statement setting out your right to a further appeal, along with instructions on how to proceed.

## APPEAL THE DECISION

If your request has again been denied, the deadline for filing a further appeal is within 60 days of receiving the original reconsideration notice. At this stage, the process will become more formal:

■ **You must file your appeal on HCFA Form 501.1,** which you should receive with the reconsideration notice. However, in some cases you may be instructed to file it by letter or by using a different format. Be sure to follow the instructions you receive with your reconsideration notice.

### SMART MOVES

If you need to have surgery performed or you require emergency treatment, it's a good idea to have a friend or family member accompany you to help you make decisions and to be sure that you understand what's being proposed by the doctors. Hospitals can be stressful places, emergency rooms may be chaotic, and when you're already in pain, keeping a clear head is difficult. Having someone to help will reduce the chance that you'll make a poor or uninformed choice.

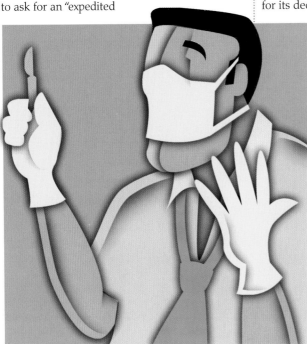

- **You must show that the amount in question is $100 or more.** An administrative law judge (ALJ) will review your appeal to decide if this threshold of requirements has been met.
  - If not, the ALJ will notify you of his decision not to allow the appeal to proceed. You then have 15 days to provide evidence showing that the ALJ's determination is mistaken.
  - If it is, you'll receive a notice from the ALJ of the date of your hearing. You should receive this notice at least 10 days before the hearing is scheduled to take place.
- **You must provide the same kind of evidence at your hearing** that you provided to the PRO in your reconsideration request. The ALJ will then evaluate this evidence along with the evidence provided by the PRO in support of its decision. After reviewing the evidence, the ALJ will issue a ruling.

## SEEK LEGAL HELP

If the ruling is not in your favor, you may still have the right to further appeals, provided the amount in question is at least $1,000. At this stage, it's wise to hire an experienced lawyer. (Your state or local bar association or organizations that provide services to older Americans can provide you with the names of lawyers who handle Medicare coverage appeals.) Your lawyer can help you appeal the ALJ's unfavorable ruling to the Social Security Appeals Council. If that ruling also goes against you or the Appeals Council refuses to hear your case, you can seek a final accounting in federal court.

Your chances of winning your appeal are good. While most people never challenge an unfavorable Medicare decision, statistics show that those who do appeal obtain a reversal of Medicare's initial ruling about half the time.

---

*Y*ou need surgery, but your HMO wants you to have it performed at one of its own hospitals, which happens to be out of state, instead of at one in your own community.

---

When it comes to medical treatment or surgery, everyone wants the best care. If you live in a small town, this may require traveling to a larger metropolitan area where there is likely to be a wider range of specialists and the most modern facilities. When health maintenance organizations, or HMOs, propose surgery in another community, though, it's usually with an eye on the bottom line—if your surgery is done in a hospital they own or have favorable contracts with, it costs them less.

But sometimes staying in your own community for surgery may be to your advantage. You and your friends, family, and primary-care doctor are nearby, and your spouse or children won't have the added expense of meals and lodging near an out-of-town hospital. In many cases, the medical treatment available in your community may be just as good as that available elsewhere.

## CALL FIRST

If you and your doctor believe that you would be better served by a local hospital, you can make a case for having your operation performed locally. First, call your HMO's customer service department and ask that it reconsider its decision to deny coverage for surgery in your own area. Next, request that your primary-care doctor and the specialists you've consulted intervene with the plan administrator on your behalf. They can point out the potential physical, emotional, and psychological problems related to your having surgery in another city.

## FILE A FORMAL GRIEVANCE

If this doesn't work, take the following steps:

- **Review the formal grievance and appeal procedure** included in your plan. By law, HMOs must have a formal written procedure by which members can appeal a plan decision without threat of discrimination. Specific procedures for appealing vary from plan to plan, but generally you must first file a form with the plan stating the decision you are objecting to and the reasons for your objection.

● The form should tell you how long you must wait before you receive an answer from the HMO, such as within 3 working days of receiving it. But if the complaint can't be resolved through the usual channels in that time period, or if an immediate decision is required, the plan should refer your complaint to the HMO's medical director or chief operating officer for a ruling.

● If your surgery isn't immediately required, the HMO's officials may have as many as 10 days in which to decide your case. You may be contacted by these company officers for more information, and you may be asked to provide additional information in support of your position. After considering all the evidence, a ruling will be issued, and you should then be provided with information about further appeals available to you.

■ **Appeal the decision to an HMO committee** if the HMO continues to rule against you. This committee will review the record of your complaint and issue its ruling within a specified time period, such as 30 days.

■ **Contact the state or federal agency** that regulates the HMO if you aren't satisfied with the committee's decision. And if the decision of the agency supports the HMO's position, you may be able to go to court to seek an order requiring the HMO to honor your request.

### WHERE TO GET HELP

When you're ill and under stress, pursuing this appeal yourself is difficult and may even be detrimental to your health. While you may want to hire a lawyer who deals with HMOs and health insurers on a regular basis, there are patient's advocacy groups across the country that can help you make your way through your HMO's procedural maze. Talk to your doctor or your employer about getting help. Doing things right is important, because a failure to follow the HMO's procedures could mean being unable to get a court to review your case.

And don't forget the power of the press. In some cases, media attention and newspaper articles about an HMO have been the catalyst for further review and ultimate approval of the case.

## YOUR RIGHTS AS AN HMO MEMBER

When you are a member of an HMO, you have a number of rights. Some of these are granted by law, but others are a matter of policy. Generally, when you belong to an HMO, you have...

✔ The right to reasonable access to medical care

✔ The right to receive preventative services, such as physical examinations, laboratory tests, wellness counseling, and health-promotion programs, such as smoking cessation courses and stress management classes

✔ The right to participate in making decisions about the care you will receive

✔ The right to refuse medical treatment

✔ The right to make your own decisions about the care provided at the end of your life

✔ The right to notify the plan administrators about problems with the care you receive without the fear of retaliation

✔ The right to a prompt and courteous response to your concerns

✔ The right to treatment that's polite, fair, honest, and respectful

✔ The right to expect that your medical records will be kept confidential and that your privacy will be protected

✔ The right to inspect and receive an explanation of your medical records.

Just about every state requires state-licensed insurers to handle claims in a timely manner. But the definition of *timely* differs from state to state, and sometimes even from case to case. Some states require insurers to pay claims within 30 or 60 days, unless the company needs additional information in order to evaluate it and determine if it falls within the limits of the policy holder's coverage. Others require only that claims be paid within a "reasonable" amount of time.

## CALL THE INSURER

If your wait stretches on, you may solve the problem by calling the insurer's toll-free customer service number. If you have to listen to a recorded menu of options, choose "inquiring about the status of your unpaid claim." (Some voice-mail systems let you short-circuit the recorded menu by pressing "0," which will put you in touch with a live operator.) Be prepared to provide the date you filed the claim, the services or treatment that the claim covers (prescriptions, follow-up care after surgery, and the like), and the amount of the claim. Take these steps:

- **If the claim hasn't been received:** Send a photocopy of the claim to the insurer. Ask the representative if you can resubmit your claim by fax, if you have access to one. This can speed up the process considerably. Whether you send the claim by fax or mail, ask for the name of the person to whom it should be sent (usually the adjuster handling your claim), and direct it to her. And if using the mail, send it certified mail, return receipt requested.
- **If the claim is still being evaluated,** ask what additional supporting material might be needed. If, for example, the insurance company needs a more detailed description of a treatment you received, you can offer to obtain it yourself from your doctor or have him forward it to the claims representative.

- **If a request for more information has already been made:** Ask for a copy of the request and look at the date it was made. In some states, health insurers have to request more information within a specified time limit or lose their right to deny coverage. For example, in New York State a request for more information about a claim must be made within 30 days of the receipt of the original claim. In that state, insurers can be required to pay interest on claims that aren't handled by the insurance company in a timely manner.

## PREVENTING FUTURE PROBLEMS

Fortunately, the majority of health insurers pay routine claims promptly. But if yours is habitually slow in paying, consider taking these steps:

- **For insurance provided by an employer,** ask the human-resources department or your company's benefits administrator to intervene on your behalf. Chances are that other employees are facing similar problems. Getting the company involved puts the insurer on notice that it may be faced with losing your employer's business when it comes to policy renewal time.

- **For coverage offered through a professional or trade association** to which you belong, request that its benefits administrators look into the matter in question.

### NOTIFY THE STATE

If even this doesn't help or if you purchase your health-care coverage on an individual basis, contact your state's department of

insurance with your complaint. While it's unlikely that the department can do much for you on an individual basis, it can contact the insurer about its claims-handling procedures and ask for an explanation of the delays. If the insurance department discovers an ongoing pattern of unreasonable or prolonged dawdling in handling its claims, the insurance company could be subject to fines, and in extreme cases, it could even lose its license to operate in the state.

### WHEN GENERIC ISN'T AS GOOD

As a cost-cutting measure, many health insurers and health-care maintenance organizations, or HMOs, require patients to accept generic drugs in place of the brand-name medications their doctors prescribe. If you're given a generic in place of a brand-name medicine, ask your pharmacist the following questions *before* you start to take it:

- **Is it a chemical equivalent of your brand-name prescription?** If it is, you shouldn't have any problem with it.

- **Is it a *therapeutic substitution* of the brand-name drug?** For many newer medicines— those still protected by patent law—there isn't a true chemical equivalent available. In these cases, your insurer may pay only for a therapeutic substitution, a drug that treats the same condition as the brand-name product but has a different chemical composition. The problem with a therapeutic substitution is that it could cause side effects or interact with other medications you take—problems that wouldn't occur with the medication your doctor prescribed.

If it's the latter, call your doctor before taking it. Your doctor should be notified of the switch before your prescription is filled, but some doctors have signed agreements with HMOs that automatically allow a substitution to be made. If there's a potentially dangerous drug interaction between the therapeutic substitution and other medication you take, he should be able to convince your insurer that the name brand medicine is medically necessary.

# Your health insurance company has rejected your claim, but you don't understand why.

You've jumped through all the hoops of filing your claim for health care you're sure is covered by your plan, only to receive the company's notice that your claim is being denied or that the company will pay only a portion of what you thought it would. This is fairly common, but it should not be accepted as the final word.

## THE EXPLANATION OF BENEFITS

The rejection of your claim will usually come on what's known as an *explanation of benefits* form that you will receive in the mail. Unfortunately, these forms are often confusing or provide little real information about the reason for the insurer's decision. Some explanation of benefits forms are coded, with an explanation of the codes used printed on the reverse side of the form. Take a look at the back of the form to determine the reason your claim was rejected. In many cases, rejections or reductions take place because…

- You have not met your deductible and must pay the bill out of pocket.
- You are required to make a copayment for the care you received.
- The bill was submitted for services that the insurer asserts aren't covered by your policy.
- The bill you submitted didn't adequately describe the services, and the insurer needs more information.
- The insurer claims that the bill you submitted was previously paid.

## CALL, THEN WRITE

If you disagree with the company's explanation, or if you don't understand it, do the following:

- **Call the insurance company's claims department.** Be sure to write down the name of the person you talk to, her title, and the dates and times of your conversations. Ask for clarification of the rejection. If, for example, the insurance company needs more information, ask the representative to tell you exactly what it requires and from whom you should obtain it. In some cases, doctors will bill for a "consultation" without indicating the reason for it. Your insurer may need to know only that it was related to a condition covered under your policy to reconsider the claim and pay it in full. If that's the case, getting your doctor to provide clarification may put an end to the problem.

- **Write to the insurer** if you can't resolve the problem over the telephone, explaining why you believe that the claim should be covered. Ask for a written explanation of the company's stand. Be sure to keep copies of all your correspondence with the company, and send all letters by certified mail, return receipt requested, so the insurance company can't claim that it never got them.

- **Write again** if the company maintains that your policy doesn't cover the claim you submitted. In your letter, ask the insurer to point out the specific provision in the policy that supports its position. If it can't, or if your understanding of the provision is different from the company's, insist that it honor its obligation to pay your legitimate claim.

## GET HELP FROM THE STATE

If the company still refuses to pay your claim, take these steps:

- **Contact the consumer protection division of your state insurance department.** Call to get the name of the person who investigates complaints like yours, then send a letter describing your problem.
  - Enclose copies of all the correspondence between you and the insurance company as well as a copy (*not* the original) of your policy.
  - Be sure to include your name and address, and a telephone number where you can be reached during the day, in case the insurance department needs to call you during business hours to ask for more information.
  - Explain why you think that your claim is covered, and ask the insurance department to contact the company about the matter. Getting the state involved doesn't necessarily mean the insurance company will change its mind, but it may convince the insurer to take another look at the matter. If the language of your policy is subject to interpretation that could reasonably be in your favor, it may decide to pay the claim in order to avoid

a fight that will be more expensive than the amount that's in dispute.

The insurance company will typically have 30 days in which to respond to the insurance department's inquiry. When it does, the insurance department should provide you with a copy of the company's response.

## CONSIDER ARBITRATION

If the response is not in your favor and your policy allows for it, you should then look into arbitration. In this process, you and the insurer appear before one or more trained professionals who hear both sides of the case and make a decision about who is right. A drawback to arbitration is that if you disagree with the arbitrator's final decision, your right to take the matter to court may then be severely limited.

## GO TO COURT

If there's no arbitration clause in your policy, you may be able to take the matter to court. Before you decide on this course of action, talk to a lawyer about your claim.

The lawyer can review your insurance policy to determine if the language there supports your claim. She can also help you figure out the costs and benefits of pursuing the matter in court, and she can also estimate the time it will take to have your case heard.

If the claim amount in question is relatively small, going to court probably isn't worth your effort and the expense of hiring a lawyer. And you may not even be able to find a lawyer who will represent you. But if the insurance company has denied a major claim and it cannot justify its refusal satisfactorily, then filing a lawsuit may be your last and best resort.

---

### AVOIDING CLAIMS HASSLES

Filing insurance claims can be a headache. Claims forms are often confusing, and if you've had a major medical incident, the sheer volume of paperwork involved can be overwhelming. Here are some tips that can help make the process easier and get claims paid more quickly:

- **Obtain complete and itemized statements from doctors** and other health-care providers. Claims that are incomplete or vague are usually rejected, and you will have to take the time to get a new, more detailed bill and resubmit your claim in order to have it paid.

- **Use care in filling out the claims forms.** Failing to include required information, such as your policy number, or not including your doctor's or pharmacist's bill will almost certainly delay your claim. Don't forget to sign and date the claims form in the appropriate place.

- **Keep photocopies of all completed forms and attachments.** Filing these forms by date in an accordion folder will help you keep track of when your claim was filed and allow you to refile quickly if a claim goes astray.

- **Follow up on a regular basis.** If you haven't heard from your insurer about a claim within 30 days, call the company's toll-free number and ask about the status of your claim. If the insurer tells you that it hasn't made a decision yet, ask for a date by which it intends to do so. Then follow up again if that date comes and goes without a response.

- **Don't delay when filing claims.** By filing claims as soon as possible, you avoid the risk of losing bills or forgetting about them. Most insurers will automatically deny claims submitted after a specified period of time has elapsed, usually six months or a year. Check your policy for the time limits that apply to you.

According to national surveys, you are not alone. It's estimated that more than 35 million Americans are without health insurance of any kind. Most of the uninsured are self-employed, or they work for small businesses that cannot afford to offer employees health-care coverage due to its expense.

While insurers are willing to provide coverage to people who don't suffer from serious health problems, those who have had major illnesses or needed surgery often have trouble getting a company to cover them. And even those who've been in good health are faced with high premiums, big deductibles, and sometimes are offered only limited benefits.

### INVESTIGATE YOUR OPTIONS

If you've tried to buy a policy on an individual basis and you've been turned down, here are other options to explore:

■ **Buy insurance as a member of an association or professional group.** Groups, such as college alumni associations, may also have arrangements that allow members to purchase at least limited coverage. In many cases, there are no limits placed on group policyholders due to preexisting conditions; in others, benefits related to the condition may be limited for the first year or two of your coverage.

> **I**t's estimated that more than 35 million Americans are without health insurance of any kind.

■ **Contact your state insurance department** to see if any companies in your state have what are known as *open enrollment periods.* During an open enrollment period, a health insurer will accept anyone as a new policyholder, regardless of preexisting medical conditions. Not all insurance companies offer this option, but your state insurance department can point you to those that do.

■ **Investigate a *risk-sharing* plan.** This is a plan that allows people who can't obtain insurance elsewhere to get coverage. The benefits are paid by private insurers licensed to do business in the state. Call your state insurance department and ask if your state authorizes this type of plan (more than half the states do). The rules of eligibility for these types of plans vary somewhat, but typically you must be a permanent resident of the state for a specified period, and you must have been turned down by at least one private insurance company.

Premiums for risk-sharing insurance plans can be hefty—sometimes as much as 25 percent or higher than the cost of an individual health insurance policy—but they may be worth it if such a plan is your only option.

# BUYING TRADITIONAL HEALTH INSURANCE

Although it's usually more expensive than participating in a health-maintenance organization (HMO), or a preferred provider organization, or PPO, traditional health insurance (also called fee-for-service insurance) does have its advantages. With traditional health insurance, there are no limits on which doctors you may see and no "gatekeepers" to get past in order to receive the care of a specialist. Here are the questions to ask when choosing a traditional health-care insurance policy:

■ **How good is the insurance company's financial condition?** Be cautious about buying coverage from an insurer that isn't highly rated by companies such as A.M. Best or Standard & Poor's. You can find ratings of insurers' financial conditions at most major libraries.

■ **What will the premium be, and what is its average rate of increase?** Premiums are locked in on an annual basis, but increases from one year to the next can be substantial. Ask about the history of rate increases during the past few years. While such information is no guarantee that there won't be a large increase next year, it may give you an idea of the kind of rate increase to expect.

■ **How much is the deductible?** Deductibles—the amount you pay before your insurance coverage kicks in—can start as low as $100 to $200, and they may be as high as $5,000. The higher the deductible, the lower the premium will be. If you and your family are in relatively good health, a higher deductible may be a good option.

■ **What is the maximum lifetime benefit of the policy?** Health insurers typically limit the amount of benefits they will pay during your lifetime. A major illness that involves surgery and a lengthy hospital stay could use up much of your policy limits. Today most experts recommend a maximum lifetime benefit of at least $1 million.

■ **What's covered?** A good fee-for-service policy will pay for...

● Hospital coverage—it includes the cost of a semiprivate room (no more than one room-mate), operating-room costs, nursing care, laboratory tests, food, and other costs related to your care while you are hospitalized. Many policies require that you get a second opinion before the insurer will approve a hospital stay or surgery.

● Doctors' fees—many policies require you to pay 20 percent of this cost (called a copayment), up to a specified amount (your stop-loss limit). After that, the insurer picks up the entire amount, subject to your policy's limits.

● Necessary medical equipment—oxygen tents, wheelchairs, or hospital beds required for home convalescence are included.

● Alternative medicine practitioners—some policies limit the number of visits to alternative providers, such as acupuncturists and chiropractors, during each policy period.

● Mental-health care—policies cover both an inpatient and outpatient basis.

● Prescription drugs—most policies provide this coverage, but they require the insured to make a copayment for each prescription, which is typically between $10 and $20.

■ **What's excluded from coverage?** Many policies exclude dental care, regular vision care, and other preventive care, such as routine physicals, vaccinations, and birth-control devices. If you have a preexisting condition, you may receive no coverage for it for a period of time. The policy should clearly set out what's not covered.

WORKPLACE WORRIES

*You lose your job and apply for unemployment pay, but you are told you aren't entitled to receive it.*

This kind of news could make a bad situation even worse. The unemployment compensation system—operated by each state—exists to provide at least some income to workers during periods when they are out of work through no fault of their own. And in some cases, you may be able to collect unemployment compensation when you quit your job voluntarily instead of being fired or laid off. But whether you can receive unemployment compensation depends on a variety of factors, including how much time you have worked, the reason for your unemployment, and the conditions of your employment.

### WHO IS ELIGIBLE

In general, you are eligible for unemployment compensation if you worked a minimum amount of time and earned a minimum amount of money during what's known as a base *eligibility period.* In most states, this means you must have worked for at least 3 of the past 12 months. The amount you must have earned varies widely among states, depending on the cost of living, and in most states it is adjusted annually to cover inflation.

### WHO MAY NOT BE ELIGIBLE

State laws don't require that every worker be covered by unemployment insurance. Those who don't have to have this kind of coverage include…

- Independent contractors
- Newspaper carriers under the age of 18
- Insurance agents paid only on commission
- Children employed by their parents
- Persons employed by their child or spouse
- Casual domestic workers and baby-sitters
- Workers on some small farms
- Students employed as part of a school-sponsored "work experience" program
- Student nurses or interns
- Students and their spouses who work for a college or university that they also attend,

as long as the spouse of a working student is informed that he or she is not eligible.

Even if you don't fall into one of these categories, you may still *not* be qualified to receive unemployment benefits. The reasons for disqualification most often include…

- **Quitting your job** without a good work-related cause.
- **Being fired for repeated misconduct** on the job.
- **Being fired for *just cause.*** For example, if you do something at work that seriously endangers another worker, your employer, or the public, or that causes a serious threat to safety or property, your employer may have just cause to dismiss you from your job, even if what you did happened only once.

### VISIT THE UNEMPLOYMENT OFFICE

Most states impose a waiting period between the time you lose your job and when you can begin to collect unemployment benefits. In order to have your claim processed, you must go to your local unemployment insurance office. (Check with your employer's human resources department or the state department of labor for the location.) Be sure to bring the following with you:

✔ Your Social Security card or a photocopy
✔ A list of your work history for the past three years, including the names, addresses, and telephone numbers of previous employers
✔ Pay stubs and other proof of wages, such as a W-2, from your most recent employer
✔ Any notice that you received from your employer regarding your dismissal.

Be prepared to wait. Initial visits to the unemployment office are often time-consuming, and you may find yourself shuttling from one line to another before you get to the person who will examine your forms and conduct an interview to find out why you're unemployed.

The unemployment office will contact your last employer to confirm the reason for your dismissal. Your employer is required to respond to this inquiry, either by confirming your account of your termination or disputing it. In some states, you won't receive your benefits until your employer responds; other states don't wait for the employer's response before starting benefit pay.

If your employer disputes your claim, you'll receive benefits while the appeal is heard. But if the employer's appeal is upheld, you may be required to repay some or all of what you've collected, depending on your ability to do so.

### APPEAL A DENIAL OF BENEFITS

If your employer contests your application and you are denied benefits by the unemployment insurance office, you will be notified in writing of the reason for the denial. At this point, you can do the following:

- **File an appeal of the unemployment office's decision.** The denial notice will tell you where to do this and the deadline. (Deadlines vary from state to state.) The unemployment insurance office will then schedule an appeal hearing.
- **Line up witnesses** and gather any evidence to support your claim. You and your employer each have the right to call witnesses and present evidence at the hearing.
- **Consider having a lawyer present** at the appeal hearing. You are allowed to represent

yourself at this hearing, but many employers, especially big companies, will be represented by a lawyer. If hiring a lawyer is out of your financial reach, contact a local law school to see if it sponsors a legal clinic where you can get help from law students supervised by a professor. In some cities, legal-aid clinics may also provide help at low cost or even no cost.

*Most states impose a waiting period between the time you lose your job and when you can begin to collect unemployment benefits.*

- **Follow the basic rules of courtesy and demeanor** at the hearing, even though this hearing is usually more informal than a courtroom procedure. Be sure to…
✔ Be on time.
✔ Be clean and neatly dressed.
✔ Be respectful of the examiner or administrative law judge (ALJ) conducting the hearing.
✔ Concentrate on the evidence and avoid personal attacks on your ex-employer.
✔ Answer questions from the hearing officer briefly and courteously.
✔ Ask for clarification when you don't understand the proceedings or a question you've been asked.

### WINNING YOUR CASE

After the hearing officer has heard the appeal, she will issue a ruling. If your employer's objection to your application is rejected, you will begin receiving benefits as soon as the hearing officer's ruling is made. Sometimes this decision is made immediately, but in other cases it may be made several days after the hearing is conducted. In either case, you will be entitled to receive benefits dating back to the day on which you first made your unemployment insurance application.

While it's possible for you or your ex-employer to file an appeal of the hearing officer's decision to the state courts, this is rarely done, in part because of the expense involved. But if your ex-employer does file a further appeal, it is essential that you get legal help to fight back.

> You were injured at work when a piece of
> equipment malfunctioned, but your employer claims you
> aren't entitled to workers' compensation.

It's the law—employers must provide workers' compensation insurance for employees. This insurance pays workers who suffer injuries or illnesses related to their work. It also pays death benefits to their dependents when they die as a result of a work-related injury or illness.

Sometimes employers dispute whether an injury is really work-related. In some cases this is

> Worker's compensation insurance pays workers who suffer injuries or illnesses related to their work.

legitimate, while in others it may be done only to keep the employer's insurance rates from increasing. To fight back and win, you need to understand when workers' compensation applies, when you may not be entitled to it, and what you must do to appeal a denial of workers' compensation.

## WHO IS NOT ELIGIBLE

Workers' compensation is generally a matter of state law. To determine if you are entitled to receive benefits, you'll need to look at your state's list of eligible workers. In general, however, coverage is *not* available to…

- Independent contractors, sole proprietors, or partners in a business
- Part-time domestic workers employed in private homes
- Federal employees, railroad employees, and those in the maritime industries, such as merchant seamen and harbor workers, who are covered by federal law
- Some farm workers
- Members of the employer's family, including a spouse and children, who live in the employer's home.

Some states also exempt small businesses, such as those with five or fewer employees, from having to provide workers' compensation coverage.

## WHAT IS COVERED

In order to receive benefits, workers' compensation laws require that your illness or injury "arise out of and in the course of employment." Usually this means you must have been injured…

- During work time
- At a place where you would reasonably have been expected to be
- While doing a task associated with or "incidental to" your job
- In circumstances that create a cause and effect between your job and your injury or illness; in other words, you wouldn't have suffered your injury except for the fact that you were at your job.

In addition, it's possible to collect workers' compensation for injuries you suffer away from work during nonworking hours. As we've already noted, state laws differ widely, and workers' compensation cases are decided on a case-by-case basis. For example, in some states you may be eligible for workers' compensation if you're struck by a car while walking across your employer's parking lot. You may also be eligible if you're injured while on your way to work, or on your way home at the end of the day. But in other states the law views these incidents differently, and you might be denied benefits under exactly the same circumstances.

Illnesses may also entitle you to workers' compensation in some states and under some circumstances. If your job is particularly stressful, for example, you may be entitled to workers' compensation if you have a heart attack or suffer a psychological illness that can reasonably be connected to your work.

## FILING A CLAIM

To file a worker's compensation claim, you must do the following:

- **Notify your employer that you are filing a claim.** In most states, you are required to do this within a day or two of being injured or learning of a work-related illness. This requirement is often waived if your employer has actual knowledge of your injury, such as when you're taken away from work in an ambulance, or when a manager or other company official saw the injury occur.

■ **File your workers' compensation claim promptly.** Strict deadlines apply when filing claims. Some states require you to file within a few days of being injured, while others give you a month or even a year or more to make your claim. In general, though, the sooner you file, the faster your case can be resolved.

■ **Provide the following information** to both your employer and the workers' compensation agency:

✔ Your name, address, and your occupation

✔ Your employer's name and business address

✔ The date of the injury or the date you became aware of a job-related illness

✔ The place at which the injury took place

✔ A description of the illness or injury and why you believe it is work related.

Be sure to keep a copy of your claim notices for your own files, and then send the original notices to your employer and the workers' compensation agency by certified mail, return receipt requested.

### If Your Claim Is Contested

If your employer challenges your workers' compensation claim, a hearing will be scheduled before an official of the state workers' compensation agency. This hearing will be relatively informal. You and your employer will each have an opportunity to present your case. Be prepared to provide medical records supporting your claim, along with company accident reports or statements from other employees who have firsthand knowledge of your injury and how it occurred. The hearing officer will then try to arrange a mutually satisfactory settlement of your claim with your employer.

If a settlement isn't reached, a formal hearing will be held at a later date, typically several weeks after the informal proceeding. At that hearing, you and your employer have the option of representing yourselves or being represented by lawyers. It's a good idea to hire a lawyer because

your employer probably will. The hearing officer will usually have the power to call witnesses and even to issue subpoenas.

It may take weeks or even months after this hearing for you to receive the decision. If you win, you will begin receiving benefits backdated to when you were first eligible to receive workers' compensation payments.

Your employer can still appeal the decision, first to the entire workers' compensation board and ultimately to the state courts. But if he loses, he can be required to reimburse the state workers' compensation fund and interest.

### What Workers' Compensation Covers

Depending on the severity of your injury or illness, you may be entitled to payment for all medical bills related to the injury or illness. You may also receive weekly benefits to help compensate you for lost wages and payment of a lump sum for any permanent disability or incapacity.

In some states, your employer will also be required to continue paying for your group health and life insurance coverage. He may also be obligated to provide you with "light-duty" work, if such work is available, when your injury no longer prevents you from working. And he can be required to allow you to return to your old job or an equivalent position once you have sufficiently recovered from your injury.

## EMPLOYEE OR INDEPENDENT CONTRACTOR?

Employers frequently try to avoid being responsible for workers' compensation, unemployment insurance, Social Security contributions, and other required payments by claiming that a worker is an independent contractor and not an employee. However, government agencies will often look beyond the label your employer gives you to decide if you are entitled to be treated as an employee. Generally, the factors they will consider are:

- Does the employer provide instruction and training on how to do the job?

- Does the employer provide the equipment and tools you use to do the job?

- Do you perform the job during hours set by the employer at the place of business?

- Do you work for a single employer, or do you have other clients as well?

- Do you receive payment on an hourly or weekly basis or by the job?

- Do you have ongoing employment with this employer, or are you hired on a job-by-job basis?

- Are you paid out of the employer's payroll account or out of its business expenses account?

- Does the employer have the right to fire you without any further liability?

- Do you have the right to quit whenever you want without any contractual liability to the employer?

*You need to use a wheelchair to get around, but the small business you work for refuses to remodel the employee lavatory to make it accessible.*

Until fairly recently, few workplaces were accessible to people with disabilities. But in the 1990s, Congress enacted the Americans With Disabilities Act (ADA) as the principal federal law protecting the rights of disabled workers.

Originally the ADA was applied to those companies with 25 or more employees, but the law now extends to companies with as few as 15 employees.

Under the ADA, a worker is considered disabled when she has a physical or mental impairment that limits one or more than one major life activity, has a record of such an impairment, or is perceived as having such an impairment. For example, someone with an infectious disease may not actually be disabled, but he may be viewed as being disabled by his coworkers and others, and as a result he is treated differently.

### WHO IS COVERED

The most important provision of the ADA is its requirement that employers provide reasonable accommodations for qualified disabled persons who can perform their job's essential functions, unless doing so would cause the employer an undue hardship.

To find out if you are covered by the ADA's protections, you need to answer these questions:

- **How many employees are there at the company?** Unless there are 15 or more, the federal law doesn't apply. However, there may be state laws that offer similar protections and that apply to companies with fewer employees—sometimes as few as one worker.

- **Are you a qualified disabled person?** You must have a disability or impairment that substantially limits your ability to work when compared with the average person with comparable qualifications. And you must also be able to perform the "essential functions" of the job regardless of whether or not an accommodation would be necessary.

Generally, deciding whether or not a particular duty is an essential function of your job is done by evaluating the amount of time spent on each task and by determining how much of a problem it would be for your employer if he couldn't require you to perform that task.

For example, if your job consists of hand-loading 100-pound containers of auto parts onto shelves in a warehouse and you use a wheelchair or walker to move about, it would essentially be impossible for you to perform the job's major task, no matter how great an effort was made by your employer to accommodate you. But if you work as a bookkeeper and you can't reach all the files you need from your wheelchair, getting the files is not an essential function of your job. Someone could retrieve the files for you, or they could simply be moved so you can reach them yourself. Doing so puts no substantial burden on your employer. If he fired you or moved you to a lower-paying position, you would be able to bring a complaint against him under the ADA.

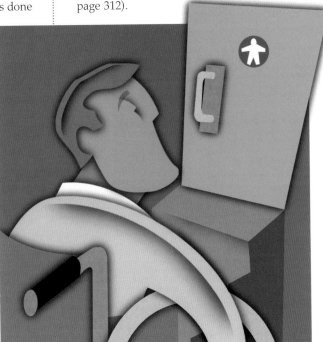

### STEPS TO TAKE

Making modifications to lavatories and other workplace facilities generally falls within the boundaries of what would be considered a reasonable accommodation, and not an undue hardship. Your employer may not be aware that he is required to offer these accommodations. Here's what you should do:

- **Find out what laws apply to your situation.** If your company employs at least 15 workers, the ADA will apply. If it is smaller than that, contact your state labor department to find out what state laws—if any—offer protection.
- **Notify your supervisor about your problem.** She may forward the complaint to your employer or help you resolve the complaint informally.
- **Call in the government** if the problem is not resolved to your satisfaction. Contact the federal Equal Employment Opportunity Commission (EEOC), if your employer is covered by the ADA, or the state agency that handles discrimination complaints. Your state labor department can direct you to the appropriate agency (see "Filing a Complaint with the EEOC," page 312).

### GO TO COURT

If the EEOC investigates your complaint and sends you a right-to-sue letter, consider hiring a lawyer. You can file suit on your own behalf, but a lawyer experienced in handling illegal workplace-discrimination cases can be a valuable asset.

She can help you decide where to file your suit. Most cases involving illegal discrimination can be brought in either the state or federal court system. A lawyer can tell you which system is most likely to reach a decision in your favor. She can also help you decide whether to ask for a jury trial or have your case heard by a judge.

If you win your case, the court can issue an *injunction,* ordering your employer to take appropriate steps to remedy the situation at work. If you were wrongfully fired, you may be reinstated with back pay and have your seniority rights and employee benefits restored. And although your employer usually can't collect attorney fees from you in the event that the court finds in his favor, you can ask the court to award "reasonable" attorney fees and court costs when you win.

## FILING A COMPLAINT WITH THE EEOC

There are federal laws prohibiting job discrimination based on race, color, religion, gender, national origin, age, or disability. They are enforced by the Equal Employment Opportunity Commission (EEOC), which can be reached at (800) 669-4000. The process is as follows:

- **First, file a formal complaint with the EEOC.** This must be done before you can bring legal action against an employer for violating an antidiscrimination law. File your complaint in person, or mail it certified, return receipt requested to the EEOC. Include in your complaint:

  ✔ A brief description of the alleged discrimination, including the date or dates it took place, and the steps you've taken to have the problem resolved

  ✔ The responses you've received from your employer, including the names and titles of those whom you've talked to about your problem

  ● Generally, you must file your complaint within 180 days of the incident, and it must be sworn to before a notary public or other official authorized to administer oaths.

- **The EEOC will notify state or local agencies** if state or local laws cover your complaint. This is to preserve any additional rights you have under these laws. These agencies have 60 days in which to act on your complaint. If they refuse to act during this period, the EEOC will take over jurisdiction of your complaint. In these cases, your time limit for filing a complaint with the EEOC can be extended to as many as 300 days.

- **The EEOC will notify your employer** within 10 days of receiving your complaint that a *charge* has been filed against it.

- **The EEOC will investigate.** It can assign the charge for *priority investigation*, if the initial facts make a strong case that a law has been violated, or for what's called *follow-up investigation*, when the initial evidence isn't strong enough to warrant a priority investigation.

- **It may make written requests** for more information; interview the employer, the complaining employee, and others; review documents and correspondence; and visit the workplace.

- **It can seek to settle the charge** within 180 days, if you and your employer agree to do so. It may also suggest mediation if both parties agree. Mediation is voluntary and confidential. If mediation doesn't work, the EEOC will resume its investigation.

- **If the EEOC finds illegal discrimination,** you and your employer will receive what's called a determination letter, explaining its finding. The EEOC will then attempt a *conciliation*, working with you and your employer to find a remedy for the illegal discrimination. If the case is resolved through conciliation, settlement, or mediation, neither you nor the EEOC can take further legal action unless your employer fails to honor the agreement.

- **If there's not enough evidence to prove illegal discrimination,** the EEOC will notify you in writing and send a *right-to-sue* letter giving you 90 days to file a lawsuit.

### If You Win
An employer found to have illegally discriminated against you can be ordered to provide you with a reasonable accommodation and to take actions to make you "whole." This can include...

✔ Rehiring or reinstatement with back pay

✔ Front pay (the difference between what you will earn upon reinstatement and what you would have earned if the employer hadn't fired you) and possibly promotion

✔ Attorney fees, court costs, and expert-witness fees

✔ Compensatory damages to recover actual monetary losses, mental anguish, and inconvenience, and possibly punitive damages.

Even in a booming economy, some companies struggle to survive. And for some of these companies, the solution is to drastically cut back on their workforce. Other companies close what they see as unproductive facilities or those where workers earn more than the company wants to pay, to try to maximize profits. But while workers once had no recourse when a company made a sudden and unexpected announcement that it was closing up shop or slashing its employment rolls, today the law provides at least some protection to workers and the communities where they live when a major job cut takes place.

## THE LAW'S PROTECTION

If you are faced with losing your job because of a mass layoff or because your employer is closing the facility where you work, you may be protected by a federal law known as the Worker Adjustment and Retraining Notification Act, sometimes called WARN. This law requires any company that has 100 or more full-time workers to provide employees with at least 60 days' notice if it reasonably expects that more than 50 employees will experience the loss of employment during a 30-day period. Under WARN, loss of employment is considered to be the following:

- Involuntary termination (except being fired "for just cause")
- A suspension or layoff from employment of more than six months
- A cutback in an employee's hours of work that's greater than 50 percent.

For WARN purposes, this does not include employees who retire or quit and aren't replaced.

## REQUIRED NOTICE

Before a mass layoff or plant closing can take place, the company must provide workers with written notice in language understandable to the employees. The notice must include…

- The name and address of the affected site
- Whether the layoff or closing is going to be permanent or temporary

- Whether the entire site will be closed
- The date that layoffs or terminations are expected to begin
- The name and telephone number of a company official who can provide employees with more information
- Whether senior employees have the right to displace junior employees in the same job category (called "bumping" rights).

Employers are also required to provide notice to the state's department of labor or department of employment and to give the same notice to the highest elected official in the town where the layoff or plant closing will occur.

## EXCEPTIONS TO THE RULE

In a few specific situations, companies are not required to meet the WARN notification requirements. Generally, companies need not provide notice if…

- **The facility to be closed is temporary or seasonal** or was used to fulfill a specific contract. But in these cases, employees must have been hired with the understanding that the work was not permanent.
- **Employees are on strike** or a legitimate lockout is in effect at that location. However, any workers who are *not* on strike must be given notice.
- **The company was attempting to obtain new business** or raise capital to continue operating, and the notice would have kept it from attracting the money it needed. Investors don't like to put their money into businesses that have already told the world that they are in financial trouble.
- **The plant closing is caused by a natural disaster,** such as a flood or earthquake.
- **The closing or layoff is the result of a sudden or unforeseeable situation** that was beyond the company's control, such as a fire or an unexpected financial setback.

## WHAT YOU CAN DO

If the above scenario happens to you, to be sure you're properly notified, take these steps:

- **If you belong to a union, contact a union representative.** The union should be able to take action against your employer if it failed to provide adequate notice, and the union rep should keep you informed of the union's intended actions.
- **Get in touch with your local government representatives.** One of the reasons WARN was enacted was because of the devastating impact a major plant closing or layoff can have on the local economy. Under WARN, the company can be fined $500 per day for a maximum of 60 days for its failure to provide employees with the required notice.
- **If there's no union where you work, call a lawyer** who is experienced in labor and management law. Your state or local bar association's referral service can provide you with a list of attorneys. Employees who aren't given the required WARN notice have a right to file suit against the company in federal district court. If you win your suit, the employer can be ordered to provide as much as three years back pay and benefits to each and every affected worker.

### SMART MOVES

Many states have laws similar to WARN designed to protect workers from unexpected layoffs and closings. They can require the company to continue to provide medical coverage and other benefits. Some cities have similar ordinances. Contact your state department of labor or an attorney experienced in this area to find out about other protections.

---

> **Y**ou complain to your employer that
> a piece of equipment at your factory is defective and
> dangerous, and she threatens to fire you.

---

At one time, workers had little legal protection from hazardous working conditions. The few laws on the books were often poorly enforced, and employees who sought the law's protection often found themselves out of a job, victims of retaliatory firing by employers.

That all changed with the enactment of the federal Occupational Safety and Health Act in 1970. Now virtually all employers are required to meet standards designed to make the workplace safer for their employees. And about half the states have laws that offer as much health and safety protection to workers as the federal laws, and sometimes more.

#### PROTECTION FROM WORK HAZARDS

The federal Occupational Safety and Health Act protects you from retaliation by your employer when you refuse to do work that you reasonably believe is unsafe. For the law to apply, the unsafe condition must pose a substantial risk of physical harm, disease, or death, and the condition must be the result of your employer's violation of established safety and health standards.

Safety and health standards are set by the Occupational Safety and Health Administration (OSHA) and fall into two categories:

- **General standards** are those that apply to every business. They require your employer to provide a workplace that is free from recognized hazards (conditions that are obviously dangerous or that are generally considered hazardous in the employer's business or that the employer knows are dangerous) that are likely to cause serious harm or death.
- **Specific standards** are those established by OSHA to cover nearly every aspect of the workplace environment. OSHA has set out these standards in minute detail, and governs

everything from general working conditions to requirements for ventilation, providing personal safety equipment to workers, and the storage and handling of toxic or hazardous materials, explosives, and flammable items.

## STAND FIRM

If you've warned your employer about a dangerous piece of equipment and were threatened with retaliation as a result, the law is on your side. OSHA prohibits employers from disciplining or discharging workers who refuse to perform work that is unreasonably unsafe. You should…

■ **Refuse to do work** that involves any of the following:
- A substantial risk that a reasonable person qualified to do your job would recognize
- A situation that can't wait for resolution through normal channels, such as filing a complaint with OSHA
- A refusal by your employer to take any action to correct the safety problem after you have brought the situation to her attention.

■ **Ask your employer to investigate your complaint;** keep a record of your conversations or correspondence. During the investigation the company should give you other work with equivalent pay. If she finds that your complaint is legitimate, she should correct the condition and return you to regular work.

## FILE AN OSHA COMPLAINT

If your employer says the equipment is safe to operate, but you believe otherwise, your next step is to file a complaint with OSHA. Call OSHA (you'll find the number under the federal government listings in the phone book).

OSHA will investigate, and if it determines that your complaint is justified, your employer will be required to fix the problem to eliminate the dangerous working condition. Your employer may also be subject to civil penalties and could be fined as much as $70,000 for each violation of OSHA requirements.

**TAKE NOTE** *Although the law allows you to file an anonymous complaint with OSHA, once your employer learns of the complaint it's likely that your identity will be known.*

## IF YOU'RE FIRED OR DISCIPLINED

Unfortunately, some companies defy the law and demote or fire workers who go to OSHA for help. Usually these employers will come up with another reason for taking action against a whistle-blowing employee, such as claiming that the worker was tardy or absent without excuse or was guilty of "insubordination."

If you're a union member, ask the union to help you challenge your dismissal or demotion. It may be able to arrange reinstatement, back pay, and the restoration of benefits and seniority rights.

### GO TO COURT

If your union can't get the company to reverse its decision, or if you work in a nonunion environment, consider suing your employer. Consult a lawyer experienced in labor and management law to assess how strong your case is and to help decide your course of action. To help a lawyer evaluate your case properly, you'll need…
- Documentation of all your conversations with your supervisors about the problem and their responses
- Information about your complaint to OSHA and OSHA's response
- Copies of any letters or disciplinary notices you received from your employer
- Copies of any commendations and any performance reviews you received

✔ Statements from coworkers or others who can help show that the discipline you were subjected to was motivated by your OSHA complaint and not by your poor performance.

If you decide to file suit, be prepared for a lengthy battle. While it's possible that your lawyer can negotiate a quick settlement if the evidence in your favor is strong, not every company is willing to settle without a fight. In some cases, months and even years have passed before an OSHA suit was finally resolved in the courts.

But if you win, it's worth the fight. You can collect back pay and benefits, and your employer can be ordered to reinstate you to your regular job. If your job was eliminated or you missed out on a promotion, the court could also award what's known as front pay, the difference between what you will earn upon reinstatement and what you would have earned if the employer hadn't retaliated.

If reinstatement is likely to result in a hostile working environment, the court could also order front pay to help put you in the same financial position you would have had except for your company's unlawful behavior. In this case, the court will order pay to cover a limited period of time, which is usually for a few years.

---

### You refuse to take an on-the-job drug test, so your employer fires you.

---

Under many circumstances, employers have the right to test their employees for illegal drug use, but employees have rights, too. Finding out whether drug testing of employees is allowed is complicated. This is because a patch-work of laws regulates an employer's right—and in some cases, its obligation—to require workers to submit to drug tests.

#### WHEN EMPLOYERS ARE ALLOWED TO DO TESTING

Generally, an employer can require current employees to take a drug test *only* if the following conditions are met:

● The employer has a written drug-testing policy that is known to employees.
● An employee under the influence of alcohol or drugs presents or could present a threat to himself or others.
● The employer reasonably suspects that drug or alcohol use is negatively affecting the employee's job performance.
● The tested employee must not be subjected to observation when providing a urine sample.
● All samples are carefully guarded to ensure their integrity.
● Any positive test results must be independently retested for accuracy.

● Test results must be kept confidential—between the employer and employee.

#### WHEN EMPLOYERS MUST TEST

Federal law *requires* that some employers test employees for drugs under certain conditions. For example, workers in safety-related jobs regulated by the Department of Transportation (DOT) are subjected to drug testing as a condition of their employment. The DOT takes a very broad approach to what jobs are "safety related." As a result, just about anyone who works for an airline, railroad, bus company, or cruise line can be tested by his or her employer.

#### GAUGE THE COMPANY'S ACTION

Even if your employer is legally permitted to conduct drug testing of current employees, it may have gone too far by firing you for refusing to cooperate. Consider the following questions to help you decide what course of action to take:

■ **Are you able to perform the essential functions of your job?** If so, your employer's request that you submit to a test may violate its own drug-testing policy.
■ **Do you pose a threat to the safety of yourself or others?** If not, asking you to take a drug test may violate company testing policy.

- **Does your employer have evidence that you were under the influence of drugs or alcohol while on the job?** Without evidence, such as a marijuana cigarette or drug paraphernalia, your employer may not be able to justify requiring a drug test.
- **Did the company follow its grievance policy?** Companies often set procedures to be observed when employees object to proposed disciplinary action. Failing to do so could prohibit your employer from dismissing you.
- **Did the company act consistently in dismissing you?** If other employees were disciplined differently or offered the opportunity to take drug education or rehabilitation that was not offered to you, your employer may have violated your rights by treating you differently.

In most cases, however, you'll have to take action on your own behalf. Begin by taking a careful look at your employee manual to see if there is a grievance procedure for challenging a termination decision. For example, you may be entitled to have the decision reviewed by a panel of arbitrators. If arbitration is called for but your employer refuses to participate, you have a better chance of getting a court to rule in your favor and order your employer to reinstate you and restore your benefits and seniority rights.

Companies often place a statement in their employee manuals stating that the manual does not create a contract between employer and employee. They hope that such a disclaimer will allow them to take disciplinary measures without the necessity of going through their own stated procedures. Don't give up if your employee manual contains this kind of statement. Some courts have held that even when such a statement is in the manual, it may not be enforceable, depending on what other promises or assurances the manual makes. Consider having a lawyer review the manual in light of decisions in the courts that may have jurisdiction over your case.

### DISCRIMINATION IN DISGUISE?

There is little the government can do for an employee who is fired or otherwise disciplined for refusing to take a drug test, unless you can show that asking you to take the test was a form of prohibited discrimination. For instance, if you are the only African-American employee at your company, and you are singled out for testing or are tested more frequently than the company's white employees, your employer could be using drug testing as a pretext to cover illegal racial discrimination. If you think this could be the case, contact the Equal Employment Opportunity Commission (EEOC) (see "Filing a Complaint with the EEOC," page 312).

### YOUR LAST RESORT

In any case, your best bet is to contact a lawyer to see what legal action might be available. Because the facts of every case vary (and decisions vary in different jurisdictions), an experienced lawyer's advice and assistance can make the difference between winning your fight and losing it.

> *You and some of your coworkers want to form a union, but your manager won't let you discuss it with other employees.*

Today about 15 percent of American workers belong to a union, but recent studies show that the interest in union membership is again on the rise. Because many employers haven't had any recent experience with the laws governing union organizing, they may not be aware of the strict limitations on what they can do to discourage union organization.

### LAWS THAT PROTECT UNIONS

The right of employees to create, join, and participate in the activities of a labor union without intimidation or retaliation from their employers is guaranteed by Section 7 and Section 8 of the National Labor Relations Act (NLRA), sometimes called the Wagner Act, and the Labor Management Relations Act, often called the Taft-

Hartley Act. Under these laws, an employer is prohibited from doing the following:

> *If your employer is violating the law by thwarting your efforts to organize a union, you can get help from unions that already represent workers in jobs similar to those where you work.*

● Interfering with or restraining employees who are exercising their rights to organize or to bargain collectively, or to engage in concerted activities for their own protection
● Interfering with the formation of any union or labor organization
● Contributing financial or other support to a labor organization (the so-called *company union*) in an effort to sabotage the process
● Encouraging or discouraging union membership through discrimination in hiring, seniority, or other kinds of employment conditions
● Discriminating against or discharging employees who file complaints or testify under the NLRA
● Refusing to sit down to bargain with the employees' majority labor organization.

## YOUR RIGHTS AT WORK

Your employer can't stop you or your fellow employees from…

● Wearing prounion messages on items such as pins and clothing
● Discussing union membership or distributing and reading union literature during nonwork hours in nonwork areas, such as an employee lounge or lunchroom
● Signing a card or petition asking your employer to recognize and bargain with a union

● Signing petitions or grievances about employment terms and conditions
● Asking your coworkers to sign petitions and grievances.

## GET ASSISTANCE

If your employer is violating the law by thwarting efforts to organize a union, do the following:

■ **Get help from unions** that already represent workers in jobs similar to those where you work. Check the Yellow Pages under "Unions" or "Labor Organizations" for the names of unions that might be interested in helping.
■ **Contact the American Federation of Labor and Congress of Industrial Organizations** (AFL-CIO) for help in finding union organizers experienced in dealing with an employer who opposes having a union representing its workers.
■ **Call the National Labor Relations Board** (NLRB) about your employer's actions. (The phone number is in the federal government listings of the phone book.) The NLRB will investigate; if it determines that your employer violated the law, it can represent you and fellow employees in administrative hearings and even go to court on your behalf to put an end to the company's illegal acts.

Companies where employees are members of labor unions are often referred to as shops, and shops generally take one of three forms:

- **A union shop:** This is a company permitted to hire workers who aren't already union members. Those who are hired must join the union within a specified time period, such as within 30 days of being employed. Under federal law, you can be fired for refusing to join the union at a union shop, but only if the union rejects or expels you for failing to pay union dues and fees. As strange as it may seem, this means that technically you don't have to join the union and can continue working as long as you pay the union dues and fees required of those who are union members. Union shops are legal only in states that haven't passed *right-to-work* laws, which allow employees to work in a unionized company without joining the union. Currently, about half the states have enacted right-to-work laws.

- **An agency shop:** In this type of company, employees may be represented by a union, but each employee gets to decide whether to become a union member. As with the union shop, you will still be required to pay dues even if you don't join. In an agency shop, the union must represent you if there's a labor problem, *even if you aren't a member.* But employees who don't join the union don't get to take advantage of other union benefits, such as grievance procedures and union-sponsored benefits. Like union shops, agency shops may be prohibited in states with right-to-work laws.

- **An open shop:** Here, a labor union may represent employees, but workers aren't required to join the union, nor are they required to pay union dues or fees.

- **A closed shop:** This type of company requires an employer to hire only applicants who are already members of a union. Under federal law, closed shops are illegal everywhere.

*Your employer's new policy requires each employee to work one Sunday per month, but your religion prohibits you from working on your Sabbath.*

Discriminating against an employee because of his religion is prohibited by a federal law—Title VII of the Civil Rights Act of 1964. In fact, this law requires an employer to make reasonable accommodations for her employees' religious practices and observances. It protects employers as well, shielding them from having to make accommodations that cause undue hardship. But court rulings have been inconsistent in defining a "reasonable accommodation" of an employee's religious practices. To make matters murkier, what constitutes an "undue hardship" is subject to interpretation.

### The Employer's Obligation

To figure out what an employer is and is not required to do to accommodate your religious practices, you must consider a number of factors, including the type of work to be performed, the size of the company, and the nature of the accommodation being requested.

For example, if you work for a company that operates around the clock seven days a week and employs several hundred customer-service representatives, it's much more likely that your employer can give you Sundays off without causing undue hardship for itself or for other employees. On the other hand, if you work for a small antiques shop that's open only on weekends, allowing you to take Sundays off could be considered an undue hardship—one that your employer wouldn't have to endure in order to accommodate you. According to the U.S. Supreme Court, an employer doesn't have to incur more than minimal costs to accommodate you. Hiring and training another employee to work Sundays could be more than minimal costs.

### FILE A COMPLAINT

If you believe that your employer is not making a reasonable attempt to accommodate your special needs, your next and best move is to file a formal complaint with the Equal Employment Opportunity Commission (EEOC) (see "Filing a Complaint with the EEOC," page 312).

### GO TO COURT

If the EEOC decides to investigate your complaint and then sends you a right-to-sue letter, it's a good idea to hire a lawyer to help you take on your employer.

You are allowed to sue on your own behalf, but having a lawyer experienced in handling illegal workplace discrimination cases improves your odds of winning your case.

**Your company requires you to work overtime, but instead of overtime pay, it offers you extra time off as compensation.**

This is the sort of practice that the Fair Labor Standards Act (FLSA) was designed to protect against. The FLSA, a federal law, governs various workplace issues, including the requirement to pay most workers at a rate of one and a half times their regular hourly rate of pay when they work more than 40 hours per week. And some states require overtime pay on any day when an employee works more than 8 hours.

But problems sometimes arise when employers suggest that employees take "comp time" in lieu of the overtime pay they are legally entitled to receive.

### WHEN EMPLOYERS STRETCH THE TRUTH

Some employers will go to great lengths to avoid providing overtime pay for work beyond the 40-hour weekly limit. They may attempt to classify employees in exempt categories when they really don't qualify for the exemption (see "Exemptions From the Overtime Rules," facing page.)

For example, one company tried to exempt a file clerk from overtime pay requirements by claiming that she was a company administrator. Evidence revealed that she had no administrative authority, wasn't allowed to take breaks or lunch without obtaining permission from her supervisor, and had no special training or experience that an administrator would normally have to

have in the business in which her employer was engaged. The state Department of Labor rejected the employer's attempt to avoid paying overtime.

### COMP TIME

Although private employers are prohibited from offering comp time instead of paying overtime, state and local government agencies are permitted to offer comp time, but with certain limitations. For example:

- Most state employees can be given time off at a rate of 1.5 hours for every hour of overtime worked.
- Once you've worked 160 hours of overtime and been granted 240 hours of comp time, the agency must pay for any additional overtime hours.
- Limits are higher for fire fighters, police, and other safety and emergency personnel; for these workers, monetary payment for overtime begins after 320 hours of overtime work.

### GO TO A HIGHER AUTHORITY

If your employer refuses to pay you for overtime and you are not an exempt employee, contact your state department of labor. The department will look into your complaint, and if it suspects that your company has violated the FLSA, it can conduct an audit of all its payroll records and payment policies. This audit will help the department determine if your employer has underpaid its other employees.

If it discovers that your coworkers have been offered comp time instead of overtime pay, it can take a variety of actions against the company, including ordering it to pay all of its affected employees for the overtime they worked. You may also receive additional damages, called *liquidated damages,* equal to the amount you should have been paid, effectively requiring your company to pay twice the amount they should have paid you and your coworkers in the first place.

## Take Legal Action

It may be difficult to convince the labor department to act aggressively on your behalf, especially if you work for a small company.

If that's the case, consider taking legal action on your own. Generally, you must file a private lawsuit within two years of discovering that your employer has violated the FLSA, but it's best not to delay, because getting your lawsuit to court can take years.

Some private employers have tried to convince their employees to sign an agreement that permits the substitution of comp time for overtime pay. But the courts have held these agreements to be illegal. You cannot waive your right to be paid for overtime, and even if you did, you are still entitled to sue your employer unless you fall into an exempt category (see "Exemptions From the Overtime Rules," below).

If your suit is successful, your employer may be required to pay the damages described above. It can be ordered by the court to pay your attorney fees and court costs.

## Exemptions From the Overtime Rules

Certain categories of employees are not covered by the FLSA's overtime provisions. Among those who *don't* have to be paid overtime are...

- **Executive, administrative, and professional employees.** Popularly referred to as *white-collar employees,* these employees usually spend their time at work managing the work of others, may have the authority to hire and fire other employees, and generally use their own discretion in the performance of their duties. To qualify for an exemption in this category, an employee must at least earn a specified amount of money each week, which varies somewhat depending on the time spent at executive, administrative, or other professional duties.

- **Computer professionals** earning above a specified amount annually (currently six and a half times the minimum wage, or about $70,000 per year in 2000) and who spend most of their work time designing, creating, or modifying computer programs or being systems analysts.

- **Outside sales representatives** who customarily spend the bulk of their day away from the office obtaining orders, making sales, or getting contracts on behalf of their employer, and who spend less than 20 percent of the time doing any other sort of work aren't covered.

- **Apprentices and trainees** working under a written apprenticeship agreement or receiving vocational training similar to what you would receive in a trade or vocational school. Apprentices must be older than 16, while trainees must be younger than 20 in order to fall into the exempt category.

- **Independent contractors** who follow a profession, trade, or business independent of that of the person employing them. Generally, this means that if you set your own hours and aren't under the employer's direction on when to work, what to do, and how to do it, you are an independent contractor and not entitled to overtime pay.

- **Miscellaneous employees,** including some disabled workers, agricultural workers, and volunteers.

*Your daughter discovers she is being paid thousands of dollars less than a male coworker for doing exactly the same job.*

Although Congress enacted the Equal Pay Act nearly 40 years ago, complaints that women are still paid less than men continue to make headlines. Under the Equal Pay Act, employers must provide equal pay to workers who perform "substantially equal work" under "similar circumstances" without regard to the sex of the employee. But determining what's substantially equal and what are similar circumstances is still decided on a case-by-case basis.

## EQUAL WORK?

In deciding cases brought under the Equal Pay Act, courts look at these factors in reaching a decision that one job is worth more than another:

● Does the job with the higher pay rate require additional experience, ability, education, or training?
● Does the higher-paying job require additional time or effort?
● If there's extra work performed, is that work really important to the job, or is it merely perfunctory?

## EXCEPTIONS TO THE EQUAL PAY ACT

Certain jobs fall under exceptions to the Equal Pay Act. By law, employers don't violate the Equal Pay Act if the difference in pay is due to seniority, a merit system, or one that's based on the quantity or quality of job production, as long as none of these are sex-based. Similarly, if you work part-time or on a temporary basis, you can be paid a lower rate than a full-time worker doing the same job.

However, if an employer hires a substantially larger percentage of women as part-time and temporary workers and pays them less than full-time male workers, the employer could be found to have done so as a pretext to illegally discriminate against female workers. The Equal Opportunity Employment Commission (EEOC) and the courts will carefully scrutinize company records to see if your daughter's employer is trying to pull a fast one so it can pay women less than men doing substantially the same work.

### NEXT STEPS

Your daughter has several options when it comes to filing a complaint, all of which need to be considered carefully.

■ **She can file suit under the Equal Pay Act, or she can file a complaint with the EEOC** about the disparity in pay. **Reasons to file under the Equal Pay Act:**
● She can sue immediately rather than waiting for the EEOC's investigative process.
**Reasons to go through the EEOC:**
● Since a violation of the Equal Pay Act could also be a violation of Title VII of the Civil Rights Act of 1964, which prohibits workplace discrimination based on gender, most legal experts and the EEOC recommend filing charges with the EEOC alleging violations under both acts.

● She'll save money by letting the EEOC take action and conduct an investigation instead of hiring an attorney herself to perform the same function. And if she does decide to sue, much of the groundwork for her case will have been done at no cost to her.

■ **Your daughter may want to remain anonymous,** even though the law prohibits any retaliation against her. The law allows for an individual, agency, or organization to file a complaint on her behalf in order to protect her identity. For example, she could take her complaint to the National Organization for Women (NOW), or a similar group with an interest in protecting women's rights, and ask them to file the complaint against her employer.

**Reasons to have a group file for her:**
● If she works for a large company, her identity may be protected.

**Reasons to file herself:**
● If her company is small, it may be impossible to protect her identity for long.

● Involving others could make it less likely that her employer will be willing to attempt to settle the charge or go to mediation.

■ **Your daughter can represent herself or hire a lawyer** in a lawsuit alleging violations of the Equal Pay Act.

**Reasons to represent herself:**
● She will save money.

**Reasons to hire a lawyer:**
● It won't cost much to have a labor lawyer review the facts of her case before she takes any action.
● A lawyer experienced in cases of this type can boost her chance of winning.

If she already has her own attorney, or if you have one, he may be able to look into the matter himself or refer you to a colleague who handles cases of this type. If not, contact your state or local bar association's referral service for the names of attorneys who practice in this area of the law.

> **Y**our employer lays you off, telling you
> that "business is slow." Later you discover he has hired
> a younger person to take your place.

**A**lthough there's an old saying that "life begins at 40," for many workers, getting older can mean diminishing job opportunities. Although federal and state laws prohibit most age-based discrimination, older employees are still offered early retirement, are laid off, or are fired in favor of younger employees, who may work for lower wages and cost less to insure.

## YOUR RIGHTS

The federal Age Discrimination in Employment Act (ADEA) protects workers from discrimination on the basis of age, as long as the employee is age 40 or older and works for a company that employs at least 20 people. State civil rights laws often give protections similar to the ADEA's to workers younger than 40. Call your state civil rights commission (check the state government section of your phone book) for information about specific laws that may apply in your state

and how to pursue a claim under state law.

As with just about all employment laws, however, there are exceptions to the ADEA. The one most often relied upon by employers is that age is what the law refers to as a *bona fide occupational qualification,* or BFOQ. For example, airline pilots can be forced to retire at age 60, because the airlines have convinced the courts that a pilot older than 60 is at greater risk of endangering the public safety because of lessened stamina, poorer eyesight and health, and slower reflexes. Although some studies suggest that this kind of generalization is inaccurate, so far the courts have allowed the airlines' age limitation to stand.

## MAKING YOUR CASE

It's likely that your employer will try to claim that your dismissal was not age related but was due to other circumstances. He may claim that economic hardship required him to release you, that your job performance warranted your dismissal, or that you were dismissed for insubordination and failing to follow the instructions of superiors.

To proceed with your discrimination case, you need to meet four requirements:

● You must show that you are in the protected age group (older than 40 under the ADEA; sometimes younger under state law).

● You must show that you were demoted, laid off, fired, or subjected to some kind of adverse decision affecting your employment.

● You must show that you were qualified to do the job—for example—by providing good job reviews, showing a history of raises or bonuses, or by presenting a record of commendations from your employer for your performance.

● You must show that termination came under circumstances suggesting age discrimination, such as being replaced by a younger person.

At one time, an employer could defeat a charge of age discrimination by hiring a younger worker who still fell within the protected age group. For example, if a company discharged a 60-year-old worker and replaced him with one who was 45, the courts often ruled that that was not age discrimination. However, the U.S. Supreme Court has ruled that replacement by a younger worker, even from within the protected

class, is often enough to meet the fourth requirement above. It's up to the employer to show that the replacement wasn't due to age discrimination.

## IF YOU SIGNED A WAIVER

Some employers try to avoid an age discrimination charge by having the employee sign a waiver of her right to sue under the ADEA. In exchange, the employee may be promised additional severance pay or told that failing to sign will result in the loss of expected benefits or pay. Under the ADEA and another law, the Older Workers Benefit Protection Act, a waiver of rights or claims is valid only if it is made "knowingly and voluntarily." Under the law, this means that the waiver…

● Has to be in writing that's easily understood by the employee
● Must refer to your ADEA rights and claims
● Can't require you to waive any rights that you may obtain after you sign the waiver
● Must give you something in exchange for your promise not to pursue your ADEA rights and claims in addition to what you were already entitled to by law and company policy
● Must contain a provision advising you to consult an attorney before signing the waiver
● Must give you 21 days to consider the agreement; 45 days if you're part of a group or class of employees receiving a retirement incentive
● Can be revoked by you for up to 7 days after you *execute*, or sign, it.

## CONTACT THE EEOC

If you decide to sue an employer for violating the ADEA, you must first file a formal complaint with the Equal Employment Opportunity Commission (EEOC), (see "Filing a Complaint with the EEOC," page 312).

## GO TO COURT

If the EEOC investigates your case and sends you a right-to-sue letter, it's a good idea to hire a lawyer. While it's possible to file your own suit, a lawyer experienced in handling illegal workplace discrimination cases can be a valuable asset.

The Equal Employment Opportunity Commission (EEOC) has set up a mediation program designed to serve as a quick and low-cost alternative to its traditional investigation and litigation procedures. In mediation, a neutral third party tries to help the employer and the complaining employee reach a voluntary solution to a discrimination charge. It gives both sides a chance to discuss the issues raised in the charge, clear up misunderstandings, and find areas of agreement that can be incorporated into a mutually acceptable settlement.

Mediation is free to the participants and strictly confidential, and the proceedings aren't transcribed or recorded in any way. Any notes taken during the mediation process are destroyed when mediation ends. Information the mediator obtains during the proceedings can't be revealed to anyone, including EEOC employees. Either party can end the mediation process at any time, and the EEOC will resume its investigation following its usual procedures.

According to the EEOC, employers and employees who have taken advantage of the mediation program have been extremely satisfied with its results, in some cases resolving charges in hours instead of the weeks or months it takes for the EEOC to conduct a full investigation. For more information about the EEOC's mediation program, call (800) 669-4000, or visit its Web site at www.eeoc.gov.

*Your supervisor tells lewd jokes and makes sexually suggestive remarks, even after you object.*

You might think that with all the media attention to the issue of sexual harassment in the workplace, the problem would be a thing of the past. Unfortunately, you would be wrong. Sexual harassment, sometimes subtle, often overt, is still a problem encountered by both men and women in many places of employment.

Although there are no federal laws that specifically prohibit sexual harassment, it is nonetheless illegal because it's considered a form of sexual discrimination, which is prohibited by the Civil Rights Act of 1964.

### THE DEFINITION OF SEXUAL HARASSMENT

In its simplest terms, sexual harassment consists of any unwelcome or uninvited sexual advance or conduct on the job that creates a hostile working environment. Sexual harassment may be non-sexual conduct that singles out a specific person or group because of gender, such as treating workers of one sex with disrespect or singling

them out for the most difficult or unpleasant tasks. Although most reported cases of sexual harassment involve men harassing women, women can also be guilty of harassing men, and same-sex sexual harassment can also occur. Sexual harassment falls into one of two categories:

- **Quid pro quo harassment:** This is the most obvious and familiar form of sexual harassment. It occurs when someone higher up the ladder promises or delivers a benefit, or threatens or follows through with a negative action, based on a subordinate's response to a sexual advance. For example, a worker is promised a raise or promotion if she agrees to sexual relations with her boss or is threatened with demotion or dismissal for refusing.
- **Hostile environment harassment:** This is subtle but no less offensive. It occurs when unwanted conduct aimed at a worker or a group of workers based on their sex is so

severe or persistent that it creates an intimidating or offensive working environment.

The law states that such harassment must be severe or persistent. A single comment by a supervisor or coworker about another worker's appearance or dress, such as "I like that skirt you're wearing," probably doesn't constitute a hostile working environment. But a history of such comments, especially after you've objected to them, may be enough to convince the Equal Employment Opportunity Commission (EEOC), a state civil rights agency, or even a court that you are being harassed. A single comment or action, if severely offensive, could constitute sexual harassment.

It's important to remember that the intentions of the harasser don't matter. What counts is whether a reasonable person of the same sex as the target of the conduct would consider the remarks, comments, or behavior intimidating or offensive.

## SPEAK UP

If you believe you're the victim of sexual harassment, here are the steps you should take:

- **Write down what the offensive behavior was,** and when and where it took place. Should it persist, this will provide a record.
- **Tell the person who has offended you** that the behavior is unwelcome. Some workers unwittingly commit acts that offend others, often because of age or cultural differences. Simply telling the offender to stop may put an end to the problem with no further action.
  ● Don't treat the matter with humor, and don't let the offender claim "it was a joke."
  ● Be direct. Tell the supervisor or coworker exactly what it was that made you uncomfortable, and insist that the behavior stop.
  ● Make it clear that if the behavior continues you will report it to company officials.
- **If it continues, report it to your supervisor** or another company official. If the problem is one that involves your supervisor, contact his superior and share your concern.
- **Contact your employer's human resources department** or benefits administrator to find out if your company has an established procedure for dealing with sexual harassment claims. If it does, follow it. Failing to do so could limit your ability to recover damages if you need to pursue legal action later. Today most companies do have policies for handling

such complaints. In fact, a few states have laws requiring companies with more than a specified number of employees to create procedures for receiving and investigating sexual harassment charges. Courts also have ordered companies with incidents of sexual harassment to create these policies and procedures to deal with problems when they arise.

Once you've filed your complaint with the appropriate company official, he should investigate the problem promptly and confidentially. The results of such an investigation should be made known to the person claiming harassment as well as to the accused person. If the accused supervisor will be suspended or have a record of the disciplinary action placed in his file, you should be notified that this will take place.

## FILE A COMPLAINT

If you're dissatisfied with the way your employer handles your claim, or if the offensive conduct doesn't stop, your next step is to file a complaint with the EEOC or with the state agency responsible for enforcing your state's fair employment laws (see "Filing a Complaint with the EEOC," page 312).

## SUE YOUR EMPLOYER

If the EEOC investigates and gives you a right-to-sue letter, you need to consider whether to file suit under the federal Civil Rights Act of 1964 or under state laws prohibiting sexual harassment.

Your choice depends, to a great extent, on the law of the state where you live. For example, federal law allows you to bring a suit only if your employer has 15 or more employees, while state law may extend protection to workers at much smaller companies. In some states, the amount of damages you may be entitled to receive will be limited to lost wages and benefits, while federal law allows recovery of some additional damages. But several states allow a plaintiff to receive greater damages than the federal law permits.

It's best to consult an experienced labor lawyer to help you decide which law is likely to provide a more favorable outcome for you if you win your case in court. You may also be able to file a lawsuit charging your supervisor and employer with a *tort*—a civil wrong. For example, some workers who have been subjected to unwanted physical contact have won lawsuits charging their employers with assault and battery, and for the intentional infliction of emotional distress. Ask your lawyer for more information.

*You quit your sales job and take a new one with your former company's competitor. Your ex-employer says he will sue you if you have contact with any of your old clients.*

When an employee who is a key part of a business quits and takes a job with a competitor, it's bound to make the former employer unhappy. Employers not only invest a lot of money in training their employees, but they also often give them access to confidential information about business operations. It's not surprising that your old boss would try to limit what you might do to take a bite out of his business.

However, unless you had a written employment agreement with your previous employer, it's unlikely that he will be able to take any action against you if you contact your old customers. The situation is trickier, though, if you signed a written agreement when you took your last position.

## EMPLOYMENT CONTRACTS

Many salespeople, managers, and employees in other essential jobs sign employment contracts when they are hired. If you signed such a contract, you may find that it contains provisions called *noncompetition* and *nondisclosure clauses.*

In most states, courts will enforce these clauses if they are reasonable in their effort to protect the previous employer's business interests. What's reasonable is usually decided on a case-by-case basis and may differ from business to business. Generally, however, courts will look at three factors to decide how reasonable noncompetition and nondisclosure clauses are. These are…

- **The scope of the restriction.** Does the contract make it impossible for you to obtain employment elsewhere, or does it merely prohibit working for direct competitors?

- **The geographical restriction.** Are you prohibited from working within 500 miles of your previous employer's location, or only within 10 miles? If it's the former, a court is more likely to find the restriction unreasonable.
- **The time period placed on the restriction.** The shorter the time period, the more likely it is that a court will enforce it. Although there are exceptions, in general a restriction for a year or two will be considered reasonable.

## PROTECT YOURSELF

If you did not have an employment contract with your previous employer, there's probably nothing he can do, although he may still attempt to convince you otherwise.

He may send you notice that he is filing a lawsuit against you. If this happens, talk to your superiors at your new job about the problem. Their legal department or lawyer may be able to contact your old company about the problem and may even be willing to defend you in court. Chances are, if your ex-employer is willing to pursue the matter against you, she will also sue your new company to prevent it from benefiting from your contacts and knowledge. Your new employer may be able to settle the matter by compensating your old employer.

But if your new company won't defend you, or if you feel your new job may be in jeopardy, get in touch with a labor lawyer who can help you. Legal advice is a must, because decisions on whether these clauses can be enforced vary widely from place to place and from industry to industry. Contact your local or state bar association's lawyer-referral program for the names of lawyers who practice labor and contract law.

You decide to take leave from your job to care for your dying mother, but your employer says that if you're gone for more than four weeks, he'll have to replace you.

Not long ago, if you needed extended time off from work to care for family needs or to recover from a serious illness, you usually lost your job. That changed in 1993, when Congress passed the Family and Medical Leave Act (FMLA), which recognizes that important life events can require employees to be away from their jobs.

### IT'S THE LAW

Under this law, all public employers and private companies that employ 50 or more workers must give each employee with more than 12 months on the job—and at least 1,250 hours on the job in the past 12 months—up to 12 weeks of unpaid annual leave for any of the following reasons:

- The birth or adoption of a child, or for foster placement of a child, provided that the leave occurs within one year of the child's arrival
- To provide care for and attention to the serious health needs of an employee's spouse, parents, or children
- To recuperate from a serious physical or psychological health condition.

### REQUIREMENTS FOR EMPLOYERS AND EMPLOYEES

If you meet the above criteria and need to take leave for medical purposes, do the following:

- **Give your employer certification** of your medical condition, or that of your family member, from a health-care provider. Your employer must give you 15 days in which to obtain certification. If you're taking leave due to your own health condition, your employer can ask for a second opinion from another doctor. The employer is responsible for the cost of obtaining the second opinion. And if the two opinions differ, your employer can ask

for a third opinion (again, at its expense), the result of which is binding on both you and your employer.

- **Give your employer advance notice** of the need to take advantage of the FMLA. This isn't hard if you're expecting a baby, but if you need to take leave because of an emergency, you need only tell your employer as soon as it's practical to do so. There's no requirement in the FMLA that an employee make a written request, nor do you have to specifically mention the FMLA in any request you do make. There is one exception—if your employer has an established policy requiring that all leave requests be put in writing, then you should comply with that policy.

While you take leave, your employer is required to:

- **Continue to make any benefit contributions,** such as premiums for health insurance, that it made before you went on leave. But your seniority rights and pension benefits won't continue to accrue during your leave.
- **Let you return to the same position** as the one you held when you left, or a similar one.

### TALK TO THE BOSS

If the above scenario happens to you, and you meet the requirements of the FMLA, point it out to your employer. He may not be aware of his responsibilities under this law. A covered employer who violates the FMLA can be required to pay backpay, damages, attorney fees, court costs, and the cost of up to 12 weeks of care for a child, spouse, or parent. State Family and Medical Leave laws are also in effect in over half the states. Contact the state or federal Department of Labor for information.

### SMART MOVES

In 2000, President Bill Clinton authorized an experimental program letting states make payments out of unemployment compensation funds to workers taking advantage of the FMLA. Ask your benefits or human resources department, or the state department of labor, if it is in effect in your state.

YOUR OWN BUSINESS

**M**any business owners form corporations or limited liability companies (LLCs) to avoid being personally responsible for claims and debts incurred by their businesses. But even with the added protection that a corporation or LLC provides, owners can sometimes find themselves being held liable.

### Work With Your Insurance Company

Your first step is to contact the company that handles your business insurance and notify them of the claim. Most business policies require you to provide timely notice as soon as you are aware of a potential claim, so delaying could jeopardize your coverage. Refer the injured customer's lawyer to your insurer's claims department, and notify the lawyer that you will not discuss the matter. This should put an end to any further contact from the customer's attorney.

Your insurer will investigate the claim, and you want to cooperate as fully as you can. To help the investigation, you should…

- **Provide a copy of any accident report** that was filed.
- **Provide the names of any witnesses** to the alleged accident and information about how to contact them.
- **Allow time for any employees** who saw the incident to meet with the investigator and recount what they saw.

Some or all of the amount that the injured customer is seeking may be paid by your insurer, or it may deny the claim. If it chooses to deny, the insurer usually has a duty to defend you if the customer files a lawsuit. But take a good look at the wording of your policy. Under the policies, the insurer agrees to pay any damages awarded by a court but limits the coverage for attorney fees. If you will be liable for the cost of your own defense, you may want to urge your insurer to reconsider its decision to deny the claim.

### If You Are Uninsured

Many businesses operate without liability insurance, hoping that they can avoid claims or that they will have the financial reserves to pay any

claims that do arise. If your business is uninsured, you will have to take on the task of negotiating with the customer's lawyer. You may need to hire an attorney to handle the negotiations.

In the event that you can't arrive at a mutually agreeable settlement, there's a chance the customer will not only sue your corporation or limited liability company, but also name you individually as a defendant. Plaintiffs' attorneys will generally name everyone they think may be potentially liable for compensating their clients.

Whether or not you can be judged personally liable depends on several factors:

- First, you may have done something in your *individual capacity* that would make you personally liable for the customer's injury. For example, if the injury was caused because you struck her with a cart while stocking store shelves or if you were delivering building materials to the customer's home and dropped a load of bricks on her, you could be personally liable—in addition to any liability that your business may incur.
- Second, you may have failed to adequately separate your personal finances from those of the corporation. Or you may not have complied with the laws for managing your corporation. As a result of your action (or inaction), the injured customer's attorney can argue that the corporation is merely a sham and that you should be held personally liable. In lawyers' terms, this is known as *piercing the corporate veil*. In order to defend yourself against this kind of claim, you must be very careful to adhere to all of your state's requirements for shareholder meetings, issuing corporate resolutions, and amending bylaws, *even if you are the only shareholder.*

Finally, if your uninsured corporation is small, be prepared to shoulder at least some of the costs. You may well find yourself spending personal funds in order to defend yourself in court.

### Call a Lawyer

Immediately get in touch with a lawyer—your company's legal representative or an experienced liability attorney—whenever you are contacted by the attorney representing a client claiming to have been injured while doing business with you. A knowledgeable attorney can advise you of your rights under the law, evaluate the strength of the claim against you, and help you weigh the costs and benefits of settling out of court verses those of fighting the case in court.

## LIMITED LIABILITY COMPANIES AND CORPORATIONS

Until a little more than a decade ago, businesses took one of three forms: a sole proprietorship, a partnership, or a corporation. The first two were relatively simple to organize and operate, but they did little to shield the owners from personal liability. Forming a corporation offered greater protection to business owners, but the many regulations for operating a corporation are time-consuming and often costly.

To make it possible for business owners to protect themselves from claims and to reduce the red tape involved in running a corporation, a new form of business entity, called a *limited liability company,* or LLC, came into being. Now available across the country, LLCs are easier to organize than corporations, provide increased tax flexibility, and still protect their owners (who are called members) from personal liability for the debts of the business, unless the member personally guarantees them.

State laws governing the way an LLC is organized vary. For example, a few states require LLCs to have two or more members, while in most states an individual can form an LLC. And in some states, certain types of businesses, such as banks, aren't entitled to LLC status.

For more information about forming an LLC in your state, contact your state's office of business development, secretary of state, or an attorney.

Publishers, software companies, and businesses that sell incorporation services sometimes over-state the benefits of forming a corporation. While there are some advantages to incorporating your business, doing so can have drawbacks as well.

Among the *advantages* of incorporating:

- It can be easier to raise funds for a corporation than for a sole proprietorship.
- There may be estate-planning benefits.
- Transferring full or partial ownership of your business will often be easier.
- Tax rates can sometimes be lower, depending on the way your corporation is organized.
- You may be able to give yourself certain employee benefits and favorable tax treatment.
- You can often attract and keep employees with an offer of stock or stock options.

Among the *disadvantages* of incorporating:

- State and local registration fees may make operating a corporation more expensive.
- Additional paperwork and record keeping also add to the cost of running your business.
- The Internal Revenue Service may limit the amount you can pay yourself.
- Going out of business can require additional steps and notice to government agencies, customers, and stockholders that aren't required of sole proprietorships.

> **Y**our business is experiencing a rash
> of bounced checks, and it's affecting your bottom line.

Take some comfort in knowing that you're not alone. According to one recent study, U.S. businesses accepted more than 400 million bad checks in just one year. And that adds up to millions of headaches for business owners.

It's often true that customers bounce checks due to honest mistakes, such as making an error when balancing the family checkbook. But there are plenty of dishonest people who intentionally forge checks, or write checks on closed accounts or on accounts that they know have insufficient funds.

Some customers also stop payment on checks when they are dissatisfied with their purchase—before giving the merchant an opportunity to offer them a repair, replacement, or refund.

The cost of bad checks can be significant. Your bank may charge a fee for each bad check you deposit into your account. If you've taken a large check that bounces, you could bounce checks drawn from your account. That will mean more fees and time spent trying to reassure your vendors about your company's financial stability. Factor in the time spent trying to contact customers who've written bad checks, and it's easy to see how expensive a single bad check can be.

### PROTECTING YOUR BUSINESS FROM ACCEPTING BAD CHECKS

While there's no law that requires any business to accept checks, the practice is so commonplace that it's unlikely you can operate a business without taking them. Here are some steps you can take to help reduce the number of bounced and bad checks your business receives.

- **Require a photo ID** from anyone offering a check as payment.
- **Match the information** on the check (the account holder's name and address) with the information on the ID.
- **Accept only checks** that have been drawn on local banks from your customers.

- **Be cautious about accepting checks** with very low check numbers. Some criminals will open a new checking account with a minimum deposit, and write checks at businesses all over town.
- **Don't accept third-party checks.** A third-party check (a payroll check, for example) is one written to your customer, endorsed by the customer and presented to you. There are ways to accept these checks so that you can recover funds from the endorser if the check bounces, but recovery is a time-consuming and often fruitless pursuit.
- **Never accept checks for more than the amount** of the customer's purchase.
- **Always indicate a customer's payment by check on the receipt** for the purchase. This precaution enables you to avoid making a cash refund to a customer before the check has had time to clear at the bank.
- **Place a notice in a conspicuous place** (near the sales counter or cash register) informing customers that you will impose a processing fee on all bounced checks.

- **Use a check verification service,** such as Telecheck. For a fee, these companies provide equipment that reads and compares coded information on checks with a database of bad checks. If you accept a bad check that your service approved, it will reimburse you for the check and take on collection.
- **Ask your local law enforcement agency for information** on ways to recognize phony checks. Computer technology makes it easy for criminals to print official-looking company checks and identification cards. In one city, a ring of check counterfeiters was able to pass nearly a million dollars in bad checks before the authorities caught on. Similar stories are told by police across the country. The local police can keep you informed about problems experienced by other local businesses.

## COLLECTING ON A BAD CHECK

In many cases, getting a customer who has written a bad check to make good on it will take only a telephone call from you. But in some instances, in order to get what you're owed, you'll need to file a lawsuit in small-claims court or in regular trial court.

Most states allow bad-check victims to collect as much as two to three times the amount of the check plus attorney fees and court costs. But even if you win your case, getting payment will require additional steps on your part.

# You extended credit to a company that is now more than a month late in paying its bill.

In today's economy, it's really an economic necessity to offer payment terms for business-to-business transactions. But some businesses, even well-intentioned ones, can fall behind on their payments to creditors. Others merely cheat unsuspecting business owners who operate with too much faith and not enough caution. Here's what you can do if you are having trouble collecting for services or goods that you provided to another business.

## STEPS TO TAKE

If you haven't billed your client for the second time recently, now's the time to do so. Send an invoice showing the amount owed (with any accrued interest your credit agreement allows you to charge) and a cover letter addressed to the person who authorized the purchase. *Don't* send this notice to the accounts payable department, which may have instructions to ignore your invoices or to continue delaying payment.

- **Be polite but firm.** Your letter should include a reference to the amount of the outstanding debt and note that it is still unpaid. For example, "Our invoice #1123454 in the amount of $3,050 is now more than 60 days past due."
- **Make a demand for payment.** Your letter should contain a statement such as "Please remit your payment to us at the address on the enclosed invoice within 5 business days."
- **Provide the name and telephone number** of someone in your office to contact about the debt if the purchaser believes it is in error or if there is a question. "Please feel free to contact our director of accounting, Jim Jones,

at 555-1212 in the event that you have any questions about this invoice."

Sign the letter and mail or fax it to the company. And keep a copy for your files.

■ **If you don't get a response,** it's time to send a formal demand letter by certified mail, return receipt requested. It will often be enough to prompt the company to send its check. But if it doesn't pay you by the deadline, you'll want to consider taking your case to court. In your demand letter you should:
 ● Include the information mentioned above.
 ● Include a statement indicating that if payment is not received by the deadline you set, you reserve the right to take further action as permitted by law.

## FILING SUIT TO COLLECT A DEBT

You may want to go to small-claims court if the debt is relatively small. To find out the limits for a small-claims suit in your state, call your county courthouse and ask to speak to the court clerk.

If the debt is within your state's small-claims limit, your next step will be to speak to the small claims court administrator and ask what forms you must complete to begin your suit and what fees you may have to pay.

Some states require a certified check to pay for filing fees, while in others, a personal or company check is acceptable. Ask first to save yourself a return trip to the courthouse.

■ **Once you have the information you need, go to the courthouse and file a complaint.** The small-claims administrator will give you a form. Read it carefully and ask the administrator to clarify anything you don't understand. Court officials can't give you legal advice, but they can provide explanations that will help you fill out your complaint form correctly.

■ **You'll probably be required** to set out the basis for your lawsuit in a paragraph or two on the form. For example, "On January 2, 2000, ABC, Inc., a corporation doing business in this state, ordered $4,000 of widgets on credit,

---

**SMART MOVES**

Many businesses are reducing billing and collections by requiring customers to use a credit card when purchasing goods or services. You'll usually pay a monthly fee and a percentage of each transaction—but it's small change compared to what a collection agency or going to court might cost. Your business banker can help set up an account with credit card companies.

---

agreeing to make payment in 30 days. To date, ABC, Inc. has not paid this debt, despite repeated attempts at collection. We ask the court to award us relief in the amount of the debt, accrued interest, court costs, and the costs of collection." There's no need to go into any more detail here.

■ **Sign the form** and give it to the administrator together with the required filing fee. The administrator will review the form, and if anything appears incomplete, she may ask you for additional information.

■ **Arrange to serve the complaint on your debtor.** In some states, local sheriffs handle this task; in others, you may be able to serve your complaint by mail. See if the procedure is included on the complaint form, or ask the court clerk or administrator to tell you about the process. (The court official, however, may be reluctant to advise you, because doing so might be considered the unauthorized practice of law.) You can always find the correct procedure under Court Rules in your state's statutes. Copies of the statutes can be found at the county courthouse and larger public libraries. Some states now put all or a portion of their statutes on-line, so you might want to do your research on the Internet.

Once you file your suit and your complaint is served on the debtor, don't be surprised if you get a check in the mail or a phone call from a company official asking for an extension of time or proposing a payment plan. Before you decide against a payment plan, be sure to consider the situation carefully. Do you think that the business's failure to pay is due to legitimate problems? Has your relationship with the company been problem-free in the past? If you think the business can remedy its problems and you want to keep the business relationship, then a payment plan—allowing the business to pay a significant portion immediately and the rest within a short period—could be a win-win solution.

**TAKE NOTE** *In some states, you can have a business debtor execute what's known as a*

Making decisions about extending credit and running your business becomes more complicated when you have one or more partners. At a minimum your partnership agreement should include:

- The name of the partnership

- The nature of the partnership—a general or limited partnership

- The purpose of the partnership and a list of its business functions

- The duration of the partnership

- The authority and duties of each partner

- The number of partners and the method for admitting new ones

- The procedure for resolving disputes among all of the partners

- The method of dissolving the partnership when disputes can't be resolved

- The contributions made by each partner to the partnership

- The partnership's bookkeeping and accounting procedures

- How title to the property used by the partnership will be held

- The methods to be used in allocating the partnership's losses and profits

- How the interest of a partner who dies, becomes disabled, or leaves the partnership will be acquired by the remaining partners.

Even the best of friends need to create a written partnership agreement when they decide to go into business together. Without something in writing, state laws governing partnerships will be applied when there's a dispute or if one of the partners wants to quit. And that could mean an outcome that makes none of the partners happy.

Judgment Note *or* Confession of Judgment. *If the firm then fails to meet its obligation, it is prevented from contesting the debt in any future court proceeding. You can sometimes find these forms at local stationery stores or in business software programs. Be sure to have any form you use reviewed first by a lawyer familiar with your state's laws to be certain it's enforceable in your state. Confessions of Judgment are prohibited in cases where the debtor is an individual consumer.*

If you think that the company is merely engaging in stalling tactics or has no intention of paying after you withdraw your suit, you will need to go forward with your case. But before you do, remember that litigation will probably mean the end of any future business dealings between you and your debtor. Our advice is to think and think again before you go to court to collect the debt.

## ALTERNATIVES TO A COURT CASE

In some states, you may be able to ask the court to appoint a mediator or arbitrator to help you resolve a problem with another business. These programs are typically less costly than going to court. They can be especially useful when the amount of the debt is too large for small-claims court and there's a dispute about whether the debt is actually owed.

You may also consider hiring a collection agency or attorney to pursue the debt. This can be costly; some collection agencies want as much as half of any amount they are able to collect. Collection attorneys are usually less expensive, but in either case, you will end up sacrificing a big chunk of what you're owed.

## GOING TO COURT

Whether you end up in the small-claims system or in the regular civil courts, winning your lawsuit will depend to a great extent on how well you document, prepare, and present your case in court—particularly in small-claims court.

■ **Documentation includes contracts**, notes, or sales agreements, and copies of correspondence with the debtor. It's best to organize them in a binder with tabs indicating which are which. The judge can then turn to any document you mention in court. Make three copies of all documents—one for the judge, one for you, and one for your opponent.

■ **Preparation involves rehearsing** your arguments ahead of time. Present them to a friend or family member and get feedback on what's unclear and on habits that could detract from your presentation, such as stammering or saying "you know." Visit the courtroom ahead of time to help you understand how the courtroom is run and give you an idea of the judge's personality.

■ **Presentation is the way you deliver your argument** to the court. Limit yourself to a chronological account of the facts of your case. Avoid personal attacks. Keep your presentation brief, answer any questions the judge asks as honestly and completely as you can, and pay attention to your opponent's defense claims. Don't interrupt if the defendant says something outrageous. In most cases, you will get a chance to rebut these statements before the judge reaches a decision.

It's not unusual for the other side to fail to appear on the court date. You will be awarded a *default judgment* if your opponent is a no-show, but getting your money could still be a hassle.

## COLLECTING THE DEBT

If the court's judgment is in your favor, you still have to collect, or execute the order. You may be able to attach the company's bank accounts or to file a lien against its real estate or equipment. The court clerk can provide forms and instructions for collecting the money. You may want an attorney to help you track down assets and collect the payment that the court has awarded.

**BE CAUTIOUS** *Collecting a debt from an individual is tricky and can expose you to more potential liability than collecting from another business. The federal Fair Debt Collection Practices Act (FDCPA) and similar state laws put severe restrictions on tactics you can use when trying to collect.*

Someone you think of as a business customer may actually be entitled to FDCPA protection. To avoid problems, it's a good idea to follow the FDCPA rules even when trying to collect a business debt. Basically this means that you should never...

● Threaten physical force or any other kind of violence
● Use profane, abusive, or obscene language
● Suggest that the debtor will be subject to criminal charges if the debt isn't paid
● Contact the debtor in a way that could be considered harassment, such as incessant phoning
● Contact the debtor during unusual hours, typically before 8 am or after 9 pm
● Contact the debtor after he notifies you that he's represented by an attorney, except to learn the attorney's identity
● Contact or threaten to contact any third parties about the alleged debt.

Your lawyer, the local chamber of commerce, Better Business Bureau, and state attorney general's office or local district attorney's office may provide you with information about other collection practices that may be restricted or prohibited.

You've sent your demand letters, filed your lawsuit, and presented your case, and now the court has awarded you damages against a business that owes you money. All that's left is to collect your judgment. Right? Not always. Believe it or not, even after winning at every step of the legal battle, you may never get a penny. A company that owes you money may be judgment proof—a business with no assets, no money, and no current business to provide income.

In other instances, when you are just one of a number of businesses owed money, a company may be able to avoid paying a judgment by filing for bankruptcy. Once it files, the court will give it an automatic stay, preventing you from taking any action to collect. Other creditors who have protected their loans by taking collateral from the company (known as secured creditors) will have precedence in getting paid out of any remaining company assets. Your judgment may be completely wiped out by the bankruptcy court.

Finally, some companies just disappear, even though the law requires them to take certain steps to satisfy their debts before going out of business. Tracking down the company's owners or shareholders and attempting to collect from them can be time-consuming and less than cost-effective. You should get the help of a lawyer experienced in working with businesses like yours when deciding how much time, money, and effort you want to expend in pursuing a debt that may ultimately be uncollectible.

*You have an idea for an invention. A company has offered to develop and market the idea for you, but they want you to pay thousands of dollars when you sign the agreement.*

Even for experienced entrepreneurs, getting a new invention to the marketplace is a difficult task. Patent applications are complicated, and it can sometimes be years before an application is approved or rejected. Only about half of all patent applications are ever approved. While dozens of companies claim to have access to thousands of companies here and abroad that will license the rights to your invention, the plain fact is that less than 2 percent of inventions ever are marketed successfully.

There *are* legitimate firms willing to take on newly invented products or processes. But the best of these concerns never will charge you fees or expenses up front. Instead, they make their money by taking a percentage of the money that the inventor earns (much like a lawyer's contingency fees).

## BE CAUTIOUS

According to the Federal Trade Commission (FTC), you may find yourself dealing with a less-than-honest company if…

● The company offers to file "preliminary documents" with the U.S. Patent and Trademark Office (PTO) for a fee of several hundred dollars. The actual cost of filing a *disclosure document* (evidence of the date you came up with your idea) is only $10—you can do it yourself.
● The company claims to have a high rate of success in licensing its clients' inventions. Ask for the exact licensing rate the firm has had in the past 12 months. Get the names, addresses, and telephone numbers of its successful inventors. Contact these inventors to

find out if they've made more money in fees than they paid to the marketing company. Chances are they haven't.

● The company accepts all or most of the ideas submitted. Legitimate companies know that the number of successful inventions is low, so they tend to reject many more submissions than they accept.

● The company offers a two-step "marketing service." The first step involves a market evaluation or research report that costs anywhere from several hundred to several thousand dollars. Invariably, this report will include a glowing and enthusiastic review of the potential market for your idea. The second step will be patent and licensing services, which can cost you several thousand dollars more, and it's payable (of course) in advance.

### PROTECTING YOURSELF

Instead of signing with a company that wants money up front, contact a marketing service that works on a contingency-fee basis. You may also want to talk to a patent attorney who can help you file with the PTO. While patent attorneys often work on an hourly basis or for a flat fee, their charges are preferable to paying a scam artist who won't promote your invention.

Get in touch with the FTC if you've already signed with a company and you suspect that it is not on the up-and-up. Contact the commission's Consumer Response Center at

(877) 382-4357, or file an on-line complaint at www.ftc.gov. The FTC has arranged for court orders against a number of questionable invention-marketing services, and in some cases the FTC has obtained refunds for customers who were cheated.

You may also get help from your state attorney general's office or consumer protection agency, especially if the company you're working with is located in the same state. The attorneys general of several states have brought legal actions that resulted in refunds for inventors.

### COPYRIGHT PROTECTION

You can protect your ownership rights in certain kinds of artistic expression by registering a copyright for the material you create. While copyright is now automatic once you've put a work in a fixed form (written on paper, for example), registering your copyright with the Library of Congress's Copyright Office will give you additional legal protections. Under current law, you can copyright the following:

● Literary works

● Dramatic works

● Musical works

● Choreographed works

● Pantomime

● Sculptural, pictorial, and graphic works

● Motion pictures and other audiovisuals

● Sound recordings

> **Y**ou paid a fee to obtain an Internet franchise, but you never get the assistance or return on your investment that you were promised.

The Internet has become a favorite way for con artists and unscrupulous businesses to take advantage of investors. People have been bilked out of thousands of dollars through phony franchise or business opportunities that promise big returns through marketing Internet services and selling Internet access.

## What You Can Do

It's possible that the franchiser you're dealing with is legitimate, so your first step will be to contact the company for help. Although it's often easier to succeed when you franchise your business rather than operating it independently, even franchised businesses require a great deal of effort from the operators to be profitable. Get in touch with the franchiser's management and ask for suggestions to help you improve your business's profitability.

However, you may not get any help. Or it may become apparent that no matter how hard you work, you won't be able to achieve the revenue that you were led to believe was within your reach. In either case, you'll need to take action to try to get your money back.

Before you sent money to the franchiser, you should have received a disclosure statement from it. Review this statement to see what it says about the franchise you purchased. Under what's known as the FTC's Franchise Rule, this disclosure statement must include information about…

- The history of the franchiser
- Litigation between the franchiser and franchisee related to their business relationship
- State or federal orders that restrict the franchiser/franchisee relationship
- Terms and conditions the franchise offers
- Information about other franchisees,

including their names, addresses, and their toll phone numbers.

The FTC Franchise Rule also requires anyone selling a franchise to…

- Have a reasonable basis for statements it makes about profits and earnings
- Accompany any of the earnings projections that it gives you with the number and percentage of its franchisees who have attained the claimed results
- Provide specific documentation that backs up all of the company's claims.

You will also have signed a franchise agreement that sets out your financial obligations and the franchiser's responsibilities to you. Look at the disclosure statement and agreement carefully. If they contain any misrepresentations by the parent company, or if the company has failed to live up to any of its responsibilities to you under your contract, you then have a couple of options to pursue.

- **Send a demand letter to the franchiser** by certified mail, return receipt requested so that you'll have proof of its delivery. In your letter, point to the portion of your agreement that you believe the franchiser has breached. For example, the agreement may have promised that the franchiser would provide advertising and also give potential customers information that would specifically direct them to your franchise. If no such advertising has been done, note this fact in your letter.
- **Give the franchiser the opportunity to** *cure,* or to correct, the breach within the specified period of time required by your contract. If no time is stated in the contract that you

### Smart Moves

Internet chat groups and "list-servs" can be valuable sources of information about the problems and pitfalls of owning a franchise business. You can learn whether other franchisees have experienced the same or similar problems. You may even be able to join forces with other disgruntled franchise owners, reducing the cost of obtaining legal help by acting as a group.

signed, the law will often imply that the parent company must be given a reasonable time to take corrective action. In your letter, give the franchiser a deadline—within 10 business days, for example. If the franchiser doesn't comply with your deadline, you will be enti-

---

*Before you sent money to the franchiser, you should have received a disclosure statement from the company. Review this statement to see what it says about the franchise.*

---

tled to pursue other remedies, either by asking for arbitration between yourself and the parent company or by seeking the termination of your agreement with the franchiser and then claiming damages by pursuing a lawsuit against it.

### THE FTC CAN HELP

If you believe that the franchiser's disclosure statement was inaccurate or if you didn't receive a disclosure statement, you should contact the FTC with your concerns. The FTC will review the documents you received and look into the claims the franchiser made.

Should the FTC find that the franchiser used deceptive or misleading information to lure you into purchasing your franchise, it can…

- Move to put an end to the company's unethical and illegal practices
- Obtain a consent decree by which the company agrees to provide refunds to unhappy franchisees and to stop selling franchises.

If a company refuses to cooperate with the FTC or violates the consent decree, the FTC can take further action on behalf of

franchisees. In one recent case, the FTC went to federal court and obtained an injunction against a company that made misleading statements that induced consumers to purchase franchises. The FTC got a court order freezing the franchiser's assets and the assets of the firm's officers. The commission also asked the court to order the company to refund franchise fees to those who had signed on with the parent company.

### FILING A PRIVATE LAWSUIT

The FTC goes to court when it believes that the federal franchise laws have been violated and that legal proceedings are in the public interest. But not every case the FTC investigates leads to a consent decree or a court order. You may, in the end, find it necessary to file a private lawsuit against the franchiser.

It's unlikely that you will want to proceed without a lawyer; in fact, you may not be able to sue—depending on the way you organized your own business. For example, if you formed a corporation to buy the franchise, you may be barred from appearing in court on behalf of the corporation, even if you're the only stockholder. In larger cities, there are usually several law firms able to help you evaluate your case and pursue a lawsuit if one is warranted. In smaller communities, finding a lawyer to take on a franchise suit may be more difficult. Contact your state bar association's referral service to obtain the names of lawyers in your area who can handle these kinds of franchise cases.

## EVALUATING A FRANCHISE

Franchises can be a great way to get into business. You have the advantage of the franchiser's established brand and its guidance in areas, such as training, bookkeeping, and picking a site for your business.

Not all franchises are created equal, however, and some companies that offer franchises are only interested in getting up-front fees and requiring you to purchase supplies from their own warehouses. When considering a franchise, here are some things to look for:

- **What kind of franchise are you getting?** In general, franchises fall into one of three categories: A *business format* franchise is one in which the franchiser develops the marketing techniques and dictates matters such as quality control but generally leaves other matters to the franchisee. A *trade name* franchise is one that gives the franchisee the exclusive right to sell the franchiser's products or services in a particular area. A *turnkey* franchise is one in which the franchiser locates the site for your business, constructs the building and the facilities, and generally exercises strict control over how your business is run.

- **How free are you to choose your own source of supplies or merchandise?** Again, some franchisers will insist that you purchase items only from them or an affiliated company. This may mean higher costs than if you're free to make your purchases on the open market.

- **How free are you to set your own prices?** Fast-food restaurants and auto-repair franchises often require franchisees to honor chain-wide advertised prices. Other franchisers will give an individual franchisee or the holder of several franchises the option of setting prices within a certain range. Still others place no controls on the prices their franchisees charge.

- **How protected is your franchise territory?** If the franchiser can sell another unit in the same trading area as yours, your ability to operate successfully will likely be diluted. In one case, some franchised sandwich-shop owners filed suit against their franchiser, claiming that the number of franchises sold made it difficult for any one franchisee to make a profit.

- **How much managerial help will you get from the franchiser?** If you're an experienced business owner, you may not need much help with matters, such as hiring, training, and making payroll. But if you're not, having a franchiser that can help with these issues can mean the difference between success and failure.

- **What's the franchise really going to cost?** In addition to the initial purchase price, you need to consider what ongoing fees will be required and whether you will have to make contributions for advertising and marketing costs.

- **How easy is it to sell or terminate the franchise?** If you find you're not suited to run a franchise business, how hard will it be to get the franchiser to approve a sale to someone else? On the other hand, how easy is it for the franchiser to cancel the agreement if it feels that you aren't bringing in the expected profits?

**You've operated a beauty parlor from your home for years, but now the city claims that you are violating zoning laws and wants you to shut down your business.**

Despite the growth of home businesses, some communities remain rigid about zoning laws. Cities and towns can be difficult when they discover a business operating in violation of zoning laws prohibiting home-based businesses. But before you comply with the city's request, investigate your options. You may be able to continue running your business from home.

OUT OF BUSINESS
DONNA'S SALON

### DEALING WITH THE ZONING BOARD

Keep in mind that zoning ordinances and regulations are a matter of local law and will differ from one community to another. A home business that may be perfectly legal in one town may be prohibited in the community on the other side of the road. But in most cases, the procedures for responding to and opposing a zoning-board complaint will be similar to the following.

Generally, anyone who lives or works in your community can file a complaint about an alleged violation of the zoning laws on your street. In most cases, a neighbor will bring the matter to the city's attention. He may be unhappy about the cars parked in your driveway, visits by customers during the early morning or late at night, or what he perceives as increased traffic or decreased parking along your street.

No matter what reason a resident may have, once a complaint is filed, the city will send an inspector to investigate the claim. If the inspector decides that your business is in violation of the zoning laws, you'll be contacted by the city and instructed to stop operating it.

If you've been contacted only informally by the city about your business, you can continue operating the business until you receive a formal written notice that you are in violation of the law. A written notice should contain…

- A statement of the zoning ordinance that you are accused of violating
- A deadline by which you must stop violating the local zoning ordinances
- A statement of the penalties for failing to comply. Penalties for continuing to violate zoning laws will vary, but usually you can face a fine for each day that you continue to ignore the zoning laws. You may be subject to jail time as well if you persist in breaking the zoning regulations.

Your notice should also include the name, address, and telephone number of the zoning board. It may include a copy of the ordinance you are accused of violating and provide information about the steps you must take to appeal.

You should review the zoning ordinances to look for anything that will bolster your appeal. A copy of current ordinances should be available at city hall or the local public library. Don't rely solely on the ordinance listed in the notice you receive.

There may be another ordinance giving you the right to continue operating because the zoning for your community was changed after you opened your home business. In some communities, businesses are grandfathered, or protected from subsequent zoning changes.

Court decisions in your state may also have modified or overruled certain zoning laws. Not every zoning board is aware of all the decisions reached by the state's courts; even when they do know the rulings, the board may feel that the court's decision doesn't apply because the facts of your case are different.

---

*In some communities, businesses are grandfathered, or protected from subsequent changes in zoning laws.*

---

You will find many court decisions listed in your state's court reports. You may also find information about court decisions listed in the annotated state statutes. Your county courthouse should have these publications available. If you live near a law school, you might also be able to search the law school's library.

Follow the steps in the notice you received to challenge the zoning board's decision, or look at the ordinances to learn what steps you must take to make your appeal. Follow the procedures carefully, and be certain to file the required documents on or before the deadline—or you could be barred from having your appeal heard.

If your appeal is successful, you should be able to continue operating your business. But if the zoning board rules against you, you may be entitled to appeal to the city council or board of aldermen. If this appeal fails and you believe that the city has misapplied the law in your situation, you may need to file suit. The help of a lawyer who handles real estate and zoning law cases is almost always required. Generally, you'll be allowed to continue operating your business while your appeal is being heard—a process that can take months or even years, depending on court calendars and your own persistence.

### ZONING-LAW CHANGES AND VARIANCES

It may become clear from the law that your business is prohibited (get a lawyer's advice before making that assumption), but don't give up. There are a couple of possible approaches that may allow you to resume your home-based business.

One method is to *get the zoning law changed.* In many parts of the country, zoning laws prohibiting home businesses are out of date. Check with the city clerk about the procedure for proposing a change to zoning ordinances. In some towns, anyone can appear before the city government or zoning board to propose a change. Other communities require that a certain number of residents sign a petition supporting the change.

If you aren't interested in changing the zoning law, you might *request a variance* to the law that would apply specifically to your situation. A variance, or "conditional use," is a license that lets you use your own property in a way prohibited to others. In either case, there will be an opportunity for members of the public to oppose your proposed change. Your chances of success will be greater if you can enlist the support of neighbors.

---

*You get a letter from a business in another city claiming that your company's name is infringing on its trademark.*

---

You may think the name you gave your business is unique, but that's rarely the case. While it's not hard to meet the legal requirements for naming a business, problems sometimes occur when a business elsewhere is already operating with the same name or a name similar to the one you've chosen.

### NAMING YOUR BUSINESS

In most states, you must file a proposed business name with the state department of revenue or the county clerk where your business is located. In some states, you are also required to place a notice in the classified section of your local newspaper. The rationale for these procedures is clear enough: the government agency can stop you from using a name that's the same as one already in use in the area or so similar to the name of an existing business that the public might not be able to tell them apart. Publishing a notice allows a local business owner who may think your business name is too close to his to object before you begin using it.

But while these procedures worked well in the past, developing technology and the rise of national and multinational businesses makes them outmoded in many instances. For example, if you open a restaurant named "McDonnell's," there's a good chance you'll soon receive a letter from the legal department at McDonald's claiming that you are infringing on its *trademark* and insisting that you change your restaurant's name—even if McDonald's has never operated a restaurant in your city.

### TRADEMARKS AND SERVICE MARKS

As defined by the U.S. Patent and Trademark Office (PTO), a *trademark* is a word, phrase, symbol, design, or combination of any of these that identifies and distinguishes the source of goods of one party from those of others. A *service mark* is the same as a *trademark* except that it identifies and distinguishes the source of a service rather than a product.

Although most of us think of trademarks as being registered with the PTO, there is common-law protection for trademarks that have been in use by a business without registration. While

registration of a trademark does help make the rights of a business owner somewhat easier to enforce, it isn't necessary, and many businesses never bother to register their trademarks or service marks. But they can still enforce the right to their mark in court. A business found guilty of infringing the trademark or service mark of another can be held liable for damages and be required to stop using the name.

### GET EXPERT HELP

Get in touch with your attorney as soon as you receive notice from the company claiming that you are infringing on its trademark. Expert legal advice and assistance is essential, and going it alone is not recommended. Some businesses have faced federal lawsuits and spent thousands of dollars trying to protect their business names and identities. Even when these efforts succeeded, the cost of litigation often meant spending money that could have been used in expanding the business and entering new markets. Your lawyer can tell you how the courts have ruled in cases similar to yours, help you weigh the pros and cons of fighting back, and advise you on your chances of successfully defending your case in court.

Before responding to the company's claim, your attorney will suggest the following:

- **Check industry directories,** trade journals, and other business and trade publications.
- **Review state and county records** to see if the other business's name is registered.
- **Review your state trademark registry**—trademarks can be registered with the office of the secretary of state or similar office in most states, giving them additional legal protection.
- **Search the federal register of trademarks** to see if the mark is registered nationally.

If you have time, you can do much of this research yourself and save legal fees, but first talk to your lawyer about how go about it and what to look for. Checking trademark records will help you and your lawyer decide what kind of a response to make to the business that is claiming infringement. For example, if the other business never registered its trademark, you may want to argue that the business began using its name after you had already been using yours.

You may also be able to argue that there is little or no possibility that consumers will confuse

> *There is common-law protection for trademarks that have been in use by a business without registration.*

your business with the complaining one, so there is no need for you to stop using your business name. For instance, you receive a demand letter from Elmer's Country Kitchen, claiming that your business, Elmer's Kountry Kabinets, infringes on

its trademark. Although the other business operates restaurants throughout a portion of the country, none are located in your state. Your business is refinishing old furniture. In this case, a court might decide that the chance of confusing your business with the other one is too remote to require you to abandon your business name.

## PROTECTING YOUR OWN BUSINESS NAME

If you win your battle to keep your company's name, consider taking steps to protect it from being infringed on by other companies. Consider registering the trademark for your business name. In most states, you can register your trademark at the state level in the office of the secretary of state. On the federal level, trademark registration is handled by the U.S. Patent and Trademark Office. You can get instructions and forms for registering by writing to: Commissioner, Patent and Trademark Office, Washington DC 20231.

> *You thought you'd hired just the right person for the job opening. But now you've discovered that your new employee falsified information on his job application.*

Studies indicate that as many as 25 percent of resumes and job applications contain inaccurate information or downright lies, and some research puts the figure even higher.

While on first glance, a few false statements may not seem to amount to much, it's important to think carefully before you overlook them. Finding one false statement on an application may mean that other, more significant ones are also present.

## TAKING ACTION IS IMPORTANT

Legally, a business owner has an obligation to protect the general public, customers, and other employees from being injured by an employee that the employer knows or reasonably should know poses a danger to others. If, for example, your employee claimed to have experience operating equipment when he really has no experience, allowing him to continue to operate the equipment could expose you to liability if he injures someone on the job.

Similarly, you could be liable if your employee has been previously convicted of a violent crime, such as sexual assault, and you let him have contact with customers in their homes (perhaps as a salesman or repairman), or you employ him as a child care worker or an attendant in a nursing home. Should he assault one of your customers, you might be the target of a lawsuit. Lawsuits for *negligent hiring* have increased in the past decade, and a number of employers have found themselves on the losing end—in some cases paying hundreds of thousands of dollars in damages.

> **ALERT** *It's often appropriate to ask an applicant about prior criminal convictions if there's a connection between the work to be done (driving a delivery truck, for example) and your inquiry ("Have you ever been convicted of driving under the influence?"). But you usually can't ask about arrests. In some states, you can't even ask an applicant about convictions for certain offenses after a specified period of time has elapsed.*

*Check with your state department of labor or a lawyer with experience in representing business owners to find out what questions are specifically disallowed in your state.*

### GETTING TO THE TRUTH

When you learn that your employee has made a false statement on his application, you can talk to him and ask him about the statement. Be sure your conversation is as confidential as possible. If he admits that the statement is false, ask if there are any other false statements on the application.

Well-designed job application forms should contain a clause warning against false statements. The warning should be above the applicant's signature. By reading this clause and signing the application, the applicant acknowledges…

- That the statements in the application are true and correct to the best of his knowledge
- That making any false statement will be cause for discharge.

If your employee signed an application with such a clause, you can probably terminate him with no further legal obligation beyond paying him for time worked. The problem gets stickier, however, if your application form didn't include a provision regarding false statements. If the employee has been on the job for any length of time, the situation can become more complicated.

Before firing an employee under these circumstances, you need to ask yourself the following questions:

> *Finding one false statement on an application may mean that other, more significant ones are also present.*

- Is the false statement significant enough to affect the safety and welfare of coworkers, customers, and others who may come in contact with the employee? A false claim of a degree in pharmacy is probably enough to allow you to fire someone you employ as a pharmacist. But it may not be relevant if he works as an Internet designer.
- Did you make any commitments when the employee was hired that would lead him to believe he could be fired only for conduct on the job?
- Do you have a written or oral contract promising employees continued employment?
- Do you have an employee manual that limits reasons for employee termination?
- Did you let others remain at work after discovering that their applications had a falsehood?

### GET LEGAL ADVICE

Although some courts have ruled against firing an employee when a lie isn't serious, other courts have taken the opposite view. In fact, courts in some states have allowed employers to use a false or incomplete job application to justify firings that might otherwise be illegal. Because state laws and court decisions on wrongful termination differ, it's important to get legal advice quickly. If you belong to a trade or professional association, it may be able to give you the names of lawyers who can provide information about the laws in your state.

Sometimes it seems as if the law is making it harder for employers to obtain enough information about job applicants to make good hiring decisions. Despite the horror stories that circulate whenever employers get together, there are plenty of questions you can ask a prospective employee. You are legally permitted to ask any job applicants…

- Their full name and whether they have ever worked for your company in the past under a different name

- Whether a spouse or relative is currently employed by your company

- Their current address and the length of time they've lived at that address

- If they are at least 18 years of age

- If they are currently eligible to work in the United States

- If they speak or write any foreign languages

- Their education and work experience

- If they have been convicted of a crime or have felony charges currently filed against them

- The name and address of a person to be contacted in case of accident or emergency.

Among other laws, the Americans With Disabilities Act (ADA) prohibits employers from asking prospective employees certain kinds of questions on job applications or in the interviewing process. According to the Equal Employment Opportunity Commission, you should avoid asking the following questions or ones that are similar in scope:

- Are there any diseases or conditions for which you've received medical treatment?

- Have you had any major illness in the last year (or the last 3, 5, or 10 years)?

- Have you ever been treated by a psychologist or psychiatrist for any mental condition, and if so, what was the condition?

- Do you currently take prescription medications, and if so, what are they?

- Have you ever been hospitalized, and if so, for what condition?

- How many days were you absent from work due to illness or injury in the past year?

- Have you ever filed for workers compensation?

- Are you an alcoholic or a drug addict, or were you treated for alcohol or drug addiction?

- Do you have any disabilities, impairments, or physical defects that would affect your ability to do the job you are seeking?

- Do you have any disabilities, impairments, or physical defects that would limit your ability to do certain kinds of work?

Other state and federal laws prohibit asking applicants about matters, such as their marital status, religious affiliation, age, and national origin. Ask your attorney for information on other questions to avoid asking job applicants in the hiring process.

---

*A* former employee claims that you gave
him a bad reference. Now he is threatening to sue you.

---

It's hard enough to deal with difficult or incompetent workers who are in your employ. Now you may have problems after they quit. It's a sad fact that more and more former employees are taking legal action when a previous employer gives them a less than enthusiastic reference when they apply for their next job. As a result of this trend, many companies now have policies that limit the information their managers can provide about previous employees as to…

- Job titles
- Salary
- Dates of their employment.

If you've given out more than the minimum information or made negative statements about a former employee of your company, you could be faced with a defamation suit. And because of a U.S. Supreme Court decision, you might even be sued for violating your former employee's civil rights if your motivation for giving a negative reference was retaliatory.

## HOW TO DEFEND YOURSELF

Keep in mind that many threats made by former employees will never lead to other action. Your first defense against such a call from a disgruntled former employee is probably to make no response to it at all.

- **Don't make any statements** to the employee that will give him more fuel for the fire.
- **Don't make any personal attacks.** Stay focused on the issues at hand.
- **Get in touch with your company's lawyer** immediately if you are contacted by the former employee's attorney or served notice of a potential lawsuit. She can help you gather the resources you'll need to defeat your ex-employee's claim. Provide your lawyer with

---

*R*emember that telling
the truth is a defense to
a charge of defamation.

---

documents related to the former employee's job performance—job reviews, disciplinary records, warnings that the employee received for failing to meet company standards, failing to comply with company policies, and other evidence that will show that your negative statements are supported.

Remember that when you tell the truth it becomes a defense to a charge of defamation. If you claimed that your ex-employee was terminated for his unexcused absences, and that's the actual reason for it, then you have a defense. When you are discussing the matter with your lawyer…

### SMART MOVES

When asked for references over the telephone, record the name of the person calling, where he works, the date and time of the call, and the nature of your comments. Some ex-employees have a friend or relative pose as an employer in an attempt to trick you into saying something negative. Others fabricate stories about obtaining negative references from you.

- Don't hide the fact that you may have made a mistake by speaking out.
- Don't deny that you may have said unflattering things about the ex-employee. Rely on your lawyer's expertise; follow her advice.

Your lawyer may be able to find case law (court decisions in your state or elsewhere) that undermines the ex-employee's claims or reduces his chance of success. She may also be able to negotiate a settlement. Remember, however, that the decision to make a settlement offer is yours.

> *Y*ou fired an employee for chronic absenteeism.
> Now she claims that she is protected by the Americans With
> Disabilities Act, and she's threatening to sue.

The Americans With Disabilities Act (ADA) has been the subject of much controversy and thousands of lawsuits since it became the law in 1990. Designed to prevent workplace discrimination on the basis of disabilities, this law (and state laws that provide similar protections) requires employers to make *reasonable accommodations* for otherwise qualified individuals with disabilities, unless doing so would cause the employer *undue hardship.* But trying to decipher what's reasonable and what constitutes an undue hardship can sometimes be mind-boggling.

## WHO IS DISABLED?

According to the ADA, a person can be considered disabled by the court when he or she:

- Has a physical or mental impairment that substantially limits a major life activity (for example, the person is a quadriplegic or amputee, or has difficulty thinking, concentrating, or interacting with others)
- Has a record of impairment, such as a past diagnosis of cancer, clinical depression, bipolar disorder, or some other disease
- Is regarded as having an impairment, such as scars or other disfiguring marks that may make others uncomfortable.

## WHAT THE ADA PROHIBITS

ADA provisions forbid employers with 15 or more employees from...

- Discriminating on the basis of most physical or mental disabilities
- Asking applicants about their current or past medical conditions
- Requiring their job applicants to take employment medical examinations before being hired
- Creating or operating a workplace that contains substantial physical barriers to the those who are physically disabled.

## MAKING REASONABLE ACCOMMODATIONS

The ADA requires you to make changes in the workplace or modify the tasks required of workers in order to make it possible for disabled employees to work. You aren't required to make changes or modifications that are unjustifiably expensive or too extreme. In deciding what is and isn't required, courts have generally looked at several factors, including...

- The cost of the accommodation
- The financial resources of the employer

- The nature of the business, including its size, number of employees, and its structure
- Accommodations that have already been made by the employer.

**ALERT** *Once an employee has told you of her need for reasonable accommodations, you must not only consider her request, but you must also propose your own accommodations. You can't just leave it up to the employee. A number of consultants and firms now help* *employers develop and implement reasonable accommodations. Check with your trade or professional association or the local chamber of commerce to find a consultant who can help you.*

## FIGHT BACK AGAINST A COMPLAINT

Before an employee can bring any legal action against her employer for violating the ADA, she must first file a formal complaint with the EEOC.

Generally, the employee must file the claim within 180 days of the incident that's the subject of the complaint. The claim must be sworn to before a notary public or some other official who is authorized to administer oaths, such as a justice of the peace.

If you live in a state with its own agencies for handling discrimination complaints, the EEOC will give the state 60 days in which to take action, and the EEOC will take over jurisdiction only if the state agency refuses to act during this period. In these cases the time limit for filing a complaint with the EEOC can be extended up to as many as 300 days.

Within 10 days of receiving the complaint, the EEOC will notify you that a charge has been filed, and the agency will begin its investigation. The EEOC is empowered to look at your company records, interview the other employees as well as company officials, and summon witnesses to testify under oath.

If the EEOC decides that a violation of the ADA has taken place, it will try to help you and your employee reach a reasonable settlement. By law, the EEOC has 180 days in which to negotiate a settlement that's acceptable to both of you.

If there is no way to reach a mutually agreeable settlement, however, the EEOC can either:

- **Bring legal action** against the company on the employee's behalf.
- **Give the employee a right-to-sue letter,** which allows her 90 days in which to file a lawsuit against you.

## PROTECT YOURSELF

Don't assume that an employee who files a claim of ADA-prohibited discrimination will always

### SMART MOVES

It's wise to carefully document problems you have with employees, their responses to problems, and disciplinary actions you take. Having written records can help rebut an employee's claim that she's been treated differently than other employees or in a way that violates federal and state antidiscrimination laws. Be sure your treatment of employees is consistent.

succeed with the claim. Here are just some of the defenses that you can raise:

- **The employee failed to follow legal procedures** and deadlines. An employee who misses the deadline for filing an ADA complaint or fails to have the complaint notarized may not be able to prevail. Similarly, an employee who fails to contact the EEOC or the appropriate state agency before the filing deadline isn't entitled to the ADA's protections.
- **Your workplace isn't covered by the ADA.** The federal law applies only to those businesses with 15 or more full- or part-time employees for at least 20 weeks during the current or previous calendar year. Also be aware that some state laws will apply to companies with fewer employers. Your local Chamber of Commerce, the state department of labor, or your attorney can give you specific information about your state's statutes concerning employees' disability rights.
- **The employee is not disabled under the terms of the ADA**. Not every physical or mental condition qualifies as a disability under the ADA. For example, some courts have held that nervousness or anxiety about meeting the public isn't a disabling condition. Other courts around the country have held that conditions that last only for a brief period don't qualify an employee for ADA protection.
- **You made reasonable efforts to accommodate the employee.** As we've already said, an employer isn't required to do everything imaginable or unreasonably expensive to accommodate a disabled worker. If her absences occurred despite your efforts to accommodate her, you may be in the clear.
- **Accommodating this employee would cause your business undue hardship.** Allowing the employee to continue missing work requires finding replacement workers and incurring added training costs, and could result in the loss of business to your firm. Taken together, these factors could add up to more than the law requires.

■ **The employee violated company policy.** If your company's stated policy requires workers to notify their supervisor when they will be absent, the employee's failure to comply with that requirement could justify her dismissal.

**TAKE NOTE** *You can get additional guidance on the ADA and the regulations that have been passed to help employers implement its provisions by going to the Department of Justice's Web site at www.usdoj.gov.*

## SO WHEN CAN YOU FIRE AN EMPLOYEE?

While it may seem as if letting an employee go is almost certain to get you into legal hot water, there are plenty of reasons the courts recognize as legitimate for firing an employee. Employees can be fired…

- For making false statements in their job application or resume
- For failing to make productivity requirements
- For excessive absenteeism or tardiness
- For engaging in criminal activity
- For failing to follow company rules
- For endangering or threatening coworkers, managers, or customers
- For fighting at work
- For gambling on the job
- For revealing company secrets or confidential information to competitors
- For drug or alcohol use at work
- For possessing dangerous weapons, such as guns or switchblade knives, in the workplace
- For stealing or dishonesty
- For failing to follow supervisors' reasonable instructions
- For sexually harassing coworkers or customers
- For misuse of company property or conducting personal business on company time
- For being convicted of a crime
- Because the business no longer requires the employee's services
- For being incapable of doing the required work due to a physical or mental disability and there is no way to provide a reasonable accommodation.

What's almost as important as your reason for dismissing an employee is how you go about it. Be sure to follow your company's rules and procedures before terminating an employee. If you've established a progressive disciplinary system that requires workers to receive a series of oral or written warnings or to have the right to a hearing before being dismissed, firing a worker without giving him or her the benefits of that system could land you in legal trouble.

You can limit the possibility of an unhappy ex-employee taking legal action by avoiding the temptation to make insulting or derogatory remarks in the firing process and by refusing to discuss reasons for the termination with other employees, business associates, and customers.

*Several of your employees are complaining
about a coworker's lewd comments and sexually explicit jokes.*

After decades of sensitivity training workshops, news reports about sexual harassment, and even the near downfall of a U.S. president, sexual misconduct in the workplace remains a problem. As an employer, you need to take decisive action if you discover that one of your employees is behaving in an unacceptable manner. Failing to investigate claims of sexual harassment, or refusing to act when investigation verifies that harassment is taking place can put you and your business at jeopardy in the courts.

You should keep the complaining employees informed about the status of the investigation you're conducting, but be careful about revealing too many details too soon. Early findings could be contradicted by something you discover later. Making derogatory comments about an employee who's later found to be innocent of the charges could open the door for a defamation lawsuit.

If your investigation discloses that the complaining employees' concerns are warranted, decide what disciplinary action to take.

- **You may have no choice** but to dismiss the worker, especially in a small company.
- **You might retrain the worker** about sexual harassment issues and assign him to another part of the company with a warning that further inappropriate conduct will result in termination.

Consider bringing in outside trainers to heighten employee awareness of what behaviors violate your company's anti-harassment policies. Doing so sends a message that your company doesn't tolerate offensive behavior or comments. Obtain information about training and awareness from the Equal Employment Opportunity Commission and your state's civil rights agency.

## WHAT YOU SHOULD DO

As soon as you are made aware of a problem involving sexual harassment, you should begin to conduct a thorough and fair investigation. That means interviewing the employees making the complaints and the one who's the source of the complaints. Conduct the interviews privately. Be sure to take notes about what you are told and to remain impartial. Don't make rash statements to the accusers about the punishment you intend to mete out; don't dismiss the seriousness of their concerns. Your first job is to determine if a problem actually exists, and not to prejudge the case.

## WHEN AN EMPLOYEE IS VIOLENT

In some cases, employees have been guilty of threatening sexual assaults or carrying them out against coworkers. In these cases, contact your company's attorney immediately and prepare for the employee's termination. Also contact local law-enforcement authorities to find out what protective orders may be available to bar a potentially violent ex-employee from the workplace. Failing to act quickly and decisively not only endangers employees and yourself, but also could leave you open to a lawsuit if the violent worker remains on the job.

RETIREMENT YEARS

---

*You've been offered early retirement,
but your employer wants you to sign a waiver and give up
your right to sue for age discrimination.*

---

All the evidence tells us that older workers have lower absentee rates, are more productive, and are cheaper to hire and train than younger workers. Yet many companies prefer to keep younger people and let older ones go when faced with a reduction in the work force.

Of course, terminating an employee's job on the basis of age is prohibited under the federal Age Discrimination in Employment Act (ADEA). The ADEA protects people older than 40 who work for companies that have at least 20 employees. Workers covered by the ADEA are entitled to file age-discrimination claims against their employers with the Equal Employment Opportunity Commission (EEOC). Similar laws in some states cover companies with fewer than 20 employees and employees younger than 40.

Unfortunately, some employers try to avoid age-discrimination claims by having an employee waive his or her right to sue under the ADEA—usually in exchange for additional severance pay (or sometimes under the threat that failing to sign the waiver will result in the loss of expected benefits or pay). Under the ADEA and also under the federal Older Workers Benefit Protection Act, an employer is permitted to ask an employee to sign such an agreement, but the waiver is valid only if it is made knowingly and voluntarily. This means that the waiver…

- Must be in writing that's easily understood by the employee
- Must specifically refer to your right to file a claim with the EEOC and also mention your right to file suit charging age discrimination, which is permissible under the ADEA
- Can't require you to waive any rights that you may obtain after you sign the waiver
- Must give you something in exchange for your promise not to pursue your ADEA rights and claims in addition to what you were already entitled to by law and company policy
- Must contain a provision advising you to consult an attorney before you sign such a waiver
- Must give you at least 21 days to consider the agreement or 45 days if you are part of a group or class of employees who are receiving a retirement incentive
- Can be revoked by you for up to 7 days after you *execute*, or sign, the waiver.

### CONSIDER THE OFFER CAREFULLY

Don't allow yourself to be bullied into signing any waiver before you're ready. If your employer is covered by the ADEA, the law is on your side.

To determine if your company's offer is a good deal for you, talk it over with your accountant, tax adviser, or attorney. Your lawyer can also review the document to make sure that it complies with the ADEA requirements and any other requirements under your state's laws.

If you're not convinced that the offer is to your benefit, you can try to negotiate a better one.

While it's possible to negotiate on your own, getting an attorney to represent you—either by letter or face-to-face with your employer—might be a cost-effective alternative. Hiring a lawyer to handle the matter will show your employer that

---

*The federal Age Discrimination in Employment Act (ADEA)...protects people over the age of 40 who work for companies with at least 20 employees.*

---

you're serious about your claim to additional pay or benefits. Besides, your employer has probably had legal assistance in deciding what to offer for your waiver. On your own, you will be up against

highly paid and experienced advisers who may have handled dozens, even hundreds, of age-discrimination situations like yours.

To find an attorney experienced in handling age-discrimination cases, ask for recommendations from your friends or business associates who have already received an offer of early retirement. You can also call your state or local bar association's lawyer-referral service to get the names of lawyers who can handle age-discrimination cases.

### WHAT IF YOU DECIDE NOT TO SIGN?

Your employer may let you go even if you don't agree to execute a waiver of your ADEA rights, and you will most likely be denied the additional benefits that were offered as an inducement to influence you to sign. If you believe you've been let go in violation of federal or state laws, you can file a complaint with the EEOC or your state's civil-rights agency (see "Filing a Complaint with the EEOC," page 312).

---

**Your 401(k) is heavily invested in your own company's stock. Now the stock is tumbling.**

---

The popularity of 401(k) retirement plans has grown rapidly in recent years. These plans are offered at companies large and small. While it's not required, a substantial number of these companies also match employee contributions, either in whole or in part—making the 401(k) a good way to increase your retirement savings quickly.

Some companies match employee contributions with stock in the company itself. For example, Coca-Cola employees have had 80 percent or more of their 401(k)s invested in company stock. If you work for a company that's employee owned through an employee stock-ownership plan (ESOP), all of your 401(k) may be invested

### SMART MOVES

Even if you can't make the maximum contribution to your 401(K), putting just a few dollars in each pay period makes sense, especially when your employer matches your contribution.

in company stock. So the value of your retirement account will pretty much depend on the success or failure of the company where you work. When things are good, the worth of your 401(k) can rise dramatically. But if your employer suffers a setback or if the company loses a valuable piece of business, your retirement account can suffer just as dramatically.

Generally, federal government regulations give employers the option of offering one of two kinds of 401(k) plans. In the first, the employer agrees to accept a *fiduciary responsibility*, requiring it to act in the best interests of its employees. With this kind of plan, an employer is free to offer any kind of investment vehicle, including only company stock. But he makes bad investment decisions and employees lose money as a result, the employer can be held liable.

In the second kind of plan, an employer can limit liability for losses by...

● Offering at least three diversified investment choices that allow employees to pick from several risk and return possibilities—for example, a plan might allow employees to invest in a mutual fund of blue-chip stocks, stocks of small U.S. companies, and still another in bonds. Employees can also be offered company stock, but this doesn't count against the three-choice minimum.
● Allowing employees to make changes in their choice of investment options at least every three months
● Providing adequate disclosure about each of the investment options
● Offering employee communication and education programs to help workers make decisions about which investments to select.

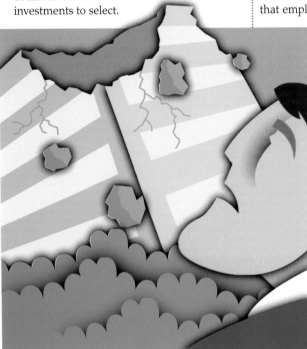

Generally, companies that meet all the requirements of this second kind of 401(k) plan won't be liable for any losses that you might suffer. But companies may still be responsible if they fail to pick good investment managers or fail to investigate the options they offer to employees to make sure that they are varied enough.

## WHAT YOU CAN DO

If your 401(k) investment is decreasing and you think the problem is serious, you should...

■ **Look at the summary plan description** of your 401(k). It should describe the type of plan in which your money is invested.
■ **Switch your money out of company stock** and into another kind of investment if your plan allows this option.
■ **Contact your plan administrator** and express your concern about the way that your contributions are being invested.
■ **Talk to your union representative**—if you're a union member—about including changes to the company's 401(k) plan in the next round of collective bargaining.

## GETTING HELP FROM THE GOVERNMENT

You can contact the U.S. Department of Labor (DOL) if you believe that your plan is being administered in a way that is violating the terms of the summary plan description for the company that employees you. The DOL can investigate the situation; if the DOL determines that the plan is being run in violation of the law, the DOL can order your employer to come into compliance. Under federal law, a plan that doesn't fully comply with the Employee Retirement Income Security Act (ERISA) can lose its tax-qualified status. If this happens, your employer can be required to pay back taxes and also pay penalties on its 401(k) contributions—a powerful incentive to make sure that everything is on the up-and-up.

## YOUR LAST RESORT

In a few cases, courts have allowed employees to sue employers when their company's 401(k) plan has been heavily weighted with company stock and the plan's trustees failed to switch to other investments when the company stock declined. In the year 2000, several lawsuits across the country alleging mismanagement and breach of the company's fiduciary responsibility are currently being litigated.

This isn't the kind of case for the average neighborhood lawyer to take on. Bringing a suit against the company you work for and the investment plan's trustees and administrators will require some very specialized legal help. You and your fellow employees will need a lawyer who has experience in practicing in the area of pension law. Contact your local bar association or law school and ask them to refer you to experienced lawyers who work in this field.

## THE SUMMARY PLAN DESCRIPTION

Under the Employee Retirement Income Security Act (ERISA), the administrator of a 401(k) plan or other pension plans is required to file what's known as a *summary plan description*, or SPD, with the U.S. Department of Labor. Every employee who participates in the plan must receive a copy of this document within 90 days of becoming a plan participant. In language that can be understood by the average plan participant, the SPD must include…

- The name of the plan

- The employer's name and address

- The employer's EIN (Employer Identification Number)

- The type of plan being offered—for example, whether the plan is a defined-contribution plan, such as a 401(k) or defined-benefit plan (such as a more traditional pension)

- The name, address, and telephone number of the plan administrator

- The name, title, and address of the plan's trustee

- The way the plan is administered

- The name and address of the plan's legal counsel

- The plan's eligibility requirements

- A statement about the plan's joint and survivor benefits

- A description of the plan's vesting requirements (that is, the time period after which you earn the right to receive benefits)

- A description of any provisions in a collective-bargaining agreement that affect your pension rights

- Sources of plan contributions, and how those contributions are calculated

- How the plan may be terminated

- Procedures to follow to make claims or seek remedies for breach of the plan

- A statement describing the ERISA rights of plan participants.

Your employer must also provide you with an updated SPD every five years describing any and all changes and amendments made to the plan.

*You need money from your 401(k) for medical expenses, but you've been told you must pay a penalty for early withdrawal.*

While a 401(k) can be a smart way to build a nest egg for retirement, you can have problems getting at your money in the meantime. Except in very limited circumstances, once the money is put into a 401(k), it can't be taken out of the plan until…

- You reach age 59½
- You leave the company
- You die or become disabled
- The plan is terminated
- The company sponsoring the plan is sold.

As a way around these limitations in some circumstances, the federal government allows (but doesn't require) plans to permit *hardship withdrawals.* Under Internal Revenue Service (IRS) regulations, hardship withdrawals are allowed *only* when you have an immediate and pressing financial need *and only* when you have exhausted all of your other financial resources.

There are four situations that can qualify you for a hardship withdrawal:

- To pay medical expenses for you, your spouse, or other dependents
- To make the down payment on a home that will be your principal residence
- To prevent foreclosure and/or eviction from your current principal residence
- To pay tuition and to pay other fees for the coming year of college for yourself, your spouse, or for dependents.

You'll be required to pay income taxes on the money you take out of your 401(k) plan, plus a penalty of 10 percent of the amount you withdraw. And you won't be allowed to make any new contributions to your 401(k) for a full year.

## A BETTER CHOICE

Instead of applying for a hardship withdrawal from your 401(k), you may be far better off borrowing from it. In fact, if your plan allows you to borrow, you're required to apply for a loan before being considered for a hardship withdrawal.

A recent study of 401(k) plans showed that more than 80 percent of companies allow 401(k) loans. You can probably borrow from your plan for just about any reason, although some needs, such as to make a down payment on a house or to pay medical expenses, are clearly better incentives than using the money for other purchases, such as for buying a more expensive car or planning and taking a vacation.

Although most rules for getting a loan from your 401(k) are set by your employer, the federal government places some limitations on how much you can borrow and the interest you will be charged. Generally, you can't borrow more than 50 percent of the value of the money in your plan, to a maximum of $50,000. In most cases, the loan must be repaid within five years (longer if it's used to purchase a principal residence). The plan must charge interest at the market rate—generally the rate a bank or savings and loan would charge its customers for a similar loan.

## SOME DRAWBACKS TO 401(K) LOANS

A loan from your 401(k) can have serious consequences. For example, most plans don't allow you to continue making your loan payments if you leave your employer or if you're fired. You must pay the entire outstanding balance in a lump sum, which can be extremely difficult if you've just lost your job.

In case you simply can't repay the balance, the IRS will treat the amount as a taxable distribution, and you are expected to pay taxes and a 10 percent penalty when you file your 1040 form. That should be reason enough to consider a 401(k) loan only for essential expenditures and not for frivolous reasons.

## HOW TO GET 401(K) FUNDS

If you're still interested in obtaining a 401(k) loan or you think you may be eligible for a hardship withdrawal, contact your company's employee-benefits administrator for information about the steps to take under the specific terms of your plan. If you are asking for a hardship withdrawal, you'll be expected to provide very clear documentation of the nature of your need—as well as information about what other resources you have and how they have been depleted—before your application can be approved.

All this time, you thought your retirement was secure. Now you learn that, for whatever reasons, your hard-earned pension money is going down the drain. Are you really back at square one? What can you do?

Under Employment Retirement Income Security Act (ERISA)—the federal law that governs the administration of most pension plans—those who manage your pension's investments are required to act *prudently,* making wise and careful investments and not commingling pension funds with other company accounts or investments. Pension-plan administrators are legally required to make plan investments *solely in the interest of the plan's participants.* That means that they can't use the money to further

their own business interests or the financial interests of family members or friends.

While the majority of pension plans are well managed, even pension administrators with the best intentions sometimes find themselves making poor choices of investment vehicles. The administrator may have invested in stocks that take a nosedive, or could have invested in real-estate ventures that fail to materialize, or in other

kinds of investments that never achieve the expected returns. Very small plans are often run by company owners, who may be tempted to raid the firm's pension fund in order to get through a business slowdown. When their business doesn't pick up, the pension funds are not reimbursed. In some cases, pension administrators intentionally misuse or embezzle pension funds. According to a study conducted in the state of New York, corrupt pension officials can steal enormous sums of pension money simply by…

- Withdrawing money in their own names or under fictitious names
- Writing checks in payment for various goods or services that were never received or to companies that do not exist
- Investing in other "businesses" that they actually secretly own or that the pension officials actually control
- Making loans to themselves, to friends, and even to organized crime figures, with the money never being repaid to the fund
- Awarding contracts for plan medical and legal benefits at inflated prices to firms that "kick back" a portion of the payment to the plan administrator.

## KNOW WHAT'S GOING ON

It's important for you to ask your pension administrator for a periodic accounting of your pension plan's assets. By law, your 401(k) plan must provide you with a *summary annual report,* or SAR. This report should include the following:

- A statement about whether the plan's investments have made or lost money, and the total amount lost or gained
- A detailed report showing a breakdown of the plan's administrative expenses for the year
- Whether any money that's been lent out from the plan has been paid back on time

● Whether there are any financial arrangements between the plan and persons closely connected to its administrators. These kinds of arrangements are generally prohibited, although in certain cases, Department of Labor (DOL) rulings allow exceptions.

Pensions administered for 100 or more employees must also file an annual statement (Form 5500) with the Department of Labor, while pensions covering less than 100 employees must file a similar, although less detailed, document every three years. You can obtain a copy of the form for your plan by requesting it in writing from the plan administrator, who is allowed to charge you a reasonable copying fee. But be on the lookout for…

● Big fees paid to investment managers, lawyers, and other consultants by the plan
● Big salaries paid to plan administrators
● Unusually high rent charged to the company for the plan-administrators' offices
● The types of investments your plan holds—these should be a diverse mix of stocks, bonds, mutual funds, and other investments. Diversity ensures than if one or more investment types go sour, the others will help to protect your plan from losing all of its accumulated value.

## What Government Can and Can't Do

Federal reporting requirements may not be enough to protect you when your pension fund begins to shrink rapidly. The Department of Labor (DOL) has only a relative handful of investigators to audit pension statements, so small-investment plans may never be reviewed by it—putting you at the mercy of your plan administrator's investment savvy, honesty, and integrity.

Most DOL investigations are triggered when a participant raises questions about fund management. The minute that you suspect that your

pension plan is experiencing financial trouble, contact the Department of Labor's Pension and Welfare Benefit Administration (PWBA), at 200 Constitution Ave., NW, Washington DC 20210, call (202) 219-8233, or visit its Web site at www.dol.gov.

The DOL can investigate, but in some cases, it may take months or even years—while your pension continues to erode. In other cases, the investigation may be perfunctory. If you, fellow employees, and retirees are not satisfied with the way the DOL handles its investigation, contact the news media. Media pressure has persuaded the DOL to reopen many closed or dormant investigations. If the DOL finds evidence of wrongdoing, it has some options:

● In the majority of cases, DOL will try to reach a voluntary agreement requiring plan administrators to return funds that are missing due to mismanagement.
● If a voluntary agreement with plan administrators can't be reached, the DOL can file a civil suit to obtain restitution for you.
● If there is theft or self-dealing, the DOL can refer the case to the Department of Justice for criminal proceedings. Plan administrators found guilty of violating federal law can be sentenced to up to five years in federal prison, fined $10,000, or both for each conviction.

You don't have to wait for the government to act. You can contact a lawyer who's experienced in pension law. Ask the lawyer to look into the possibility of filing a private lawsuit on your behalf against pension administrators. In several cases, courts have awarded multimillion dollar judgments against pension administrators who stole or embezzled funds from the plans they ran. A court could find that an honest but inept plan administrator had failed to meet obligations to the plan by making a series of poor investments.

### SMART MOVES

In addition to the DOL, consider contacting the Internal Revenue Service's Intelligence Unit. If your pension administrator has been engaged in self-dealing or embezzlement, there's a good chance he hasn't reported the money on his tax return. As a whistleblower, you may be entitled to receive a percentage of any back taxes the IRS collects.

*You disagree with the amount of the pension your company's employee-benefits department says you will be paid.*

You've done the addition and it appears as if your pension will fall short of your expectations. But don't assume that your figures are wrong without checking into it.

In most pension plans, the administrator is required to provide you with an *individual-benefit statement* at your written request.

By law, your plan administrator must respond to your written request within 30 days. Your individual benefit statement will include information about the following topics:

● The plan's vesting requirements (see "Pensions and Your 'Vested' Interest," page 368)
● Whether or not you are vested in your pension plan, either partially or fully
● How much your annual retirement pension would be at age 65 if you were to leave your company as of the date of the statement.

This statement may not answer all the questions you have about your pension, and if the figures it contains don't jibe with your calculations, you'll want to ask more questions.

### WHAT YOU SHOULD DO

You'll need to ask your retirement-pension plan administrator for enough information to help you determine if your benefit statement is correct. Be sure to find out:

■ **If the benefit shown is what you will receive** as a single or a married retiree. Under the federal Retirement Equity Act (REA), if you're married at the time you begin receiving benefits, the amount you receive will be reduced in order to provide a pension benefit for your spouse if you die first, unless your spouse agrees in writing to give up the benefit.

■ **The formula that was used to calculate your benefit**—In some cases, your pension plan may show your projected benefit if you continued working for the company until retirement age. This figure can be quite different from what you'll actually get, especially if you won't be reaching retirement age soon. Long before you receive benefits, your employer might alter the method used to calculate benefits, such as ending automatic cost-of-living adjustments, fire you or lay you off, terminate the pension plan, or the company could even go out of business.

■ **If your company's pension plan integrates benefits with the amount you'll receive from Social Security.** For example, your plan may project that you'll get $3,500 per month upon retirement, but the plan may estimate that you'll be receiving $1,200 from Social Security. This means your actual pension benefit would be $2,300 per month.

Your pension benefit could also be less than you expect if you had a *break in service* with your employer that lasted at least five years and was longer than the period of time you worked for the employer before you took the break. For instance, if you took a six-year break after working for the company for only five years—working for another company, for example, or going back to college—the benefits you accrued during the earlier period of employment may be lost.

> **TAKE NOTE** *Military service in time of war or national emergency or a year off work to care for a newborn or newly-adopted child cannot be counted toward a break in eligible service. Other break-in-service rules are complicated, and companies can be more generous than the law requires when setting these rules.*

Your union representative or a lawyer experienced in pension law can help you review your retirement plan to determine if the benefit your plan projects is being estimated accurately. If you're still not satisfied, or if you run into roadblocks obtaining an individual-benefit statement, you can contact the nearest office of the Department of Labor's Pension and Welfare Benefit Administration for professional help.

---

**Y**ou receive a statement of benefits from Social Security, but it doesn't reflect all of your earnings over the years.

---

**Y**ou'll probably be pleasantly surprised to learn how much money you've earned since you got your first job. In the year 2000, the Social Security Administration (SSA) began sending a *personal earnings and benefits statement* to everyone age 25 and over. Generally, this computer-generated form includes all of the earnings that have been credited to your account up to a date shown on the form. Using these figures, the SSA will estimate what you would be entitled to receive at retirement in current dollars.

As with all computerized data, however, mistakes happen, and there's the possibility that the form won't show all earnings for a certain year. The usual reason is a mistake your employer made in reporting your wages—for example, transposing digits in your Social Security number or using someone else's number. In some cases,

the error might be due to a mistake in entering information into the system—leaving a zero off your account so that the $30,000 you earned appears as $3,000 in the statement you receive. The SSA admits that about one percent of all earnings records contain errors, and some experts think there may be even more.

### CORRECTING ERRORS

It's important to review your statement when you receive it from the SSA. If you discover an error, getting it corrected isn't always difficult, but it can take some patience. Here's what to do:

■ **Call the SSA** at the toll-free number shown on the form and report the error. In a few cases, the SSA telephone representative may be able to correct the problem by telephone.

- **Ask the telephone representative** exactly what documentation you must provide to get the error corrected, and be sure to get her name and title for your records. In most cases you'll have to send a letter notifying the SSA of the problem.
- **Include a request to the SSA in your letter** asking that the SSA update your records and provide you with a new statement so that you can be sure the correction has been entered into your records.
- **Keep a copy of your letter** and copies of any supporting documents you send to the SSA.

Generally, you can expect to wait about six to eight weeks for a reply and a new benefit statement. If you don't have a response by then, call the SSA again and ask the same representative to follow up on your request. Eventually, your record should be corrected to show the correct amount of earnings you were paid.

### IF THE PROBLEM PERSISTS

It's possible that the SSA won't accept your claim that you're entitled to higher benefits. But you have a couple of options that you can pursue to get the SSA's decision changed.

- **Contact your local Social Security office** for a reconsideration. You'll find it in the federal government pages of your telephone directory, or call (800) 772-1213. Find out what steps you must take (such as providing additional evidence) to have the decision reviewed.
- **Ask for a hearing** if you can't get the SSA to see things your way; you have the right to a hearing before an administrative law judge (ALJ). If you are still dissatisfied, you can ask for a hearing by the SSA's appeals council. Finally, you can file suit against the SSA in federal-district court.

It's unlikely that you'll need to attend these procedures, but if so, talk to a lawyer experienced in Social Security appeals. Even if he doesn't appear at hearings or in court, he can provide guidance to you if you handle matters yourself.

**ALERT** *If you're not yet 25 years of age, you won't automatically receive a benefits statement from the SSA. However, you can request an Earnings and Benefits Estimate Statement by writing to the SSA and requesting it, by visiting your nearest Social Security office, or by making your request on-line at www.ssa.gov.*

---

## THE INCREDIBLE RISING RETIREMENT AGE

For decades, workers knew that they could receive their maximum Social Security retirement benefits when they reached age 65. But beginning in 2000, you'll have to stay on the job after your 65th birthday in order to get all the Social Security benefits you're entitled to. According to the Social Security Administration, here's when you can expect to qualify for your full benefits:

| Year of Birth | Age to Receive Full Benefits | Year of Birth | Age to Receive Full Benefits |
|---|---|---|---|
| pre-1938 | 65 years 0 months | 1955 | 66 years 2 months |
| 1938 | 65 years 2 months | 1956 | 66 years 4 months |
| 1939 | 65 years 4 months | 1957 | 66 years 6 months |
| 1940 | 65 years 6 months | 1958 | 66 years 8 months |
| 1941 | 65 years 8 months | 1959 | 66 years 10 months |
| 1942 | 65 years 10 months | 1960 and later | 67 years 0 months |
| 1943–1954 | 66 years 0 months | | |

> **Y**ou get a letter offering to help you
> obtain your Social Security benefits—in return for a fee.

For decades, older Americans have been besieged with letters from individuals and companies with official-sounding names regarding their retirement benefits. These companies offer to get estimates of Social Security benefits, obtain benefit payments, and

---

*If you are contacted by a company claiming it can get you more benefits or offering to obtain your Social Security benefits statement in return for a fee, call the Social Security Administration and report the solicitation.*

---

even increase the amount you will receive from Social Security when you retire. Typically, the fee for this so-called "service" is relatively low, usually about $15 to $20.

These offers are almost always worthless, and you should avoid them. Getting your benefits estimate is now automatic if you are age 25 or older. You'll receive a report from the SSA each year. You can check your benefits more often at the Social Security Administration's Web site: www.ssa.gov.

There isn't any way for a company to obtain higher benefits for you than your earnings record or the earnings record of your spouse will allow. Checking your annual benefits estimate will tell you if the SSA has incorrectly recorded your earnings.

### GETTING YOUR BENEFITS

Obtaining your retirement benefits is something only you can do. The process is really simple, although it

can take some time. Social Security offices are often busy. Experts suggest that you avoid visiting or calling Social Security during the first week of the month, on Mondays and Fridays, and in the middle of any day.

The steps you need to follow to start receiving your benefits include…

- **Beginning the process three months before you retire.** Otherwise, you may not receive a check in the month you stop working, although you will receive it later.
- **Calling your local Social Security office.** You'll find it listed in the federal government pages of your telephone directory, or you can call (800)-772-1213 for information. Get the office hours. Ask whether you can schedule an appointment with a Social Security representative or if new applicants are accepted only on a walk-in basis.

When you visit the office to apply for your benefits, be sure to bring:

- Your Social Security number, or better yet, the card, if you can locate it

• Proof of your age, such as a certified copy of your birth certificate or baptismal certificate

• Evidence of your past two years' earnings, such as W-2 forms from your employer or your income-tax return if you are self-employed. If the latter is the case, be sure to bring your Form SE to show your most recent Social Security contributions.

• Information about the account into which you want your payments deposited. Although some recipients still get their benefit checks by mail, applicants must use direct deposit. That's all there is to it. Your Social Security payment should be deposited into your bank account on the same date each month.

## FIGHTING OFF SOLICITORS

If you are contacted by a company claiming that it can get you more benefits or offering to obtain your Social Security benefits statement in return for a fee, call the Social Security Administration and report the solicitation.

You may also want to file a complaint with Postal Service inspectors. Your local post office can provide you with information about the exact steps to take in order to file your complaint.

## GET HIGHER SOCIAL SECURITY BENEFITS BY DELAYING RETIREMENT

Most of us know that retiring *before* the normal Social Security retirement age results in a permanent reduction of monthly benefits. It's not as well known that Social Security rewards those who wait until *after* normal retirement age to begin collecting their checks. The extra amount is being increased on a graduated basis: for example, a worker born in 1943 who waits until age 67 to begin collecting Social Security benefits instead of retiring at age 66 will get a permanent increase of 8 percent. Wait until age 68, and the extra amount is nearly 17 percent, because the 8 percent increase compounds annually.

Should you consider waiting an extra few years in order to boost the size of your Social Security check? You need to compare the increase in monthly checks with the shorter length of time you're likely to receive them. But if you're in good health and earning a high salary (which will also result in a higher retirement benefit when you do begin collecting from Social Security), or if you can make it for a year or two after you retire without Social Security benefits, delaying signing up for Social Security may be a strategy worth considering. Talk to your accountant or other financial adviser for specific advice about your retirement plan.

---

*You're about to turn 62, and you want
Social Security benefits based on your ex-husband's work record.*

Under federal law, a divorced spouse is entitled to receive Social Security benefits based on an ex-spouse's earnings.

In order to be entitled to these benefits, however, you must have been married for at least 10 years before your divorce took place. You can begin receiving these benefits when you reach age 62, provided that your ex-husband is at least 62 years old. You're entitled to receive them even if he continues to work, provided that the divorce took place at least two years before you file your claim. You can receive the benefits even if your "ex" has remarried, although they will usually make you ineligible, or terminate, if you remarry.

Think very carefully before you file a claim. If you apply for benefits at age 62, you'll be subject to a *permanent reduction* in the amount you receive from Social Security. Instead of being eligible for half of your ex-husband's benefit, you'll be entitled to slightly more than a third of his benefit amount. For example, suppose your ex-husband's benefit would be $1,500 at retirement age. If you were to begin collecting benefits at age 65, you'd get a monthly Social Security payment of $750 a month. But if you begin taking your payments at age 62, you'll get only $562.50. And as the normal retirement age increases from 65 to 67, the reduction in payments will be greater.

### How to Start Collecting

Assuming that you'll need to begin receiving Social Security benefits at age 62, you will apply just as if you were seeking benefits based on your own work record.

You need to provide your own Social Security card, a certified copy of your birth certificate, and proof of your earnings over the past two years, such as W-2 forms or your federal 1040 forms. In addition, you must provide some additional documentation to the Social Security Administration:

● A certified copy of your original marriage certificate
● A copy of your divorce decree to prove how long you were married and how long ago you were divorced.

---

**You will apply just as if you were seeking benefits based on your own work record.**

---

Provide all of the above documentation, and you shouldn't have any trouble getting benefits based on your ex-husband's earnings. But as with any bureaucracy, it's possible for things to go wrong. Application forms can be misfiled, addresses can be entered incorrectly, Social Security numbers can be transposed. To protect yourself against a Social Security snafu, be sure to get the name, title, and telephone number of any Social Security employee with whom you communicate. Make a log of the dates and times of all of your conversations, note the substance of those conversations in a paragraph or two, and keep the log in your files.

Make and keep copies of all the applications and other documents you supply to the Social Security Administration. If a document goes astray, you can supply a copy quickly and help minimize processing delays.

Write your Social Security number at the top of each page of documents you submit to the administration. The reason?

The administration files all of its documents by Social Security numbers; putting your Social Security number on each page will make it easier for Social Security employees to get a document's pages back in the right place if one becomes separated from the rest of your file.

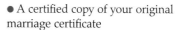

> *Years ago, you worked for a company that promised you a pension. Now you've retired, but you can't claim your benefits because you can't locate the company.*

Having more than 40 or 50 years of employment behind you means that you've probably worked for several companies. But it's not always easy to keep track of an employer who promised you pension benefits back in the early days of your career. Companies change their names, merge with former competitors, are acquired by companies from unrelated industries, or take over other businesses and assume their names. Workers move from town to town and state to state, get married, change their names, remarry and change their names again. A worker dies, and his or her spouse doesn't know that a pension exists. According to one lawyer, thousands of American workers or their survivors are entitled to pension benefits that they aren't receiving, either because the company can't find them or because they can't find the company.

### SEARCHING FOR A PAST EMPLOYER

If you believe you were promised a pension from a previous employer but can't find the company in order to claim it, here's what to do:

- **Check your home files** for a summary plan description, benefits booklet, pension account statement, or anything else from your old employer that describes the plan you were enrolled in and that contains the employer's, name, address, and telephone number.
- **Call or write former coworkers** and ask them to help you locate your old employer.
- **Contact the local government where the company was located.** City records may contain information about successor companies or the company's address after it moved.
- **Check with the secretary of state's office** in the state where you live. It can search its records to see if the company is still authorized to do business in the state, and if so, it can provide you with an address. If the company was in a different state, you must contact the Secretary of State's office in the state where the business was located.
- **Write to the Pension Benefit Guaranty Corporation** (PBGC) or visit its Web site at www.pbgc.gov to see if it has any information. The PBGC's pension search program is

designed for situations just like yours. The PBGC maintains a free on-line directory of people who are owed pension benefits by plans that have been terminated and the names of the companies that sponsored those plans. When contacting the PBGC either by email or letter, be sure to provide as much information as possible, including...

- ✔ Your name, address, and telephone number
- ✔ Your date of birth
- ✔ Your Social Security number
- ✔ The name of the company you think may be holding benefits for you, if you know it
- ✔ The dates you were employed there
- ✔ Any other information that could be helpful, such as an Employer Identification Number or even a copy of an old pay stub.

For more information about the PBGC's pension search program, request a free copy of its booklet entitled "Finding a Lost Pension"—also available on-line at www.pbgc.gov.

### OTHER PLACES TO LOOK

Not all pensions are regulated by the PBGC, but don't give up yet. You can contact the Pension and Welfare Benefit Administration (PWBA) of the federal Department of Labor (DOL). Write or visit the nearest PWBA regional office (listed in the federal government blue pages of your telephone directory) or check the DOL Web site at www.dol.gov. Again, you'll need to provide as much specific information as you can. While the PBWA doesn't keep records on individuals, it does maintain records on most retirement plans, so it may be able to provide you with the correct contact information for a former employer even if the company has moved, merged, or been acquired by another company.

Finally, you can contact your state treasurer or the secretary of state's office which keeps records on abandoned or unclaimed property. If your pension was administered by a bank or an insurance company, it may have turned your benefits over to the state. Most states list the unclaimed property they hold on their Web sites and also publish lists periodically in major newspapers.

**ALERT** *Beware of companies that offer to find unclaimed property in return for an up-front fee. Many of these companies are pure-and-simple scams. Once you send your money off, you never hear another thing from them. Searching state unclaimed property records isn't hard, especially if you have Internet access, and there's no cost for you to do the search.*

## WHEN YOUR PERSISTENCE PAYS

Your search has paid off, and you've found the company that you think is holding your pension benefits. It's time to write to the company's human-resources department or employee-benefits department, and claim what's owed you. Be sure to call first and get the name of the specific person and department to contact.

In your letter, you'll want to include the dates you worked for the company and the location where you were employed. Your letter should also include a request for information about…

● The amount of money being held for you by the pension plan
● How that money is available to be paid, such as whether it's going to be paid in a lump sum or as a monthly benefit
● The steps you must take to claim it.

Include your full name and the name you used when you were working, if your name was different when you worked there. Include your current address and a daytime telephone number where the company can reach you. Keep a copy of your letter for your files and send the original by certified mail, return receipt requested.

Give the company time to process your request, but don't let matters drag on. Following up with a telephone call after two to three weeks have passed may help speed the process and help you obtain the benefits you're entitled to. If delays persist, however, get in touch with the government agencies mentioned above for assistance.

---

### PENSIONS AND YOUR "VESTED" INTEREST

Under federal law, your employer can require you to stay on the job for a specified period of time before you're guaranteed to receive any benefits from the company pension plan. This process is referred to as *vesting* and falls into two categories:

■ **Gradual vesting** takes place, well, gradually. Federal law requires that you be at least 20 percent vested (entitled to 20 percent of your total retirement benefit) within three years of joining the plan and fully vested within seven years.

■ **Cliff vesting** allows employers to make you wait five years before you have any vested interest in your pension plan. But at the end of that period, you are 100 percent vested. Leave before the five years is up, and you get nothing from the pension plan.

Any money *you* put into a pension plan is considered fully vested as soon as you contribute it. No matter when you leave the company, you're entitled to take that money with you. But your employer's matching contributions will vest only according to one of the methods described above. Check your pension's summary-plan description (SPD) or contact your plan administrator for information on your company's pension-vesting provisions.

Few things in life are more difficult than the failing health or mental deterioration of a spouse. After years of working, planning, saving, and investing together, you now face handling legal and financial matters on your own. Add the emotional and psychological strain of caring for a spouse with a debilitating illness, and the results can even threaten your health.

## PREVENTING A PROBLEM

If your husband created a *durable power of attorney,* you may be able to sell the house without his signature. In a durable power of attorney, an individual (called the *principal*) appoints someone else (the *attorney-in-fact*) to handle his financial matters and to act on the principal's behalf when he is unable to do so. Many times married couples appoint each other as attorney-in-fact.

In some states, the law allows individuals to create a *springing power of attorney.* While a durable power of attorney allows the attorney-in-fact to act on behalf of the principal even when he could act for himself, a springing power of attorney takes affect only when some triggering event occurs—for example, when the principal is declared mentally incompetent by two physicians.

The first steps to take to find out if your husband executed a power of attorney are…

- **Make a careful search** of all of your family's financial files for the document.
- **Look in any safe-deposit boxes** you hold jointly with your husband.
- **Check with your family lawyer;** he may have your husband's power of attorney among his files.

Even with a power of attorney, however, you may not be entirely out of the woods. Some banks and mortgage lenders won't accept a power of attorney unless it's on one of their forms, and these forms can vary from one lender to another. If you have trouble getting your husband's durable power of attorney accepted, you may want to have your lawyer contact the lender and attempt to convince them that the document is acceptable under state law.

## GUARDIANSHIP AND CONSERVATORSHIP

If your husband never executed a durable power of attorney or if the one he created isn't acceptable for real-estate transactions, you may need to establish a guardianship or conservatorship for him. As your husband's legal guardian or conservator—the terminology differs from state to state and also depends on the responsibilities you take on—you can act on his behalf; handling his financial affairs.

> *In a durable power of attorney, an individual … appoints someone else … to handle financial matters and to act on… [his] behalf*

To become your husband's guardian or conservator, you must file a petition in state court. Call the local courthouse or check with a lawyer to find out which court handles legal guardianship and conservatorship cases. Your state's department on aging may also assist you.

Once you've filed, the court will schedule a hearing to determine whether your husband is truly in need of a guardian. You need to show evidence, such as doctors' evaluations and perhaps a social worker's statement that your husband is no longer competent to handle his affairs.

In some cases, your petition could be opposed by another family member—an adult child, for example, who may feel that she is better equipped than you to handle your husband's financial matters. And if your husband isn't convinced that he's incompetent, he also has the right to be heard by the court.

Once the court has heard all the evidence and determined that naming you as guardian is in your husband's best interest, it will issue an order to that effect. With a copy of this order, you will be able to enter into contracts on behalf of your husband, including the sale of your house.

*You were paying for your wife's nursing home expenses, but your funds are exhausted and Medicaid has taken over. The home now suggests that she may have to move to another facility.*

For someone living in a nursing home, being involuntarily transferred or discharged is deeply troubling and stressful. Some studies suggest that residents who are forced to leave nursing homes against their will have a death rate five times higher than others of the same age and health who are not subjected to moving.

Generally, nursing homes prefer residents who don't need a lot of care, who don't rock the boat with demands for activities and services, and who don't require much attention from the home's staff. They also like private-pay patients, who typically pay much more for their nursing-home stay than Medicaid's rate. In some states, Medicaid reimbursement to nursing homes falls short by as much as $100 *per day* of the actual costs of a resident's care. Even though nearly two-thirds of nursing-home residents rely on Medicaid, nursing homes sometimes try to limit the number of the Medicaid-covered residents in their facilities.

### REGULATING NURSING HOME DISCHARGES

By law, nursing-home residents can be moved out of a facility only under one of the following five conditions:

- The resident no longer needs nursing-home care because his or her condition improved.
- The resident needs medical care that cannot be provided in the nursing-home setting.
- The resident presents a threat to the health or safety of other individuals in the home.
- A private-pay patient failed to pay for care for a specified length of time. Some states, however, legally prohibit a nursing home from evicting a resident for nonpayment.
- The nursing home is planning to go out of business.

Under federal law, a nursing home isn't required to accept new residents who are covered by Medicaid. But it cannot evict a private-pay patient who converts to Medicaid, even if the home later drops out of the Medicaid program. The nursing home must continue to provide care and accept Medicaid reimbursement to all its residents covered by Medicaid at the time the home decides to withdraw from Medicaid.

**TAKE NOTE** *An eviction or transfer is never permitted if it would be more harmful to the resident's health than would allowing her to stay in the present facility.*

### TRANSFER PROCEEDINGS AND RESIDENTS' RIGHTS

Some nursing-home operators have attempted to circumvent Medicaid laws by claiming that the eviction is for legally permissible reasons. For example, the nursing home may claim that your wife's condition no longer warrants a stay in a nursing home and that she would be better off if she were living at home.

The law offers strong protections to nursing-home residents to avoid being surprised by a sudden eviction notice. Generally, a nursing home must provide written notice to the resident, the resident's guardian or conservator, or a legally liable relative at least 30 days before the proposed move. This notice must include…

- The reason for the transfer or discharge
- The date of the proposed transfer or discharge of the resident
- The location to which the nursing home intends to transfer the resident
- The right to a hearing to oppose the resident's transfer or discharge
- A description of the procedures to follow to request a hearing
- The deadline by which the request for a hearing must be made
- Residents' rights to represent themselves or to have a lawyer, relative, friend, or any other person represent them at the hearing
- The name, address, and telephone number of the state's long-term-care ombudsman, who may be able to intervene on the Medicaid resident's behalf.

If the nursing home is proposing to transfer your wife to a hospital, it must also provide information about holding her bed at the home and the procedures for readmission to the nursing home when her health has sufficiently improved.

Medicaid laws also require the nursing home to develop a written discharge plan before evicting or transferring a resident. Except in an emergency, the nursing home must provide the plan to the resident or the person responsible for the resident. This new plan must be developed by the resident's doctor or by the nursing facility's medical director and other medical staff. It must include a written evaluation of the effects of the transfer on the resident as well as a statement of the steps the nursing home will take to make the transfer less disturbing. It must also outline the kinds of services and care the resident will need after being moved.

## APPEALING AN EVICTION

Nursing home residents have the right to appeal, but they must act quickly. Generally, an appeal can be filed within 30 days of receiving the transfer or discharge notice. If the appeal is filed within 10 days, the resident cannot be moved until a hearing is held and a written decision is issued.

The hearing will be conducted by a state employee. Typically it's an official of the state department of social services, human services, or public aid (the exact department can vary from state to state).

At the hearing, the burden of proof is on the nursing home to show that the reason for the move is legally permitted. If the proposed move is based on the nursing home's assessment of the resident's medical condition, the hearing officer is usually authorized to arrange to have an independent medical exam of the patient conducted at the state's expense.

In most cases, the hearing officer will issue a written decision. If the transfer is considered permissible, the law generally gives the resident 15 days before the move can take place.

## GOING TO COURT

Even if the state's hearing officer finds in favor of the nursing home, you can still appeal your wife's case in state court, and in many states the court is required to take the case on an expedited basis.

You can also file a private lawsuit against the nursing home if it has failed to provide you with adequate notice or tried to evict your wife in violation of the law. The court can impose a

variety of sanctions against a nursing home that acted illegally, including…

- Issuing an injunction to stop a resident's proposed transfer
- Ordering the facility to readmit someone who has already been evicted
- Requiring the nursing-home operator to reimburse the resident for any costs that were incurred as a result of your wife's eviction.

Nursing homes are prohibited from taking any retaliatory action against a resident who opposes a transfer or discharge, or who takes action to exercise the rights guaranteed by law. In some states, a nursing-home operator who attempts to discriminate or retaliate can be liable for triple damages to the injured party.

**ALERT** *Because Medicaid programs are administered by the states, the benefits and rules for eligibility differ from one state to another. It's always best to get expert advice when facing a problem involving Medicaid services. Every state has a Medicaid ombudsman to serve as a resource for people on Medicaid. Many private attorneys and social workers can also answer your questions and guide you through the maze of Medicaid laws and regulations. The local legal-aid society and groups such as AARP can also be valuable resources when dealing with Medicaid.*

## PICKING A LONG-TERM-CARE INSURANCE POLICY

According to the U.S. Government Accounting Office, a typical nursing-home stay will last more than three years. With the average annual cost of nursing-home care at around $40,000—even more in some parts of the country—you may consider purchasing an insurance policy to help protect your retirement savings if you or your spouse must enter a nursing home.

The longer you wait to buy long-term-care insurance, the more expensive the premiums will be. For example, one company charges almost twice as much annually for a policy that you buy at age 65 than it does for one you buy at age 55.

A number of companies now offer long-term-care insurance. Look for a policy with a company that's highly rated by at least two insurance-rating agencies such as A.M. Best, Standard & Poor's, or Weiss Services. The company you choose should have offered long-term-care policies for at least three years.

Be sure to ask about the company's past record of premium increases. While premiums are usually projected to remain unchanged, there's often no guarantee that rates won't rise. A look back at the company's premium history can be a good predictor of potential increases.

The benefits that long-term-care policies offer and the premiums vary widely. A good long-term-care policy should...

● Be written in language that's easy to understand

● Clearly describe the "triggering events" for receiving benefits—many policies will begin payment when you can no longer perform the functions of everyday living (dressing, bathing, eating, and so forth) without assistance. Others kick in when you suffer "cognitive impairment" such as memory loss. In either case, you'll usually need a doctor's certification that you are eligible for benefits. Make sure that the policy will accept your own doctor's certification and doesn't require you to use a doctor hired by the insurer.

● Include a "free look" period that allows you to review the policy for a specified period (30 days, for example) after you've purchased it—be sure you can get a refund if you aren't satisfied or simply change your mind.

● Include a "waiver of premium" provision that will keep the coverage in force with no more premium payments due once you begin receiving benefits

● Include coverage for assisted living and home-health care in addition to nursing-home care

● Reimburse 100 percent of your actual expenses, not just "reasonable and customary" or "prevailing" charges

● Include coverage for Alzheimer's disease, Parkinson's disease, dementia, senility, and related illnesses

● Offer a premium discount if you are married or if you are in above-average health.

**ALERT** *Some long-term-care policies require that you or your spouse be hospitalized for a period of time before beginning to collect benefits. But in many cases, the need for a long-term-care facility or home health care isn't preceded by an illness that requires a hospital stay. You're better off with a policy that doesn't include a hospitalization requirement.*

> *Your wife recently died. You just got a call from a salesman who tells you that the special family Bible she ordered for you is ready for delivery.*

One of the lowest forms of human life is the con artist who preys on the elderly—especially one who victimizes an older person who has recently suffered the loss of a spouse. Some of these crooks regularly scan the obituaries in the local newspaper for potential victims, looking for the names of persons affiliated with a church group or congregation.

By using the phone directory, they can also locate the address and telephone number of the widow or widower. They call the surviving spouse and claim that the deceased person had ordered a Bible from their firm as a surprise for the family. Feigning shock and sympathy, the scam artist then asks if the bereaved spouse still wants the specially imprinted Bible.

Few people in the early stages of grief can refuse such a request, and most will send off a check to the Bible salesman. If a Bible ever arrives at all, it's usually worth far less than the price the con artist charged. Often when the surviving spouse recognizes that he's been cheated, he's often too embarrassed to admit falling for a scam.

## TAKE ACTION NOW

It does no good to hide the fact that you've been contacted or taken advantage of by a con artist. In fact, once you fall for a con artist's scam and do nothing about it, you're more likely to become the target of other scams by other criminals in the future.

If you receive a call from someone asking you to buy a Bible or some other sentimental item, such as jewelry or a picture that the caller claims your dead spouse ordered but hadn't paid for, you should get the name, address, and telephone number of the caller. Then ask for a copy of the signed order your spouse placed for the item. Chances are, this will end the matter, because there is no order for you to review.

Report the scam to your local police department. The police can use your information—as well as information from other victims and potential victims—in their investigation and may be able to track down the criminal. If you were taken in by a con artist, it's even more important to contact the police. If the Bible or other item was sent to you by mail, you should also report the scheme to U.S. Postal Service inspectors.

Act quickly. With quick action, you'll be able to help law enforcement authorities locate the criminal before he can change addresses or move on to another town or another scam. If caught, the con artist can be charged with state and federal crimes and may also be fined, imprisoned, and ordered to make restitution.

Whatever the outcome, you'll feel a lot better when you take positive action, because you had the courage to stand up and protect yourself and others in grief from con artists.

> **Y**our deceased husband left you a large retirement account. Now you're being hounded by financial advisers who want to help you manage your money.

These days, it seems as if there's a financial planner behind every bush. A good adviser can be a real help in organizing and making the most of your retirement money. But a bad one can drain your retirement accounts by recommending investments that aren't suitable for a retired person. This isn't the time of life to take on high-risk investments; rather, it's time to invest in a way that will provide you a comfortable living—and maybe leave something for you to pass on to the next generation.

---

### Get a written agreement that clearly sets out all of the terms of the arrangement with the financial planner.

---

Unfortunately, financial planners aren't highly regulated, and just about anyone can call himself a financial planner. Some of these so-called "experts" may be little more than salespeople, earning a commission by selling you the very products they recommend. Others use a one-size-fits-all approach to financial planning, instead of tailoring a plan to meet your specific needs. But you won't be taken in if you know what to look for in a financial planner.

### SET UP SOME INTERVIEWS

Begin your search for a qualified financial planner by interviewing a number of potential candidates. Contact several of the planners who have already contacted you, or get names from your friends and family members.

But think about the source of any referral carefully. If your son's financial planner is helping him to build a portfolio of small-company, high-risk stocks, that planner may not be right for you, if you are seeking long-term growth.

Before your interview takes place with each candidate, you should…

- **Compile a brief summary** of all of your assets, income, and debts.

- **Take some time to consider exactly** what you want a financial adviser to do for you. Do you merely want a review of your current investments and some suggestions about other investments to consider, or do you want the planner to take a more hands-on approach to managing your investments? Do you want the planner to help you with noninvestment financial issues, such as obtaining long-term-care insurance?

- **Prepare a list of questions** for the candidate you are interviewing. You'll want to know…
  - The planner's personal experience and training as a financial planner and what kind of work he did before entering financial planning. This will help you discover any biases the planner has. For example, someone with a background in insurance sales may tend to favor annuities or cash-value life insurance, which may not be what you need.
  - The history of the firm he works for and the experience and background of his associates. (Do they have experience in areas where the planner you are considering may be weak?)
  - The size of the average portfolio the planner manages. If she's used to handling multi-million dollar plans, will she be interested in one that's significantly smaller? Will you be a low priority for her?
  - How the planner will be compensated. Some financial planners work for "fee only" and are likely to provide advice that's designed to be in your best interest. Others earn their living from the commissions on the products and services they sell. Since some investments pay higher commissions than others, there's a greater potential that the planner will choose investment vehicles that earn more for her. Some planners charge fees and earn commissions—an arrangement that's good for them, maybe not so good for you.

Get a written agreement that clearly sets out all of the terms of the arrangement with the financial planner. Don't feel compelled to sign immediately. You'll still have more interviews to conduct. You may want to have your lawyer look over any agreement to be sure that all the promises made during your interview are included. And check the planner's references. Get at least three names and call each person and ask how satisfied he or she is with the services.

## LOOK FOR CERTIFICATION

Although state and federal regulation of financial planners is relatively weak, several private organizations do offer financial-planning accreditation programs. Look for an adviser with one or more of the following designations:

● CHFC, or Chartered Financial Consultant, which means the planner has received accreditation from the American College in Bryn Mawr, Pennsylvania

● CFP, or Certified Financial Planner, which denotes that the advisor is accredited by the International Board of Standards for Certified Financial Planners in Denver, Colorado

● PFS, or Personal Financial Specialist; the planner has been awarded such status by the American Institute of Certified Public Accountants in New York City, New York.

**TAKE NOTE** *Even with these designations, you must be diligent about checking references; accrediting organizations don't pass judgment on the wisdom of the strategies of planners they accredit. Check with your state's securities commission and the federal Securities and Exchange Commission (SEC) to learn if a planner you're considering has been the subject of complaints.*

---

**You've been getting Social Security benefits, but Social Security now says you aren't eligible to receive them.**

---

Getting Social Security benefits isn't normally complicated, but there are exceptions. Occasionally, a dispute arises about whether a recipient is entitled to continued payments. For example, your retirement benefits can be discontinued if you are in prison or if you are deported; disability benefits can be stopped if you refuse to participate in a rehabilitation program or if the Social Security Administration (SSA) says you are no longer disabled.

Under federal law, you have up to 60 days to appeal an adverse decision about Social Security benefits, such as a denial, reduction, or termination. Be sure to get a written explanation of the SSA's decision—a verbal statement doesn't count. Don't miss the deadline to appeal, because you will lose forever your right to have the initial decision reviewed.

Your first step is to file a *written request* for reconsideration. Your original application will be reviewed by an SSA employee other than the one who made the decision. You are allowed to add the necessary additional documents in order to bolster your claim.

You'll receive written notice of the reconsideration decision within 30 days. Since a large number of claims denials are reversed at this point, you could begin receiving benefits again with no further difficulties. But if you're still unhappy with the SSA's decision, you can file a written request for an administrative hearing.

---

**Under federal law, you have 60 days to appeal an adverse decision about Social Security benefits.**

---

You have 60 days in which to file this request. A hearing will be scheduled, but because the SSA's hearing calendar is often full, you should expect to wait several months before your hearing actually takes place.

At the hearing you can either represent yourself or be represented by an attorney or even a lay advocate. An administrative law judge (ALJ) will conduct the hearing, and the SSA will be represented there by one of its employees, but it will not be represented by a lawyer.

You can expect the ALJ's decision within 60 to 90 days, and if your appeal is successful, you'll be entitled to benefits from the date you would originally have been eligible. But if you lose, you can still file an appeal with the SSA Appeals Council, located in Washington, D.C. You won't appear in person at this proceeding, which consists of a review of the earlier proceedings and any additional written information you have included in your file.

If you still can't convince the SSA to change its decision, you can file an appeal in federal district court. But talk first to a lawyer experienced in handling Social Security appeals. He can help you weigh the costs of a court case against the value of the benefits you are claiming.

## GOOD NEWS FROM SOCIAL SECURITY

Until recently, your Social Security benefits could be reduced if you continued working after you began to collect benefits. In 1999, for example, if you were between 65 and 70 years of age, your benefit would be reduced by $1 for every $2 you earned from work once you made more than $9,600 during that year—and an additional $1 for every $3 you earned in excess of $15,500. Only when you turned 70 could you earn as much as you wanted without having your Social Security benefits reduced.

The good news for you is that Congress removed these limitations in the year 2000. You can now collect your full Social Security benefits no matter how much you earn from work at any age. As before, there's no reduction in benefits because of money earned from your pensions, investments, dividends, and interest.

---

## You signed a prenuptial agreement that waived your right to your wife's pension. But you're having second thoughts.

Prenuptial agreements can be useful for couples embarking on a second or third marriage—especially if husband and wife both have assets that they want to preserve for children from earlier marriages, to pay for the care of their aging parents, or to avoid a struggle over how assets will be divided in a divorce.

Prenuptial agreements are regulated by state laws, but your right to receive a pension benefit after your spouse dies is regulated at the federal level. Under the federal Employee Retirement Income Security Act (ERISA), you cannot waive your right to receive a pension benefit from your wife through a prenuptial agreement. You must make a waiver of that right after you're married,

under the provisions of the Retirement Equity Act (REA). This law requires a worker to get his or her spouse's written consent to give up what's called a *qualified joint and survivor annuity,* or QJSA. Unless you waive your QJSA, you remain entitled to the spousal benefit provided by your wife's pension benefits. Likewise, she is entitled to benefits from any plan your employer provides unless she executes a waiver.

### THERE'S A CATCH

While ERISA and REA apply to all defined benefit plans, there's a loophole that could end up depriving you of benefits from your spouse's defined contribution plan, 401(k), profit-sharing plan, Simplified Employee Pension, or Employee Stock Ownership Plan. These plans don't have to provide a QJSA if the entire vested benefit is payable to the surviving spouse when the working spouse dies.

But many of these plans also allow employees to take the entire amount of their benefits and roll it over into an individual retirement account (IRA) when they retire.

Nothing in REA, however, requires the retiring worker to name his or her spouse as the beneficiary of his IRA. So if your wife names someone other than you as her IRA beneficiary, you could still end up with nothing—even if you hadn't signed the prenuptial agreement. If your wife's pension is covered by REA, there really isn't any-

thing you must do. No matter what your prenuptial agreement says, you will receive a benefit from your wife's pension when she dies. But it might be worthwhile to have the prenuptial agreement modified, just to clarify matters and to protect your right to your wife's IRA, Keogh, or other non-ERISA plan if she dies. Just as you did when you made out your original prenuptial agreement, you and your spouse should make a full disclosure of all the benefits you are entitled to receive when you retire. Then you can contact the lawyer who drew up the agreement.

Either you can have the original agreement canceled entirely and a new postnuptial agreement created, or you can amend the relevant parts of your old agreement.

## WHEN PENSIONS AREN'T PROTECTED

Not every pension is covered by the provisions of the Employee Retirement Income Security Act (ERISA) or other federal pension laws. For example, your pension usually isn't protected under ERISA unless it's offered by a private employer. Federal, state, and local government plans are not covered.

If you left your employer before 1976—the year ERISA took effect—your pension benefits probably aren't protected under federal law. And if your plan is a *defined contribution plan* instead of a *defined benefit plan*, then your pension isn't insured by the Pension Benefit Guaranty Association.

Finally, survivor benefits from a pension plan weren't automatically protected until 1984, when the federal Retirement Equity Act took effect. If your spouse retired before then, she may have chosen an option that paid out only until her death and made no provision for survivor benefits for spouse or family members after she passed away.

*You and your husband are getting a divorce, but you can't agree how to split up his retirement benefits.*

**W**hen a marriage falls apart, it's hard enough dealing with issues, such as child custody, support, and visitation that are very much in the here and now. Battling over something that seems in the distant future

can seem less important, and many divorcing women find themselves agreeing to receive none or only some of the retirement benefits that they may be entitled to from their ex-husband's pension plan. But the future will arrive sooner than you may expect. Knowing what the law allows and how to negotiate for what you need can make the difference between a comfortable retirement and one that's a financial struggle.

## GENDER-NEUTRAL LAWS RULE

It's important to keep in mind that laws about the distribution of property during a divorce don't recognize a difference between the sexes. Just as you may be entitled to receive a portion of your husband's retirement benefits, he may also be entitled to receive a portion of the benefits from your plan.

In most states, divorce courts are mandated to divide a couple's assets using a concept called *equitable distribution.* This means that the court looks at the contributions each party made to the marriage, both financial and otherwise (such as by staying home and raising the family's children). The court calculates the assets of the marriage and then tries to arrive at a formula that's fair to both husband and wife.

Unfortunately, the decisions of divorce courts vary widely, both from state to state and sometimes within the same courthouse. One judge might award a spouse half or more of the other spouse's pension benefits, while another judge ruling in a similar case may award nothing at all. In any case, your chances of getting an award of pension benefits can be increased considerably, if you know what to do.

## STEPS TO TAKE

Before you do anything else, you'll need to know exactly what benefits your soon-to-be ex-spouse is entitled to from his current and past employers. Your husband should provide you with information about all the plans he has any interest in, including any 401(k), defined benefit pensions, and profit-sharing plans.

If your husband is reluctant to provide this information, you may need to have the court order him to turn it over to you and your lawyer. You'll need to get the summary plan descriptions (SPDs) and copies of your husband's individual benefit statements for every plan.

Once you've gathered all the information, you'll need to calculate the value of your husband's benefits—not always an easy thing to do. For instance, if your husband is enrolled in a defined-benefit plan at his current employer, the value of his benefits will depend on factors, such as his age, salary level, and length of service with that employer.

After you have a sense of what your husband's pension benefits are worth, it's time to begin negotiations. It's far better to arrive at a mutually agreeable settlement than to drag things out in a lengthy court battle, especially when the outcome is uncertain. Many states now require divorcing couples to use mediators in an attempt to settle disputes before they can bring their claims to court. Mediation can be faster and much less expensive than litigation; you and your husband should consider mediation carefully as a solution.

If you're able to agree on a fair figure, you will include this in the documents you file with the court. The judge will review the amount that you present. Unless it's blatantly unfair to you or your husband, the judge will almost certainly incorporate it unchanged into your divorce decree.

## METHODS OF PAYMENT

There are several ways in which you can obtain your share of your ex-husband's pension benefits:

■ **Ask the court to award you a percentage** of his retirement benefits when he reaches retirement age. This can be a good option if your husband's pension is a defined benefit plan and he is in a job where his wages—and therefore his pension—are expected to increase substantially in the future.

- **Take the cash equivalent of your share at the time of your divorce.** Using a *Qualified Domestic Relations Order,* or QDRO (pronounced "QUAH-dro"), the court can order your husband's pension administrator to release money from his plan that you can roll over into an IRA. You can even take the money without rolling it over and avoid the usual penalty from the IRS. Taking a lump-sum cash equivalent means that you don't run the risk that your husband's plan will be terminated and it also relieves you of having to deal with the plan administrator for years until you actually begin receiving benefits.

## WHAT GOES IN A QDRO

Federal law is very specific about what a QDRO must contain. Some pension-plan administrators now provide a model form that you can use in order to be sure that your QDRO meets all the legal requirements. The Pension Benefit Guaranty Corporation also has a model form that your husband's plan may accept. The QDRO must include the following information:

- The name and last known address of the plan participant
- The name and address of the *alternate payee.* In most cases, that's you, but some divorce decrees also allow children to acquire a right to a parent's pension benefits. If so, their names and addresses must also be shown.
- The name of each pension plan covered by the QDRO
- The time period the QDRO covers or the number of payments to be made
- The amount—or the percentage—of the participant's benefits to be paid to each alternate payee
- The method the plan administrator must use when calculating payments to each alternative payee.

**ALERT** *The requirements for drafting a QDRO are extremely rigid, and this is not a task for the average person. In fact, even when lawyers draft QDROs, they can make mistakes that cause the pension-plan administrator to reject the order, causing unnecessary delay and added expense. Have your attorney talk to the plan administrator before drafting the QDRO in order to determine exactly what must be included.*

### SMART MOVES

Ask your lawyer to retain an actuary to help calculate the value of a defined-benefit program. Many divorce lawyers work with actuaries on a regular basis in cases where assessing a pension's value is complex.

## PROBLEMS WITH LUMP-SUM DISTRIBUTIONS

Even though a lump-sum distribution from your husband's plan may sound like the best way to get your share of his pension benefits, it may not be so easy. A pension plan may be prohibited by law from releasing the full amount you agreed to because your husband is too far away from retirement age. As a result, your husband may be forced to pay you the equivalent in cash out of his other assets, if he has any.

Or he may offer to purchase an annuity equal in value to the amount you've agreed to accept as your fair share of his pension benefits.

## SUBMITTING YOUR QDRO

Whether your QDRO calls for a lump-sum payment or benefits paid out over years, it won't become effective until authorized by the judge and delivered to your ex-husband's plan administrator. The plan administrator then has a reasonable period of time to determine whether the QDRO meets the requirements of the law. If the QDRO is acceptable, the administrator must honor its terms.

But if the administrator doesn't believe the QDRO is in legal compliance—for example, it fails to clearly state how money is to be apportioned among alternate payees—the administrator can refuse to accept the order.

In this event, either you can appeal the decision through the plan's ERISA procedures, or you can redraft the QDRO and go back to court to have the new QDRO approved before submitting it to the plan administrator.

As you can see, getting retirement benefits from an ex-spouse's pension plan can be an arduous task. It requires careful research on your part, expert legal help, and plenty of persistence. In some cases, delays in getting benefits can take months, even when you've done everything to comply with the law. But with patience and the assistance of a lawyer experienced in handling QDRO orders, you can, in fact, win the benefits you will need in your later years.

## RETIREMENT PLANS FOR THE SELF-EMPLOYED

If you're one of the millions of Americans now working on your own, you should be aware of three major programs to help you put money away for your retirement.

Keogh plans are the original retirement-investment plan approved by Congress for the self-employed. With a Keogh, your contributions are fully tax deductible, and there's no tax on the plan's earnings until you begin making withdrawals. You're eligible to open a Keogh account even if you have another job and participate in your employer's pension plan—provided that you get income from any of the following:

- As owner of a full-time or part-time small business that you own as sole proprietor or that is incorporated

- As a partner in a business

- As a self-employed professional—a doctor, lawyer, engineer, and so forth

- As a freelance worker, writer, speaker, or business consultant.

Depending on the kind of Keogh you choose, you can invest much more of your self-employment income than you can in an IRA—up to 25 percent of your net self-employment earnings to a maximum of $30,000 annually. If you set up a profit-sharing plan, you decide whether to contribute (and how much) each year. With a money-purchase plan, you'll contribute the same percentage of income each year. Setting up and maintaining a Keogh takes a lot of paperwork, and you probably need an accountant or financial adviser to get your plan established.

A SEP-IRA (Simplified Employee Pension—Individual Retirement Account) is a much simpler method of managing your retirement funds, but it has some drawbacks. For example, with a SEP-IRA, you can contribute up to only 15 percent of your net annual self-employment earnings, to a maximum of $22,500—far less than with a Keogh plan. If you have eligible employees, you must make contributions to their plans in any year that you make a contribution to your own.

On the plus side, you can vary your contributions each year, and you're not required to make a contribution at all during the year (a big help when your business is slow and income is low). There's only one form to fill out in order to start a SEP-IRA—and no ongoing reports to submit. Because your employees manage their own SEP-IRA investments, your business avoids the responsibility and potential liability for bad investments.

Finally, a Savings Incentive Match Plan for Employees (SIMPLE) plan is available for small businesses with up to 100 employees and can also be used by a self-employed person. As with a Keogh plan, you can have a SIMPLE plan and also be covered by a plan offered by your employer. But you cannot have a Keogh and a SIMPLE.

The maximum annual contribution to a SIMPLE plan is $6,000, even if that's all your net self-employment income. As with a traditional IRA, SIMPLE contributions are tax deductible, earnings are tax deferred, and there's a penalty (as much as 25 percent in some circumstances) if you take money out before you reach age 59½.

These plans are offered by mutual-fund companies, brokerage houses, and banks. For specific information about setting up these accounts, contact your accountant, banker, or broker.

WILLS & ESTATE PLANNING

You and your long-time partner have never married. Although your grown son promises to "take care" of her when you die, you aren't convinced that he will.

When someone dies *intestate* (without a will), provisions in the law protect spouses and other family members but not unmarried partners. And while your family may have a great deal of affection for your partner, when it comes to sharing your estate, that affection is likely to have limits. In thousands of cases, unmarried domestic partners have been forced out of the homes they shared with their loved one and have suffered a steep and sudden decline in lifestyle.

## PROVIDE FOR YOUR PARTNER

There are some simple steps you can take to protect your domestic partner's interests:

- **Write a will.** A will allows you to designate the kind and amount of property your partner will receive. Without one, the state will decide how to distribute your estate—with none of it going to your unmarried partner. Afterward, review it from time to time to be sure that it accurately reflects your living situation and your financial status (see "When to Revise Your Estate Plan," page 389).
- **Create a trust.** A living trust might be a good option in this situation, especially if you want to protect the privacy of your partner and your relationship. Unlike a will, which becomes a public document when submitted to the *probate court*, which is the court with jurisdiction over wills and estates, a trust remains confidential.

### SMART MOVES

Today, around 80 million Americans have access to *legal plans*, which offer free or reduced-cost legal services, such as having a simple will drawn up each year. Talk to your human resources department, union representative, or the membership department of your association to see if this benefit is available to you. Some plans are also available inexpensively to individuals.

- **Prepare a durable power of attorney,** also called attorney-in-fact, which authorizes a person of your choice to make legal and health-care decisions for you if you become unable to do so. If you want to assure that your partner will be able to make financial and health-care decisions for you, you should name her as your attorney-in-fact while you are competent. This can short-circuit another family member's attempt to step in and make decisions for you if you are unable to act on your own behalf.
- **Buy life insurance.** While federal tax law allows all of your estate to pass to your spouse tax-free, that isn't the case when

you leave your property to an unmarried domestic partner. If your estate would be subject to federal estate taxes, buying life insurance through an *irrevocable life insurance trust* can provide funds to pay estate taxes without adding the value of the insurance to your taxable estate.

By taking a few careful steps now, you can be sure that your partner will be taken care of the way you would want her to be—without having to depend on the promises of others, who may change their minds about honoring your requests after you pass away.

> **TAKE NOTE** *Probate court can have a different name in different states. It might be called the probate registry, registry of wills, surrogate court, circuit court, or probate office. To find out the exact name of the probate court in your state, call the county courthouse and ask for the court that handles wills and estates.*

> # *Without your knowledge, your late cousin named you as executor in his will. But you have no idea what's required of you or whether you can handle it.*

In most cases, it comes as no surprise that a person has been named to execute someone's will (distribute the person's assets after his or her death), since it's common to get the executor's consent before assigning her this important task. But no matter whether you agreed in advance or had the news sprung on you after the fact, you are not *obligated* to serve as executor. Many wills provide for an alternate executor to take on the responsibility of shepherding the will through probate—the legal process of administering the will—if the first choice is unable or unwilling to do so.

## WHO CAN BE AN EXECUTOR

Even if there's no alternate named, or the alternate also declines to serve, there are other options. State laws provide a list of preferences for naming someone to do the job, often in the following order:

- The surviving spouse of the testator (the person who wrote the will)
- Another family member, such as an adult child
- A person selected by the surviving spouse
- Another beneficiary, such as a friend of the testator who is named in the will
- A person selected by a beneficiary named in the will
- A creditor of the estate.

## IF YOU DECLINE

If you don't feel qualified to handle the tasks that face an executor, you can file a *renunciation* with the probate court, which will release you of responsibilities for handling the estate. But be sure to do this before taking actions, such as writing checks on the estate's account, which could be seen as an acceptance of the executor's duties.

> ## *No matter whether you agreed in advance or had the news sprung on you after the fact, you are not obligated to serve as executor.*

## IF YOU ACCEPT

If you decide to serve as your cousin's executor, you must present the will to the probate court and provide notice to any interested parties. In general, interested parties include the deceased's spouse, other next of kin, anyone named in the will as a beneficiary, *heirs at law* (individuals who would receive property from the deceased if there were no will but who may not be mentioned in the will), and creditors of the deceased. When you provide notice, you let these parties know that the testator has died, that a will has been presented for probate, that an executor has been named, and that probate is about to get under way. You'll need to include the following in the notice you send to interested parties:

- A copy of the will
- A copy of the petition seeking to have the will admitted into probate
- Information about whether a hearing will be held before the will is admitted, and if so, when and where it will take place
- Information about how an interested party may object to having the will admitted.

While at first glance this may not seem very complicated, in some cases tracking down all the interested parties can be quite a chore. For example, say your cousin, in his will, left his prized 1966 Mustang to his old friend Bill Smith. Neither you nor other family members know Bill Smith or where he lives. You will need to take a number of steps to try to locate Bill, including going through your late cousin's address books and old correspondence; contacting your cousin's employers, social clubs, and trade or professional organizations; or even hiring a firm that specializes in tracking down missing beneficiaries.

## ABC's OF EXECUTING AN ESTATE

To fulfill your role as your cousin's executor, these are the steps to take:

- **Receive letters of appointment** (in some states called *letters testamentary*) from the probate court, if the interested parties have no objections to the will or to your serving as executor. These give you the power to begin taking actions on behalf of the estate.
- **Notify banks, mortgage companies, stock brokerages,** and others that you are now officially authorized by the probate court to act on behalf of your cousin's estate. You will need to include a letter of appointment in your written correspondence.
- **Put together an inventory** of your late cousin's assets as well as his debts. You'll be ahead of the game if he kept good records; otherwise, it can be a time-consuming and complicated task to assemble all the necessary information. The inventory will list the property and its value, so you need to arrange for appraisals of items such as artwork, furniture, antiques, and jewelry. Don't delay; many states require the executor to provide an inventory within a relatively short period of time—often as little as three months.

- **Open a checking account in the name of your cousin's estate.** You will be responsible for making mortgage payments and paying credit-card bills, utility bills, and other debts as they come due. You'll also have to pay any property taxes owed.
- **Return any Social Security, Railroad Retirement, or veteran's benefits checks** that were received in the month of your cousin's death, *even if he died on the last day of the month.* If the check was cashed before he died, you will have to repay that amount to the government out of the assets of the estate.
- **File federal tax returns,** including a final Form 1040 for the tax year in which your cousin passed away, and a Form 1041, *U.S. Income Tax Return for Estates and Trusts,* in which you'll report income earned by the estate after your cousin's death. You may also have to file Form 706, *United States Estate (and Generation-Skipping Transfer) Tax Return* if his gross estate exceeded the amount exempt from estate tax in the year of his death (see "New Estate Tax Limits," facing page), or if he left a large amount of money or assets to a grandchild. And depending on other circumstances, you could be required to file dozens of other forms and schedules with the Internal Revenue Service and state tax departments. Unless you're experienced in filing complex returns, you'll need to hire a professional to negotiate the maze of laws and regulations.

## SAFEGUARDING ESTATE ASSETS

You will also be responsible for managing and caring for your late cousin's property. In some cases, you'll have to decide who is entitled to have custody of certain property. Since your cousin left his 1966 Mustang to Bill Smith, it may seem to make sense to let Bill take possession of the car now, rather than waiting until the probate process ends. But if you do, be sure to get a written acknowledgment from Bill that he understands that you may need to reclaim the car if circumstances require it and that letting him have the car now doesn't guarantee that he will get to keep it. You'll also need to make sure that the car and your cousin's other property are adequately insured against loss or damage.

## WHO GETS WHAT?

At last, it's time to figure out how to distribute your late cousin's property according to the terms of his will. In most cases, this part of the probate process goes smoothly. But in a few instances, there can be problems.

For example, suppose your cousin's will states that he leaves his Persian carpets to a neighbor. Unfortunately, your cousin sold the carpets a year before his death. As a result, the gift to the neighbor is said to have been *adeemed,* and the neighbor gets nothing.

Another problem occurs when there aren't enough assets to fulfill all the bequests your cousin made in his will. Suppose he left $5,000 to each of his 12 nephews and nieces, for a total of $60,000. But the assets of the estate are only $40,000. In this case, the law imposes what's known as an *abatement* on the gifts, eliminating them entirely for some of the beneficiaries or reducing them proportionally, depending on the state where the will is being probated.

It's also possible that your cousin left gifts to someone who preceded him in death. If so, you need to look to the language of the will regarding the gift and to state law to determine if the gift was eliminated, or if it could be passed to the intended recipient's descendants.

## APPROACHING THE FINISH

As the end of the probate process draws near, you will be required to file an accounting with the court. The court will use it to authorize distribution of the estate's assets. This document lists the original assets, their increase or decrease in value, and will act as a record of income and expenses incurred during the estate's administration.

You must also put a notice in a local newspaper to inform the public that the estate is about to be closed—and send written notice to all of the interested parties as well. If there are no objections, the court will authorize the distribution of assets. You will need to get a receipt from each beneficiary and a release absolving you of personal liability.

## THE FINISH

Only after you've performed all of the required duties, received the approval of the court, distributed the property from the estate, and obtained receipts and releases from the beneficiaries will you be relieved of your responsibilities as your late cousin's executor. It can be a daunting task, and while you are entitled to compensation for your services and permitted to hire lawyers, accounts, and other advisers to help you, *you* are ultimately responsible if things go wrong. Think carefully before taking on an executor's duties.

## NEW ESTATE TAX LIMITS

Until a few years ago, only estates valued at $600,000 or less were exempt from paying estate taxes to the federal government. Thanks to the Taxpayer Relief Act of 1997, however, these limits increased to $675,000 in the years 2000-2001 and will continue to increase until 2006, when the exemption will hit the $1 million mark.

Here's a look at exemptions between now and then:

| Year of Death | Exemption |
| --- | --- |
| 2002 | $700,000 |
| 2003 | $700,000 |
| 2004 | $850,000 |
| 2005 | $950,000 |
| 2006 | $1,000,000 |

While $1 million may seem like a tremendously large estate, keep in mind that life insurance policies, the success of the stock market, and the rapid increase in the price of real estate during the past several years now make it far more likely that thousands of Americans will leave estates valued at or near this threshold in the next decade. In addition, Congress has already proposed eliminating the federal estate tax entirely. Although a recent effort to do away with the tax failed, it's very likely that the estate tax abolition will be proposed again in the near future. Talk to your attorney or financial adviser for details.

## CHECKLIST FOR EXECUTORS

While it can seem like an honor to be named as someone's executor or personal representative, there's plenty of work involved as well. Here's a list of the duties you'll be expected to perform:

✔ Find the will.

✔ Apply to appear as the personal representative in probate court.

✔ Contact the beneficiaries named in the will.

✔ Hire lawyers, accountants, and other professionals to help you with estate administration.

✔ Mail notices to each known creditor of the deceased.

✔ Publish notices in newspapers to inform unknown creditors of the death of the testator.

✔ Notify the post office, banks, credit-card issuers, utility companies, and the Social Security Administration of the testator's death.

✔ Contact the deceased's employer and obtain any salary owed, and collect any employee insurance benefits.

✔ File for Social Security, Railroad Retirement, and veteran's benefits.

✔ Claim life insurance benefits.

✔ Make an inventory of and value all of the estate's assets.

✔ Obtain appraisals of assets whose value isn't immediately apparent.

✔ Collect any debts owed to the estate.

✔ Pay valid claims against the estate.

✔ Distribute the estate's assets to the beneficiaries named in the will.

✔ File federal, state, and local income tax returns, and federal and state estate tax returns.

✔ Obtain the court's permission to close the estate and relieve you of your executor's duties.

*Your father named his attorney as executor of his will. Now the probate process is dragging on and on, and the lawyer's fees continue to mount.*

One of the great fears people have about probate is that a lot of time will pass between the death of the *testator* (the person who made the will) and the date that the estate is closed and the date on which assets are distributed to the beneficiaries and the estate is closed. It takes at least six months to probate an estate. That's because the executor has a variety of duties that he is legally required to perform.

If the executor fails to fulfill those requirements, he can be held personally responsible for any claims raised as a result of his failure (for a list of those duties, see "Checklist for Executors," above).

The probate process can run into roadblocks due to the following problems:

- **Lost property**. Your father's executor may be unable to locate all of the property in the estate.
- **Questionable claims on the estate**. The executor may be investigating a claim from someone that the estate owes them money.
- **Valid wills**. Other family members could delay the process—and reduce the size of your father's estate—if they believe that the will the executor presented for probate isn't valid.
- **Liquidating assets.** Your father's will may have instructed the executor to *liquidate* certain assets (exchange them for cash), but he hasn't been able to find a buyer.

Your father's executor also has what's referred to as a *fiduciary* responsibility, which means he must act for the benefit of others—following the instructions left for him in the will and taking all appropriate steps to maximize the value of the estate for the beneficiaries. This can be a tough balancing act; if the executor invests estate assets in risky ways and loses money, he can be personally liable for the loss in the assets' value. But if he holds non-income-producing assets without the will's authorization to do so, he could also be held liable for the loss of potential income.

## HOW TO SPEED THINGS ALONG

To find out what's holding things up, try the following:

- **Ask the executor the reason for the delay.** As a matter of course, most executors communicate with a will's beneficiaries on a regular basis during the probate process to keep them up to date on the latest developments. But some executors are more diligent about communicating than others, so it may be up to you to initiate the contact.
- **Find out how long the delay will continue.** If the executor claims that the press of other business or obligations is keeping him from moving your father's will through the probate process, ask him if those problems will

continue for the foreseeable future or if they're about to come to an end. If the worst is past, getting a new executor appointed can only add to the delay. But if there's no end in sight, it might be worth asking the executor to step aside in favor of someone who can do the job more efficiently.

---

*Your father's executor has what's referred to as a fiduciary responsibility, which means he must act for the benefit of others.*

---

- **Inquire about a partial distribution.** If you're struggling to make ends meet and could benefit from receiving a portion of what your father left to you in his will, find out if your state's probate process allows for partial distributions. If the executor tells you that partial distributions are prohibited or are allowed only to a surviving spouse or dependent children, ask him to cite the state law that sets this out.

## GET AN INDEPENDENT REVIEW

If you think that you're getting the runaround or that the executor is dragging things out simply to earn a

bigger fee, it's a good idea to ask another lawyer to review the situation. (Your father's will is a public document once it's admitted to probate, so if you can't get the executor to provide you with a copy, you can obtain one—for a fee—from the probate court.)

If the lawyer's review indicates that there's no good reason for the delays, consider asking the probate court to appoint an administrator in place of the executor. If the will names a successor executor—who would take the place of the current one if he was unable or unwilling to serve—you may be able to convince the court that it is in everyone's best interest to relieve your father's lawyer of his duties. The court might also appoint another lawyer or financial professional to take over. An independent review could uncover a more sinister motive for the delay.

In a few cases, executors have been known to "borrow" cash or other assets from the estate they're administering. When they can't repay the money, they may take even more in hopes of recovering all the losses through a big score in the stock market or at the casino.

If you suspect misconduct on the executor's part, consider talking to your attorney about filing a lawsuit charging the executor with breach of his fiduciary duty. If you win, the executor can be required to reimburse the estate and pay damages for lost income opportunities.

If the executor has already been replaced when the misconduct is discovered, the current executor also has the right to sue the former executor on behalf of the estate. In either case, don't try this on your own; you'll need competent legal advice to pursue the matter in court.

> **Y**our widowed mother remarried just before she died. Although her will doesn't mention her new spouse, he claims he's entitled to everything she owned.

**W**hile your mother's new husband is probably entitled to *something* from her estate, he's in for a rude awakening if he believes that all of her property will pass to him. And under certain circumstances, he may not be entitled to anything.

### What the Law Says

Generally, the law works like this. Your mother's new husband is entitled to what's known as an *elective share* or *statutory share* of her estate. That means he can take an amount that's allowed by state law to a surviving spouse who either isn't mentioned at all in the will or is left an amount that's less than what the law permits.

In most states, the surviving spouse has traditionally been allowed to take between one-third and one-half of the total amount of the estate. But some states have declared it unfair that someone who married shortly before their new spouse died should receive such a large portion of the deceased spouse's property. As a result, certain states have revised their laws so

that the elective share is on a sliding scale—the longer the couple was married, the more the surviving spouse is entitled to receive.

> **I**n most states, the surviving spouse has traditionally been allowed to take between one-third and one-half of the total amount of the estate.

### Prenuptial and Postnuptial Agreements

It's possible that your mother and her new husband had a prenuptial or postnuptial agreement that legally limited the amount of property he would receive under her will. People who remarry often sign these contracts as a way of protecting their children's inheritance. Unless it can be shown that the agreement was entered into under duress or because of fraud, or that your mother failed to adequately disclose the extent of her property, it's likely that the court will enforce the contract's terms. Check with your mother's attorney to see if she executed one of these agreements with her new husband.

## CALL A LAWYER

If you are the executor for your mother's estate, and your mother's husband seems bent on a fight, ask an attorney to write him a letter explaining how the law in your state works. In most cases, once the facts are set out, you can avoid more serious problems. A lawyer's help will also be needed if your mother's husband threatens to contest—or challenge—the will in court.

## WHEN TO REVISE YOUR ESTATE PLAN

Diamonds may be forever, but an estate plan shouldn't be. To keep your estate plan current, it's a good idea to sit down at least once a year and consider your financial situation and your relationships with potential beneficiaries of your estate. You may need to change your plan if:

- You've married or divorced.

- You've had children or a child has reached the age of majority (legal adulthood).

- You've moved to another state.

- State or federal law has changed in a way that affects taxation of your estate.

- You've acquired major new assets, such as a home, or received a substantial inheritance of your own.

- You've purchased or sold a business.

- The mental or physical condition of one of your beneficiaries has changed significantly (for example, one of your children has become disabled).

- A beneficiary has died.

- Your executor or trustee has died, become disabled, or moved away, or your relationship with that person has changed significantly.

Any one of the above can mean it's time to revise your estate plan to reflect the changes in circumstances. A minor change in your will can be made by executing what's known as a *codicil*, but be sure that you execute it with all the formalities called for under state law, such as signing it at the end and having it witnessed. For major changes, it's best to write a new will that contains the new provisions as well as a statement specifically revoking all your previous wills.

Changing a trust usually requires creating a new page for each change you make, such as replacing a trustee, removing assets from the trust, or changing beneficiaries.

*Never* make changes to a trust or a will by removing old pages and replacing them with new ones. Doing so will open the door to challenges from beneficiaries who are unhappy with the changes you made.

You are the executor of your late brother's will,
which names his ex-wife as a beneficiary. She insists you pay her
immediately, or she will take you to court.

Being an executor can be a difficult task, but it becomes especially challenging when someone named in the will may not actually be entitled to receive property. In many states, for example, a divorce automatically revokes the will of each spouse. In others, the divorce revokes only those provisions in the will that directly affect the ex-spouse of the testator, the person who wrote the will. So no matter what the will says about providing for your brother's ex-wife, you may be legally prohibited from honoring those terms *unless the will was made after your brother and his ex-wife divorced.*

CHECK YOUR STATE LAW

Assuming that the will was written before the divorce, your first step is to find out what the law in your state says about the effect a divorce has on a will written before the end of the marriage. You can look in your state's statute books under the probate code to find out what is revoked— the entire will or the provisions concerning your

brother's ex-wife. Even if the estate is relatively small, it's a good idea to talk to an experienced estate-planning lawyer who can confirm what the law says. Your next move depends on which of the following applies:

■ **If the will is entirely revoked due to the divorce:** Now you have another set of problems, since, in the eyes of the law, your brother died *intestate* (without a will). As a result, you may not be able to serve as executor. When a person dies intestate, the distribution of his estate is left in the hands of an administrator rather than an executor or personal representative. An administrator performs all the functions of an executor and has the same level of fiduciary responsibility. Generally, state laws rank potential administrators in the following order of preference:

● A surviving spouse
● Other family members entitled to inherit under the laws of intestacy, such as children, parents, or siblings
● Independent administrators unrelated to the deceased (these are usually appointed only when no family member is willing to serve).

■ **If only the provisions that affect your brother's ex-wife are revoked** due to the divorce—in this case, the property that would have been hers under the terms of the will instead becomes a part of the *residuary* estate—the amount left over after all of the specific gifts have been made.

Finally, you will need to examine the terms of your late brother's divorce decree to determine if he was required to leave certain property to his ex-wife. If so, the law will view this as a contract, and you will be required to honor that contract as your brother's executor.

## HIRE A LAWYER

While it may be tempting to offer your former sister-in-law something from the estate in order to avoid a battle, *don't do it.* You could find yourself being sued by the other beneficiaries of the will for breaching your responsibility as the will's executor.

Consult a lawyer about the legitimacy of the ex-wife's claims. If the lawyer concludes that her claim is invalid, having the lawyer write her a letter may be enough to put an end to her claims. But if she goes so far as to file a claim against the estate in probate court, as executor you have the responsibility of defending the will. The probate court will look to the law in your state to decide the consequences of your brother's divorce. The cost of defending a will against a challenge

---

*In many states a divorce automatically revokes the will of each spouse.*

---

is usually deducted from the estate, but if the challenge is frivolous, consult your lawyer about seeking reimbursement of legal fees and costs.

---

*Your widowed father passes away. You discover he had written a new will leaving everything to the leader of a religious group he joined just before his death.*

---

It's a common misconception that parents are legally obligated to leave their property to family members, such as children, grandchildren, or siblings. Except in the state of Louisiana, where children usually do have a claim to at least a portion of their parents' estates, there's no obligation for a parent to leave anything to family members.

However, the law *does* prohibit beneficiaries of a will from taking advantage of the *testator* (the person making a will). In some cases, wills have been contested and overturned when the probate court discovered that a bequest was made as a result of undue influence or fraud, or because the person making the will lacked the capacity to do so.

### UNDUE INFLUENCE AND FRAUD

In order to convince the probate court that a will should be overturned because of undue influence, there must be evidence that trickery, coercion, or force was used to overcome the free will of the testator and that otherwise the will would have been made out differently. Undue influence claims are frequently brought by family members when a will favors one child more than the others, but they can also be brought against those who had a relationship of trust with the testator, such as an accountant, a lawyer, or a member of the clergy. Charges against these individuals are most often brought when the testator makes a "deathbed" will that gives a large amount of the estate to the adviser.

Fraud charges fall into one of two categories:

- **Fraud in the inducement** takes place when someone influences a testator to make a bequest through deception. For example, suppose your sister claims that her husband is desperately ill and that he will need expensive care for the rest of his life. In fact, he has no such illness, but your father changes his will to provide additional funds to your sister. Your sister is guilty of fraud in the inducement, and the terms of your father's will could be challenged.
- **Fraud in the execution** occurs when someone misrepresents the contents of a will to the testator. For example, suppose your father's religious adviser brought him a document that he claimed was a pledge form but that was actually a will leaving everything to the leader's church. This is fraud in the execution and grounds for challenging the will.

## FORGERY

Charges of outright forgery of a testator's signature are less common than those claiming undue influence or fraud, but they do occur. Some court cases have held that a person who is physically incapable of signing a will can have someone else sign it on his behalf provided that he acknowledges the signature as his own. But there have been cases when a person clearly unaware of what was happening had his hand "guided" by someone who stood to benefit greatly if the will was accepted as valid.

When this happens, the testimony of the will's official witnesses will be crucial in determining whether the will is enforceable. But the testimony of other witnesses, such as doctors, nurses, and visitors to the testator, may also be considered in reaching a decision on whether to accept or reject the will.

## LACK OF CAPACITY

This is the reason most often used to challenge a will. By law, a person making a will must have what's known as *testamentary capacity*. To have this capacity, the testator must…

■ **Understand the nature and extent of the property** he owns. While this doesn't mean that the testator has to have a detailed knowledge of every account number and the legal description of all his real estate, it does mean that he must know that he owns such assets as well as some general sense of how much his estate is worth.

■ **Recognize the "natural objects of his bounty"**—that is, he must be able to remember his family and who they are. This is sometimes difficult for people suffering from Alzheimer's disease or other forms of dementia, who may not remember all of their children, or that a child has died.

■ **Understand that he is making a will** (in legal terms, understand the *"testamentary act"*). This means that the testator has to understand that the document he is signing will dispose of his property after his death.

■ **Understand the way each of the three elements above relates to the other.** That doesn't mean that he must leave his property to family members, but it does mean that he must understand that he isn't leaving them anything.

## CONTEST THE WILL

If you believe that your father lacked the capacity to make a will, or if you think he was subjected to undue influence or was the victim of fraud, you can go to court to contest, or challenge, the will's provisions. In most states, only an "interested party" can contest a will; that means someone who stands to gain if the will's provisions are overruled.

Don't delay taking action, since in most states will contests must take place within a very short period of time after the will is offered for probate—often for no more than several months.

You will have the burden of proof in court, which means you will be required to convince the court that your father's will is invalid. In many states, you must meet the standard of *clear and convincing evidence*—not as hard as proving your case *beyond a reasonable doubt,* but more difficult than proving your case by a *preponderance of the evidence,* or merely showing that the position you take is more likely than not to be correct.

You will have to show that your father lacked capacity or was the victim of fraud, coercion, or undue influence at the time the will was made. The testimony of the witnesses to your father's will is given great weight by the probate court, but it may also hear from others who had knowledge of your father's state of mind or the circumstances surrounding the execution of his will. For example, if your father was in a nursing home when the will was written and signed, the home's medical director and nursing staff members could be called to testify.

While it's possible that the probate court may reach a speedy resolution of your claim, be prepared for a lengthy battle; will contests have been known to drag on for years, especially when the estate is sizable. And remember that not only does the executor have a duty to defend the will's validity in court, but he must pay for the costs of that defense out of the estate's assets. A drawn-out court fight can take a significant toll on the size of the estate. If you are offered a settlement by the executor, it may make more sense to accept it than to allow the contest to continue indefinitely. Your lawyer can help you evaluate a settlement offer in light of the success of other cases like yours and the strength of the evidence you present, but ultimately the decision to accept or reject a settlement will be yours.

## IF YOU SUCCEED

If the probate court agrees that your father's will is invalid, there are two possible outcomes. In many states, if your father had made a will previous to the one that has been overturned,

that will is revived and its provisions take effect. In others, or if your father had no previous will, his estate will be distributed according to the state's laws of intestate succession and divided among surviving children, or their descendants.

---

*In most states, only an "interested party" can contest a will.*

---

## IN TERROREM CLAUSES

Some testators attempt to head off will contests by including an *in terrorem* clause in the will that prohibits an unsuccessful challenger from receiving anything from the estate.

If, for example, you receive a smaller share of your father's estate than your brother and only sibling gets, and you contest the will and lose, this clause would prevent you from getting anything from your father's estate—your brother would get everything.

In the belief that doing so might help perpetuate fraud, not every state enforces *in terrorem* clauses when good-faith challenges to wills are made. Your lawyer can tell you about the validity of *in terrorem* clauses in your state.

---

*You know that your mother wrote a will, but you aren't able to locate it.*

---

Finding a will is usually easy, especially when a deceased person is survived by a spouse.

But when the person who died lived alone, or was secretive, locating a will can pose a problem. And sometimes a will can't be found because it was concealed or destroyed by a potential heir who stood to gain less than she would receive under the state's laws of intestate succession (see "When a Will Is Destroyed," page 395).

## HOW TO SEARCH

If your mother's spouse is still living, he's the first person to ask about the will's whereabouts.

But be sure to be sensitive; dealing with a grieving spouse can be a difficult. He may be angry, disoriented, or disorganized—not to mention concerned about his own future. A gentle approach is best in these circumstances.

If your mother lived alone at the time of her death or if her husband isn't able to help, these steps may help you locate her will:

- **If you know the name of her attorney or accountant,** call him to see if he knows where your mother put the original or if he has a copy of the will in his files.

- **If your mother belonged to a prepaid legal service plan,** contact the plan's administrator or the attorney who actually provided service to her. Ask if will safekeeping was a benefit of the plan.
- **If you don't know who your mother's lawyer is,** look through the files she maintained at home. Contact her siblings, in-laws, business associates, and friends for any leads about the will's location.

### SAFETY-DEPOSIT BOXES: HANDLE WITH CARE

If the will still doesn't turn up, start contacting banks where your mother had accounts to see if she had a safe-deposit box. Many older people keep important documents in a safe-deposit box. You should also ask at other institutions located in the area where your mother lived. Banks may require you to put your request in writing and to provide a copy of your mother's death certificate.

---

*Many states will allow the safe-deposit box to be opened for a will search provided that it's opened in the presence of a bank officer and no other items are removed from the box.*

---

If you discover that your mother had a safe-deposit box, you'll need to do some research before trying to open it. State laws differ dramatically about who is allowed to open a safe deposit box after the death of the box holder. Some states allow a spouse who was the joint holder of a safe-deposit box access at any time after a spouse's death, but may deny access to a sibling or child who was a joint tenant. In other states, the law requires the bank to seal the box upon the death of any holder, to be opened in the presence of local tax authorities. But many states will allow the box to be opened for a will search, provided that the box is opened in the presence of a bank officer and no other items are removed from the box.

Unless you are absolutely certain that there's no legal obstacle to entering a safe-deposit box

held by a deceased relative, check with a lawyer about the legality of doing so before taking action. If you are a joint tenant and enter the box shortly after your mother's death, for example, you could be subject to civil or criminal charges if state law prohibited access. And in some cases, people who enter the safe-deposit boxes of deceased family members find themselves accused of theft by other beneficiaries and heirs of the deceased.

### TAKE OUT AN AD

Finally, consult your attorney about placing an ad in a legal newspaper, seeking information about any will your mother may have written. It's possible that a lawyer who formerly worked in the neighborhood where your mother lived has moved to another location. If the lawyer sees the advertisement, he can contact you with information that could be helpful in locating the will, or he may even have a copy in his files.

### WHEN A WILL DOESN'T LOOK LIKE A WILL

Most of us think of a will as a formal, typewritten document. And in fact, courts are usually very strict in enforcing state laws that set out the criteria for a valid will. But a will can take several different forms, and in some states, documents that are very informally created have been given full force and effect in the probate courts.

In a few states, a simple statement in your mother's handwriting disposing of her property (called a *holographic will*) would be considered every bit as valid as a lengthy document produced by a major law firm. Older people sometimes create these documents during a hospital stay or while in a nursing home. A holographic will that has been properly witnessed is legal in every state.

To be sure that you don't overlook a document that a court could accept as your mother's will, look closely at all of the papers in her files. Even documents written on scraps of paper have been upheld in some state probate courts. If you find something in writing that might be considered a will, get legal advice about its potential validity from an experienced attorney.

In a few states, an oral will made during the testator's last illness (called a *nuncupative will*) can be allowed to pass on items of the deceased's personal property, but it isn't valid to transfer title to real estate. And while movies and television shows depict wills made on videotape, videos are no substitute for a written document, although they can be used as evidence in a will contest to confirm the mental stability of the testator at the time a written will was executed. If your mother made a video, ask a lawyer if the court in your state will consider it as evidence that a written will was created.

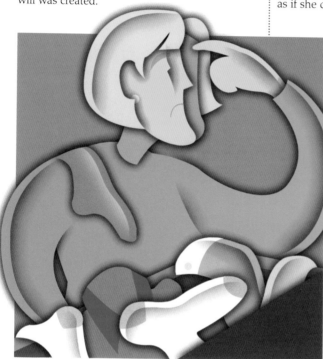

In some cases, no matter how hard you search, you won't be able to find a copy of anything that could be considered your mother's will. If so, you'll have to have your mother's estate probated as if she died without having made one. Under these circumstances, your mother's estate will pass to the next heir according to the state law of intestate succession. Although these laws vary from state to state, generally they provide one-third to one-half of the estate to any surviving spouse, with the rest going to the children or their descendants. A few states also provide for a share of the estate to go to the deceased's surviving parents.

While there's usually no time limit for opening an estate under intestacy laws, it's a good idea to get the process started as soon as it's clear that there is no will. Talk to a lawyer if there's a possibility that a will could turn up later. If you begin administering the estate according to state law, and a valid will is discovered, the complications and expenses needed to straighten things out can cause enormous headaches.

## WHEN A WILL IS DESTROYED

In some cases, family members have been known to hide or destroy a will that left them less than what they'd receive under the state's laws of intestacy. While the law requires anyone who has possession of a person's will to deliver it to the executor as soon as they learn of the testator's death, in practice it can be hard to prove that a will was destroyed.

If you suspect that someone has hidden or destroyed the will of a deceased relative:

- **Contact the people you believe witnessed the will,** such as friends or business associates of the testator. They may be able to provide information about when and where the will was written, and even who had possession of it.

- **Notify the probate court administrator** if you get confirmation that a will was written. She can tell you how to proceed.

- **Talk to your local prosecutor's office** about the matter. But be forewarned that unless you have extremely strong proof against a specific individual, it's unlikely that the prosecutor's office will take much of an interest.

> *Y*our grandfather created a trust to provide for your education, with the balance to be paid to you at age 25. Upon your 25th birthday you learn that the money is gone.

**M**ost trustees manage the balancing act of satisfying both the trust's beneficiaries and its legal requirements. But some circumstances can make it virtually impossible to keep a trust's beneficiaries happy.

### WHY PROBLEMS OCCUR

Like executors, trustees have a variety of responsibilities, including…

- Acting in the best interest of the trust beneficiaries
- Avoiding commingling trust funds with their own money
- Making the trust's assets productive
- Managing the trust's assets responsibly to avoid waste and preserve the trust fund.

But suppose that your grandfather established your trust with $10,000 shortly before his death. The terms of the trust require the trustee to pay out a portion of the trust each year to fund your college education. The trustee successfully invests the assets, doubling the trust fund. But the cost of your higher education is more than $5,000 per year, so he must reduce the original principal and accumulated growth in order to pay for your schooling. As a result, at the end of your four years in college, the entire trust fund is exhausted.

But that doesn't mean you didn't get anything. In fact, you got just what the trust your grandfather established called for: payment for your education, with any remaining funds released to you when you turn 25.

### IS IT INCOMPETENCE OR FRAUD?

On the other hand, not every trustee is capable, and a few may be downright dishonest. If your grandfather funded your education trust with $100,000 instead of $10,000 and the trustee still claims that the fund has been used up, alarm bells should be going off.

Some trustees simply don't have the experience to handle the tasks required of them. Others may have suffered a physical or mental illness that affects their capacity to perform their duties. In some cases, trustees may have problems with substance abuse, alcoholism, or personal finances that may tempt them to dip into trust funds for their personal use.

Generally, it's not an easy task to remove a trustee simply because he hasn't had a great deal of success investing the trust's assets. But your chances of dismissing the trustee and recovering losses are greater if the trustee has been guilty of fraud, negligence, or self-dealing (such as investing trust funds in a business he owns or controls).

### HOW TO FIGHT BACK

As the date for ending the trust nears, you should receive an accounting from the trustee of how funds were distributed, how investments were made, and the amount of money left for distribution. If you haven't received this accounting, request one in writing from the trustee. Take this statement to an accountant for an independent review. An objective examination may show that the trustee has fulfilled all of his responsibilities as required and that the fund is depleted through no fault of the trustee.

On the other hand, if the accountant finds discrepancies in the accounting, you should take the following steps:

■ **Discuss the matter with the trustee.** Ask him for a written explanation of any problems that the accountant noted. Keep a log of the dates of your conversations with the trustee and the responses you receive.

■ **Make a written request for clarification** if your informal request doesn't produce a satisfactory answer or if the trustee simply refuses to discuss the matter with you. At this stage, you don't want to be accusatory; there may be a good explanation for the reduced trust fund. Be sure to set a deadline for the trustee to respond to your request, and send your letter by certified mail, return receipt requested.

■ **Consult an attorney** who practices in the field of wills and trusts if you can't get a satisfactory answer after your written request. She can take a look at the entire set of circumstances, including the terms of the trust, the accounting provided by the trustee, and the opinion of the accountant. By evaluating all of these factors in light of state law, the attorney can tell you what recourse, if any, you may have against the trustee.
  ● The lawyer may be able to write a letter demanding that the trustee restore missing funds to the trust.
  ● If the trustee refuses, you may be able to file suit in state court charging the trustee with breach of his duty.

**TAKE NOTE** *In some cases, trustees may be required to post a bond designed to protect them from having to pay losses out of their own pocket. Look into the possibility that there is a bonding company that should be notified of your claim against the trustee.*

## A TRUSTEE'S DUTIES

Trustees need a variety of skills to perform their duties successfully. As a trustee, you will be expected to...

  ✔ Notify the beneficiaries that you are the trustee.

  ✔ Provide a copy of the trust document to each beneficiary.

  ✔ Notify financial institutions holding trust property that you are the trustee.

  ✔ Inventory all of the trust's assets and collect trust income.

  ✔ Make appropriate investments of trust funds.

  ✔ File federal and state tax returns and make tax payments.

  ✔ Distribute trust property to beneficiaries as required.

  ✔ Prepare a final accounting and distribute all the trust assets when the trust terminates.

While in most cases you can hire professionals to help you with the management of the trust, keep in mind that you bear the ultimate responsibility for decisions affecting the trust and could find yourself personally liable if investments go sour or beneficiaries successfully challenge the decisions you made. Think long and hard before agreeing to take on the task of serving as a trustee.

**Y**our son has never handled his finances very successfully, and you are concerned that money you leave him when you die will be squandered.

It's difficult when grown children act irresponsibly with money, and it's even more troubling to consider that the property and assets you've worked so hard to accumulate could be gone in the blink of an eye once you pass away.

Fortunately, there is a legal way to help preserve the value of your estate to provide for your son after you're gone. By establishing a *spendthrift trust*, you can benefit your son even though you believe he can't or won't manage his inheritance wisely. And you can also help protect your estate from being decimated by your son's creditors.

### CHOOSING A TRUSTEE

While it's common for someone establishing a trust to name a family member or personal friend as trustee, in some situations that may not be the best path to take. A family member could fall prey to the entreaties or threats of another family member who is the beneficiary of a spendthrift trust, releasing more funds from the trust than is wise or than you believe your son can handle. If the trustee does this, not only does she defeat the purpose of the spendthrift trust, but she also could end up being sued by your son for failing to act in his best interest.

In a case like this, it might be a good idea to use a professional trustee, such as a bank or trust company. A professional trustee can administer your trust more impersonally and is unlikely to violate the terms of the trust. Professional trustees (sometimes called *institutional trustees* or *corporate fiduciaries*) can provide other benefits as well. They offer full-time management of your trust fund, and a trust-fund officer who will have hands-on responsibility for your trust is usually well versed in the law, in making investments, and in distributing trust funds to beneficiaries. In addition, she will be able to call on other employees of the trust company or bank for assistance when a matter calls for special expertise.

Contact several different banks and trust companies before selecting one to act as your trustee. You'll want to find out what kinds of investment, accounting, or tax-preparation services they offer.

Once the trust company or bank takes over as trustee, it will be entitled to collect a fee for its services out of the trust's assets. Be sure you understand in advance how that fee will be calculated. And remember that professional trustees have the right to decline to serve as your trustee, just as an individual would. If your estate is relatively small, the professional trustee may not feel that it makes financial sense to take on the task of administering your trust.

You responded to an advertisement for an estate-planning seminar. Now you're being pressured by a salesperson to purchase a living-trust kit from the seminar company.

According to AARP and various consumer protection agencies across the country, living- trust scams are a growing area of consumer fraud. Charging anywhere from $500 to $5,000 for living-trust kits, con artists are making millions of dollars annually peddling a product that many Americans don't really need or that won't provide the benefits that are promised.

### WHAT IS A LIVING TRUST?

A living trust is a document that allows you to transfer ownership of your assets before you die. In the living trust, you (referred to as the *settlor* or the *grantor* of the trust) name a *trustee* to manage the property according to the terms contained in the trust document. You can name just about any adult to act as your trustee, such as a friend, spouse, or family member, or designate a bank or other financial institution to do the job. In most cases, you can also name yourself as trustee of your own trust and name someone else to take over when you die or become incapacitated.

### WHAT TO WATCH OUT FOR

Typically, living-trust scam artists concentrate on those who are 50 or older and have accumulated assets that they are concerned about protecting from estate taxes. You may be contacted through the mail or by a telemarketer. Some living-trust salespeople work door-to-door, while others invite you to attend free estate-planning workshops, which usually turn out to be little more than high-pressure sales meetings. They may offer a "free" living will or power of attorney as an added inducement to get you to attend. But these documents are generally the same fill-in-the-blank forms you can purchase for a few dollars at your local stationery store.

### PHONY CLAIMS ABOUT LIVING TRUSTS

Living-trust scam artists play on the mistrust many Americans have of the legal system in general and lawyers in particular. You'll often hear them making false or misleading statements designed to frighten older people about the cost and delays of the probate process. These are some typical false claims made by living trust salespeople:

---

*Typically, living-trust scam artists concentrate on those who are 50 or older and have accumulated assets that they are concerned about protecting from estate taxes.*

---

- **Living trusts save taxes.** In fact, a revocable living trust won't save any more taxes than a carefully constructed will.
- **Living trusts let you avoid paying your creditors.** Not true. While you're alive and after you die, the assets in a living trust can be subject to creditors' claims.
- **Living trusts can't be contested the way a will can.** A living trust can be attacked for most of the same reasons a will can, including

claims of fraud, undue influence, or lack of capacity (the mental ability to create the trust).

- **Living trusts are the only way to avoid probate.** Actually, there are a number of other methods available to transfer property outside the probate process, including joint tenancy with right of survivorship, custodial accounts for minor children, annuities, and pay-on-death (POD) accounts. And even with a living trust, you could still face probate of any assets that haven't been properly placed in the trust, so you'll need a will anyway.
- **Probate typically takes years to complete.** While there have been some famous cases in which probate dragged on for many years (like that of Howard Hughes and Marilyn Monroe), but in most cases it does not take a great deal of time to take most estates through the probate process. And simplified probate procedures for small estates are in place in most states to help expedite matters even further.
- **Probate costs and legal fees will eat up most of your estate.** Probate costs for most estates aren't large—typically, only a few thousand dollars. Simplified probate procedures for smaller estates are even less expensive, and they don't always require a lawyer's involvement. When a lawyer is involved, fees are always negotiable.

### HIDDEN DANGERS IN LIVING-TRUST KITS

On top of the fact that these living-trust kits don't deliver the results they promise, they can even make matters more complicated, not less. Most of these kits are full of what lawyers call *boilerplate*—one-size-fits-all language, which may not apply to your own estate-planning circumstances. For example, some widowed individuals have purchased living-trust kits that were written for a married couple.

In other cases, the language within the trust document may be confusing. One trust stated that the trust would end when the grantor's grandchildren reached the age of 18, but in another paragraph the age was set at 21. To get the matter straightened out, your loved ones may have to hire an attorney and go to court, further reducing the amount left for your beneficiaries.

Another reason to avoid living trusts is that

---

**SMART MOVES**

If you have a living trust naming a spouse as beneficiary, that provision could stay in effect even after you divorce. Check with your attorney about the law in your state and the steps you must take to amend the living trust.

---

creating one may actually reduce your eligibility for Medicaid coverage of nursing-home care. Generally, assets such as your home and automobile are exempted when calculating your

> **A**nother reason to avoid living trusts is that creating one may actually reduce your eligibility for Medicaid coverage of nursing-home care.

assets and determining eligibility. But when these assets are transferred to a living trust, they are often included in figuring your assets, and you could end up being denied Medicaid coverage as a result. State laws differ in the way they treat certain assets for Medicaid purposes. Talk to a lawyer about the specific rules in your state.

Similarly, homestead laws exempt at least some of your home's value from creditors' claims. In some states, these laws also protect you and your spouse from being forced out of your home. Putting title to your home in a trust could deprive you of this important legal protection.

Finally, unless your estate is large, the costs associated with creating and administering a trust may equal or exceed any benefits derived. It's not enough just to fill in the blanks or use a computer program to create the trust documents.

There's also the time and expense involved in changing title to the property you own as an individual and transferring that title to the trust. If you don't take this step, the property won't become part of the trust fund, and it will pass by the terms of your will (if you have one) or the law of intestate succession (if you don't have a will).

### INVESTIGATE THE CLAIMS

Con artists will often depend on high-pressure sales tactics to get you to sign on the dotted line and purchase a living trust kit. But if you think a living trust might be worth considering, don't

allow yourself to be strong-armed into making a purchase. Instead:

- **Ask for the credentials of the attorney** who designed the kit being offered. State laws vary, and the plan you're being offered should be drawn up by a lawyer licensed in your state.
- **Contact the Better Business Bureau** and your state's office of consumer protection to find out about any complaints against the company.
- **Talk to your accountant,** banker, financial planner, or attorney about how a living trust might benefit you.
- **Never allow yourself to be pressured** into "acting now." If the offer is a good one and the company has a legitimate product, you should be able to buy it after you've had time to investigate the company, consult with professionals you trust, and weigh the pros and cons carefully for yourself.

Recently, law enforcement officials and state bar associations have taken a greater interest in pursuing claims against companies that sell boilerplate living trusts, charging them with making misleading claims in order to frighten older Americans into purchasing a kit, or investigating them for the unauthorized practice of law. If you feel that you have been conned into purchasing a living trust, contact the consumer protection division of your state attorney general's office, or your local bar association, for assistance.

## WHEN A LIVING TRUST *DOES* MAKE SENSE

Living trusts may not be for everyone, especially those with relatively modest estates. But they can be a good estate-planning tool under certain circumstances. Generally, you might want to consider a living trust if…

■ **You have very specific goals** for how your money will be divided among your beneficiaries.

■ **You own property in a state other than the one in which you live.** Having a trust hold title to that real estate could avoid the costs and complications associated with what are known as "ancillary" probate proceedings. For example, if the bulk of your estate is located in Colorado, but you own some land in Ohio, you will have to have a personal representative appointed to transfer ownership of that property to your heirs. That usually means hiring another lawyer licensed in the state where the land is located in addition to the one handling matters in your home state.

■ **You want to appoint someone who lives out of state** to administer your estate. Some states place restrictions on out-of-state executors that don't apply to a trustee.

■ **You are tired of managing your own property** and want to hand that task over to a professional trustee or a trusted friend or family member.

■ **You want to protect the privacy of your decisions** about how your property is to be distributed. Unlike a will, which becomes a public document when it's presented to the probate court, a trust remains sheltered from public view.

It's worthwhile to speak with an experienced estate-planning attorney about your specific financial situation. In most cases, having a living trust drawn up by a lawyer isn't as expensive as you might expect, and in many cases it's even less expensive than the living-trust kits being peddled by companies at seminars and door-to-door.

A *sales clerk at a boutique in town asks you to put your home address and telephone number on a credit-card sales slip. When you decline, she says you can't make a purchase unless you agree.*

In most cases, this practice is not allowed—either by credit-card issuers or by the law. Many credit-card issuers don't authorize merchants to do anything more than compare the signature on the card to the signature on the sales slip. And in a number of states, it's actually illegal for a merchant to record any identifying information when a credit card is used.

## SOME EXCEPTIONS MAY APPLY

Depending on the law in your state, you could be required to provide some identifying information, such as your telephone number and address, when you use your credit card for the following reasons:

- To make a deposit on an item you are renting
- To obtain a cash advance
- When the information is required for an incidental purpose, such as for shipping goods
- When you provide your credit-card number but don't have the actual card in your possession
- If a federal or state law requires identification (for example, when purchasing a firearm).

In addition, some states allow merchants to request photo identification, such as a driver's license or a state-issued ID card.

## TALK TO THE BOSS

If the above scenario happens to you, you can probably resolve the matter by talking to the manager or owner of the shop. Tell him that you object to providing personal information. In many cases, this will be the end of the matter.

If the manager or store owner insists, however, ask him what his agreement with the credit-card issuer says about collecting personal data. He may not know it, but he may be violating his contract with the credit-card company by asking for personal information.

You should also ask him if the law allows him to collect personal information for a simple credit-card purchase. If he claims that the law in your state permits this, ask him to provide you with the statute that authorizes him to do so. Of course, he won't be able to because there is no such law.

## COMPLAIN TO HIGHER AUTHORITIES

If the merchant persists in demanding that you give her additional information, consider whether to walk away from the purchase or to provide the information she wants. In either case, there are steps you can take after you leave the store to help protect your privacy and that of other customers.

- **Notify your credit-card company.**
  A representative can contact the merchant and remind him that asking for additional identification or personal information may be a violation of their agreement.

- **File a complaint** with your state attorney general's office of consumer protection. This agency can investigate the store's practices, and if it's received similar complaints from a number of other consumers, it can file suit. If the merchant is found to have violated state law, he may be subject to a variety of penalties, including fines for each violation and a court order prohibiting him from violating the law in the future.

## YOUR LAST RESORT

Depending on your state law, you may be able to file a private lawsuit to collect monetary damages from the merchant. In some states, you can collect the actual damages you suffer or an amount set out in the statutes, whichever is greater.

You may also be able to file a class-action lawsuit if it appears that the merchant has broken the law against many customers in the same way. You'll need an attorney's help for a class-action

> *In a number of states, it's actually illegal for a merchant to record any identifying information when a credit card is used.*

suit. An attorney will usually meet with you to evaluate your case for no charge or for a small fee. (Be sure to ask if there is a charge for an initial consultation, and what that charge will be.)

## WARRANTY CARDS INVADE YOUR PRIVACY

Nowadays, everything from blenders to bowling balls comes with a warranty card that you're urged to return to the manufacturer to "register your purchase." But in addition to asking for your name, address, and telephone number, these cards often ask you to reveal:

- ✔ Your age
- ✔ Your income
- ✔ Hobbies and interests
- ✔ Your e-mail address
- ✔ How you learned about the product
- ✔ Where you purchased the product
- ✔ What other major purchases you've recently made.

In fact, none of this information is related in any way to the warranty on the product you've purchased. The cards are simply a way to collect data that can be rented or shared with other manufacturers and merchants. Answer the questions, and chances are your mailbox will soon be flooded with offers from companies selling products geared to your demographic group.

There's no need to return one of these cards to the manufacturer in order to protect your warranty rights. All you have to do is keep the original receipt from your purchase, along with the information enclosed with the product about how to obtain warranty repairs or a replacement. Don't get suckered into revealing more information about yourself than necessary by filling out and returning a warranty card.

Your local supermarket introduces a new "shopper's club card." But to get the store's best discounts, you are required to reveal personal information on the card application.

**M**ajor supermarket chains first introduced VIP and preferred shopper cards in the 1990s, and they caught on like wildfire. Shoppers like them because they get special savings on selected items throughout the store without the chore of collecting coupons. Supermarkets like shopper cards because they keep customers coming back. But they serve an additional purpose. Every time you use your shopping card, you're disclosing information about your buying habits to the store.

### Your Buying Habits

Buying baby food? Your store may make you a "special offer" on diapers or offer a discount on a child-care book. Loading your cart with cupcakes and candy? The store might send you information about its "healthy eating" options.

Retailers call this *database marketing*. Merchants use it to learn about the kinds of customers who shop in their stores and to target consumers with advertisements in the mail. They claim that the use of database marketing allows them to improve the services they provide, to stock their shelves with more of the goods consumers want, and to develop customer loyalty.

What's the harm in it? Some critics cite these potential problems:

- **Grocery chains may sell or give information** about your buying habits to other merchants and marketers. Although most supermarket operators claim that they have no intention of doing this, there is nothing to stop them if they want to.
- **Law enforcement authorities may subpoena shopping-card records** in the course of investigating suspected criminal activity. In several states, Drug Enforcement Administration (DEA) agents have subpoenaed records to review customer purchases of certain cold medications that contain an ingredient used in the manufacture of illegal drugs.

- **Lawyers in a private lawsuit may subpoena shopping-card records** to see if they contain information that could be used against you. For example, if you are fighting for child custody, your ex-spouse's attorney could get a court order and review your purchasing history to see if you are buying alcoholic beverages, cigarettes, or contraceptives, all of which could help support a claim that you are not fit to have custody of your children.
- **The store may use the information to shield itself** from liability if you are injured on the store's premises. In one case, a shopper who slipped and fell in a grocery store was allegedly told that if he pursued a lawsuit against the store, it was prepared to reveal in court that the customer frequently purchased alcoholic beverages, implying that he was intoxicated at the time of the accident.

### Protect Your Privacy

If you don't want the store to have personal information about you, here's what you can do:

- **Don't give identifying information.** It isn't publicized, but according to officials at several supermarket chains that issue shopping cards, you aren't *required* to provide personal information when applying for a card. You may be given a card linked to a title, such as "Valued Customer" rather than one linked to your name or other personal information. Store personnel may not be aware of the company's policy in this regard, so talk to a store manager if you want to have your card issued this way.

### Smart Moves

Always check receipts to be sure you received the special savings you're entitled to when using your shopping card. Faulty scanners and computer programming can result in higher-than-advertised prices. If so, tell the store manager or customer service representative.

Find out if the store has a policy of giving mispriced items to customers at no charge.

■ **Ask before you tell.** If your favorite supermarket insists on having you fill out an application completed with a name, address, telephone number, and other

---

*Every time you use your shopping card, you're disclosing information about your buying habits.*

---

identifying information, ask the store manager the following questions:

✔ What information is required and what will it be used for?

✔ What benefits will you receive for providing your personal information?

✔ What is the company's policy on sharing information with other merchants, manufacturers, and service providers?

✔ Is the company's privacy policy in writing, and can the policy be changed without notifying you first?

■ **Change stores.** Some local grocery stores and a few national chains still offer discounts to all their customers and don't require a store-issued card in order for a shopper to take advantage of special offers and sale prices. Patronizing these stores is a good way to "vote with your pocketbook." Stores that lose money because of their data-collection practices may be forced to change the way they do business.

■ **Consider using a pseudonym.** If you aren't satisfied with the answers you receive, but you still want to get the special prices offered only to card members, consider using a false name, address, and telephone number on your card application. The clerk who takes your application is unlikely to question the information you provide, and this way you get the benefits of using the store's card without revealing any identifying information about yourself.

**TAKE NOTE** *Under federal regulations, your telephone company cannot block your number from being identified when you call a merchant's 800, 888, or a 877 toll-free telephone number.*

---

*You've moved into a new home, and the local utility company wants your Social Security number before it will turn on the electricity.*

---

Whether you're applying for insurance, visiting a new doctor or dentist, or even taking your pet to a new veterinarian for a checkup, chances are you'll be asked to provide your Social Security number on the forms you fill out. Social Security numbers have become a form of national identification.

While many of us provide this number without giving it a second thought or because we think we're legally required to do so, in fact only a few places need our Social Security numbers. You must reveal the number only to the following:

● The Internal Revenue Service and the state taxation departments
● Banks, home lenders, and stock brokerages

● Your employer, for income-tax withholding
● State licensing agencies for assisting in collection of child support.

On the other hand, there's no law prohibiting businesses or other government agencies from asking you to provide your Social Security number. But because it's linked to your bank accounts, financial records, and credit report, letting the number fall into the wrong hands could make you the victim of identity fraud.

### WHAT YOU SHOULD DO

If you would prefer not to provide your Social Security number to a private business of any kind, here are some steps to take:

- **Ask why the business needs your Social Security number.** If you're told that it's "required by company policy," ask to see the written policy statement. Chances are there isn't one.
- **Offer to provide an alternative number** that can be used for identification purposes. More and more businesses are becoming aware of the problem of identity fraud and are willing to work with their customers to prevent it.
- **Ask to talk to a supervisor** if you still can't convince the company's representative. Lower-level employees may not be empowered to let you use a different number.

- **Keep working your way up the chain of command** if the supervisor can't help. It's likely that someone at a higher level can use his or her authority to honor your request.
- **Contact your state or local consumer protection agency.** It may be able to convince the business that it can use a different method of identifying you in its records.

**ALERT** *While it may be tempting to make up a number when asked for your Social Security number, don't do it. You could give someone else's number—someone whose credit and payment history aren't as solid as yours. And you could even find yourself being investigated for identity theft.*

**Y**ou learn that your state's Department of Motor Vehicles is considering selling information about licensed drivers to an out-of-state insurance company.

**Y**our state Department of Motor Vehicles (DMV) knows a surprising amount about you. After all, in order to obtain a driver's license, you are asked to provide not only your name, address, and telephone number but also your Social Security number, a photograph, and medical information as well. For years, many states helped to fill their coffers by selling some or all of this information to individuals and businesses, in most cases, without their residents ever knowing about it.

### POTENTIAL PROBLEMS

For the most part, this information was purchased by legitimate businesses, such as insurers, automobile manufacturers, and other companies that used the data to customize sales materials they sent to potential customers. But others had less benign motives. In 1989, a young actress named Rebecca Schaeffer was stalked and murdered by a man who had obtained her address and telephone number from her state's DMV. Some victims of domestic violence were confronted by ex-partners who learned of their whereabouts from state DMV records. And a few extreme antiabortion organizations used DMV records to

find the home addresses of doctors and other medical personnel involved in performing abortions, then harassed them at home.

### FEDERAL PROTECTION

In response to these problems, Congress enacted the Drivers' Privacy Protection Act of 1994 (DPPA), which limits the ability of a state DMV to release a driver's personal information without the driver's consent. This law restricts the ability of the DMV in a state to release the following information:

- ✔ Your photograph
- ✔ Your Social Security number
- ✔ Your driver identification number
- ✔ Your name, address, and telephone number
- ✔ Your medical records
- ✔ Information about a disability

But that's not the end of the problem. Many critics of the DPPA claim that the law is so loaded down with exceptions that it's still far too easy for someone to get your personal information from the DMV without your knowledge or consent. For example, states can still provide your information:

✔ To an insurer and their agents, employees, and contractors for purposes of underwriting and rating policyholders

✔ To licensed private investigators and security services for certain purposes

✔ To tow-truck and impound-lot operators

✔ For use in research studies and for statistical reports

✔ To a host of other businesses and to individuals for a number of approved uses.

## YOUR OPTIONS

Contact your state DMV and ask it about its current privacy policy. If the DMV tells you that it does sell information for use by marketers or in solicitations, these are the steps to take:

■ **Ask to "opt out"** of having your personal information disclosed. Under the DPPA, states must implement methods that give you this option.

■ **Contact the Department of Justice** if you find out that your state has no easy system for opting out. A state DMV that is found to be in "substantial noncompliance" with the DPPA can be fined as much as $5,000 for each day that it doesn't comply with the law.

■ **Express your concerns to your elected state representatives,** and urge them to sponsor or support legislation that would strictly prohibit the release of your personal driver's license information.

---

*Many critics of the DPPA claim that the law is so loaded down with exceptions that it's still far too easy for someone to get your personal information*

---

## GO TO COURT

Check with an attorney or privacy advocacy group about filing a civil lawsuit in the federal district court against any company or individual that obtains your personal information from the DMV in violation of the DPPA. If you win your case, you could be awarded actual damages, but no less than $2,500. You could also get punitive damages if you prove that the information was obtained with willful or reckless disregard for the law. In addition, you may recoup the costs of reasonable attorney fees and other costs of pursuing your case in court as well as other relief that the court finds appropriate, such as a temporary or permanent injunction prohibiting the use of any data collected.

**TAKE NOTE** *The DPPA prohibits not only the release of your driver's license information but also personal information related to your license plates, title to your car, and automobile registration papers.*

**ALERT** *For years, many states put Social Security numbers on their licenses as an additional method of identification. But under federal law, you no longer have to allow your Social Security number to be displayed on your license.*

> **A**fter you apply for a job, your prospective employer conducts a background check without your consent.

Today an increasing number of employers are investigating job applicants' backgrounds before they hire them. They do this in the hope of weeding out troublesome applicants before they're on the job, rather than run the risk of discovering a problem after they hire them, then facing potential legal problems when they dismiss them. There are dozens of companies whose sole purpose is to conduct these investigations for companies of all sizes.

### WHAT'S WRONG WITH THIS PICTURE

Unfortunately, some employers and the companies that conduct background checks go overboard in their investigations. They may look at factors that they aren't supposed to consider when deciding whom to hire and whom to reject. For example, some have investigated applicants to determine…

- Marital status
- Age, race, national origin, and religion
- Number of dependents
- Medical history
- Worker compensation claims made in the past
- Union activity involvement.

Employers often seek access to a potential employee's credit records as well. Under the federal Fair Credit Reporting Act, a company that wants to ask a credit-reporting agency for information about you must notify you in writing within three days of the inquiry. In addition, the credit-reporting agency must alert you that a credit investigation is being made and must tell you that you have a right to ask the employer about the nature and the scope of the investigation.

### YOUR NEXT MOVE

Before considering what actions to take regarding the employer's unauthorized background check,

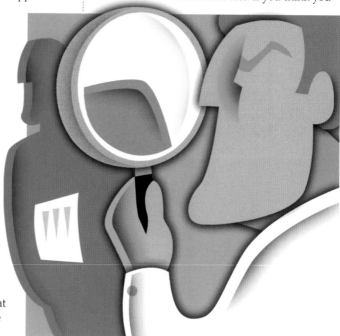

ask yourself if the company's actions have actually damaged you in any way. For example, if you get the job, how will filing a complaint or seeking legal help affect your employment situation? On the other hand, if you're being offered a supervisory position, you could be exposing yourself to potential legal problems if you're asked to engage in the same sort of practices once you're on the payroll.

However, if you *don't* get the job, the reason may be that the employer discovered something in your background that led it to unlawfully discriminate against you. There are a host of federal laws to protect people from illegal discrimination in the workplace, including Title VII of the Civil Rights Act of 1964, the Age Discrimination in Employment Act, and the Americans With Disabilities Act. If you think you

are a victim of illegal discrimination, you should file a complaint with the federal Equal Employment Opportunity Commission (EEOC). You may also be entitled to file suit under state antidiscrimination and civil rights laws.

With a few exceptions, the federal Employee Polygraph Protection Act now prohibits most private employers from requiring job applicants or employees to submit to polygraph (lie detector), voice stress, and psychological stress evaluator tests. The act even prohibits asking them to take one. And anyone who refuses to submit to an illegal lie detector test cannot be disciplined, discharged, or discriminated against for doing so.

Federal law *does* allow an employer to ask an employee to submit to a polygraph test under certain limited circumstances. You can be asked to submit to a lie detector test when:

- Your employer is investigating a specific incident, such as theft or embezzlement.

- You had access to the missing property or money.

- Your employer has a reasonable suspicion that you were involved in the incident.

- You have been given written notice of the proposed examination, the incident being investigated, and the reason you are suspected at least 48 hours in advance.

Federal, state, and local government agencies and certain companies, such as those in the security industry and drug and pharmaceutical firms, are exempt from this federal law. Companies that provide services to the Department of Defense and FBI are also exempt.

Most states have also enacted laws similar in scope to the federal law; in some of these states, you have even greater protection than the federal law provides. Union contracts may also put additional restrictions on an employer's ability to ask you to take a polygraph test. Check with an attorney or your union representative for information about the law in your state.

# $Y$our employer begins monitoring your telephone calls and e-mail at work.

Employers are caught between a rock and a hard place when it comes to employee privacy. On the one hand, a company could be found liable for illegal discrimination or sexual harassment if it doesn't stop employees from making offensive communications on the company's computers. On the other hand, employers can find themselves faced with lawsuits if they unreasonably invade their employees' privacy.

Striking a balance between these two competing interests can be difficult. But if you discover that your employer is monitoring your telephone calls or reading your e-mail, there are ways to protest. And in some situations, you may even be able to put an end to the practice.

## WHAT THE LAW SAYS

Laws regarding the privacy of employee communications vary from state to state, and federal laws that address this issue have been interpreted differently by different courts. For example, the federal Electronic Communications Privacy Act (ECPA) makes it illegal for anyone to intentionally intercept or attempt to intercept any "electronic communications." But in at least one case, a federal court ruled that e-mail stored in a company's computers was no longer an electronic communication, so the law did not prohibit reading e-mail once it had been received.

The ECPA also contains several important exceptions that employers have come to rely on to help them justify reading employee e-mail. These exemptions include:

- **The "prior consent" exemption.** If an employee is informed that the company will monitor e-mail, she cannot then complain that the company's actions constitute an invasion of privacy.
- **The "business use" exemption.** This allows an employer to intercept electronic communications made in the ordinary course of business and in the course of the worker's employment. What this means is that an employer can look at an e-mail address and subject line to determine if the communication is business-related or personal, but it can't read or disclose the e-mail's actual content.
- **The "systems provider" exemption.** This exemption allows the provider of an e-mail system (such as America Online, Earthlink, or Compuserve) to read and disclose the contents of e-mail carried over its system. Some employers have also tried to use this exemption to justify monitoring employee e-mail, claiming that they are the providers of their company's e-mail system.

State laws about employee e-mail privacy generally follow the provisions of the ECPA, but in a few states employees have additional rights. In Colorado, for example, employers are required to have written policies about e-mail and company monitoring of employees' electronic communications. In Georgia, state law makes it an invasion of privacy for an employer to reveal the contents of an employee's e-mail messages.

## WHEN PRIVACY IS INVADED

An invasion of privacy occurs when someone intentionally intrudes into the solitude or seclusion of another, or into another's personal affairs. In deciding whether an employer might be liable for invading an employee's privacy by reading her e-mail, courts will usually consider if the intrusion…

- Was intentional
- Was warranted because of the location and nature of the activity
- Would be highly offensive to any reasonable person
- Was legitimate.

## REPORT THE PROBLEM

If you find your calls and e-mails being monitored, take the following steps:

- **Talk directly to the person causing the problem.** Ask your supervisor for a meeting to discuss why the company is monitoring your communications and to express your concern about the policy.
- **Report the problem to the appropriate company official** if someone unauthorized is monitoring your e-mails. For example, if your boss is accessing your e-mail without authorization, report his actions to the human resources manager.
- **Contact your union steward or representative** about filing an official grievance if you are a union member. The procedure for filing a grievance will be set out in your union's collective bargaining agreement with your employer.

## GET LEGAL HELP

Although several lawsuits have been brought to various courts around the country claiming invasion of privacy, the courts have generally sided with the employers. The courts have given employers great leeway in monitoring employee e-mail and take the stand that an employer has a legitimate need to know about the communications being carried from its computers.

Still, it may be possible to convince a court that a company's actions constitute an invasion of privacy if the company's conduct was unwarranted. Consider discussing your situation with an attorney who handles labor law cases. The local chapter of the American Civil Liberties Union (ACLU) may also be able to provide you with guidance and the names of attorneys who might be interested in taking on your case.

## LOBBY TO CHANGE THE LAW

It's a good idea to express your concerns to your state legislator as well as your senator and representative. Although employees have some legal rights to privacy in their telephone and e-mail communications, stronger protections could be enacted—but only if employees let their elected representatives know about the problems.

**EMPLOYER MONITORING ALERT** *Not only do many employers now monitor their workers' e-mail, but they're also taking advantage of software that lets them track the Web sites that employees visit on company computers. So be careful: Workers have been terminated for spending company time to visit on-line casinos, pornographic Web sites, and other Internet destinations that aren't related to their work.*

## SIX WAYS TO PROTECT YOUR IDENTITY ONLINE

You may not realize it, but the more time you spend visiting the World Wide Web, the more likely it is that you'll unwittingly reveal enough information about yourself to help others discover your identity. Here are six simple steps you can take to help protect your privacy online.

- **Stay private by going public.** Almost all public libraries now offer on-line services, and print and copy shops may also have Internet service available. Using these facilities helps avoid connecting your Internet use to your home address.

- **Be "browser smart."** Some browsers ask you for information such as your name and telephone number when you "register" the browser software. But all the browser software needs to operate properly is the name of your Internet Service Provider (ISP) and your e-mail address. If you can't make the software work with just this information, use another browser.

- **Use an on-line "post office box."** If you use a local ISP, it's easy for someone to determine what part of the country you live in, and using your company's e-mail lets them know where you work. Consider opening a free e-mail account with companies such as juno.com, Hotmail, or Yahoo!.

- **Stay away from web-site contests.** While it may be tempting to enter a contest to win a trip overseas, a new car, or cash, most contests are designed primarily to get personal information about you that the contest sponsor can then rent or sell to others. Although the old saying may be "You can't win if you don't enter," in this case just the opposite may be true.

- **Change your address.** Changing screen names and e-mail addresses from time to time will help you stay ahead of identity thieves and "spammers" (companies and individuals that send unsolicited e-mail ads).

- **Ignore the so-called spam you do get.** Many Internet spammers offer you the option to be removed from their mailing lists. Do yourself a favor and simply delete the e-mail. Many advertisers consider any response a positive one (it means you read the e-mail they sent you), and that usually means more so-called spam, not less.

> ## You discover that a neighbor has been listening in on calls you make on your cordless phone.

You may not realize it, but it's a snap for others to listen in on calls made or received on cordless and cellular phones. Cordless telephones are essentially miniature radio stations, sending signals from the base to the handset and back again. These signals can be received by other cordless phones, police scanners, radios, and even baby monitors, sometimes as far as a mile or more away.

Cellular telephones also transmit radio signals to transmitters, usually within a range of 10 miles. As you travel from one place to another, this signal is transferred to the nearest transmitter. It can be picked up by radio scanners, although the Federal Trade Commission (FCC) now prohibits the manufacture or importing of scanners that tune in to cellular-telephone frequencies.

In most cases, conversations on cellular or cordless telephones are unintentionally overheard, but there are a number of cases on record in which people have purposely eavesdropped on and have even recorded these calls.

Those who do can face penalties ranging from fines to imprisonment, or both, depending on the nature of the offense and whether there have been repeat offenses.

---

### Federal law makes it illegal to eavesdrop on cordless and cellular telephone conversations.

---

Laws in many states offer similar protections. For example, California law makes an intentional eavesdropper subject to a penalty of $2,500 or one year of imprisonment, or both, for a first offense, and fines up to as much as $10,000 and a year in prison for repeat offenders. That state's statutes also allow anyone victimized by a telephone eavesdropper to sue the offender for damages of up to $5,000 or three times the amount of actual damages that the victim suffers.

### THE EXCEPTIONS

Generally, state laws provide some exceptions. For example, eavesdropping on cellular or cordless telephone conversations may not result in criminal prosecution if the eavesdropping is conducted by law-enforcement officials or citizens in order to obtain evidence of certain crimes, such as:

- Kidnapping
- Extortion
- Bribery
- Threats of violence
- Ethnic intimidation or hate crimes
- Any violent felony.

### REPORT THE PROBLEM

You may never know that someone is listening in on your conversations unless they tell someone else about it and it gets back to you. If it does, take the following steps:

### LEGAL PROTECTION FOR CALLERS

Federal law makes it illegal to eavesdrop on cordless and cellular telephone conversations.

- **Contact your local law-enforcement authorities *immediately*.** They will investigate your claim, and if they can verify that the eavesdropping took place, they'll file the appropriate charges in criminal court. Be persistent: law-enforcement officials may look on eavesdropping as a minor crime and give it a low priority. You might need to enlist the aid of a sympathetic newspaper reporter or the consumer advocate at a local television or radio station in order to prod the prosecutor into taking action.
- **Protect yourself from future eavesdropping** by a neighborhood snoop.
  - Look into advanced cordless phones that use digital technology. This makes it more difficult for your calls to be intercepted.
  - Investigate digital cellular networks. They also provide added protection.
  - Use a corded phone if you're not in a position to invest in new technology.

## A WORD OF CAUTION

When using a cordless or cellular phone, be wary about the information you reveal. For example, using a cordless phone to make a credit-card purchase could make it easy for someone who is listening in on your call use your card number and expiration date to commit credit-card fraud.

Discussing very personal matters over a cordless or cellular telephone, such as medical conditions, or talking to your psychologist on a cordless phone or an older-model cellular phone could lead to others learning information that you would prefer to keep private.

Finally, remember that other devices that operate on radio frequencies can also be listened in on. These include walkie-talkies, baby monitors, and wireless home intercom systems. It's a good idea to turn these items off when they're not in use just to make sure that your private conversations stay that way.

**TAKE NOTE** *While it's easier to eavesdrop on a cordless or cellular telephone call than one made over an old-fashioned wired phone, don't forget that those calls can also be recorded without your knowledge or consent. In many states, as long as one party to the conversation knows that a recording is being made, there's no legal recourse available to someone who didn't realize that a call was being taped. If you're concerned that someone may be taping your telephone calls (such as an ex-spouse hoping to gather evidence for a change in custody), check with your local-law enforcement agency and talk to your attorney about the specific law where you live.*

---

*Y*ou ended your relationship, but now
your old boyfriend is showing up at your place of work and
making menacing calls at all hours of the night.

---

**S**talking victims, the vast majority of whom are women, live in constant fear for their personal safety. Although stalking is a crime in every state, and the Interstate Stalking Punishment and Prevention Act now makes stalking a person across state lines a federal crime, the problem continues. By one recent estimate, more than 1 million Americans have been the victim of a stalker.

While penalties for stalking can include prison sentences or fines, or both, the fact remains that many stalkers are undeterred by the punishment the law metes out. And while you can obtain a

restraining order against someone who stalks you, many stalkers ignore these orders, sometimes with fatal consequences for their victims. Some experts suggest that getting a court order may only make things worse, acting as a trigger for violent behavior. Talk to the local police, a lawyer, or a victims' support group if you have concerns about getting a restraining order.

## HOW TO PROTECT YOURSELF

Your first step, of course, is to contact the police if you feel that you are being stalked. Keep in mind that the law in most states defines a stalker as someone who willfully, maliciously, and repeatedly follows or harasses another and makes a threat that places the victim and/or the victim's family in fear for their safety.

To help bolster your case, keep a log of all contacts your ex-boyfriend makes with you either in person or by telephone. Save any letters or items sent through the mail, and make copies of answering machine tapes that contain messages from the stalker. Make a log of all your contacts with law-enforcement officials about the problem, writing down the names of those you speak to and a summary of your conversations.

Your local police or district attorney's office can help you get in touch with support and advocacy groups and may even be able to arrange for you to leave your home and take up residence in a shelter. This usually isn't a permanent solution, however, and it may be necessary to move to a new home if you feel unsafe in your current residence.

Here are some other steps you should consider that can help put you out of a stalker's reach:

■ **Change your mailing address to a private post office box.** Private boxes provide more protection of your identity than those offered by the U.S. Postal Service (USPS), since most private box operators require a court subpoena before releasing information about their box holders. But the USPS merely requires confirmation from an attorney that a case is pending against a box holder, which is relatively easy to fabricate. Use the private post office box address on your checks, and don't use your home address for anything mailed or shipped to you.

■ **Get an unpublished, unlisted telephone number.** Even if your number isn't published in the local telephone directory, it could still be available from directory assistance. Never print your telephone number on your checks—if asked to write it on, either make up a number or simply refuse to provide one.

■ **Get Caller ID and Call Blocking services from the telephone company.** Caller ID allows you to see the telephone number where calls originate, while Call Blocking prevents your number from being displayed when you make a telephone call to someone who has Caller ID.

■ **Contact your state's Department of Motor Vehicles** (DMV), and ask it to suppress the release of any information from your auto registration or driver's license records. You'll probably have to provide a police report or other evidence that you are being stalked, such as a restraining order, in order to have the DMV honor your request. Your local DMV office or victims' assistance police officer can help with this process. Tip: Depending on state law, you may be able to have your private post office box listed as your address on your driver's license.

■ **Avoid verifying personal information over the telephone.** Some stalkers have been known to enlist others in their pursuit of their victims. If someone calls you to verify your address for delivery purposes or because they claim to have money or a prize for you, be wary. Get a telephone number you can call back, and talk to the police before returning the call.

■ **Be aware of your surroundings when away from home.** Stay away from isolated locations where a stalker could attack you. Carry a cellular telephone so you can call for help quickly if your stalker does appear. Keep car doors locked, and ask for an escort when leaving a mall, restaurant, and other locations after dark. Some stalking victims carry pepper spray, but in some cases these sprays have ended up being used against the victim by a stalker who surprised and overpowered them.

## GETTING HELP

Stalking has become such a pervasive problem that a number of organizations now exist to help victims of stalkers. The National Center for Victims of Crime can be reached at (800) 394-2255, or by visiting www.ncvc.org. The National Domestic Violence Hotline offers a variety of resources to stalking victims, and can be reached at (800) 799-7233, or by visiting its Web site, www.ndvh.org. And nearly every major city and many smaller ones now have local support groups for stalking victims and their families.

*You get a call from a "bank officer" who asks for your ATM card's PIN in order to help trap a thief at the bank.*

When you answer the telephone, a voice on the other end of the line tells you: "Mr. Smith, I'm calling about a problem we've discovered here at the bank. We think one of our employees is illegally accessing our customers' accounts, and we'd like your help in catching her. We'll need you to verify the account number and the Personal Identification Number (PIN) of your Automated Teller Machine (ATM) card, but you can be assured that information will be kept strictly confidential. You'll be performing a great service to us and to our other customers. Won't you please help?"

If you ever get a phone call like this one—and thousands of Americans already have—*don't fall for it for a second.* This is a scam, designed to give a bank-card counterfeiter access to your savings and checking accounts so that he can drain them while you're busy congratulating yourself on being such a good citizen.

## GETTING HELP

Instead of giving the caller what he wants, do the following:

■ **Tell the caller that you will have to confirm his identity** before agreeing to provide any information. It's likely that the con man will simply hang up once he suspects that you're on to his scam, but he may actually offer to provide you with a telephone number that's a "direct line" to the bank's security department. In reality, calling this number will connect you only with one of his confed-

erates in crime. Write down the number and tell the caller that you will get back in touch with him.

■ ***Immediately* call your local police department** and report the call. Provide the officers with as many details as you can about the call, including any telephone number that the caller gave you.

■ **Call your bank and ask to speak to a manager.** Tell the manager about the call, and ask that the bank place a notation in your files. That way, the bank will be alerted if someone calls pretending to be you and asks to have money transferred out of your account. You'll also be helping the bank to warn other customers about the problem, because the bank can then contact the media and ask for their assistance in getting word out to the public.

■ **Consider getting a new ATM card** and changing your PIN, in case the criminal who called you has already obtained access to your account information. For example, some consumers who were contacted by con men asking for their PINs complied with the request because the caller already knew their ATM card numbers. What the consumers didn't realize is that the caller had stolen a new ATM card from their mail or had taken it out of a purse or wallet left overnight in an unlocked car. By the time the worried consumers realized that their ATM cards were missing, the thieves had taken some or all of the money from the bank accounts linked to the card.

## PROTECTING YOUR CREDIT BY PREVENTING MAIL THEFT

Mailbox theft is a fast-growing problem in America. According to the U.S. Postal Service (USPS), it may be the number-one type of white-collar crime in this country. And while many mailbox thieves are looking for cash or checks, an increasing number are looking for credit-card statements, bank account numbers, and other financial information that can be used to steal your identity. In some cases, it may be weeks or months before you even discover the problem. Once you do figure out what's happened, it can take many more months to get things straightened out and your credit rating restored.

Although it's virtually impossible to completely eliminate the possibility of mail theft (drug addicts have been known to take crowbars to Postal Service mail-collection boxes, and a number of criminal cases have been filed against USPS workers), there are steps you can take to protect yourself:

- **If you don't receive a check or a bill** when it's expected, contact the issuing bank or company immediately.

- **Remove your mail as soon as possible** from your mailbox. If you don't already know approximately what time your mail is delivered, ask your mail carrier.

- **Always deposit outgoing mail in a Postal Service mailbox** or in the slot at the post office. Don't put outgoing mail in your curbside mailbox or in an area where it can easily be stolen, such as an apartment building hallway.

- **Report any suspicious activity** near mailboxes to local law enforcement authorities and Postal Service inspectors. Some criminals drive through neighborhoods and take mail from unsecured mailboxes, especially on days when pension checks and welfare payments may be due.

- **Consider replacing an older mailbox** with one that provides greater security, such as a drop slot into a locked box. Check with your local postmaster for information about United States Postal Service (USPS)-approved mailboxes.

- **When you move,** be sure to send a change-of-address form to everyone you do business with and to notify the post office of the change.

- **Have your mail picked up** by a trustworthy neighbor, friend, or family member if you will be away from home for more than a day or two. You can ask the post office to hold your mail until your return, but this can alert a dishonest postal worker to your absence, letting her select credit-card applications, bank statements, or other items that can give her access to your identity.

- **If you belong to a neighborhood watch group,** ask the local post office to provide your group with a speaker to discuss problems in the community and furnish additional tips on how to protect your mail.

> ***Y**our purse is missing from the locker at the health club and you're afraid that it's been stolen. It contains credit cards and other items that could be used to steal your identity.*

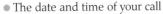

It's a heart-stopping experience to discover that your wallet or purse is gone. And with identity theft on the increase—up to as many as 600,000 cases are now reported annually to just one of the major credit bureaus—the odds are that not only will you lose whatever cash you may have been carrying, but that you'll also face a problem down the road when someone uses your credit cards, driver's license, and other items to perpetrate identity fraud. With one stolen item, a criminal can apply for credit cards, forge checks, access your bank accounts, and destroy your good credit.

### ALERT THE POLICE

Your first step is to call the police immediately. If possible, get the police to come to the health club to take a report, and be sure to get a copy of it. In some communities, you may not be able to get an officer to visit the scene of the loss. Instead, you'll have to give your statement over the phone. If this happens, be sure to write down…

- The name and badge number of the officer to whom you spoke

- The date and time of your call
- The nature of the information you provided (make sure that everything that was in your purse is listed on the report, including credit cards, checkbooks, ATM cards, your Social Security card, library card, video store membership card, employee ID card—*anything* that a thief could use to impersonate you)
- The name and badge number of the officer who will investigate your case, if this is someone other than the officer taking the report
- The case number for your report.

Ask the officer to mail you a copy of the report. You'll need this to help clear your name if the thief uses your identity to obtain merchandise, money, or credit.

In most cases, you'll receive the police report within a week or so, but be persistent if you don't. In one case, a victim of such a theft waited more than three months before receiving the police report, making it difficult for her to convince businesses that she was truly a victim. If you don't get the report in a few weeks and you live near the police department that took your report, call the police officer handling your case and ask if you can come to the station and pick up a copy.

### CALL, THEN WRITE

Next, you need to contact financial institutions, credit-card companies, and others about your loss. Keep a log of all conversations, and the names, titles, mailing addresses, and telephone numbers of those you talk to about the loss of your purse and its contents. Then send letters confirming the details of your conversations by certified mail, return receipt requested. Don't forget to keep copies of all letters, claim forms, and other documents related to your loss. Here's what you should do:

■ **Call your bank** and tell the customer service representative that your purse, identification, checkbook, and ATM card have been stolen. The representative can close your accounts and open new ones. Don't forget to cancel any overdraft protection you have, or you could end up having checks honored even after you close your account.

■ **Stop payment on checks** you've written on the now closed accounts that haven't yet cleared the bank, and write replacement checks from your new account. Be sure to notify the payees about the problem and ask them not to cash or deposit the checks they've received.

■ **Cancel all the credit cards and other cards** that were in your purse. This includes telephone calling cards and auto club membership cards. And don't forget to call the video store and library, or you could end up being billed for items checked out on your card and never returned.

■ **Call your state Department of Motor Vehicles** (DMV) or go to the nearest office and explain that your driver's license has been stolen. In some states, you'll be issued a new license number immediately; in others, you may not get a new number until after your old one is used fraudulently. The DMV clerk can explain the procedure in your state.

■ **Contact the nearest Social Security Administration (SSA) office** if you carried your Social Security card in your purse. You can also call the SSA at (800) 269-0271. You'll get a new card, although not necessarily a new number, and information on what to do if someone misuses your old card.

### NOTIFY THE CREDIT BUREAUS

Next, call the three major credit-reporting companies. These are...

✔ TransUnion, at (800) 680-7289
✔ Equifax, at (800) 526-6285
✔ Experian, at (888) 397-3742.

Ask to speak to a fraud representative. Report the theft of your credit cards and other documents, then request that a fraud alert be placed on your file. With a fraud alert in place, a merchant or credit grantor will contact you by telephone before giving credit to someone using your name or other information to verify the applicant's identity. Ask how long the alert will remain in effect. It should last for at least a year, and you should renew it when it expires.

You should also ask for a copy of your credit report to determine if anyone has already applied for credit using your identity. (This report should be free if you request it because of possible credit fraud.) If someone has used your identity to apply for credit, you can put a statement in your file

---

*Get the police to take a report, and be sure to get a copy of it.*

---

explaining the problem; for example, "My identification was stolen on January 1, 2001, and has been used to apply for credit fraudulently. Contact me at (720) 555-1212 for information and to verify all credit applications." Ask the credit bureaus to delete any credit inquiries from your record that are related to a fraudulent application.

Follow up your telephone calls to the credit bureaus in writing, and ask that they provide you with copies of your report periodically or when inquiries are made about your credit record.

If credit has already been given to someone using your identity, get the telephone number of the creditor from the credit bureau and contact it to explain the problem. As always, get the name, title, and mailing address of the person you speak to about the problem, and be sure to follow up your telephone conversation with a letter.

### LEGAL ACTION

Even with all these precautions, the person who stole your identification could run up debts in your name, and you could find yourself getting calls and letters from collection agencies or even being threatened with legal action. If this happens, don't ignore it. It won't go away on its own, and even though you are innocent, you could find yourself being rejected for credit when you really need it. Respond to every inquiry in writing, and include a copy of the police report of the theft. Send all correspondence by certified mail, return receipt requested.

If problems persist, it might be worthwhile to contact an attorney, to help you straighten matters out. Your local legal-aid society or a law school's student clinic program may also be able to help you untangle the mess an identity thief can create.

According to the Federal Trade Commission (FTC), the problem of identity theft grows and grows. In one recent four-month period, calls to the FTC's Identity Fraud Hotline (877) ID-THEFT more than doubled. The Better Business Bureau estimates that more than 1,000 Americans fall victim to ID theft every day. Here's what you can do to reduce your chances of becoming a victim of this crime:

- **Never carry your Social Security card** with you.

- **Don't imprint your Social Security number** or driver's license number on your checks.

- **Leave credit cards at home** unless you plan to use them that day.

- **Store credit cards in a secure place** in your home and check from time to time to make sure that none are missing.

- **Make separate lists** of credit-card numbers and the telephone numbers to call if they are stolen or lost. But don't keep these two lists in the same place.

- **Tear up or shred any papers** that may contain identifying information, such as credit-card receipts and old bills, before discarding them. Do the same with any credit-card offers you receive through the mail.

- **Change ATM passwords and PINs** often, and don't write them on the ATM card.

- **Avoid easy-to-guess passwords and PINs,** such as your birthday or the number of your address. Instead, use a random combination of numbers and letters.

- **Review all your bills** when they arrive, and question immediately any charges that you don't recognize. If bills don't arrive on time, contact your creditors.

- **Check your credit report** at least once a year. Always review it before making a major purchase on credit, and challenge any accounts that are listed incorrectly as soon as possible.

*You learn that your lawyer's secretary has been talking about your pending divorce to a mutual friend.*

**G**etting involved in any legal matter can be stressful, and it's even more so when what you discuss with your lawyer is repeated for public consumption. Under the Rules of Professional Responsibility that govern attorney conduct, lawyers have a duty to safeguard the confidences and secrets of their clients. They also have an ethical duty to prevent their employees from divulging confidential information that they learn about on the job. Unfortunately, in some cases a lawyer's office staff may violate this duty, sometimes intentionally, but more often unthinkingly.

### TALK TO THE BOSS

Contact your attorney immediately and explain the problem that you've encountered. It's probably best *not* to have the lawyer's secretary present for this meeting. Insist that your lawyer inform her secretary that the discussion of your confidential legal matters is inappropriate and a violation of your rights as the lawyer's client.

## FILE A COMPLAINT

Next, file a complaint with the state's attorney disciplinary committee. Contact your state's Supreme Court or the local bar association for the exact procedure to follow to file a complaint. Many states have forms, which will be sent to you with instructions for completing them, along with a pamphlet about the disciplinary process.

*Lawyers have a duty to safeguard the confidences and secrets of their clients.*

If your state's disciplinary committee doesn't have a form, send a letter describing the problem you've experienced. Write a brief state-

ment about the secretary's violation of your confidences and what response the attorney made when you approached her directly about the problem. Include your name, address, and a daytime telephone number. Be sure to include the name of anyone willing to verify your complaint, such as the mutual friend who your lawyer's secretary told about your case.

Your complaint to the state's disciplinary committee will set in motion the following process:

■ **The disciplinary committee will review your complaint,** and if it finds that a violation of the ethical rules may have occurred, it will contact your lawyer and ask for her written response to your claim.

■ **Once the committee receives this response,** in many cases it will consider the case closed, provided that the lawyer has taken appropriate measures to ensure that no further confidences are revealed. For example, the lawyer may state that she has disciplined the legal secretary for her misconduct and required her to attend a seminar on attorney-client privilege, which she completed successfully.

■ **If your lawyer does not respond** to the committee's inquiry, or if the committee believes that the response is inadequate, it may schedule a hearing. In general, disciplinary hearings are rare—by some estimates, only 1 in 10 client complaints ever reach the hearing stage.

■ **After the hearing,** the committee will decide one of two things: either to dismiss your complaint, or to subject your lawyer to a variety of punishments. These can include…
  ● An informal admonition from the disciplinary committee
  ● A private written reprimand
  ● A public reprimand published in the state's court records
  ● A requirement that the lawyer submit to supervision by another attorney
  ● A temporary suspension of the lawyer's license to practice
  ● Disbarment, the permanent removal of the lawyer's license to practice.

■ **The state's highest court will review the recommendation** of the disciplinary committee, and in most cases it will impose the recommended punishment. But in some cases, the court can decide on a different punishment than the one that has been suggested to it by the disciplinary committee, either by reducing the penalty it imposes due to mitigating circumstances (for example, the lawyer was experiencing a family problem or a personal illness at the time that made it difficult for her to supervise her office personnel) or increasing it (as was the case when a lawyer had received similar complaints from other clients and had failed to take appropriate action).

*Your preteen daughter is receiving e-mails, so-called spam, and junk mail from Web sites she has visited.*

There's no denying that kids love exploring the Internet, and there are thousands of sites that provide information and entertainment aimed at preteens. There is also a law designed to safeguard the privacy of children using the Internet. This law, the Children's Online Privacy Protection Act (COPPA), requires Web sites directed primarily at children younger than 13 and general-audience sites that knowingly collect personal information from children to post privacy policies and to obtain parental consent before requesting information from juveniles.

### How the Law Works

To determine whether a Web site is directed primarily at children younger than 13, the Federal Trade Commission (FTC) looks at a number of factors, including…

- The site's subject matter
- Video and audio content on the site
- The age of models featured on the site
- Language used on the site
- Whether advertising on the site is directed at children
- Whether animated characters or other child-oriented features are present
- Information provided by the operator about the age of the site's intended audience.

An operator of a site aimed at children younger than 13 is allowed to collect identifiable information about a child (such as her name, address, e-mail address, and telephone number) and to use that information to market products and services to the child. But it is required to obtain the permission of the child's parents *before* doing so. The Web site operator must also post a clear and prominent link on its site's home page describing its information practices as well as at each area of the site where it collects personal information from preteens. An operator of a general-audience site with a separate children's area must post a link to its notice on the home page of the children's area. The FTC recommends that site operators use a larger font, different color type, or a different color background to enhance the visibility of this notice.

### The Privacy Notice

In addition to being clearly written and prominently displayed, the Web site's privacy notice must also include the following information:

- **The name of and contact information** about (address, telephone number, and e-mail address) all operators collecting or maintaining children's personal information through the Web site or on-line service.
- **The kinds of personal information** being collected from children, such as their names, e-mail addresses, and hobbies and interests, and how this information is collected—directly from the child or passively with "cookies." (See "Keeping Out of the Cookie Jar," page 425.)
- **The uses of the information collected,** such as for marketing back to the child or in order to notify contest winners.
- **Whether the operator discloses information** to third parties. If it does, it must also disclose the kinds of businesses those third parties are engaged in, the general purposes for which the information will be used, and whether the third parties have agreed to maintain the confidentiality and security of the information.
- **That the parent has the option** to agree to the collection and use of the child's information without allowing the Web site to disclose the information to third parties

### Smart Moves

To learn how the federal government can help protect your children from being taken advantage of on the Internet, visit the FTC's Web page at www.ftc.gov/kidzprivacy. You'll find out how to complain about Web sites that are collecting personal data about your children without the required authorization, and your children will find tips on surfing the Web safely.

- **That the operator cannot require a child** to disclose more information than is reasonably necessary to participate in an activity.
- **That the parent can review the child's personal information,** have it deleted, and refuse to allow any further collection or use of previously collected information, as well as the procedures for the parent to follow.

### HOW PARENTS GIVE CONSENT

A privacy notice must also state the methods by which the parent can provide consent. This notice can be sent by a variety of methods, including sending an e-mail or a written request through regular mail.

The Web site operator must obtain verifiable parental consent before it uses the information it collects. What's acceptable as verifiable consent varies according to the use that the Web site operator plans to make of the information.

For example, if the Web site intends to use the information only internally, the operator may be able to use an e-mail if it confirms the parent's consent with a telephone call or letter. But if the operator intends to disclose the information it gathers to third parties, such as other Web sites or merchants, a more reliable method of obtaining and confirming the parent's consent must be used, such as:

- Getting a signed form from the parent by fax or through the U.S. Postal Service

- Accepting and verifying a credit-card number from the parent
- Accepting toll-free telephone calls to obtain parental consent
- Accepting an e-mail accompanied by a digital signature.

### EXCEPTIONS TO COPPA

Prior parental consent isn't always required for some very popular on-line activities that children may want to participate in. For example, an operator can obtain a child's e-mail address *without* parental consent when the purpose is to:

- **Provide notice** and obtain consent.
- **Respond to a onetime request** and then delete the child's e-mail address from its records.
- **Respond more than once to a specific request,** such as to provide a subscription to a newsletter. However, in this case the operator must notify the parent that it is communicating with the child and give the parent an opportunity to stop the ongoing communication before sending a second communication to the child.
- **Protect the child's safety,** such as when an adult is posing as a child in a chat room for kids. In this situation, the operator must notify the parent and give him or her the chance to prevent any further use of the information.
- **Protect the security of the site** or respond to a law enforcement request.

### REPORTING A COPPA VIOLATION

Although Web site operators have had plenty of time to take steps to ensure their compliance with COPPA, the FTC recently reported that more than half of all Web sites aimed at children failed to take adequate steps to protect the children's on-line privacy.

If you believe that a Web site has collected or distributed information about your preteen child in violation of COPPA, call the FTC's Consumer Response Center at (877) 382-4357, or write to it at 600 Pennsylvania Ave., NW, Washington, DC 20580. The FTC can take a variety of enforcement actions against Web site operators who violate COPPA regulations, including imposing fines and obtaining orders prohibiting an operator from continued violations of the law.

**TAKE NOTE** *Some on-line service providers, such as America Online (AOL), allow members to create a profile that can be viewed by others using the same service. In some instances, sexual predators have been able to take advantage of the information in these profiles to strike up relationships with children, and some have even gone so far as to arrange personal meetings with the young people they meet on-line. Be sure to caution your children about the dangers of posting too much personal information in an on-line profile, especially their full name, age, and address. And have them tell you if an adult offers to meet with them for any reason. Contact your local law-enforcement agency immediately if you discover that your child has been contacted by an adult trying to arrange a meeting or has been the recipient of sexually explicit e-mails.*

## KEEPING OUT OF THE "COOKIE" JAR

Many Web sites use what are known as "cookies" in order to track your movements and activity on their site. A cookie is an identifier—a unique, personal service number—that a Web server places on your computer and can be used to retrieve your records from the Web site's database. In some cases, these cookies are stored on your hard drive for only a brief period. In others, they may last 25 years or more.

Web sites can also "synchronize" their cookies, exchanging data they collect from you with companies that advertise on their site. For example, if you sign up to receive an e-mailed newsletter on California wines, that information may be shared with other companies that sell wine or other alcoholic beverages, offer tours to California, or sell other products or services that are somehow connected to your original area of interest.

In essence, once any Web site identifies you, others may also know your identity anytime you visit their site. And you can find yourself the target of junk e-mail, or so-called so-called spam, sent to you by other advertisers who rent this identifying information from the sites you've visited.

Fortunately, you can prevent most cookies from entering your hard drive through steps you can take on your browser.

■ **Set your browser to warn you** about cookies as they are sent to your computer and decide whether or not to accept them. But this can be time-consuming—some Web sites will have four or five cookies on each page of the site.

■ **Refuse or disable all cookies directed to your computer.** This is an option available with most newer browsers. Take a look at the Options or Edit menu on your browser, or contact your Internet Service Provider (ISP) for information on how to do this.

■ **Consider switching to a different ISP** if yours doesn't offer this option. Let your current ISP know that you are switching to a company that does a better job of protecting your privacy.

Although federal legislation has been proposed to require Web site operators to disclose the use of cookies on their sites, or to give users warnings when cookies are being received, at present no laws have been enacted. Contact your senator and representative to let them know if you object to the use of cookies to track your Internet use.

Your teenage son is involved in an altercation at school. In the aftermath, his school records are released to the media without your permission.

Although some comedians tell funny stories of their school misconduct and bad grades going on their "permanent records," in fact it's no joke. While many of us may believe that our school records contain only information about which schools we've attended and what grades we've earned, in reality that's not all there is.

### WHAT'S ON A SCHOOL RECORD

These records can contain a host of other information, including…

- The results of personality and IQ testing
- Comments from teachers and administrators about students' attitudes and aptitudes
- Conversations students had with counselors and advisers about personal problems
- Medical records and visits to school nurses
- Comments from school personnel about students' home life, real or suspected drug use, religious beliefs and practices, and even their sexual activities.

In many ways, this information does form a "permanent record." The data contained in school records can influence a college or university's decision to accept or reject an applicant, and it can be used by employers when a job applicant is just starting his career to help them decide whether to make a job offer.

### LEGAL PROTECTION

In 1974, Congress enacted the Family Educational Rights and Privacy Act, more commonly referred to as the Buckley Amendment, after the senator who sponsored it. The Buckley Amendment applies only to schools that receive federal funding, which means it does not apply to most private or parochial schools. Under the Buckley Amendment, school records cannot be released without the prior consent of the student or the student's parents, with some exceptions. For example, no prior consent is needed when a student's records are released to:

- Officials within the school the student is currently attending who have a legitimate

interest in seeing them, such as a disciplinary administrator, or a principal
- Officials of another school where the student intends to enroll

The data contained in school records can be used by employers when a job applicant is just starting his career to help them decide whether to make a job offer.

- State and federal education officials, but only for the purpose of enforcing state or federal programs, and only on the condition that no personally identifiable information is disclosed to anyone but the officials and the information is destroyed after it is used
- Officials who require financial-aid information to determine student eligibility for loans, grants, and other assistance and to enforce the terms and conditions of any aid already being received.

Under the Buckley Amendment, disciplinary actions taken for violations of school rules are considered school records, and their release is subject to the same kinds of restrictions that are described above.

### FILING SUIT

Any school that violates the provisions of the Buckley Amendment may lose its federal funding. You may file a complaint with the office of the Secretary of Education, which will investigate the matter and decide what action to take, if any.

While the Buckley Amendment doesn't authorize lawsuits brought by individual students against the school that released records in violation of the law, a number of students have been able to file suit against their school in federal court for violating their civil rights.

In addition, some students have been able to file suit under the federal Privacy Act. If such a suit is successful, the court can issue an injunction against the school prohibiting future violation of the act and award the student damages, attorney fees, and court costs. The federal Privacy Act also includes criminal penalties for those who willfully violate its antidisclosure provisions. A person convicted under the Privacy Act is guilty of a misdemeanor and can be fined as much as $5,000 per violation.

Most states also have provisions in their statutes that protect the privacy of student records, and that usually provide for penalties similar to those imposed for violation of the Buckley Amendment.

## SEEK LEGAL HELP

Figuring out which laws to follow and which court to pursue a lawsuit in is complicated, and you will probably need an attorney's help to make the right decision. Although your state or local bar association may be able to provide you with the names of several lawyers who could help, don't forget to contact organizations, such as the American Civil Liberties Union (ACLU). You should also speak with the local prosecuting attorney about filing a criminal complaint under state laws that may make the unauthorized release of student records a criminal violation.

---

### WHEN SCHOOL RECORDS ARE WRONG

The Family Educational Rights and Privacy Act (also known as FERPA, or the Buckley Amendment) gives parents and older students a variety of rights regarding school records:

- **The right to see school records.** Parents or legal guardians of students younger than age 18 have the right to see their children's school records. Students 18 or older or those attending post-secondary schools have the right to see their own records. In some states, students are entitled to see their records at an even earlier age—as young as age 14 in Delaware.

- **The right to ask for any part of a record to be changed.** Sometimes school records are incomplete or in error when describing student conduct or the evaluations of teachers, counselors, or administrators. If there's information in your child's records that you think is unfair, inaccurate, or irrelevant, you can ask to have that information deleted or changed.

- **The right to a formal hearing** before an impartial third party if school administrators refuse to make the changes you request. The hearing officer will listen to your reasons for requesting a change as well as the school officials' reasons for opposing your request.

- **The right to place a dissenting statement in the records** if the hearing officer makes a decision denying your request. You may put a statement in the records that you believe that the information they contain is inaccurate or unfair. This statement will become a part of the record themselves, and must be released along with the records when requested or when the law requires their release.

Check with an attorney or your local branch of the American Civil Liberties Union for assistance if you encounter opposition to a request to view, challenge, or change your child's school records.

## WHEN PUBLIC SCHOOLS PLAY "BIG BROTHER"

You may not be aware of it, but some public schools around the country are collecting and storing data about you, your child, and the rest of your family in ways that some people find alarming. For example, some social science classes now ask students to provide information about matters such as family income; their parents' political beliefs and affiliations, whether the family ever used public transportation; and whether a close family member had ever suffered from drug addiction, alcohol abuse, or mental illness. When challenged, school administrators have defended the class by claiming that it was designed to open the lines of communication between students and their parents.

In a midwestern school district, junior high school students were asked to respond to questions such as:

- Does your family own or rent your home?
- How much does it cost per month?
- How did your family earn the money to pay for it?
- What are your family's monthly household expenses?
- What decorative and heirloom objects are there in your home?
- How much energy does your family consume?
- How much waste does your family generate?
- Do you lock the door to your home at night?
- Does your family take vacations, and if so, where do they go and when?

Although school officials assured concerned parents that the answers their children gave to these questions would be kept confidential, it's easy to see how the information gleaned from these students could be beneficial to thieves and burglars if it was to fall into the wrong hands.

To find out if your children are being asked to answer questions about personal and family matters, ask them to inform you if their teachers or school administrators require them to participate in assignments like those described above. And check with your children's school administrators and the local school board to learn if these kinds of inquiries are being made and to voice your opposition to them.

*The junior high principal wrongfully accused your daughter of possessing drugs. Despite your daughter's protests, she had her strip-searched by a female instructor.*

Under the Fourth Amendment to the U.S. Constitution, everyone, including students, is protected from "unreasonable searches and seizures." Generally, it means that a search conducted without prior approval from a judge or magistrate is illegal, and any evidence that is obtained as a result of the search can't be used against the person in criminal proceedings. This amendment helps protect what courts call a *reasonable expectation of privacy.*

But as the U.S. Supreme Court has stated, the protection offered by the Fourth Amendment isn't absolute. For example, searches and seizures can take place without a warrant under certain clearly established exceptions, such as…

- When a person gives consent to the search
- When evidence will be lost or destroyed while a warrant is obtained
- When contraband (a legally prohibited item) is in plain view
- When a person is arrested.

## SPECIAL RULES FOR SCHOOLS

In addition to the exceptions above, the Supreme Court also held that the Fourth Amendment's ban against unreasonable searches and seizures isn't as far reaching when it comes to actions of school officials. Students have expectations of privacy, but their rights must be balanced with the legitimate needs of the school to maintain a learning environment. While a search must still be reasonable, it isn't subject to the requirement that officials have probable cause to believe that the student being searched violated a law.

## SO WHAT'S REASONABLE?

Although courts have reached different conclusions in cases that seem very similar, in most cases a school can…

- Bring in drug-sniffing dogs to patrol hallways and parking lots, and identify lockers and automobiles that may contain illegal drugs
- Search the purses or wallets of students for cigarettes, marijuana, and other drugs and drug paraphernalia
- Require students to enter the school building through metal detectors
- Conduct periodic searches of school lockers when the lockers are identified as being the property of the school and not the student.

## WHAT'S NOT PERMITTED?

The answer to this question varies from state to state, but searches are generally not permitted…

- **Unless they are based on facts,** information, or circumstances that would lead a reasonable person to conclude that evidence of a violation of the law or school rules will be found. (For example, it would be reasonable to search a student for alcohol if the student's breath smelled of it.)
- **When the search is unreasonable in scope.** (For example, looking in a student's wallet for a handgun would be unreasonable—looking in her locker or in a backpack wouldn't.) In addition, a number of states have enacted laws that specifically prohibit strip searches of students by school officials.

Even in states where such searches are allowed, they can be conducted only under the most extreme circumstances. For example, a search to locate a weapon used in an attack on a student or on a teacher may be permissible in order to protect other at the school from immediate danger. But a strip search of a student when another complains that $5 is missing from his desk would almost certainly be found to have violated the searched student's Fourth Amendment rights.

## HOW TO FIGHT BACK

Contact the school administrators immediately to find out all the circumstances surrounding the strip search of your daughter. You should be informed in writing of the reasons for the search. If the administrators refuse to respond to your request or if their response isn't satisfactory, you should get in touch with an attorney who handles students' rights cases. Your local bar association or the state chapter of the American Civil Liberties Union (ACLU) can help you find a lawyer willing to review your daughter's situation and advise you about your legal options.

Depending on the facts of the case and the state in which you live, you may be able to file a lawsuit on behalf of your daughter in state or federal court, seeking damages for violation

of prohibitions on strip searches and for the emotional distress she suffered. In a number of cases, students who were strip-searched have been awarded significant financial settlements from the schools they attended. Teachers and administrators who conduct illegal strip searches may also be disciplined by the local school board and could even be subject to criminal charges. Your lawyer can tell you what specific penalties may apply in cases of prohibited strip searches in your community.

> $Y$ou have reason to believe that a federal agency has been keeping records about you, but you don't know how to get access to them to see what they are and whether they're accurate.

**M**any of us are concerned about the information that businesses collect about us, but state and federal government agencies also have billions of records about us. By some estimates, U.S. government computers contain the equivalent of more than 15 records for every man, woman, and child in the country. Unfortunately, many of these records contain information that is inaccurate. Your name may be confused with that of someone who has been involved in antigovernment protests, or you may have been denied government benefits you are entitled to because of incorrect information about your eligibility.

### REQUESTING YOUR RECORDS

In 1974, Congress enacted the Privacy Act, which allows Americans to examine records that U.S. government agencies maintain on them and to correct records that contain errors or are incomplete, outdated, or irrelevant. Another federal law passed at the same time, the Freedom of Information Act (FOIA), allows anyone to

obtain certain federal records from government agencies. When trying to obtain these records, it's best to file a request to see them under both laws.

If you know which federal agency has records about you (for example, the Department of Veteran Affairs or Department of Justice), write to that agency asking for your personal files. Address your letter to the agency's Freedom of Information officer. (You can get the name by calling the agency's Washington telephone number or visiting its Web site.) Your letter should include…

- Your date and place of birth
- Your Social Security number
- Your maiden name, nicknames, or other names you may have used previously
- The contacts you may have had with the agency that would have led to the creation of records about you (for example, if you are a veteran, note your dates of service, the nature of your discharge, and any correspondence you may have had with the Department of Veteran Affairs about veterans' benefits)

**SMART MOVES**

Be as specific as possible about the information you want an agency to provide. Making a request for "all records" that an agency may have usually isn't the best strategy. It can run up costs, and it may give the agency an excuse to drag its feet in responding to your request.

• A statement that you are making your request under the Freedom of Information Act and the Privacy Act of 1974

• A statement about the costs you are willing to pay, or a request of a fee waiver because the information you are requesting is for your personal use. Under the FOIA, you can be charged for the cost of a search, the agency's review of the records to see if they should be included in the agency's response, and the cost of photocopying; under the Privacy Act, you can be charged only for the cost of duplicating records. (You'll find a sample FOIA and Privacy Act letter for requesting government records on page 466.)

If you don't know which agency to contact, you'll have to send a request for information to each agency you believe may have records about you. The local office of your senator or congressional representative can often help you determine which agencies to contact and provide you with the appropriate names and addresses. Your public library may also have a directory of federal agencies available in its reference section.

You'll need to send your request through the mail, since e-mail requests are generally not accepted. And be sure to keep a copy of the letter as well as of any correspondence you receive from the agency.

## THE WAITING GAME

Once you've sent your request, these are the next steps:

■ **Be prepared to wait** for a reply. By law, federal agencies must respond within 10 working days. But some agencies are so overwhelmed with these requests that it may take them much longer to research yours. If so, you should receive a letter from the agency within about two weeks of making your request, stating that your request has been received and is acknowledged, a search for your records has begun, and the agency is in the process of determining the fees for your request.

■ **Find out the agency's fees.** Fees for FOIA requests vary from agency to agency and sometimes even within an agency itself. Generally, however, you cannot be charged for the first two hours spent searching records,

or for the first 100 pages provided in response to an FOIA request. The FOIA office can give you a copy of its current fee schedule.

■ **If the agency informs you that it can't meet your request** within the time allowed by law, contact the FOIA office to try to get a deadline by which the agency will commit to making a response, such as within 30 working days. You can make this request by letter or by talking to an agency FOIA officer on the telephone. If you call, be sure to record the name of the officer and her title, the date and time of your conversation, and whatever commitment the officer gives you. Then send her a letter confirming the details of your conversation.

■ **If you haven't received a response by the deadline** agreed to by the FOIA office, you have the right to go to court to force the agency to release your files to you, because in the eyes of the law, excessive delay equals denying your request.

But it may be better to first write a follow-up letter to the FOIA officer, informing her that her agency has missed the deadline and telling her that unless you have a response within 10 working days, you will take the agency to court. (You'll find a sample follow-up letter on page 457.)

## NEGATIVE RESPONSES

It's possible that when the agency that you've contacted does respond to your request, it won't provide the information you expect. For example, the agency may claim that…

■ **The requested records don't exist.** If you know that there must be records in the agency's files, restate your request more explicitly, giving the agency additional time to search its records. Talking to an FOIA officer at the agency may help you make your request in a more useful way.

---

*In 1974, Congress enacted the Privacy Act, which allows Americans to examine records that U.S. government agencies maintain on them.*

---

■ **Your description of the requested materials is inadequate.** Contact the agency's FOIA office to see if it can help you redefine your request in a way that will allow it to locate the records you are seeking.

■ **The material you are requesting is exempt from disclosure.** As with just about every law, there are exceptions to the FOIA that protect some records from being disclosed. Generally, you cannot obtain records that contain…

● Information that would compromise national security

● Information that other statutes protect from being disclosed, such as identifiable census information or federal income-tax returns

● Business information such as trade secrets, commercial or financial information, and confidential information provided to an agency

● Internal government memos, such as those covered by attorney-client privilege, or that involve advice, recommendations, and opinions that were part of the government's decision-making process

● Information on private matters, such as personnel files or medical files

● Information regarding most law enforcement activities, especially if they would reveal investigative techniques, disclose the identity of a confidential informant, or compromise an ongoing criminal investigation

● Information regarding the regulation of financial institutions, such as banks and savings and loans

● Information that describes or reveals the location of oil wells.

The agency you're seeking records from may use one or more of the exemptions listed above to deny your request. If so, it must give you the reason for the denial and inform you that you have the right to appeal directly to the head of the agency. If you do, and your appeal is denied, you must then be informed of your right to appeal to the federal courts.

## GOING TO COURT

To take a federal agency to court for refusing to comply with an FOIA or Privacy Act request, you'll need professional guidance. A number of advocacy groups, such as the American Civil Liberties Union (ACLU), provide advice and assistance to individuals whose requests for federal records have been denied. Federal law also allows an individual who wins an appeal of a denial in court to recover reasonable attorney fees and court costs.

**TAKE NOTE** *While the laws and procedures discussed here apply only to records kept by federal agencies, every state has similar laws regarding access to records that are maintained by state agencies. You can find these laws in state statute books, which are available at your county or local courthouse, at most public libraries, at law schools, or at your state's Internet site. Your state representative's office can also help you find out how and where to file a request for access to records containing information about you that are kept by the state government.*

CRIME & PUNISHMENT

*The police caught the burglars who broke into your house and stole your valuables—too late. The crooks had already sold your property and spent the money.*

The burglars will get their day in court, but what about you? Is there any way to recover your losses on what was taken? You may be in luck, assuming the thieves are convicted. In most states, a person convicted of a crime that causes financial harm to the victim can be ordered to make *restitution*. Courts order restitution not only as a way to help victims but also to impress on the criminal that his actions have consequences. Making restitution is intended to be part of a criminal's rehabilitation.

*Court-ordered restitution is similar to getting a judgment in your favor in a civil lawsuit.*

## ASK FOR RESTITUTION

When a person has been convicted of a crime, the court will impose a sentence that can include a fine, jail or prison time, probation, and a restitution order if the victim asks for it. Depending on the law in your state, there are several ways to seek restitution:

● File a written request with the court.
● Attend the sentencing hearing and make your request in person.
● Make your request at a restitution hearing in states where these proceedings are held separately from the sentencing hearing.

Be sure to ask the prosecuting attorney handling the case how to go about initiating restitution procedures in your state. She can also help you obtain any necessary forms or assist you in preparing your testimony to take to court.

## GETTING RESTITUTION

Getting a court to order restitution is one thing; getting the convicted criminal to make good on it is often more difficult. Courts can, however, impose unappealing punishments on criminals who fail to pay. Generally, most state laws offer several methods for enforcing a restitution order:

● If the criminal is sentenced to prison, some or all of the money that he earns while employed in prison work programs can be used to pay restitution to his victim.
● If the criminal is paroled, the parole board can make continuing restitution payments a condition of his parole. A criminal who does not meet this condition can have his parole revoked and be returned to prison.
● If the criminal is granted probation, failing to make court-ordered restitution payments could violate his probation terms and lead to his imprisonment.

Court-ordered restitution is similar to getting a judgment in your favor in a civil lawsuit, and in most states, you have the same tools available to help you collect your money. You have the right to seize money in the criminal's bank accounts, levy against his real estate, and garnish his wages. A few states also allow victims to add interest to the unpaid restitution. In several other states, you can add the cost of legal fees and court costs that you incur as a result of filing liens or obtaining garnishment orders. Ask the prosecuting attorney in your area to list your options.

**Your cousin borrowed your car. She was stopped by the police and charged with drug possession. Now the police have seized your car and won't return it.**

A number of state and federal laws now make it relatively easy for the government to seize your car, your money, and even your home when law-enforcement officials believe these items are involved in a crime or are the fruits of criminal activity. Forfeited property may be used or sold by law enforcement agencies, and in some cases, the proceeds can be shared with other government agencies. According to some critics, this process of *civil forfeiture* is too tempting for the authorities to resist and too easy for police departments and other law enforcement agencies to abuse.

> *Congress [has] enacted a statute that places greater limits on the federal government's power to seize private property.*

Currently, more than 100 federal statutes authorize civil forfeiture. Federal agencies that can confiscate property include the Drug Enforcement Administration (DEA), the Federal Bureau of Investigation (FBI), the U.S. Customs Service, the Department of Justice, the Internal Revenue Service (IRS), and even the U.S. Fish and Wildlife Service. State and local laws also give these agencies the right to seize your property without any advance notice or a hearing.

In many states, forfeiture laws allow law enforcement officials to keep seized property even when the person who owns the property is never convicted or even charged with a crime. These laws require the property owner to file a lawsuit to force the return of the property.

Some state laws require owners to prove…

- That the property wasn't involved in the alleged criminal activity, *or*
- That the property in question was purchased with legally obtained funds.

To critics, this shift in *burden of proof* from the government to the individual makes it difficult and expensive for those who've been wronged by the government to defend themselves.

### GET A LAWYER FAST

If property, such as your car, has been seized, it's essential to *get legal help immediately*. Filing deadlines to reclaim your property are often short, and a lawyer can help you with this, and also to get a hearing in the appropriate court.

If you can't afford a private lawyer or can't find one willing to handle your case, contact the local office of the American Civil Liberties Union (ACLU). The ACLU has taken on some forfeiture cases on a *pro bono* basis, handling the matter at no charge to the individual client. Even if it isn't able to represent you, the ACLU can probably direct you to a private attorney willing to take your case on a reduced-fee basis.

**TAKE NOTE** *Some states require an innocent party to post a bond equal to a portion of the value of the seized property in order to have his day in court. For a person who has had his home or vehicle taken, meeting this burden can be* *difficult, and in some cases it has prevented a property owner from pursuing the matter in court.*

## CHANGES IN FEDERAL LAW

Until recently, serious attempts to reform the federal forfeiture laws have been thwarted by opposition from the very agencies that benefit from the current system. In the year 2000, however, Congress enacted a statute that places some limits on the federal government's power to seize private property. This new legislation:

■ **Shifts the burden of proof** to the government. The government must now prove a connection between the seized property and the suspected crime, rather than requiring, as in the past, that the property owner prove that there was no connection.

■ **Allows a court to order the property returned** to its owner in cases of hardship. For example, the operator of a delivery service could have his truck returned to him during the forfeiture proceedings.

■ **Provides for reimbursement** of attorney fees in cases when property owners are successful in defeating the government's claim.

## DOES DOUBLE JEOPARDY APPLY?

Some people who had property seized as a result of alleged criminal activity have argued that forfeiture is a form of *double jeopardy* (when a person is punished twice for the same crime), which is forbidden by the U.S. Constitution. But the U.S. Supreme Court has ruled that civil forfeiture is not punishment as envisioned in the Constitution and therefore is not prohibited. Double jeopardy doesn't apply.

---

### CIVIL FORFEITURE HORROR STORIES

Just being a "law-abiding citizen" doesn't protect you from civil forfeiture laws. Take a look at some real-life stories involving persons who were never convicted—and in some cases never even charged with a crime.

■ **A Georgia businesswoman's** three automobiles were seized by the FBI, which claimed that her husband had used the cars' telephones to place illegal sports bets.

■ **A Chicago pizzeria owner** had more than $500,000 seized by local police. The money was seized after police arrested one of the owner's employees, a crack-cocaine addict who claimed that he used the restaurant to store stolen property. Although none of the stolen property was found at the restaurant, police took the money from the owner's safe. The money was returned only after the restaurant owner spent more than four years and thousands of dollars in legal fees contesting the seizure.

■ **A private charter pilot** flew a passenger carrying more than $2 million in cash in his plane. When the plane landed, both the pilot (who had no knowledge of the contents of his passenger's luggage) and the passenger were arrested by Drug Enforcement Administration (DEA) agents. Although charges against both men were dropped, the DEA seized the plane and kept it for more than two years. The DEA finally agreed to sell the plane back to the pilot, but only after he had incurred more than $80,000 in legal fees.

■ **A 60-year-old mother of seven** suffered from serious medical problems and spent most of her days confined to bed in her home, which she owned outright. Unknown to the mother, several of her grown children who lived in her house were suspected of using and selling illegal drugs. Police executed a search warrant and discovered a small quantity of marijuana and several hundred dollars in cash in the house. They immediately seized the house, arguing that it was the scene of criminal activity and had been paid for with the profits from drug transactions. Although the house had been paid for years before and no criminal charges were ever brought against the mother, she was forced to leave her home. Because she had no money and few other resources, she couldn't find a lawyer who would contest the seizure. Her house was sold by the government, and the money split between local police and the federal DEA.

The financial stress is literally adding insult to your injuries. Yet there may be help to pay for lost wages, medical expenses, counseling, and rehabilitation—even when there's little or no hope of obtaining restitution from the person who commits a crime. By applying to the *state victim compensation fund,* you can get at least a portion of these expenses paid.

## ARE YOU ELIGIBLE FOR BENEFITS?

Although the law differs from state to state, in general you are eligible for compensation if...

- You are the victim of a violent crime and you suffered physical harm.
- You are the spouse or minor child of a victim of a violent crime who is unable to work as a result of injuries suffered during the crime or died as a result of the crime.

But you may *not* be eligible for payment of benefits if...

- Your claim is very small. Some states won't consider claims that fall below a minimum dollar amount, such as $250.
- You have a high net worth.
- You are on parole or probation for a crime.
- Payment would in some way benefit the perpetrator of the crime. For example, if your husband abused you and you continue to live in the same household, the compensation-fund board could decide that he would benefit from any payment you receive.
- You refuse to cooperate with law enforcement authorities in the arrest and conviction of the person who committed the crime.

## ELIGIBLE EXPENSES

Victim compensation funds pay out "reasonable and necessary" expenses related to a victim's medical care. These expenses include...

- ✔ Hospital costs, doctors' bills, and the cost of ambulance services
- ✔ Prescription drugs and medications
- ✔ Eyeglasses, dentures, and prosthetic devices
- ✔ Chiropractic care, and physical and occupational therapy
- ✔ Psychological and psychiatric services.

In some states, you may be compensated for severe mental anguish and for pain and suffering, or for property damage or loss connected with a violent crime. For example, if the police hold your clothes as evidence, you may be entitled to collect up to $100 for replacement clothing. Compensation from the fund may be limited if you received money from insurance to pay for medical expenses or if you've received disability payments from an insurance company or government agency.

Your family members may be entitled to payment for loss of your income or for the cost of obtaining domestic services that you need—housekeeping or child care, for example. If you die, then the state may pay for some or all of the funeral or cremation costs and for any counseling services provided to your immediate family.

### FILE YOUR CLAIM ON TIME

Victim compensation funds are usually administered by a victim compensation commission or victim compensation board. Your local police department can direct you to the appropriate agency in your state. It's important to make your claim quickly. To qualify, you must report the crime within a period specified by the law in your state, such as 72 hours after the crime was committed. Then you must file your compensation claim within another time period, usually within one year of the crime. In a few states, special provisions in the law allow children who are the victims of sexual assault to make their claim within a year of reaching age 18.

In most states, you will receive a form from the board to complete and return together with documentation in support of your claim.

- **Check the form** carefully, because failing to provide necessary documents can delay consideration or lead to the denial of your claim.
- **Provide evidence** of your expenses and losses. This includes…
  ✔ Copies of medical bills and other health care expenses
  ✔ Information about lost wages and other losses resulting from the crime
  ✔ A copy of the police report or other evidence that a crime occurred.

You may be asked to sign a medical release allowing the compensation board to review your medical records. And the board may also ask you to undergo some additional medical examinations to verify the validity of your claim.

**TAKE NOTE** *Get legal advice before allowing the board to look at your complete medical history. If there's sensitive information in your records (for example, an abortion or treatment for*

*depression before the crime occurred), you may be able to limit the information the board receives to what is directly connected to the crime.*

---

*Victim compensation funds have helped thousands of crime victims pick up the pieces and get back on their feet after a violent crime.*

---

In most cases, your claim will be handled entirely through the mail, but if there's a question about your claim, a *hearing* may be held.

In a hearing, you are entitled to appear on your own behalf, and you may also be allowed to call witnesses or present other documents in support of your claim. Usually the hearing panel has the power to issue a subpoena—a court order compelling reluctant witnesses to attend the hearing—and to make them provide pertinent documents that are in their possession.

Victim compensation funds have helped thousands of crime victims pick up the pieces and get back on their feet after experiencing a violent crime. Don't hesitate to take advantage of these programs to help you handle the costs that often accompany being a victim of a crime.

**VICTIM ALERT** *Every state sets limits on how much compensation a crime victim can receive. In some cases, this may be far lower than the victim's actual expenses. What's more, in a few states, victim compensation funds have actually run out of money in a given year. In these states, claims have been carried over to the next year and settled in chronological order based on the date that the claim was filed. To avoid this kind of a delay in being paid, you'll want to file your claim for compensation as soon as possible.*

> **You were arrested in a case of mistaken identity. The charges were dropped, but you've just discovered that the arrest is still on your record.**

You did nothing wrong, yet your reputation is at stake. Court records—including arrests, indictments, and convictions—are generally available for public review. In a world where information about you is readily accessible, an arrest record can hurt you in dozens of ways—from getting a loan to getting a job. In some cases, however, courts have the power to prohibit or limit access to your record. As a person who has been a party to a court action, you can ask the court to have your record *sealed.*

## SEALING YOUR RECORD

Although the steps vary from state to state, you usually begin the process by filing a petition with the court in the district where records are located.

- If you were arrested in your town, file your petition in the court located there.
- If you were arrested elsewhere, file your petition in the court that has jurisdiction in the area where the arrest took place.

The court can provide you with the forms you need. Unless you can show that you have no assets or income, you'll have to pay a fee when you file the petition with the court.

In order for a petition to succeed, the records must involve a criminal offense for which…

- You were not charged.
- All charges were dismissed.
- You were acquitted.

If the court grants your petition, it will order that your arrest record be sealed. Once this happens, you are not usually required to disclose any information in the sealed records to employers, state or local governments, educational institutions, and the like. On job applications or in interviews where you are asked about criminal

records, you can legally claim that no records exist (presuming this arrest was your only record).

> *If the court grants your petition, it will order that your arrest record be sealed.*

## COVERING YOUR TRACKS

You need to follow up to be sure that your record is cleared. For example, you may need to provide the law enforcement agency that arrested you with a copy of the court's order. The agency should then contact the FBI with a request to return any fingerprint cards and photos they have as a result of your arrest. When this material is returned, your name will be removed from the National Crime Information Center's computer records in regard to the arrest.

**TAKE NOTE** *When you petition to have your arrest record sealed, make sure that you ask the court to seal the record of the proceeding as well. Otherwise, someone investigating your background may obtain the record of your court proceeding, which also contains information about the arrest.*

## DO YOU NEED A LAWYER TO PETITION?

You don't necessarily need a lawyer to petition to have your criminal and court proceeding records sealed, but lawyers who handle criminal cases can help you navigate your way through the process and avoid paperwork mistakes that can delay having your petition granted. Many lawyers who specialize in this area of the law will also take on these cases for a relatively low fee.

**Y**ou were the victim of a violent assault, and the perpetrator has been tried and convicted. But you're afraid he'll receive a light sentence for the crime.

**A**s a victim, you want justice, and now you can speak out. In most states, a presentence investigation is required before a person convicted of a serious crime is sentenced. Major consideration is given to the impact of the crime on the victim, and many states give the victim a voice in the proceedings.

### APPEARING IN COURT

Nearly every state gives victims the right to be notified about the date of the sentencing, and many give victims the right to speak at the hearing. Depending on state law, you may be required to testify under oath or merely be asked to address the court with a statement about the crime and its impact on your life.

In a few states, the law allows a crime victim to make a videotaped statement, which the court will view and take into consideration in determining the sentence. This option is especially useful for victims who are emotionally or psychologically distressed at the prospect of facing their attacker again. A videotaped statement provides the court with a more personal impression of the victim and of his suffering than a written statement can convey.

### THE VICTIM IMPACT STATEMENT

In order to impress upon the court the seriousness of the crime and its negative effect on the victim, a victim impact statement—whether written, delivered in person, or recorded on videotape—should include...

● A description of any physical injury suffered by the victim including information about the severity of the injuries and any permanent disability that resulted

● A description of financial losses due to the crime and costs to the victim, including:

✔ Hospital and medical costs

✔ Psychiatric treatment or other counseling costs

✔ Costs for physical or occupational therapy and other rehabilitation services

✔ Loss of or damage to the victim's property

✔ Lost earnings, and loss of future earnings

✔ The costs of required therapeutic devices, such as crutches, walkers, and wheelchair

● A description of any negative effect the crime has had on the victim's personal, business, and family relationships

● A description of the impact on the victim's family members, and any resulting counseling

● The victim's recommendation in regard to sentencing.

Most courts also require you to include mitigating information, such as receiving insurance payments to compensate for financial losses or restitution paid by the perpetrator.

> *Your daughter was raped. The rapist was tried and convicted, but now he is up for parole. Your daughter is terrified, and you are outraged.*

Your daughter worries that she may be victimized again. Your whole family wants the rapist to serve his full term behind bars for committing such a terrible crime. But who will listen to you?

*Parole* is a process by which some prisoners may be released from prison before they complete their sentences, although they remain under the supervision of the prison system. But in most states, you have the right to object. Before a parole is granted, the state will notify the victims of serious crimes of the convict's impending release and of their right to object.

### A Victim's Right to Be Heard

The parole board is an administrative agency that is part of the state penal system. If you've kept your current address on file with the authorities, you should receive *written notification* in advance of the convict's appearance before the parole board. State laws vary:

- In some states, notification is automatic.
- In other states, the victim or the victim's representative must ask *at the time the convict is sentenced* for notification.

To protect your right to be heard, you should keep the parole board, the department of corrections, or the state attorney general's office informed about your current residence and any change in your address.

Your daughter, as the victim of the crime, is the person who will have the greatest influence on the parole board's decision. However, if your daughter is a minor or is incompetent or disabled, you or another representative may be able to object to the parole on her behalf.

While your daughter can contest the rapist's parole in writing, a letter is rarely as effective as a personal appearance. In most states, she or her representative can appeal before the parole board in person; in a handful of states, victims may make a videotaped statement to the parole board.

In deciding whether or not to release a prisoner, the parole board will consider a variety of factors. The board may take into account…

- The prisoner's conduct in prison
- The prisoner's expressions of remorse
- Rehabilitative efforts the prisoner has made, such as attending counseling sessions and taking advantage of educational opportunities
- The seriousness of the crime
- The victim's statement.

### When Parole Is Granted

In most states, the victim of a crime has the right to receive notice of the parole board's decision, especially if parole is granted. Depending on state law, the victim may also be entitled to know…

✔ The date the convict will be released
✔ Where the release will take place
✔ The terms of the parole.

Although a paroled convict has been freed from prison, he will remain under the supervision of the Department of Corrections for a specified amount of time. A parolee who violates the terms of his parole (see "Parole, Probation, and Pardons," page 442) can be sent back to prison to complete the original term of his sentence.

### When the Prisoner Gets Out

Whether the parole board decides on early release or the prisoner serves a full sentence, most convicts eventually get out of prison—and away from official scrutiny. Most states notify victims of a serious crime when the convict is about to be released or when his parole supervision is ending. In the latter case, many states give victims the right to appear before the parole board to object to the end of supervision. Convicted sex offenders also may have to register with local law enforcement agencies where they live.

## PAROLE, PROBATION, AND PARDONS

Although the terms parole, probation, and pardon are similar-sounding, there are differences in when each takes place and what each entails.

■ **Parole** involves the release of a prisoner from prison under certain restrictions and conditions. Parole usually involves *stricter supervision* than probation. The parolee typically has to:

● Report to a parole officer on a regular basis

● Inform the parole officer of his address, place of employment, and any travel plans, which will normally be restricted

● Avoid use of alcohol or illegal or unapproved drugs

● Submit to random testing for drugs and alcohol

● Make court-ordered restitution

● Wear a surveillance device that allows a parole officer to monitor the parolee's movements

● Refrain from contact with the victim, the victim's family, witnesses who testified in the criminal case against the parolee, and other convicted criminals.

While a court hearing is required before probation can be revoked, parolees are entitled only to a hearing before the parole revocation board. The government doesn't have to have a high burden of proof to meet in this hearing, and the parolee generally has no right to cross-examine government witnesses or to present witnesses to testify on his behalf.

■ **Probation** is sometimes imposed instead of prison or jail time. Probation is more likely to be granted when…

● The crime is a first offense

● The crime is nonviolent

● The criminal is willing to make restitution to the victim or has begun making restitution

● The criminal doesn't present a danger to society.

Persons placed on probation must meet conditions imposed by the court, such as reporting to a probation officer on a regular basis, submitting to alcohol and drug testing, and accepting surprise visits and drug searches by probation officers. Violating these provisions can lead to having probation revoked and jail time imposed.

■ **Pardons** are granted when the state discovers that a person was wrongly convicted of a crime. The governor grants a pardon in a state criminal case; the president of the United States grants one when the crime is a federal offense. A pardoned convict is not placed under supervision, and the pardon will usually wipe out any record of the arrest and conviction.

In the bad old days, this kind of treatment of victims was all too common. At one time, sexual-assault victims were even asked to take a lie detector test (polygraph) to help police and prosecutors decide whether to pursue charges against an alleged assailant.

Times have changed, and the vast majority of today's law enforcement officers and prosecutors are sensitive and caring in their treatment of victims of rape and sexual assault. There are still a few, however, who can be callous and unfeeling. Sometimes these unprofessional law-enforcement officials will ask questions about the victim's prior sexual conduct, with her assailant or with others, or imply that she may have provoked the attack by her behavior or the style of clothing she was wearing.

## ASK THE POLICE TO PUT YOU IN CONTACT WITH AN ADVOCATE

It can be hard to stand up for yourself when you're already feeling vulnerable and victimized. In many communities, an advocates program for victims of sexual assault can be a great comfort to victims. An advocate will help you through the difficult days immediately following the assault and provide support during the often lengthy period of time between the arrest of the perpetrator and the trial. If the police officer on your case behaves in an offensive manner, or he hasn't put you in touch with an advocate, you should:

- **Speak to the police officer's superior** and ask that another officer be assigned to your case. Tell the supervisor the reason for your request. If the officer's conduct was very offensive, you may want to consider filing a formal complaint against him. Your complaint will be investigated by the police department's internal affairs division, which can recommend a variety of disciplinary measures against the officer and order additional training to help avoid similar problems in the future.

- **Ask for the phone number of a victim-advocacy agency** or have another officer contact the advocacy agency on your behalf. An advocate can help you obtain counseling and medical treatment and can provide step-by-step information on the legal process.

If the behavior of the lawyer who interviewed you was offensive, you may also consider filing a complaint against him with the prosecutor's office. It may be possible to have a different attorney handle the remainder of the case, and if you file the complaint, you will be providing a public service by making the prosecutors aware of a problem in their office.

### LAWS THAT PROTECT RAPE VICTIMS

In the past several decades, laws have been enacted in nearly every state that are designed to help rape survivors. These laws vary from state to state, and victims' advocates can provide information about specific protections. In general, protections include provisions stating that...

- The defendant in a rape case cannot introduce evidence of the alleged victim's prior sexual conduct or behavior unless it also involved the defendant.

- Victims cannot be required to submit to lie detector (polygraph) testing by the police or prosecutors, because the results of such tests are inadmissible as evidence.

> **Y**ou teach, and you have good reason
> to suspect that one of your students is being abused at home.
> But your principal tells you to keep quiet.

**T**he principal may be right about a lot of things, but in this case, she's flat wrong. *Mandatory reporting laws* enacted in every state now require certain persons to inform law enforcement authorities when they believe a child is the victim of physical or sexual abuse or of neglect. As a teacher, your obligation is to contact the authorities about your suspicions.

### WHO MUST REPORT?

The laws vary from state to state, but in general, professionals who come in contact with children during the course of their work are mandated to report abuse or neglect to legal authorities. These professionals include:

- Doctors, nurses, and hospital personnel
- Psychologists, psychiatrists, and counselors
- Teachers, principals, and other school employees
- Day-care providers.

In some states, the law requires film processors and developers, firefighters, and even dog-catchers to report potential child abuse.

Reports must be made either to the police or to the state agency with the authority to investigate child abuse and neglect claims. This agency is called the Department of Social Services or the Child Protective Services Agency or a similar name.

### ABUSE VS. NEGLECT

Although the exact terminology may differ somewhat, states generally define *abuse* as the behavior of a caretaker that constitutes…

- Extreme and repeated cruelty
- Physical or psychological abuse
- Sexual abuse or exploitation
- Nonaccidental physical injury
- Conduct that creates the substantial possibility of disfigurement, physical or

psychological impairment, illness, or death of a child. *Neglect* is often defined as:
—The failure or refusal to protect the child from abuse
—The failure, refusal, or continuing inability to provide food, shelter, clothing, and medical care for the child
—The failure, refusal, or continuing inability to provide for the child's mental, emotional, or educational needs.

### YOUR LEGAL OBLIGATIONS

If you suspect abuse or neglect, under the law you should…

- **Call the state child-abuse hotline.** You'll find toll-free numbers listed in the government pages of the phone book, or you can call your local police department.
- **Be prepared to file** a written report, which is usually required within a day or two of calling.
- **Obtain feedback** from the child-protective agency. In most states, the agency conducting

the investigation must report the outcome to the individual who made the report.

There are, however, some actions that could put you or the child at risk.

- **Don't attempt to investigate** or prove the suspected abuse by yourself. You may endanger yourself and the child.
- **Don't contact the child's parent or caretaker** unless you are requested to do so by law enforcement officials or the child protective agency. Even then, you are not required to do so. Consider such a request carefully before agreeing to it, because of exposure to potential physical harm either to the child or to yourself.

## PENALTIES FOR NOT REPORTING

In most states, a person failing to make a mandated report can be charged with a misdemeanor. If convicted, he can be fined or jailed, or both. Your principal can be subject to similar penalties if she interferes with your reporting. And both of you could be subject to a civil lawsuit by the child or the child's court-appointed guardian for failing to report the suspected abuse or neglect.

## YOUR LEGAL PROTECTIONS

If you're required by state law to report suspected abuse or neglect, usually you must give your name and the capacity in which you serve. However, the law also provides that your name

---

*A*s a teacher, your obligation is to contact the authorities about your suspicions.

---

will be held in confidence by the child protective agency. As a further protection, your identity can be made public only by court order.

Also, state laws generally provide immunity from lawsuits to any person making a report of suspected child abuse or neglect. The exception is when the report is made maliciously or in bad faith.

In some states, the government maintains a fund to pay some or all legal fees for anyone who is required to report and is subsequently sued.

---

*Y*ou were charged with a crime. Your lawyer wants you to accept a plea bargain, but you want to fight the charge in court.

---

**G**uilty or innocent, when you face criminal charges, you need good legal advice and assistance. But remember—if your lawyer or the prosecutor raises the possibility of your accepting a plea bargain, *the decision is yours.* Taking a plea bargain means that you accept some degree of guilt, so you want to consider carefully the positives and the negatives.

## THE PLUSES OF PLEA BARGAINS

Plea bargains can be a good deal for a defendant for a number of reasons. With a plea bargain, the defendant can gain certain advantages:

- **Less time in prison.** By pleading guilty to a reduced charge or to a single charge, instead of facing trial on a serious charge or facing

multiple charges, the defendant serves less time in prison—or perhaps no time.

- **Quicker disposition of the case.** If the plea bargain involves probation or a sentence of community service, the defendant can be released as soon as the bargain is approved by the court (instead of waiting in jail until the appointed trial date).
- **A "cleaner" record.** The defendant's criminal record shows conviction for a lesser crime than the original charge. This can be important. For example, some states revoke the professional license of anyone convicted of a felony. By pleading guilty to a misdemeanor instead of risking a felony conviction, a defendant may be avoid losing his license (see "Why Plea Bargains Exist," page 447).

### THE MINUSES OF PLEA BARGAINS

Even if you reach a plea bargain agreement with the prosecutor that is acceptable, there's often no guarantee that the judge assigned to your case will approve it. While a judge can't force the prosecutor to charge you with a specific crime, she can impose a sentence that's greater than the one that you and the prosecutor had previously agreed to.

*Taking a plea bargain means that you accept some degree of guilt, so you want to consider carefully the positives and the negatives.*

Usually a judge will indicate her disapproval of the plea bargain before the matter gets to court. That gives both parties the chance to renegotiate the deal. Sometimes, however, a judge may simply impose a harsher sentence than the prosecutor's offer. When this happens, you may be able to withdraw your guilty plea to the lesser charge and go to trial instead. But in some cases, especially if you were warned beforehand that the judge might not go along with the prosecutor's recommended sentence, you may have no right to withdraw your guilty plea.

Plea bargains can have unintended consequences. For example, in one case a resident alien who pleaded guilty to a charge of domestic battery against his wife received probation from the court. But the guilty plea attracted the attention of the U.S. Immigration and Naturalization Service, which began deportation proceedings based on the criminal conviction.

Acknowledging guilt for a crime that you did not commit may seem like the easy way out,

but it can have far-reaching consequences. You could find yourself unable to get certain jobs or to rent an apartment because of the conviction on your record. If you plead guilty to a sex-related charge (for example, you plead guilty to a charge of molestation instead of rape), you could be placed on a list of convicted sex offenders and you could then be required to report your movements to the government for years to come.

### BEFORE YOU DECIDE

If you're offered a plea bargain by the prosecuting attorney, you will want to ask your lawyer the following questions before deciding to accept or reject the offer.

- **Is this the best offer the prosecutor is likely to make?** Some prosecutors will make a relatively conservative first offer and are open to further negotiations. Others use a "take it or leave it" approach. If you reject the initial offer, there won't be another.
- **How likely is the judge to accept this plea bargain?** As mentioned, some judges will impose a harsher sentence than the prosecutor offered in his plea bargain. Your lawyer should know the judge's record of accepting or rejecting bargains for particular types of crimes. For example, a judge may be willing to accept the prosecutor's recommendation on nonviolent crimes but may be less likely to do so in cases of domestic violence or cases of sexual assault.
- **What are the chances of acquittal if we proceed to trial?** While it's impossible for any lawyer to predict the exact outcome of a case, your lawyer can advise you about matters, such as the strength of the testimony and other evidence that's presented against you. If the bargain you've been offered isn't much better than you could expect if you're found guilty, going to trial may make more sense than accepting the prosecutor's offer.

Judges and prosecutors often encourage plea bargains to reduce the court calendar and to lighten the prosecutors' workloads. By eliminating trials, plea bargains also enable prosecutors to concentrate their resources on more serious crimes. Since a plea bargain is counted as a conviction, prosecutors who must stand for election include them when campaigning on their successful conviction record.

Sometimes public defenders are just as eager to propose plea bargains on behalf of their clients. Most public defenders carry enormous caseloads, and plea bargains are one way to dispose of some of their cases. For some public defenders, it seems the more plea bargains they can arrange, the better. A plea bargain is a kind of compromise between a criminal defendant and a prosecutor. The person charged with a crime may…

- Plead guilty to a lesser crime

- Plead guilty to one of several charges in return for having the related charges dropped

- Plead guilty or no contest to the crime as charged in return for the prosecutor's promise to seek a reduced sentence or probation.

## *Your teenage daughter is arrested and interrogated by the police. Neither you nor a lawyer is present.*

Someone tells you that your daughter has been taken to the police station. You rush to be with her, only to learn that she has been in custody and under interrogation for several hours. What are her rights—and yours?

Until a few decades ago, juveniles charged with crimes were entitled to very few of the rights normally granted to adults. While court decisions and statutes now give juveniles more protection than they had in the past, your actions can be crucial to your child's legal defense.

### STOP THE INTERROGATION

As soon as you find out that your daughter is in police custody, you should…

- **Speak to the officers conducting the interrogation.** Inform them that you want the questioning stopped immediately and that you want the opportunity to speak with your child.
- **Ask to meet the watch commander** or other officer in charge if the interrogating officers

refuse your requests. Repeat your request that the interrogation be stopped and that you be allowed to speak with your child.

> *While court decisions and statutes now give juveniles more protection than they had in the past, your actions can be crucial to your child's legal defense.*

In most cases, this will put an end to the questioning. The police don't want to jeopardize the case by continuing the interrogation.

On the other hand, the police may claim that your child has waived her right to remain silent. If this happens, contact a criminal defense lawyer as quickly as possible. The attorney can meet with your daughter after the interrogation and determine if her waiver was voluntary or if it even existed.

For example, the lawyer may be able to show that your child was too young to understand the Miranda warnings (see "The Legal Rights of Juveniles," below) or that the police continued their questioning after your child asked to speak with you. Any information obtained in this way cannot be used in court.

**TAKE NOTE** *Some juvenile court cases don't require a lawyer's help. When a minor offense, such as shoplifting an inexpensive item from a discount store or spraying graffiti on a fence, is the first offense of a juvenile with an otherwise spotless record, a lawyer's help may not be necessary. Such cases can often be handled informally. In fact, some judges take a dim view of juvenile offenders being represented by attorneys, because these judges believe that defense lawyers will tend to complicate matters.*

## THE LEGAL RIGHTS OF JUVENILES

Like adults charged with a crime, juveniles have certain rights. The police should advise your child of these rights by providing what are known as Miranda warnings. These warnings will tell your child that:

- She has the right to remain silent.

- Anything she says may be used against her in court proceedings.

- She has the right to an attorney.

- If she cannot afford an attorney, one may be appointed to defend her at no charge.

A minor can ask to speak with a lawyer or with her parents or legal guardian before making a statement to the police. A minor charged with a serious crime should never make any statements to the police until she's had the chance to speak with a lawyer or her parent or guardian.

Once your child exercises her right to remain silent, the police cannot continue to question her. If they do, any information they obtain as a result of that questioning is inadmissible in court.

The right to a court-appointed attorney applies to the minor no matter what her family's financial condition. But if you have the money to pay for an attorney, you can almost always provide your child with a far better defense than she is likely to get from the public defender's office.

## *Your 14-year-old son has been accused of a serious crime, and the prosecutor plans to charge him as an adult.*

Increasingly, young people who are accused of serious crimes—especially those involving violence—find their cases transferred out of the juvenile court system and into regular criminal courts. In some states, the age range at which young people can be charged as adults is being reduced—to as low as age 13.

In most cases, however, the transfer of a juvenile to adult criminal court requires a hearing before a juvenile court judge.

## Your Child Needs a Lawyer

When your child faces possible transfer to the adult court system, *get legal help immediately.* You want your son to avoid time in an adult prison if at all possible. A lawyer experienced in handling criminal cases, including juvenile cases, can identify the best methods for ensuring that your son's case remains in the juvenile system. If you don't already have a lawyer, ask family members or friends for a referral, or contact your state or local bar association's attorney referral service for assistance.

## How You Can Help Your Child

There are also things you can do to help your son avoid transfer to the adult court system. Rally the support of family members, friends, and others who will testify on your son's behalf at the transfer hearing. You want to be able to show the court that…

- Your son has made a mistake that's out of character with his usual behavior.
- He acted impulsively and has since expressed remorse.

- He doesn't present an ongoing threat to society.
- He's more likely to benefit from treatment and rehabilitation in the juvenile justice system than from a prison sentence.

---

*R*ally the support of family members, friends, and others who will testify on your son's behalf at the transfer hearing.

---

In some courts, supporters of the accused can appear in person. In others, the court may consider letters written on his behalf. In either case, it's important to provide specific examples of facts and circumstances showing that your son's criminal behavior is an aberration—and not a true indication of his character or potential to be a productive member of society.

## How Your Son Can Help Himself

The juvenile court will also consider your child's demeanor and behavior while he is in custody and during his court appearances. Your son can increase his chances of avoiding a transfer to adult court by…

- **Being respectful** to law enforcement and court personnel, including police officers, intake officers, bailiffs, clerks, and the judge. Avoid using profanity and displaying any "attitude" that seems contemptuous of the judicial system.
- **Dressing neatly and conservatively.** A purple mohawk haircut and a nose ring may be valid means of self-expression, but the impact on the juvenile court judge is doubtless going to be negative.

## THE TRANSFER HEARING

Before a case involving a minor can be transferred from juvenile court to adult criminal court, a hearing must be held to determine if the transfer is warranted. Transfer hearing procedures may vary, but in general the process involves the following:

- A showing of *probable cause* by the prosecutor is when evidence is introduced to show that there is at least a reasonable basis for suspecting that the minor committed the crime for which he is charged.

- The admission of evidence regarding the minor's family and background, any prior juvenile record, and the way in which the minor responded to the court's disposition of any previous cases must be shown.

- Consideration of the nature of the offense and whether the juvenile system offers appropriate penalties must be given.

After hearing testimony and attorney's arguments concerning all of the above, the juvenile court judge will issue a decision about whether the juvenile's case should be transferred.

In some states, statutes require that minors older than a certain age (usually 16) who are charged with crimes such as sexual assault or murder automatically have their cases transferred to the regular criminal court. Even in these states the minor is entitled to a transfer hearing. But the burden is on the juvenile to prove that his case would be better suited to the juvenile justice system.

*Y*our grown son was arrested and charged with a felony, but that was months ago, and his case still hasn't come to trial.

The Sixth Amendment to the U.S. Constitution guarantees those accused of crimes the right to a *speedy trial*. Unfortunately, the amendment doesn't provide any more guidance, so courts in different jurisdictions have different concepts of what constitutes a "speedy trial." For example, many states give the defendant in a criminal case the right to demand a trial within 60 or 90 days of his arrest. Under federal law, the U.S. government must begin trial proceedings no more than 70 days after charging someone with a crime.

### A MULTITUDE OF EXCEPTIONS

Although these time limits are established by statute, courts generally have great leeway in calculating the time that passes before delays violate a defendant's constitutional rights. For example, if a key witness in the government's case is missing, the court may be able to extend the time before the clock begins to run. Defendants' representatives may request extensions and delays in order to prepare defenses, but a defendant can't ask the court to delay trial, and then claim that there's been a violation of his right to a speedy trial.

### TO FILE OR NOT TO FILE?

Your son should talk to his attorney about filing a *motion for a speedy trial.* This motion will force the prosecutor to obey the statutory time limits or risk having the charges against your son dismissed. Before insisting on this motion, however, ask your son's lawyer if the delay in bringing his case to trial is really a detriment to his case.

Some criminal defense attorneys are reluctant to seek a speedy trial because delays can often benefit the defendant. In some instances, cases not brought to trial for months have been dismissed because…

- Prosecution witnesses were no longer as certain of their testimony.
- Witnesses had moved away and were unavailable to testify.
- Evidence had been misplaced by the police during the delay.

In other cases, the opposite is true, and insisting on a speedy trial is the smart strategy. With prosecutors often handling large caseloads, the government may not have enough time to prepare its case carefully. Prosecutors may not be able to thoroughly sift through all the evidence.

Insisting on a speedy trial may also prompt an unprepared prosecutor to decide it's in his interest to negotiate a plea bargain.

Knowing which course to follow will depend to a great extent on the advice of your son's lawyer. Based on her experience in dealing with local prosecutors and judges, the lawyer will advise your son about the pros and cons of filing a motion for a speedy trial.

But ultimately the decision will rest with your son. If he's still in jail awaiting trial because he was unable to make bail, getting the case resolved more quickly may be more important to him than taking a more patient approach. If he's free on bail, however, letting the matter drag on can be annoying to others involved in the case, but it may ultimately be in his best interest.

## ALTERNATIVES TO DOING JAIL TIME

With prison populations at an all-time high, some judges are now employing alternatives to jail time when sentencing a convicted criminal.

- **Alternative sentences**—some of these have been challenged as a form of cruel and unusual punishment, but for the most part their validity has been upheld on appeal. Some alternatives the courts have devised require…

  - Drivers convicted of driving under the influence of alcohol or illegal drugs (DUI) to put bumper stickers on their cars informing the public of their conviction

  - DUI offenders to visit morgues and hospitals to view victims of DUI automobile accidents

  - Convicted criminals to serve time in jail on weekends

  - Criminals to write letters of apology to their victims

  - Convicts to submit to wearing monitoring devices that alert law enforcement officers if the convict strays beyond a prescribed distance

  - Landlords convicted of repeated or serious building code violations to live in their own buildings for a period of time.

- **Diversion programs.** One alternative to a trial when charged with certain crimes is participation in a diversion program. These programs offer defendants a kind of probation and usually require them to participate in rehabilitation programs or to obtain counseling. In some cases, a defendant can be required to move into a residential-treatment center. If the defendant completes the program successfully, the prosecutor will drop charges, allowing the defendant to avoid a criminal conviction on his record, but not erasing the record of an arrest.

  The guidelines for participation vary from place to place, but diversion programs are generally available to people charged with minor drug- or alcohol-related offenses, nonviolent misdemeanors, and traffic-law violations. Guilty parties have to pay for the cost of the treatment and may also be required to pay an administrative fee to the court.

**Y**our sister was arrested and is being held in the county jail, and she can't make bail. She needs your help to get out.

**N**aturally you want to get your sister out of jail. But your decision to "stand bail" depends on understanding how the system works and what your obligations will be (see "What Is Bail and How Is It Set," facing page).

### PAYING THE BAIL

If the amount is small, you can post the bail with the court, paying with cash or by writing a check. But if the judge sets a high bail, you will probably need to use the services of a bail bondsman to get your sister released. When bail is high, the bondsman will normally ask for collateral to protect him from losses if your sister fails to appear in court ("jumps bail"). If your sister owns her home or other property, such as a car, boat, or motorcycle, she can use her own property as collateral. But if she owns no valuable property, you may be tempted to offer your own to guarantee your sister's bond.

Think carefully before offering your property as collateral. While your sister's case is pending, any property that you offer as collateral cannot

> **Y**our decision to "stand bail" for her depends on understanding how the system works and what your obligations will be.

be sold. If you are planning to sell your house, for example, you won't be able to sell it until your sister's case is concluded.

■ **Consider your sister's reliability.** Are there good reasons for the court's suspicions that she won't return to stand trial? Many well-intentioned people have lost their homes when someone they trusted jumped bail.

■ **Consider your sister's financial position and character before proceeding**. If she does make her required court appearances, will she be willing or even able to reimburse you for the cost of the bondsman's fee?

Keep in mind that jumping bail is an offense that is separate from the original charge that your sister faces. Even if she is acquitted of the initial charges, your sister could still end up serving time for having failed to appear in court.

## WHAT IS BAIL AND HOW IS IT SET?

Bail is a payment or pledge of payment that you make to the court to obtain the release of a criminal defendant awaiting the outcome of a case. Courts may impose a very high bail or even deny it completely, but they cannot do so arbitrarily or without justification. Bail isn't supposed to be a punishment or penalty—defendants are innocent until proven guilty and cannot be punished until then. The only purpose of bail is to ensure that the defendant will appear in court as required. While the Eighth Amendment to the U.S. Constitution includes a prohibition against "excessive bail," decisions about what's excessive are usually made on a case-by-case basis.

Laws generally require bail hearings within 48 hours of being *booked,* or charged with a crime. But these laws don't take weekends and holidays into consideration when calculating the elapsed time. So if someone is arrested on the Friday evening of Memorial Day weekend, for example, she may not get a bail hearing until the following Wednesday.

In most jurisdictions, judges set the amount of bail at the bail hearing. Many courts have standardized bail schedules—the more serious the crime, the more substantial the amount of bail that's likely to be required. In some parts of the country, police don't even involve judges when setting bail, but instead use the schedules set out by the local court. In these jurisdictions, a defendant pays the set amount in order to get out of jail.

Judges normally have the right to vary from standard bail schedules, however. For example, if a person has few ties to the community or has been convicted on serious charges in the past, the judge may impose a higher bail amount than that listed on the schedule. On the other hand, if a defendant has no prior arrest record, has a stable work history, and has family ties that make her unlikely to flee, the judge may be willing to lower the bail amount. Judges may even release a defendant *on her own recognizance*—the defendant's written promise to appear for court proceedings as required.

■ **The role of the bail bondsman** comes into play when bail is set too high for the defendant or her family to pay. At this point, many people turn to a bail bondsman. The bail bondsman will post a bond with the court for the full amount of the bail. If the defendant fails to appear for court proceedings, the bondsman will forfeit the full amount to the court (bail bondsmen are easy to find—their offices are usually clustered around the courthouse, and their telephone numbers are listed in the Yellow Pages).

Bail bondsmen typically charge 10 percent of the bail. This fee isn't refundable, even if the defendant shows up for trial and is acquitted. If a defendant jumps bail, the bondsman may hire a "bounty hunter" to locate and return her to police custody. Bounty hunters don't need a warrant, and they don't have to inform a bail jumper of his or her right to remain silent. They are usually armed, and are allowed to use force as needed to apprehend a defendant.

*O*n a visit to a foreign country you are arrested for spitting out gum. You had no idea that it was against the law. What should you do?

**B**eing charged with a crime while visiting a foreign country can be enormously stressful. Laws in many other countries give an accused person far fewer rights than do the U.S. Constitution and American laws. If you are arrested in a foreign country…

■ **State that you are a citizen of the United States** and ask that the police notify the U.S. embassy or consulate of your arrest. The consulate doesn't have the power to obtain your release, but it can take certain steps to help you, including informing family and friends at home of your arrest and providing you with the names of local lawyers.

■ **Don't make any statements to the police** until after you've spoken to a lawyer. In many countries, the police are under no obligation to inform you of your right to remain silent, and anything you say may ultimately be used against you in court.

■ **Hire a translator** if you're in a country where English is not spoken. Even if you speak the local language fairly well, you'll probably need a translator in order to understand the legal proceedings. Your lawyer or the U. S. Consulate should be able to provide you with the names of experienced translators.

■ **Be wary of officials who request money** in order to get you out of jail or to pay for items such as food and medicine. Bribery is a fact of life in some countries, even when illegal. Don't offer payments to police or jail personnel unless your lawyer advises you to do so.

■ **Be prepared for a lengthy jail stay.** In many countries, there is no right to bail, and you could remain incarcerated until your trial.

**TAKE NOTE** *Crimes that might be considered petty offenses or misdemeanors in the United States—possessing a small amount of marijuana for personal use, for example—can lead to serious criminal charges in many foreign countries. If you find yourself convicted of a crime in another country, you could face years in prison there for something that might have brought only a fine or probation at home. Think twice and even three times before doing anything that could land you in any trouble with another country's laws.*

# SAMPLE COMPLAINT LETTER

*You can adapt this letter to just about any kind of consumer complaint you have. This letter should be used only when less formal attempts at getting satisfaction have failed. Remember to be brief but thorough, and be sure to state the solution you expect—such as a repair, replacement, or a refund.*

Month, date, year

Name of contact
Business name
Address
City/state/zip code

Dear [contact's name]:

On [date of purchase] I bought a [describe the item; for example, "a Sukkitup vacuum cleaner, model J-22"] at [give the location of the purchase; for example "your Mockingbird Hills Mall store"]. A copy of my receipt for this purchase is enclosed.

Unfortunately, [describe the problem; for example, "this vacuum cleaner has failed to perform as promised, even though the motor and all belts have been replaced twice. Your store's service manager now informs me that no further repairs will be made under warranty."]

In order to put an end to this problem, [state your proposed solution; for example, "I request that your company arrange to pick up the vacuum cleaner from my home and provide me with a full refund of the purchase price."]

I look forward to your response within 10 business days from the date of this letter. Please feel free to contact me at the telephone number listed below.

Thank you for your prompt attention to this matter.

Sincerely,

(Signature)

Your name
Your address
Your city/state/zip code
Your telephone number

## Sample First Demand Letter

Month, date, year

Name of contact
Business Name
Address
City/state/zip code

Dear [contact's name]:

On [date of incident], [state the problem; for example, "your company installed new prefinished wood floors in the kitchen and hallway of my home. However, in the process of installation, your employee Jon Dough damaged my living room carpet, ripping it in several places. Despite numerous assurances by Mr. Dough and other employees of your company that my carpet would be repaired, no repairs have been made at this time."]

Therefore, unless [state the solution you want; for example, "my carpet is repaired or replaced to my satisfaction within 10 business days of the date of this letter"], I will contact another company to make the repairs and hold you responsible for any costs I incur in doing so.

I look forward to your prompt response.

Sincerely,

(Signature)

Your name
Your address

Your city/state/zip code
Your telephone number

# SAMPLE FINAL DEMAND LETTER

Month, date, year

Name of contact
Business name
Address
City/state/zip code

Dear [contact's name]:

Because you failed to take any action in response to my earlier letter regarding the damage caused to my carpet by your employee Jon Dough (a copy of which is enclosed), I have had the repairs done by the Carpet Magik Company. The cost of repairs was $500. A copy of the invoice for these repairs is enclosed.

I hold your company responsible for the damage caused to my carpet. In order to avoid any legal action in this matter, please reimburse me for the cost of these repairs within 10 business days of the date of this letter.

Sincerely,

(Signature)

Your name
Your address
Your city/state/zip code
Your telephone number

## SAMPLE FIRST LETTER TO A NEIGHBOR ABOUT A PROBLEM

Month, date, year

Neighbor's name
Address
City/state/zip code

Dear [neighbor's name]:

As we discussed last week, I'm concerned that your elm tree has a dead limb that hangs into my yard. The limb is about to fall into the side of my house. If it does, I'm afraid it will cause considerable damage, which I'm sure you don't want to have to pay for. Please trim this limb immediately to eliminate the potential damage it may cause. I appreciate your prompt attention to this problem.

Sincerely,

(Signature)

Your name
Your address
Your city/state/zip code

# Sample Final Letter to a Neighbor About a Problem

Month, date, year

Neighbor's name
Address
City/state/zip code

Dear [neighbor's name]:

On [date], the dead limb from your elm tree fell and landed on the roof and side of my house, causing damage in the amount of $____. I'm enclosing a copy of the invoice from the repair company for your review.

Despite my earlier warnings about this tree's dangerous condition, you took no action to have the dead limb removed. You have also failed to respond to my previous request for reimbursement of the cost of repairs to my home.

Unless I receive payment from you in the amount of $____ within 10 days of the date of this letter, I will have no choice but to pursue legal action in this matter.

Sincerely,

(Signature)

Your name
Your address
Your city/state/zip code

## LETTER REQUESTING INFORMATION ABOUT AN INSURER

*Use this kind of letter after you've been injured or suffered property damage in an accident and don't know the name of the responsible party's insurer.*

Month, date, year

Name of person
Address
City/state/zip code

Dear [responsible party's name]:

On January 15, 2001, at approximately 3 P.M., I was injured when a limb from the aspen tree in your front yard broke while you were trimming it, and the limb fell into my driveway striking me and breaking my arm.

Please call or write me with the name, address, and telephone number of your homeowner's insurance company and your policy number. This will enable me to provide your insurer with information about my injuries, in order to allow it to begin processing my claim. I am also enclosing an additional copy of this letter, and I ask that you forward it to your insurance company.

I look forward to receiving this information by [set a deadline, such as one week from the date of your letter]. Thanks for your prompt response to this request.

Sincerely,

(Signature)

Your name
Your address
Your city/state/zip code
Your telephone number

## SAMPLE CLAIM LETTER TO AN INSURANCE COMPANY

*Use this letter if you live in a state without no-fault insurance.*

Month, date, year

Claims Department
Insurance company name
Address
City/state/zip code

Dear [name of Claims Adjuster]:

This letter is to inform you that I was involved in an automobile accident on [date] at [location of accident], with your insured, [name of other driver], whose address is [address/city/state/zip code]. At the time of the accident, [other driver] was driving a [year/color/make/model], license number _____.

In this accident I suffered [bodily injuries/sustained damage to my car/both bodily injuries and damage to my own car].

Please be advised that at this time I intend to proceed against [name of other driver]. However, I reserve the right to file a claim under my own insurance coverage, if I choose.

Sincerely,

(Signature)

Your name
Your address
Your city/state/zip code
Your telephone number

## SAMPLE CLAIM LETTER TO AN INSURANCE COMPANY

*Use this letter if you live in a state with no-fault insurance.*

Month, date, year

Claims Department
Insurance company name
Address
City/state/zip code

Dear [name of Claims Adjuster]:

This letter is to inform you that I was involved in an automobile accident on [date] at [location of accident]. In this accident I [sustained bodily injuries/damage to my car/both bodily injuries and damage to my own car].

The other driver involved in this accident was [name of other driver], whose address is [address/city/state/zip code]. At the time of the accident, [other driver] was driving a [year/color/make/model], license number _____.

Please be advised that at this time I intend to proceed against the Personal Injury Protection coverage included in my policy. However, I also reserve the right to proceed as well against others responsible for this accident, if I choose.

Sincerely,

(Signature)

Your name
Your address
Your city/state/zip code
Your telephone number
Your auto insurance policy number

Month, date, year

Name of adjuster
Insurance company name
Address
City/state/zip code

Dear Mr./Ms./ [name of Claims Adjuster]:

As you know, I have considered your offer of $____, which you made [by telephone on/in your letter of month/date/year], and which I told you on [month/date/year] was unacceptable.

Since I have heard nothing further from you since then, I can only assume that you are no longer interested in negotiating a good faith settlement that will adequately compensate me for the injuries and property damage I experienced, as well as for my continuing expenses, pain, and suffering.

Unless I hear from you within 10 business days with an offer that will provide me with fair compensation, I will have no choice but to turn this matter over to an attorney in order to obtain a just settlement of my claim.

I will look forward to your response to this letter by [date].

Sincerely,

(Signature)

Your name
Your address
Your city/state/zip code
Your telephone number

## LETTER REQUESTING CREDIT REPORT

*Call the agency in advance to find out what fee, if any, you will be charged.*
*Remember that in several states you are entitled to one free report annually]*

Month, date, year

Credit reporting agency
Address
City/state/zip code

Re: Request for Credit Report

As provided for under the federal Fair Credit Reporting Act, I hereby make written
request for a copy of my credit report. Please include information regarding the
source of any information contained in my file, as well as the name and address of
any organization or individual that has received information about my credit history
from you, either orally or in writing.

I enclose my check for $ ___ as payment in full for this report.

*or*

I have been denied credit within the past 30 days. I request that you provide me with
this information at no charge, as provided for under the Fair Credit Reporting Act.

(Optional): To further assist you in locating my file, I was formerly known as [for
example, your maiden name]. From [date] to [date], I resided at [previous address, if
you've been in your current home for less than two years].

Please contact me at [your telephone number, including area code] for any additional
information you may require to fulfill this request. Thank you for your attention to
this matter.

Sincerely,

(Signature)

Your name
Your Social Security number
Your address
Your city/state/zip code
Your telephone number

# LETTER CORRECTING A CREDIT REPORT ERROR

Month, date, year

Credit reporting agency
Address
City/state/zip code

Re: Credit Report Correction

A review of my credit file reveals that it contains the following incomplete/erroneous information:

[Describe the error you found. For example, "The report states that I have an open MasterCard account with the A-Z Bank of Delaware. This account was closed at my request on January 1, 2000."]

In accordance with the provisions of the federal Fair Credit Reporting Act, please take the appropriate steps to correct this error and to notify any individuals or organizations that have requested a copy of my credit report within the past six months that this information is erroneous.

Thank you for your prompt attention to this matter.

Sincerely,

(Signature)

Your name
Your Social Security number
Your address
Your city/state/zip code
Your telephone number

## FREEDOM OF INFORMATION AND PRIVACY ACT REQUEST

Month, date, year

Name of Freedom of Information officer
Name of federal agency
Agency address
City/state/zip code

Dear Mr./Ms. [name of FOI Officer]:

This letter constitutes my request under the Freedom of Information Act and The Privacy Act of 1974 for information you may have about me.

I request that a copy of the following documents be provided to me: [describe the information you want the agency to provide. For example, "records kept by your agency in regard to my political activities while attending classes at the University of XYZ during the period from 1972 to 1976"].

To help you determine what fees to assess, you are hereby notified that I am an individual seeking this information for my personal use. I will pay all reasonable costs associated with this request. However, if costs are expected to be in excess of $____, please inform me of the anticipated total cost in advance.

*or*

I request a waiver of all fees because disclosure of the information I request is in the public interest, since it will contribute significantly to public understanding of government operations and activities, and it is not being sought for any commercial purpose.

Yours truly,

(Signature)

Your name
Your address
Your city/state/zip code
Your daytime telephone number (optional)

**American Association of Retired Persons (AARP)**
601 E St. NW, Washington DC 20049
Phone (800) 424-3410   Phone (202) 434-2277
Web site www.aarp.org

**American Society of Travel Agents**
1101 King St., Suite 200, Alexandria VA 22314
Phone (703) 739-2782
Web site: www.astanet.com

**Consumer Credit Counseling Service**
**National Foundation for Credit Counseling**
8611 Second Ave., Suite 100, Silver Spring MD 20910
Phone (800) 388-2227
Web site: www.nfcc.org

**Department of Housing and Urban Development**
451 Seventh St. SW, Washington DC 20410
Phone: (800) 669-9777
Web site: www.hud.gov

**Direct Marketing Association**
**Mail Preference Service**
P.O. Box 9008, Farmingdale NY 11735-9008
Web site: www.the-dma.org

**Environmental Protection Agency**
Ariel Rios Building
1200 Pennsylvania Ave. NW, Washington DC 20460
Phone (202) 260-2090
Web site www.epa.gov

**Equal Employment Opportunity Commission**
**(EEOC)**
1801 L St. NW, Washington DC 20507
Phone (800) 669-4000   Phone (202) 663-4900
*TTY (202) 663-4494
Web site: www.eeoc.gov

**Federal Communications Commission**
445 12th St. SW, Washington DC 20554
Phone (888) 225-5322   Phone (202) 418-0190
*TTY (888) 835-5322

**Federal Deposit Insurance Corporation (FDIC)**
**Office of Consumer Affairs**
550 17th St. NW, Washington DC 20429
Phone (800) 934-3342
Web site: www.fdic.gov

**Federal Reserve System**
20th St. & Constitution Ave. NW, Washington DC 20551
Phone (800) 827-3340
Web site: www.federalreserve.gov

**Federal Trade Commission**
6th St. and Pennsylvania Ave. NW
Washington DC 20580
Phone (202) 326-2222
Web site: www.ftc.gov

**Food and Drug Administration**
5600 Fishers Lane, Rockville MD 20857
Phone (800) 463-6332
Web site: www.fda.gov

**Health Care Financing Administration**
6325 Security Blvd., Baltimore, MD 21207
Phone (800) 638-6833
Web site www.hcfa.gov

**National Adoption Information**
**Clearinghouse (NAIC)**
330 C St. SW, Washington DC 20447
Phone (888) 251-0075   Phone (703) 352-3488
Web site www.calib.com/naic

**National Center for Home Equity Conversion**
360 North Robert #403, St. Paul MN 55101
Phone (651) 222-6775
Web site: www.reverse.org

**National Information Center for Children**
**& Youth With Disabilities**
P.O. Box 1492, Washington DC 20013
Phone (800) 695-0285
Web site: www.nichcy.org

**Occupation Safety and Health Administration**
**U. S. Department of Labor**
200 Constitution Ave. NW, Room N3647
Washington DC 20210
Phone (800) 321-6742   Phone (202) 693-1999
Web site: www.osha.gov

**Pension and Welfare Benefit Administration**
**U. S. Department of Labor**
200 Constitution Ave. NW, Washington DC 20210
Phone (202) 219-8771   Phone (202) 219-8776
Web site: www.dol.gov/dol/pwba

**Securities and Exchange Commission**
450 Fifth St. NW, Washington DC 20549
Phone (800) 732-0330   Phone (202) 942-7040
Web site: www.sec.gov

**Small Business Administration**
409 Third St. SW, Suite 7600, Washington DC 20416
Phone (800) 827-5722   Phone (202) 205-6744
Web site: www.sba.gov

**Social Security Administration**
6401 Security Boulevard, Room 4-5-C Annex
Baltimore MD 21235
Phone (800) 772-1213   *TTY (800) 325-0778
Web site: www.ssa.gov

**Telephone Preference Service**
P.O. Box 9014, Farmingdale NY 11735-9014
Web site: www.the-dma.org

**U.S. Department of Labor**
200 Constitution Ave. NW, Washington DC 20210
Phone (202) 693-4650
Web site: www.dol.gov

**CREDIT REPORTING AGENCIES**
**Equifax**
P.O. Box 740256, Atlanta GA 30374
Phone (800) 685-1111   Phone (888) 532-0179
Web site: www.equifax.com

**Experian**
P.O. Box 9595, Allen TX 75013
Phone (888) 397-3742
Web site: www.experian.com

**TransUnion**
P.O. Box 2000, Chester PA 19022
Phone (800) 680-7289
Web site: www.transunion.com

*Hearing-impaired phone number

INDEX

INDEX

# Q

# R

INDEX

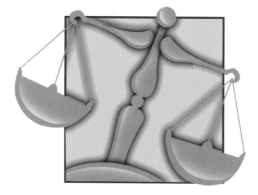